THE
PARTHA CHATTERJEE
OMNIBUS

OUP India's Omnibus collection offers readers a comprehensive coverage
of works of enduring value, woven together by a new introduction,
attractively packaged for easy reference and reading.

THE
PARTHA CHATTERJEE
OMNIBUS

COMPRISING

Nationalist Thought and the Colonial World

The Nation and Its Fragments

A Possible India

OXFORD
UNIVERSITY PRESS

OXFORD
UNIVERSITY PRESS

YMCA Library Building, Jai Singh Road, New Delhi 110001

Oxford University Press is a department of the University of Oxford. It furthers
the University's objective of excellence in research, scholarship, and education
by publishing worldwide in

Oxford New York
Auckland Cape Town Dar es Salaam Hong Kong Karachi
Kuala Lumpur Madrid Melbourne Mexico City Nairobi
New Delhi Shanghai Taipei Toronto

With offices in
Argentina Austria Brazil Chile Czech Republic France Greece
Guatemala Hungary Italy Japan Poland Portugal Singapore
South Korea Switzerland Thailand Turkey Ukraine Vietnam

Oxford is a registered trade mark of Oxford University Press
in the UK and in certain other countries

Published in India by Oxford University Press, New Delhi

ISBN-13: 978-0-19-565156-0
ISBN-10: 0-19-565156-1

Jacket Photograph: Sanjiv Saith

Printed in India at Rashtriya Printers, Delhi 110 032
Published by Manzar Khan, Oxford University Press
YMCA Library Building, Jai Singh Road, New Delhi 110 001

Preface to the Omnibus Edition

The writings compiled in this omnibus volume have been discussed, criticized, praised, distorted, misunderstood and appropriated in so many places and on so many occasions since their first appearance that, for me, they have taken on a certain quality of remoteness. While participating in some of these discussions, I have often been startled to discover that I had been thinking about these books as though they had been written by someone else. I must also confess that a few times, exasperated by my failures to get through to my interlocutors—both critics and supporters—I have claimed, somewhat opportunistically, that the author of these texts was dead.

Given this background, I do not intend to use this occasion to cast on these writings the light of later reflection. In their own ways, they bear the marks of the time when they were written. To the extent that they are still referred to in current discussions, they probably remain relevant at least to some of the present concerns of scholars in the field. However, in this omnibus form of a single volume, the three books have now acquired a corporeality that they did not possess before. Looking at them together, it strikes me that it might be worthwhile here to point out some of those things that these writings did try to achieve and, perhaps more importantly, what they did not try to do.

The principal object of study in all three books is the actually existing nation-state officially called 'India, that is Bharat'. That was the starting point of *Nationalist Thought and the Colonial World*: to write the 'ideological history' of the Indian nation-state from its conception to its fruition. The narrative structure of that book, that of a journey: departure, manoeuvre, arrival, clearly obtained its shape from the fact that the end of the story—the birth of the Indian nation-state—was what was immediately known and needed to be problematized. *The Nation and Its Fragments* abandoned the linear narrative for a series of interventions in different disciplinary fields. But they all converged from different directions upon the same object—the Indian nation-state as it had developed after four decades of its post-colonial career. The linear narrative was restored in *A Possible India*, but this time it was written alongside the events described, as in a diary, rather than after the fact, so that the end of the story was not already known before its telling. This made for a more strategic and contingent, and hence more actively political, engagement with my object of analysis—namely, the present career and crisis of the Indian nation-state.

Defining the object in this somewhat 'presentist' fashion has its limitations. It takes as given the immediate conditions and limits of politics as they have been set by the instituted processes of the nation-state from within which the criticism emanates. Even a political project of surmounting those given conditions and limits must, so to speak, work 'from within'. This means that I rule out *ab initio* all speculation about political futures that appeals to a history-as-it-should-have-been or a utopia without national borders. I acknowledge the power of both kinds of speculation, but they do not have a place within my conception of a 'politics from within'. (I have recently elaborated on this conception in the article 'Beyond the Nation? Or Within?', *Economic and Political Weekly*, 4–11 January 1997 and *Social Text*, (Fall 1998), pp. 57–69.)

I have been particularly reminded of this consciously chosen limit of my work by my critics from Pakistan who have pointed out, with justification, that all three books, including the two that are 'historical', take the partition of India and the creation of Pakistan in 1947 as already given facts. They have found these writings 'unhelpful' in thinking of political futures that start from a radical questioning of the very historicity of those facts. I accept the criticism and can only reply that even in alliance, our locations in political practice must remain, for the present, different.

Taken together, all three books investigate the relation between rulers and peoples within the imagined-into-reality framework of the Indian nation. I emphasize '*rulers* and peoples', because in the recent lamentations over the crisis of governability in India, what is being often forgotten is the elementary truth, known to all perceptive political thinkers from Machiavelli to Marx, that behind every proposal for the good governance of all lies the need to ensure the rule of the few.

I am grateful to Rukun Advani and Nitasha Devasar of Oxford University Press, Delhi, for suggesting the idea of this omnibus volume and to Zed Books, London, and Princeton University Press for granting the necessary permissions to bring the idea into reality.

P.C.
Calcutta

March 7, 1999

Contents

NATIONALIST THOUGHT
AND
THE COLONIAL WORLD
A Derivative Discourse?

Preface

In the last scene of Bertolt Brecht's *Life of Galileo*, the scientist is quoted as having said, 'If there are obstacles the shortest line between two points may well be a crooked line.' Given the abstract neatness of the theoretical world of classical mechanics, the statement carries a ring of irony. In the much less well-ordered world of politics, however, it would seem to be a truism.

Yet it is remarkable how seldom political theorists have taken seriously the fact that 'politics' necessarily operates in an ideological world in which words rarely have unambiguous meanings; where notions are inexact, and have political value precisely because they are inexact and hence capable of suggesting a range of possible interpretations; where intentions themselves are contradictory and consequences very often unintended; where movements follow winding and unpredictable paths; where choices are strategic and relative, not univocal and absolute. And still, this inexact world of ambiguity and half-truth, of manipulation and deception, of dreams and illusions, is not wholly patternless, for here, too, objectives are realised, rules established, values asserted, revolutions accomplished and states founded.

This book is about a political revolution, but one whose course cannot be described by selecting from history two points of origin and culmination and joining them by a straight line. The critical viewpoint reveals that it is a revolution which at the same time, and in fundamental ways, is not a revolution. It is in the shifts, slides, discontinuities, the unintended moves, what is suppressed as much as what is asserted, that one can get a sense of this complex movement, not as so many accidental or disturbing factors but as constitutive of the very historical rationality of its process. And it is by examining the jagged edges that we can find clues to an understanding of the political relevance today of the ideological history of nationalism.

I wanted to call this book *Crooked Line*. But friends more knowledgeable than I in the ways of the publishing world have persuaded me that that would not be the best way to reach my potential readers. I have deferred to their judgment.

I began writing this book in the 1981-82 academic year which I spent at St Antony's College, Oxford. I am grateful to the Nuffield Foundation, London, for a travelling fellowship. I continued the work during my short stay in 1982-83 as a Visiting Fellow at the Research School of Pacific Studies, Australian

National University, Canberra, and completed it on my return to Calcutta. I am grateful to the staff of the Bodleian Library in Oxford, the ANU Library in Canberra, the National Library in Calcutta, the Department of History Library of the University of Calcutta and, of course, the Library of the Centre for Studies in Social Sciences, Calcutta, for their help.

Among those who have read and commented on earlier drafts of this book are Anouar Abdel-Malek, Shahid Amin, Jasodhara Bagchi, Dipesh Chakrabarty, John Dunn, Omkar Goswami, Ranajit Guha, Tapati Guha Thakurta, Sudipta Kaviraj, Rudrangshu Mukherjee, Gyan Pandey, Abhijit Sen and Asok Sen. I thank them all for their criticisms and suggestions.

I have presented and discussed different parts of this book in seminars at Algiers, Oxford, Canberra, Baroda, Paris and Calcutta. My thanks to all participants at those seminars.

I am grateful to Kinhide Mushakoji and Anouar Abdel-Malek of the United Nations University, Robert Molteno and Anna Gourlay of Zed Books, London, and Ravi Dayal and Rukun Advani of Oxford University Press, New Delhi, for their help in the publication of this book. My thanks also to May McKenzie and Margaret Hall for preparing the typescript.

Finally, I take this opportunity to record my gratitude to Gouri for her support and understanding.

Partha Chatterjee
Calcutta

December 1985

1. Nationalism as a Problem in the History of Political Ideas

> To trouble oneself with the task of dealing with something
> that has been adequately dealt with before is superfluous,
> a result of ignorance, or a sign of evil intent.
> Abu Bakr Muhammad Ibn Bajjah [Avempace],
> *Tadbir al-mutawaḥḥid*

I

In one of his less celebrated articles, John Plamenatz has talked about 'two types' of nationalism:[1] in both, nationalism is 'primarily a cultural phenomenon' although it often takes a 'political form'. One type is 'western', having emerged primarily in Western Europe, and the other 'eastern', to be found in Eastern Europe, in Asia and Africa, and also in Latin America. Both types depend upon the acceptance of a common set of standards by which the state of development of a particular national culture is measured. In the first type, however, although there is the feeling that the nation is at a disadvantage with respect to others, it is nevertheless already 'culturally equipped' to make the attempt to remove those deficiencies. Thus, although the new global standard of progress may have been set for the rest of the world by France or Britain, they were based upon a set of ideas 'about man, morals and society' which, in their social and intellectual origins, were West European generally. Britain and France may have been the cultural, economic and political pace makers, and may have been envied or admired for this reason, but simultaneous with the process of their emergence as world leaders, there had emerged a 'comity of nations' in Western Europe 'which had already learned to think of itself as ahead of all the others'. Consequently, when nationalism emerged in the other countries of the West, despite the fact that it was the product of a sense of disadvantage with respect to the standards of progress set by the pace makers, there was no feeling that the nation was not culturally equipped to make the effort to reach those standards. Germans or Italians, for instance, already had the necessary linguistic, educational and professional skills that were deemed necessary for a 'consciously progressive civilisation'. They had therefore 'little need to equip themselves culturally by appropriating what was alien to them'. That is to say, although the acceptance of a universal standard of progress had produced an

1

awareness of disadvantage, that universal standard itself was not seen in any fundamental way as being alien to the national culture.

'Eastern' nationalism, on the other hand, has appeared among 'peoples recently drawn into a civilisation hitherto alien to them, and whose ancestral cultures are not adapted to success and excellence by these cosmopolitan and increasingly dominant standards'. They too have measured the backwardness of their nations in terms of certain global standards set by the advanced nations of Western Europe. But what is distinctive here is that there is also a fundamental awareness that those standards have come from an alien culture, and that the inherited culture of the nation did not provide the necessary adaptive leverage to enable it to reach those standards of progress. The 'Eastern' type of nationalism, consequently, has been accompanied by an effort to 're-equip' the nation culturally, to transform it. But it could not do so simply by imitating the alien culture, for then the nation would lose its distinctive identity. The search therefore was for a regeneration of the national culture, adapted to the requirements of progress, but retaining at the same time its distinctiveness.

The attempt is deeply contradictory: 'It is both imitative and hostile to the models it imitates . . .' It is imitative in that it accepts the value of the standards set by the alien culture. But it also involves a rejection: 'in fact, two rejections, both of them ambivalent: rejection of the alien intruder and dominator who is nevertheless to be imitated and surpassed by his own standards, and rejection of ancestral ways which are seen as obstacles to progress and yet also cherished as marks of identity'. This contradictory process is therefore deeply disturbing as well. 'Eastern nationalism is disturbed and ambivalent as the nationalisms of Herder and Mazzini were not.'

Unlike much of his other work, this article by Plamenatz is neither rigorously argued nor particularly profound. But in making the distinction between the two types of nationalism, it states with sufficient clarity the premises of what may be called the liberal-rationalist dilemma in talking about nationalist thought. The same dilemma can be seen in the standard liberal histories of nationalism, most notably in the work of Hans Kohn.[2] This historiography accepts nationalism as an integral part of the story of liberty. Its origin is coeval with the birth of universal history, and its development is part of the same historical process which saw the rise of industrialism and democracy. In its essential aspects, therefore, nationalism represents the attempt to actualize in political terms the universal urge for liberty and progress. And yet the evidence was undeniable that it could also give rise to mindless chauvinism and xenophobia and serve as the justification for organized violence and tyranny. Seen as part of the story of liberty, nationalism could be defined as a rational ideological framework for the realization of rational, and highly laudable, political ends. But that was not how nationalism had made its presence felt in much of recent history. It has been the cause of the most destructive wars ever seen; it has justified the brutality of Nazism and Fascism; it has become the ideology of racial hatred in the colonies and has given birth to some of the most irrational revivalist movements as well as to the most oppressive political regimes in the contemporary world. The evidence was indeed overwhelming that nationalism and liberty could often be quite irreconcilably opposed.

The distinction between the two types of nationalism is an attempt to come to terms with this liberal dilemma. Indeed, Kohn also made a distinction of this sort, between 'western' and 'non-western' nationalisms,[3] and later between 'good' nationalism and 'evil' nationalism.[4] The distinction is designed to explain how a profoundly liberal idea could be so distorted as to produce such grossly illiberal movements and regimes. It does this by constructing a dichotomy, between a normal and a special type. The normal is the classical, the orthodox, the pure type. This type of nationalism shares the same material and intellectual premises with the European Enlightenment, with industry and the idea of progress, and with modern democracy. Together they constitute a historical unity, defined with a fair degree of clarity in both geographical and chronological terms. This gives the liberal-rationalist his paradigmatic form in which nationalism goes hand-in-hand with reason, liberty and progress. The special type emerges under somewhat different historical circumstances. It is, therefore, complex, impure, often deviant; it represents a very difficult and contradictory historical process which can be very 'disturbing'. There is nothing in it, the liberal-rationalist would argue, that is necessarily illiberal. But being a special type, operating in unfavourable circumstances, it can often be so. 'No doubt,' says Plamenatz, 'nationalists have quite often not been liberals, but this, I suggest, is largely because they have so often been active in conditions unpropitious to freedom, as the liberal understands it. I see no logical repugnance between nationalism and liberalism.' Indeed, the very fact that nationalists of the 'eastern' type accept and value the ideal of progress — and strive to transform their inherited cultures in order to make them better suited for the conditions of the modern world — means that archaic forms of authority are destroyed, conditions are created for the growth of a certain degree of individual initiative and choice, and for the introduction of science and modern education. All this cannot but be liberating in a fundamental historical sense. Consequently, even when this kind of nationalism appears in the form of revivalist movements or oppressive regimes, it still represents an urge for progress and freedom.

> We must see this nationalism as part of a social, intellectual and moral revolution of which the aspirations to democracy and personal freedom are also products. It is connected with these aspirations, and even serves to strengthen them and to create some of the social conditions of their realisation, even though it so often also perverts them.

Thus the liberal-rationalist saves the purity of his paradigm by designating as deviant all those cases which do not fit the classical form. Even in these deviant cases, he would argue, one can still discern the basic historical urge to attain the classical ideals. The deviations themselves are to be explained by the special circumstances in which this attempt has to be made in countries where conditions are 'unpropitious to freedom'. That is to say, the deviations are to be explained *sociologically*, by grouping and classifying the various empirical

3

cases and then constructing coherent sets of sociological conditions which may be said to be the cause for each particular type of deviation.[5]

The argument could then start, to take one example,[6] by recognizing first of all the world-wide sweep of 'the tidal wave of modernisation', but distilling its essence in the awareness of man's 'capacity to contribute to, and to profit from, industrial society'. It would then proceed to describe the erosion of the 'structure' of traditional society, conceived as a system of role relationships, and its replacement by the 'culture' of industrial society, in which the classification of people by culture is the classification by nationality. The argument would then take in the fact of the notorious 'unevenness' of the process of industrialization, in terms of geographical and cultural regions. Not only does industrialization disrupt traditional society, it disrupts it unevenly. But now there is also a common standard by which the states of advancement of different regions can be compared. The perception of uneven development creates the possibility for nationalism; it is born when the more and the less advanced populations can be easily distinguished in cultural terms. 'Nationalism is not the awakening of nations to self-consciousness: it invents nations where they do not exist — but it does need some pre-existing differentiating marks to work on . . .' The two crucial social groups which carry the struggle forward are the proletariat and the intelligentsia. The intellectuals 'will exchange second-class citizenship for a first-class citizenship plus greater privileges based on rarity'. The proletarians will exchange 'hardships-with-snubs for possibly greater hardships with national identification'. The dilemma of a choice between imitation and identity? 'Superficially', the intellectuals

> always face the crucial dilemma of choosing between 'westernising' and a *narodnik* tendency . . . But the dilemma is quite spurious: ultimately the movements invariably contain both elements, a genuine modernism and a more or less spurious concern for local culture . . . By the twentieth century, the dilemma hardly bothers anyone: the philosopher-kings of the 'underdeveloped' world all act as westernisers, and all talk like *narodniks*.

Thus the liberal dilemma is circumvented by a positive sociology. The urge for modernization is a positive fact of contemporary history. If the struggles in the backward parts of the world 'to lift onself by one's own shoelaces, economically', mean a certain repressive attitude, that too is a sociological fact, to be understood and explained. But it is on the whole a good thing that these struggles are being conducted within a framework of nationalism. There are, first of all, the 'psychological blessings' of dignity and self-respect, of the elimination of inferior grades of citizenship. There is also the fortunate consequence that these political convulsions 'do not need to be re-imported into the developed, previously imperial, territories'. They can be fought out at a distance, with a certain degree of autonomy. If the liberal conscience of the West adopts the right moral attitude of sympathy and non-interference, these backward nations will find their own chosen paths to independence, freedom and progress.

An elaboration of this sociological understanding of the phenomenon of nationalism would then inevitably proceed towards a teleology, i.e. a theory of political development. And once this step is taken, the empirical relation between nationalism and illiberal regimes can even be justified by a theory of the stages of development. Thus, it could be argued that given the very special sociological circumstances in which the new nations have to struggle to modernize themselves, it might be a perfectly rational strategy for them, in a sense, to postpone the democratic consummation of their efforts until the economic structures of their society are sufficiently industrialized and their social institutions modernized.[7] An empiricist sociology can do wonderful things to resolve the moral dilemmas of a liberal conscience.

Indeed, armed with his sociological explanation of the 'conditions' which give rise to nationalist movements, the liberal theorist can even assert that nationalism poses only a very trivial problem for the history of political ideas. 'It is not so much,' runs the self-complacent judgment of Ernest Gellner,

> that the prophets of nationalism were not anywhere near the First Division, when it came to the business of thinking . . . It is rather that these thinkers did not really make much difference. If one of them had fallen, others would have stepped into his place . . . The quality of nationalist thought would hardly have been affected much by such substitutions. Their precise doctrines are hardly worth analysing.[8]

Why? Because given the 'conditions' in which nationalism made its appearance, there was little scope for genuine doctrinal innovation or philosophical defence. Or more precisely, the necessary philosophizing had already been done, in a different context — that of the rise of 'industrialism'. (Gellner quaintly refers to Hume and Kant as the ones who 'explored, with unparalleled philosophical depth . . . the general logic of the new spirit . . .'[9]) By the time nationalism came on the scene, mankind was 'irreversibly committed to industrial society, and therefore to a society whose productive system is based on cumulative science and technology'. This commitment necessarily meant coming to terms with the requirements of industrial society, namely a cultural homogeneity and its convergence with a political unit. Cultural homogeneity was an essential concomitant of industrial society, 'and we had better make our peace with it. It is not the case . . . that nationalism imposes homogeneity; it is rather that a homogeneity imposed by objective, inescapable imperative eventually appears on the surface in the form of nationalism.'[10]

Thus nationalist thought did not even need to investigate 'the general logic' of the kind of society it was trying to build: that logic was given to it objectively. It did, of course, have to confront the problem of selecting from pre-existing cultures in agrarian society some of the distinctive elements of this new homo-geneous national culture. Nationalism 'uses some of the pre-existent cultures, generally transforming them in the process, but it cannot possibly use them all'.[11] It often defines itself in the name of some putative folk culture. But this is a myth, a piece of self-deception: that is not what it really does. In reality,

> nationalism is, essentially, the general imposition of a high culture on society, whose previously low cultures had taken up the lives of the majority, and in some

cases of the totality, of the population. It means that generalized diffusion of a school-mediated, academy-supervised idiom, codified for the requirements of reasonably precise bureaucratic and technological communication. It is the establishment of an anonymous, impersonal society, with mutually substitutable atomized individuals, held together above all by a shared culture of this kind, in place of a previous complex structure of local groups, sustained by folk cultures reproduced locally and idiosyncratically by the micro-groups themselves. That is what *really* happens.[12]

What if the new high culture happens to be the product of an alien imposition? Can it then effectively supersede the various folk cultures and become a truly homogeneous national culture? Is there not a problem of incommensurability and inter-cultural relativism which the new national culture must overcome? Gellner recognizes that there is a problem here, but it is not one which he thinks needs to be taken seriously. The fact is that with the universal acceptance of the imperative of industrialism, every national culture does manage to overcome incommensurability and relativism.

> The question concerning just *how* we manage to transcend relativism is interesting and difficult, and certainly will not be solved here. What is relevant, however, is that we somehow or other do manage to overcome it, that we are not hopelessly imprisoned within a set of cultural cocoons and their norms, and that for some very obvious reasons (shared cognitive and productive bases and greatly increased inter-social communication) we may expect fully industrial man to be even less enslaved to his local culture than was his agrarian predecessor.[13]

Nationalist thought, in other words, does not pose any special problems for either epistemology or political philosophy. All its problems can be reduced to the sociological requirements of industrial society whose universal sway provides the context for the understanding of nationalism.

It is by a recourse to sociology, in fact, that the liberal-rationalist can first identify in positive terms, and then 'sympathetically' understand, the difficult conditions under which the poor and oppressed nations of the world have to strive in order to attain those universal values of reason, liberty and progress which the latter have, at last, learnt to cherish. There is unfortunately a great historical lag which they must make up. The knowledge of backwardness is never very comforting. It is even more disturbing when its removal means a coming to terms with a culture that is alien. But that is the historical destiny of the backward nations. There can be no merit, as Plamenatz gently chides 'Western critics of nationalism', in expressing distaste for the failings of these backward peoples. 'In a world in which the strong and rich people have dominated and exploited the poor and the weak peoples, and in which autonomy is held to be a mark of dignity, of adequacy, of the capacity to live as befits human beings, in such a world this kind of nationalism is the inevitable reaction of the poor and the weak.'[14]

II

'Guilt!' an unrepentant critic of nationalism like Elie Kedourie will say: '. . . guilt, indignation, and moral passion'; '. . . powerful and corrosive feelings of guilt'.[15] This merciless self-accusation has been propagated in recent years by European publicists, and their audience, always so keen to be fair and considerate to the underdogs, have accepted the charge without protest. The very idea of nationalism being a rational and self-conscious attempt by the weak and poor peoples of the world to achieve autonomy and liberty is demonstrably false. Nationalism as an ideology is irrational, narrow, hateful and destructive. It is not an authentic product of any of the non-European civilizations which, in each particular case, it claims as its classical heritage. It is wholly a European export to the rest of the world. It is also one of Europe's most pernicious exports, for it is not a child of reason or liberty, but of their opposite: of fervent romanticism, of political messianism whose inevitable consequence is the annihilation of freedom.

Kedourie's is a severe indictment of nationalism, and one against which liberal defenders of the doctrine have been hard put to it to state their case. Of course, Kedourie's own brand of conservative politics, the ground from which he has launched his powerful attack, could easily be dismissed as archaic and irrelevant. For instance he states his belief in the essential fairness and nobility of the true principles of empire. He believes that those who rule and those who are ruled are 'different species of men' and that it is most conducive for political order when those distinctions are clearly maintained. He believes in a style of politics in which emotions and passions are kept to a minimum, where interests are not given the illusory form of moral principles, where governance is not compromised by the fickle determinations of a plebiscite. These ideas may seem quaint or bizarre, depending on one's particular taste for such old-world wisdoms. But they can be dismissed quite easily.

Why, then, the continuing debate with Kedourie, and the hesitant, almost timid, defence of the liberal's case? Anthony Smith, for instance, objects that Kedourie's description of the consequences of nationalism is a one-sided misrepresentation.[16] It overlooks 'the advantages and blessings of nationalist revivals': Dvořák and Chopin, for example, or Césaire, Senghor, 'Abduh and Tagore. Nationalism has often had a great humanizing and civilizing influence. Besides, it is misleading to portray nationalist politics merely as secret conspiracy and terrorism or nihilism and totalitarianism.

> Nobody would dispute that these have been features of some nationalisms . . . But it is only fair to recall the extreme situations in which they operated . . . Kedourie forgets the uses of nationalism in developing countries, the way in which they can legitimate new regimes desirous of maintaining political stability and keeping a fissiparous population under a single and viable harness. He forgets too the examples of nationalism providing an impetus to constitutional reforms, as in India or Ottoman Turkey, not to mention its uses in legitimising sweeping social change and modernisation . . .

This, of course, is a rather feeble rejoinder, conceding at the very start a great deal of empirical ground: 'Nobody would dispute that these have been features of *some* nationalisms . . .', but *not of all*. Smith then goes on to construct a defensible case by stating a 'core doctrine of nationalism', itself 'incomplete' and 'unstable', but capable of being rounded out by 'specific' theories that can encompass particular sets of empirical cases of movements conventionally called nationalist. The core doctrine 'fuses three ideals: collective self-determination of the people, the expression of national character and individuality, and finally the vertical division of the world into unique nations each contributing its special genius to the common fund of humanity'.[17] As such, this doctrine can be regarded 'as a not unreasonable application of Enlightenment principles to the complexities of modern politics and societies . . . it constitutes a necessary condition for the search for realistic conditions of liberty and equality, not to mention democracy, in an already divided world'.[18] About the 'specific' theories which are additionally necessary to encompass the many particular cases of nationalist movements, Smith's submission is that they are the products of very specific historical circumstances and are therefore 'morally highly variegated', and it would be wrong to make 'a *simpliste* ascription of all these concrete manifestations to the *unmediated* effects of "nationalism" '.

The problem of the 'specific', or rather the 'deviant', cases is thus consigned to the domain of the historically contingent, to be explained by a suitable sociological theory, and therefore not requiring a moral defence. The core doctrine, however, does assert a moral claim, made up of three separate but related parts: self-determination, expression of national character, and each nation contributing its special genius to the common fund of humanity. This is how the often contentious claim to national autonomy is reconciled with the ideal of universal liberty and fraternity. But in specifying this application of Enlightenment principles to the conditions of modern politics, the liberal defender of nationalism must invariably play straight into Kedourie's hand. For this specification will have to be in terms of the idea of progress, of the spread of science and rationality, of modernization and industrialization, and probably equality and democracy as well. And this will immediately destroy the central moral claim of the 'core doctrine' of nationalism, namely, the autonomy of national self-consciousness.

Now Kedourie can retort by beginning from the very first sentence of his book: 'Nationalism is a doctrine invented in Europe at the beginning of the nineteenth century.'[19] Every part of the nationalist doctrine, he will argue, can be taken apart and shown to have been derived from some species of European thought. It is totally alien to the non-European world: 'it is neither something indigenous to these areas nor an irresistible tendency of the human spirit everywhere, but rather an importation from Europe clearly branded with the mark of its origin'.[20] For the non-European world, in short, nationalist thought does not constitute an autonomous discourse.

Once that position has been surrendered, Kedourie can fire volley after volley directed at the spurious claims of a liberal doctrine of nationalism. The argument that culture, and more specifically, language, uniquely defines a nation is an invention of 19th century European writers, particularly Herder, Schlegel, Fichte and Schleiermacher, which has been subsequently taken up by nationalist intellectuals of the East. The emphasis, again, on history as a distinct mode of thought in which the life of the nation can be represented and indeed experienced is also a European innovation subsequently absorbed into the intellectual life of the new nationalisms. 'Nationalist doctrine . . . decrees that just as nations exist, so nations by definition must have a past.'[21] So every nationalism has invented a past for the nation; every nationalism speaks through a discourse, 'historical in its form but apologetic in its substance', which claims to demonstrate the rise, progress and efflorescence of its own particular genius. Modern European intellectual fashion not only decrees that a nation must have a past, it also demands that it have a future. Have faith in the historical progress of man, it preaches, and history will not let you down. The idea of progress, once again a European invention, 'is a secularized and respectable version of the medieval millennium'.[22] It goes hand in hand with an extremist, millennial style of politics, made respectable all over the world in the years following the French Revolution. 'This frenzied meliorism, which in its religious form was long suppressed and disreputable, in its secular form became the dominant strand of the political tradition first of Europe and then of the whole world.'[23] The antipathy which one often notices in nationalist revivals in Asia and Africa, the superficial rejection of things Western, is not really a rejection at all. It is part and parcel of this extremist style of politics, where the leaders of the revolution will use any means available to reach their goals, including 'conscious and deliberate manipulation of what [is], in their eyes, primitive superstition'.[24] Thus, when Bipin Chandra Pal glorifies Kāli, the dark goddess of destruction with a garland of human heads round her neck, blood dripping from the severed heads, he is 'in a line of succession from Robespierre's conjunction of virtue and terror'. '. . . the mainspring of nationalism in Asia and Africa is the same secular millennialism which had its rise and development in Europe and in which society is subjected to the will of a handful of visionaries who, to achieve their vision, must destroy all barriers between private and public'.[25] Yet another element of this extremist style of politics exported from Europe is the 'pathetic fallacy', known and demonstrated as false in the classical texts on power in every non-European civilization, which asserts 'that a government is the same as the subjects and is flesh of their flesh' and 'that the aims and interests of government are the very same as those for which the governed work and struggle'.[26] The new claimants to power in the nations of Asia and Africa constantly and profitably use this fallacy in a 'rhetoric of the heart', a fervent, impassioned, romantic, and inherently false, discourse.

'Resentment and impatience, the depravity of the rich and the virtue of the poor, the guilt of Europe and the innocence of Asia and Africa, salvation through violence, the coming reign of universal love':[27] those are the elements of nationalist thought. Each of them is an export from Europe, like the printing press, the radio, and television. Nationalist opposition to European rule is driven by a faith in a theory. Yet the theory itself, and indeed the very attitude of faith in a theory, are the gifts of Europe to the rest of the world. Nationalism sets out to assert its freedom from European domination. But in the very conception of its project, it remains a prisoner of the prevalent European intellectual fashions.

III

The last sentence is not really a paraphase of Kedourie, because he does not pose the problem in those terms. But it would be a logical implication of his critique of the liberal doctrine of nationalism if it was situated in the context of a different theoretical problem. What Kedourie does not see, and his liberal antagonists do not recognize, are the far-reaching implications of the argument that nationalist thought does not, and indeed cannot, constitute an autonomous discourse. Kedourie merely uses the argument as a convenient stick with which to beat the liberals, by showing that nationalism is an inauthentic and misguided attempt to reach illusory ideals that can never be reached and that its only consequence is violence, destruction and tyranny. The liberal, on the other hand, can object, quite justifiably, that this characterization of nationalism as something essentially irrational and illiberal is unwarranted. He then points to the specific socio-historical conditions in which most of these nationalist movements occur and suggests that one adopt a charitable view and try to understand these movements as more or less rational attempts made under difficult conditions to pursue the now universally accepted ideals of enlightenment and progress. If the conditions are right, there is reason enough to believe that these nationalisms would succeed in finding their way towards that goal. The liberal-rationalist, in other words, refuses to pose the lack of autonomy of nationalist discourse as a theoretical problem.

Indeed, to put it plainly, the Enlightenment view of rationality and progress and the historical values enshrined in that view are shared by both sides in the debate. But starting from this premise the conservatives argue, whether explicitly like Kedourie or in the form of a more implicit structure of assumptions as in a great deal of European historiography on nationalist movements in the colonial world — which sees them as a congeries of factions, patron–client relationships, traditional loyalties clothed in the garb of modern political organizations, etc. — that the non-European peoples are culturally incapable of acquiring the values of the Enlightenment. The liberals, on the other hand, assert that these irrational and regressive features are only a hangover from the past, that these countries too are involved in the historical task of modernization, and once the conditions which are detrimental to progress are removed there is no reason why they should not also proceed to approximate the values that have made the West what it is today. But neither side can pose the problem in a form in which the question can be asked: why is it that non-European colonial countries have no historical alternative but to try to approximate the given attributes of modernity when that very process of approximation means their continued subjection under a world order which only sets their tasks for them and over which they have no control?

I will now argue that it is not possible to pose this theoretical problem within the ambit of bourgeois-rationalist thought, whether conservative or liberal. For to pose it is to place thought itself, including thought that is supposedly rational and scientific, within a discourse of *power*. It is to question the very universality, the 'givenness', the sovereignty of that thought, to go to its roots and thus radically to criticize it. It is to raise the possibility that it is not just military might or industrial strength, but thought itself, which can dominate and subjugate. It is to approach the field of discourse, historical, philosophical and scientific, as a battleground of political power.

From such a perspective, the problem of nationalist thought becomes the particular manifestation of a much more general problem, namely, the problem of the bourgeois-rationalist conception of knowledge, established in the post-Enlightenment period of European intellectual history, as the moral and epistemic foundation for a supposedly universal framework of thought which perpetuates, in a real and not merely a metaphorical sense, a colonial domination. It is a framework of knowledge which proclaims its own universality; its validity, it pronounces, is independent of cultures. Nationalist thought, in agreeing to become 'modern', accepts the claim to universality of this 'modern' framework of knowledge. Yet it also asserts the autonomous identity of a national culture. It thus simultaneously rejects and accepts the dominance, both epistemic and moral, of an alien culture. Is knowledge then independent of cultures? If not, can there be knowledge which is independent of power? To pose the problem thus is to situate knowledge itself within a dialectic that relates culture to power.

In order to show a little more clearly the generality of this problem, it will be worth our while to digress into a recent debate about the cognitive status of anthropology as a science of cross-cultural understanding.[28] The problem is posed most sharply within the discipline of anthropology because here, as one participant in the debate puts it, the scientist consciously 'sets himself to understand a culture which is not his own'.[29] The anthropologist, consequently, must answer the question whether, and in what ways, culture differences affect cognition.

The most familiar problem which the Western anthropologist faces when trying to understand non-Western cultures is when beliefs held by other peoples turn out to be manifestly irrational and false when judged in terms of Western criteria of rationality or truth. The question then arises: how is one to interpret the fact that large numbers of people collectively hold beliefs that are false? Is it fair, or legitimate, or valid, to proceed by designating such beliefs as false and then to try and find out why, or how, such irrational beliefs are communally held? Would that not involve the bias of ethnocentrism? Several alternative answers have been proposed to this question. One of them seeks to apply what is called 'the principle of charity', derived from a proposal put forward by the philosopher Donald Davidson[30] which suggests that when confronted by large sets of communal beliefs which apparently seem false by our standards of rationality, we should be charitable in our interpretation and 'take it as given that most beliefs are correct'. Among the set of alternative interpretations of these beliefs, then, we (in this case, the anthropologist) should select the one which makes the largest possible number of beliefs true; that is to say, the strategy of interpretation should be to maximize the area of agreement between the anthropologist and the people he is studying. The underlying assumption is, of course, that it is only when such an area of agreement exists that interpretation becomes possible.

The pragmatic argument in favour of this principle is that even when other cultures seem vastly different from our own, the principle of charity can make large areas of those cultures open to interpretation in terms of the specific social circumstances in which those people live, especially in the area of beliefs which inform practical activity. The reason is that for any community with an ongoing social process, it is very unlikely that their everyday practical activities will be guided by large-scale communal error. There is, therefore, or so it is argued, good reason to think that the principle of charity (or its variants such as the 'principle of humanity'[31]) may yield fairly satisfactory results in at least those areas of cross-cultural understanding which involve practical activity.

Already we notice the parallels between the debate on nationalism and this one on anthropology, including a profusion of such enchantingly liberal sentiments as 'charity' and 'humanity'. The difficulty with these principles is, first of all, to decide what it means to specify adequately the social circumstances in which a community lives. Can this be done at all? Second, can we identify the particular outcomes which the community desires when it engages in particular acts, so that we can judge whether those acts, or the beliefs informing them, are rational or not? Most practising anthropologists do not seem to think that either of these is feasible. The dominant orientations in the discipline do not therefore explicitly subscribe to either of these principles. Instead they are in favour of either rejecting any search for rationality or proclaiming that there can be several alternative rationalities.

An influential approach which asserts the irrelevance of rationality in cross-cultural understanding is functionalism. Here the object of understanding is not to judge whether particular beliefs or actions are rational or not, but to discover in what ways they contribute to the functioning and persistence of the social system as a whole. Thus, whether or not particular acts are intelligible to us in terms of the avowed objectives for which they are performed, their continued performance may still be satisfactorily explained in terms of the (perhaps unintended) consequences of those acts which promote the maintenance of the social system.

The second anthropological approach which also denies the usefulness of looking for rational explanations of behaviour is the one which claims that apparently strange behaviour should be interpreted as symbolic acts: their meaning should be sought for in terms of their place within an entire symbolic pattern, whose fundamental structure may also be latent in consciousness, by which man's perception of nature, of his relations with nature and with other men, are ordered. The anthropologist's task is to discover this latent structure of the symbolic order, which will then make particular beliefs or actions meaningful in relation to other beliefs or actions within that order.

Many substantive problems have been raised about the validity and the usefulness of both functionalist and symbolist (structuralist) explanations in anthropology, but these need not concern us here. We are more interested in what the 'rationalists' have to say about these approaches. Their main argument is that both functionalism and symbolism skirt around the crucial question: why do people continue to hold beliefs which seem to us to be patently false? What, in other words, are the reasons for their acting in this apparently absurd way? And if those reasons can indeed be attributed to the specific social circumstances in which the beliefs are held, and not merely explained away by referring to the functional requirements of a social system or the internal logic of the symbolic order, then why should we not be justified in holding on to the superior cognitive status of the criteria of scientific rationality and attempting to interpret other cultures from that cognitive position?

Here there is a clear division within the rationalist camp, because one group has replied that what seems to us as an intelligible reason for acting may not be so for others. That is to say, although the actions of others may not seem rational to us, they may be perfectly rational according to entirely different criteria of rationality. The radical assertion then is: the notion of rationality may not be cross-cultural; other cultures may have their own, and equally valid because incommensurable, standards of rationality. By trying to judge other cultures according to our criteria of rationality and pronouncing them irrational, we are being unjustifiably ethnocentric, because there is no single cross-culturally valid standard of rationality: rationality is relative.

Now, there can be a strong argument of relativism which insists that each culture could have its own distinctive categorical scheme for ordering reality and its own distinctive system of logic which would make the beliefs held by people living in that culture thoroughly incommensurable with beliefs held in other cultures. This, of course, would invalidate any attempts at cross-cultural understanding, because no interpretation from outside a culture would be justified. However, the argument also depends crucially on our being able to determine the cognitive boundaries of a culture, and this is by no means a straightforward procedure. If the thought-system of a culture is indeed incommensurably different from those of others, we would not even have the background of consensus necessary to recognize the differences. This would make relativism completely unintelligible. Further, the argument applies not only to cases of judging cultures from the outside. If cognitive boundaries of cultures are indeterminate, we cannot reliably know whether we are inside or outside a culture when we attempt to interpret it. In other words, a strictly relativist position would have to be based on a holistic conception of cultures which would make any kind of interpretation, whether from within or without a culture, impossible, because our own perception of the full cognitive map of a culture — even the one which we belong to — can only be partial, and in many respects individually specific.

But most of those who have argued for a 'relativist' position on the matter of cross-cultural understanding do not seem to favour so strong an interpretation of their case. And curiously enough, many of those who think that a strictly relativist philosophical position would destroy any viable basis for a scientific understanding of society, also assert that weakly interpreted, as a basis for a sympathetic and imaginative understanding of other cultures, the relativist case says a lot of important things about an undogmatic, non-ethnocentric methodology of the social sciences. We are back, it would seem, to some kind of 'principle of charity', however formulated.

This leaves us with a somewhat paradoxical view of the debate. The 'relativist' argument originates in a critique of 'rationalist' methods of interpretation in which the main attack is directed against exaggerated claims of universal validity for those standards of evaluating social beliefs which are only specific to modern industrial society in the West. The 'relativist' thus accuses the 'rationalist' of holding an essentialist view of his own culture as a result of which he uses elements of his own belief-system to judge beliefs held in other cultures and pronounces the latter, either explicitly or by implication, to be erroneous or inferior, overlooking the fact that his own beliefs are the product of a specific socio-historical context which is different from the contexts of other cultures. This constitutes the unjustifiable ethnocentric bias in 'rationalist' attempts at cross-cultural understanding. On the other hand, the 'non-relativist' argues that relativism, in so far as it can claim a distinctive philosophical foundation, itself rests on an essentialist conception of cultures which militates against the validity of any scientific attempt at cross-cultural understanding. Each side, it would appear, ends up by accusing the other of the same crime: ahistorical essentialism.[32]

I will argue that this paradoxical situation is in fact an accurate reflection of the spurious philosophical premises on which the debate has been conducted in Anglo-American social science. A cultural essentialism has been germane to the very way in which the sciences of society have developed in the West in the post-Enlightenment period, at least since the early 19th century. It is an essentialism which is much more deep-rooted than the obvious cultural arrogance of colonial anthropology or the inept policy prescriptions of neo-Weberian modernization theory. It is indeed an aspect of the post-Enlightenment view of the world in which the idea of rational knowledge assumes a very definite form. The sciences of nature become the paradigm of all rational knowledge. And the principal characteristic of these sciences as they are now conceived is their relation to an entirely new idea of man's *control* over nature — a progressive and ceaseless process of the appropriation of nature to serve human 'interests'. By extension, a notion of 'interests' also enters into the conception of the new sciences of society. The rational knowledge of human society comes to be organized around concepts such as wealth, productive efficiency, progress, etc. all of which are defined in terms of the promotion of some social 'interests'. Yet 'interests' in society are necessarily diverse; indeed, they are stratified in terms of the relations of power. Consequently, the subject–object relation between man and nature which is central to the new conception of the sciences of nature is now subtly transferred, through the 'rational' conception of society, to relations between man and man. Thus, the sciences of society become the knowledge of the Self and of the Other. Construed in terms of rationality, it necessarily also becomes a means to the *power* of the Self over the Other. In short, knowledge becomes the means to the domination of the world.

And yet, the notion of rationality which is involved in the problem of universality and relativism is not a simple problem of positive science. If the question is 'Are the beliefs held by particular groups of people true or false?' a reasonable approach would seem to be to answer the question by reference to the currently accepted methods, procedures and theories in the particular scientific discipline to which the belief relates. Thus, the question of whether Kalabari beliefs about the curative properties of particular herbs are true or not can be answered within the theoretical knowledge currently provided by medical science, including considerations of possible psychosomatic effects of the particular procedures by which the drugs are administered in Kalabari society. However, it is clear that not all beliefs in society will admit a meaningful scientific answer as to whether they are true or not. There are large classes of beliefs for which the criteria true/false make little sense in terms of science as we know it today. However, to the extent that questions of this sort are at all answerable within currently established scientific theories, ethnicity or culture will be in principle an irrelevant consideration.

But, by pointing out that answers to such questions are only meaningful within 'currently accepted' scientific methods or theories, or that they can or cannot be answered only in terms of science 'as we know it today', we are acknowledging the historicity of scientific methods themselves -- the fact that they rest only on the currently prevailing consensus among scientists, with a broad penumbra where they are subjects of varying degrees of contention, that even currently accepted methods are subject to change, including paradigmatic changes of the Kuhnian type, and that they too are affected (assuming we are not prepared to go so far as to say 'determined') by the socio-historical processes in the societies in which they appear. Again, when we say that in answering questions of this sort, ethnicity or culture are 'in principle' irrelevant, we recognize the possibility that this may not actually be the case in every instance of scientific practice. There can be, for example, a major problem of determining precisely *what* a particular belief is, because it may involve a complicated and not unproblematical exercise of trying to unravel the *meaning* of particular utterances or acts or behaviour of particular people. Here, the question of culture may well be considered crucial, and a host of problems would have to be sorted out before we can say that we have identified a belief which is held by a particular group of people. But these are problems which arise *before* the stage where we can ask whether a belief is true or not.

The second way in which ethnicity becomes relevant to scientific practice concerns the social structure of scientific research itself, in this case in the international or inter-cultural dimension. It could be argued that a given structure of the scientific profession — its pattern of funding, its assignment of research priorities, its very choice of problems for investigation and, inevitably, therefore, its judgment of what does or does not constitute a legitimate or worthwhile subject for scientific research — may be so biased in geographical, and hence cultural, terms that it overlooks, ignores· or dogmatically rejects insights into the nature of the physical or social world which may have been developed in supposedly 'non-scientific' cultures. These insights may form a part of the technological practices of various people in various parts of the world; or of the expressive or symbolic ordering of their relations with nature and with one another; or of their pre-theoretical practical guides to the activities of everyday life; or of their speculative philosophies about the nature of the world; or (who knows?) of their theoretical formulations about specific physical or social processes which have been overlooked or ignored by the currently dominant international structure of science because they were embedded within larger speculative systems of philosophy that were deemed irrational, archaic or morally repugnant. In this sense, ethnocentrism does affect the development of scientific knowledge.

But when one raises the question of whether people in other cultures are rational or not, one does not simply mean whether their beliefs are true in relation to currently accepted scientific theories. Anyone with even a modicum of awareness of the philosophical problems involved in answering the question 'Is such and such a statement scientifically true?' will realize that it is only in very rare cases that one can obtain even a reasonably unambiguous answer in the affirmative. If this was the meaning of the concept of rational belief, then the problem of rationality in sociological theory would be reduced to one of very minor importance, because very few beliefs held in societies anywhere in the world, including the contemporary Western world, would, by this definition, qualify as rational. No, rationality as the notion is used in current debates is wider than mere scientific truth. It is seen as incorporating a certain way of looking at the properties of nature, of ordering our knowledge of those properties in a certain consistent and coherent way, of using this knowledge for adaptive advantage vis-à-vis nature. It is, as Max Weber would have put it – and it does not matter if present-day votaries of rationality do not agree with his definition of its precise content — an ethic. Rationality becomes the normative principle of a certain way of life which is said to promote a certain way of thinking, namely, science. Hence, the question of culture does become relevant.

It is important to note, however, that the stricter definition of scientific truth is now contained within the wider notion of rationality as an ethic. So much so that the ethic of rationality is now seen to be characteristic of 'scientifically-oriented' or 'theoretically-oriented' cultures. And thus, by a conceptual sleight of hand, the epistemic privilege which is due to 'scientific truth' is appropriated by entire cultures. What results is an *essentialism*: certain historically specific correspondences between certain elements in the structure of beliefs in European society and certain, albeit spectacular, changes in techno-economic conditions of production are attributed the quality of essences which are said to characterize Western cultures as a whole. It is an essentialism which, when imposed on historical time, divides up the history of Western society into pre-scientific and scientific, and casts every other culture of the world into the darkness of unscientific traditionalism. Initially, this essentialism enjoys a straightforwardly ethnic privilege: the superiority of the European people. Later, it is given a moral privilege, encompassing as in the post-Enlightenment theories of progress — positivism, utilitarianism, Weberian sociology — a historically progressive philosophy of life. And finally, when all of these privileged positions are challenged with the spread of anti-colonial movements, it is the epistemic privilege which has become the last bastion of global supremacy for the cultural values of Western industrial societies. It is a privilege which sanctions the assertion of cultural supremacy while assiduously denying at the same time that it has anything to do with cultural evaluations. Relativist or rationalist, each one is keen to outdo the other in the radicalness of his stand against ethnocentric bias.

It is not trivial to point out here that in this whole debate about the possibility of cross-cultural understanding, the scientist is always one of 'us': he is a Western anthropologist, modern, enlightened and self-conscious (and it does not matter what his nationality or the colour of his skin happens to be). The objects of study are 'other' cultures — always non-Western. No one has raised the possibility, and the accompanying problems, of a 'rational' understanding of 'us' by a member of the 'other' culture — of, let us say, a Kalabari anthropology of the white man. It could be argued, of course, that when we consider the problem of relativism, we consider the relations between cultures in the abstract and it does not matter if the subject–object relation between Western and non-Western cultures is reversed: the relations would be isomorphic.

But it would not: that is precisely why we do not, and probably never will, have a Kalabari anthropology of the white man. And that is why even a Kalabari anthropology of the Kalabari will adopt the same representational form, if not the same substantive conclusions, as the white man's anthropology of the Kalabari. For there is a relation of power involved in the very conception of the autonomy of cultures. That is, in fact, why the problem of nationalist thought is only a particular manifestation of this much more general problem. If nationalism expresses itself in a frenzy of irrational passion, it does so *because* it seeks to represent itself in the image of the Enlightenment and *fails* to do so. For Enlightenment itself, to assert its sovereignty as the universal ideal, needs its Other; if it could ever actualize itself in the real world as the truly universal, it would in fact destroy itself. No matter how much the liberal-rationalist may wonder, the Cunning of Reason has not met its match in nationalism.[33] On the contrary, it has seduced, apprehended and imprisoned it: that is what this book is all about.

IV

So far I have argued that the problems of a liberal doctrine of nationalism can be traced back to a much more fundamental question about the moral and epistemic status of a bourgeois-rational conception of universal history. However, I cannot hope to settle the matter simply by designating it as a problem of 'bourgeois' knowledge. For we see much the same sorts of problems appearing in Marxist discussions of nationalism as well.

I will not go into the issue of what Marx himself had to say about nationalism.[34] However, what can be said quite definitely on this subject is that in his own work Marx never directly addressed himself to nationalism as a theoretical problem. Much of the debate on this question is about the implications of his general theoretical scheme, or about inferences from the various comments he made on the subject during a very active literary and political career. We are more concerned here about the more influential interpretations of Marxism addressed to what has come to be called 'the national question', and more particularly the problem of nationalism in the non-European world where it has taken the compendium form of 'the national *and* colonial question'.

The question was long debated in the Second and Third Internationals.[35] The most remarkable contribution came from Lenin who, working out his ideas from the immediate practical problems facing the revolution in a huge multi-ethnic empire, highlighted the central question of political democracy as the keystone of Marxist analyses of nationalism. It was this emphasis which led him to formulate his famous thesis on the rights of nations to self-determination.[36] But Lenin's proposals were not directed towards the construction of a general theoretical paradigm for the study of nationalism, and in the tumultuous period of national liberation movements since the 1930s, Marxists have continued to argue about the question.

Horace B. Davis has recently attempted a summarization of several of these arguments.[37] He too acknowledges that there are two types of nationalism,[38] one the nationalism of the Enlightenment which 'was by and large rational rather than emotional', and the other 'based on culture and tradition', developed by German romantic writers such as Herder and Fichte, which asserted that the nation was a natural community and therefore 'something sacred, eternal, organic, carrying a deeper justification than the works of men'. But even this second type was European in origin. 'This idea of the nation as preceding the state and eventually leading to its formation is very distinctly European; it has no relevance to the problems of newly formed nations such as most of those in Africa, where the state preceded the nation and conditioned its whole existence.'[39]

What then about nationalism in the non-European world? The national question here is, of course, historically fused with a colonial question. The assertion of national identity was, therefore, a form of the struggle against colonial exploitation. Yet an assertion of traditional cultural values would often be inconsistent with the conditions of historical progress. There is thus a very real dilemma: 'whether to consider nationalism a rationalist, secular, modern movement, or whether to emphasize the more distinctively national elements, many of which are frankly atavistic and irrelevant to modern conditions'.[40] But no matter how tormenting the dilemma for those in the thick of the struggle, the outcome itself was historically determined. Between the modern and the traditional trends within nationalism, 'the one that wins out in the end is the modernizing, Westernizing element, but it may be only after a prolonged struggle'.[41]

The question therefore was not one of taking a moral position with respect to nationalism qua nationalism, but one of judging its probable historical consequences. 'Nationalism, then, is not in itself irrational, but it may be irrationally applied. Atavistic nationalism cannot be condemned out of hand; when considered as part of a movement for a people to regain its pride and self respect, it has a constructive aspect. But belligerent, aggressive, chauvinistic nationalism is a menace and thus irrational from the point of view of humanity as a whole.'[42] Nationalism had to be looked at in its instrumental aspect: whether or not it furthered the universal movement of historical progress. 'Nationalism', Davis says,

> is not a thing, even an abstract thing, but a process, an implement . . . One does not take a position for or against a hammer, or a can opener, or any other implement. When used for murder, the hammer is no doubt a weapon; when used for building a house, it is a constructive tool. Nationalism considered as the vindication of a particular culture is morally neutral; considered as a movement against national oppression, it has a positive moral content; considered as the vehicle of aggression, it is morally indefensible.[43]

This book by Davis may be a particularly unsubtle example of Marxist thinking on the subject of nationalism. If so, let us take a more recent, and in every way more sophisticated, treatment of the subject and see where it gets us: I have in mind Benedict Anderson's *Imagined Communities*.[44] Anderson's intervention is highly unorthodox, because far from following the dominant tendency in Marxist discussions on the 'national question', typically represented by Stalin's oft-quoted formulation,[45] he refuses to 'define' a nation by a set of external and abstract criteria. On the contrary, he fundamentally subverts the determinist scheme by asserting that the nation is 'an imagined political community'. It is not uniquely produced by the constellation of certain objective social facts; rather, the nation is 'thought out', 'created'.

At first glance, this may seem to be fairly close to Gellner's position: 'Nationalism is not the awakening of nations to self-consciousness: it invents nations where they do not exist.' But Anderson is quick to mark the difference. For Gellner 'invent' means 'fabrication' and 'falsity', a piece of historical disingenuousness; he cannot regard the thinking out of a nation as genuine creation.[46] What does 'creation' mean? Let us follow Anderson's argument.

Historically, the political community of nation superseded the preceding 'cultural systems' of religious community and dynastic realm. In the process there occurred 'a fundamental change . . . in modes of apprehending the world, which, more than anything else, made it possible to "think" the nation'.[47] It was the 'coalition of Protestantism and print-capitalism' which brought about this change. 'What, in a positive sense, made the new communities imaginable was a half-fortuitous, but explosive, interaction between a system of production and productive relations (capitalism), a technology of communications (print), and the fatality of human linguistic diversity.'[48] The innumerable and varied ideolects of pre-print Europe were now 'assembled, within definite limits, into print-languages far fewer in number'. This was crucial for the emergence of national consciousness because print-languages created 'unified fields of exchange and communications' below Latin and above the spoken vernaculars, gave a new fixity to language, and created new kinds of 'languages-of-power' since some dialects were closer to the print-languages and dominated them while others remained dialects because they could not insist on their own printed form.

Once again historically, three distinct types or 'models' of nationalism emerged. 'Creole nationalism' of the Americas was built upon the ambitions of classes whose economic interests were ranged against the metropolis. It also drew upon liberal and enlightened ideas from Europe which provided ideological criticisms of imperialism and *anciens régimes*. But the shape of the new imagined communities was created by 'pilgrim creole functionaries and provincial creole printmen'. Yet as a 'model' for emulation, creole nationalism remained incomplete, because it lacked linguistic communality and its state form was both retrograde and congruent with the arbitrary administrative boundaries of the imperial order.

The second 'model' was that of the linguistic nationalisms of Europe, a model of the independent national state which henceforth became 'available for pirating'.

> But precisely because it was by then a known model, it imposed certain 'standards' from which too-marked deviations were impossible . . . Thus the 'populist' character of the early European nationalisms, even when led, demagogically, by the most backward social groups, was deeper than in the Americas: serfdom had to go, legal slavery was unimaginable — not least because the conceptual model was set in ineradicable place.[49]

The third 'model' was provided by 'official nationalism' — typically, Russia. This involved the imposition of cultural homogeneity from the top, through state action. 'Russification' was a project which could be, and was, emulated elsewhere.

All three modular forms were available to third world nationalisms in the 20th century. Just as creole functionaries first perceived a national meaning in the imperial administrative unit, so did the 'brown or black Englishman' when he made his bureaucratic pilgrimage to the metropolis. On return,

> the apex of his looping flight was the highest administrative centre to which he was assigned: Rangoon, Accra, Georgetown, or Colombo. Yet in each constricted journey he found bilingual travelling companions with whom he came to feel a growing communality. In his journey he understood rather quickly that his point of origin — conceived either ethnically, linguistically, or geographically — was of small significance . . . it did not fundamentally determine his destination or his companions. Out of this pattern came that subtle, half-concealed transformation, step by step, of the colonial-state into the national-state, a transformation made possible not only by a solid continuity of personnel, but by the established skein of journeys through which each state was experienced by its functionaries.[50]

But this only made possible the emergence of a national consciousness. Its rapid spread and acquisition of popular roots in the 20th century are to be explained by the fact that these journeys were now made by 'huge and variegated crowds'. Enormous increases in physical mobility, imperial

'Russification' programmes sponsored by the colonial state as well as by corporate capital, and the spread of modern-style education created a large bilingual section which could mediate linguistically between the metropolitan nation and the colonized people. The vanguard role of the intelligentsia derived from its bilingual literacy. 'Print-literacy already made possible the imagined community floating in homogeneous, empty time . . . Bilingualism meant access, through the European language-of-state, to modern Western culture in the broadest sense, and, in particular, to the models of nationalism, nation-ness, and nation-state produced elsewhere in the course of the nineteenth century.'[51]

Third-world nationalisms in the 20th century thus came to acquire a 'modular' character. 'They can, and do, draw on more than a century and a half of human experience and three earlier models of nationalism. Nationalist leaders are thus in a position consciously to deploy civil and military educational systems modelled on official nationalism's; elections, party organizations, and cultural celebrations modelled on the popular nationalisms of 19th century Europe; and the citizen–republican idea brought into the world by the Americas.' Above all, the very idea of 'nation' is now nested firmly in virtually all print-languages, and nation-ness is virtually inseparable from political consciousness.

'In a world in which the national state is the overwhelming norm, all of this means that nations can now be imagined without linguistic communality — not in the naive spirit of *nostros los Americanos*, but out of a general awareness of what modern history has demonstrated to be possible.'[52]

Anderson's chief contribution to the Marxist debate on the national question is to emphatically pose the ideological creation of the nation as a central problem in the study of national movements. In doing this he also highlights the social process of creation of modern language communities. Yet, instead of pursuing the varied, and often contradictory, *political* possibilities inherent in this process, Anderson seals up his theme with a sociological determinism. What, if we look closely, are the substantive differences between Anderson and Gellner on 20th century nationalism? None. Both point out a fundamental change in ways of perceiving the social world which occurs before nationalism can emerge: Gellner relates this change to the requirements of 'industrial society', Anderson more ingeniously to the dynamics of 'print-capitalism'. Both describe the characteristics of the new cultural homogeneity which is sought to be imposed on the emerging nation: for Gellner this is the imposition of a common high culture on the variegated complex of local folk cultures, for Anderson the process involves the formation of a 'print-language' and the shared experience of the 'journeys' undertaken by the colonized intelligentsia. In the end, both see in third-world nationalisms a profoundly 'modular' character. They are invariably shaped according to contours outlined by given historical models: 'objective, inescapable imperative', 'too-marked deviations . . . impossible'.

Where in all this is the working of the imagination, the intellectual process of creation? For Gellner the problem does not arise, because even when nations are 'invented', it is out of necessity: some distinguishing cultural marks simply have to be chosen in order to identify the nation, and it is not a particularly interesting problem for him to study the intellectual process by which this is done. But Anderson? He too confines his discussion to the 'modular' character of 20th century nationalisms, without noticing the twists and turns, the suppressed possibilities, the contradictions still unresolved. Consequently, in place of Gellner's superciliousness, Anderson has to conclude on a note of unmitigated political pessimism: 'No one imagines, I presume, that the broad masses of the Chinese people give a fig for what happens along the border between Cambodia and Vietnam. Nor is it at all likely that Khmer and Vietnamese peasants wanted wars between their peoples, or were consulted in the matter. In a very real sense these were "chancellery wars" in which popular nationalism was mobilized after the fact and always in a language of self-defence.'[53] Thus, it is all a matter of a vanguard intelligentsia coming to state power by 'mobilizing' popular nationalism and using the 'machiavellian' instruments of official nationalism. Like religion and kinship, nationalism is an anthropological fact, and there is nothing else to it.

Marxists have found it extremely hard to escape the liberal dilemma we described in the previous section. More often than not, they have adopted exactly the same methods as those of the liberals — either a resort to *sociologism*, i.e. fitting nationalism to certain universal and inescapable sociological constraints of the modern age, or alternatively, reducing the two contending trends within nationalism, one traditional and conservative and the other rational and progressive, to their sociological determinants, or invoking a *functionalism*, i.e. taking up an appropriate attitude towards a specific nationalism by reference to its consequences for universal history. The problem can be even better illustrated if we shift our sights from general theoretical treatments to the analysis of particular nationalist movements. I will refer to a debate about India, a country where Marxist historiography has had to establish itself by trying to confront a nationalist intellectual orthodoxy.

V

To start with, Marxist historians in India had taken their cue from a well-known remark by Marx in his 1853 article on 'British Rule in India':

> England, it is true, in causing a social revolution in Hindustan, was actuated only by the vilest interests, and was stupid in her manner of enforcing them. But that is not the question. The question is, can mankind fulfil its destiny without a fundamental revolution in the social state of Asia? If not, whatever may have been the crimes of England she was the unconscious tool of history in bringing about that revolution.[54]

Here too, as in the liberal history of nationalism, history becomes episodic, marked by one Great Event which is in every sense the watershed, dividing up historical time into past and future, tradition and modernity, stagnation and development — and inescapably, into bad and good: despotism and liberty, superstition and enlightenment, priestcraft and the triumph of reason. For India, the Great Event was the advent of British rule which terminated centuries of despotism, superstition and vegetative life and ushered in a new era of change — of 'destruction' as well as 'regeneration', destruction of antiquated tradition and the emergence of modern, secular and national forces.

A whole generation of Marxist historians of India,[55] despite the many political differences among them, agreed that the intellectual history of India in the 19th and 20th centuries was a history of the struggle between the forces of reaction and those of progress. The approach was both sociological and functional. There was the attempt to reduce 'traditional-conservative' and 'rational-modernist' ideas to their social roots, i.e. to 'reactionary' and 'progressive' classes, respectively. At the same time, there was the attempt to judge the effectivity of these ideas in terms of their consequences, i.e. whether or not they furthered the national democratic struggle against colonial domination and exploitation. And the results of these two simultaneous inquiries often turned out to be contradictory. The national was not always secular and modern, the popular and democratic quite often traditional and even fanatically anti-modern.

The 1970s saw several attempts to question the earlier applications of Marxism to Indian intellectual history. In 1972 official celebrations were held to mark the bicentenary of the birth of Rammohun Roy (1772-1833), the first great 'modernizer' and father of the 19th century 'renaissance' in Indian thought. A volume of critical essays[56] brought out on the occasion contained several contributions in the earlier genre, but there were others which questioned the whole premise of the characterization of the 'renaissance' and even the categories of tradition/modernity. The main theoretical ground on which these critiques were located was a reassessment of the nature of the relationship between culture and structure or, to use an orthodox Marxist terminology which already in the very thrust of the critique seemed to lose some of its theoretical value, between superstructure and base. It was all very well, these critics argued, to pick out the many undoubtedly modern elements in the thought of the 19th century social reformers and ideologues, but what significance do these elements of modernity acquire when looked at in the context of the evolving colonial economy of the same period, of massive deindustrialization and destitution, of unbearable pressures on the land leading to a virtually irreversible process of regressive rent-exploitation and stagnation in levels of productivity, of the crushing of peasant resistance, of the growing social gulf rather than bonds of alliance between a modernized, western-educated, urban elite and the rest of the nation? In what sense can this modernity be reconciled with any meaningful conception of the national–popular?

These questions were posed from within a Marxist framework, but earlier Marxist formulations on the 19th century renaissance were severely criticized. Sumit Sarkar,[57] for instance, showed that Indian Marxists in interpreting the evolution of Indian thought as a conflict between two trends, 'westernist' or 'modernist' on the one hand and 'traditionalist' on the other, had, notwith-standing the many analytical intricacies, wholeheartedly plumped for westernism as the historically progressive trend. He then argued: 'An unqualified equation of the "westernizers" . . . with modernism or progress almost inevitably leads on to a more positive assessment of British rule, English education, and the nineteenth-century protagonists of both . . .' In fact, the entire 'tradition–modernization' dichotomy served as a cover under which 'the grosser facts of imperialist political and economic exploitation [were] very often quietly tucked away in a corner'. As facts stand, Rammohun Roy's break with tradition was 'deeply contradictory', accommodating within the same corpus of thinking numerous compromises with orthodox, Hindu-elitist and, by his own enlightened standards, clearly irrational ways of thought and practice, and in any case it was a break only 'on the intellectual plane and not at the level of basic social transformation'. In his economic thinking, he accepted *in toto* the then fashionable logic of free trade and seemed to visualize 'a kind of dependent but still real bourgeois development in Bengal in close collaboration with British merchants and entrepreneurs'. This was an utterly absurd illusion, because colonial subjection would never permit full-blooded bourgeois modernity but only a 'weak and distorted caricature'.[58]

The argument was therefore that while there were elements of modernity in the new cultural and intellectual movements in 19th century India, these cannot become meaningful unless they are located in their relation, on the one hand, to the changing socio-economic structure of the country, and on the other, to the crucial context of power, i.e. the reality of colonial subjection. When thus located, the achievements of early 19th century 'modernizers' such as Rammohun seemed limited within a Hindu-elitist, colonial, almost comprador, framework.

This argument was stated at much greater length in Asok Sen's study[59] of the career of another 19th century social reformer of Bengal, Iswar Chandra Vidyasagar (1820-1891). Sen placed the problem in the theoretical context of Antonio Gramsci's discussion of the relation of intellectuals to more fundamental forces of social transformation. The mere acceptance of new ideas or their original structure of assumptions and implications did not in themselves mean much; major changes in thought and attitude were, in fact, brought about 'by the capacity of nascent social forces to achieve goals of transformation [often] not entirely clarified in the original postulates of reasoning or speculation'.[60] What was crucial, therefore, was a fundamental class striving for class hegemony and advance of social production. Without such a class, 'the cultural influence of intellectuals is reduced to an essentially abstract phenomenon giving no consistent direction of significant social renewal; their influence is limited to tiny intellectual groups who have no creative bonds with a broader social consensus'.[61]

In the specific context of 19th century Bengal, the middle class was not a fundamental class in this sense, nor were its intellectuals organic to any fundamental project of social transformation or conquest of hegemony. The new middle class was a product of English education. But in an economy under direct colonial control, in which there was little prospect for the release of forces of industrialization, the attempt 'to achieve through education what was denied to the economy' was utterly anomalous.

> The new intelligentsia was stirred by various elements of western thought — the ideas of liberal freedom, rational humanism and scientific advance. But the learned aspirations of the middle class were undone by its dysfunctional role in the process of production; the former called for goals which the latter necessarily precluded. Hence, modernity could hardly be a force of objective social achievement . . . For a middle class with no positive role in social production, the theories of Locke, Bentham and Mill acted more as sources of confusion about the nature of the state and society under colonial rule . . . the middle class had neither the position, nor the strength to mediate effectively between polity and production. There lay the travesty of imported ideas of individual rights and rationality.[62]

Vidyasagar's own attempts at social reform, for instance, placed great reliance upon liberal backing by the colonial government. The failure of those attempts showed that his hopes were misplaced. On the other hand, he did not find any effective support for his schemes from within his own class. When arguing for reform, Vidyasagar, despite his own professed disregard for the sanctity or reasonableness of the *śāstra*, felt compelled to look for scriptural support for his programmes. He did not think it feasible to attempt to create a 'nonconformism outside the bond of canonical orthodoxy'. In fact, this remained a major ideological anomaly in all 19th century attempts to 'modernize' religion and social practice — 'a spurious conciliation of Indian idealism and imported liberal sanctions' — which led to a major backlash after 1880 in the form of movements to 'revive tradition', movements that were openly hostile to the earlier decades of 'reason and enlightenment'.

> Thus, a reformation with no entrenchment in conditions of mass hegemony failed not only to produce its Anabaptist complement, but the reaction, when it inevitably set in, hastened the reformation to its day of burial.[63]

In Sen, therefore, the argument becomes sharper. The 19th century intelligentsia may have genuinely welcomed the new ideas of reason and rationality, and some may even have shown considerable courage and enterprise in seeking to 'modernize' social customs and attitudes. But the fundamental forces of transformation were absent in colonial society. As a result, there was no possibility for the emergence of a consistently rational set of beliefs or practices. Liberalism stood on highly fragile foundations; 'reason dwindled to merely individual means of self-gratification without social responsibility'.[64] The half-heartedness and ambiguity was part of the very process of bourgeois development in a colonial country. '. . . the dialectics of loyalty and opposition' did not permit 'a clear division among the native bourgeoisie or the entire middle class into two exclusive categories of collaborators and opponents of imperialism'.[65] In India, bourgeois opposition to imperialism was always ambiguous.

The attempt to relate developments in thought to the evolving socio-economic structure of a colonial country inevitably led, therefore, to the problem of power: the subjection of a colonial country and the question of loyalty or opposition to the imperial power. And once put in that perspective, the modern and the national seemed to diverge in fundamental ways.

It is the problem of power which is placed at the centre of another critique of the 19th century 'renaissance' — Ranajit Guha's analysis of a play on the 1860-61 Indigo Uprising in Bengal by the playwright Dinabandhu Mitra.[66] This play has always been regarded in nationalist circles in Bengal as a remarkably bold indictment of the depredations of English planters in the Indian countryside and as a classical portrayal of the bravery and determination of the peasantry in their resistance to colonialism. But Guha shows the innately liberal-humanitarian assumptions underlying Dinabandhu's criticism of the planters, assumptions he shared with virtually the whole of the new intelligentsia of the 19th century. Thus, underlying the criticism of the lawlessness of the planters and of the action of a few foolish and inconsiderate English officials, there was an abiding faith in the rationality and impartiality of English law and in the good intentions of the colonial administration taken as a whole. Never did the thought occur in the minds of these newly enlightened gentlemen, despite their fondness for justice and liberty, to question the legitimacy of British rule in India. In fact, it was the very existence of British power in India that was regarded as the final and most secure guarantee against lawlessness, superstition and despotism. Not only that, the image of the resolute peasant defending his rights against the predatory planter, as represented in elite accounts such as Dinabandhu's *Nil Darpan*, is that of an enlightened liberal, conscious of his rights as an individual, willing to go to great lengths to defend those rights against recalcitrant officials, even succumbing to 'brief, intermittent bursts' of violence, but all the while believing in the fundamental legitimacy of the social order. This was a far cry from any truly revolutionary appreciation by a progressive intelligentsia of the strength of peasant resistance to colonialism and of its potentials for the construction of a new 'national–popular' consciousness. What the play does reveal is, in fact, an attitude of collaboration, between a colonial government and its educated native collaborators, sealed by the marriage of law and literacy. The sympathy of the intelligentsia for the victims of violence of indigo planters and the support by large sections of the rich and middling sorts of people in town and countryside for the cause of the peasants are explained by a specific conjuncture of interests and events. In the overall estimate, such opposition only opened up

> an immense hinterland of compromise and reformism into which to retreat from a direct contest for power with the colonial masters . . . And, thus, 'improvement', that characteristic ideological gift of nineteenth-century British capitalism, is made to pre-empt and replace the urge for a revolutionary transformation of society.

The formulation of the problem now encompasses a great deal of complexity in the relations between thought, culture and power. First of all, there is the question of the effectiveness of thought as a vehicle of change. If the imperatives, conditions and consequences of change have been thought out within an elaborate and reasonably consistent framework of knowledge, does this itself indicate that the social potentials exist for the change to occur? The assumption here would be that if the conditions did not exist at least potentially, then the theory could not have been thought. Or is the more crucial element the existence of determinate social forces, in the form of a class or an alliance of classes, which have the will and strength to act as agents of transformation, perhaps even without the aid of an elaborately formulated theoretical apparatus to think out the process of change? The sociological determinist would say that the conditions for the emergence of a nationalist ideology for the transformation of an agrarian into an industrial society are present universally. The only point of interest for particular nationalisms is the specific cultural demarcation of a national identity which wills for itself a distinct political unit. Yet the historical evidence marshalled in the above debate suggests that the social forces which could be said to have favoured the transformation of a medieval agrarian society into a rational modern one were not unambiguously nationalist, while those that were opposed to colonial domination were not necessarily in favour of a transformation.

Second, there is the question of the relation of thought to the existing culture of the society, i.e. to the way in which the social code already provides a set of correspondences between signs and meanings to the overwhelming mass of the people. What are the necessary steps when a new group of thinkers and reformers seek to substitute a new code in the place of the old one? Do they set up a radical group of nonconformists, or do they gradually 'modernize' the tradition? If such a cultural transformation does take place, what is the role of an ideological leadership — a vanguard intelligentsia — in bringing it about?

Third, there is the question of the implantation into new cultures of categories and frameworks of thought produced in other — alien — cultural contexts. Is the positive knowledge contained in these frameworks neutral to the cultural context? Do they have different social consequences when projected on different socio-cultural situations? Even more interestingly, do the categories and theoretical relations themselves acquire new meanings in their new cultural context? What then of the positivity of knowledge?

Fourth, when the new framework of thought is directly associated with a relation of dominance in the cross-cultural context of power, what, in the new cultural context, are the specific changes which occur in the original categories and relations within the domain of thought? That is to say, if relations of dominance and subordination are perceived as existing *between* cultures, which is what happens under colonial rule, what are the specific ways in which frameworks of thought conceived in the context of the dominant culture are received and transformed in the subordinate culture?

Finally, all of the above relations between thought and culture have a bearing on still another crucial question — the changing relations of power *within* the society under colonial domination. And here, even if we grant that the social consequences of particular frameworks of thought produced in the metropolitan countries would be drastically different in the colonized culture, i.e. the historical correspondence between thought and change witnessed in the age of Enlightenment in the West would not obtain in the colonized East, we would still have to answer the question, 'What are the specific relations between thought and change which do obtain in those countries?'

Unlike the sociological determinist who is satisfied with the supposedly empirical 'fact' that all nationalist leaderships manage 'somehow or other' to transcend the problems of cross-cultural relativism inherent in the colonial situation, we will need to pose this as a matter of fundamental significance for an understanding, first, of the relationship between colonialism and nationalism, and second, of the specific structure of domination which is built under the aegis of the post-colonial national state.

The critique of the 1970s seriously damaged the old structure of assumptions about the Indian 'renaissance'. It emphasized at numerous points the impossibility of making the distinction between a progressive and a conservative trend within the 19th century intelligentsia. It showed, in fact, that on most fundamental questions virtually the whole intelligentsia shared the same presuppositions. But those presuppositions were neither unambiguously modern, nor unambiguously national. Liberal, secular and rational attitudes were invariably compromised by concessions to scriptural or canonical authority or. even more ignominiously, by succumbing to pressures for conformity or to enticements of individual material advancement. On the other hand, sentiments of nationality flowed out of an unconcealed faith in the basic goodness of the colonial order and the progressive support of the colonial state. All this reflected the absence of a fundamental social class infused by a revolutionary urge to transform society and to stamp it with the imprint of its own unquestioned hegemony. The Indian 'renaissance' had no historical links with the revolutionary mission of a progressive bourgeoisie seeking to create a nation in its own image.

Interestingly, however, even in their critique of the 'renaissance' argument, the historians of the 1970s did not relinquish the analogy with European history as their basic structure of reference. Indeed, the critique was possible only by reference to that analogue. The point of the critique was, in fact, to show that if modern Europe is taken as the classic example of the progressive significance of an intellectual revolution in the history of the emergence of the capitalist economy and the modern state, then the intellectual history of 19th century India did not have this significance. As the harbinger of a bourgeois and a national revolution, the Indian 'renaissance' was partial, fragmented; indeed, it was a failure. Thus, what was meant to be modern became increasingly alienated from the mass of the people. What seemed to assert greater ideological sway over the nation were newer forms of conservatism. And yet those seemingly conservative movements in thought were themselves premised on the same presuppositions — 'modern' presuppositions — as those of the 'renaissance'.

VI

The Indian debate has brought up these questions within the ambit of Marxist theory, but more specifically within the relations between culture and politics suggested in the writings of Antonio Gramsci. In so doing, it has brought to the foreground of the discussion several problems with the conventional Marxist approach to the 'national and colonial question'. Recent European discussions on Gramsci have highlighted the importance of his ideas not merely in the context of revolutionary politics in Europe, but for problems such as the national and colonial questions or the nature of the post-colonial state in the countries of Asia, Africa and Latin America. Leonardo Paggi, for instance, has argued:

> If, beginning in 1924, Gramsci's position is characterised by an emphasis on the specificity of the Western European situation with regard to czarist Russia, his contribution cannot be reduced to the recognition of this specificity . . . The most favourable conditions do not always necessarily exist in those countries where the development of capitalism and industrialism has reached the highest level . . . To theorise this possibility was not merely a matter of claiming the existence of conditions favourable to a revolutionary development *even* in countries which have not yet reached capitalist maturity, but also, and more importantly, to have completely changed the analytical tools. It meant primarily the abandonment of the traditional interpretation of historical materialism which had shown itself inadequate not only in the East, but also in the West . . . In the East as well as the West, marxism had to reject the interpretative scheme based on the relation of cause and effect between structure and superstructure. It had to reintroduce the concept of the social relations of production in political science, according to Gramsci's analysis of power relations.[67]

It is Gramsci's conception of the state as 'coercion plus hegemony' and of the struggle for power as 'domination plus intellectual–moral leadership' which enabled the Indian critics to examine afresh the so-called 'renaissance' in 19th century India in terms of the aspirations of a new class to assert its intellectual–moral leadership over a modernizing Indian nation and to stake its claim to power in opposition to its colonial masters. But the examination also demonstrated how, under the specific conditions of the economy and polity of a colonial country, this domination necessarily rests on extremely fragile foundations and the intellectual–moral leadership of the dominant classes over the new nation remains fragmented.

Even more specifically, Gramsci's writings provide another line of enquiry which becomes useful in the understanding of such apparently deviant, but historically numerous, cases of the formation of capitalist nation-states. In his famous 'Notes on Italian History',[68] Gramsci outlines an argument about the 'passive revolution of capital'. Contrasting the history of the formation of the Italian state in the period of the Risorgimento with the classic political revolution in France in 1789, Gramsci says that the new claimants to power in Italy, lacking the social strength to launch a full-scale political assault on the old dominant classes, opted for a path in which the demands of a new society would be 'satisfied by small doses, legally, in a reformist manner — in such a way that it was possible to preserve the political and economic position of the old feudal classes, to avoid agrarian reform, and, especially, to avoid the popular masses going through a period of political experience such as occurred in France in the years of Jacobinism, in 1831, and in 1848.'⁶⁹ Thus in situations where an emergent bourgeoisie lacks the social conditions for establishing complete hegemony over the new nation, it resorts to a 'passive revolution', by attempting a 'molecular transformation' of the old dominant classes into partners in a new historical bloc and only a partial appropriation of the popular masses, in order first to create a state as the necessary precondition for the establishment of capitalism as the dominant mode of production.

Gramsci's ideas provide only a general, and somewhat obscurely stated, formulation of this problem. To sharpen it, one must examine several historical cases of 'passive revolutions' in their economic, political and ideological aspects. On the face of it, the Indian case seems a particularly good example, but the examination of modern Indian history in terms of this problematic has only just begun. What I will outline here is an analytical framework in which the ideological history of the Indian state can be studied. The framework attempts to locate, within a historical context of 'passive revolution', the problem of the autonomy of nationalist discourse as a discourse of power..

Nationalist texts were addressed both to 'the people' who were said to constitute the nation and to the colonial masters whose claim to rule nationalism questioned. To both, nationalism sought to demonstrate the falsity of the colonial claim that the backward peoples were culturally incapable of ruling themselves in the conditions of the modern world. Nationalism denied the alleged inferiority of the colonized people; it also asserted that a backward nation could 'modernize' itself while retaining its cultural identity. It thus produced a discourse in which, even as it challenged the colonial claim to political domination, it also accepted the very intellectual premises of 'modernity' on which colonial domination was based. How are we to sort out these contradictory elements in nationalist discourse?

Notes

1. John Plamenatz, 'Two Types of Nationalism' in Eugene Kamenka, ed., *Nationalism: The Nature and Evolution of an Idea* (London: Edward Arnold, 1976), pp.23-36.

2. Hans Kohn, *The Idea of Nationalism* (New York: Macmillan, 1944); *The Age of Nationalism* (New York: Harper, 1962); *Nationalism, Its Meaning and History* (Princeton, NJ: Van Nostrand, 1955).

3. For a discussion of this distinction in Kohn, see Aira Kemiläinen, *Nationalism* (Jyväskylä: Jyväskylä: Kasvatusopillinen Korkeakoulu, 1964), pp.115ff.

4. See Ken Wolf, 'Hans Kohn's Liberal Nationalism: The Historian as Prophet', *Journal of the History of Ideas*, 37, 4 (October-December 1976),

pp.651-72. Carlton Hayes, the American historian of nationalism, proposed a theory of the 'degeneration' of nationalism from a liberal, humanitarian and peaceful form to a reactionary, egoistic and violent form. Carlton J.H. Hayes, *The Historical Evolution of Modern Nationalism* (New York: R.R. Smith, 1931) and *Nationalism: A Religion* (New York: Macmillan, 1960). More recently, Seton-Watson has written a comparative history of nationalist movements based on a distinction between 'old' and 'new' nations. 'The old are those which had acquired national identity or national consciousness before the formulation of the doctrine of nationalism'. Such nations were the English, Scots, French, Dutch, Castilians, Portuguese, Danes, Swedes, Hungarians, Poles and Russians. 'The new are those for whom two processes developed simultaneously: the formation of national consciousness and the creation of nationalist movements. Both processes were the work of small educated political elites.' Hugh Seton-Watson, *Nations and States: An Enquiry into the Origins of Nations and the Politics of Nationalism* (London: Methuen, 1977).

5. Thus for example, Karl W. Deutsch, *Nationalism and Social Communication* (Cambridge, Mass: MIT Press, 1966); or Anthony D. Smith, *Theories of Nationalism* (London: Duckworth, 1971); or most recently, John Breuilly, *Nationalism and the State* (Manchester: Manchester University Press, 1982).

6. Ernest Gellner, *Thought and Change* (London: Weidenfeld and Nicholson, 1964), pp.147-78.

7. Thus, for example, David E. Apter, *The Politics of Modernization* (Chicago: University of Chicago Press, 1965); Samuel P. Huntington, *Political Order in Changing Societies* (New Haven, Conn: Yale University Press, 1969).

8. Ernest Gellner, *Nations and Nationalism* (Oxford: Basil Blackwell, 1983), p.124.

9. Ibid., p.20.

10. Ibid., p.39.

11. Ibid., p.48.

12. Ibid., p.57. Gellner's typology of nationalism, despite a rather elaborate attempt at model-building, coincides with the 'two types' of Plamenatz, with the addition of a third type, that of 'diaspora nationalism'.

13. Ibid., p.120.

14. John Dunn is somewhat less gentle:

if nationalism as a political force is in some ways a reactionary and irrationalist sentiment in the modern world, its insistence on the moral claims of the community upon its members and its emphasis that civic order and peace is not a force but an achievement which may well have to be struggled for again is in many ways a less superstitious political vision than the intuitive political consciousness of most capitalist democracies today.

It is in this sense broadly true that the populations of most if not all capitalist democracies today espouse a relaxed and peaceful economic nationalism but shrink back rather from the stridencies and the violence of those whose nations still appear to them to require liberation, to be still *unfree*. And it is natural for them to see the former versions of nationalism as harmless and the latter as purely damaging, fit conduct for Palestinians. Yet both of these more or less reflex judgements are disastrously inadequate. The relaxed economic nationalism of operating states, although it is a natural outcome of the dynamics of the world economy, poses a real threat to the future of the species, while the terrorist politics of national liberation, unprepossessing though it certainly is in itself,

31

is premised upon very deep truths about the human political condition which it is wildly imprudent for us to ignore.

Western Political Theory in the Face of the Future (Cambridge: Cambridge University Press, 1979), p.71.

15. 'Introduction' in Elie Kedourie, ed., *Nationalism in Asia and Africa* (London: Weidenfeld and Nicolson, 1970), p.2.

16. Anthony Smith, *Theories of Nationalism*, pp.12-24.

17. Ibid., p.23.

18. Ibid., p.15.

19. *Nationalism* (London: Hutchinson, 1960), p.9.

20. *Nationalism in Asia and Africa*, p.29.

21. Ibid., p.36.

22. Ibid., p.103.

23. Ibid., p.105.

24. Ibid., p.76.

25. Ibid., p.106.

26. Ibid., p.135.

27. Ibid., pp.146-7.

28. A representative selection of the different arguments in this debate can be found in Bryan R. Wilson, ed., *Rationality* (Oxford: Basil Blackwell, 1970).

29. Martin Hollis, 'Reason and Ritual', *Philosophy*, 43 (1967), 165, pp.231-47.

30. Davidson's argument is that the idea that there can be two 'conceptual schemes', both largely true but not translatable from one to the other, rests on a holistic theory of meaning, viz., that to give the meaning of any sentence or word in a language we need to give the meaning of every sentence or word in that language. This is false. If so, then Davidson shows that there can be no intelligible basis for saying that another scheme is different from our own in the sense of being untranslatable. And if we cannot say schemes are different, neither can we intelligibly say they are the same. Hence, the only intelligible procedure would be to maintain that most of the beliefs in a scheme are true and that every other language is in principle translatable into our own. Donald Davidson, 'On the Very Idea of a Conceptual Scheme', *Proceedings of the American Philosophical Association*, 17 (1973-4), pp.5-20.

31. The 'principle of humanity' suggests that instead of attempting to maximize agreement, one should try to minimize disagreement, specifically in those cases in which we find the beliefs apparently unintelligible. Here the underlying assumption is that of the unity of human nature, from which basis it is argued that, except for a small number of bizarre cases, it should be possible to explain most cross-cultural differences in beliefs or actions in terms of the varying circumstances in which other peoples live. That is to say, one assumes a certain universal instrumental rationality for all human beings and then asks: are the particular beliefs according to which a particular group of people act in a certain way in order to achieve certain outcomes rational *within* their specific social circumstances? If so, then their beliefs and behaviour would become intelligible to us. We would then in effect be saying that had we been placed in exactly the same circumstances, we would have held the same beliefs.

32. Consider for instance, the following exchange:

Alasdair MacIntyre: .... at any given date in any given society the criteria in current use by religious believers or by scientists will differ from what they are at other times and places. Criteria have a history . . . It seems to me that one could only hold the belief of the Azande rationally *in the absence* of any practice of science and technology in which criteria of effectiveness, ineffectiveness and kindred notions have been built up. But to say this is to recognize the appropriateness of scientific criteria of judgment from our standpoint. The Azande do not intend their belief either as a piece of science or as a piece of non-science. They do not possess those categories. It is only *post eventum*, in the light of later and more sophisticated understanding, that their belief and concepts can be classified and evaluated at all.

This suggests strongly that beliefs and concepts are not merely to be evaluated by the criteria implicit in the practice of those who hold and use them.

Alasdair MacIntyre, 'Is Understanding Religion Compatible with Believing?' in Wilson, ed., *Rationality*, pp.62-77.

Peter Winch: . . . far from overcoming relativism, as he claims, MacIntyre himself falls into an extreme form of it. He disguises this from himself by committing the very error of which, wrongly as I have tried to show, he accuses me: the error of overlooking the fact that 'criteria and concepts have a history'. While he emphasizes this point when he is dealing with the concepts and criteria governing action in particular social contexts, he forgets it when he comes to talk of the criticism of such criteria. Do not the criteria appealed to in the criticism of existing institutions equally have a history? MacIntyre's implicit answer is that it is in ours; but if we are to speak of difficulties and incoherencies appearing and being detected in the way certain practices have hitherto been carried on in a society, surely this can only be understood in connection with problems arising *in* the carrying on of that activity. Outside that context we could not begin to grasp what was problematical . . . MacIntyre criticizes, justly, Sir James Frazer for having imposed the image of his own culture on more primitive ones; but that is exactly what MacIntyre himself is doing here. It is extremely difficult for a sophisticated society to grasp a very simple and primitive form of life: in a way he must jettison his sophistication, a process which is itself perhaps the ultimate sophistication. Or, rather, the distinction between sophistication and simplicity becomes unhelpful at this point.

Peter Winch, 'Understanding a Primitive Society', *American Philosophical Quarterly*, 1 (1964), pp.307-24.
33.

Nationalism is the starkest political shame of the twentieth century . . . The degree to which its prevalence is still felt as a scandal is itself a mark of the unexpectedness of this predominance, of the sharpness of the check which it has administered to Europe's admiring Enlightenment vision of the Cunning of Reason. In nationalism at last, or so it at present seems, the Cunning of Reason has more than met its match.

John Dunn, *Western Political Theory*, p.55.
34. There exists a set of notebooks by Marx, which Engels called the 'Chronological Notes', containing Marx's researches in the years 1881-2 into the history of the emergence of the bourgeoisie, the formation of nation-states and peasant rebellions in Europe in the period of transition. There has been little discussion on these notes. The only account I know is in Boris Porshnev, 'Historical Interest of Marx in his Last Years of Life: The Chronological Notes' in

E.A. Zeluvoskaya, L.I. Golman, V.M. Dalin and B.R. Porshnev, eds., *Marks Istorik* (Moscow: Academy of Sciences, 1968), pp.404-32. A Bengali translation of this article is available in *Baromas*, 7, 1 (Autumn 1985), pp.1-12.

35. For a short review, see Michael Löwy, 'Marxists and the National Question', *New Left Review*, 96 (March-April 1976), pp.81-100. Also see the remarkable note by Roman Rosdolsky, 'Worker and Fatherland: A Note on a Passage in the *Communist Manifesto*', *Science and Society*, 29 (1965), pp.330-7.

36. See in particular, V.I. Lenin, 'Critical Remarks on the National Question', *Collected Works* (Moscow: Progress Publishers, 1964), vol.20, pp.17-54; 'The Right of Nations to Self-determination', *Collected Works*, vol.20, pp.393-454; 'The Socialist Revolution and the Right of Nations to Self-determination', *Collected Works*, vol.22, pp.143-56; 'The Discussion on Self-determination Summed Up', *Collected Works*, vol.22, pp.320-60.

37. *Toward a Marxist Theory of Nationalism* (New York: Monthly Review Press, 1978).

38. Ibid., p.29.

39. Ibid.

40. Ibid., p.24.

41. Ibid., p.25.

42. Ibid.

43. Ibid., p.31.

44. *Imagined Communities: Reflections on the Origin and Spread of Nationalism* (London: Verso, 1983).

45. J.V. Stalin, 'Marxism and the National Question', *Works*, vol.2 (Calcutta: Gana-Sahitya Prakash, 1974), pp.194-215. Stalin's definition runs as follows:

> A nation is a historically constituted, stable community of people, formed on the basis of a common language, territory, economic life, and psychological make-up manifested in a common culture . . . none of the above characteristics taken separately is sufficient to define a nation. More than that, it is sufficient for a single one of these characteristics to be lacking and the nation ceases to be a nation.

46. *Imagined Communities*, p.15.

47. Ibid., p.28.

48. Ibid., p.46.

49. Ibid., pp.78-9.

50. Ibid., p.105.

51. Ibid., p.107.

52. Ibid., p.123.

53. Ibid., p.146.

54. Karl Marx, 'The British Rule in India' in K. Marx and F. Engels, *The First Indian War of Independence 1857-1859* (Moscow: Foreign Languages Publishing House, 1959), p.20.

55. See, for instance, R.P. Dutt, *India Today* (Bombay: People's Publishing House, 1949); S.C. Sarkar, *Bengal Renaissance and Other Essays* (New Delhi: People's Publishing House, 1970); A.R. Desai, *Social Background of Indian Nationalism* (Bombay: Popular Book Depot, 1948); Bipan Chandra, *The Rise and Growth of Economic Nationalism in India* (New Delhi: People's Publishing House, 1966); Arabinda Poddar, *Renaissance in Bengal: Search for Identity* (Simla: Indian Institute of Advanced Study, 1977).

56. V.C. Joshi, ed., *Rammohun Roy and the Process of Modernization in*

India (Delhi: Vikas, 1975).

57. Sumit Sarkar, 'Rammohun Roy and the Break with the Past', ibid., pp.46-68.

58. Similar arguments were put forward in three other articles in the same volume: Asok Sen, 'The Bengal Economy and Rammohun Roy'; Barun De, 'A Biographical Perspective on the Political and Economic Ideas of Rammohun Roy'; and Pradyumna Bhattacharya, 'Rammohun Roy and Bengali Prose'; and in Sumit Sarkar, 'The Complexities of Young Bengal', *Nineteenth Century Studies*, 4 (1973), pp.504-34; Barun De, 'A Historiographical Critique of Renaissance Analogues for Nineteenth-Century India' in Barun De, ed., *Perspectives in the Social Sciences I: Historical Dimensions* (Calcutta: Oxford University Press, 1977), pp.178-218.

59. Asok Sen, *Iswar Chandra Vidyasagar and his Elusive Milestones* (Calcutta: Riddhi-India, 1977).

60. Ibid., p.75

61. Ibid., p.86.

62. Ibid., pp.152, 155-6.

63. Ibid., pp.106-7.

64. Ibid., p.157.

65. Ibid., p.xiii.

66. Ranajit Guha, 'Neel Darpan: The Image of the Peasant Revolt in a Liberal Mirror', *Journal of Peasant Studies*, 2, 1 (October 1974), pp.1-46.

67. Leonardo Paggi, 'Gramsci's General Theory of Marxism' in Chantal Mouffe, ed., *Gramsci and Marxist Theory* (London: Routledge and Kegan Paul, 1979), pp.113-67.

68. Antonio Gramsci, *Selections from the Prison Notebooks*, tr. Q. Hoare and G. Nowell Smith (New York: International Publishers, 1971), pp.44-120.

69. Ibid., p.119.

2. The Thematic and the Problematic

> Do not conduct a war before studying the layout of
> the land — its mountains, forests, passes, lakes, rivers, etc.
> *The Art of War*, a treatise on Chinese military science
> compiled about 500 BC

I

In his book *Orientalism*,[1] Edward W. Said has shown how the post-Enlightenment age in Europe produced an entire body of knowledge in which the Orient appeared as a 'system of representations framed by a whole set of forces that brought the Orient into Western learning, Western consciousness, and later, Western empire'. As a style of thought, Orientalism is 'based upon an ontological and epistemological distinction made between "the Orient" and (most of the time) "the Occident" '. On this basis, an 'enormously systematic discipline' was created 'by which European culture was able to manage — and even produce — the Orient politically, sociologically, militarily, ideologically, scientifically, and imaginatively during the post-Enlightenment period'. Orientalism *created* the Oriental; it was a body of knowledge in which the Oriental was '*contained* and *represented* by dominating frameworks' and Western power over the Orient was given the 'status of scientific truth'. Thus, Orientalism was 'a kind of Western projection onto and will to govern over the Orient'.

The central characteristics of this dominating framework of knowledge have been described by Anouar Abdel-Malek as follows,[2] and this characterization has been adopted by Said. Abdel-Malek identified the *problematic* in Orientalism as one in which the Orient and Orientals were

> an 'object' of study, stamped with an otherness — as all that is different, whether it be 'subject' or 'object' — but of a constitutive otherness, of an essentialist character . . . This 'object' of study will be, as is customary, passive, non-participating, endowed with a 'historical' subjectivity, above all, non-active, non-autonomous, non-sovereign with regard to itself: the only Orient or Oriental or 'subject' which could be admitted, at the extreme limit, is the alienated being, philosophically, that is, other than itself in relationship to itself, posed, understood, defined — and acted — by others.

At the level of the *thematic*, on the other hand, there was an

> essentialist concept of the countries, nations and peoples of the Orient under study, a conception which expresses itself through a characterized ethnist typology . . .
>
> According to the traditional orientalists, an essence should exist — sometimes even clearly described in metaphysical terms — which constitutes the inalienable and common basis of all the beings considered: this essence is both 'historical', since it goes back to the dawn of history, and fundamentally a-historical, since it transfixed the being, 'the object' of study, within its inalienable and non-evolutive specificity, instead of defining it as all other beings, states, nations, peoples, and cultures — as a product, a resultant of the vection of the forces operating in the field of historical evolution.
>
> Thus one ends with a typology — based on a real specificity, but detached from history, and, consequently, conceived as being intangible, essential — which makes of the studied 'object' another being with regard to whom the studying subject is transcendent; we will have a homo Sinicus, a homo Arabicus (and why not a homo Aegypticus, etc.), a homo Africanus, the man — the 'normal man', it is understood — being the European man of the historical period, that is, since Greek antiquity.

Abdel-Malek does not elaborate on the precise meaning of his distinction between the problematic and the thematic. Presumably, he uses them in the sense in which the terms *problématique* and *thématique* (or *thétique*) have been used in post-War French philosophy, especially in the 'phenomeno-logical' writings of Jean-Paul Sartre or Maurice Merleau-Ponty. However, it is worth pursuing the possibilities opened up by his distinction of 'levels' within the structure of a body of knowledge, because this could give us a clue to the formulation of our problem in which nationalist thought appears to oppose the dominating implications of post-Enlightenment European thought at one level and yet, at the same time, seems to accept that domination at another.

Let us then recall that in Aristotelian logic, the term 'problematic' is used to indicate the mode or modality of a proposition. A problematic proposition is one that asserts that something is possible; it will contain modal terms like 'possible' or 'may'. We need not, of course, restrict ourselves to the syllogistic framework of Aristotelian logic. But let us open our analytic towards the ground for play that this definition offers. We also know the sense in which the term 'problematic' has been used in contemporary philosophy of science, viz. to indicate the common thrust or direction of theoretical inquiry implied by the posing of a whole group or ensemble of problems in a particular scientific discipline. Finally, we have the sense in which Louis Althusser has used the term, to mean the theoretical or ideological framework in which a word or concept is used, to be recovered by a 'symptomatic reading' of the relevant body of texts.[3]

The term 'thematic', on the other hand, has been used in widely varying senses. In Greek logic, 'themata' are rules of inference, i.e. rules which govern the construction of arguments out of arguments. In contemporary linguistics, the 'theme' or the 'thematic' is used in the analysis of sentences (or, by extension, of discourse) to refer to the way in which the 'relative importance' of the subject-matter of a sentence (or discourse) is identified. In Sartre or Merleau-Ponty, the 'thematic' is that which poses something as an intentional object of mental activity, whether implicitly in a non-reflective mode or explicitly in the reflective mode of thought. But these are merely fragments from the history of this philosophical term, which we can cite so as to indicate the range of meaning it can suggest; we need not be bound by any of the stricter definitions of the term as they occur in particular logical or theoretical systems.

Our present concern is to make a suitable distinction by which we can separate, for analytical purposes, that part of a social ideology, consciously formulated and expressed in terms of a formal theoretical discourse, which *asserts* the existence, and often the practical realizability, of certain historical possibilities from the part which seeks to *justify* those claims by an appeal to both epistemic and moral principles. That is to say, we wish to separate the claims of an ideology, i.e. its identification of historical possibilities and the practical or programmatic forms of its realization, from its justificatory structures, i.e. the nature of the evidence it presents in support of those claims, the rules of inference it relies on to logically relate a statement of the evidence to a structure of arguments, the set of epistemological principles it uses to demonstrate the existence of its claims as historical possibilities, and finally, the set of ethical principles it appeals to in order to assert that those claims are morally justified. The former part of a social ideology we will call its *problematic* and the latter part its *thematic*. The thematic, in other words, refers to an epistemological as well as ethical system which provides a framework of elements and rules for establishing relations between elements; the problematic, on the other hand, consists of concrete statements about possibilities justified by reference to the thematic.

By applying this distinction to our material, we will find that the problematic in nationalist thought is exactly the reverse of that of Orientalism. That is to say, the 'object' in nationalist thought is still the Oriental, who retains the essentialist character depicted in Orientalist discourse. Only he is not passive, non-participating. He is seen to possess a 'subjectivity' which he can himself 'make'. In other words, while his relationship to himself and to others have been 'posed, understood and defined' by others, i.e. by an objective scientific consciousness, by Knowledge, by Reason, those relationships are not acted by others. His subjectivity, he thinks, is active, autonomous and sovereign.

At the level of the thematic, on the other hand, nationalist thought accepts and adopts the same essentialist conception based on the distinction between 'the East' and 'the West', the same typology created by a transcendent studying subject, and hence the same 'objectifying' procedures of knowledge constructed in the post-Enlightenment age of Western science.

There is, consequently, an inherent contradictoriness in nationalist thinking, because it reasons within a framework of knowledge whose representational structure corresponds to the very structure of power nationalist thought seeks to repudiate. It is this contradictoriness in the domain of thought which creates the possibility for several divergent solutions to be proposed for the nationalist problematic. Furthermore, it is this contradictoriness which signifies, in the domain of thought, the theoretical insolubility of the national question in a colonial country, or for that matter, of the extended problem of social transformation in a post-colonial country, within a strictly nationalist framework.

II

At first sight, the distinction between the thematic and the problematic might seem analogous to the distinction in structural linguistics between *langue* and *parole*, where the former refers to the language system shared by a given community of speakers while the latter is the concrete speech act of individual speakers. It might also appear analogous to the distinction in the analytical philosophy of language between an understanding of meaning in terms of the subjective *intentions* that lie behind particular speech acts and meaning as codified in linguistic *conventions*. Thus, it might seem that what we are trying to suggest about the lack of autonomy of nationalist discourse is simply that it puts forward certain propositions about society and politics whose syntactic and semantic structure — more generally, whose meaning — is fully governed by the rules of the 'language' of post-Enlightenment rational thought. In other words, nationalist texts are 'meaningful' only when read in terms of the rules of that larger framework of thought; the former, therefore, merely consists of particular utterances whose meanings are fixed by the lexical and grammatical system provided by the latter. Alternatively, it may be supposed that what we are trying to establish at the level of the problematic are the subjective 'reasons' behind particular assertions made in nationalist texts, to establish *why* nationalist writers wrote what they wrote, the 'meaning' of those assertions, of course, being established only in terms of the 'conventions' laid down at the level of the thematic, i.e. the theoretical framework of post-Enlightenment rational thought.

These are not, however, the sort of problems we will need to tackle here. Our particular distinction between the thematic and the problematic must serve a purpose which the seemingly analogous distinctions in other fields are not designed to serve.

First of all, a strictly linguistic study will be premature if we have not adequately delineated the particular conceptual or theoretical field in which our nationalist texts are located. Given the sort of problems we have raised in the previous chapter, it is obvious we will need to find our preliminary answers by looking directly in the field of political–ideological discourse. Although this field will be constituted for us by the material provided in a variety of ideological texts, a linguistic study of these texts cannot immediately be of much use for us. That is to say, even if we assume that we can give to a body of ideological texts a reasonable macro-structural semantic form (which itself is a very large assumption because the linguistic study of discourse is still concerned with short sequences of sentences[4]), a strictly linguistic study can only give us the general syntactic and semantic conditions determining to what extent this discourse is well-formed or interpretable. But before one can proceed to that level of textual analysis, one must first constitute the discursive field in its own theoretical terms, viz. in the terms of a *political* theory. That, therefore, is the first requirement which our proposed analytical framework must fulfil.

Second, to address ourselves to the interpretation of nationalist texts as a body of writings on political theory necessarily means to explore their meaning in terms of their implicit or explicit reference to things, i.e. their logical and theoretical implications. It means, in other words, to conduct our analysis not at the level of language, but at the level of *discourse*. It would not do to prejudge the issue by declaring straightaway that since this discourse is only a product of ideology, its content must be purely tautological and thus unworthy of being studied as content. On the contrary, it is precisely the relation between the content of nationalist discourse and the kind of politics which nationalism conducts which will be of central concern to us.

What will be required, therefore, is an explicitly critical study of the *ideology* of nationalism. Both sociological determinism and functionalism have sought to interpret nationalist ideology by emptying it of all content — as far as nationalist politics is concerned, their assumption is that 'thinkers did not really make much difference'. Our position, however, is that it is the content of nationalist ideology, its claims about what is possible and what is legitimate, which gives specific shape to its politics. The latter cannot be understood without examining the former.

Indeed, our approach in this study admits an even stronger formulation: nationalist ideology, it will be evident, is inherently polemical, shot through with tension; its voice, now impassioned, now faltering, betrays the pressures of having to state its case against formidable opposition. The polemic is not a mere stylistic device which a dispassionate analyst can calmly separate out of a pure doctrine. It is part of the ideological content of nationalism which takes as its adversary a contrary discourse — the discourse of colonialism. Pitting itself against the reality of colonial rule — which appears before it as an existent, almost palpable, historical truth — nationalism seeks to assert the feasibility of entirely new political possibilities. These are its political claims which colonialist discourse haughtily denies. Only a vulgar reductionist can insist that these new possibilities simply 'emerge' out of a social structure or out of the supposedly objective workings of a world-historical process, that they do not need to be thought out, formulated, propagated and defended in the battlefield of politics. As a matter of fact, it is precisely in the innovative thinking out of political possibilities and the defence of their historical feasibility that the unity is established between nationalist thought and nationalist politics. The polemical content of nationalist ideology *is* its politics.

It is this aspect that we seek to identify at the level of what we have called the problematic. It is the level, let us recall, where nationalist discourse makes certain claims regarding the historical possibilities which it thinks are feasible; it also makes claims regarding the practical forms through which those possibilities could be realized. *Historical* possibilities, *practical* realization. The claims of the ideology are directly located on the terrain of politics, the field

40

of contest for power, where its claims are challenged by others emanating from an opposite discourse. It is at the level of the problematic then that we can fix the specifically historical and the specifically political character of nationalist discourse. It is there that we can connect the ideology to its 'social bases', relate its theoretical claims to the state of the social structure and its dynamics, to the 'interests' of various social classes, their opposition as well as their coming together. It will also become evident that the problematic need not remain fixed and unchanging. As 'historical conditions' change, so are new political possibilities thought out; the problematic undergoes a transformation within the same structure of discourse. With the help of the problematic, then, we seek to establish the political location as well as the historicity of nationalist discourse.

But political–ideological discourse does not consist only of claims: those claims also have to be justified by appeal to logical, epistemological and above all ethical principles. In politics, people have to be persuaded about not only the feasibility but also the legitimacy and desirability of ends and means. Consequently, along with its claims, political–ideological discourse also has its structures of justification. It must present credible evidence in support of its political claims, build a logical structure of argument to show how that evidence supports the claims, and try to convince that the claims are morally justified.

It is at this level that we can consider the content of nationalist discourse as having logical and theoretical implications. The sociological determinist, of course, ignores this aspect of nationalist ideology altogether, dogmatically asserting that in this respect its logical principles and theoretical concepts are wholly derived from another framework of knowledge — that of modern Western rational thought. It will be a major task of this study to show that this dogmatic refusal to take seriously the content as well as the logical and theoretical forms of nationalist thought not only leads one to miss out on the fascinating story of the encounter between a world-conquering Western thought and the intellectual modes of non-Western cultures, it also results in a crucial misunderstanding of the true historical effectivity of nationalism itself.

At the level of the thematic we will be necessarily concerned with the relation between nationalist discourse and the forms of modern Western thought. But this, we will show, is not a simple relation of correspondence, even of derivation. First of all, nationalist thought is selective about what it takes from Western rational thought. Indeed it is deliberately and necessarily selective. Its political burden, as we have said, is to oppose colonial rule. It must therefore reject the immediate political implications of colonialist thought and argue in favour of political possibilities which colonialist thought refuses to admit. It cannot do this simply by asserting that those possibilities are feasible; the quarrel with colonialist thought will be necessarily carried into the domain of justification. Thus nationalist texts will question the veracity of colonialist knowledge, dispute its arguments, point out contradictions, reject its moral claims. Even when it adopts, as we will see it does, the modes of thought characteristic of rational knowledge in the post-Enlightenment age, it cannot adopt them in their entirety, for then it would not constitute itself as a *nationalist* discourse.

Taken together, in its dialectical unity, the problematic and the thematic will enable us to show how nationalism succeeds in producing a *different* discourse. The difference is marked, on the terrain of political–ideological discourse, by a political contest, a struggle for power, which nationalist thought must think about and set down in words. Its problematic forces it relentlessly to demarcate itself from the discourse of colonialism. Thus nationalist thinking is necessarily a struggle with an entire body of systematic knowledge, a struggle that is political at the same time as it is intellectual. Its politics impels it to open up that framework of knowledge which presumes to dominate it, to displace that framework, to subvert its authority, to challenge its morality.

Yet in its very constitution as a discourse of power, nationalist thought cannot remain only a negation; it is also a *positive* discourse which seeks to replace the structure of colonial power with a new order, that of national power. Can nationalist thought produce a discourse of order while daring to negate the very foundations of a system of knowledge that has conquered the world? How far can it succeed in maintaining its difference from a discourse that seeks to dominate it?

A different discourse, yet one that is dominated by another: that is my hypothesis about nationalist thought. It is, on the face of it, a paradoxical formulation. But surely that is what ought to emerge from a critical study of a body of ideological doctrine which claims for itself a certain unity and autonomy. The object of the critique is not to produce a new 'theory' which presumes to explain nationalist ideology by reducing it to something else. Rather, the object is to ask: 'What does nationalist discourse presuppose? Where is it located in relation to other discourses? Where are the cracks on its surface, the points of tension in its structure, the contrary forces, the contradictions? What does it reveal and what does it suppress?' These are the types of questions with which I propose to conduct this study, not with a positive sociological theory.

There is a second reason why the relation between nationalist thought and the framework of colonialist knowledge cannot be a simple one. This reason has to do with the very historicity of thought. Like all other systems of ideological doctrine, nationalist thought has evolved over time. Hence, there is a *historical* process through which nationalist discourse constitutes itself. At the level of the problematic, the political opposition to colonial rule goes through specific programmatic phases, marked by innovations in political objectives, in strategy and tactics, in selecting the types of issues on which to focus its ideological sights and concentrate its polemical attack. Shifts at the level of the problematic may well call for a reconsideration of the logical or theoretical underpinnings of the ideology. It could lead to a change in the sorts of theoretical ideas which nationalist thought had borrowed from Western rationalism, giving up older theories and adopting, even devising, new ones. There could be new theoretical resources which become available at the level of the thematic, for like nationalist thought Western rationalism too has a continuing history. On the other hand, the very logical and theoretical structure of the thematic may influence the formulation of the problematic, constrain the identification of political possibilities, make some possibilities appear more desirable or feasible than others. Indeed, the thematic will tend to apply a closure on the range of possibilities, and many possibilities will be ignored and some not even recognized. At the same time, this process of mutual influence between the thematic and problematic of nationalist discourse — the periodic dissociations and coming together — could even produce at critical junctures a thoroughgoing critique of the thematic itself, points at which nationalist thought will seem to be on the verge of transcending itself.

The complexity in the relation between nationalist and colonialist thought therefore must also be tackled in terms of a theory of *stages* in the constitution of a nationalist discourse — not necessarily chronological stages, but rather a logical sequence in the evolution of its full ideological structure. But is a theory of stages not one which assumes a certain linearity of evolution, a certain teleology? We need to face this question, because it has to do quite centrally with the way in which we propose to relate a political theory of nation-state formation with the ideological history of that state.

III

We have already introduced at the end of the previous chapter Gramsci's concept of 'passive revolution'. Since this is the central concept around which we will build our political analysis of 20th century nationalism, it is necessary to explore the location of this concept within the Marxist theory of state and revolution, and its possible uses in our field of inquiry. In particular, we will need to show how, given the contradictions between the problematic and the thematic of nationalism, passive revolution becomes the historical path by which a 'national' development of capital can occur without resolving or surmounting those contradictions.

Antonio Gramsci himself locates this concept on the theoretical ground defined by two propositions stated by Marx in his Preface to *The Critique of Political Economy*: 'No social order ever perishes before all the productive forces for which there is room in it have developed; and new, higher relations of production never appear before the material conditions of their existence have matured in the womb of the old society itself. Therefore mankind always sets itself only such tasks as it can solve . . .'[5] Gramsci applies the two propositions to the history of bourgeois-national movements in late 19th century Europe, particularly the history of the Italian Risorgimento, and is led to the identification, in all their concreteness, of two inseparably related aspects of those movements: one, the historical impediments to bourgeois hegemony, and two, the possibilities of marginal change within those limits.

What are these limits? Gramsci analyses them in terms of three moments or levels of the 'relation of forces'.[6] The first is that of the objective structure, 'independent of human will'. In countries such as Italy in the second half of the 19th century, the level of the development of the material forces of production and the relative positions and functions of the different classes in production were not such as to favour the rapid emergence of a fully developed system of capitalist production. The political position of the older governing classes; a backward agrarian economy; the weakness of the national capitalist class in relation to the advanced levels of productive organization in the world capitalist economy — all of these were constraints at the level of the 'objective structure'.

The second moment is the relation of political forces, 'the degree of homogeneity, self-awareness and organization attained by the various social classes'. Here the question of ideology and organization is not simply that of the economic–corporate organization of particular productive groups or even the solidarity of interests among all members of a social class. The crucial level is the 'most purely political' one where 'one becomes aware that one's own corporate interests, in their present and future development, transcend the corporate limits of the purely economic class, and can and must become the interests of other subordinate groups too'. It is at this level that

> previously germinated ideologies become 'party', come into confrontation and conflict, until only one of them, or at least a single combination of them, tends to prevail, to gain the upper hand, to propagate itself throughout society — bringing about not only a unison of economic and political aims, but also intellectual and moral unity, posing all the questions around which the struggle rages not on a corporate but on a 'universal' plane, and thus creating the hegemony of a fundamental social group over a series of subordinate groups. It is true that the State is seen as the organ of one particular group, destined to create favourable conditions for the latter's maximum expansion. But the development and expansion of the particular group are conceived of, and presented, as being the motor force of a universal expansion, of a development of all the 'national' energies. In other words, the dominant group is coordinated concretely with the general interests of the subordinate groups, and the life of the State is conceived of as a continuous process of formation and superseding of unstable equilibria (on the juridical plane) between the interests of the fundamental group and those of the subordinate groups — equilibria in which the interests of the dominant group prevail, but only up to a certain point, i.e. stopping short of narrowly corporate economic interests.[7]

This is the 'moment' to which Gramsci paid the greatest attention in his *Notebooks*, analyzing in concrete detail the political history of the Risorgimento to show how the ideology and organization of bourgeois hegemony in its twin aspects of coercive power embodied in the state and intellectual–moral leadership in society at large necessarily remained incomplete and fragmented.

The third 'moment' is that of the relation of military forces, consisting of the technical military configuration as well as what might be called the 'politico-military' situation. In the case of the direct political occupation of a country by a foreign armed power, for instance,

> this type of oppression would be inexplicable if it were not for the state of social disintegration of the oppressed people, and the passivity of the majority of them; consequently independence cannot be won with purely military forces, it requires

both military and politico-military. If the oppressed nation, in fact, before embarking on its struggle for independence, had to wait until the hegemonic State allowed it to organise its own army in the strict and technical sense of the word, it would have to wait quite a while . . . The oppressed nation will therefore initially oppose the dominant military force with a force which is only 'politico-military', that is to say a form of political action which has the virtue of provoking repercussions of a military character in the sense: 1. that it has the capacity to destroy the war potential of the dominant nation from within; 2. that it compels the dominant military force to thin out and disperse itself over a large territory, thus nullifying a great part of its war potential.[8]

In this aspect too Gramsci noted 'the disastrous absence of politico-military leadership' in the Italian Risorgimento.

Considering together all three 'moments' of the political situation, the conclusion becomes inescapable that in conditions of a relatively advanced world capitalism, a bourgeoisie aspiring for hegemony in a new national political order cannot hope to launch a 'war of movement' (or 'manoeuvre') in the traditional sense, i.e. a frontal assault on the state. For such a bourgeoisie, a full-scale, concentrated and decisive attack on the existing structure of political rule in the fashion of the French Revolution or the Revolutions of 1848 is impossible. Instead, it must engage in a 'war of position', a kind of political trench warfare waged on a number of different fronts. Its strategy would be to attempt a 'molecular transformation' of the state, neutralizing opponents, converting sections of the former ruling classes into allies in a partially reorganized system of government, undertaking economic reforms on a limited scale so as to appropriate the support of the popular masses but keeping them out of any form of direct participation in the processes of governance.

This is the 'passive revolution', a historical phase in which the 'war of position' coincides with the revolution of capital. But this 'interpretative criterion' Gramsci applies 'dynamically' to the history of the Italian Risorgimento. In the process, he is able to make some observations of great significance in the analysis of the emergence of nation-states in the period of a relatively advanced world capitalism.

Talking about the relationship between Cavour, a classic exponent of the 'war of position', and Mazzini who represented to a much greater extent the element of popular initiative or 'war of movement', Gramsci asks: 'are not both of them indispensable precisely to the same extent?'[9] The answer is: yes, but there is a fundamental asymmetry in the relation between the two tendencies. Cavour was aware of his own role; he was also aware of the role being played by Mazzini. That is to say, Cavour was not only conscious that the change he was seeking to bring about was a partial, circumscribed and strictly calibrated change, he was also conscious of how far the other tendency, that of a more direct challenge to the established order by means of popular initiative, could go. Mazzini, on the other hand, was a 'visionary apostle', unaware both of his own role and that of Cavour. As a result, the Mazzinian tendency was in a sense itself appropriated within the overall strategy of the 'war of position'. 'Out of the Action Party and the Moderates, which represented the real "subjective forces" of the Risorgimento? Without a shadow of doubt it was the Moderates, precisely because they were also aware of the role of the Action Party: thanks to this awareness, their "subjectivity" was of a superior and more decisive quality.'[10] On the other hand, if Mazzini had been more aware of Cavour's role and that of his own, 'then the equilibrium which resulted from the convergence of the two men's activities would have been different, would have been more favourable to Mazzinianism. In other words, the Italian State would have been constituted on a less retrograde and more modern basis.'[11] Instead, what happened was that the forces of 'moderation' succeeded in appropriating the results of popular initiative for the purposes of a partially reorganized and reformist state order. The dialectic was blocked, the opposition could not be transcended. The passive revolution allowed

> the 'thesis' to achieve its full development, up to the point where it would even succeed in incorporating a part of the antithesis itself — in order, that is, not to allow itself to be 'transcended' in the dialectical opposition. The thesis alone in fact develops to the full its potential for struggle, up to the point where it absorbs even the so-called representatives of the antithesis: it is precisely in this that the passive revolution or revolution/restoration consists.[12]

In exploring the relation between passive revolution and the 'war of position', therefore, Gramsci is not proposing some invariant, suprahistorical 'theory' of the formation of nation-states in the period of advanced world capitalism. Indeed, he begins from the premise that there are two contrary tendencies within such movements — one of gradualism, moderation, molecular changes controlled 'from the top', the other of popular initiative, radical challenge, war of movement. The equilibrium that would result from the struggle between these two tendencies was in no way predetermined: it depended on the particular 'moments' of the relation of forces, especially on the relative quality of the 'subjective forces' which provided political-ideological leadership to each tendency.

If we are to apply this 'interpretative criterion of molecular changes' to anti-colonial movements in the non-European parts of the world, movements seeking to replace colonial rule with a modern national state structure, we would be led into identifying at the level of the overall political-ideological strategy the two conflicting and yet mutually indispensable tendencies. The specific organizational forms in which the two tendencies appear in particular national movements, the manner in which the struggle takes place between them, the particular form of resolution of the struggle — all of these could be documented and analysed in order to provide a more varied and comprehensive treatment of the problem of the formation of national states in recent history. For the case of the Risorgimento, Gramsci illustrates the fundamental asymmetry between the two tendencies by noting that while conditions did not exist for the popular initiative to take the form of a 'concentrated and instantaneous' insurrection, it could not even exert itself in the 'diffused and capillary form of indirect pressure'.[13] Consequently, while there did exist 'the enormous importance of the "demagogic" mass movement, with its leaders thrown up by chance . . . it was nevertheless in actual fact taken over by the traditional organic forces — in other words, by the parties of long standing, with rationally-formed leaders . . .'[14] It would be an interesting exercise in itself to explore what form this relation between 'demagogic' and 'rationally-formed' leaderships takes in a non-Western cultural context in which the very notion of a 'rational' structure of political power is likely to be associated with the ideology of colonial rule.

But there is another aspect to this asymmetry between the 'subjective forces' in the passive revolution which is of even greater significance in understanding the ideological history of nation-state formation in colonial countries. Besides the relative quality of the two leaderships in the Risorgimento, Gramsci also relates the asymmetry to certain 'organic tendencies of the modern state' which seem to favour the forces which carry out a protracted, many-faceted and well-coordinated 'war of position' rather than those which think only of an instantaneous 'war of movement'. And it is at this level of his argument that Gramsci draws out the implications of his analysis of the Risorgimento in relation to the political struggle of the proletariat against the capitalist order.

These 'organic tendencies of the modern state' are set under historical conditions in which the question of socialism and the possibility of socialist revolution have been already raised and demonstrated. Thus, in a fundamental historical sense, the capitalist state can no longer retain the same character as before. What it does now is intervene in the process of production in a far more direct way than was the case under the classical liberal state. The state now 'finds itself invested with a primordial function in the capitalist system, both as a company . . . which concentrates the savings to be put at the disposal of private industry and activity, and as a medium and long-term investor . . .' Once the state assumes this function, it is then inevitably led

> to intervene in order to check whether the investments which have taken place through State means are properly administered . . . But control by itself is not sufficient. It is not just a question of preserving the productive apparatus just as it is at a given moment. It is a matter of reorganising it in order to develop it in parallel with the increase in the population and in collective needs.

Besides, there are other elements which also compel the state to become interventionist: 'increasing protectionism and autarkic tendencies, investment premiums, dumping, salvaging of large enterprises which are in the process, or in danger of going bankrupt; in other words, as the phrase goes, the "nationalisation of losses and industrial deficits" . . .'[15]

Gramsci of course discusses this interventionist capitalist state in the context of 'Americanism' and 'Fordism'. Here the state retains the formal character of a liberal state, 'not in the sense of a free-trade liberalism or of effective political liberty, but in the more fundamental sense of free initiative and of economic individualism which, with its own means, on the level of "civil society", through historical development, itself arrives at a regime of industrial concentration and monopoly.'[16] Gramsci then continues the argument about the interventionist capitalist state into the stage where it attains the specific form of fascism.

We need not concern ourselves here with the debate on the relevance of Gramsci's analysis for an understanding of the state in the advanced capitalist countries of today. Instead, let us piece together some of these fragments of his analysis into an argument about the historical character of capitalist nation-states which have emerged from successful anti-colonial movements in countries of the non-European world.

First of all, at the level of the 'objective structure', an aspiring bourgeoisie in a colonial country faces the two-fold problem, now well known in the literature on 'underdevelopment', of a low level of development of the forces of production at home as well as the overwhelming dominance, both economic and political, of an advanced metropolitan capitalism. The problem takes on a particularly intractable structural form in countries with a large and backward agrarian economy. The principal task for a nationalist bourgeoisie in such a country becomes one in which it must find for itself sufficient room for a certain degree of relatively independent capitalist development. For this it must engage in a political struggle with the colonial power as well as with forces at home which impede the structural transformation of the domestic economy. How can it project this two-fold struggle as something going beyond the narrow corporate interests of the bourgeoisie and give to it the form of a 'national' struggle? That becomes its principal political-ideological task.

The task is still more formidable if at the 'politico–military' level the possibility of a 'concentrated and instantaneous' armed assault on the colonial state is remote. Thus if the 'politico–military' basis of the colonial state itself is strong enough not to permit the formation of a rival armed force, then the nationalist leadership will not have before it the viable option of a purely military solution. It must rely on a 'politico–military' strategy based on the coordinated, and perhaps protracted, action of very large sections of the popular masses against the colonial state.

The nationalist leadership in such situations cannot resort to a 'war of movement'; a 'war of position' becomes inevitable. To conduct this 'war of position' it must bring under the sway of a nationalist ideology and political programme the overwhelming part of the popular elements in the nation, and particularly the vast mass of peasants. It is here that the politico–ideological problem would get intertwined with a more fundamental cultural problem. The structural 'underdevelopment' of the agrarian economy would be associated with the cultural 'backwardness' of the peasantry — its localism, immobility, resistance to change, subjection to a variety of pre-capitalist forms of domination, etc. Will the 'war of position' be one in which a 'modernization' of these cultural institutions precedes the phase of independent capitalist development and formation of the nation-state, or is the replacement of the colonial state by a national one itself the precondition for capitalist development and 'modernization'?

The characteristic form of 'passive revolution' in colonial countries follows the second path. That is to say, the 'war of position' implies a political–ideological programme by which the largest possible nationalist alliance is built up against the political rule of the colonial power. The aim is to form a politically independent nation-state. The means involve the creation of a series of alliances, within the organizational structure of a national movement, between the bourgeoisie and other dominant classes and the mobilization, under this leadership, of mass support from the subordinate classes. The project is a reorganization of the political order, but it is moderated in two quite fundamental ways. On the one hand, it does not attempt to break up or transform in any radical way the institutional structures of 'rational' authority set up in the period of colonial rule, whether in the domain of administration and law or in the realm of economic institutions or in the structure of education, scientific research and cultural organization. On the other hand, it also does not undertake a full-scale assault on all pre-capitalist dominant classes; rather, it seeks to limit their former power, neutralize them where necessary, attack them only selectively, and in general to bring them round to a position of subsidiary allies within a reformed state structure. The dominance of capital does not emanate from its hegemonic sway over 'civil society'. On the contrary, it is its measure of control over the new state apparatus which becomes a precondition for further capitalist development. It is by means of an interventionist state, directly entering the domain of production as a mobilizer and manager of investible resources, that the foundations are laid for the expansion of capital. Yet the dominance of capital over the national state remains constrained in several ways. Its function of representing the 'national–popular' has to be shared with other governing groups and its transformative role moderated to reformist and 'molecular' changes. It is thus that the passive revolution acquires the dual character of 'revolution/restoration'.

IV

To be sure, there are many differences in the specific forms which the post-colonial state has taken in various countries of Asia, Africa and Central and South America. There also exists a large literature which explores these forms from the standpoint of political economy or political sociology. Even if one were to look at the character of the dominant ideologies associated with these state forms, one would find diverse mixes of free enterprise/state control, electoral democracy/authoritarianism and a variety of populist doctrines. An empirical description or classification of these forms would justify the comparative methods of study on which much of this sociological literature has been based.

What I propose here, however, is a study of the ideological history of the post-colonial state by taking as *paradigmatic* the most developed form of that state. That is to say, I give to nationalist thought its ideological unity by relating it to a form of the post-colonial state which accords most closely to the theoretical characterization I have made above of the passive revolution. I trace the historical constitution of this unity in terms of certain stages, which I will call *moments*, each having a specific form of combination of the thematic and the problematic and each bearing certain distinct historical possibilities in terms of the relation of 'subjective forces'. I use as my material certain nationalist texts from India, but the theoretical import of the argument is general.

In fact, to sustain my analytical framework, I will need to argue that 'passive revolution' is the *general* form of the transition from colonial to post-colonial national states in the 20th century. The various stages of movement in the realm of ideas which accompany the historical process of this passive revolution are also an aspect of this general argument. The precise historical location of the transitions from one stage to another, or even the specific ideological content of each stage, will of course need to be fixed separately for each particular nationalist movement. I do not even try to locate, in comparative terms, some of these specific variants even for illustrative purposes, because I do not have the same familiarity with nationalist texts from any other country. But the theoretical structure of my argument must stand or fall at the general level, as an argument about nationalist thought in colonial countries and not as an argument about Indian nationalism. That is one of the main theoretical uses to which I wish to put Gramsci's remarks on 'the organic tendencies of the modern state'.

The question of identifying the different ideological strands or 'subjective forces' in nationalist thought cannot, however, be answered by applying any simple criterion such as progressive/reactionary, elitist/populist or indirect/direct assault on the colonial state. In fact, even Gramsci's interpretative criterion of war of position/war of movement cannot be used to separate out two distinct and opposed ideological tendencies in all nationalist movements. In one of his stray remarks on India, for instance, Gramsci himself says: 'India's political struggle against the English . . . knows three forms of war; war of movement, war of position and underground warfare. Gandhi's passive resistance is a war of position, which at certain moments becomes a war of movement, and at others underground warfare.'[17] Here, therefore, a straightforward identification of the two 'subjective forces', as in the case of Cavour and Mazzini in the Italian Risorgimento, is not possible. We will consequently need to devise other, more general, analytical means to make sense of the various ideological ensembles we will encounter in our study of nationalist thought.

I tackle this problem by breaking up the presumed unity of nationalist thought into three stages or moments. I call these, respectively, the moments of departure, manoeuvre and arrival. The argument is that for nationalist thought to attain its paradigmatic form, these three are *necessary* ideological moments.

The *moment of departure* lies in the encounter of a nationalist consciousness with the framework of knowledge created by post-Enlightenment rationalist thought. It produces the awareness — and acceptance — of an essential cultural difference between East and West. Modern European culture, it is thought, possesses attributes which make the European culturally equipped for power and progress, while such attributes are lacking in the 'traditional' cultures of the East, thus dooming those countries to poverty and subjection. But the nationalist's claim is that this backwardness is not a character which is historically immutable: it can be transformed by the nation acting collectively, by adopting all those modern attributes of European culture. But would this not obliterate those very differences which mark the national culture as something distinct from Western culture? Nationalist thought at its moment of departure formulates the following characteristic answer: it asserts that the superiority of the West lies in the materiality of its culture, exemplified by its science, technology and love of progress. But the East is superior in the spiritual aspect of culture. True modernity for the non-European nations would lie in combining the superior material qualities of Western cultures with the spiritual greatness of the East. I illustrate this moment in the formation of nationalist thought by a study of the writings of Bankimchandra Chattopadhyay, an early nationalist thinker.

This ideal, however, necessarily implies an elitist programme, for the act of cultural synthesis can only be performed by the supremely refined intellect. Popular consciousness, steeped in centuries of superstition and irrational folk religion, can hardly be expected to adopt this ideal: it would have to be transformed from without. This is where the central political–ideological dilemma of capitalist transformation occurs in a colonial country, whose solution, as we have outlined above, is passive revolution. It requires the mobilization of the popular elements in the cause of an anti-colonial struggle and, at the same time, a distancing of those elements from the structure of the state. This is achieved at the *moment of manoeuvre*, a crucial moment with many contradictory possibilities. It combines in one inseparable process elements of both 'war of movement' and 'war of position'. It consists in the historical consolidation of the 'national' by decrying the 'modern', the preparation for expanded capitalist production by resort to an ideology of anti-capitalism — in other words, 'the development of the thesis by incorporating a part of the antithesis'. This moment I illustrate in the course of a discussion of the thought of Mohandas Karamchand Gandhi.

The *moment of arrival* is when nationalist thought attains its fullest development. It is now a discourse of order, of the rational organization of power. Here the discourse is not only conducted in a single, consistent, unambiguous voice, it also succeeds in glossing over all earlier contradictions, divergences and differences and incorporating within the body of a unified discourse every aspect and stage in the history of its formation. This ideological unity of nationalist thought it seeks to actualize in the unified life of the state. Nationalist discourse at its moment of arrival is passive revolution uttering its own life-history. I illustrate this final point in the argument with a study of the writings of Jawaharlal Nehru.

At each stage, I attempt to use the distinction between the level of the problematic and that of the thematic to point out the inherent contradictions in the structure of the ideology, the range of possibilities and the logic of the development towards the next moment. True enough, assertions and justifications lie intertwined in the same body of doctrine. Indeed, this is precisely what gives to an ideology its unity, for it is also a characteristic of ideological thinking that the solution is already thought of at the same time as a problem is formulated.

But, for that very reason, it is by following the disjunctures between the claims and their justifications that I propose to identify the ambiguities and contradictions in the doctrine of nationalism, show how the assertion of political possibilities conditions the choice of a structure of justification, how on the other hand the justificatory structure itself may condition the identification of possibilities, how some possibilities are emphasised, others erased, how the marks of disjuncture are suppressed and the rational continuity of a progressive historical development established.[18] The distinction between the thematic and the problematic will offer us a means of access into the internal structure of nationalist discourse and the relation between its theory and practice. It will also give us a standpoint for the critical analysis of the complex relation between nationalist thought and the discourse of colonialism.

This critique, as I have said before, is not one which stems from an alternative theory claiming to provide better answers to the problems which nationalism poses for itself. Rather, the object is to look into the manner in which those problems were posed by nationalist thought. In a sense, therefore, we too will need to locate texts in their own historical contexts, an interpretative procedure which some recent historians of political thought have recommended in opposition to the view that the classic texts of politics can be read as part of some timeless discourse of human wisdom.[19] But we will need to do more. We will not attempt to suppress the marks of our own engagement in a political–ideological discourse. The critical analysis of nationalist thought is also necessarily an intervention in a political discourse of our own time. Reflecting on the intellectual struggles of nationalist writers of a bygone era, we are made aware of the way in which we relate our own theory and practice; judging their assessment of political possibilities, we begin to ponder the possibilities open to us today. Thus, analysis itself becomes politics; interpretation acquires the undertones of a polemic. In such circumstances, to pretend to speak in the 'objective' voice of history is to dissimulate. By marking our own text with the signs of battle, we hope to go a little further towards a more open and self-aware discourse.

Notes

1. Edward W. Said, *Orientalism* (London: Routledge and Kegan Paul, 1978).
2. Anouar Abdel-Malek, 'Orientalism in Crisis', *Diogenes*, 44 (Winter 1963), pp.102-40.
3. Louis Althusser, *For Marx*, tr. Ben Brewster (London: Allen Lane, 1969); Louis Althusser and Étienne Balibar, *Reading Capital*, tr. Ben Brewster (London: New Left Books, 1970).
4. See for a survey of linguistic research on this subject, Teun A. van Dijk, *Text and Context: Explorations in the Semantics and Pragmatics of Discourse* (London: Longman, 1977).
5. Karl Marx, 'Preface to *A Contribution to the Critique of Political Economy*'

in K. Marx and F. Engels, *Selected Works*, vol.1 (Moscow: Progress Publishers, 1969), p.504.

6. Antonio Gramsci, *Selections from the Prison Notebooks*, pp.180-5. For discussions on Gramsci's concept of passive revolution, see Christine Buci-Glucksmann, 'State, Transition and Passive Revolution' in Mouffe, ed., *Gramsci and Social Theory*, pp.113-67; Buci-Glucksmann, *Gramsci and the State*, tr. David Fernbach (London: Lawrence and Wishart, 1980), pp.290-324; Anne Showstack Sassoon, 'Passive Revolution and the Politics of Reform' in Sassoon, ed., *Approaches to Gramsci* (London: Writers and Readers, 1982), pp.127-48.

7. Antonio Gramsci, *Selections from the Prison Notebooks*, pp.181-2.

8. Ibid., p.183.

9. Ibid., p.108.

10. Ibid., p.113.

11. Ibid., p.108.

12. Ibid., p.110.

13. Ibid., p.110.

14. Ibid., p.112.

15. Ibid., pp.314-5.

16. Ibid., p.293.

17. Ibid., p.227.

18. This kind of exercise in the history of ideas has now become much more acceptable than before in academic circles, not only because of the impact of hermeneutic philosophy and the writings of that diverse group of French intellectuals clubbed together under the ungainly label of 'post-structuralists', but also because of the many uncertainties even among Anglo-American professional philosophers regarding the 'givenness' of *a* scientific method. See for instance, Richard Rorty, *Philosophy and the Mirror of Nature* (Oxford: Basil Blackwell, 1980). It is only proper for me to acknowledge the influence on my thinking of the works of many of the former group of writers, in particular Hans-Georg Gadamer, Paul Ricoeur, Roland Barthes, Michel Foucault and Jacques Derrida. I cannot, of course, attempt here a systematic discussion of these writings or of the relation which they bear to the historical method of Marxism. But I must state that my intellectual attitude towards the relation between nationalism and the universalist claims of 'science' stems from a completely different source, namely, the cultural predicament of one whose practice of science means not only a separation from his own people but also invariably the intellectual legitimation of newer and ever more insidious forms of domination of the few over the many.

19. See, for instance, Quentin Skinner, 'Meaning and Understanding in the History of Ideas', *History and Theory*, 8 (1969), pp.3-53; Skinner, 'Some Problems in the Analysis of Political Thought and Action', *Political Theory*, 2 (1974), pp.277-303; John Dunn, 'The Identity of the History of Ideas' in P. Laslett, W.G. Runciman and Q. Skinner, eds., *Philosophy, Politics and Society*, Series IV (Oxford: Oxford University Press, 1972), pp.158-73; Dunn, 'Practising History and Social Science on "Realist" Assumptions' in C. Hookway and P. Pettit, eds., *Action and Interpretation: Studies in the Philosophy of the Social Sciences* (Cambridge: Cambridge University Press, 1978), pp.145-75.

3. The Moment of Departure: Culture and Power in the Thought of Bankimchandra

> . . . the Bengali is a creature of his circumstances;
> circumstances do not come under his control.
> (*Kapālkuṇḍalā*, I, ch.8)

Bankimchandra Chattopadhyay (1838-94), novelist, satirist, and easily the most acclaimed man of letters in the Calcutta of his day,[1] was one of the first systematic expounders in India of the principles of nationalism. He was widely read in European literature, particularly in 19th century sociology and political economy, and was greatly influenced, according to his own admission, by positivism as well as utilitarianism. He wrote a great deal on social and political questions, using several literary forms. It makes no sense to try to present here anything like a fair assessment of the richness and complexity of his thought, often clothed in the colourful garb of banter and satire, subtly combining within a highly formal discursive prose the earthiness of popular colloquialisms, much of it quite untranslatable. All we can do here is concentrate on some of his essays dealing directly with the issues we have raised in the preceding chapters. Specifically, we look at the ways in which his thought relates culture to power in the particular context of a colonial country.

I

Let us begin with the question of power: why has India been a subject nation for such a long time? Bankim first considers one obvious answer to this question: because Indians lack physical strength and courage; because, as the Europeans always allege, the 'Hindoos' are 'effeminate'. Yet this answer is obviously false, because although the Hindus are notorious for their negligence in the writing of their own history, the accounts left behind by chroniclers accompanying the victorious Greek and Muslim armies speak of the bravery and strength of the Hindus. Even as recently as the early decades of the 19th century, the English had taken a beating from the Marathas and the Sikhs. The question is not, therefore, of the lack of strength or valour. There are two great reasons, Bankim thinks, for India being a subject nation. The first is that Indians lack a natural desire for liberty. Some Indians probably nurse a vague feeling that independence is better than subjection, but never has this feeling become a compelling desire; never have the majority of Indians fought for their liberty.

For more than three thousand years, Aryans have fought against Aryans, or Aryans against non-Aryans, or non-Aryans against non-Aryans — Magadh has fought Kanauj, Kanauj has fought Delhi, Delhi has fought Lahore, Hindus have battled against Pathans, Pathans against Mughals, Mughals against the English — all of these people have fought against one another and continually stoked the fires of war in this country. But all of these were battles among kings; the bulk of Hindu society has never fought for or against anyone. Hindu kings or the rulers of Hindustan have been repeatedly conquered by alien people, but it cannot be said that the bulk of Hindu society has ever been vanquished in battle, because the bulk of Hindu society has never gone to war.[2]

And this led directly to the second great reason for the subjection of India: the lack of solidarity in Hindu society. National solidarity, Bankim says, is crucially dependent on two kinds of attitudes. One is the conviction that what is good for every Hindu is good for me; that my opinions, my beliefs, my actions must be combined and made consistent with those of every other Hindu. The other attitude is a single-minded devotion to the interests of my nation, if necessary even at the cost of the interests of other nations. It is true that such an attitude leads to a lot of misery and bitter warfare, as the history of Europe clearly shows. But such are the realities of national feeling and the love of liberty. Hindus have always lacked this feeling and today, with diverse nationalities living in this country, separated by habitat, language, race and religion, national solidarity is completely absent.

However, argues Bankim, it is because of our contacts with the English that we have discovered for the first time the true basis of liberty and national solidarity. We know that the reason for our subjection does not lie in our lack of physical strength. We have seen in the examples of Shivaji and Ranjit Singh what can be achieved by the spirit of fraternity and united action. If only Hindus become desirous of liberty, if they can convince themselves of the value of liberty, they can achieve it.

Thus, Bankim's explanation of the subjection of India is not in terms of material or physical strength. It is an explanation in terms of *culture*. More specifically, it is an explanation which proceeds from a premise of cultural difference: an essential difference from all those attributes which make the European culturally equipped for power and for progress. Consequently, India, and the people of India, are defined as the 'Other' of the European. Sometimes it is the Bengali, sometimes the Hindu; sometimes Bankim is talking of the *bhāratvarṣīya*, the inhabitants of India. There is no attempt here to define the boundaries of the Indian nation *from within*. This definition of the Bengali, the Hindu or the Indian as the 'Other', the 'subject', is then extrapolated backwards into the historical past. In talking about the subjection of India, Bankim encapsulates into his conception of the cultural failure of the Indian people to face up to the realities of power a whole series of conquests dating from the first

Muslim invasions of India and culminating in the establishment of British rule. To Bankim, India has been a subject nation for seven centuries.

II

The crucial cultural attribute which, according to Bankim, stands out as the major reason for India's subjection is the Hindu attitude towards power. In a long essay on 'Sāṅkhya Philosophy',[3] he argues that the central philosophical foundation of the overwhelming part of religious beliefs in India, including Buddhism, lies in the philosophy of Sāṅkhya. And the chief characteristic of the philosophy is its emphasis on *vairāgya*.

> The present state of the Hindus is a product of this excessive other-worldliness. The lack of devotion to work which foreigners point out as our chief characteristic is only a manifestation of this quality. Our second most important characteristic — fatalism — is yet another form of this other-worldliness derived from the Sāṅkhya. It is because of this other-worldliness and fatalism that in spite of the immense physical prowess of the Indians, this land of the Aryans had come under Muslim rule. And it is for the same reason that India remains a subject country till this day. It is for the same reason again that social progress in this country slowed down a long time ago and finally stopped completely.[4]

> Philosophically, the Sāṅkhya (which, incidentally, was the only system of Indian philosophy Bankim says he had studied in any depth up to this time in his life[5]) was 'perhaps the only system of belief known in the whole world which accepts a Revelation and rejects a God'. It was a thoroughly sceptical and atheistic philosophy which nonetheless asserted, perhaps not very sincerely, the ultimate authority of the Vedas. This specific combination of religion and philosophy had 'disastrous consequences'.

> These consequences must in every case be, that philosophy moving within the narrow circles of orthodoxy, would develop into systems of error; and the errors of national and sectarian creeds, which would otherwise die out of their own rottenness, would receive strength and life from the subtle and illusory arguments of philosophy. This mischievous tendency of an alliance between religion and philosophy, was never so conspicuous as in the case of the Sāṅkhya. The Sāṅkhya is remarkably sceptical in its tendency; many antiquated or contemporaneous errors were swept away by its merciless logic. Carried to its legitimate consequences, a wise scepticism might have contributed to the lasting benefit of the Hindū progress. And yet the Sāṅkhya is as great a mass of errors as any other branch of Hindū philosophy — even inferior, perhaps, to the Nyāya and Vaiśeshika in intrinsic worth. This was the result of its uniform display of a tendency to support the authority of the Vedas. God himself could be denied, but not the authority of the Vedas. There is every reason to believe that this veneration for the Vedas was by no means a very sincere feeling with the sceptical philosopher; but whether that feeling was sincere or hollow, the authority of the Vedas appears to have set the limits beyond which thought was not allowed to range.[6]

It is not as though the Sāṅkhya philosophers did not recognize the need for gaining a knowledge of the world. But the goal of knowledge was salvation.

'Knowledge is power': that is the slogan of Western civilisation. 'Knowledge is salvation' is the slogan of Hindu civilisation. The two peoples set out on the same road bound for two different goals. The Westerners have found power. Have we found salvation? There is no doubt that the results of our journeys have been dissimilar.

Europeans are devotees of power. That is the key to their advancement. We are negligent towards power: that is the key to our downfall. Europeans pursue a goal which they must reach in this world: they are victorious on earth. We pursue a goal which lies in the world beyond, which is why we have failed to win on earth. Whether we will win in the life beyond is a question on which there are differences of opinion.[7]

It will be noticed here that Bankim's critique of the state of religious beliefs in India during its period of subjection, and perhaps also the period of decline beginning a few centuries before its actual subjection, is founded on a specific conception of the relation between culture and power. Certain cultural values are more advantageous than others in the real-political world of power relationships. Those which are advantageous imply a certain rational evaluation of the importance of power in material life, and indeed of the material bases of power in society, and attempt to sustain and extend those bases. Other cultures do not make such a rational evaluation and are consequently thrown into subjection. The critique of Indian culture is here, in every way, a 'rationalist' critique, and so is the critique of Sāṅkhya philosophy.

The argument is further clarified in another article: here Bankim considers the allegation that the Bengalis are a weak people. Discussing several possible reasons as to why this should be so — the fertility of the land, the hot and humid climate, the food habits, customs such as child marriage, etc., Bankim does not find adequate scientific grounds for believing that these establish sufficient conditions for the continued physical weakness of a people. But whether or not these reasons are adequate, they can only point to the lack of physical strength of a people. Yet physical strength is not the same thing as force or power. Power, or the lack of it, is a social phenomenon; power results from the application on physical strength of four elements: enterprise, solidarity, courage and perseverance. The Bengalis as a people have always lacked these elements, which is why they are a powerless people. But these are cultural attributes; they can be acquired.

If ever (i) the Bengalis acquire a compelling desire for some national good, (ii) if this desire becomes compelling in every Bengali heart, (iii) if this compulsion becomes so great that people are prepared to stake their lives for it, and (iv) if this desire becomes permanent, then the Bengalis would certainly become a powerful people.[8]

The theoretical position implied in Bankim's discussion — and this is a position which recurs in much of his writing — involves, then, the following line of reasoning: 1) force or power is the basis of the state; 2) the liberty or subjection of a nation is ultimately a question of force or power; 3) but power is not something that is determined by material (environmental or technological) conditions; 4) power can be acquired by the cultivation of appropriate national–cultural values.

Let us stop for a moment and fix the location of this argument within our frame of reference. The entire mode of reasoning in Bankim involves an attempt to 'objectify'; the project is to achieve positive knowledge. The 'subject' is a scientific consciousness, distanced from the 'object' which is the Indian, the Bengali, the Hindu (it does not matter which, because all of them are defined in terms of the contraposition between the Eastern and the Western). The material is the archive — historical documents, literary texts, archaeological finds —and the archivist (helpless as he feels about this, there is nothing he can do about it!)[9] the Orientalist scholar — William Jones, H.H. Wilson, Thomas Colebrooke, Albrecht Weber, Friedrich Max Müller, and all the rest of them. Of course, he often quarrels with their interpretations — these Europeans do not really have a good enough knowledge of India — but when he does, it is always as another scientist with a superior command over the facts (or else, he is alleging that the European might have special reasons for misrepresenting the facts); he never questions the 'objectivity' of the facts themselves or that they could be 'objectively' represented. And the procedures for objective representation were, for him, laid down in the Great Science of Society of which the three greatest architects were Auguste Comte, John Stuart Mill and Herbert Spencer.

III

Bankim's method, concepts and modes of reasoning are completely contained within the forms of post-Enlightenment scientific thought. One major characteristic of this thought is its celebration of the principle of historicity as the essential procedure for acquiring 'objective' knowledge. The study of social institutions or beliefs, for instance, had to consist of a description of their own internal histories — of their origins and processes of evolution — just as the study of non-human or inanimate beings became the field of natural history. History, indeed, was seen as reflecting on its surface the scientific representation of the objective and changing world of being.

To Bankim this was axiomatic. In his mind, for instance, the self-awareness of a people consisted of the knowledge of its own history. One might indeed say that to him a nation existed in its history. Thus, his distress at what he saw as the ignorance of the Hindus of their own history, indeed their apathy towards it, and his anger at the 'falsifications' of Hindu history at the hands of foreign (including Muslim) historians, are hardly surprising. And his repeated exhortations to the Indian peoples for urgent efforts to 'discover' their true histories are entirely in keeping with this 'scientific' mode of thought.

When he attempted, for instance, to set down in one of his last books, *Krsnacaritra* (1886), a full statement of his ethical philosophy in the form of an appreciation of the character of Krishna, the first task he set for himself was to establish the historicity of the character. He accepted, of course, that Sanskrit literary texts consisted of an abundance of myths and legends, but this did not mean that they were entirely useless as historical sources. The accounts of Livy and Herodotus or Ferishta contained much that was patently mythical; yet they were still regarded as useful sources of history. And

> no matter what modern European critics may say, ancient Greeks or Romans did not regard Livy or Herodotus as unhistorical. On the other hand, there may well come a day when Gibbon or Froude will be dismissed as unhistorical. And despite the protests of modern critics, no history of Rome or Greece has yet been written without using Livy or Herodotus as sources.[10]

The fact was, of course, that the texts on the life of Krishna as handed down to the present day contained numerous additions, abridgements and recensions on the 'original', carried out by unknown and unidentifiable editors over a period of many hundreds of years. The first task, therefore, was to select out and brush aside these later alterations and reach the 'original historical account' of the life of Krishna. To do this Bankim devised several criteria, all of them strictly scientific and rational. Some of these criteria were formal and textual, having to do with continuity, stylistic consistency, uniformity of conception, and so on. But more important were the substantive criteria, because according to him, the formation of these texts as they now existed consisted of an original core of historical truth overlaid by subsequent layers of 'legends, fables and fantastic imaginings'. What is truly historical in a book such as the *Mahābhārata* must lie in its *original* text; the myths and fables were merely the dross of time. Therefore, if one followed the strict criterion of refusing to accept all 'unreal, impossible and supernatural events', it would become possible to extract the rationally acceptable historical core of the *Mahābhārata*.

It is a different matter altogether to judge whether Bankim performed this hermeneutic task with any reasonable degree of technical competence. The more important point is that he should have felt that a discourse on ethical principles, arguing in favour of the exemplariness of the character of Krishna as an ideal for modern man, *required* a demonstration of the historicity of Krishna. Equally important is the fact that all those attributes which, according to him, went to make the character of Krishna an ideal for modern man were the ones which he showed to be part of the 'original historical core' of the *Mahābhārata*, and all those which make the Krishna of folk belief 'an object of contempt and ridicule in the eyes of educated Indians and foreigners' the creations of fable-makers. History, to him, was the receptacle of rational truth; conversely, the validation of truth had to lie in a rational demonstration of its historicity.

It is also significant that when Bankim quarrels with the Orientalists about their assessment of the quality of the sources of Indian history and the way these should be used, he does so from a thoroughly rationalist position. From that position, he accuses his adversaries of ethnocentric bias and racial prejudices which, when they were not plain ignorant, deflected them from a strictly rational examination of the evidence. Albrecht Weber, for instance, had argued that the *Mahābhārata* could not have existed in the 4th century BC because Megasthenes did not mention it in his accounts. This, Bankim says, is 'deliberate fraud' on the part of Weber, because Weber knew perfectly well that only fragments of the original accounts of Megasthenes had survived, and in any case it was sheer prejudice to place such overwhelming reliance on Megasthenes's evidence merely because he was European.

Many Hindus have travelled to Germany and have returned to write books about that country. We have not come across the name of Mr Weber in any of their accounts. Shall we conclude then that Mr Weber does not exist?[11]

In one of the episodes in *Kamalākānter Daptar*, that brilliant product of Bankim's penchant for 'nonsense [which] I can create ad libitum',[12] the narrator Kamalakanta, a sparkling combination of acerbic wit and opium-induced wisdom, talks to the Plateetud bird which had flown from Europe to the warm climes of Bengal in order to preach its profound rallying cry: 'Plateetud, plateetud!' The bird explains to Kamalakanta its own origins: how it used to live near the shores of the Black Sea; only then it was not a bird but a pig, wallowing in the swamps off the coast. And then some fierce two-legged beasts called humans arrived and mistook the pigs for eels. What follows must go down as one of the earliest rationalist critiques of structuralist anthropology, written fifty years before Lévi-Strauss was born!

I. How could they mistake pigs for eels?
Bird. Well, pigs scavenge in the swamps, so do eels. Therefore, pigs and eels are the same thing.
  I knew my Whateley's *Logic*. Immediately I objected, 'But that's a fallacy of the undistributed middle!' 'Tut, tut,' the bird said. 'Fallacy of the undistributed middle! That's logic! This is Antiquities! What does logic have to do with Antiquities? Study Antiquities for a few days, read the books of Mr Weber, and you'll never ask questions like that!'[13]

What Bankim identifies here as an incorrect or incomplete application of the principles of rational scientific investigation, he can explain only as a case of racial prejudice.

It is impossible for one whose ancestors were only the other day barbarians roaming the forests of Germany to accept the reality of India's glorious past. Consequently, he is ever keen to prove that civilisation in India is only a recent phenomenon.[14]
  . . . These pundits of Europe and America . . . attempt to construct historical theories out of ancient Sanskrit texts, but they cannot accept that the subject and powerless people of India were ever civilised, or that this civilisation dates from very ancient times.[15]

Later in his life, he formulated the problem as one of an irreconcilable difference in points of view, arising out of the fact that Hindu scriptures or religious practices had a significance for European scholars that was fundamentally different from its significance for Indians.

European scholars, like Professor Max Müller, have been very eloquent on the importance of the study of the Vedas, but their point of view is exclusively the European point of view, and fails to represent the vastly superior interest Vedic studies possess of us, natives of the country. The Vedas are nothing less than *the basis of our entire religious and social organisation.*[16]

He even brought up the question of the fundamental impossibility of adequate translation in cross-cultural understanding.

> Let the translator be the profoundest Sanskrit scholar in the world — let the translation be the most accurate that language can make it, still the disparity between the original and the translation will be, for practical purposes, very wide. The reason is obvious. You can translate a word by a word, but behind the word is an idea, the thing which the word denotes, and this idea you cannot translate, if it does not exist among the people in whose language you are translating. . . . And who is best qualified to expound the ideas and conceptions which cannot be translated — the foreigner who has nothing corresponding to them in the whole range of his thoughts and experiences, or the native who was nurtured in them from his infancy? . . . [A European] will fail in arriving at a correct comprehension of Hinduism, as — I say it most emphatically — *as every other European who has made the attempt has failed.*[17]

Thus, he would assert: 'A single hour of study of the Sakuntala by a Bengali writer, Baboo Chandranath Bose, is worth all that Europe has had to say on Kalidasa, not excepting even Goethe's well-known eulogy.'[18] Drawn into debate, Bankim was even prepared to question the sovereignty of European knowledge, to challenge

> that monstrous claim to omniscience, which certain Europeans — an extremely limited number happily — put forward for themselves. No knowledge is to them true knowledge unless it has passed through the sieve of European criticism. All coin is false coin unless it bears the stamp of a Western mint. Existence is possible to nothing which is hid from their searching vision. Truth is not truth, but noisome error and rank falsehood, if it presumes to exist outside the pale of European cognisance.[19]

Yet, even at this point, Bankim's critique of Orientalist knowledge is not epistemological, or even methodological. His charge is still one of prejudice, from which 'certain Europeans — an extremely limited number happily' suffered. It does not occur to Bankim that these distortions in Orientalist knowledge might actually be a much more fundamental and systematic feature of the *content* of many of the theories which made up the rational sciences of society, even in those aspects not directly related to the subject of Indian civilization. His critique of Orientalist scholarship remains at the level of technical criteria, showing how *a priori* prejudices could vitiate a truly objective enquiry. It does not extend to questioning the cognitive or explanatory status of the framework of concepts and theoretical relations which defined the science of society. Here he accepted entirely the fundamental methodological assumptions, the primary concepts and the general theoretical orientation of 19th century positivist sociology and utilitarian political economy. He wholly shared the Enlightenment belief in the perfectibility of man and agreed with the positivist view of looking at the history of social institutions as evolving from less developed and imperfect forms to more developed and perfect ones. 'In worldly matters I accept the teachings of science in demonstrating that the world is evolving gradually from an incomplete and undeveloped state towards a complete and developed form.'[20]

He accepted, for instance, that free trade was a more developed form of economic organization than anything that had existed previously, including protectionism, because it represented a rational scheme of division of labour and was beneficial to all parties involved in economic exchange.

> The gravely erroneous theory of protectionism has been superseded by the modern theory of free trade, a feat for which Bright and Cobden will always be remembered in history. Napoleon III has now established this theory as the basis of official policy in France. Yet many in Europe still hold on to the earlier erroneous beliefs. Is it surprising then that ordinary people in our country should also believe in this mistaken theory? If you wish to learn what harm was caused to Europe by protection, read Buckle. If you wish to know why the theory is false, read Mill.[21]

Trade between Britain and India, he thought, had led to an expansion of agricultural activity in India.

> What we buy from England we pay for by exporting agricultural commodities, such as rice, silk, cotton, jute, indigo, etc. It goes without saying that as trade expands, the demand for such agricultural commodities will also increase by the same proportion. As a result, agriculture will expand in this country. Ever since the establishment of British rule, the trade of this country has increased, leading to a demand for more exportable agricultural products and hence to an expansion of agriculture.[22]

But had this not also meant a destruction of indigenous manufacturing, as many people in Bengal were already alleging? Perhaps, is Bankim's reply, but this did not necessarily mean that Indians were becoming less prosperous. If it was becoming difficult for Indian weavers to compete with imported textiles, the logical course to adopt would be for them to shift to those activities which were expanding as a result of this trade.

> The weaving trade may have collapsed, but why does not the weaver move to another occupation? . . . He may not be able to feed himself by weaving cloth, but there is no reason why he cannot do so by cultivating rice. Social theorists have shown that the rate of return from all productive activities is, on the average, equal. If the weaver had earned five rupees a month by weaving, he could do the same by cultivating rice instead.[23]

The real reason weavers were not seizing the opportunities opened up by expanded agricultural activities was cultural: the inertia of backward and outmoded social customs.

> People in our country are reluctant to give up their hereditary trades. This is unfortunate for our weavers, but it does not mean a loss of wealth for the country. The import of foreign cloth results in a corresponding increase in agricultural

incomes — this is inevitable. What happens is merely that this income goes not to the weaver but to somebody else. The misery of the weaver does not indicate a loss of national wealth.[24]

Thus, Bankim's devotion to what he regarded as the fundamental principles of a rational science of economics makes it impossible for him to arrive at a critique of the political economy of colonial rule, even when the evidence from which such a critique may have proceeded was, in a sense, perfectly visible to him. He could not, for instance, formulate a problem in which the axiomatic equality of all exchange relations may have been called into question, in spite of the fact that late in his life he admitted that substantial wealth was probably being transferred to Britain in the form of payments to colonial administrators for which India was getting nothing in return.[25] He was aware of the fact of deindustrialization, but did not possess, and could not construct for himself, a conceptual apparatus by which this could be interpreted in any way other than free trade, increasing specialization and division of labour, and hence inevitable progress and prosperity. It is indeed ironic that his infinitely less sophisticated and obviously prejudiced antagonists in the journal *Samājdarpan*, who thought that Bengal was being impoverished by the trade policies of the colonial government, were, in a quite unreflective perceptual sense, correct.

On agrarian matters, again, Bankim's keen and sympathetic perception of the poverty of the majority of Bengal's peasantry is made sensible to him only after it is filtered through the conceptual grid of 19th century political economy. It is the Permanent Settlement which he thinks is to blame, but only because it was made with a class of unproductive landlords.

> We consider the Settlement of Cornwallis erroneous, unjust and harmful, not because the English relinquished their rights to the land and gave it to the people of this country or because they gave up the right to increase the revenue — this we do not think can be criticised, because it was wise, just and conducive to social welfare. Our argument is that the Permanent Settlement should have been made not with the zamindar but with the tenant.[26]

It was a land settlement which could only have worked if the landlords were kind and sympathetic to their tenants, but this of course was an unrealistic expectation, and what had happened to the Bengal peasantry was only the result of the greed and rapacity of a certain section of landlords, instances of which he catalogued at great length in his essay on 'The Bengal Peasantry' and later incorporated into his book *Sāmya* [Equality]. It was idle, and perhaps impolitic, he thought, to now attempt to reverse the Permanent Settlement. The only course open was for landlords to mend their ways.

> We request the British Indian Association to pay heed to this task. If they can control the wicked landlords, they will do a service to the country which will be remembered in history for all time to come . . . If this is not done, there is no hope for the prosperity of Bengal.[27]

That is all he could suggest as a remedy for the poverty of Bengal's peasants.

Besides the rapacity of landlords who sought to skim off by force every available pice out of a submissive and helpless peasantry, the other great reas n for the misery of the peasants was — and this again is part and parcel of Malthusian political economy — 'the increase in population'.[28] Bankim narrates an imaginary conversation with Ramdhan Pod, a typical Bengal peasant, who announces to him his plans for his son's marriage.

I asked him, 'You cannot feed the mouths you've already collected around you. Why do you want to add more?' . . . Ramdhan got angry. He said, 'Who doesn't want to get his son married? Everyone does, whether he can feed himself or not'. I said, 'But is it good for someone who can't feed his family, to get his son married?' Ramdhan said, 'The whole world does it'. I said, 'Not the whole world, Ramdhan. Only in this country. There is no more ignorant country in the world'. Ramdhan replied, 'Why blame me when the whole country is at fault?' How do I convince someone as ignorant as this? I said, 'If the whole country hangs itself, will you do the same?'[29]

Reasoning from within his rational world of thought, made up of received concepts and objective criteria of validation, there was no way in which Bankim could arrive at anything other than a positive assessment of the overall social effects of British rule in India. Comparing the colonial order in India with a historical reconstruction of the Brahmanical order, he had to admit that British rule had established a fairer and more impersonal legal and judicial system, greater access — at least in principle — for the lower castes to positions of power and status, and had made available the means for Indians to acquire the benefits of Western science and literature. All this had regenerated the conditions for social progress. The position of the upper classes may have declined somewhat because of the loss of liberty, but as far as the lower classes were concerned — well, 'for one who is oppressed, it makes no difference whether the oppressor is one's compatriot or whether he is foreign'.[30] If anything, the position of the lower classes in India had improved slightly under British rule.

Some may become displeased with me and ask, 'Are you then saying that liberty or subjection makes no difference? Why then does every nation on earth fight for its liberty?' To these critics we can only reply, 'We are not engaged in settling that question. We are a subject people, and will remain that way for a long time to come: let us not get involved in fruitless debate. All that we set out to discuss was whether ancient Indians were in general better off because of their liberty than the people of modern India. We have concluded that the condition of the upper classes such as Brahmans and Kshatriyas has declined, but that of Sudras or ordinary people has improved.'[31]

IV

Bankim indeed undertakes the same classificatory project as the Orientalist, and arrives at precisely the same typologies under which the Oriental (the Hindu, the Bengali) is stamped with an essentialist character signifying in every aspect his difference from modern Western man.

What Bankim does not accept, however, is the immutability of this character.

There is, he argues, a subjectivity that can *will* a transformation of this culturally determined character. This is the National Will, which can be summoned into existence by the nation acting collectively. But how? How are these national–cultural values to be cultivated? One way is to imitate those who have demonstrated their capacities as powerful and freedom-loving nations. A perennial problem this has been in all nationalist thinking: how does one accept what is valuable in another's culture without losing one's own cultural identity? Rajnarayan Bose, in a public address entitled 'Then and Now' (1874), had castigated the newly educated classes of Bengal for aping English manners and life-styles. This was only one in a whole series of attacks on overt Westernization which was in the 19th century the staple of social satire in the popular literature and the visual and performing arts of Bengal. But Bankim's answer to the question is curiously half-hearted and ambiguous. 'Is all imitation bad?', he asks, in an uncharacteristically gentle rejoinder to Rajnarayan's speech.

> That cannot be. One cannot learn except by imitation. Just as children learn to speak by imitating the speech of adults, to act by imitating the actions of adults, so do uncivilised and uneducated people learn by imitating the ways of the civilised and the educated. Thus it is reasonable and rational that Bengalis should imitate the English.[32]

Of course, mere imitation can never produce excellence. That is the product of genius. But imitation is always the first step in learning. It is true that there have been nations such as the Greeks who have become civilised on their own, but that is a matter of protracted evolution. It is much quicker to learn from others who are more advanced.

> Such imitation is natural, and its consequences can be most beneficial. There are many who are angry at our imitating English habits in food and dress; what would they say of the English imitating the French in their food and dress? Are the English any less imitative than Bengalis? At least we imitate the rulers of our nation; who do the English imitate?[33]

But almost as soon as Bankim has made this characteristic thrust of logic, he feels compelled to backtrack: 'Of course, we agree that it may not be entirely desirable for the Bengalis to be as imitative as they now are.'[34]

We can see Bankim's predicament here. He accepts that the reasons for India's subjection, and those for her backwardness, are to be found in her culture. He accepts that there exist historically demonstrated models embodying superior cultural values. His project is to initiate 'progress' by transforming the backward culture of his nation. But does this not necessarily imply losing the essential character of his culture which, within the thematic of nationalism, is defined in opposition to Western culture? Bankim does not have an answer.

There did, however, exist an answer, and Bankim was to find it in the later years of his life. This is the answer which he spent many pages in explaining in his last books. It is also an answer which is characteristic of nationalist thought at its moment of departure.

The answer can be found within the thematic and problematic of nationalist thought. It does no violence to its theoretical framework where the thematic of

65

Orientalism is dominant, while it still provides a specific subjectivity to the East in which it is active, autonomous and undominated.

The superiority of the West was in the materiality of its culture. The West had achieved progress, prosperity and freedom because it had placed Reason at the heart of its culture. The distinctive culture of the West was its science, its technology and its love of progress. But culture did not consist only of the material aspect of life. There was the spiritual aspect too, and here the European Enlightenment had little to contribute. In the spiritual aspect of culture, the East was superior — and hence, undominated.

This answer did not conflict in any way with the fundamental classificatory scheme of Orientalist thought. All it did was to assert a cultural domain of superiority for the East and, in time, to tie this assertion with the national struggle against Western political domination.

Let us see how Bankim formulates this answer. In 1888 he wrote a long tract entitled *The Theory of Religion* in the form of a dialogue between a teacher and his pupil, in which he set out his concept of *anuśīlan* or practice. *Anuśīlan*, he said, was a 'system of culture', more complete and more perfect than the Western concept of culture as propounded by Comte or, more recently, by Matthew Arnold. The Western concept was fundamentally agnostic, and hence incomplete.[35] *Anuśīlan* was based on the concept of *bhakti* which, in turn, implied the unity of knowledge and duty. There were three kinds of knowledge: knowledge of the world, of the self and of God. Knowledge of the world consisted of mathematics, astronomy, physics and chemistry, and these one would have to learn from the West. Knowledge of the self meant biology and sociology, and these too one would have to learn from the West. Finally, knowledge of God, and in this field the Hindu *śāstra* contained the greatest human achievements — the *Upaniṣad*, the *darśana*, the *Purāṇa*, the *itihāsa*, but principally the *Gītā*.[36]

But mere knowledge would not create *bhakti*; for that, knowledge would have to be united with duty. Duty meant the performance of acts without the expectation of reward. To eat is a duty; so is the defence of one's country. But these acts had to be performed because they should be performed, not because they might produce beneficial results.[37] This non-possessive, non-utilitarian concept of duty was the core of *dharma* or religion.

Teacher. The day the European industries and sciences are united with Indian *dharma*, man will be god . . .
Pupil. Will such a day ever come in the life of man?
Teacher. It will if you Indians are prepared to act. It is in your hands. If you will it, you can become master and leader of the whole world. If you do not aspire to it, then all my words are in vain.[38]

In fact, that day was not far off.

Teacher. Soon you will see that with the spread of the doctrine of pure *bhakti*, the Hindus will gain new life and become powerful like the English at the time of Cromwell or the Arabs under Muhammad.[39]

Here then was a cultural ideal which retained what was thought to be distinctively Indian, while subsuming what was valuable in the culture of the West. The aim was to produce the complete and perfect man — learned, wise, agile, religious and refined — a better man than the merely efficient and prosperous Westerner.

But once again, the striking fact here is not so much the distinction between the material and the spiritual spheres of culture. What is remarkable is that this distinction should be defended on the most thorough rationalist grounds afforded by 19th century European philosophy. There are two planks on which Bankim builds his defence. One was the rationalist critique of Christianity which Bankim uses to demolish the claims of European religion as a suitable moral philosophy for man living in a modern scientific age and, by implication, to expose the irrationality of reformist attempts to 'Christianize' in some form or other the popular religious practices and beliefs in Indian society. The second referred to the contemporary philosophical debates in Europe about the finite limits of empirical science which Bankim employs to demonstrate the rational validity of a suitable philosophy of spirit and then to turn this argument around to show the much greater accordance of a purified Hindu philosophy of spirit with the rational scientific temper of the modern age. Bankim advances some strikingly ingenious arguments on both these points, and it is worth looking into some of them in detail in order to appreciate the subtle and immensely complex interplay between the thematic and the problematic in some of the philosophically most sophisticated variants of nationalist thought.

Bankim spelled out one part of the argument in an essay which was originally entitled 'Mill, Darwin and Hindu Religion' when it was first published in 1875 in *Bangadarsan*, and later changed to 'What Science Has to Say About the [Hindu] Trinity' when it was reprinted in his collected essays. Here Bankim considers the common Hindu conception of Brahmā, Viṣṇu and Maheśvara — Creator, Preserver and Destroyer — as the three distinct forms of the Divine, and asks how far this conception accords with the findings of modern scientific investigations. For a start, he takes the three posthumously published essays of J.S. Mill on religion[40] in which Mill assesses the validity of the 'intelligent creator' argument for the existence of an omnipotent, omniscient and all-merciful God. Mill argues that if the evidence for the existence of the omniscient creator lies in the massive intricacy of the skills involved in the act of creation, then the obvious imperfections of the products of creation — susceptibility to injury and pain, mortality, decay — would seem to militate against the creator's omniscience. Of course, it could be argued that it is not a lack of omniscience, but rather certain limits to his powers which result in these imperfections in God's creation. Here, Mill advanced two explanations, both of which he held in different periods of his life. The first is the argument that God was not a creator, but only a constructor, working on material which was already in existence, and it was the imperfection of those materials which have resulted in the imperfections in the final products of creation. This, therefore, saves both the omniscient and the omnipotent qualities of God, but reduces him from the role of creator to that of a mere constructor. The other argument is that there is another power distinct from God which acts as an impediment to his actions, and it is as an effect of this antagonistic power that imperfections appear in the acts of creation. Mills' arguments, therefore, raise considerable doubts about the existence of an omniscient and omnipotent creator; moreover, they indicate the existence of two distinct forces — one, the preserver, and the other, the destroyer.

But what about the creator? Here Bankim brings in the results of Darwin's researches on evolution. Darwin had shown that the powers underlying creation cannot ensure survival; many more creatures are born in nature than are able to survive. Hence a principle of natural selection had to operate in order to ensure that those who were the fittest would survive. This scientific principle could be interpreted to imply the existence of two distinct forces in nature — one, the creator, and the other, the preserver. It could, of course, be objected that this was not the implication at all. There was no need to think of the creator and the preserver as distinct entities. The principle of natural selection could easily be interpreted as the consequence of the acts of a destructive force which impeded the acts of the creator who was at the same time the preserver. But this argument is fallacious, because it requires one to believe in an omniscient creator–preserver who creates much more than he knows can be preserved. It is much more logical to conceive of a creator whose sole intention is to create, a preserver whose sole intention is to preserve, and a destroyer who seeks to destroy what has been created.

Having advanced this argument, Bankim then establishes very clearly what he thinks its cognitive status is in relation to an empiricist epistemology. In the first place, he says this argument does not prove the existence of God. It was, therefore, open to one to believe in God in the absence of an empirical proof either in favour or against his existence. If one did believe in God, however, the question would arise of the nature or form of the Divine. It is as a reply to this question that the argument establishes the logical accordance of the Hindu conception of the Trinity with the findings of modern science. Second, the argument does not assert that the founders of the Hindu religion had these scientific considerations in mind when they conceived of the Trinity. Third, although the argument establishes a natural basis for the religious belief in the Trinity, it does not purport to be a scientific proof of the existence of the Trinity, nor does it justify a belief in their existence in tangible physical forms. What the argument does imply, however is the following:

it is true that there is no scientific proof of the existence of the Trinity. But it must be admitted that in comparison with Christianity, the religion followed by those great practitioners of science, the European peoples, the Hindu worship of the Trinity is far more natural and in accordance with scientific theories. The worship of the Trinity may not be founded in science, but it is not in opposition to it. On the other hand, Mill's arguments have shown conclusively that the Christian belief in an omnipotent, omniscient and all-merciful God is entirely contrary to scientific principles. The Hindu philosophies of *karma* or *māyā* are far more consistent with science.

Science is showing at every step that there exists everywhere in this universe an infinite, inconceivable and inscrutable power — it is the cause of all being, the inner spirit of the external world. Far be it for us to deny the existence of this great force; on the contrary, we humbly pay our respects to it.[41]

The second argument which Bankim uses to defend a rational philosophy of spirit is based on the notion of finite limits to positive knowledge. He develops this argument in the course of his commentary on the *Gītā*. Science, he says, admits of two sorts of proof: one, direct sense–perception and two, inference based on sense–perception. Neither is sufficient to prove the existence of the soul. Hence, empirical science is incapable of constructing a true philosophy of spirit.

It cannot, because it is beyond the power of science. One can only go as far as one is able. The diver tied by a rope to his boat can only search the bottom of the sea as far as his rope will permit him; it is beyond his powers to gather all the treasures which the sea holds. Science is tied to its epistemic leash; how can it find a philosophy of spirit which lies beyond its range of proof? Where science cannot reach, it has no privilege: it can consider itself beholden by resting on the lowest steps of that stairway which leads up to the higher reaches. To look for scientific proof where it cannot apply is a fundamentally mistaken search.[42]

Scientists could object here and say that since only empirical proof provides valid basis of knowledge, all we can say about the existence of the soul is that we neither know that it exists nor that it does not. Only a thoroughly agnostic position would be consistent with science.

To this, Bankim says, there can be two answers: one is provided in Indian philosophy which admits two other kinds of proof, namely, analogy and revelation. Analogy, we now know from the findings of science, is a very uncertain basis of knowledge and can lead to numerous errors. Revelation, if one accepts it as a valid basis of knowledge, can eliminate all uncertainty since, unlike human perception or inference, God can never be wrong. However, revelation can only be accepted by the believer; a scientist can hardly be expected to admit it as a method of proof. The second answer, however, has been given in German philosophy. Kant has argued that besides phenomenal knowledge arising out of sense–perception or inference based on perception, there is also a transcendental knowledge based on concepts which are true in themselves. Of course, Kant's philosophy is not universally accepted.

However, I am obliged to state here what I, in accordance with my own knowledge and beliefs, consider true. I firmly believe that if all one's mental faculties are suitably developed, the knowledge of this philosophy of spirit becomes transcendentally true.

. . . I have engaged in this extended discussion because many use the findings of a limited and imperfect science to ridicule the philosophy of spirit. They ought to know that the philosophy of spirit is beyond the limits of Western science, not opposed to it.[43]

V

The contrast with Christianity also brings out another crucial aspect of Bankim's philosophical system: the centrality of a rational philosophy of *power* within an entire moral project of national regeneration. In *Kṛṣṇacaritra*, Bankim discusses the rival claims of Buddha, Christ and Krishna as ideal characters. It is true, he says, that Krishna's life does not show the same concern for redeeming the fallen as do the lives of Jesus or Gautama. But the latter were men whose sole occupation was the preaching of religion — a most noble occupation, and Gautama and Jesus both revealed themselves in that occupation as great human beings. But their lives could hardly serve as complete ideals for all men, because the truly ideal character must retain its ideal quality for all men of all occupations.

> The true fulfilment of human life consists of the fullest and most consistent development of all human faculties. He whose life shows this full and consistent development is the ideal man. We cannot see it in Christ; we can in Sri Krishna. If the Roman Emperor had appointed Jesus to govern the Jews, would he have succeeded? No, because the requisite faculties were not developed in him . . . Again, suppose the Jews had risen in revolt against Roman oppression and elected Jesus to lead them in their war of independence, what would Jesus have done? He had neither the strength nor the desire for battle. He would have said, 'Render unto Caesar what is due to Caesar', and walked away. Krishna too had little taste for war. But war was often justified in religion. In cases of just war, Krishna would agree to engage in it. When he engaged in war, he was invincible . . . Krishna is the true ideal for man. The Hindu ideal is superior to the Christian ideal . . .
>
> Krishna himself was householder, diplomat, warrior, law-giver, saint and preacher; as such, he represents a complete human ideal for all these kinds of people . . . We cannot appreciate the comprehensiveness of the Hindu ideal by reducing it to the imperfect standards of the Buddhist or Christian ideals of mercy and renunciation.[44]

What, in fact, had happened in Europe was a complete divorce between its religion and its political practice. Europe's religion idealizes the humble, peace-loving and merciful renunciator. Yet its politics is the battlefield of violent forces wholly dedicated to the amoral pursuit of worldly goods. A similar fall had occurred in Indian society too, from the supreme ideal represented by the Krishna of the *Mahābhārata* to the Krishna celebrated in popular cults and festivities. What was needed above all for a national regeneration in India was the re-establishment of a harmonious unity of religion and politics, harmony between a comprehensive ethical ideal and the practice of power.

Bankim then brings up what he thinks is the central problem in the field of law and politics: the establishment of a criterion based on a judicious combination of force and mercy. The two are opposed in their consequences. A show of mercy to all offenders would ultimately lead to the destruction of social life. On the other hand, a society based entirely on force would reduce human life to a state of unmitigated bestiality. Modern and civilized Europe had hardly succeeded in finding the right balance between the two. The politics of modern Europe had overwhelmed its religion, which is why mercy had disappeared from European life and force reigned supreme in every sphere. In the Udyogaparva of the *Mahābhārata*, however, Krishna raises precisely this question: the right combination of force and mercy. Faced with the dilemma, the strong prefer a solution based on force and the weak appeal for mercy. But what is the answer for one who is both powerful and compassionate? That would be the ideal answer, and Krishna provides it in the Udyogaparva.

Bankim's interpretation of these passages in the *Mahābhārata* strongly emphasises a concept of duty which embodies what Bankim regards as a rational as well as an ethical philosophy of power. One element here is the notion of moral right.

> I will not desire a paradise given to the pursuit of immoral pleasures. But at the same time, I will not relinquish to the swindler a single grain of what is morally due to me. If I do so, I may not harm myself too much, but I will be guilty of the sin of adopting a path that will bring ruin upon society.[45]

Another element consists of the notions of rightful self-defence and just war.

> It is moral to wage war in defence of myself and of others. To shy away from doing so is grave immorality. We, the people of Bengal, are bearing the consequences of our immorality for seven hundred years.[46]

But self-defence and just war are totally opposed to the European conceptions of conquest and glory.

> Apart from the bloodthirsty demons who pursue glory, anyone else will realise that there is only a small difference between *glorie* and theft: the conqueror is a great robber, others are petty thieves.[47]

And here Bankim adds with unconcealed disingenuousness:

> Of course, we are told that there exist other considerations when foreign lands are conquered for the good of the aliens. I am unable to judge this question, because I do not claim to be an expert in politics.[48]

In any case, moral philosophers would agree in principle that it is ethically right to defend oneself against small as well as big thieves.

> The English name for self-defence against petty theft is Justice, while defence against the great robber is called Patriotism. The Indian name for both is *dharma*.[49]

The third element is the concept of *ahiṃsā* or non-violence, but it is a concept entirely in keeping with the ideas of moral right, self-defence and just war. *Ahiṃsā* does not enjoin one to abhor violence at all times and under all circumstances. It is impossible to conduct even the ordinary acts of human living without in some form or other doing violence to other creatures. With every drink of water we gulp down a million microscopic germs; every step we take, we trample under our feet, a thousand little creatures. If it is said that these are unintended acts of violence, then many other instances can be given where conscious violence is the only protection to life. When a tiger prepares to spring upon me, I must pull the trigger as quickly as possible because if I do not destroy it, it will destroy me. There are situations where violence is moral. The main consideration here is the following:

> the supreme moral duty is to refrain from violence except when it is demanded by *dharma*. To use violence to prevent one who does violence is not immoral; on the contrary, it is the highest moral duty.[50]

However, the duty of non-violence, i.e. refraining from violence except when morally justified, is a higher duty than considerations such as honesty or truth. That is to say, there are situations where it is moral to utter falsehood in order to avoid unjustified violence. Bankim is particularly harsh here on Westernized moralists who pretend that there can be nothing more precious than honesty and who regard any compromise with that principle a licence for chicanery and deviousness. In the first place, Bankim says, nowhere in the public life of Europe is honesty given that kind of privilege: the entire corpus of Western jurisprudence shows, for instance, that a murderer is treated as a much greater offender than a liar. Second, such adulation, whether hypocritical or merely sentimental, of honesty and plain-speaking is precisely the result of the divorce between religious ideals and political practice which is the hallmark of European civilization today.

> If there is any moralist who says, 'Kill if need be, but do not lie', then we say to him, 'Keep your religion to yourself. Let India remain unacquainted with such a hellish religion.'[51]

The fourth important element in the concept of duty is the principle of control over the senses. Bankim is very careful here to distinguish this principle from both asceticism and puritanism. The philosophy of *dharma* is not an ascetic philosophy. It does not advocate the renunciation of sensual pleasure. It is a worldly philosophy which makes it a duty to achieve control over the senses. On the other hand, unlike puritanism, it does not set up a moral ideal as a result of which human life is constantly torn by an unnatural, and irreconcilable, opposition between sensual pleasure and spiritual salvation. Puritanism is opposed to sensual pleasure: the *dharma* of the *Gītā* advocates neither desire nor abhorrence: '. . . no room for hypocrisy here'.[52]

Bankim's concept of *dharma* attempts to reconcile a philosophy of spirit with a rational doctrine of power. In the process, the interplay between the thematic and the problematic of nationalist thought results in a curious transposition of the supposed relation between a puritan ethic and the rationalization of social life in the modern age. Bankim's nationalism leads him to the claim that a purified and regenerated Hindu ideal is far superior as a rational philosophy of life than anything that Western religion or philosophy has to offer.

VI

We have in Bankim a reversal of the Orientalist problematic, but within the same general thematic. It is only in this sense that nationalist thought is opposed to colonialist (Orientalist) thought. Bankim then seeks a specific subjectivity for the nation, but within an essentialist typology of cultures in which this specificity can never be truly historical. Within the domain of thought thus defined, however, it seems a valid answer. The West has a superior culture, but only partially; spiritually, the East is superior. What is needed, now, is the creation of a cultural ideal in which the industries and the sciences of the West can be learnt and emulated while retaining the spiritual greatness of Eastern culture. This is the national–cultural project at its moment of departure.

An elitism now becomes inescapable. Because the act of cultural synthesis can, in fact, be performed only by a supremely cultivated and refined intellect. It is a project of national–cultural regeneration in which the intelligentsia leads and the nation follows. The national–cultural ideal of the complete and perfect man was to be aspired for and approximated by practice, that is, *anuśilan*. And it was not likely that large masses of people would reach this perfection. Bankim states this quite clearly: 'I do not entertain much hope at this time that the ordinary Hindu would understand the religion of *anuśilan*.' But, 'a national character is built out of the national religion . . . I do expect that if intellectuals accept this religion, a national character will finally be built.'[53]

Bankim's doctrine of power, in fact, drew him towards a singularly elitist project for a new national politics. Compared to the various forms of nationalist political movements in 20th century India, Bankim's ideas were, of course, much less clearly specified in organizational terms. There was little in them from which one could derive anything by way of a nationalist political programme. But in accordance with the fundamental unity in his conception of power between a doctrine of force and the need for an organic moral authority incorporated into a national religion or culture, he became an unsparing opponent of the principal form of elite-nationalist politics of his times, viz. social reform through the medium of the legislative institutions of the colonial state. It is not as though he disagreed with the reformers' critique of various Hindu customs and practices; in fact, he seldom did. But he vehemently questioned both the mode of reasoning employed by the reformers and their means for achieving the reform. Relentlessly, he poured scorn and ridicule on their attempts, on the one hand, to persuade British administrators to legislate on social questions by appealing to enlightened reason and rationality, and on the other, to neutralize conservative opinion by a highly selective interpretation of Hindu scriptures in order to show that the reforms were sanctioned by the *śāstra*. This he thought hypocritical, because it implied a wholly opportunistic ambivalence with regard to the moral foundations of reform — rationality for some, scriptural infallibility for others. Moreover, and somewhat paradoxically in the context of his general sympathy for utilitarian social theory, he had little faith in the efficacy of legislation to bring about a genuine reform of social institutions. Reform, in order to succeed, must flow from a new moral consensus in society. To the extent that this new morality was an inevitable consequence of changes in the basic economic and social conditions of living in the modern age, a new pattern of beliefs and practices would emerge on its own, and reform by legislation would become redundant. This was, for instance, Bankim's reading of the issue of polygamy. It was clear, he thought, that polygamy, to the extent that it was ever common in Hindu society, was rapidly on the decline. This decline had come about without state legislation or injunctions by religious leaders. Given the changes in social conditions, its ultimate disappearance was inevitable. Consequently, he thought there was little difference between the efforts of reformers like Vidyasagar and those of Don Quixote.[54]

More fundamentally, however, Bankim's conception of power, unlike the reformers' faith in the general accordance of British rule of law with the universal principles of reason and rationality, could hardly allow him to disregard the great and unbridgeable gulf which separated the colonial state from the rest of Indian society. The colonial state was founded on a superiority of force; its *raison d'être* lay in the maintenance and extension of British imperial power. In the process, many of the fundamental elements of the conditions of social life in India were undergoing rapid change. But the original superiority of force was the product of a superior culture which shaped and directed the British national project in the world. To match and overcome that superiority, Indian society would have to undergo a similar transformation. And the key to that transformation must lie in a regeneration of national culture embodying, in fact, an unrivalled combination of material and spiritual values. To Bankim, therefore, the remedy for cultural backwardness was not reform, but a total regeneration of national culture, or as he preferred to call it, the national religion. Indeed, mere reform negates the nationalist problematic itself, for it assumes that the Oriental (the Indian, the Hindu) is non-autonomous, passive, historically non-active, indeed for that very reason ahistorical, and therefore ever in need to be acted upon by others. Bankim's doctrine of power, as we have seen, is premised on a reversal of this historical relationship.

This autonomous subjectivity of the nation, now, would have to be provided by a new national religion. Its elements were all there. If religion, as Comte defined it, 'in itself expresses the state of perfect unity which is the distinctive mark of man's existence both as an individual and in society, when all the constituent parts of his nature, moral and physical, are made habitually to converge towards one common purpose', then Bankim's burden was to show that 'Hinduism is the greatest of all religions'.[55] All that was necessary was to 'sweep it clean of the dross that had accumulated over the centuries',[56] to interpret its tenets in the light of contemporary social conditions.

> For religion is universal, and its relation to society immanent. It cannot be in accordance with the intentions of God that his words must apply only to a particular society or to specific social conditions, and that if those conditions change they would not apply any more, and that, consequently, society must be kept static. As times change, it is necessary to reinterpret the words of God in accordance with the new social conditions and the advances in social knowledge.[57]

And to do this one would need to set up a new moral ideal to be accepted and followed by the intellectual leaders of society. Their practice of the national religion would lead to the establishment of the new national character.

> The national religion can bring under its fold and shape the lives even of those who understand nothing of religion. Few people ever understand the subtle intricacies of religious thought. Most merely accept and imitate the example set by those who do understand. That is how the national character is determined.[58]

Why this new national religion had to be based on a purified 'Hindu' ideal is, of course, an interesting question and one that has embarrassed 'secular nationalists' in 20th century India who have given to Bankim an important place in the pantheon of nationalist heroes. Hinduism was not the only religion practised in India and in Bankim's home province of Bengal more than half the population was Muslim. But for India as a whole, the majority of people could be said to have practised some form or other of Hinduism. However, now the very definition of a 'Hindu' religion had become enmeshed in the complex interplay between the thematic and problematic of nationalism. For the national–cultural project was not only to define a distinct cultural identity for the nation and to assert its claim to modernity, it was also to find a viable cultural basis for the convergence of the national and the popular. In the Indian case, unlike that of many countries in central and southern Europe, neither language nor racial distinctiveness was a suitable criterion for defining national solidarity. Rather, within this thematic and problematic, two elements combined to identify Hinduism as a likely candidate which could provide Indian nationalism with a viable cultural foundation of nationhood: first, the possibility of a large popular basis, and second, the very identification by modern Orientalist scholarship of the great spiritual qualities of classical Hinduism.

Bankim in fact identified both these elements quite clearly. In an unfinished manuscript entitled 'Letters on Hinduism', he attempted to state his definition of the 'modern Hindu religion'. He accepted straightaway that there were a great many differences in the religious beliefs and practices of groups of people who were generally called Hindu. 'It is no exaggeration to say that there is greater affinity between Mohamedanism and Christianity than between the Saktaism of the Tantras and the Vaisnavism of Chaitanya.'[59] In fact, the very designation of something called a 'Hindu religion' was the work of foreigners.

> Search through all the vast written literature of India, and you will not, except in modern writings where the Hindu has sought obsequiously to translate the phraseology of his conquerors, meet with any mention of such a thing as the *Hindu religion*. Search through all the vast records of pre-Mohamedan India, nowhere will you meet with even such a word as *Hindu*, let alone Hindu religion. Nay more. Search through the whole of that record, and nowhere will you meet with a word such as *religion*. The word *Dharma*, which is used in the modern vernaculars as its equivalent, was never used in pre-Mohamedan India in the same sense as *Religion*.
> ... There is no Hindu conception answering to the term 'Hinduism', and the

question with which I began this letter, what is Hinduism, can only be answered by defining what it is that the foreigners who use the word mean by the term.[60]

The thematic now begins to take shape. The Hindu is defined by those who are *not* Hindu. He is also defined by a *difference*, as possessing in common with all other Hindus something that was essentially different from all other religions. What is this esential commonness? Two features stand out, says Bankim. First, the various religions which are designated as Hindu 'are all sprung from a common source, and therefore hold many doctrines in common'. Second, 'they are all supported by sacred scriptures in Sanskrita, or in some other language sprung from the Sanskrita'.[61] But these characteristics are not sufficient to define the religious beliefs held in common by all modern Hindus; there are more substantive features of commonness. And in identifying these substantive doctrinal and religious elements which make up modern Hinduism, European scholars are guilty of several errors.

First of all, by tracing their origins to a common source, the religions of India are often credited with a homogeneity which they do not possess. The error is the result of a lack of knowledge of the specific differences between the various faiths. It is like saying that Judaism and Christianity are the same religion because they are both derived from a common source. Second, the Hindu religion is often regarded as having had the same form since its inception. The fact that it has undergone considerable change through the ages is completely ignored. Third, a great deal that is not religious at all, but purely secular, is often treated as part and parcel of Hindu religion. Thus, principles of social ethics, politics, aesthetics, law, folklore, popular observances — 'everything Hindu is merged into that whirlpool of things — the Hindu religion'.[62] Finally, this compendious 'religion' is also made to include diverse beliefs and practices which have nothing to do with Hinduism — non-Aryan customs and observances, fetishism, popular superstitions, beliefs which are to be found in every country irrespective of its religion: 'a monstrous caricature of a national faith is thus manufactured and described in eloquent language, "as a tangled jungle of gods, ghosts, demons and saints" '.[63]

The result is a completely erroneous ethnology. Bankim clinches his argument with a brilliant reversal of the anthropological problem of cross-cultural understanding:

Suppose a Hindu, ignorant of European languages, travelled through Europe, and like most Europeans in his situation, set about writing an account of his travels. What would be his account of Christianity? Observing the worship of the Virgin and the Saints in Catholic countries, he would take Christianity to be a polytheism. The worship of images would lead him to believe, that Christianity was an idolatry also, and the reverence paid to the crucifix would induce him to think that there was also a leaven of fetishism in it. Protestant Christianity he would account to be a dualism, a religion of the good and evil principles — a religion of God and the Devil. And if he mixed well enough with the ignorant peasantry of Christendom, he too would meet with that tangled jungle of ghosts and demons which it has been Sir Alfred Lyall's lot to meet with in India. And who shall say that the Hindu's account of Christianity would be wider of the truth than many an account of Hinduism by European or native?[64]

But of course this reversal does not lead Bankim to a critique of the Orientalist thematic. What it does instead is strengthen his assertion about the superiority of a reformed Hindu religion as a complete 'system of culture', a 'theoretic body of doctrines' as well as a 'basis of practical life' which provides a far more adequate ethic for the modern Indian than the purely materialistic ideal of modern Europe. This ideal is that of a 'reformed, regenerated and purified' Hinduism, cleansed of 'the rubbish of the ages'. It is not a return to old and archaic types: 'that which was suited to people who lived three thousand years ago, may not be suited to the present and future generations . . . The great principles of Hinduism are good for all ages and all mankind . . . but its non-essential adjuncts have become effete and even pernicious in an altered state of society.'[65]

It is this ideal, the essential principles of a modern national religion for India, which Bankim described in his last works. It combined a rational theory of power with a non-possessive spirituality. It was an ideal which contained the potential for unifying within a single national culture the vast majority of the inhabitants of India. It was this ideal, once again, which produced in Bankim a barely concealed hostility towards Islam. He recognized in Islam a quest for power and glory, but he saw it as being completely devoid of spiritual or ethical qualities, a complete antithesis to his ideal religion, irrational, bigoted, devious, sensual and immoral. It is perfectly possible that apart from the prevalent cultural prejudices of the upper-caste Hindu Bengali elite of his time, Bankim's opinion was also shaped to a great extent by the stereotypes of post-Enlightenment European historiography. He shows little awareness of, let alone enthusiasm for, the rationalism of early medieval Islamic scholarship and its explorations in Greek philosophy, long before the European Renaissance of which Bankim was so appreciative.

The main task in establishing this national religion was a 'reformation' of Hinduism, 'not an unprecedented necessity for an ancient religion.'[66] The true *dharma* had to be extracted out of the impurities of folk religion and then disseminated among the people. The crucial medium here, according to Bankim, was education. At times, of course, he made the most exaggerated and hollow claims on its behalf, as for instance in the conclusion of his book *Sāmya* in which he called it 'the means to eliminate all social evils', including foreign economic exploitation, the poverty of the peasantry and the oppression of women.[67] But elsewhere, he is more specific. At one level, Bankim is concerned with elite education — the advancement of rational learning among those who would be the cultural and intellectual leaders of society, the new synthesizers of the best of the West and the best of the East. But he was not particularly impressed by the 'filtration' theory of education.

The argument is that it is only necessary for the upper classes to be educated; there is no need for a separate system of instruction for the lower classes . . . The porousness of the newly educated class will guarantee that the ignorant masses will soon be soaked with knowledge! . . . . We do not, however, have much faith that this will happen.[68]

It was necessary, Bankim thought, for the intellectual leadership to engage in a much more conscious programme of national education. A first step in this programme was to make available the results of modern learning in the Indian vernaculars. In his own case, it could certainly be said that his entire literary career was devoted to this single pursuit. Further, he was quite specific about the kinds of people to whom this popular literature in the vernaculars had to be addressed.

> The artizan and the shopkeeper who keep their own accounts, the village zemindar and the mofussil lawyer, the humbler official employé whose English carries him no further than the duties of his office, and the small proprietor who has as little to do with English as with office, all these classes read Bengali and Bengali only; all in fact between the ignorant peasant and the really well-educated classes. And if to these be added the vast numbers who are likely to benefit by a system of vernacular education, extended and developed so as to suit the requirements of the country, we may be in a position to appreciate fully the importance of a literature for the *people* of Bengal; for these classes constitute the *people*.[69]

But even more than this formal medium of the written word, Bankim was concerned with reviving the many cultural institutions of popular instruction which had long existed in India but which were rapidly dying out because of the exclusive concern of the upper classes with English education.

> It is not true that in our country there was always this lack of means of popular instruction. How else did Śākyasimha teach the Buddhist religion to all of India? Just think of it; even our modern philosophers find it excruciatingly difficult to unravel the complex arguments of Buddhist philosophy! Max Müller did not understand it at all . . . Yet Śākyasimha and his disciples taught this . . . immensely difficult doctrine to one and all . . . And then Śaṅkarācārya demolished this firmly established, world-conquering, egalitarian religion and taught all of India the Śaiva faith. How, if there were no means of popular instruction? Much more recently, Caitanya converted all of Orissa to the Vaiṣṇava religion. No means of popular instruction? But in our day, from Rammohun Roy to the latest hordes of college students, three and a half generations have been peddling Brahmoism, and yet the people do not accept their teachings. Before there used to be means of popular instruction; they do not exist any more.[70]

In the case of Bengal, Bankim was particularly impressed by the historical example of the Vaiṣṇava cultural efflorescence of the 14th and 15th centuries. In contrast to his consistently derisive reference to the efforts of the 19th century intelligentsia for religious and social reform, Bankim unhesitatingly located the 'renaissance' in Bengali culture in that earlier period of Bengal's history.

> How long has Europe been civilised? In the fifteenth century — only four hundred years ago — Europe was more uncivilised than we were. One event brought civilisation to Europe. Suddenly Europe rediscovered the long-forgotten

culture of the Greeks . . . Petrarch, Luther, Galileo, Bacon: suddenly there seemed to be no end to Europe's good fortune. But there was a similar age in our history as well. The rise of Caitanya in Nabadwip, followed by Rūpa, Sanātana and countless other poets and theologians; Raghunātha Śiromaṇi, Gadādhara, Jagadīśa in philosophy; in law, Raghunandana and his followers. And then there was a new wave of Bengali poetry: Vidyāpati and Candīdāsa came before Caitanya, but the poetry which followed him is unparalleled in the whole world. Where did all this come from?

How did our Renaissance happen? Where did our nation get this sudden enlightenment? . . . Why did this light go out? Perhaps it was because of the advent of Mughal rule — the land revenue settlement of the Hindu Raja Todar Mal. Gather the evidence and find out all of these things.[71]

This was, in fact, a major part of Bankim's project for a national history of Bengal. The hallmark of the 'renaissance' was its popular character. And this would have to be the character of the new national–cultural revival as well. It called for a very specific relationship between the intellectual leaders of society and the rest of the nation. The intellectual–moral leadership of the nation was based not on an elitism of birth or caste or privilege or wealth, but of excellence. The leaders were leaders because through *anuśilan* they had attained an exemplary unity of knowledge and duty. Their relationship with the masses must, therefore, be one of sympathy on the one side and deference on the other: 'The English have a good name for it: Subordination . . . Not fear, but respect.'[72]

VII

This is the characteristic form of nationalist thought at its moment of departure. It is born out of the encounter of a patriotic consciousness with the framework of knowledge imposed upon it by colonialism. It leads inevitably to an elitism of the intelligentsia, rooted in the vision of a radical regeneration of national culture. In Bankim's time, the heyday of colonial rule, this vision could not find any viable political means to actualize itself. Instead, it became a dream: a utopian political community in which the nation was the Mother, once resplendent in wealth and beauty, now in tatters. Relentlessly, she exhorts a small band of her sons, those of them who are brave and enlightened, to vanquish the enemy and win back her honour. Imprisoned within the rationalist framework of his theoretical discourse and powerless to reject its dominating implications, Bankim lived out his dreams of liberation in his later novels. In form, *Ānandamaṭh* (1882), *Devī Caudhurāṇī* (1884) and *Sītārām* (1887) are historical romances, but they are suffused with a utopianism which, by the power of the particular religious semiotic in which it was expressed, had a deep emotional influence on the new intelligentsia. It is not surprising that in the history of political movements in India, Bankim's direct disciples were the 'revolutionary terrorists', the small groups of armed activists drawn from the Hindu middle classes, wedded to secret underground organization and planned assassination.

Literary critics have often explained this overtly spiritualist and conservative turn in Bankim's last novels in terms of a tussle between a rationalism and an emotionalism, a conflict of the mind and the heart. His intellect, they have argued, was attracted by the rationality, historicity and scientific temper of the European Enlightenment. But his heart remained in the mysterious, dreamy world of the past. 'Irrational emotionalism on the one hand, dispassionate rationalism on the other: Bankim's mental world was lashed violently by these opposing currents.' His rationalism persuaded him that it was necessary to implant the scientific and historically progressive values of Western civilization in his own culture. But his heart refused to accept this solution; it kept pulling him back towards the imaginary authenticity of a glorious Hindu past. 'As a result, he mistook a relation between the present and the past for a relation of the present with the future.' This surrender to a backward-looking emotionalism was, according to these critics, an aberration in the onward march of rationalist and progressive thinking in modern India. It did sway some people for a time, particularly around the turn of the century, but the predominant trend was resumed soon after.[73]

This manner of interpreting the so-called 'conservative' trend in Indian nationalism misses the most crucial point of tension in *all* nationalist thought. It was not a question of a forward-looking rationality being swamped by a flood of archaic emotionalism. Much of this conservatism in fact rejected, as Bankim certainly did, any wishful dreams of a return to the past. To treat 'Hindu orthodoxy' of this kind as a backward-looking emotionalism would be to miss its very source of ideological strength, namely, its proclamation of a rational and modern religion suitable for the nation. Unlike the liberal reformers of the 19th century who could think of no way of 'modernizing' the antiquated institutions of their society except to rely on the legislative and administrative powers of the colonial state, it was the so-called 'conservative' or 'revivalist' trend which confronted for the first time the crucial question of power in the historical project of nationalism. Rather, the point of tension lay embedded in the contradictions of the thematic and the problematic of nationalism itself at its moment of departure. Both the so-called rationalism and the so-called emotionalism, progressive as well as conservative tendencies, proceeded from this point. Neither conservatives nor progressives were able to resolve the divergence between the *modern* and the *national* in any historically specific way, because the specificity of the modern and the specificity of the national remained distinct and opposed. But this was so because both conservatives and progressives were equally prisoners of the rationalism, historicism and scientism of the nationalist thematic. Theoretically, the modern and the national could be synthesised only in the ideal of the complete man, the true intellectual. But it was hardly possible to devise programmatic steps to achieve that ideal in the realm of politics. At its moment of departure, all nationalist thought remained trapped in this unresolved contradiction.

It was this contradiction which served as the basis for divergent political programmes within the national movement. An emphasis on the modern meant arguing for a period of tutelage until the leaders of the country and its material bases had been sufficiently 'modernized'. For a long time this meant a continuation of colonial rule, a sharing of power between colonial officials and a modernized elite, and an emphasis on state action to reform traditional institutions and bring into being modern ones. It also meant, and indeed still means, a continued period of 'collaboration' with the West. Usually a political programme of this sort has been associated with liberal, constitutionalist and pro-Western circles. On the other hand, a more uncompromising position on the question of colonial rule has meant an ideological emphasis on what is distinctly national, i.e. culturally distinct from the Western and the modern. This is seen to be characteristic of revivalist or fundamentalist cultural movements, usually of a religious–communal nature. Both possibilities are inherent in Bankim's unresolved problem.

The narrow elitism of the intelligentsia could hardly resolve the central problem of nationalist politics in a large agrarian country under colonial rule. To represent the nation as a political entity within a colonial state process which clearly possessed considerable resources to broaden its bases of legitimacy by intervening directly in the agrarian class struggle, it was necessary above all to take nationalist politics to the peasantry. Without this an emergent Indian bourgeoisie could never hope to pose an adequate challenge to colonial rule. Similarly, without devising suitable ways of establishing an intellectual–moral leadership over the vast masses of the peasantry, the organic functions of the new intelligentsia in building a national consensus for self-government were doomed to failure.

The problem, however, lay precisely in the insurmountable difficulty of reconciling the modes of thought characteristic of a peasant consciousness with the rationalist forms of an 'enlightened' nationalist politics. Either peasant consciousness would have to be transformed, or else it would have to be appropriated. The former would require a total transformation of the agrarian economy, the abolition of pre-capitalist forms of production and the virtual dissolution of the peasantry as a distinct form of the social existence of labour. Given the conditions of the colonial economy even in the early 20th century, this could hardly seem a viable political possibility. The other possibility then was an appropriation of peasant support for the historic cause of creating a nation-state in which the peasant masses would be represented, but of which they would not be a constituent part. In other words, passive revolution.

This is where the moment of manoeuvre occurs. To understand the significance of this moment in the historical constitution of a nationalist discourse, we must extricate the problem from questions of subjective motivations, influences, manipulations, who used whom to gain what, etc. Those are valid historical questions, but they lie at an entirely different analytical level. It is at this moment of manoeuvre — this critical moment in the task of constituting a historical bloc to achieve a 'passive revolution of capital' in India — that we examine the significance of the Gandhian intervention in Indian politics.

Notes

1. For biographical details, see Brajendranath Bandyopadhyay and Sajanikanta Das, *Sāhitya Sādhak Caritmālā*, vol.2 (Calcutta: Bangiya Sahitya Parishad, 1945), and most recently, Sisir Kumar Das, *The Artist in Chains: The Life of Bankimchandra Chatterji* (New Delhi: New Statesman, 1984).

2. 'Bhāratvarṣa parādhīn kena?' *Baṅkim Racanābalī*, ed. Jogesh Chandra Bagal, vol.2 (Calcutta: Sahitya Samsad, 1965) [hereafter BR], p.239. All translations from the Bengali are mine.

3. *BR*, pp.221-34.

4. 'Sāṅkhyadarśan', *BR*, p.222.

5. Letter to Sambhu Chandra Mookerjee, 28 December 1872, in 'The Secretary's Notes', *Bengal Past and Present*, 8, part 2, 16 (April-June 1914).

6. 'Buddhism and the Sāṅkhya Philosophy', *Calcutta Review*, 53 (1871), 106, pp.191-203.

7. 'Sāṅkhyadarśan', *BR*, p.226.

8. 'Baṅgālīr Vāhubal', *BR*, p.213.

9.

If the English go out to shoot birds, a history is written of the expedition. But Bengal has no history! . . . There is a specific reason why Indians have no history. Partly because of the environment, partly the fear of invaders, Indians are greatly devoted to their gods . . . As a result of this way of thinking, Indians are extremely modest: They do not think themselves the subjects of their own actions; it is always the gods who act through them . . . It is this modesty of attitude and devotion to the gods which are the reasons for our people not writing their own history. The Europeans are extremely proud. They think that even when they yawn, the achievement should be recorded as a memorable deed in the annals of world history. Proud nations have an abundance of historical writing; we have none.

'Baṅgālār Itihās', *BR*, p.330.

10. *Kṛṣṇacaritra*, in *BR*, p.411.

11. Ibid., *BR*, p.413.

12. Letter to Sambhu Chandra Mookerjee, op.cit.

13. 'Kākātuyā', *BR*, p.110.

14. *Kṛṣṇacaritra*, in *BR*, p.413.

15. Ibid., *BR*, p.410.

16. 'Vedic Literature: An Address', *Baṅkim Racanabālī (English Works)*, ed. Jogesh Chandra Bagal (Calcutta: Sahitya Samsad, 1969), p.150.

17. 'European Versions of Hindoo Doctrine: An Exchange with Mr. Hastie', ibid., pp.204-5.

18. 'The Intellectual Superiority of Europe: An Exchange with Mr. Hastie', ibid., p.212.

19. Ibid., p.210.

20. *Kṛṣṇacaritra*, in *BR*, p.434.

21. 'Baṅgadeser kṛṣak', *BR*, p.311.

22. Ibid., *BR*, p.289.

23. Ibid., *BR*, p.312.

24. Ibid.

25. When not bound down by the formal analytical requirements of a theoretical

discourse, Bankim was of course capable of considerable scepticism about the 'philanthropic' aspects of colonial rule. About his own work as a government official, he wrote to a friend:

> I have been doing right royal service to the State by trying to fill its coffers, so that it may rebuild the Jagur barracks and indulge in other magnificent pastimes, to the edification of the tax-paying public. What the devil do niggers want their money for? they had better pay in their all at the Government Treasuries, and Government will do them an immense deal of good by erecting uninhabitable barracks and abolishing slavery in Zanzibar. You see my work is genuine philanthrophy.

Letter to S.C. Mookerjee, op.cit.

26. Ibid., *BR*, p.310.
27. Ibid., *BR*, p.298.
28. Ibid., *BR*, p.301.
29. 'Rāmdhan Pod', *BR*, p.380.
30. 'Bhāratvarṣer svādhīnatā evaṃ parādhīnatā', *BR*, p.244.
31. Ibid., *BR*, p.245.
32. 'Anukaraṇ', *BR*, p.201.
33. Ibid., *BR*, p.203.
34. Ibid.
35. *Dharmatattva*, in *BR*, p.585.
36. Ibid., *BR*, p.630.
37. Ibid., *BR*, pp.628-9.
38. Ibid., *BR*, p.633.
39. Ibid., *BR*, p.647.
40. John Stuart Mill, *Nature, The Utility of Religion, and Theism* (London: Watts, 1904).
41. 'Tridev sambandhe vijñānśāstra ki bale', *BR*, p.280.
42. *Śrīmadbhagavadgītā*, in *BR*, pp.699-700.
43. Ibid., *BR*, p.701.
44. *Kṛṣṇacaritra*, in *BR*, pp.516-7.
45. Ibid., *BR*, p.529.
46. Ibid., *BR*, p.495.
47. Ibid., *BR*, p.533.
48. Ibid., *BR*, p.533.
49. Ibid., *BR*, p.534.
50. Ibid., *BR*, p.562.
51. Ibid., *BR*, p.563.
52. *Śrīmadbhagavadgītā*, in *BR*, p.744.
53. *Dharmatattva*, in *BR*, p.651.
54. 'Vahuvivāha', *BR*, p.315.
55. *Dharmatattva*, in *BR*, p.676.
56. Ibid., *BR*, p.668.
57. *Śrīmadbhagavadgītā*, in *BR*, p.695.
58. *Dharmatattva*, in *BR*, p.651.
59. 'Letters on Hinduism', *Bankim Racanābalī (English Works)*, p.230.
60. Ibid., pp.230-1.
61. Ibid., p.232.
62. Ibid., p.233.

63. Ibid.
64. Ibid., p.235.
65. Ibid., p.235-6.
66. Ibid., p.235.
67. *Sāmya*, in *BR*, pp.405-6.
68. 'Bangadarśaner patrasūcanā', *BR*, p.282.
69. 'A Popular Literature for Bengal', *Bankim Racanābalī (English Works)*, p.97.
70. 'Lokaśikṣā', *BR*, p.377.
71. 'Bāngālār itihās sambandhe kayekti kathā', *BR*, p.339.
72. *Dharmatattva*, in *BR*, p.619.
73. See in particular, Arabinda Poddar, *Bankim-mānas* (Calcutta: Indiana, 1960), especially pp.80, 111, 165-7.

4. The Moment of Manoeuvre: Gandhi and the Critique of Civil Society

> My language is aphoristic, it lacks precision.
> It is therefore open to several interpretations.
> 'Discussion with Dharmadev', *The Collected Works of Mahatma Gandhi*, vol.53, Appendix III, p.485.

I

Although Gandhi's *Collected Works* will finally run into nearly ninety thick volumes, there exist few texts in which he can be seen attempting a systematic exposition of his ideas on state, society and nation. One of the first, and perhaps the fullest, is entitled *Hind Swaraj*, written in Gujarati in 1909 and published in an English translation in Johannesburg in 1910 after the original edition was proscribed by the Government of Bombay. It contains a statement of some of the fundamental elements of Gandhi's politics. Romain Rolland, one of his first sympathetic but critical commentators, saw in this book a reflection of the central features of Gandhi's thought: 'the negation of Progress and also of European science'.[1] A more recent commentator, Raghavan Iyer, sees it as 'a severe condemnation of modern civilzation' and 'the *point d'appui* of Gandhi's moral and political thought'.[2] I prefer to read it as a text in which Gandhi's relation to nationalism can be shown to rest on a fundamental critique of the idea of civil society.

On the surface, it is indeed a critique of modern civilization, 'a civilization only in name'.[3] And the argument proceeds, as it does in Bankim, from a consideration of the question: Why is India a subject nation? To start with, Gandhi's answer too seems to run along the same lines. He too is concerned more with locating the sources of Indian weakness than putting the blame on British avarice or deceit. But the emphasis is not so much on the elements of culture. Gandhi points much more forcefully to the moral failure.

> The English have not taken India; we have given it to them. They are not in India because of their strength, but because we keep them . . . Recall the Company Bahadur. Who made it Bahadur? They had not the slightest intention at the time of establishing a kingdom. Who assisted the Company's officers? Who was tempted at the sight of their silver? Who bought their goods? History testifies that we did all this . . . When our Princes fought among themselves, they sought the

assistance of Company Bahadur. That corporation was versed alike in commerce and war. It was unhampered by questions of morality . . . Is it not then useless to blame the English for what we did at the time? . . . it is truer to say that we gave India to the English than that India was lost.[4]

It was a moral failure on the part of Indians that led to the conquest of India. And in exploring the reasons behind this moral failure, Gandhi's answer becomes diametrically opposed to that of Bankim. It is not because Indian society lacked the necessary cultural attributes that it was unable to face up to the power of the English. It is not the backwardness or lack of modernity of India's culture that keeps it in continued subjection. And the task of achieving freedom would not be accomplished by creating a new modern culture for the nation. For Gandhi, it is precisely because Indians were seduced by the glitter of modern civilization that they became a subject people. And what keeps them in subjection is the acceptance by leading sections of Indians of the supposed benefits of civilization. Indeed, as long as Indians continue to harbour illusions about the 'progressive' qualities of modern civilization, they will remain a subject nation. Even if they succeed physically in driving out the English, they would still have 'English rule without the Englishman', because it is not the physical presence of the English which makes India a subject nation: it is civilization which subjects.

There then follows an indictment of modern civilization as it has emerged in the West and as it has been imported into India. Fundamentally, Gandhi attacks the very notions of modernity and progress and subverts the central claim made on behalf of those notions, viz. their correspondence with a new organization of society in which the productive capacities of human labour are multiplied several times, creating increased wealth and prosperity for all and hence increased leisure, comfort, health and happiness. Gandhi argues that far from achieving these objectives, what modern civilization does is make man a prisoner of his craving for luxury and self-indulgence, release the forces of unbridled competition and thereby bring upon society the evils of poverty, disease, war and suffering. It is precisely because modern civilization looks at man as a limitless consumer and thus sets out to open the floodgates of industrial production that it also becomes the source of inequality, oppression and violence on a scale hitherto unknown in human history.

Machinery, for instance, is intended to increase the productivity of labour and thus to satisfy the never-ending urge for consumption. But it only whets the appetite, it does not satisfy it. What it does instead is bring exploitation and disease to the industrial cities and unemployment and ruin to the countryside.

> When I read Mr Dutt's *Economic History of India*, I wept; and as I think of it again my heart sickens. It is machinery that has impoverished India. It is difficult to measure the harm that Manchester has done to us. It is due to Manchester that Indian handicraft has all but disappeared.[5]

The driving social urge behind industrial production is the craving for excessive consumption. It is in this context that Gandhi interprets the modern spirit of scientific inquiry and technological advance; a tendency to let the mind wander uncontrolled and chase the objects of our passions.

> We notice that the mind is a restless bird; the more it gets the more it wants, and still remains unsatisfied. The more we indulge our passions, the more unbridled they become. Our ancestors, therefore, set a limit to our indulgences. They saw that happiness was largely a mental condition . . . Observing all this, our ancestors dissuaded us from luxuries and pleasures. We have managed with the same kind of plough as existed thousands of years ago. We have retained the same kind of cottages that we had in former times and our indigenous education remains the same as before. We have had no system of life-corroding competition . . . It was not that we did not know how to invent machinery, but our forefathers knew that if we set our hearts after such things, we would become slaves and lose our moral fibres. They, therefore, after due deliberation decided that we should only do what we could with our hands and feet.[6]

Hence, his solution to the social evils of industrialism is not just to remove its defects, because he thinks these so-called defects are germane to the very fundamentals of the modern system of production. His solution is to give up industrialism altogether: 'instead of welcoming machinery as a boon, we should look upon it as an evil'.[7] It is only a complete change in moral values that will change our perception of our social needs and thus enable us once again to set deliberate limits to social consumption. Nothing short of this will succeed.

> A certain degree of physical harmony and comfort is necessary, but above a certain level it becomes a hindrance instead of help. Therefore the ideal of creating an unlimited number of wants and satisfying them seems to be a delusion and a snare. The satisfaction of one's physical needs, even the intellectual needs of one's narrow self, must meet at a certain point a dead stop, before it degenerates into physical and intellectual voluptuousness.[8]

Clearly, then, Gandhi's critique of British rule in India attempted to situate it at a much more fundamental level than Bankim, or indeed any other nationalist writer of his time. Where they were criticizing merely the excesses of Western notions of patriotism and national glory which inevitably pushed those countries towards the pursuit of colonial conquests and victories in war, Gandhi has no doubt at all that the source of modern imperialism lies specifically in the system of social production which the countries of the Western world have adopted. It is the limitless desire for ever-increased production and ever-greater consumption, and the spirit of ruthless competitiveness which keeps the entire system going, that impel these countries to seek colonial possessions which can be exploited for economic purposes. Gandhi stated this position quite emphatically as early as in *Hind Swaraj* and held on to it all his life. It was, in fact, in many ways the most crucial theoretical foundation of his entire strategy of winning *svarāj* for India.

> Napoleon is said to have described the English as a nation of shop-keepers. It is a fitting description. They hold whatever dominions they have for the sake of their commerce. Their army and their navy are intended to protect it. When the Transvaal offered no such attractions, the late Mr Gladstone discovered that it was not right for the English to hold it. When it became a paying proposition,

resistance led to war. Mr Chamberlain soon discovered that England enjoyed a suzerainty over the Transvaal. It is related that someone asked the late President Kruger whether there was gold on the moon. He replied that it was highly unlikely because, if there were, the English would have annexed it. Many problems can be solved by remembering that money is their God . . . If you accept the above statements, it is proved that the English entered India for the purposes of trade. They remain in it for the same purpose . . . They wish to convert the whole world into a vast market for their goods. That they cannot do so is true, but the blame will not be theirs. They will leave no stone unturned to reach the goal.⁹

Thus, in the case of modern imperialism, morality and politics are both subordinated to the primary consideration of economics, and this consideration is directly related to a specific organization of social production characterized not so much by the nature of ownership of the means of production but fundamentally by the purposes and the processes of production. That is to say, whereas Gandhi is in this particular historical instance talking about the capitalist system of production in Britain, his characterization of the type of economy which leads to exploitation and colonial conquest is not necessarily restricted to capitalism alone, because as long as the purpose of social production is to continually expand it in order to satisfy an endless urge for consumption and as long as the process of production is based on ever-increased mechanization, those consequences would follow inevitably. And the purposes and processes of production take on this particular form whenever production is primarily directed not towards the creation of articles of immediate *use* but towards *exchange* — exchange between town and country and between metropolis and colony. Any kind of industrialization on a large scale would have to be based on certain determinate exchange relations between town and country, with the balance inevitably tipping against the latter whenever the pace of industrialization quickens. This would lead to unemployment and poverty in the villages or, which amounts to the same thing, to the exploitation of colonial possessions.

Industrialization on a mass scale will necessarily lead to passive or active exploitation of the villagers as the problems of competition and marketing come in. Therefore we have to concentrate on the village being self-contained, manufacturing mainly for use.¹⁰

The mere socialization of industries would not alter this process in any way at all.

Pandit Nehru wants industrialization because he thinks that, if it is socialized, it would be free from the evils of capitalism. My own view is that evils are inherent in industrialism, and no amount of socialization can eradicate them.¹¹

In fact, Gandhi's argument was that there is no feasible way in which *any* process of industrialization can avoid the creation of exploitative and inhuman relations of exchange between town and country. He states this quite clearly when he argues that *khādī* is the only sound economic proposition for India.

'Khadi is the only true economic proposition in terms of the millions of villagers until such time, if ever, when a better system of supplying work and adequate wages for every able-bodied person above the age of sixteen, male or female, is found for his field, cottage or even factory in every one of the villages of India; or till sufficient cities are built up to displace the villages so as to give the villagers the necessary comforts and amenities that a well-regulated life demands and is entitled to.' I have only to state the proposition thus fully to show that khadi must hold the field for any length of time that we can think of.[12]

It is true, of course, that in the midst of continuing controversy about the economic policies of the Congress, and especially the programme of *khādī*, Gandhi increasingly tended to emphasize the strict economic argument against heavy industrialization in a large agrarian economy with an abundance of underemployed labour. During the 1920s and 1930s, the period of the growth of the national movement, he would often in fact prefer to suspend the debate about the larger moral issues of mechanization *per se* in order to win his point on the infeasibility of heavy industrialization in the particular context of India. 'I have no partiality,' he would say, 'for return to the primitive methods of grinding and husking for the sake of them. I suggest the return, because there is no other way of giving employment to the millions of villagers who are living in idleness.'[13] At times he even conceded that mechanization might have an economic logic in situations of labour scarcity.

Mechanization is good when the hands are too few for the work intended to be accomplished. It is an evil when there are more hands than required for the work, as is the case in India . . . The problem with us is not how to find leisure for the teeming millions inhabiting our villages. The problem is how to utilize their idle hours, which are equal to the working days of six months in the year . . . spinning and weaving mills have deprived the villagers of a substantial means of livelihood. It is no answer in reply to say that they turn out cheaper, better cloth, if they do so at all. For, if they have displaced thousands of workers, the cheapest mill cloth is dearer than the dearest khadi woven in the villages.[14]

But this was only a debating point, an attempt to bring round to the cause of his economic programme those who did not share his fundamental philosophical premises. Because ever so often, even as he argued about the practical economic necessity of *khādī*, he would remind his readers where exactly he stood with regard to the fundamental moral issues.

If I could do it, I would most assuredly destroy or radically change much that goes under the name of modern civilization. But that is an old story of life. The attempt is undoubtedly there. Its success depends upon God. But the attempt to revive and encourage the remunerative village industries is not part of such an attempt, except in so far as every one of my activities, including the propagation of non-violence, can be described as such an attempt.[15]

Even when it came to a question of the fundamental principles of organization of economic life, Gandhi would unhesitatingly state his opposition to the concept of the *homo oeconomicus*, to the supposed benefits of the social division of labour, and to the current faith in the laws of the marketplace transforming private vices into public virtues.

> I am always reminded of one thing which the well-known British economist Adam Smith has said in his famous treatise *The Wealth of Nations*. In it he has described some economic laws as universal and absolute. Then he has described certain situations which may be an obstacle to the operation of these laws. These disturbing factors are the human nature, the human temperament or altruism inherent in it. Now, the economics of khadi is just the opposite of it. Benevolence which is inherent in human nature is the very foundation of the economics of khadi. What Adam Smith has described as pure economic activity based merely on the calculations of profit and loss is a selfish attitude and it is an obstacle to the development of khadi; and it is the function of a champion of khadi to counteract this tendency.[16]

And thus one comes back to Gandhi's condemnation of what he calls 'modern civilization', which in fact is a fundamental critique of the entire edifice of bourgeois society: its continually expanding and prosperous economic life, based on individual property, the social division of labour and the impersonal laws of the market, described with clinical precision and complete moral approbation by Mandeville and Smith; its political institutions based on a dual notion of sovereignty in which the people in theory rule themselves, but are only allowed to do so through the medium of their representatives whose actions have to be ratified only once in so many years; its spirit of innovation, adventure and scientific progress; its rationalization of philosophy and ethics and secularization of art and education. As early as in *Hind Swaraj*, Gandhi launches a thoroughgoing critique against each of these constitutive features of civil society.

Parliament, for instance, he calls 'a sterile woman and a prostitute', the first because, despite being a sovereign institution, it cannot enact a law according to its own judgment but is constantly swayed by outside pressures, and the second because it continually shifts its allegiance from one set of ministers to another depending on which is more powerful. But basically, Gandhi objects to an entire structure of politics and government in which each individual is assumed to have his own individual interest, individuals are expected to come together into parties and alliances in terms of those self-interests, these combinations of interests are then supposed to exert pressure on each other by mobilizing public opinion and manipulating the levers of the governmental machinery, and legislative enactments are then expected to emerge as choices made on behalf of the whole society.

> It is generally acknowledged that the members [of Parliament] are hypocritical and selfish. Each thinks of his own little interest. It is fear that is the guiding motive . . . Members vote for their party without a thought. Their so-called discipline binds them to it. If any member, by way of exception, gives an independent vote, he is considered a renegade . . . The Prime Minister is more concerned about his power than about the welfare of Parliament. His energy is concentrated upon securing the success of his party. His care is not always that

Parliament should do right . . . If they are considered honest because they do not take what are generally known as bribes, let them be so considered, but they are open to subtler influences. In order to gain their ends, they certainly bribe people with honours. I do not hesitate to say that they have neither real honesty nor a living conscience.[17]

And the process by which support is mobilized on behalf of particular leaders or parties or interests is equally unworthy of moral approval.

To the English voters their newspaper is their Bible. They take their cue from their newspapers which are often dishonest. The same fact is differently interpreted by different newspapers, according to the party in whose interests they are edited . . . [The] people change their views frequently . . . These views swing like the pendulum of a clock and are never steadfast. The people would follow a powerful orator or a man who gives them parties, receptions, etc.[18]

Once again, Gandhi's criticism is aimed against the abrogation of moral responsibility involved in the duality of sovereignty and the mediation of complex legal–political institutions which distance the rulers of society from those they are supposed to represent. He does not accept the argument that if effective combinations are formed among individuals and groups sharing a set of common self-interests, then the institutions of representative democracy will ensure that the government will act in ways which are, on the whole, in the common interest of the entire collectivity. His argument is, in fact, that the dissociation of political values, based on self-interest, from social morality, based on certain universal ethical values shared by the whole community, leads to a structure and process of politics in which the wealthy and the powerful enjoy disproportionate opportunities to manipulate the machinery of government to their own sectional interests. Besides, the legal fiction of equality before the law and the supposed neutrality of state institutions only have the effect of perpetuating the inequalities and divisions which already exist in society: politics has no role in removing those inequalities or cementing the divisions. In fact, this very process of law and politics which thrives on conflict creates a vested interest among politicians, state officials and legal practitioners to perpetuate social divisions and indeed to create new ones.

[The lawyers'] duty is to side with their clients and to find out ways and arguments in favour of their clients, to which they (the clients) are often strangers . . . The lawyers, therefore, will, as a rule, advance quarrels instead of repressing them . . . It is within my knowledge that they are glad when men have disputes. Petty pleaders actually manufacture them.[19]

Similarly, the colonial state in India, by projecting an image of neutrality with regard to social divisions within Indian society, not only upholds the rigours of those divisions, such as the ones imposed by the caste system, but actually strengthens them.[20]

By contrast, it is only when politics is *directly* subordinated to a communal morality that the minority of exploiters in society can be resisted by the people and inequalities and divisions removed. As a political ideal, therefore, Gandhi counterposes against the system of representative government an undivided concept of popular sovereignty, where the community is self-regulating and political power is dissolved into the collective moral will.

> The power to control national life through national representatives is called political power. Representatives will become unnecessary if the national life becomes so perfect as to be self-controlled. It will then be a state of enlightened anarchy in which each person will become his own ruler. He will conduct himself in such a way that his behaviour will not hamper the well-being of his neighbours. In an ideal State there will be no political institution and therefore no political power.[21]

In its form, this political ideal is not meant to be a consensual democracy with complete and continual participation by every member of the polity. The utopia is *Rāmarājya*, a patriarchy in which the ruler, by his moral quality and habitual adherence to truth, always expresses the collective will.[22] It is also a utopia in which the economic organization of production, arranged according to a perfect four-fold *varṇa* scheme of specialization and a perfect system of reciprocity in the exchange of commodities and services, always ensures that there is no spirit of competition and no differences in status between different kinds of labour.[23] The ideal conception of *Rāmarājya*, in fact, encapsulates the critique of all that is morally reprehensible in the economic and political organization of civil society.

The argument is then extended to other aspects of civil society. The secularization of education, for instance, has made a 'fetish' of the knowledge of letters and has thereby both exaggerated and rationalized the inequalities in society. It ignores completely the ethical aspect of education and the need to integrate the individual within the collectively shared moral values of the community, and instead cultivates 'the pretension of learning many sciences'. The result is a pervasive feeling of dissatisfaction, of moral anarchy, and a license to individual self-seeking, to 'hypocrisy, tyranny, etc'.[24] It also rationalizes, by ascribing an economic logic to it, one of the fundamental aspects of the social division of labour in modern industrial society: the distinction between mental and manual work. It denies that intellectual labour is an aspect not of the creation of wealth but of human self-fulfilment and must, therefore, be made available to every human being, and this can only be done if all share equally in providing the needs of the body.

> May not men earn their bread by intellectual labour? No . . . Mere mental, that is, intellectual labour is for the soul and is its own satisfaction. It should never demand payment.[25]
> . . . Bodily sustenance should come from body labour, and intellectual labour is necessary for the culture of the mind. Division of labour there will necessarily be, but it will be a division into various species of body labour and not a division into intellectual labour to be confined to one class and body labour to be confined to another class.[26]

The spirit of scientific inquiry and technological innovation too is aimed more towards physical self-indulgence and luxury than towards the discovery of truth. The science of medicine, for instance, on whose behalf the tallest claims are made by the propagators of modernity, concerns itself more with enabling people to consume more than with the removal of disease.

> I overeat, I have indigestion, I go to the doctor, he gives me medicine, I am cured. I overeat again, I take his pills again. Had I not taken the pills in the first instance, I would have suffered the punishment deserved by me and I would not have overeaten again. The doctor intervened and helped me to indulge myself.[27]

And this, of course, only perpetuates the disease; it does not cure it. The modern science of medicine is satisfied by treating illnesses merely at the surface level of physical causality. The scientific spirit, divorced as it is from considerations of morality, does not feel obliged to look deeper into the true causes of diseases which must lie in the very mode of social living.

II

What appears on surface as a critique of Western civilization is, therefore, a total moral critique of the fundamental aspects of civil society. It is not, at this level, a critique of Western culture or religion,[28] nor is it an attempt to establish the superior spiritual claims of Hindu religion. In fact, the moral charge against the West is not that its religion is inferior, but that by whole-heartedly embracing the dubious virtues of modern civilization, it has forgotten the true teachings of the Christian faith. At this level of thought, therefore, Gandhi is not operating at all with the problematic of nationalism. His solution too is meant to be universal, applicable as much to the countries of the West as to nations such as India.

Not only that; what is even more striking, but equally clear, is that Gandhi does not even think within the thematic of nationalism. He seldom writes or speaks in terms of the conceptual frameworks or the modes of reasoning and inference adopted by the nationalists of his day, and quite emphatically rejects their rationalism, scientism and historicism. As early as in *Hind Swaraj*, Gandhi dismisses all historical objections to his project of freeing India, not by the strength of arms but by the force of the soul, by saying, 'To believe that what has not occurred in history will not occur at all is to argue disbelief in the dignity of man.'[29] He does not feel it necessary to even attempt a historical demonstration of the possibilities he is trying to point out. Indeed, he objects that the historical mode of reasoning is quite unsuitable, indeed irrelevant, for his purpose. History, he says, is built upon the records not of the working of the force of the soul but of its exact opposite. It is a record of the interruptions of peace.

> Two brothers quarrel; one of them repents and re-awakens the love that was lying dormant in him; the two again begin to leave in peace; nobody takes note of this. But if the two brothers, through the intervention of solicitors or some other reason take up arms or go to law — which is another form of the exhibition of brute force — their doings would be immediately noticed in the Press, they would be the talk

of their neighbours and would probably go down in history. And what is true of families and communities is true of nations.[30]

History therefore, does not record the Truth. Truth lies outside history; it is universal, unchanging. Truth has no history of its own.

It is instructive to compare the method Gandhi follows in his attempts to reinterpret the scriptures with those followed by practically every other nationalist reformer of the time — Bankim or Tilak or Dayanand, for example. Not only does he not attempt a historical examination of the authenticity of scriptural texts or of the historicity of the great characters of sacred history, he quite explicitly states that such exercises were quite irrelevant to the determination of truth. In *Anāsaktiyoga*, his commentaries on the *Gītā*, Gandhi does not bother at all about the history of the text itself or about the historicity of Krishna, although he was quite aware of the debates surrounding these questions. Mahadev Desai, in his introductory note to the English translation of *Anāsaktiyoga*, mentions the debate about the 'original' text of the *Gītā* and says,

> One may however say that, even when this original is discovered, it will not make much difference to souls like Gandhiji, every moment of whose life is a conscious effort to live the message of the Gita. This does not mean that Gandhiji is indifferent to the efforts of scholars in this direction. The smallest questions of historical detail interest him intensely as I can say from personal knowledge . . . But his attitude is that in the last analysis it is the message that abides, and he is sure that no textual discovery is going to affect by a jot the essence or universality of that message. The same thing may be said about questions of the historical Krishna and the genesis and history of the Krishna Vasudeva worship . . .[31]

Further, Gandhi did not regard the *Gītā*, or even the *Mahābhārata* of which it appears as a part, as a historical narrative. The historical underpinnings were merely a literary device; the message had nothing to do with history.

> Even in 1888-9, when I first became acquainted with the Gita, I felt that it was not a historical work, but that, under the guise of physical warfare, it described the duel that perpetually went on in the hearts of mankind, and that physical warfare was brought in merely to make the description of the internal duel more alluring. This preliminary intuition became more confirmed on a closer study of religion and the Gita. A study of the Mahabharata gave it added confirmation. I do not regard the Mahabharata as a historical work in the accepted sense. The *Adiparva* contains powerful evidence in support of my opinion. By ascribing to the chief actors superhuman or subhuman origins, the great Vyasa made short work of the history of kings and their peoples. The persons therein described may be historical, but the author of the Mahabharata has used them merely to drive home his religious theme.[32]

Indeed, whenever he was confronted with a historical argument about the great Indian epics, trying to point out, for instance, the reality of warfare and violence in human life and of the relevance of a text such as the *Gītā* as a practical consideration of the ethics of power politics, Gandhi would insist that the truth of the *Mahābhārata* or the *Rāmāyaṇa* was a 'poetic truth', not historical; the epics were allegories and not theoretical or historical treatises. 'That they most probably deal with historical figures does not affect my proposition. Each epic describes the eternal duel that goes on between the forces of darkness and light.'[33]

To discover the truth, one would, of course, have to interpret the text to the best of one's knowledge and belief.

> Who is the best interpreter? Not learned men surely. Learning there must be. But religion does not live by it. It lives in the experiences of its saints and seers, in their lives and sayings. When all the most learned commentators of the scriptures are utterly forgotten, the accumulated experience of the sages and saints will abide and be an inspiration for ages to come.[34]

There might, of course, be conflicting interpretations of the epics and the scriptures. But such a dispute could never be resolved theoretically. Only the living practice of one's faith could show whether or not one's interpretation was correct. Gandhi mentions, for instance, the difference between his interpretation of the *Gītā* and the one followed by those who believed in armed violence.

> The grim fact is that the terrorists have in absolute honesty, earnestness and with cogency used the *Gita*, which some of them know by heart, in defence of their doctrine and policy. Only they have no answer to my interpretation of the *Gita*, except to say that mine is wrong and theirs is right. Time alone will show whose is right. The *Gita* is not a theoretical treatise. It is a living but silent guide whose directions one has to understand by patient striving.[35]

Gandhi's argument was exactly the same when dealing with questions such as scriptural sanctions for all those social practices which he thought were unjust and immoral. He would not admit that the mere existence of scriptural texts was proof that they must be a constituent or consistent part of true religion. Nor would he agree to submit his case to a historical examination of the origins or evolution of particular social institutions. On the caste system, for instance, his position was as follows:

> Caste has nothing to do with religion. It is a custom whose origin I do not know and do not need to know for the satisfaction of my spiritual hunger. But I do know that it is harmful both to spiritual and national growth.[36]

When his critics argued that caste practices were quite explicitly sanctioned by the *śāstra*, his emphatic reply was: 'Nothing in the Shastras which is manifestly contrary to universal truths and morals can stand.'[37] So also on the question of the social status of women as described in the canonical *smṛti* texts:

> it is sad to think that the *Smritis* contain texts which can command no respect from men who cherish the liberty of woman as their own and who regard her as the mother of the race . . . The question arises as to what to do with the *Smritis* that contain texts . . . that are repugnant to the moral sense. I have already

suggested . . . that all that is printed in the name of scriptures need not be taken as the word of God or the inspired word.[38]

Gandhi's position, then, is that the true principles of religion or morality are universal and unchanging. There do exist religious traditions which represent the attempts by various people through the ages to discover and interpret these principles. But those traditions were the products of history; they could not be taken to represent a corpus of truths.

The true dharma is unchanging, while tradition may change with time. If we were to follow some of the tenets of *Manusmriti*, there would be moral anarchy. We have quietly discarded them altogether.[39]

Not only did Gandhi not share the historicism of the nationalist writers, he did not share their confidence in rationality and the scientific mode of knowledge. He would repeatedly assert that the knowledge unearthed by the sciences was applicable only to very limited areas of human living. If one did not acknowledge this and pretended instead that rational inquiry and a scientific search for truth would provide the solution for every problem in life, one would be either led to insanity or reduced to impotence.

Nowadays, I am relying solely on my intellect. But mere intellect makes one insane or unmanly. That is its function. In such a situation Rama is the strength of the weak. My innermost urge is for pure non-violence. My weakness is that I do not know how to make it work. I use my intellect to overcome that weakness. If this intellectual cleverness loses the support of truth, it will blur my vision of non-violence, for is not non-violence the same as truth? Mere practical sense is but a covering for truth. 'The face of truth is hidden by a golden lid.' The reasoning faculty will raise a thousand issues. Only one thing will save us from these and that is faith.[40]

Perhaps the most celebrated public controversy over Gandhi's preference for instinctive faith over the claims of scientific reasoning was when he pronounced that the devastating earthquakes in Bihar in 1934 were a 'divine chastisement' for the sin of untouchability. Rabindranath Tagore reacted very strongly and criticized Gandhi not only for implying that God, in inflicting punishment upon sinners, was unable to distinguish between the guilty and the innocent, since an earthquake is indiscriminate in its destruction, but also for strengthening the forces of unreason which fostered the belief that cosmic phenomena had something to do with the fate of human beings on earth.[41] Gandhi stuck to his position with characteristic firmness, but there was a somewhat unusual touch of acerbity in his reply.[42] He refused to entertain questions about the rationality of divine action.

I am not affected by posers such as 'why punishment for an age-old sin' or 'why punishment to Bihar and not to the South' or 'why an earthquake and not some other form of punishment'. My answer is: I am not God. Therefore I have but a limited knowledge of His purpose.[43]

He reiterated his belief 'that physical phenomena produce results both physical and spiritual. The converse I hold to be equally true.'[44] He admitted that his belief was 'instinctive' and that he could not prove it. 'But I would be untruthful and cowardly if, for fear of ridicule, when those that are nearest and dearest to me are suffering, I did not proclaim my belief from the house-top.'[45] In any case, there were very few things which we understood well enough to be able to prove by the use of reason. And 'where reason cannot function, it is faith that works'. Some physical phenomena were intricately related to our ways of living, and since we had only an 'infinitesimal' knowledge of the rational working of physical laws, the proper attitude would be to not remain content with this partial knowledge but to take a unified moral view of those relations.

> Rain is a physical phenomenon; it is no doubt related to human happiness and unhappiness; if so, how could it fail to be related to his good and bad deeds? We know of no period in human history when countless people have not related events like earthquakes to sinful deeds of man. Even today, religious-minded people everywhere believe in such a relationship.[46]

Such faith was based on firm principles of morality. It was not, therefore, superstitious.

> I beseech you not to laugh within yourself and think I want to appeal to your instinct of superstition. I don't. I am not given to making any appeal to the superstitious fears of people. I may be called superstitious, but I cannot help telling you what I feel deep down in me . . . You are free to believe it or to reject it.[47]

But by believing it, one could turn a human catastrophe into a social good. It did not matter what the correct scientific explanation was for such phenomena; by taking a firm moral attitude towards it, one could strengthen one's resolution to fight all of those things which were evil in human life.

> If my belief turns out to be ill-founded, it will still have done good to me and those who believe with me. For we shall have been spurred to more vigorous efforts towards self-purification, assuming, of course, that untouchability is a deadly sin.[48]

To Gandhi, then, truth did not lie in history, nor did science have any privileged access to it. Truth was moral: unified, unchanging and transcendental. It was not an object of critical inquiry or philosophical speculation. It could only be found in the experience of one's life, by the unflinching practice of moral living. It could never be correctly expressed within the terms of rational theoretical discourse; its only true expression was lyrical and poetic.[49] The universalist religiosity of this conception is utterly inconsistent with the dominant thematic of post-Enlightenment thought.

III

From this evidence, it is tempting to characterize Gandhism as yet another example of that typical reaction of the intelligentsia in many parts of the world to the social and moral depredations of advancing capitalism: romanticism. For instance, Gandhi's descriptions of the ideal moral order and the standpoint of his moral critique of civil society suggest strong similarities with that aspect of Russian *narodnichestvo* which Lenin called 'economic romanticism'.[50] In Gandhi too, there seems to be the vision of a utopia — 'a backward-looking petty-bourgeois utopia' — and an idealization of pre-capitalist economic and social relations. One could, of course, concede to Gandhi, as indeed Lenin did to the Populists, that despite the backwardness of his solution to the fundamental problems of a society in the throes of capitalist penetration, he nevertheless took 'a big step forward' by posing, comprehensively and in all its economic, political and moral aspects, the democratic demand of the small producers, chiefly the peasants. But in the theoretical sense, Gandhian ideology would still be 'reactionary', since, as Lenin pointed out in the case of the Russian Populists, not only is there simply a romantic longing for a return to an idealized medieval world of security and contentment, there is also 'the attempt to measure the new society with the old patriarchal yardstick, the desire to find a model in the old order and traditions, which are totally unsuited to the changed economic institutions'.[51] In spite of conceding the 'democratic points' in Gandhi's thought, therefore, the Leninist would have to pronounce that it is based on a false, indeed reactionary, theory of the world-historical process, or else that it refuses to acknowledge a theory of history at all. In either case, it would be a variant of romanticism.

This characterization gains further weight when one considers the sources of literary influence, explicitly acknowledged by Gandhi himself, which went into the formulation of his ideas on state and society. There was, for instance, Edward Carpenter's *Civilisation: Its Cause and Cure* which greatly influenced Gandhi's ideas on the corrupting effects of science, especially modern medicine. On the social consequences of the processes of industrial production, perhaps the greatest influence was John Ruskin's *Unto This Last*, that intensely moralistic critique of 'the modern *soi-disant* science of political economy'. On the fundamentally repressive nature of the powers of the state, and on the moral duty of peaceful resistance, a strong formative influence came from the political works of Tolstoy. It is true, of course, that Gandhi was highly eclectic in his borrowings, a task made easier in his case by the fact that he was unhampered by the formal theoretical requirements of scientific disciplines and philosophical schools. But there is little doubt that he was inherently sympathetic to many of the strands of argument put forward by 19th century European romantics and critics of rationalism and industrial progress.

A detailed examination of this question of influences would take us a long way from the central argument of this chapter. But the point about Gandhi's selectiveness in picking ideas from his favourite authors can be illustrated a little more in order to lead on to my next proposition that the fundamental core of the Gandhian ideology does not lie in a romantic problematic. For instance, Gandhi liked Edward Carpenter's argument about how the limitless increase of man's powers of production, brought on by the advent of modern science and technology, draws him away '(1) from Nature, (2) from his true Self, (3) from his Fellows', and how it works 'in every way to disintegrate and corrupt man —

literally to corrupt — to *break up* the unity of his nature'.[52] But Carpenter's critique of modern-day civilization was also based on a somewhat idiosyncratic reading of the anthropological theories in Lewis Morgan's *Ancient Society* and Frederick Engels's *The Origin of the Family, Private Property and the State*. This, in fact, was the main theoretical foundation on which Carpenter built his argument about how civilization, by transforming the nature of 'property', destroys man's unity with nature. Yet Carpenter's theoretical efforts do not seem to have made any impression on his more illustrious reader.

So also with Ruskin: Gandhi accepted Ruskin's cricitism of that 'political economy founded on self-interest' which had made 'mammon service' the new religion of society. He particularly liked the idea that although there had to be different professions, such as those of the soldier, the physician, the pastor, the lawyer or the merchant, their incomes must only be a payment to them from society, a means of their livelihood, and 'not the objects of their life'. He approved of Ruskin's suggestion that 'that country is richest which nourishes the greatest number of noble and happy human beings; that man is richest who, having perfected the functions of his own life to the utmost, has also the widest helpful influence, both personal, and by means of his possessions, over the lives of others'.[53] But Ruskin was also a historicist, influenced in important ways by German idealism and particularly by Hegel. Despite the contradictoriness which he shared with all the other critics of industrial civilization in Victorian Britain, Ruskin was, in the fundamental elements of his thought, a 'modernist'. Collingwood points out, for instance, that 'he cared intensely for science and progress, for political reform, for the advancement of knowledge and for new movements in art and letters'.[54] His critique of political economy was meant to show the painful contradictions between the dictates of a supposedly rational science and those of altruistic morality, and to suggest that there was something fundamentally wrong with that 'so-called science'. It was never meant to be a call for the abandonment of Reason. He was aware of the limits of the intellect but never supposed 'that "conscience" or "faith" may guide us where "intellect" breaks down'.[55]

All of these concerns were quite far removed from Gandhi's theoretical world. The critique of civil society which appears on the pages of *Hind Swaraj* does not emerge out of a consideration of the historical contradictions of civil society *as perceived from within it*. Quite unlike any of the European romantics, Gandhi is not torn between the conflicting demands of Reason and Morality, Progress and Happiness, Historical Necessity and Human Will. His idealization of a peaceful, non-competitive just and happy Indian society of the past could not have been 'a romantic longing for the lost harmony of the archaic world', because unlike romanticism, Gandhi's problem is not conceived at all within the thematic bounds of post-Enlightenment thought. He was not, for instance, seriously troubled by the problems of reconciling individuality with universalism, of being oneself and at the same time feeling at one with the infinite variety of the world. Nor was his solution one in which the individual, without merging into the world, would want to embrace the rich diversity of the world in himself. Indeed, these were concerns which affected many Indian 'modernists' of Gandhi's time, perhaps the most illustrious of them being Rabindranath Tagore. Gandhi shared neither the spiritual anguish nor indeed the aestheticism of these literary romantics of his time. Instead, his moral beliefs never seemed to lose that almost obdurate certitude which men like Tagore, or even Jawaharlal Nehru, found so exasperating.

The critique of civil society which forms such a central element of Gandhi's moral and political thinking is one which arises from an epistemic standpoint situated *outside* the thematic of post-Enlightenment thought. As such, it is a standpoint which could have been adopted by any member of the traditional intelligentsia in India, sharing the modes and categories of thought of a large pre-capitalist agrarian society, and reacting to the alien economic, political and cultural institutions imposed on it by colonial rule. But if this is all there was to Gandhism, it could hardly have acquired the tremendous power that it undoubtedly did in the history of nationalism in India and in the formation of the contemporary Indian state. It would indeed be a gross error to regard Gandhi as merely another 'peasant intellectual'; despite the inherently 'peasant–communal' character of its critique of civil society, the correct perspective for understanding the Gandhian ideology *as a whole* would be to study it in relation to the historical development of elite-nationalist thought in India. For Gandhism, like Russian populism, was not a direct expression of peasant ideology. It was an ideology conceived as an intervention in the elite-nationalist discourse of the time and was formed and shaped by the experiences of a specifically national movement. It is only by looking at it in that historical context that it becomes possible to understand the unique achievement of Gandhism: its ability to open up the possibility for achieving perhaps the most important historical task for a successful national revolution in a country like India, viz., the political appropriation of the subaltern classes by a bourgeoisie aspiring for hegemony in the new nation-state. In the Indian case, the largest popular element of the nation was the peasantry. And it was the Gandhian ideology which opened up the historical possibility for its appropriation into the evolving political structures of the Indian state.

In its critique of civil society, Gandhism adopted a standpoint that lay entirely outside the thematic of post-Enlightenment thought, and hence of nationalist thought as well. In its formulation of the problem of town–country economic exchanges, of the cultural domination of the new urban educated classes, and above all, of the legitimacy of resistance to an oppressive state apparatus, it was able to encapsulate perfectly the specific political demands as well as the modalities of thought of a peasant–communal consciousness. If one wishes to pursue the point about European influences on the formation of Gandhi's thought, it is in fact Tolstoy who emerges as the most interesting comparison. For unlike the Russian Populists, and particularly unlike N.K. Mikhaïlovskiï, against whom Lenin directed one of his first major polemical attacks,[56] Tolstoy was a consistent anarchist in his critique of the bourgeois political order, and this from a standpoint which, as Andrzej Walicki has pointed out, was 'genuinely archaic': unlike any of the Populists, Tolstoy was 'apparently more easily able to identify himself with the world outlook of the primitive, patriarchal villagers'.[57] Tolstoy, like Gandhi, believed that 'the cause of the miserable position of the workers' was not something specific to capitalism: 'The cause must lie in that which drives them from the villages'.[58] He, too, argued against the determinism inherent in the assumptions of economic science which was 'so sure that all the peasants have inevitably to become factory operatives in towns' that it continually affirmed 'that all the country people not only are not injured by the transition from the country to the town, but themselves desire it, and strive towards it'.[59] Even more significant was Tolstoy's characterization of the entire edifice of the state as the institutionalized expression of morally unjustifiable violence. His answer to state oppression was complete and implacable resistance. One must not, he said, 'neither willingly, nor under compulsion, take any part in Governmental activity . . . nor, in fact, hold any office connected with violence', nor should one 'voluntarily pay taxes to Governments' or 'appeal to Governmental violence for the protection of his possessions'.[60] This thoroughgoing anarchism in Tolstoy was not accompanied by any specific political programme. There was simply a belief that the exemplary action of a few individuals, resisting the state by the strength of their conscience, would sway the people towards a massive movement against the institutions of violence.

> Men who accept a new truth when it has reached a certain degree of dissemination always do so suddenly and in a mass . . . The same is true of the bulk of humanity which suddenly, not one by one but always in a mass, passes from one arrangement of life to another under the influence of a new public opinion . . . And therefore the transformation of human life . . . will not come about solely by all men consciously and separately assimilating a certain Christian conception of life, but will come when a Christian public opinion so definite and comprehensible as to reach everybody has arisen and subdued that whole inert mass which is not able to attain the truth by its own intuition and is therefore always swayed by public opinion.[61]

In one aspect of his thought, Gandhi shared the same standpoint; but his thought ranged far beyond this specific ideological aspect. And it is here that the comparison with Tolstoy breaks down, because Gandhism also concerned itself with the practical organizational questions of a political *movement*. And this was a *national* political movement, required to operate within the institutional processes set up and directed by a colonial state. In its latter aspect, therefore, Gandhism had perforce to reckon with the practical realities of a bourgeois legal and political structure as indeed of the organizational issues affecting a bourgeois political movement. It was the unique achievement of Gandhian thought to have attempted to reconcile these two contradictory aspects which were, at one and the same time, its integral parts: a nationalism which stood upon a critique of the very idea of civil society, a movement supported by the bourgeoisie which rejected the idea of progress, the ideology of a political organization fighting for the creation of a modern national state which accepted at the same time the ideal of an 'enlightened anarchy'. Clearly there are many ambiguities in Gandhism. And a proper understanding of its history must go into a detailed examination of how these ambiguities created the possibility for those two great movements that form part of the story of the formation of the new Indian state: on the one hand, the transformation, in its own distinctive way in each region and among each strata, of the demands of the people into 'the message of the Mahatma',[62] and on the other, the appropriation of this movement into the structural forms of a bourgeois organizational, and later constitutional, order. But that is the task of modern Indian historiography; for the present, we can only indicate the elements in Gandhian thought which made possible the coexistence of these contradictory aspects within a single ideological unity. Here, we must turn to the celebrated concepts of *ahiṃsā* and *satyāgraha* and their epistemic basis in a conception that can only be described, fully in accordance with Gandhian terminology, as 'experimental'.

IV

'Truth,' wrote Gandhi to Mirabehn in 1933, 'is what everyone for the moment feels it to be.'[63] It was a decidedly personal quest, but it did not for that reason imply a moral anarchy. A few days before, in another letter, he had explained to her:

> We know the fundamental truth we want to reach, we know also the way. The details we do not know, we shall never know them all, because we are but very humble instruments among millions of such, moving consciously or unconsciously towards the divine event. We shall reach the Absolute Truth, if we will faithfully and steadfastly work out the relative truth as each one of us knows it.[64]

More publicly, in the Introduction to the *Autobiography* in 1925, Gandhi had written:

> for me, truth is the sovereign principle, which includes numerous other principles. This truth is not only truthfulness in word, but truthfulness in thought also, and not only the relative truth of our conception, but the Absolute Truth, the Eternal Principle, that is God. There are innumerable definitions of God . . . But I worship God as Truth only. I have not yet found Him, but I am seeking after Him . . . But as long as I have not realized this Absolute Truth, so long must I hold by the relative truth as I have conceived it. That relative truth must, meanwhile, be my beacon, my shield and buckler.[65]

There did exist an Absolute Truth, absolute and transcendental; to discover it was the purpose of our lives. But one could only proceed to find it in the experience of living, through an unswerving moral and truthful practice. At every stage, one had to be firmly committed to the truth as one knew it. At the same time, one had to be prepared to learn from experience, to put one's belief to the test, to accept the consequences and revise those beliefs if they were found wanting. Only then would one have for one's moral practice an epistemic foundation that was both certain and flexible, determinate and yet adaptable, categorical as well as experiential.

So much has now been written about Gandhi's 'truths' — the Absolute Truth, which must be sought for, and the various relative truths of our conception — that it is difficult to talk about the subject without referring to various current interpretations of those concepts. But once again, this will take us away from the central line of my argument. I must, therefore, accept the risk of inviting charges of distortion and oversimplification, and without explaining its relation to the vast body of Gandhian literature, simply proceed to state my own understanding of the conception of 'truth' in the overall structure and effectivity of the Gandhian ideology. In *Hind Swaraj*, the critique of modern civilization, and the plea for a return to the simple self-sufficiency of 'traditional' village life were based on the idea that it was the very changelessness of Indian civilization, its timeless ahistoricity, which was proof of its truth. India was resistant to change because it was not necessary for it to change: its civilization had found the true principles of social organization.

> It is a charge against India that her people are so uncivilized, ignorant and stolid, that it is not possible to induce them to adopt any changes. It is a charge really against our merit. What we have tested and found true on the anvil of experience, we dare not change.[66]

All that was necessary now was to find a way of protecting that social organization from the destructive consequences of colonial rule and of eliminating the poverty that had been brought upon the people. The answer was a rejection of the entire institutional edifice of civil society, uncompromising resistance to its economic, cultural and political structures. There was no specific conception yet of a political process of struggle, of its organizational procedures, norms of practice, strategic and tactical principles. As Gandhi explained later in the *Autobiography*, 'In [*Hind Swaraj*] I took it as understood that anything that helped India to get rid of the grinding poverty of her masses would in the same process also establish swaraj.'[67] It was only in the context of the evolution of the political movement that the Gandhian ideology became something more than a utopian doctrine. It acquired a theory of the political process within which the movement was to function; it developed its own organizational principles of political practice. In course of the full working out of Gandhian thought, the sheer tactical malleability of the 'experimental' conception of truth became the principal means by which all the seemingly irreconcilable parts of that ideology were put together.

Consider *satyāgraha*, that celebrated Gandhian form of mass political action. In 1917 Gandhi explained that *satyāgraha* was not mere passive resistance. It meant 'intense activity' — political activity — by large masses of people. It was a legitimate, moral and truthful form of political action by the people against the injustices of the state, an active mass resistance to unjust rule. It was not aimed at the destruction of the state, nor was it — as yet — conceived as part of a political process intended to replace the functionaries of the state.

> We can . . . free ourselves of the unjust rule of the Government by defying the unjust rule and accepting the punishments that go with it. We do not bear malice towards the Government. When we set its fears at rest, when we do not desire

to make armed assaults on the administrators, nor to unseat them from power, but only to get rid of their injustice, they will at once be subdued to our will.[68]

Satyāgraha, at this stage, was intended to articulate only a 'negative consciousness'. It is, therefore, easy to recognise why it could express so effectively the characteristic modes of peasant–communal resistance to oppressive state authority.[69] It was true, of course, that peasant resistance to injustice was not always restricted to non-violent forms: there was much historical evidence to this effect. But at this stage, Gandhi was quite dismissive of these objections.

It is said that it is a very difficult, if not an altogether impossible, task to educate ignorant peasants in satyagraha and that it is full of perils, for it is a very arduous business to transform unlettered ignorant people from one condition into another. Both the arguments are just silly. The people of India are perfectly fit to receive the training of satyagraha. India has knowledge of dharma, and where there is knowledge of dharma, satyagraha is a very simple matter . . . Some have a fear that once people get involved in satyagraha, they may at a later stage take arms. This fear is illusory. From the path of satyagraha, a transition to the path of *a-satyagraha* is impossible. It is possible of course that some people who believe in armed activity may mislead the satyagrahis by infiltrating into their ranks and later making them take to arms. This is possible in all enterprises. But as compared to other activities, it is less likely to happen in satyagraha, for their motives soon get exposed and when the people are not ready to take up arms, it becomes almost impossible to lead them on to that terrible path.[70]

Nor was the question of leadership, and of the relation between leaders and the masses, seen as being particularly problematical in the political sense:

People in general always follow in the footsteps of the noble. There is no doubt that it is difficult to produce a satyagrahi leader. Our experience is that a satyagrahi needs many more virtues like self-control, fearlessness, etc., than are requisite for one who believes in armed action . . . The birth of such a man can bring about the salvation of India in no time. Not only India but the whole world awaits the advent of such a man. We may in the meantime prepare the ground as much as we can through satyagraha.[71]

It was this faith in the relatively spontaneous strength of popular resistance to injustice that lay behind the call to the nation to join in the agitations in 1919 against the Rowlatt Bill. There was little concern yet about the distinction between leader and *satyāgrahī* or the *satyāgrahī* and the masses, or about the precise degree of maturity before the masses could be asked to join a *satyāgraha*, or about the organizational and normative safeguards against the inherent unpredictability of a negative consciousness playing itself out in the political battleground. In March 1919, Gandhi was still able to say to the people:

whether you are satyagrahis or not, so long as you disapprove of the Rowlatt legislation, all can join and I hope that there will be such a response throughout the length and breadth of India as would convince the Government that we are alive to what is going on in our midst.[72]

All this, of course, changed after the experience of the Rowlatt *satyāgraha*: 'a rapier run through my body could hardly have pained me more'.[73] He had made a massive error of judgment and there was, he admitted, some truth in the charge that he had ignored a few obvious lessons of political history.

> I think that I at least should have foreseen some of the consequences, specially in view of the gravest warnings that were given to me by friends whose advice I have always sought and valued. But I confess that I am dense. I am not joking. So many friends have told me that I am incapable of profiting by other people's experiences and that in every case I want to go through the fire myself and learn only after bitter experience. There is exaggeration in this charge, but there is also a substance of truth in it. This denseness in me is at once a weakness and a strength. I could not have remained a satyagrahi had I not cultivated the quality of stubborn resistance and such resistance can only come from experience and not from inference.[74]

But the experience of his first political agitation on a national scale brought in Gandhi a 'new realization'. He now became aware of the fundamental incompatibility of political action informed solely by a negative consciousness with the procedural norms of a bourgeois legal order. The ethics of resistance, if it was to be relevant to a bourgeois political movement, would have to be reconciled with a theory of political obedience. 'Unfortunately,' he said,

> popular imagination has pictured satyagraha as purely and simply civil disobedience, if not in some cases even criminal disobedience . . . As satyagraha is being brought into play on a large scale on the political field for the first time, it is in an experimental stage. I am therefore ever making new discoveries. And my error in trying to let civil disobedience take the people by storm appears to me to be Himalayan because of the discovery I have made, namely, that he only is able and attains the right to offer civil disobedience who has known how to offer voluntary and deliberate obedience to the laws of the State in which he is living.[75]

And from this fundamental discovery flowed a new organizational principle; as he later explained in the *Autobiography*:

> I wondered how I could have failed to perceive what was so obvious. I realized that before a people could be fit for offering civil disobedience, they should thoroughly understand its deeper implications. That being so, before restarting civil disobedience on a mass scale, it would be necessary to create a band of well-tried, pure-hearted volunteers who thoroughly understood the strict conditions of satyagraha.[76]

Thus was born the *political* concept of the *satyāgrahi* as leader. In the course of his evidence before the Hunter Committee appointed to inquire into the Rowlatt Bill agitations, Gandhi was asked about his conception of the relation between leaders and followers.

C.H. Setalvad. I take it that your scheme, as you conceive it, involves the determination of what is the right path and the true path by people who are capable of high intellectual and moral equipment and a large number of other people following them without themselves being able to arrive at similar conclusions by reason of their lower moral and intellectual equipment?

Gandhi. I cannot subscribe to that, because I have not said that. I do not say that they are not to exercise their judgment, but I simply say that, in order that they may exercise their judgment, the same mental and moral equipment is not necessary.

C.H.S. Because they are to accept the judgment of people who are capable of exercising better judgment and equipped with better moral and intellectual standard?

G. Naturally, but I think that is in human nature, but I exact nothing more than I would exact from an ordinary human being.[77]

While mass resistance to unjust laws was the final and only certain guarantee against state oppression, the people would have to depend on their leaders for guidance.

Jagat Narayan. My point is, having regard to the circumstances, a sort of sanctity attaches to the laws of the Government of the time being?

Gandhi. Not in my estimation . . .

J.N. That is not the best check on the masses?

G. Not a blind adherence to laws, no check whatsoever. It is because either they blindly adhere or they blindly commit violence. Either event is undesirable.

J.N. So as every individual is not fit to judge for himself, he would have to follow somebody?

G. Certainly, he would have to follow somebody. The masses will have to choose their leaders most decidedly.[78]

The point was further clarified when Gandhi was asked about his understanding of the reasons why the agitations had become violent. Soon after the events in Ahmedabad, Gandhi had told a mass meeting: 'It seems that the deeds I have complained of have been done in an organized manner. There seems to be a definite design about them, and I am sure that there must be some educated and clever man or men behind them . . . You have been misled into doing these deeds by such people.'[79] Elaborating on what he meant by 'organized manner', Gandhi said to the Hunter Committee:

In my opinion, the thing was organised, but there it stands. There was no question whether it was a deep-laid conspiracy through the length and breadth of India or a deep-rooted organisation of which this was a part. The organisation was hastily constructed; the organisation was not in the sense in which we understand the word organisation . . . If I confined that word to Ahmedabad alone, to masses of absolutely unlettered men, who would be able to make no fine distinctions — then you have got the idea of what that organisation is . . . There were these poor deluded labourers whose one business was to see me released and see Anasuyabai released. That it was a wicked rumour deliberately started by somebody I have not the slightest doubt. As soon as these things happened the people thought there should be something behind it. Then there were the half-educated raw youths. This is the work of these, I am grieved to have to say. These youths possessed themselves with false ideas gathered from shows, such as the cinematograph shows that they have seen, gathered from silly novels and from the political literature of Europe . . . it was an organisation of this character.[80]

The direct physical form in which the masses appeared in the political arena was always that of a mob. It had no mind of its own.[81] Its behaviour was determined entirely by the way it was led: 'nothing is so easy as to train mobs, for the simple reason that they have no mind, no premeditation. They act in a frenzy. They repent quickly.'[82] For this reason, they were as susceptible to manipulation by mischief-makers as they were open to enlightened leadership. In order, therefore, to undertake mass political action, it was necessary first of all to create a selfless, dedicated and enlightened group of political workers who would lead the masses and protect them from being misguided.

Before we can make real headway, we must train these masses of men who have a heart of gold, who feel for the country, who want to be taught and led. But a few intelligent, sincere, local workers are needed, and the whole nation can be organized to act intelligently, and democracy can be evolved out of mobocracy.[83]

This was the problematic which lay at the heart of what soon evolved into the other celebrated concept in the Gandhian ideology — the concept of *ahiṃsā*. In its application to politics, *ahiṃsā* was also about 'intense political activity' by large masses of people. But it was not so much about resistance as about the *modalities* of resistance, about organizational principles, rules of conduct, strategies and tactics. *Ahiṃsā* was the necessary complement to the concept of *satyāgraha* which both limited it and, at the same time, made it something more than 'purely and simply civil disobedience'. *Ahiṃsā* was the rule for concretizing the 'truth' of *satyāgraha*. 'Truth is a positive value, while non-violence is a negative value. Truth affirms. Non-violence forbids something which is real enough.'[84] *Ahiṃsā*, indeed, was the concept — both ethical and epistemological because it was defined within a moral and epistemic practice that was wholly 'experimental' — which supplied Gandhism with a theory of *politics*, enabling it to become the ideology of a national political movement. It was the organizing principle for a 'science' of politics — a science wholly different from all current conceptions of politics which had only succeeded in producing the 'sciences of violence', but a science nevertheless — the 'science of non-violence', the 'science of love'. It was the moral framework for solving every practical problem of the organized political movement.

The 'science of non-violence', consequently, dealt with questions such as the requirements for being a political *satyāgrahī*, his rules of conduct, his relations with the political leadership as well as with the masses, questions about the structure of decision-making, lines of command, political strategies and tactics, and about the practical issues of breaking as well as obeying the laws of the state. It was as much a 'science' of political struggle, indeed as much a military science, as the 'sciences of violence', only it was superior because it was a science not of arms but of the moral force of the soul. At this level, in fact, it was not a utopian conception at all. There was no assumption, for instance, of collective consensus in the making of decisions, for that would be wishing away the existence of a practical political problem. Decisions were to be taken by 'a few true satyagrahis'. This would provide a far more economic and efficient method of political action than that proposed by the 'sciences of violence': 'we would require a smaller army of satyagrahis than that of soldiers trained in modern warfare, and the cost will be insignificant compared to the fabulous sums devoted by nations to armaments'.[85] Second, the practice of this 'experimental science' of mass political action was not conditional upon the masses themselves understanding all its principles or their full implications.

> A soldier of an army does not know the whole of the military science; so also does a satyagrahi not know the whole science of satyagraha. It is enough if he trusts his commander and honestly follows his instructions and is ready to suffer unto death without bearing malice against the so-called enemy . . . [The satyagrahis] must render heart discipline to their commander. There should be no mental reservation.[86]

Third, the political employment of *ahiṃsā* did not depend upon everyone accepting it as a creed. It was possible for it to be regarded as a valid political theory even without its religious core. This, in fact, was the only way it could become a general guide for solving the practical problems of an organized political movement.

> Ahimsa with me is a creed, the breath of life. But it is never as a creed that I placed it before India or, for that matter, before anyone except in casual or informal talks. I placed it before the Congress as a political weapon, to be employed for the solution of practical problems.[87]

And thus we come to an explicit recognition, within the overall unity of the Gandhian ideology as it took shape in the course of the evolution of the national movement, of a *disjuncture* between morality and politics, between private conscience and public responsibility, indeed between Noble Folly and *Realpolitik*. It was a disjuncture which the 'experimental' conception of *ahiṃsā* was meant to bridge. And yet, it was a disjuncture the steadfast denial of whose very existence had been the foundation of the original conception of *Hind Swaraj*. Now, however, we see the spinning wheel, for instance, coming to acquire a dual significance, located on entirely different planes, and it is no longer considered politically necessary for the personal religion to be identified with a political programme.

> I have never tried to make anyone regard the spinning-wheel as his *kamadhenu* or universal provider . . . When in 1908 . . . I declared my faith in the spinning-wheel in the pages of *Hind Swaraj*, I stood absolutely alone . . . I do regard the spinning-wheel as a gateway to *my* spiritual salvation, but I recommend it to others only as a powerful weapon for the attainment of swaraj and the amelioration of the economic condition of the country.[88]

In 1930, on the eve of the Dandi March, we find Gandhi telling his colleagues that he did not know what form of democracy India should have. He was not particularly interested in the question: 'the method alone interests me, and by method I mean the agency through which the wishes of the people are reached. There are only two methods; one is that of fraud and force; the other is that of non-violence and truth.'[89] It did not matter even if the goal was beyond reach. The first responsibility of the political leader was to strictly adhere to his principles of morality.

> What I want to impress on everyone is that I do not want India to reach her goal through questionable means. Whether that is possible or not is another question. It is sufficient for my present purpose if the person who thinks out the plan and leads the people is absolutely above board and has non-violence and truth in him.[90]

And once there is a recognition of the disjuncture, the failure of politics to reach Utopia could be attributed to the loftiress of the ideal, noble, truthful and inherently unreachable, or else, equally credibly, to the imperfections of the human agency. The vision of a non-violent India could be 'a mere day-dream, a childish folly'.[91] Or else, one could argue with equal validity that the problem lay not with the ideal but with one's own deficiencies.

> I do not think it is right to say that the principles propounded in *Hind Swaraj* are not workable just because I cannot practise them perfectly . . . not only do I refuse to excuse myself, but positively confess my shortcoming.[92]

The result, of course, was that under the moral umbrella of the quest for utopia, the experimental conception of politics could accommodate a potentially limitless range of imperfections, adjustments, compromises and failures. For the authority of the political leader derived not from the inherent reasonableness of his programme or the feasilibility of his project, not even from the accordance of that programme or project with a collective perception of common interests or goals. It derived entirely from a moral claim — of personal courage and sacrifice and a patent adherence to truth. So much so that the supreme test of political leadership was death itself. That was the final proof of the leader's claim to the allegiance of his people. At Anand, in the middle of the Dandi March, Gandhi said,

> This band of satyagrahis which has set out is not staging a play; its effect will not be merely temporary; even through death, it will prove true to its pledge — if death becomes necessary . . . Nothing will be better than if this band of satyagrahis perishes. If the satyagrahis meet with death, it will put a seal upon their claim.[93]

And when Jairamdas Doulatram was injured in a police firing in Karachi during the Civil Disobedience movement, Gandhi sent a telegram to the Congress office saying:

> CONSIDER JAIRAMDAS MOST FORTUNATE. BULLET WOUND THIGH BETTER THAN PRISON. WOUND HEART BETTER STILL. BAPU.[94]

Gandhism finally reconciled the contradictions between the utopian and the practical aspects of its political ideology by surrendering to the absolute truthfulness and supreme self-sacrifice of the *satyāgrahī*. It had gained its strength from an intensely powerful moral critique of the existing state of politics. In the end, it saved its Truth by escaping from politics.

V

And yet, as Gandhi himself put it, 'politics encircle us today like the coil of a snake'.[95] The historical impact of the Gandhian ideology on the evolution of Indian politics was of monumental significance.

The 'science of non-violence' was the form in which Gandhism addressed itself to the problematic of nationalism. That was the 'science' which was to provide answers to the problems of national politics, of concretizing the nation as an active historical subject rejecting the domination of a foreign power, of devising its political organization and the strategic and tactical principles of its struggle. In its specific historical effectivity, Gandhism provided for the first time in Indian politics an ideological basis for including the *whole people* within the political nation. In order to do this, it quite consciously sought to bridge even the most sanctified cultural barriers that divided the people in an immensely complex agrarian society. Thus, it was not simply a matter of bringing the peasantry into the national movement, but of consciously seeking the ideological means for bringing it in *as a whole*. This, for instance, is how one can interpret the strenuous efforts by Gandhi to obliterate the 'sin' of the existing *jāti* divisions in Indian society, and the 'deadly sin' of untouchability in particular, and to replace it by an idealized scheme based on the *varṇa* classification.[96] 'Do you not think', Gandhi was asked, 'that the improvement of the condition of starving peasants is more important than the service of Harijans? Will you not, therefore, form peasant organizations which will naturally include Harijans in so far as their economic condition is concerned?' 'Unfortunately,' Gandhi replied,

> the betterment of the economic condition of peasants will not necessarily include the betterment of that of the Harijans. The peasant who is not a Harijan can rise as high as he likes and opportunity permits him, but not so the poor suppressed Harijan. The latter cannot own and use land as freely as the *savarna* peasant . . . therefore, a special organization for the service of Harijans is a peremptory want in order to deal with the special and peculiar disabilities of Harijans. Substantial improvement of these, the lowest strata of society, must include the whole of society.[97]

Whether this idiom of solidarity necessarily referred to a cultural code that could be shown to be 'essentially Hindu', and whether that in turn alienated rather than united those sections of the people who were not 'Hindu', are of course important questions, but not strictly relevant in establishing the ideological intent behind Gandhi's efforts.

Thus, while the search was for an ideological means to unite the whole people, there was also a determinate political structure and process, specific-

and historically given, within which the task had to be accomplished. And here it was the 'experimental' conception of truth, combining the absolute moral legitimacy of *satyāgraha* with the tactical considerations of *ahiṃsā*, which made the Gandhian ideology into a powerful instrument in the historical task of constructing the new Indian state.

For now one could talk, within the overall unity of that ideology, of the constructive relation of the national movement to the evolving institutional structure of state power. Gandhi could say, on the one hand, 'I shall retain my disbelief in legislatures as an instrument for obtaining swaraj in terms of masses', and in the same breath go on to argue,

> But I see that I have failed to wean some of the Congressmen from their faith in council-entry. The question therefore is whether they should or should not enforce their desire to enter legislature as Congress representatives. I have no doubt that they must have the recognition they want. Not to give it will be to refuse to make use of the talents we possess.[98]

Indeed, the truth of the moral conception of utopia was for ever safe, no matter what compromises one had to make in the world of practical politics.

> The parliamentary work must be left to those who are so inclined. I hope that the majority will always remain untouched by the glamour of council work. In its own place, it will be useful. But . . . Swaraj can only come through an all-round conciousness of the masses.[99]

Similarly, the acceptance of ministerial office by Congressmen in 1937, an act apparently in complete contradiction with the spirit of non-cooperation enshrined in the Congress movement in 1920, now became 'not a repudiation but a fulfilment of the original, so long as the mentality behind all of them remains the same as in 1920'.[100] And if the disharmony between the act and the mentality became much too gross, the final moral act that would save the truth of the ideal was withdrawal. When the evidence became overwhelming that Congressmen as officers of the state were not exhibiting the selflessness, ability and incorruptibility that was the justification for their being in office, Gandhi's plea to Congressmen was to make a choice:

> either to apply the purge I have suggested, or, if that is not possible because of the Congress being already overmanned by those who have lost faith in its creed and its constructive programme on which depends its real strength, to secede from it for its own sake and proving his living faith in the creed and programme by practising the former and prosecuting the latter as if he had never seceded from the Congress of his ideal.[101]

Then again, the ideal of property as trust was 'true in theory only'. Like all other ideals, it would

> remain an unattainable ideal, so long as we are alive, but towards which we must ceaselessly strive. Those who own money now are asked to behave like trustees holding their riches on behalf of the poor. You may say that trusteeship is a legal fiction . . . Absolute trusteeship is an abstraction like Euclid's definition of a

point, and is equally unattainable. But if we strive for it, we shall be able to go further in realizing a state of equality on earth than by any other method.

Q. But if you say that private possession is incompatible with non-violence, why do you put up with it?

A. That is a concession one has to make to those who earn money but who would not voluntarily use their earnings for the benefit of mankind.[102]

Sometimes the justification for this concession was crassly empirical: 'I am quite clear that if a strictly honest and unchallengeable referendum of our millions were to be taken, they would not vote for wholesale expropriation of the propertied classes.'[103] At other times, it would seem to rest on a fairly sophisticated reading of the lessons of political history: the zamindars

> must regard themselves, even as the Japanese nobles did, as trustees holding their wealth for the good of their wards, the ryots . . . I am convinced that the capitalist, if he follows the Samurai of Japan, has nothing really to lose and everything to gain. There is no other choice than between voluntary surrender on the part of the capitalist of superfluities and consequent acquisition of the real happiness of all on the one hand, and on the other the impending chaos into which, if the capitalist does not wake up betimes, awakened but ignorant, famishing millions will plunge the country and which not even the armed force that a powerful Government can bring into play can avert.[104]

But in considering questions of this sort, having to do with the practical organizational issues of a bourgeois political movement, Gandhism would inevitably slip into the familiar thematic of nationalist thought. It would argue in terms of categories such as capitalism, socialism, law, citizenship, private property, individual rights, and struggle to fit its formless utopia into the conceptual grid of post-Enlightenment social-scientific thought.

> Let us not be obsessed with catchwords and seductive slogans imported from the West. Have we not our own distinct Eastern traditions? Are we not capable of finding our own solution to the question of capital and labour? . . . Let us study our Eastern institutions in that spirit of scientific inquiry and we shall evolve a truer socialism and a truer communism than the world has yet dreamed of. It is surely wrong to presume that Western socialism or communism is the last word on the question of mass poverty.[105]
>
> . . . Class war is foreign to the essential genius of India which is capable of evolving a form of communism broad-based on the fundamental rights of all and equal justice to all.[106]

Sometimes, in trying to defend his political strategy of nationalist struggle, Gandhi would even feel forced to resort to some of the most naive cultural essentialisms of Orientalist thought:

> By her very nature, India is a lover of peace . . . On the other hand, Mustafa Kamal Pasha succeeded with the sword because there is strength in every nerve of a Turk. The Turks have been fighters for centuries. The people of India have followed the path of peace for thousands of years . . . There is at the present

time not a single country on the face of the earth which is weaker than India in point of physical strength. Even tiny Afghanistan can growl at her.[107]

These difficulties are symptomatic of the curious relationship between Gandhism and the thematic and problematic of nationalist thought. In its historical effectivity, we would be perfectly justified in characterizing the entire story of the Gandhian intervention in India's nationalist politics as the moment of manoeuvre in the 'passive revolution of capital' in India. But that is not something that can be read directly from the ideological intent expressed in Gandhian texts. Rather, we must identify the possibility of manoeuvre, the result of the struggle of social forces in the battlefield of politics, in the very tensions within Gandhism — in the fundamental ambiguity of its relation to nationalist thought, in the way in which it challenged the basic premises on which the latter was built and yet sought at the same time to insert itself into the process of a nationalist politics.

There was, as we have seen, a fundamental incompatibility between the utopianism which shaped the moral conception of Gandhian politics and the realities of power within a bourgeois constitutional order. It is not as though Gandhism was unaware of this disjunction; it did not dogmatically deny the existence of the gap nor did it insist that it could be bridged with ease. What it suggested was a certain method of political practice — imperfect but innately truthful, flexible and yet principled. But once the groundswell of popular upsurge had subsided and the nationalist state leadership knew that power was within its reach, it was not easy to determine what this truthful political practice was now going to be. What was the duty of the true servant of the Congress: take up the new responsibilities of running the state or stay outside it and continue the struggle towards what was known to be an unreachable goal?

Gandhi's belief was that the true *satyāgrahī* would always choose the latter. True non-violent *svarāj* would only come by pursuing the programme of rural construction; the parliamentary programme could at best bring 'political swaraj' which was not true *svarāj*.[108] As late as November 1945, Gandhi instructed members of the All India Spinners' Association, the central body of *khādī* workers, not to take part in elections or any other political activity of that sort.[109] But by 1945-6 many of his closest and most trusted associates in the constructive work programme were being asked by the Congress to enter government, and when they turned to him for advice his replies were curiously hesitant, sometimes even petulant: 'I do not want to dampen your interest. You have the aptitude for it. Nor would I consider your going into the Assembly a bad thing. After all someone has to go there. What I mean is that neither you nor anyone else can ride two horses at the same time.'[110] 'As regards the Provincial Assembly you may take it that I am not interested. But if you are inclined that way and have the ability for it, and if all others agree, please do go.'[111] In several cases he qualified his permission by a reminder about the importance of non-attachment in the life of a leader of the people:

Because all your friends want it, you may seek election to the Assembly if it can be done without any exertion on your part and on the clear understanding that it will be a bed of thorns and not of velvet . . . Refrain from all arguments and discussions, observe silence, and if even then people elect you go to the Assembly. You should not make any effort on your part to get elected.[112]

. . . You can give your name for the Provincial election on the condition that you would neither beg for votes from the electorate nor spend any money. If you can get elected on this condition you may enter the Assembly.[113]

Later he issued a general message for all Congressmen:

I believe that some Congressmen ought to seek election in the legislatures or other elected bodies. In the past I did not hold this view. I had hoped that the boycott of legislatures would be complete. That was not to be. Moreover times have changed. Swaraj seems to be near. Under the circumstances it is necessary that Congress should contest every seat in the legislatures. The attraction should never be the honour that a seat in a legislature is said to give . . . Moreover those that are not selected by the Board should not feel hurt. On the contrary, they should feel happy that they are left there to render more useful service. But the painful fact is that those who are not selected by the Board do feel hurt.

The Congress should not have to spend money on the elections. Nominees of a popular organization should be elected without any effort on the latter's part . . .

Let us examine the utility value of legislatures . . . He who can tell the people why they become victims of the Government . . . and can teach them how to stand up against Government wrongs renders a real service. The members cannot do this essential service, for their business is to make people look to them for the redress of wrongs. [The Gujarati version of this article has a much stronger sentence: 'Councils are, have been and will be, an obstruction in this work.']

The other use of legislatures is to prevent undesirable legislation and bring in laws which are useful for the public, so that as much help as possible can be given to the constructive programme.[114]

Thus, even while conceding that many Congressmen must now enter the business of running the state machinery, Gandhi still appeared to see them in a largely oppositional role, pointing out the misdeeds of government and preventing the enactment of bad laws. The only positive role he could envisage for the national government was the support it might provide for the constructive programme. In mid-1946 he even made some specific suggestions in this regard:

The Government should notify the villagers that they will be expected to manufacture khaddar for the needs of their villages within a fixed date after which no cloth will be supplied to them. The Governments in their turn will supply the villagers with cotton seed or cotton wherever required, at cost price and the tools of manufacture also at cost, to be recovered in easy instalments . . .

The villages will be surveyed and a list prepared of things that can be manufactured locally with little or no help and which may be required for village use or for sale outside . . . If enough care is taken, the villages, most of them as good as dead or dying, will hum with life and exhibit the immense possibilities they have of supplying most of their wants themselves and of the cities and towns of India.[115]

In addition to these, Gandhi suggested two other areas in which the government could help: the preservation of cattle wealth and the spread of basic education. A few weeks later, he also proposed a modality of work: the ministers, he said, should pick out from the bureaucracy 'honest and incorruptible men' and put them under the guidance of organizations such as the All India Spinners' Association, the All India Village Industries Association and the Hindustani Talimi Sangh. The official notification regarding the stopping of mill cloth and the exclusive use of *khādī* in villages should include both villagers and mill-owners as parties to the scheme. 'The notification will show clearly that it is the people's measure, though bearing the Government stamp.' Visualizing himself in the role of minister in charge of the revival of villages, Gandhi posed the basic decision problem which he thought the new national government must face: 'The only question for me as minister is whether the AISA has the conviction and capacity to shoulder the burden of creating and guiding a khadi scheme to success. If it has, I would put my little barque to sea with all confidence.'[116]

Thus, even while identifying a specific role for the state in the programme of national construction, Gandhi was not abandoning his fundamental belief that the state could never be the appropriate machinery for carrying out this programme. What he was suggesting in fact was that the national state should formally use its legislative powers to *abdicate* its presumed responsibility of promoting 'development' and thus clear the ground for popular non-state agencies to take up the work of revitalizing the village economies.

Was he then advocating a sort of *laissez-faire* policy? If the state was to abandon its controlling role in the national economy, would it not leave the field open for exploiters and powerful vested interests to take an even firmer control over the means of economic exploitation? Now that the popular nationalist forces had come to power, was not a certain degree of intervention, even coercion, necessary and desirable in order to check those exploitative interests? This was the ideological argument which the increasingly dominant section of the nationalist state leadership offered against Gandhian 'visionaries'. For the national state to abandon its economic responsibilities, these leaders argued, would be a reactionary step.

Faced with this argument, Gandhi's response was to reassert the claims of his moral conception. The immediate political battle against colonial rule had been virtually won. Now the question of the relation between the nation and the state was posed more sharply than ever before. Having acceeded to the political compulsions of bourgeois politics for two and a half decades, Gandhi in the last years of his life resumed the struggle for Utopia.

Now he insisted with renewed conviction that mere 'political swaraj' could never be a substitute for 'true swaraj'. He reasserted the ideal of *Rāmarājya* and defined it concretely as 'independence — political, economic and moral':

'Political' necessarily means the removal of the control of the British army in every shape and form.
    'Economic' means entire freedom from British capitalists and capital, as also

their Indian counterparts . . . This can take place only by capital or capitalists sharing their skill and capital with the lowliest and the least.

'Moral' means freedom from armed defence forces. My conception of *Ramarajya* excludes replacement of the British army by a national army of occupation. A country that is governed by even its national army can never be morally free.[117]

While the existence of the state remained a practical reality, the true ideal of the stateless society needed to be posited with renewed emphasis, now that the immediate political battle had been won and yet the task of reconstructing the national society remained unaccomplished. The question was not whether statelessness could ever be actually achieved; the question was whether one's political practice should rest on a firm moral principle or whether the principle should be relinquished.

Would there be State power in an ideal society or would such a society be Stateless? I think the question is futile. If we continue to work towards the building of such a society, to some extent it is bound to be realized and to that extent people will benefit by it. Euclid has defined a straight line as having no breadth, but no one has yet succeeded in drawing such a line and no one ever will. Still we can progress in geometry only by postulating such a line. This is true of every ideal.

We might remember though that a Stateless society does not exist anywhere in the world. If such a society is possible it can be established first only in India. For attempts have been made in India towards bringing about such a society. We have not so far shown that supreme herosim. The only way is for those who believe in it to set the example.[118]

But no matter how relentlessly Gandhi insisted on a renewal of the moral battle, it had by then become patently obvious that the main body of the Congress leadership was now fully engaged in the task of running a modern state machinery on a national scale, using the full range of its coercive instruments. Gandhi saw this as a moral failure on the part of the political leadership, a surrender to the forces of violence. 'Congressmen think that now it is their government . . . Everywhere Congressmen are thus scrambling for power and favours . . . A government seems to have only military power behind it, but it cannot run on the strength of that power alone.'[119] Repeatedly in the last months of his life he spoke of his helplessness, a feeling that acquired greater poignancy in the midst of the mad violence of communal strife which marked the transfer of power.

Whatever the Congress decides will be done; nothing will be according to what I say. My writ runs no more. If it did the tragedies in the Punjab, Bihar and Noakhali would not have happened. No one listens to me any more. I am a small man. True, there was a time when mine was a big voice. Then everyone obeyed what I said; now neither the Congress nor the Hindus nor the Muslims listen to me. Where is the Congress today? It is disintegrating. I am crying in the wilderness.[120]

In sorrow not unmixed with anger Gandhi suggested that henceforth the Congress should stop talking about truth and non-violence and that it should remove the words 'peaceful and legitimate' from its constitution. 'I am convinced that so long as the army or the police continues to be used for conducting the administration we shall remain subservient to the British or some other foreign power, irrespective of whether the power is in the hands of the Congress or others.'[121] By not claiming to follow 'peaceful and legitimate' means, the Congress would at least not be hypocritical.[122]

Once again, therefore, Gandhism sought to explain the defeat of its utopian quest by putting the blame on the moral failings of those who claimed to be leaders of the people. But in truth Gandhism as a political ideology had now been brought face to face with its most irreconcilable contradiction. While it insisted on the need to stay firm in the adherence to its ideal, it was no longer able to specify concretely the modalities of implementing this as a viable *political* practice. Now that there were powerful and organized interests *within* the nation which clearly did not share the belief in the Gandhian ideal, there was no way in which the Gandhian ideology could identify a social force which would carry forward the struggle and overcome this opposition in the arena of politics.

VI

Nowhere was this basic ideological problem highlighted more clearly than in Gandhi's final battle for *khādī*. In 1944 Gandhi proposed a 'New Khadi Philosophy'. He had, he said, thought a great deal about *khādī* during his period of detention and was convinced that there was something fundamentally wrong about the way the work had been carried out for so long. 'The fault is not yours but mine' he told an assembly of *khādī* workers in September 1944. The main difficulty was that the programme so far had been guided exclusively by practical considerations; the principle had been lost sight of. 'I did not lay the necessary stress on the requisite outlook and the spirit which was to underlie it. I looked at it from its immediate practical aspect . . . But today I cannot continue to ask people to spin in that manner.'[123]

The new *khādī* 'philosophy' which Gandhi kept explaining over the next two years was based on the fundamental principle that rural production must be primarily for self-consumption and not for sale. This had not been followed in the *khādī* programme so far, because the emphasis was more on providing a little additional employment to the rural poor and most *khādī* was spun in return for wages. Besides, most of the *khādī* cloth produced from this yarn was sold in the cities. This was not in keeping with the fundamental objective of the *khādī* philosophy which was to create an economic order in which the direct producer would not have to depend on anyone else for his basic necessities. If villagers continued to spin only in order to sell the yarn to *khādī* organizations, then despite the popularity of *khādī* cloth in the cities the entire programme would be founded on wrong economic principles. 'An economics which runs counter to morality cannot be called true economics.'[124]

What was this morality? The moral significance of the *khādī* programme lay in its relation to the true conception of *svarāj*. It was a mistake to regard *khādī* as any other industry and to work out its economics in terms of the principles of the marketplace.

> If khadi is an industry it would have to be run purely on business lines. The difference between khadi and mill-cloth would then be that while a mill provides employment to a few thousand people in a city, khadi brings a crore of rupees to those scattered about in fifteen thousand villages. Both must be classified as industries, and we would hardly be justified in asking anybody to put on khadi and boycott mill-cloth. Nor can such khadi claim to be the herald of swaraj. On the other hand we have claimed that the real significance of khadi is that it is a means for uplifting the villages and thereby generating in the people the spontaneous strength for swaraj. Such a claim cannot then be sustained. It will not do to continue to help the villagers by appealing to the philanthropic sentiments of city-dwellers . . . If we encouraged mills, the nation might get sufficient cloth. And if mills are nationalized cloth prices may also come down, people may not be exploited and may earn adequate wages. But our reason for putting forward khadi is that it is the only way to redeem the people from the disease of inertia and indifference, the only way to generate in them the strength of freedom.[125]

Thus Gandhi was now quite explicitly moving away from the 'practical' argument about the economic necessity of *khādī* with which for more than two decades he had sought to persuade those who did not share his moral presuppositions. Now he was reasserting the primacy of the moral objectives. In practical terms, the existing *khādī* programme had probably succeeded in providing some additional income to poor villagers. Many of his fellow workers were arguing that some 'decentralization' had also been achieved since cloth production was being carried out in village homes. But Gandhi was unwilling to accept this claim.

> Even in Lancashire some cloth is made at home, not for the use of the home but for the use of the masters. It would be outrageous to call this decentralization. So also in Japan everything is made at home; but it is not for the use of the home; it is all for the Government which has centralized the whole business . . . I would certainly not call this decentralization.[126]

What Gandhi suggested now was a complete change in the *modus operandi* of the *khādī* programme. An attempt should be made immediately to stop the spinning of yarn for sale. Instead *khādī* workers should persuade and educate people to spin for their own use. Villagers should not be encouraged to produce yarn on payment of wages and to use that income to buy mill-made cloth. It was this dependence of the small producer on the market which the *khādī* programme must attempt to break. The present terms of exchange between town and country must be reversed.[127] Now every village should produce the entire yarn needed to meet its cloth requirements and *khādī* should be put 'beyond commercial competition'.[128] Only in this way would it be possible to put an end to the growing inequality among the mass of the people, a process in which only the few who were lucky enough to find employment in industry had a chance to survive and the rest were doomed to starvation.[129] To make *khādī* the instrument for attaining *pūrṇa svarāj* [complete independence], it would have to be extricated from the cycle of money exchange; the only currency which could be permitted in the buying and selling of *khādī* was yarn.[130]

When Srikrishnadas Jaju, Secretary of the AISA, pointed out that this would mean that 300,000 spinners who were now in contact with the *khādī* organizations would lose their additional income and that probably not more than 30,000 could be persuaded to spin for self-sufficiency in cloth, Gandhi admitted that this might be the case at first, but 'these thirty thousand would later grow into three crores. Be it as it may, I at least will not be guilty of betraying the cause.'[131]

Even if Gandhi was able to convince his associates in *khādī* work that this was the right thing to do in principle, not many were sure that it was a practical or even a judicious step. The entire organizational structure of the *khādī* programme would be disrupted, and few believed that large numbers of rural people could be persuaded to spin all the yarn required for their own clothes. As a result, the *khādī* stores in the cities which were doing very well would have to close down. But Gandhi was insistent: 'Close them down,' he said, 'We cannot maintain khadi bhandars [stores] to sell khadi. You will say that if khadi bhandars in the city close down we shall have to sell khadi in the villages and that khadi cannot sell in the villages as it can in the cities. I agree that khadi cannot sell in the villages and it should not. Khadi is not to be sold in the villages, it is to be worn there. It is to be spun and worn.'[132] When his colleagues pointed out that there were not enough workers in the *khādī* programme who had the ability to do the new work being demanded of them, Gandhi replied: 'If that is our attitude there can be no swaraj through non-violence . . . I would then go my own way even if I have to work all alone . . . It is quite possible that people may not follow us . . . We should then renounce the tall claim we have made . . . Without hesitation, without flattering ourselves we must declare that we are weak like everybody else and that we are in no way better.'[133]

Why did Gandhi decide to demand so insistently that this drastic change be brought about in a programme built up with such care and hard work over so many years? The answer lay in the very nature of the historical conjuncture which the nationalist movement in India had reached, a conjuncture of which the predominant characteristic was a general anticipation of power. The Congress state leadership was clearly preparing to take up the reins of national power; its main concerns now were to formulate in concrete terms the economic and political details of a programme of 'national development'. The people too had anticipated a collapse of the established order and had set up during the revolt of 1942-3 a large number of localized centres of rebel authority, of varying sizes and duration, in forms characteristic of mass insurgency. Gandhi was also anticipating a transition of power, but he could not approve either the plans of development which his erstwhile Congress colleagues were chalking out in order to build a modern industrial nation or the forms of insurgent violence, disorderly and innately hateful, which was the basis of armed rebellion. In his determined, even frenetic, insistence on commencing a new programme of reconstruction aiming at an economy of self-sufficient small producers not having to enter into large-scale commodity exchange or sale of labour, Gandhi was emphasizing the historical urgency of resuming his original task, the task he had formulated in *Hind Swaraj*. The transition of power would create new possibilities. The national state leadership might decide, as Gandhi dearly wished but could not entirely believe, to abdicate its coercive authority in the field of social development and leave it to popular agencies consisting of trained and committed volunteers to carry out the work of economic reconstruction. In that case, the task of setting up those agencies and training the constructive workers would have to be taken up right away. On the other hand, the national state might decide to follow the path begun in the period of British rule, in which case the struggle would have to go on, in opposition to the state. In his discussions with *khādī* activists in 1944, Gandhi virtually put the problem in so many words:

> We may be expected to clothe the whole country with khadi after getting political power. Should we not therefore make such an arrangement from today so that we may be able to make the country self-sufficient in clothing in case the future government of free India were to provide the requisite facilities to the A.I.S.A. and ask it, as an expert body, to do this task? But if the government of the day were to close all its mills, and to charge us with this responsibility, we are apt to fail as things are today.[134]

On the other hand, if the state did not provide this opportunity, then the battle for *khādī*, a means for obtaining true *svarāj*, must be carried out in opposition to it.

> To be an instrument of swaraj, naturally [the spinning-wheel] must not flourish under Government or any other patronage. It must flourish, if need be, even in spite of the resistance from Government or the capitalist who is interested in his spinning and weaving mills. The spinning-wheel represents the millions in the villages as against the classes represented by the mill-owners and the like.[135]

Gandhi, in other words, now fully anticipated the possibility of manoeuvre. The historic battle for freedom had reached a stage where 'political swaraj' was within the reach of a nationalist leadership. It was possible that this could form a new basis for the struggle for 'real swaraj', if the political leadership was prepared to participate in the struggle. It was also possible that the state leadership would not cooperate with any degree of sincerity, in which case 'political swaraj' would itself become a major impediment in the way towards 'real swaraj' and the manoeuvre would have been accomplished. In either case, Gandhism was now called upon to resume its original quest and to clearly mark its differences with what it regarded as the narrow 'political' objectives of nationalism.

The new *khādī* programme was to be the spearhead of this struggle which would gradually bring within its fold a more extended plan of rural economic reconstruction encompassing the whole range of village artizanal production, animal husbandry and basic education.[136] The object was a 'decentralization' of power in society. The very nature of industrial production required a centralization of power in the hands of the state so that the overall conditions within which a national economy functioned could be controlled. Decentralization, on the other hand, would ideally mean that each individual producer would be entirely self-sufficient in the matter of providing his essential needs; with regard to non-essentials which too were a part of social life he would cooperate with others, not as an exchanger of commodities but in the way in which members of a family help one another.[137]

The crucial social unit in this scheme of decentralization was the village which would be self-sufficient not merely in economic matters but also in ruling and defending itself:

> Independence must begin at the bottom. Thus, every village will be a republic or *panchayat* having full powers. It follows, therefore, that every village has to be self-sustained and capable of managing its affairs even to the extent of defending itself against the whole world. It will be trained and prepared to perish in the attempt to defend itself against any onslaught from without.[138]

Within the village, each individual will try to be as self-sufficient as possible and will accept cooperation from others only to the extent that it is free and voluntary, not in the false sense in which commodity exchange is described as free but in the full moral sense of collective cooperation.

Beyond the unit of the self-sufficient village, society would be organized in the form of expanding circles — a group of villages, the taluka, the district, the province, and so on, each self-reliant in its own terms, no unit having to depend on a larger unit or dominate a smaller one.[139] Towns will not disappear completely, but only a small surplus, much smaller than at present, will go out of the villages[140] and the 700,000 villages of India will dominate 'the centre with its few towns'.[141]

> In this structure composed of innumerable villages, there will be ever-widening, never-ascending circles. Life will not be a pyramid with the apex sustained by the bottom. But it will be an oceanic circle . . . the outermost circumference will not wield power to crush the inner circle but will give strength to all within and derive its own strength from it.[142]

Of course, this was an ideal construction, a 'picture', but, as Gandhi put it using his favourite analogy, 'like Euclid's point . . . it had an imperishable value . . . We must have a proper picture of what we want, before we can have something approaching it.'[143] He acknowledged that in conceiving of this system of self-sufficient village republics, he was thinking of the ancient Indian village system as described by Henry Maine.[144] 'The towns were then subservient to the villages. They were emporia for the surplus village products and beautiful manufactures.' But this was only 'the skeleton of my picture'. The ancient village system had many grave defects, most notably that of caste and probably also of the despotism of the state, and these could have no place in the ideal structure of society.[145]

But how would the struggle be carried out in leading society to the path towards this ideal state? The period of colonial rule had resulted in the entrenchment on an unprecedented scale of the forces of corruption and violence deep within the foundations of Indian society. And now after the strength of popular resistance against colonialism had been aroused and mobilized, it was tending to give birth to a new political order which, far from seeking to eliminate those entrenched forces, was building itself on the same bases. How were these overpowering forces to be resisted? Who will resist?

Gandhism's answer, as we have seen, was a moral one. The ideal must be pursued, even if it was a quest that could never end, or end only in death. Those who were convinced of the truth of the ideal must pursue it, alone if necessary. The success of the struggle depended not just crucially but entirely on the selflessness, courage and moral will of the leaders of the people. Firm in its adherence to the principle of a truthful political practice, the Gandhian ideology asserted to the very end its faith in a moral theory of mediation. If the unswerving moral practice of a few did not appear to produce quick results in the broader arena of politics, that was no reason for giving up the quest . Echoing Tolstoy, Gandhi would say, 'History provides us with a whole series of miracles of masses of people being converted to a particular view in the twinkling of an eye.'[146]

But the theory of mediation remained an abstract theory. The success of mediation depended entirely on the morality of the mediator, not on the way his programme could be brought into conformity with a concrete set of collective ethical norms which an identifiable social force within the nation might be expected to hold. Explaining his idea of the *samagra grāmsevak*, the ideal constructive worker, Gandhi said:

> He will so win over the village that they will seek and follow his advice. Supposing I go and settle down in a village with a *ghani* (village oil-press), I won't be an ordinary *ghanchi* (oil-presser) earning 15-20 rupees a month. I will be a Mahatma *ghanchi*. I have used the word Mahatma in fun but what I mean to say is that as *ghanchi* I will become a model for the villagers to follow. I will be a *ghanchi* who knows the Gita and the Koran. I will be learned enough to teach their children . . . Real strength lies in knowledge. True knowledge gives a moral standing and moral strength. Everyone seeks the advice of such a man.[147]

The people, then, would *follow* the mediator because of his moral authority, which would be a consequence of his knowledge, which in turn would be obtained as a result of his unflinching moral practice. If the people were unwilling to listen to him, it would be because he had failed to attain the moral standing required of him. Seeking to launch its final battle for Utopia, the only concrete means of mediation which Gandhism could suggest was the *individual* moral will of the mediator.

> When the critics laugh at [the constructive programme], what they mean is that forty crores of people will never co-operate in the effort to fulfil the programme. No doubt, there is considerable truth in the scoff. My answer is, it is still worth the attempt. Given an indomitable will on the part of a band of earnest workers, the programme is as workable as any other and more so than most. Anyway, I have no substitute for it, if it is to be based on non-violence.[148]

The inadequacy of the theory as a *political* theory of mediation soon became obvious. For instance, in 1946 when T. Prakasam's government in Madras decided that in order to promote *khādī* it would not permit the setting up of any new cotton mills or the expansion of existing ones, industrial interests were not unexpectedly alarmed. Responding to their vociferous criticism of Prakasam, Gandhi wrote:

It is hardly an honourable pastime to dismiss from consideration honest servants of the nation by dubbing them idealists, dreamers, fanatics and faddists.

Let not capitalists and other entrenched personages range themselves against the poor villagers and prevent them from bettering their lot by dignified labour . . .

Let it be remembered that the existing Madras mills will not be touched at present. That the whole mill industry will be affected if the scheme spreads like wildfire, as I expect some day such a thing must, goes without saying. Let not the largest capitalist rue the day when and if it comes.

The only question then worth considering is whether the Madras Government are honest and competent. If they are not, everything will go wrong. If they are, the scheme must be blessed by all and must succeed.[149]

Yet mere honesty and competence could hardly ensure that such a scheme would be 'blessed by all'. There was decidedly a question of overcoming a serious political opposition. Here to attribute the likely failure of the scheme to the lack of honesty and competence of the government was to evade the fact that the scheme was not backed by a political programme which either anticipated the opposition or suggested the means of overcoming it.

In fact, whenever the contradiction between the political implications of modern industry and *khādī* was directly posed, as it now was with respect to the policies to be followed by the national state, the Gandhian ideology could not easily provide a political answer. It could not admit that capitalists must be coerced into surrendering their interests. Consequently, while asserting the urgency of the new *khādī* programme, Gandhi would immediately say: 'At the same time I believe that some key industries are necessary. I do not believe in armchair or armed socialism.'[150] On the other hand, asked how to explain how the competition between industrial manufactures and *khādī* was to be avoided, Gandhi's answer was that 'mill-cloth should not sell side by side with khadi. Our mills may export their manufactures.'[151] But this clearly violated a fundamental Gandhian premise about the need to eliminate competition and dependence between nations. Gandhism had no answer.

The same problem appeared when the question of suggesting a concrete structure of self-government for the village arose. Despite his fundamental disbelief in the institutions of representative government, Gandhi suggested that election by secret ballot was perhaps the only practicable step. Yet the dangers were obvious: 'While exercising centralized power over the country, the British Government has polluted the atmosphere in the villages. The petty village officials have become masters instead of being servants. So great care has to be taken to ensure that these gangster elements do not get into the panchayats.' But how was this to be ensured if they could by force or trickery elicit the required electoral support? 'They should be debarred.' How, except by a contrary coercive force? 'They should themselves keep out' was the final unconvincing reply.[152] If that was possible, the problem of power would not exist; to insist on this reply was to wish away the political problem.

Beginning its journey from the utopianism of *Hind Swaraj*, and yet picking up on the way the ideological baggage of a nationalist politics, Gandhism succeeded in opening up the historical possibility by which the largest popular element of the nation — the peasantry — could be appropriated within the evolving political forms of the new Indian state. While it was doubtless the close correspondence of the moral conception of Gandhi's *Rāmarājya* with the demands and forms of political justice in the contemporary peasant–communal consciousness which was one of the ideological conditions which made it possible for those demands to be transformed into 'the message of the Mahatma', the historical consequence of the Gandhian politics of non-violence was, in fact, to give to this process of appropriation its moral justification and its own distinctive ideological form. While it was the Gandhian intervention in elite-nationalist politics in India which established for the first time that an authentic national movement could only be built upon the organized support of the whole of the peasantry, the working out of the politics of non-violence also made it abundantly clear that the object of the political mobilization of the peasantry was not at all what Gandhi claimed on its behalf, 'to train the masses in self-consciousness and attainment of power'. Rather the peasantry were meant to become willing participants in a struggle wholly conceived and directed *by others*. Champaran, Kheda, Bardoli, Borsad — those were the model peasant movements, specific, local, conducted on issues that were well within 'their own personal and felt grievances'. This, for instance, was the specific ground on which Bardoli was commended as a model movement:

> The people of Bardoli could not secure justice so long as they were afraid of being punished by the Government . . . They freed themselves from its fear by surrendering their hearts to their Sardar.
>
> From this we find that the people require neither physical nor intellectual strength to secure their own freedom; moral courage is all that is needed. This latter is dependent on faith. In this case, they were required to have faith in their Sardar, and such faith cannot be artificially generated. They found in the Sardar a worthy object of such faith and like a magnet he drew the hearts of the people to himself . . . This is not to say that the people had accepted non-violence as a principle or that they did not harbour anger even in their minds. But they understood the practical advantage of non-violence, understood their own interest, controlled their anger and, instead of retaliating in a violent manner, suffered the hardships inflicted on them.[153]

While the national organization of the dominant classes could proceed to consolidate itself within the institutional structure of the new Indian state, '*kisans* and labour' were never to be organized 'on an all-India basis'.[154] Thus, forced to mark its differences with a nationalist state ideology, Gandhism could only assert the superiority of its moral claim; it could not find the ideological means to turn that morality into an instrument of the *political* organization of the largest popular elements of the nation against the coercive structures of the state.

And so we get, in the historical effectivity of Gandhism as a whole, the conception of a national framework of politics in which the peasants are mobilized but do not participate, of a nation of which they are a part, but a national state from which they are for ever distanced. How this possibility, which emerged from the very tensions within Gandhism, was identified by the nationalist analytic of a mature bourgeois ideology, and the Gandhian intervention in Indian politics turned into the moment of manoeuvre in the 'passive revolution of capital', are questions we will discuss in the next chapter. But it will remain a task of modern Indian historiography to explain the historical process, in its specific regional and organizational forms, by which these political possibilities inherent in the Gandhian ideology became the ideological weapons in the hands of the Indian bourgeoisie in its attempt to create a new state structure. The 'message of the Mahatma' meant different things to different people. As recent researches are beginning to show,[155] what it meant to peasants or tribals was completely different from the way it was interpreted by the literati. Operating in a process of class struggle in which the dominance of the bourgeoisie was constantly under challenge and its moral leadership for ever fragmented, the great historical achievement of the nationalist state leadership in India was to reconcile the ambiguities of the Gandhian ideology within a single differentiated political structure, to appropriate all its meanings in the body of the same discourse.

Yet the logic of Utopia could be irreconcilably ambiguous. Thomas More has been read as the author of a text that laid the moral foundations for the political demands of a rising, but still far from victorious, bourgeoisie. He has also been regarded as the progenitor of utopian socialism, that inchoate articulation of the spirit of resistance of the early proletariat in Europe.[156] It is not surprising, therefore, that in the unresolved class struggles within the social formation of contemporary India, oppositional movements can still claim their moral legitimacy from the message of Mahatma.

Notes

1. Romain Rolland, *Mahatma Gandhi: A Study in Indian Nationalism*, tr. L.V. Ramaswami Aiyar (Madras: S. Ganesan, 1923), p.30.

2. Raghavan N. Iyer, *The Moral and Political Thought of Mahatma Gandhi* (New York: Oxford University Press, 1973), p.24.

3. *Hind Swaraj* in *The Collected Works of Mahatma Gandhi* (New Delhi: Publications Division, 1958-   ) [hereafter *CW*]. vol.10, p.18.

4. *Hind Swaraj*, *CW*, vol.10, pp.22-3.

5. Ibid., p.57.

6. Ibid., p.37.

7. Ibid., p.60.

8. Discussion with Maurice Frydman, 25 August 1936, *CW*, vol.63, p.241.

9. *Hind Swaraj, CW*, vol.10, p.23.

10. Discussion with Maurice Frydman, *CW*, vol.63, p.241.

11. Interview to Francis G. Hickman, 17 September 1940, *CW*, vol.73, pp.29-30.

12. 'Is Khadi Economically Sound?', *CW*, vol.63, pp.77-8.

13. 'Why Not Labour-Saving Devices', *CW*, vol.59, p.413.

14. 'Village Industries', *CW*, vol.59, p.356.

15. 'Its Meaning', *CW*, vol.60, pp.54-5.

16. 'New Life for Khadi', *CW*, vol.59, pp.205-6.

17. *Hind Swaraj, CW*, vol.10, pp.17-8.

18. Ibid., p.18.

19. Ibid., p.33.

20. Letter to David B. Hart, 21 September 1934, *CW*, vol.59, p.45.

21. 'Enlightened Anarchy: A Political Ideal', *CW*, vol.68, p.265.

22. For example, *CW*, vol.35, pp.489-90; *CW*, vol.45, pp.328-9.

23. For example, *CW*, vol.59, pp.61-7; *CW*, vol.50, pp.226-7.

24. *Hind Swaraj, CW*, vol.10, p.36.

25. 'Duty of Bread Labour', *CW*, vol.61, p.212.

26. Discussion with Gujarat Vidyapith Teachers, *CW*, vol.58, p.306.

27. *Hind Swaraj, CW*, vol.10, p.35.

28. 'It is only a critique of the "modern philosophy of life"; it is called "Western" only because it originated in the West'. *CW*, vol.57, p.498.

29. *Hind Swaraj, CW*, vol.10, p.40.

30. Ibid., p.48.

31. Mahadev Desai, *The Gospel of Selfless Action or the Gita According to Gandhi* (Ahmedabad: Navajivan, 1946), p.6.

32. Ibid., pp.123-4.

33. 'Teaching of Hinduism', *CW*, vol.63, p.339.

34. 'Dr. Ambedkar's Indictment-II', *CW*, vol.63, p.153.

35. 'The Law of Our Being', *CW*, vol.63, pp.319-20.

36. 'Dr. Ambedkar's Indictment-II', *CW*, vol.63, p.153.

37. 'Caste Has to Go', *CW*, vol.62, p.121.

38. 'Woman in the Smritis', *CW*, vol.64, p.85.

39. Letter to Ranchhodlal Patwari, 9 September 1918, *CW*, vol.15, p.45. Or, again,

> Khan Abdul Ghaffar Khan derives his belief in non-violence from the Koran, and the Bishop of London derives his belief in violence from the Bible. I derive my belief in non-violence in it. But if the worst came to the worst and if I came to the conclusion that the Koran teaches violence, I would still reject violence, but I would not therefore say that the Bible is superior to the Koran or that Mahomed is inferior to Jesus. It is not my function to judge Mahomed and Jesus. It is enough that my non-violence is independent of the sanction of scriptures.

Interview with Dr Crane, *CW*, vol.64, p.399.

40. Speech at Gandhi Seva Sangh Meeting, 28 March 1938, *CW*, vol.66, p.445.

41. For Tagore's statement, see Appendix I, *CW*, vol.57, pp.503-4.

42. To Vallabhbhai Patel he wrote: 'You must have read the Poet's attack. I am replying to it in *Harijan*. He of course made amends afterwards. He gets excited and writes, and then corrects himself. This is what he does every time.' Letter to

Vallabhbhai Patel, 13 February 1934, *CW*, vol.57, p.155.

43. 'Bihar and Untouchability', *CW*, vol.57, p.87.

44. 'Superstition v. Faith', *CW*, vol.57, pp.164-5.

45. Ibid., p.165.

46. 'Why Only Bihar?', *CW*, vol.57, p.392.

47. Speech at Reception by Merchants, Madura, 26 January 1934, *CW*, vol.57, p.51.

48. 'Superstition v. Faith', *CW*, vol.57, p.165.

49. 'Ramanama to me is all-sufficing . . . In the spiritual literature of the world, the *Ramayana* of Tulsidas takes a foremost place. It has charms that I miss in the *Mahabharata* and even in Valmiki's *Ramayana*.' *CW*, vol.58, p.291. Also, 'Power of "Ramanama" ', *CW*, vol.27, pp.107-12.

50. Thanks to the historical researches of Boris Pavlovich Koz'min and Andrzej Walicki, our present understanding of the complexities of Russian Populism has made us aware of many of the polemical excesses of Bolshevik criticism of the Narodniks. But this has sharpened, rather than obscured, the central theoretical opposition between Leninism and Populism.

51. V.I. Lenin, *A Characterisation of Economic Romanticism* in *Collected Works*, vol.2 (Moscow: Foreign Languages Publishing House, 1957), pp.129-265, esp. p.241.

52. Edward Carpenter, *Civilisation: Its Cause and Cure and Other Essays* (London: George Allen and Unwin, 1921; first edn. 1889), pp.46-9.

53. John Ruskin, *Unto This Last* (London: W.B. Clive, 1931; first edn. 1862), p.83.

54. R.G. Collingwood, *Ruskin's Philosophy* (Chichester, Sussex: Quentin Nelson, 1971; first edn. 1922), p.20.

55. Ibid., p.28.

56. V.I. Lenin, *What the 'Friends of the People' Are and How They Fight the Social-Democrats* in *Collected Works*, vol.1, pp.129-332.

57. Andrzej Walicki, *The Controversy over Capitalism: Studies in the Social Philosophy of the Russian Populists* (Oxford: Clarendon Press, 1969), p.66. Also, Walicki, *The Slavophile Controversy: History of a Conservative Utopia in Nineteenth Century Russian Thought*, tr. Hilda Andrews-Rusiecka (Oxford: Clarendon Press, 1975), p.280.

58. Leo Tolstoy, *The Slavery of Our Times*, tr. Aylmer Maude (London: John Lawrence, 1972; first edn. 1900), p.18.

59. Ibid., p.21.

60. Ibid., p.57.

61. Leo Tolstoy, 'The Kingdom of God is Within You' in *The Kingdom of God and Other Essays*, tr. Aylmer Maude (London: Oxford University Press, 1936; first edn. 1893), pp.301-2.

62. For a study of this process, see Shahid Amin, 'Gandhi as Mahatma: Gorakhpur District, Eastern U.P., 1921-1922' in Ranajit Guha, ed., *Subaltern Studies III* (Delhi: Oxford University Press, 1983), pp.1-61.

63. Letter to Mirabehn, 20 April 1933, *CW*, vol.54, p.456.

64. Letter to Mirabehn, 11 April 1933, *CW*, vol.54, p.372.

65. *An Autobiography* in *CW*, vol.39, p.4.

66. *Hind Swaraj*, *CW*, vol.10, p.36.

67. *Autobiography*, *CW*, vol.39, p.389.

68. 'Satyagraha — Not Passive Resistance', *CW*, vol.13, p.523.

69. For an explanation of the concept of negative consciousness, see Ranajit Guha, *Elementary Aspects of Peasant Insurgency in Colonial India* (Delhi. Oxford University Press, 1983), pp.18-76.

70. 'Satyagraha — Not Passive Resistance', *CW*, vol.13, p.524.

71. Ibid., pp.524-5.

72. Speech on Satyagraha Movement, Trichinopoly, 25 March 1919. *CW*, vol.15, p.155.

73. Speech at Mass Meeting, Ahmedabad, 14 April 1919, *CW*, vol.15, p.221.

74. Letter to Swami Shraddhanand, 17 April 1919, *CW*, vol.15, pp.238-9.

75. 'The Duty of Satyagrahis', *CW*, vol.15, p.436.

76. *Autobiography*, *CW*, vol.39, p.374.

77. Evidence before the Disorders Inquiry Committee, *CW*, vol.16, p.410.

78. Ibid., vol.16, p.441.

79. Speech at Mass Meeting, Ahmedabad, 14 April 1919, *CW*, vol.15, pp.221-2.

80. Evidence, *CW*, vol.16, pp.391-2.

81. Alexander Herzen, often regarded as one of the progenitors of Russian Populism, wrote about the crowd: 'I looked with horror mixed with disgust at the continually moving, swarming crowd, foreseeing how it would rob me of half of my seat at the theatre and in the diligence, how it would dash like a wild beast into the railway carriages, how it would heat and pervade the air.' Quoted in Walicki, *The Controversy over Capitalism*, p.11. Horror and disgust were the feelings which overwhelmed Gandhi too when he first encountered the Indian masses in a third-class railway carriage. See *Autobiography*, *CW*, vol.39, p.305.

82. 'Democracy v. Mobocracy', *CW*, vol.18, p.242.

83. 'Some Illustrations', *CW*, vol.18, p.275.

84. 'Meaning of the "Gita" ', *CW*, vol.28, p.317.

85. 'What Are Basic Assumptions?', *CW*, vol.67, p.436. It is quite remarkable how frequently Gandhi uses the military metaphor when talking about the 'science of non-violence'.

86. Ibid., pp.436-7.

87. Speech at AICC Meeting, Wardha, 15 January 1942, *CW*, vol.75, p.220.

88. 'Cobwebs of Ignorance', *CW*, vol.30, pp.450-1.

89. 'Answers to Questions', *CW*, vol.43, p.41.

90. Ibid.

91. 'A Complex Problem', *CW*, vol.40, p.364.

92. Letter to Labhshankar Mehta, 14 April 1926, *CW*, vol.30, p.283.

93. Speech at Anand, 17 March 1930, *CW*, vol.43, p.93.

94. Telegram to N.R. Malkani, 18 April 1930, *CW*, vol.43, p.282.

95. 'Neither a Saint nor a Politician', *CW*, vol.17, p.406.

96. Late in his life, Gandhi even seemed to suggest that the concept of *varṇāśrama* should also be dropped because it had acquired the connotation of differing privileges for different *varṇa*: '. . . in our present condition . . . our dharma lies in becoming Ati-Shudras voluntarily'. Foreword to 'Varnavyavastha', *CW*, vol.80, p.223.

97. 'Harijan v. Non-Harijan', *CW*, vol.58, pp.80-1.

98. Speech at AICC Meeting, Patna, 19 May 1934, *CW*, vol.58, pp.9-10.

99. Ibid., p.11.

100. 'My Meaning of Office-Acceptance', *CW*, vol.66, p.104.

101. 'Choice Before Congressmen', *CW*, vol.67, p.306.

102. Interview to Nirmal Kumar Bose, 9 November 1934, *CW*, vol.59, p.318.

103. 'Answers to Zamindars', *CW*, vol.58, p.247.

104. 'Zamindars and Talukdars', *CW*, vol.42, pp.239-40.

105. 'Discussion with Students', *CW*, vol.58, p.219.

106. 'Answers to Zamindars', *CW*, vol.58, p.248.

107. 'Divine Warning', *CW*, vol.22, pp.426-7.

108. Speech at AISA Meeting, Sevagram, 24 March 1945. *CW*, vol.79, p.297.

109. 'The Charkha Sangh and Politics', *CW*, vol.82, pp.17-9.

110. Letter to Purnima Bannerjee, 1 January 1946. *CW*, vol.82, pp.331-2. See also, Letter to Rameshwari Nehru, 15 January 1946, *CW*, vol.82, p.424; and to Sucheta Kripalani, 19 January 1946, *CW*, vol.82, p.440.

111. Letter to Shriman Narayan, 3 January 1946. *CW*, vol.82, p.341.

112. Letter to Dada Dharmadhikari, 28 December 1945. *CW*, vol.82, pp.290-1.

113. Letter to R.K. Patil, 1 January 1946. *CW*, vol.82, p.322. See also, Letter to Shankarrao Deo, 1 January 1946. *CW*, vol.82, p.323.

114. 'The Lure of Legislatures', *CW*, vol.83, pp.95-6.

115. 'Ministers' Duty', *CW*, vol.84, pp.44-5.

116. 'If I Were the Minister', *CW*, vol.85, pp.210-2.

117. 'Independence', *CW*, vol.84, pp.80-1.

118. 'Congress Ministries and Ahimsa', *CW*, vol.85, pp.266-7.

119. Speech at Prayer Meeting, Bikram, 21 May 1947. *CW*, vol.87, p.513.

120. Speech at Prayer Meeting, New Delhi, 1 April 1947. *CW*, vol.87, p.187.

121. 'Congress Ministries and Ahimsa', *CW*, vol.85, p.266.

122. Ibid. See also, 'Do Not Eliminate Truth and Nonviolence', *CW*, vol.85, pp.351-2; and 'Answers to Questions', *CW*, vol.85, p.364.

123. Speech at AISA Meeting, Sevagram, 1 September 1944. *CW*, vol.78, pp.62-7.

124. Discussion with Srikrishnadas Jaju, 11 October 1944. *CW*, vol.78, p.174.

125. Discussion with Srikrishnadas Jaju, 13 October 1944. *CW*, vol.78, pp.192-3.

126. Ibid., p.190.

127. 'Khadi in Towns', *CW*, vol.84, pp.438-9.

128. Speech at AISA Meeting, Sevagram, 24 March 1945. *CW*, vol.79, pp.299-300.

129. 'Why Khadi for Yarn and Not for Money?' *CW*, vol.81, pp.56-7.

130. 'Yarn Donation', *CW*, vol.81, p.137.

131. Discussion with Srikrishnadas Jaju, 13 October 1944. *CW*, vol.78, p.194.

132. 'Why the Insistence on the Yarn Clause', *CW*, vol.82, pp.122-3.

133. Discussion with Srikrishnadas Jaju, 13 October 1944. *CW*, vol.78, pp.194-5.

134. Ibid., p.190.

135. 'The Missing Link', *CW*, vol.81, p.89.

136. 'Ministers' Duty', *CW*, vol.84, p.45.

137. 'Answers to Questions', *CW*, vol.81, p.133, and Speech at Congress Workers' Conference, Sodepur, 6 January 1946, *CW*, vol.81, p.369.

138. 'Independence', *CW*, vol.85, p.32.

139. 'Decentralization', *CW*, vol.85, pp.459-60.

140. Discussion with Shriman Narayan, 2 June 1945. *CW*, vol.80, p.244.

141. Interview to P. Ramachandra Rao, before 19 June 1945. *CW*, vol.80, p.353.

142. 'Independence' *CW*, vol.85, p.33.

143. Ibid.

144. Henry Sumner Maine, *Ancient Law* (1861; New York: Dutton, 1931).

145. Speech at Meeting of Deccan Princes, Poona, 28 July 1946. *CW*, vol.85, p.79.

146. Discussion with Director of British Daily, before 28 October 1946. *CW*, vol.86, p.50.

147. Answers to Questions at Constructive Workers' Conference, Madras, 29 January 1946. *CW*, vol.83, p.46.

148. Foreword to 'Constructive Programme — Its Meaning and Place', *CW*, vol.82, p.67.

149. 'Handspun v. Mill Cloth', *CW*, vol.85, pp.472-4.

150. 'Alternative to Industrialism', *CW*, vol.85, p.206.

151. Discussion at Hindustani Talimi Sangh Meeting, Patna, 22 April 1947. *CW*, vol.87, p.330.

152. Talk with Village Representatives, Bir, 19 March 1947. *CW*, vol.87, pp.121-2.

153. 'Government's Power v. People's Power', *CW*, vol.37, pp.190-1.

154. 'Constructive Programme: Its Meaning and Place', *CW*, vol.75, pp.159-60.

155. See, for example, Shahid Amin, 'Gandhi as Mahatma'.

156. Martin Fleisher, *Radical Reform and Political Persuasion in the Life and Writings of Thomas More* (Geneva: Librairie Droz, 1973); Karl Kautsky, *Thomas More and his Utopia*, tr. H.J. Stenning (1890; London: Lawrence and Wishart, 1979).

5. The Moment of Arrival: Nehru and the Passive Revolution

> There is something very wonderful about the high
> achievements of science and modern technology . . .
> *The Discovery of India*, p.415.

I

In September 1932, at a time when the Congress organization lay stunned and scattered after the massive repression unleashed by the Government on the Civil Disobedience movement, Gandhi announced from Yeravda prison in Poona that he would go on a 'fast unto death' to protest against Ramsay Macdonald's grant of a separate electorate to the 'Depressed Classes' in India. Jawaharlal Nehru was then in Dehra Dun jail, and the news came to him like a 'bombshell'. He was greatly annoyed with Gandhi

> for choosing a side-issue for his final sacrifice — just a question of electorate. What would be the result of our freedom movement? Would not the larger issues fade into the background, for the time being at least? . . . After so much sacrifice and brave endeavour, was our movement to tail off into something insignificant?
>
> I felt angry with him at his religious and sentimental approach to a political question, and his frequent references to God in connection with it. He even seemed to suggest that God had indicated the very date of his fast. What a terrible example to set![1]

Nehru was at this time much distressed by what he saw as the lack of clarity with regard to the political objectives of the national movement. It is a complaint that runs all the way through the *Autobiography* written in prison in 1934-5. It was not as though he did not approve of the association of social and economic questions with the demands of nationalism. In fact, he was one of the foremost leaders of the Congress Left which consistently demanded that nationalism be given a more definite 'economic and social content'. But the objective of all such campaigns had to be clear: it was the establishment of a sovereign national state. That was the political objective; the social and economic issues were necessary to mobilize the masses in the movement towards that goal. If the political objective was not kept firmly in mind, all attempts at social reform would flounder, energies would be wasted, and the movement would play into the hands of the foreign government now holding power. In fact, as far as the success of these social movements was concerned, the attempts at social reform could be successful only after power had been captured and a national state established.

> The real reason why the Congress and other non-official organisations cannot do much for social reform goes deeper . . .
>
> Past experience shows us that we can make little social progress under present conditions . . . for generations past the British Government has crushed initiative and ruled despotically, or paternally, as it has itself called it. It does not approve of any big organised effort by non-officials, and suspects ulterior motives. The Harijan movement, in spite of every precaution taken by its organisers, has occasionally come in conflict with officials. I am sure that if Congress started a nation-wide propaganda for the greater use of soap it would come in conflict with Government in many places.
>
> I do not think it is very difficult to convert the masses to social reform if the State takes the matter in hand. But alien rulers are always suspect, and they cannot go far in the process of conversion. If the alien element was removed and economic changes were given precedence, an energetic administration could easily introduce far-reaching social reforms.[2]

Nehru's reaction to Gandhi's Harijan movement stemmed from an entirely novel ideological reconstruction of the elements of nationalist thought that was then being undertaken in the final, fully mature, stage of the development of nationalism in India — its moment of arrival. It was a reconstruction whose specific form was to situate nationalism within the domain of a *state ideology*. Given the historical constraints imposed on the Indian bourgeoisie within the colonial social formation, its intellectual–moral leadership could never be firmly established in the domain of civil society. Of historical necessity, its revolution had to be passive. The specific ideological form of the passive revolution in India was an *étatisme*, explicitly recognizing a central, autonomous and directing role of the state and legitimizing it by a specifically nationalist marriage between the ideas of progress and social justice.

This mature ideological form of nationalist thought can be clearly demonstrated in the writings of Jawaharlal Nehru. Nehru was a far less systematic writer than Bankimchandra, and his writings do not have the same kind of logical strength born out of solid moral convictions which one finds in Gandhi. His two major books, the *Autobiography* and *The Discovery of India*, both written during long periods of imprisonment, are rambling, bristling with the most obvious contradictions, and grossly overwritten, the latter, by his own admission, coming to an end only because his supply of paper ran out.[3] But it is in the writings of this principal political architect of the new Indian state that one can find, more clearly than anywhere else, the key ideological elements and relations of nationalist thought at its moment of arrival.

To make my presentation easier, let me first summarize what I think is the crucial line of reasoning that holds together this final ideological reconstruction of natio: alism. It is an ideology of which the central organizing principle is the autonomy of the state; the legitimizing principle is a conception of social justice.

The argument then runs as follows: social justice for all cannot be provided within the old framework because it is antiquated, decadent and incapable of dynamism. What is necessary is to create a new framework of institutions which can embody the spirit of progress or, a synonym, modernity. Progress or modernity, according to the terms of the 20th century, means giving primacy to the sphere of the economic, because it is only by a thorough reorganization of the systems of economic production and distribution that enough wealth can be created to ensure social justice for all. But the latest knowledge built up by the modern social sciences shows clearly that it is not possible to undertake an effective reorganization of the economic structures of society if the state does not assume a central coordinating and directing role. And the colonial state, in accordance with its imperial interests, will never take up this role; in fact, it has consistently acted as the chief impediment to all attempts at such a restructuring. Hence the principal political task before the nation is to establish a sovereign national state. Once established, this state will stand above the narrow interests of groups and classes in society, take an overall view of the matter and, in accordance with the best scientific procedures, plan and direct the economic processes in order to create enough social wealth to ensure welfare and justice for all.

Let us now see how Nehru attempts to establish this argument as the main constitutive principle of the mature ideological form of nationalist thought in India.

II

'The East bow'd low before the blast
In patient, deep disdain;
She let the legions thunder past,
And plunged in thought again.'

In *The Discovery of India*, Nehru quotes Matthew Arnold, and immediately proceeds to contradict him:

But it is not true that India has ever bowed patiently before the blast or been indifferent to the passage of foreign legions. Always she has resisted them, often successfully, sometimes unsuccessfully, and even when she failed for the time being, she has remembered and prepared herself for the next attempt. Her method has been twofold: to fight them and drive them out, and to absorb those who could not be driven away . . . The urge to freedom, to independence, has always been there, and the refusal to submit to alien domination.[4]

A few pages later, he offers a more direct rebuttal of the essentialist dichotomy between Eastern and Western cultures.

Ancient Greece is supposed to be the fountainhead of European civilisation, and much has been written about the fundamental difference between the Orient and the Occident. I do not understand this; a great deal of it seems to be vague and unscientific without much basis in fact. Till recently many European thinkers

133

imagined that everything that was worth while had its origin in Greece or
Rome . . . Even when some knowledge of what peoples of Asia had done in the
past soaked into the European mind, it was not willingly accepted. There was an
unconscious resistance to it . . . If scholars thought so, much more so did the
unread crowd believe in some essential difference between the East and the
West. The industrialization of Europe and the consequent material progress
impressed this difference still further on the popular mind, and by an odd process
of rationalization ancient Greece became the father or mother of modern Europe
and America.[5]

But this difference was only about industrialization and lack of industrialization;
it had nothing to do with ancient cultural traditions.

I do not understand the use of the words Orient and Occident, except in the sense
that Europe and America are highly industrialized and Asia is backward in this
respect. This industrialization is something new in the world's history . . . There
is no organic connection between Hellenic civilization and modern European
and American civilization.[6]

In fact, the spirit and outlook of ancient Greece were much closer to those of
ancient India and ancient China than of the nations of modern Europe.

They all had the same broad, tolerant, pagan outlook, joy in life and in the
surprising beauty and infinite variety of nature, love of art, and the wisdom that
comes from the accumulated experience of an old race.[7]

The real reason why we do not see these similarities and instead fall into the trap
of confused thinking is that those who teach us are interested in having us think
that way.

India, it is said, is religious, philosophical, speculative, metaphysical, uncon-
cerned with this world, and lost in dreams of the beyond and the hereafter. So we
are told, and perhaps those who tell us so would like India to remain plunged in
thought and entangled in speculation, so that they might possess this world and
the fullness thereof, unhindered by these thinkers, and take their joy of it.[8]

At last, it would seem, nationalist thought has come to grips with the
Orientalist thematic; it is now able to criticize it. It has got rid of those cultural
essentialisms that had confined it since its birth and, at last, it is able to look at the
histories of the nation and of the world in their true specificities. But wait! What
does it make of its own past, now that it has shed the old thematic? What is the
new framework of historical understanding which it adopts?

From Nehru's recounting of India's past, it would appear that there are two
great movements in the nation's history, consisting of a long cycle and a short
cycle. The long cycle begins with the earliest known historical period, that of the
Indus Valley civilization, and ends with the first Turko–Afghan invasions of the
11th century. It is a period which saw the flowering of a great civilization, rich
and vigorous, marked by some astonishing achievements in the fields of
philosophy, literature, drama, art, science and mathematics. The economy
expanded and prospered, and there were widespread trade and cultural contacts

with many other parts of the world. And yet, well before the close of the millennium,

> an inner weakness seems to seize India which affects not only her political status but her creative activities. There is no date for this, for the process was a slow and creeping one, and it affected North India earlier than the South.[9]

The evidence is clear enough: there is no great work in philosophy after Śaṅkara, or in literature after Bhavabhūti, both in the 8th century; the great era of foreign trade ends in the same period; emigrations for colonial settlement in south-east Asia continue from the South until the 9th century; the Cholas are finished as a great maritime power in the 11th century.

> We thus see that India was drying up and losing her creative genius and vitality . . . What were the causes of this political decline and cultural stagnation? Was this due to age alone . . . ? Or were external causes and invasions responsible for it? . . . But why should political freedom be lost unless some kind of decay has preceded it? . . . That internal decay is clearly evident in India at the close of those thousand years.[10]

The most significant evidence of this decay was in 'the growing rigidity and exclusiveness of the Indian social structure as represented chiefly by the caste system'.[11]

> Life became all cut up into set frames where each man's job was fixed and permanent and he had little concern with others . . . Thus particular types of activity became hereditary, and there was a tendency to avoid new types of work and activity and to confine oneself to the old groove, to restrict initiative and the spirit of innovation . . . So long as that structure afforded avenues for growth and expansion, it was progressive; when it reached the limits of expansion open to it, it became stationary, unprogressive, and, later, inevitably regressive.
> Because of this there was decline all along the line — intellectual, philosophical, political, in technique and methods of warfare, in knowledge of and contacts with the outside world, in shrinking economy, and there was a growth of local sentiments and feudal and small-group feeling at the expanse of the larger conceptions of India as a whole.[12]

And thus the long cycle came to an end because India shrank within its shell, became rigid and lost its earlier creativity and innovativeness. But it did not mean the death of Indian civilization. Some vitality remained, and even as it succumbed to a whole series of invasions, there was a historical continuity as India moved into its second, this time a somewhat shorter, cycle of efflorescence.

> Yet, as later ages were to show, there was yet vitality in the old structure and an amazing tenacity, as well as some flexibility and capacity for adaptation. Because of this it managed to survive and to profit by new contacts and waves of thought, and even progress in some ways. But that progress was always tied down to and hampered by far too many relics of the past.[13]

135

The second cycle occurs in the period of the Islamic empires, reaching its peak during the reign of the Mughal Emperor Akbar. It takes the form of a new cultural synthesis between indigenous and Turkish, Afghan, Iranian and Arabic elements, and attains great brilliance in art, architecture, literature, music, and even some synthetic religious cults and philosophies. But to Nehru, the movement is very much a state-sponsored effort, the personality of the Emperor in particular playing a crucial role. Akbar was by far the most remarkable figure in this movement, 'an idealist and a dreamer but also a man of action and a leader of men who roused the passionate loyalty of his followers'.[14] With wise statesmanship and imaginative patronage, he sought to unite the country politically and culturally. 'In him, the old dream of a united India again took shape, united not only politically in one state but organically fused into one people.'[15]

Yet the overall effects of this cultural synthesis were not deep enough to change in any fundamental way the structure of society or the ways of life of the people. The effects 'were more or less superficial, and the social culture remained much the same as it used to be. In some respects, indeed, it became more rigid.'[16] Despite the courage and imagination of imperial efforts to change society, the outlook was inherently limited and the methods far too unsubtle and unappreciative of the complexities of the task.

> Akbar might have laid the foundations of social change if his eager, inquisitive mind had turned in that direction and sought to find out what was happening in other parts of the world. But he was too busy consolidating his empire, and the big problem that faced him was how to reconcile a proselytizing religion like Islam with the national religion and customs of the people, and thus to build up the national unity. He tried to interpret religion in a rational spirit, and for the moment he appeared to have brought about a remarkable transformation of the Indian scene. But this direct approach did not succeed as it has seldom succeeded elsewhere.
>
> So not even Akbar made any basic difference to that social context of India, and after him that air of change and mental adventure which he had introduced subsided, and India resumed her static and unchanging life.[17]

Thus, despite a short period of state-sponsored cultural dynamism, 'life' itself did not change. The same historical period was seeing the most far-reaching and revolutionary changes in Europe, but 'Asia, static and dormant, still carried on in the old traditional way relying on man's toil and labor.'[18] On the eve of the European conquest of the East, therefore, there did exist a quite fundamental difference between the attitudes and outlook on life of the European nations, searching out in new directions, breaking the fetters of tradition and dogma and subjugating the whole world to their will and domination, and those of the peoples of Asia, bound by the customs and institutions of a bygone era, paralysed in body and spirit. That explains why the Asian nations succumbed to the European onslaught. They could not resist because they had lost their inner vigour and vitality.

And so we come back again to the Orientalist thematic. Only now the difference between East and West is reduced from the essential to the conjunctural. There is nothing organic or essential in European civilization which has made it dynamic and powerful: it is just that at a certain point in history it suddenly found a new spirit, new sources of energy and creativity. And similarly, there is nothing organic or essential in Asian civilizations which has made them static and powerless: after a long period of magnificent growth, the old springs of vitality and innovation had gradually dried up. It was at this historical conjuncture that the clash had occurred between West and East: the West conquered, the East submitted.

In this new nationalist reinterpretation of the colonial impact, therefore, historical time itself becomes episodic. Every civilization, it is now argued, has its periods of growth and periods of decay. There are no essential or organic, or insuperable, connections between them. Each is explained by a set of conjunctural factors: economic, political, intellectual, whatever. Further, the cultural values, or the 'spirit', which go with a particular sort of growth are capable of being extracted from their particular civilizational context and made universal historical values. Then they are no longer the 'property' of any particular culture, nor are they essentially or organically tied with that culture.

Thus, past and present can be separated out of the histories of particular nations and represented as the progression of a universal 'spirit of the age'. That determined the norm of world-historical development in relation to which particular nations could be shown to be advanced or backward, and the particular stage of that cycle explained in terms of specific conjunctural factors. Thus, the lack of modernity in colonial India had nothing to do with any essential cultural failings of Indian civilization. The particular historical conjuncture at which India had come under foreign subjugation was one where the European nations were forward-looking and dynamic while Indian society was in a stage of stultification. The subsequent failure of Indian society to match up to the universal historical norm of development was explicable entirely by the circumstances of colonial rule: it was because the dominant foreign power consistently impeded the growth of the forces of modernity that Indian society was finding it impossible to develop.

> When the British came to India, though technologically somewhat backward she was still among the advanced commercial nations of the world. Technical changes would undoubtedly have come and changed India as they had changed some Western countries. But her normal development was arrested by the British power. Industrial growth was checked, and as a consequence social growth was also arrested. The normal power relationships of society could not adjust themselves and find an equilibrium, as all power was concentrated in the alien authority, which based itself on force and encouraged groups and classes which had ceased to have any real significance . . . They had long ago finished their role in history and would have been pushed aside by new forces if they had not been given foreign protection . . . Normally they would have been weeded out or diverted to some more appropriate function by revolution or democratic process. But so long as foreign authoritarian rule continued, no such development could take place.[19]

The fact, then, that India's Present seemed to be so dominated by the Past had nothing to do with anything inherent in its culture. It was the consequence of a particular political circumstance, whose removal constituted the principal political task before the nation. By accomplishing that task, the Indian nation would take the first significant step towards coming in tune with the 'spirit of the age'. That is why the political convulsions in India represented 'the anonymous and unthinking will of an awakening people, who seem to be outgrowing their past'.[20]

It also followed that by looking for its Present not in its own past, but Elsewhere, in the universal representation of the 'spirit of the age', the Indian nation was only attempting to work back into the trajectory of its 'normal' development. This did not necessarily represent any threat to its distinctive cultural identity.

> We in India do not have to go abroad in search of the Past and the Distant. We have them here in abundance. If we go to foreign countries it is in search of the Present. That search is necessary, for isolation from it means backwardness and decay.[21]

III

But what is it that is so distinctive about this 'spirit of the age', this Present which exists Elsewhere and therefore has to be found Elsewhere? Nehru attempts to define it:

> The modern mind, that is to say the better type of the modern mind, is practical and pragmatic, ethical and social, altruistic and humanitarian. It is governed by a practical idealism for social betterment. The ideals which move it represent the spirit of the age, the Zeitgeist, the *Yugadharma*. It has discarded to a large extent the philosophical approach of the ancients, their search for ultimate reality, as well as the devotionalism and mysticism of the medieval period. Humanity is its god and social service its religion . . .
> We have therefore to function in line with the highest ideals of the age we live in . . . Those ideals may be classed under two heads: humanism and the scientific spirit.[22]

Is this, then, a return to Bankim's problematic? For does not this definition of the spirit of the age depend on the same sort of distinction between the material and the spiritual? And is not Nehru saying that in order to become a modern nation we must learn the material skills from the West without losing our spiritual heritage? At times, Nehru does indeed say exactly this:

> India, as well as China, must learn from the West, for the modern West has much to teach, and the spirit of the age is represented by the West. But the West is also obviously in need of learning much, and its advances in technology will bring it little comfort if it does not learn some of the deeper lessons of life, which have absorbed the minds of thinkers in all ages and in all countries.[23]

More generally, the distinctions between the scientific and the unscientific, the rational and the irrational, the practical and the metaphysical, are exactly those which, in their most general terms, had come to dominate post-Enlightenment rationalist, and more specifically positivist, thought in Europe. It accepted the 'givenness' of science, as a body of knowledge with its distinctive methodological principles and techniques of practical application that had demonstrated its usefulness, and hence its validity. The 'spirit of science' or the 'scientific temper' meant, therefore, not just a rationalism, but a rationalism solidly based on 'empirical facts', on 'empirically verifiable truths'. It meant a concern with 'practical' questions and a refusal to engage in 'excessive' and 'fruitless' speculation. For speculative philosophy

> has usually lived in its ivory tower cut off from life and its day-to-day problems, concentrating on ultimate purposes and failing to link them with the life of man. Logic and reason were its guides, and they took it far in many directions, but that logic was too much the product of the mind and unconcerned with fact.[24]

Science, on the other hand, looks 'at fact alone'.[25] Whatever its limits, therefore, it is science alone which offers us a reliable body of knowledge for practical living.

> It is better to understand a part of the truth, and apply it to our lives, than to understand nothing at all and flounder helplessly in a vain attempt to pierce the mystery of existence . . . It is the scientific approach, the adventurous and yet critical temper of science, the search for truth and new knowledge, the refusal to accept anything without testing and trial, the capacity to change previous conclusions in the face of new evidence, the reliance on observed fact and not on preconceived theory, the hard discipline of the mind — all this is necessary, not merely for the application of science but for life itself and the solution of its many problems.[26]

But apart from these general implications of post-Enlightenment rationalism, the 'scientific method' and the 'scientific approach to life' also meant something much more specific to Nehru than it did to someone like Bankim. At its most general level, in fact, Nehru could even assert, like Bankim, that ancient Indian thought was much closer in spirit to the scientific attitude than the overall cultural values of the modern West.

> Science has dominated the Western world and everyone there pays tribute to it, and yet the West is still far from having developed the real temper of science. It has still to bring the spirit and the flesh into creative harmony . . . the essential basis of Indian thought for ages past, though not its later manifestations, fits in with the scientific temper and approach, as well as with internationalism. It is based on a fearless search for truth, on the solidarity of man, even on the divinity of everything living, and on the free and co-operative development of the individual and the species, ever to greater freedom and higher stages of human growth.[27]

But this is not what is most distinctive about the mature reconstruction of nationalist ideology. To Nehru, the 'scientific method' also meant quite specifically the primacy of the sphere of the economic in all social questions. This in particular was what men like Nehru believed to be the distinctively modern, or 20th century, way of looking at history and society. Whether it was a question of political programmes, or economic policy, or social and cultural issues, a 'scientific' analysis must always proceed by relating it to the basic economic structure of society. The correct solutions to such problems must also be searched for in terms of a restructuring of those economic arrangements of society. 'If there is one thing that history shows,' declared Nehru, 'it is this: that economic interests shape the political views of groups and classes. Neither reason nor moral considerations override those interests.'[28]

This now becomes the new theoretical framework for a reconstructed nationalism. It supplies to it the key to a whole new series of rationalist positions on the vital political questions facing it: its assessment of colonial rule, defining the boundaries of the nation, the role of traditional social institutions, of religion, the scale and the pace of industrialization, and above all, the role of the state. From these positions, it is even able to appropriate for purely nationalist purposes 'the scientific method of Marxism' as the most advanced expression yet of the rationalism of the European Enlightenment.

The theory and philosophy of Marxism lightened up many a dark corner of my mind. History came to have a new meaning for me. The Marxist interpretation threw a flood of light on it, and it became an unfolding drama with some order and purpose, however unconscious, behind it . . .

The great world crisis and slump seemed to justify the Marxist analysis. While other systems and theories were groping about in the dark, Marxism alone explained it more or less satisfactorily and offered a real solution.

As this conviction grew upon me, I was filled with a new excitement and my depression at the non-success of civil disobedience grew much less. Was not the world marching rapidly towards the desired consummation? . . . Our national struggle became a stage in the longer journey . . . Time was in our favour.[29]

This appropriation of Marxism was, of course, deliberately selective, as we will see in a moment. But it provided a new scientific legitimation to a whole set of rationalist distinctions between the modern and the traditional, the secular and the religious, the progressive and the obscurantist, the advanced and the backward. In every case, the argument was as follows: in the present day and age, there is but one general historically given direction in which the economy must move: the direction of rapid industrialization. The position of each social group or class *vis-à-vis* the requirements for such a rapid industrialization of the economy determined the 'real economic interests' of that group or class. Those whose real economic interests are in accordance with those requirements are 'progressive' classes; those whose interests are opposed to those requirements are 'reactionary classes'. However, quite apart from the real economic interests, there also existed subjective beliefs and ideologies in society which prevented particular groups and classes from perceiving their real economic interests and acting in accordance with them. These were the backward ideologies — primordial loyalties, sectarian sentiments, religious obscurantisms. etc. — and those reactionary classes which were opposed to progressive changes often perpetuated their otherwise obsolete domination by playing upon these subjective social beliefs.

Thus, for example, that ubiquitous problem of 'communalism' which has consistently dogged Indian nationalism in the 20th century. In theory, the problem as Nehru saw it was simple enough: the fundamental political requirement was the legal guarantee of full and equal rights of citizenship, irrespective of religious, linguistic or other cultural differences. That was the basic liberal premise on which individual civil rights would be established. In addition, there had to be a consideration of welfare or social justice:

> every effort should be made by the state as well as by private agencies to remove all invidious social and customary barriers which came in the way of the full development of the individual as well as any group, and that educationally and economically backward classes should be helped to get rid of their disabilities as rapidly as possible. This applied especially to the depressed classes. It was further laid down that women should share in every way with men in the privileges of citizenship.[30]

It was true, of course, that the colonial state was hardly interested in providing these conditions for the full growth of citizenship. It was an external political force, intervening in the political conflicts in India in order to further its own particular interests, and therefore 'playing off' one side against the other by distributing special privileges on a sectarian basis. But that was all the more reason to conclude that a solution of the 'communal' problem required, as a first step, the elimination of the colonial state and the creation of a true national state.

But once these premises of the national state were granted there could not exist a 'communal' problem any more. The only problems which would then be real were economic problems.

> Having assured the protection of religion and culture, etc., the major problems that were bound to come up were economic ones which had nothing to do with a person's religion. Class conflicts there might well be, but not religious conflicts, except in so far as religion itself represented some vested interest.[31]

And once again, it was clear enough that a solution of these 'real economic problems' would require a fundamental restructuring of the economic processes of society, so that a massive increase in the social product could yield sufficient resources to satisfy the urge for equitable distribution and welfare of all groups. No true solution to the 'communal' problem could be found by attempting to tinker with the existing structure.

> Only by thinking in terms of a different political framework — and even more so a different social framework — can we build up a stable foundation for joint action. The whole idea underlying the demand for independence was this: to make people realise that we were struggling for an entirely different political structure ...
>
> But almost all our leaders continued to think within the narrow steel frame of the existing political, and of course the social, structure. They faced every problem — communal or constitutional — with this background, and inevitably, they played into the hands of the British Government, which controlled completely

that structure . . . the time had gone by when any political or economic or communal problem in India could be satisfactorily solved by reformist methods. Revolutionary outlook and planning and revolutionary solutions were demanded by the situation . . .

The want of clear ideals and objectives in our struggle for freedom undoubtedly helped the spread of communalism. The masses saw no clear connection between their day-to-day sufferings and the fight for swaraj.[32]

Yet, while all this might be clear enough from a 'scientific' analysis of the problem, the subjective beliefs held by the people did not necessarily allow them to see the solution in such a clear light. 'They fought well enough at times by instinct, but that was a feeble weapon which could be easily blunted or even turned aside for other purposes. There was no reason behind it.'[33] And then there was fear:

Fear that bigger numbers might politically overwhelm a minority . . . people had grown so accustomed to think along lines of religious cleavage, and were continually being encouraged to do so by communal religious organizations and government action, that the fear of the major religious community, that is the Hindus, swamping others continued to exercise the minds of many Moslems . . . fear is not unreasonable.[34]

The masses did not act according to 'reason' because they had not been taught to do so. They acted by 'instinct' and were therefore susceptible to 'religious passions'. Thus, although the demands of 'communalism' were quite clearly those of a very small reactionary upper class within each community, the political support those demands received from the community at large were, by any standards of rational explanation, quite 'extraordinary'.

It is nevertheless extraordinary how the bourgeois classes, both among the Hindus and the Muslims, succeeded, in the sacred name of religion, in getting a measure of mass sympathy and support for programmes and demands which had absolutely nothing to do with the masses, or even the lower middle class. Every one of the communal demands put forward by any communal group is, in the final analysis, a demand for jobs, and these jobs could only go to a handful of the upper middle class. There is also, of course, the demand for special and additional seats in the legislature, as symbolising political power, but this too is looked upon chiefly as the power to exercise patronage. These narrow political demands, benefiting at the most a small number of the upper middle classes, and often creating barriers in the way of national unity and progress, were cleverly made to appear the demands of the masses of that particular religious group. Religious passion was hitched on to them in order to hide their barrenness.

In this way political reactionaries came back to the political field in the guise of communal leaders, and the real explanation of the various steps they took was not so much their communal bias as their desire to obstruct political advance.[35]

Within the new 'scientific' construction of society and politics the problem of the subjective beliefs of the masses, as distinct from their 'objective economic interests', was not one which could be rationally comprehended, for these beliefs were located in the realm of 'unreason', of 'passions', of 'spontaneity'. All that could be comprehended were the motivations and interests of political leaders and organizations which sought to manipulate the masses by playing upon their religious passions. And so, understanding the politics of 'communalism' becomes a problem of identifying which group of politicians used which particular isses to mislead which sections of the people. Sir Syed Ahmed Khan, who launched a movement in the late 19th century to popularize Western education among Indian Muslims, was not a 'reactionary' because without this education, Muslims would have remained backward. 'The Muslims were not historically or ideologically ready then for the *bourgeois* nationalist movement as they had developed no *bourgeoisie*, as the Hindus had done. Sir Syed's activities, therefore, although seemingly very moderate, were in the right revolutionary direction.'[36] (Incidentally, the unstated assumption here is that the Muslims needed a 'Muslim bourgeoisie' in order to become historically ready for the national movement; an 'Indian bourgeoisie' would not have served the purpose.) However, in the early 20th century, when the Aga Khan emerged as a leader of the Muslims, it meant 'the lining up of the Muslim landed classes as well as the growing *bourgeoisie* with the British Government' by using the religious issue to forestall any potential threat to the stability of British rule or to the vested interests of the upper classes.[37] Still 'the inevitable drift of the Muslim *bourgeoisie* towards nationalism' could not be stopped.

Following World War I, the Ali brothers, M.A. Ansari, Abul Kalam Azad, 'and a number of other *bourgeois* leaders . . . began to play an important part in the political affairs of the Muslims'. Soon most of them were 'swept' by Gandhi into the Non-cooperation movement.[38] But the 'communal and backward elements, both among the Hindus and the Muslims' came back into the picture. There was 'a struggle for jobs for the middle-class intelligentsia'. There was also the special problem in Punjab, Sind and Bengal where the Hindus were 'the richer, creditor, urban class' and the Muslims 'the poorer, debtor, rural class'. 'The conflict between the two was therefore often economic, but it was always given a communal colouring.' There was communalism on the part of Hindu politicians as well, masquerading 'under a nationalist cloak' but really seeking to protect upper-class Hindu interests.[39] But in each of these cases, there was a particular political leadership or organization which played upon the religious sentiments of the masses in order to gather support for particular policies or interests affecting only the upper classes. When those policies were in favour of the broad goals of a united national movement, they were 'progressive'; when not, they represented the activities of 'a small upper class reactionary group' which had set out to 'exploit and take advantage of the religious passions of the masses for their own ends'.[40]

Take another vital question of the Indian national movement: the question of industrialization. Here again, Nehru's argument is similar: the spirit of the age demanded industrialization; without it, not only would the basic economic problems of poverty remain unsolved, but even the political foundations of independent nationhood would be threatened. It was not, therefore, a matter of moral or aesthetic choice. It was a simple fact of modern life, determined globally by the conditions of modern-day economic production.

> It can hardly be challenged that, in the context of the modern world, no country can be politically and economically independent, even within the framework of international interdependence, unless it is highly industrialized and has developed its power resources to the utmost. Nor can it achieve or maintain high standards of living and liquidate poverty without the aid of modern technology in almost every sphere of life. An industrially backward country will continually upset the world's equilibrium and encourage the aggressive tendencies of more developed countries.[41]

Thus, the question of a choice between two alternative paths of economic development, one based on large-scale heavy industry and the other on decentralized small-scale industry, simply did not arise. A political choice of this sort must proceed by granting a primacy to the economic determinants. And in that area, the choice had already been made — Elsewhere, by History, by 'the spirit of the age'.

> Any argument as to the relative merits of small-scale and large-scale industry seems strangely irrelevant today, when the world and the dominating facts of the situation that confront it have decided in favor of the latter.[42]

On the question of industrialization, therefore, there was, on the one hand, a consideration of national power, of the economy, i.e. an industrialized economy, providing the key to the economic and political independence of the nation. An economy based on cottage and small-scale industries was 'doomed to failure' because it could only 'fit in with the world framework' as a 'colonial appendage'.[43] But by the same logic, there was also the implication that the requisite level of industrialization for the nation would always have to be set by global standards. For science set its own technological standards, its own standards of efficiency and obsolescence; and science, of course, was a universal value. Thus the progression of Time in the domain of science was also something which took place Elsewhere. The question of small-scale and large-scale industry was not, therefore,

> a mere question of adjustment of the two forms of production and economy. One must be dominating and paramount, with the other complementary to it, fitting in where it can. The economy based on the latest technical achievements of the day must necessarily be the dominating one. If technology demands the big machine, as it does today in a large measure, then the big machine with all its implications and consequences must be accepted . . . the latest technique has to be followed, and to adhere to outworn and out-of-date methods of production, except as a temporary and stop-gap measure, is to arrest growth and development.[44]

Within the ideological framework of mature nationalism, therefore, the path of economic development was clearly set out in terms of the 'scientific' understanding of society and history. There were three fundamental requirements: 'a heavy engineering and machine-making sector, scientific research institutes, and electric power'.[45] It is also worth pointing out that when this nationalist understanding appealed to 'the scientific outlook of Marxism', it found ready theoretical support in the Bolshevik understanding of the problem of economic development, popularized in particular in the phase of Soviet industrialization. Nationalists like Nehru found in 'the primacy of the economic' a particularly useful theoretical foothold from which they could reach out and embrace the rationalist and egalitarian side of Marxism, leaving its political core well alone. Whether the Bolshevik understanding itself provided the theoretical conditions for such a selective appropriation is, of course, another matter.[46]

The historically determined and scientifically demonstrated need for national industrialization having been established, all that remained was to identify the political forces, and the policies, which were either in favour of or against such industrialization. The fundamental obstacle was, of course, the colonial state. It was true that the values of modernity and industrialization were historically established in India in the period of colonial rule and in the process of the colonial impact. But that was only a reflection of the fact that in the given historical era it was Britain, or more generally the West, which represented the universal spirit of the age. The specific consequences of colonial rule, however, were wholly injurious to Indian nationhood. In fact, at the time when Britain conquered India, there were, according to Nehru, 'two Englands'. One was 'the England of Shakespeare and Milton, of noble speech and writing and brave deeds, of political revolution and the struggle for freedom, of science and technical progress'. The other was 'the England of the savage penal code and brutal behaviour, of entrenched feudalism and reaction'. 'Which of these two Englands came to India?' he asks. The two were, of course, fused into a single entity, and one could hardly be separated from the other. 'Yet in every major action one plays the leading role, dominating the other, and it was inevitable that the wrong England should play that role in India and should come in contact with and encourage the wrong India in the process.'[47]

With respect to the industrial economy, the 'wrong' England represented the narrow and regressive interests of British capital. Having first destroyed the traditional industrial base of the country in the early phase of conquest, not only was the colonial state in its later phase not interested in Indian industrial development, it actively impeded such growth in order to protect the dominant interests of British industrial and commercial capital. Whatever facilities were conceded to Indian capital were because of special circumstances, such as wartime compulsions. Consequently, Indian industry had grown as far as it had 'in spite of the strenuous opposition of the British government in India and of vested interests in Britain'.[48] Secondly, the colonial state in India had consistently propped up an obsolete feudal order in the countryside and was thus preventing a solution of the massive agrarian problem without which no country can industrialize on a stable basis.

Hence, the most desirable national policy of industrialization would be, first of all, to replace the colonial state with a truly national state; second, to eradicate feudalism in the countryside and undertake fundamental land reforms; and third, to carefully plan the industrial development of the country, under the central coordinating aegis of the state, using the best available scientific and technical expertise and taking the broadest possible view of the range of interrelated social consequences. The performance of Indian industry in the years of World War II had shown 'the enormous capacity of India to advance with rapidity on all fronts. If this striking effort can be made under discouraging conditions,' Nehru wrote in 1944, 'and under a foreign government which disapproved of industrial growth in India, it is obvious that planned development under a free national government would completely change the face of India within a few years'.[49]

IV

The ideological reconstruction undertaken by nationalist thought at its moment of arrival placed the idea of the national state at its very heart. It is a state which must embrace the whole people, give everyone an equal right of citizenship, irrespective of sex, language, religion, caste, wealth or education. In particular, it must be based on a consciousness of national solidarity which includes, in an active political process, the vast mass of the peasantry. This was the central political objective of the Indian national movement in its mature phase.

Often as I wandered from meeting to meeting I spoke to my audience of this India of ours, of Hindustan and of Bharata, the old Sanskrit name derived from the mythical founder of the race. I seldom did so in the cities, for there the audiences were more sophisticated and wanted stronger fare. But to the peasant, with his limited outlook, I spoke of this great country for whose freedom we were struggling, of how each part differed from the other and yet was India, of common problems of the peasants from north to south and east to west, of the *Swaraj*, the self-rule that could only be for all and every part and not for some . . .

Sometimes as I reached a gathering, a great roar of welcome would greet me: *Bharat Mata ki Jai* — Victory to Mother India! I would ask them unexpectedly what they meant by that cry, who was this *Bharat Mata*, Mother India, whose victory they wanted? My question would amuse them and surprise them, and then, not knowing exactly what to answer, they would look at each other and at me. I persisted in my questioning. At last a vigorous Jat, wedded to the soil from immemorial generations, would say that it was the *dharti*, the good earth of India, that they meant. What earth? Their particular village patch, or all the patches in the district or province, or in the whole of India? And so question and answer went on, till they would ask me impatiently to tell them all about it. I would endeavour to do so and explain that India was all this that they had thought, but it was so much more. The mountains and the rivers of India, and the forests and the broad fields, which gave us food, were all dear to us, but what counted ultimately were the people of India, people like them and me, who were spread out all over this vast land. *Bharat Mata*, Mother India, was essentially these millions of people, and victory to her meant victory to these people. You are parts of this *Bharat Mata*, I told them, you are in a manner yourselves *Bharat Mata*, and as this idea slowly soaked into their brains, their eyes would light up as if they had made a great discovery.[50]

We do not have at hand any corresponding texts that record the peasants' perception of this explication by Jawaharlal Nehru of the idea of *Bharat Mata*; we must, therefore, reserve our judgement on how far the idea 'soaked into their brains'. But this remarkable passage tells us a great deal more about the ideological presuppositions of the new nationalist state leadership. To this leadership, the representation of the nation as Mother carried little of the utopian meaning, dream-like and yet passionately real, charged with a deeply religious semiotic, with which the nationalist intelligentsia had endowed it in its late 19th century phase of Hindu revivalism. It conveyed none of that sense of anguish of a small alienated middle class, daily insulted by the realities of political subjection and yet powerless to hit back, summoning up from the depths of its soul the will and the courage to deliver the ultimate sacrifice that would save the honour of the nation. We do not have here a Bankim of *Ānandamaṭh*[51] or a Rabindranath Tagore in his Swadeshi phase.[52] We have instead a state-builder, pragmatic and self-conscious. The nation as Mother comes to him as part of a political language he has taught himself to use; it is just another political slogan which had gained currency and established itself in the meeting-grounds of the Congress. It does not figure in his own 'scientific' vocabulary of politics. But he can use it, because it has become part of the language which the masses speak when they come to political meetings. So he interprets the word, giving it his own rationalist construction: the nation was the whole people, the victory of the nation meant the victory of the whole people, 'people like them and me'.

Men like Jawaharlal Nehru were acutely conscious of the immense cultural gap which separated the 'them' from the 'me'; in *The Discovery of India*, Nehru had written:

India was in my blood and there was much in her that instinctively thrilled me. And yet, I approached her almost as an alien critic, full of dislike for the present as well as for many of the relics of the past that I saw. To some extent I came to her via the West and looked at her as a friendly Westerner might have done. I was eager and anxious to change her outlook and appearance and give her the garb of modernity. And yet doubts rose within me. Did I know India, I who presumed to scrap much of her past heritage?[53]

The process of 'knowing' India too began quite accidentally, 'almost without any will of my own'[54] when in 1920, Ramachandra, the peasant leader of Uttar Pradesh, came with two hundred peasants to Allahabad to 'beg' the great Congress leaders to come with them to Partabgarh district.[55]

They showered their affection on us and looked on us with loving and hopeful eyes, as if we were the bearers of good tidings, the guides who were to lead them to the promised land. Looking at them and their misery and overflowing gratitude, I was filled with shame and sorrow, shame at my own easy-going and comfortable life and our petty politics of the city which ignored this vast multitude of semi-naked sons and daughters of India, sorrow at the degradation and overwhelming poverty of India. A new picture of India seemed to rise before me, naked, starving, crushed, and utterly miserable. And their faith in us, casual visitors from the distant city, embarrassed me and filled me with a new responsibility that frightened me.[56]

It was 'responsibility' that was the feeling which determined the attitude of the new nationalist state leadership towards the peasantry. This feeling of responsibility was not self-consciously paternalistic, for that was the attitude, condescending and inherently insulting, of the hated British administrator. Rather it was mediated by a whole series of concepts, scientific and theoretical, about politics and the state, about the principles of political organization, about relations between leaders and the masses in political movements, about strategies and tactics. The masses had to be 'represented'; the leaders must therefore learn to 'act on their behalf' and 'in their true interests'.

It was this concept of 'responsibility' as mature and self-conscious *political representation* which shaped Nehru's ideas on the place of the peasantry in the national movement and, by extension, in the new national state. Left to their own devices, peasants often rebelled. These upheavals were 'symptoms of a deep-seated unrest'.[57] While they lasted, the countryside would be 'afire with enthusiasm'[58] and the peasants would seem 'to expect strange happenings which would, as if by a miracle, put an end to their long misery'.[59] But the uprisings were always spontaneous and localized. 'The Indian *kisans* have little staying power, little energy to resist for long.'[60] And that is why leaders such as Ramachandra, who rise up on the crest of 'spontaneous' upheavals of this kind, turn out to be 'irresponsible'.

> Having organised the peasantry to some extent he made all manner of promises to them, vague and nebulous but full of hope for them. He had no programme of any kind and when he had brought them to a pitch of excitement he tried to shift the responsibility to others . . . he turned out later to be a very irresponsible and unreliable person.[61]

Peasants were 'ignorant' and subject to 'passions'. They were 'dull certainly, uninteresting individually, but in the mass they produced a feeling of overwhelming pity and a sense of ever-impending tragedy'.[62] They needed to be led properly, controlled, not by force or fear, but by 'gaining their trust', by teaching them their true interests. Thus when peasants caused 'trouble' in Rae ·Bareli in 1921 by demanding that some of the villagers who had been arrested recently by the police be released, and the local authorities refused permission to Nehru to address them and instead resorted to shooting, Nehru was 'quite sure that if I or someone [the peasants] trusted had been there and had asked them to do so they would have dispersed. They refused to take their orders from men they did not trust.'[63]

But even for a leadership which had gained the trust of the peasantry, the problem of control was not necessarily a simple one. The very domain of this kind of politics lay in a zone where a great deal was unknown and unpredictable. Often the sense of responsibility towards the peasantry would compel this leadership even to cooperate with an alien state power in order to prevent or control the sudden outbursts of peasant violence. At other times, in periods of widespread agrarian unrest, it became necessary to coordinate and control a series of localized and sporadic agitations in order to put maximum pressure on the colonial government. But the irrationality of the emotions which drove these movements and the unpredictability of their course made it very difficult for even a sympathic leadership to keep a tight grip over its peasant followers. The chapter on 'Agrarian Troubles in the United Provinces'[64] in Nehru's *Autobiography* is, for instance, interspersed with a series of questions such as 'What could they do? What could we do? What advice could we give? What was to be done to them? What would happen then?' many of the questions in fact repeated several times. At one point, when the peasants came to the Congress leaders 'complaining bitterly', Nehru confesses that he 'felt like running away and hiding somewhere, anywhere, to escape this dreadful predicament'.[65]

The problems of incomprehension and unpredictability were compounded by the fact that at moments of agrarian unrest, the peasants were often in such a state of excitement that they could easily be misled into acting in ways totally contrary to their best interests. In Fyzabad in 1921, for instance, the peasants had looted the property of a landlord at the instigation of the servants of a rival landlord.

> The poor ignorant peasants were actually told that it was the wish of Mahatma Gandhi that they should loot and they willingly agreed to carry out this behest, shouting 'Mahatma Gandhi ki jai' in the process.
>
> I was very angry when I heard of this and within a day or two of the occurrence I was on the spot . . . within a few hours five or six thousand persons had collected from numerous villages within a radius of ten miles. I spoke harshly to them for the shame they had brought on themselves and our cause and said that the guilty persons must confess publicly. (I was full in those days of what I conceived to be the spirit of Gandhiji's Satyagraha). I called upon those who had participated in the looting to raise their hands, and strange to say, there, in the presence of numerous police officials, about two dozen hands went up. That meant certain trouble for them.
>
> When I spoke to many of them privately later and heard their artless story of how they had been misled I felt very sorry for them and I began to regret having exposed these foolish and simple folk to long terms of imprisonment . . . full advantage was taken of this occasion to crush the agrarian movement in that district. Over a thousand arrests were made . . . Many died in prison during the trial. Many others received long sentences and in later years, when I went to prison, I came across some of them, boys and young men, spending their youth in prison.[66]

Faced with a situation like this, perhaps not all nationalist leaders would have exhibited quite the same amount of self-righteousness in the presence of police officials, or later regretted the consequences with the same degree of equanimity. But the underlying conception about peasants and politics would have been the same. Peasants are poor and ignorant, unthinking and subject to unreasonable excitements. They must be controlled and led by responsible leaders who would show them how they could fit, entirely in accordance with their true and rational interests, into the national movement. To do this, the nationalist political programme must highlight the main agrarian issues and show how the creation of a truly national state would mean a convincing and rational solution of the agrarian problem.

But no matter how comprehensive and scientific this understanding of the social and economic bases of a united national movement, the practical experience of agrarian upheavals repeatedly demonstrated the incomprehensibility of peasant consciousness within the conceptual domain of bourgeois rationality. When Nehru first came in touch with the widespread peasant agitation in Awadh in 1920, he found it amazing that 'this should have developed quite spontaneously without any city help or intervention of politicians and the like'.[67] Left to themselves, such upheavals were 'notoriously violent, leading to *jacqueries*', because at times like these the peasants were 'desperate and at white heat'.[68] To turn the springs of localized and spontaneous resistance by the peasantry into the broad stream of the national struggle for political freedom was the task of the organized national movement. Yet the task could never be accomplished by acting according to the rational principles of political organization. This, according to Nehru, was the principal reason for the failure of the Communist Party in India to mobilize the peasantry. They were in the habit of judging the Indian situation from 'European Labour standards'.[69] They did not realize that socialism in a country in which the peasants formed the overwhelming part of the population was 'more than mere logic'.[70] To control and direct the peasantry within an organized nation-wide movement, it was of course necessary to constantly keep in the foreground of one's rational political understanding the importance of agrarian issues for a comprehensive programme of mobilization. But this mobilization could never be achieved by a rational programme alone. It required the intervention of a political genius: it required the 'spellbinding' of a Gandhi.[71]

Indeed, on reading the many pages Nehru has written by way of explaining the phenomenon of Gandhi, what comes through most strongly is a feeling of total incomprehension. Here was a political leader who acted 'on instinct', for surely that is what it was and not what Gandhi called it, an 'inner voice' or an 'answer to prayer'.[72] Yet he had 'repeatedly shown what a wonderful knack he has of sensing the mass mind and of acting at the psychological moment'.[73] His economic and social ideas were obsolete, often idiosyncratic, and in general 'reactionary'. 'But the fact remains that this "reactionary" knows India, understands India, almost *is* peasant India, and has shaken up India as no so-called revolutionary has done.'[74] He effected, Nehru says, an almost miraculous 'psychological change, almost as if some expert in psychoanalytical method had probed deep into the patient's past, found out the origins of his complexes, exposed them to his view, and thus rid him of that burden'.[75] But this is only a very tentative image, and immediately it turns out to be an inappropriate one, because Gandhi's 'knack' was not derived from any clinical expertise in a science of mass psychotherapy. It was more in the nature of magic: 'how can I presume to advise a magician?' Nehru had once written to Gandhi at a point of extreme ideological disagreement.[76] In fact, Gandhi's appeal was not primarily to the faculty of reason; on the contrary, the appeal was essentially hypnotic, calling for a suspension of reason.

> His calm, deep eyes would hold one and gently probe into the depths; his voice, clear and limpid, would purr its way into the heart and evoke an emotional response. Whether his audience consisted of one person or a thousand, the charm and magnetism of the man passed on to it, and each one had a feeling of communion with the speaker. This feeling had little to do with the mind, though the appeal to the mind was not wholly ignored. But mind and reason definitely had second place. The process of 'spell-binding' was not brought about by oratory or the hypnotism of silken phrases . . . It was the utter sincerity of the man and his personality that gripped; he gave the impression of tremendous inner reserves of power. Perhaps also it was a tradition that had grown up about him which helped in creating a suitable atmosphere. A stranger, ignorant of this tradition and not in harmony with the surroundings, would probably not have been touched by that spell, or, at any rate, not to the same extent.[77]

And so the explanation proceeds, bending and weaving its way over an unfamiliar terrain, seeking a rational answer in some supreme expertise in the science of mass psychology, giving it up for a description in terms of magical powers, but skipping back at the very next moment to an account of the 'tradition' that had been built up around the person. But how was this 'tradition' built up? Was it the appeal to religion, the fact that the masses regarded him as a supremely religious man and therefore endowed him with an unassailable spiritual authority? To be sure, there was a lot of this in Gandhi. His politics was based on 'a definitely religious outlook on life'. But in that case it could only have been a reactionary politics; the whole movement was, in fact, 'strongly influenced' by his religious outlook and 'took on a revivalist character so far as the masses were concerned'.[78] And yet Gandhi's politics was highly revolutionary in its consequences. Was it the case, then, that there was a difference between the politics and the language, between the action and the theory that it was overtly based on? Could the metaphysical assumptions be separated from the political consequences, and the latter supported while ignoring the former?

> I used to be troubled sometimes at the growth of this religious element in our politics . . . I did not like it at all . . . |The| history and sociology and economics appeared to me all wrong, and the religious twist that was given to everything prevented all clear thinking. Even some of Gandhiji's phrases sometimes jarred upon me — thus his frequent reference to *Rama Raj* as a golden age which was to return. But I was powerless to intervene, and I consoled myself with the thought that Gandhiji used the words because they were well known and understood by the masses. He had an amazing knack of reaching the heart of the people . . .
>
> He was a very difficult person to understand, sometimes his language was almost incomprehensible to an average modern. But we felt that we knew him well enough to realise he was a great and unique man and a glorious leader, and having put our faith in him we gave him an almost blank cheque, for the time being at least. Often we discussed his fads and peculiarities among ourselves and said, half-humorously, that when Swaraj came these fads must not be encouraged.[79]

Once again, this remarkable passage tells us much less in terms of explaining the phenomenon of Gandhi than it does about the politics of the nationalist state leadership. For it lays down in the space of a few sentences the entire strategy of the passive revolution in India. To start with, it sets out the contrast between 'we', on the one hand, and 'Gandhi' on the other. Thus, on the one hand, it states that

1) we *know* the correct history, sociology and economics, but
2) we are *powerless* to intervene. On the other hand,
3) Gandhi operates with a religious element, i.e. he has a wrong history, sociology and economics. He has fads and peculiarities. His language is almost *incomprehensible*. But
4) Gandhi uses words that are well known and understood by the masses. He has an amazing *knack* of reaching the heart of the people. Therefore,
5) Gandhi is a great and *unique* man and a glorious leader. It follows as an unstated deduction that
6) Gandhi has the power to mobilize the masses towards Swaraj. The strategy then follows:
7) We *know* him well enough.
8) We give him an almost blank cheque *for the time being*.
9) *After* Swaraj, his fads and peculiarities must not be encouraged.

The argument, in other words, is that whereas our very knowledge of society tells us that 'we' are powerless, Gandhi's unique and incomprehensible knack of reaching the people makes him powerful; however, for that very reason, our knowledge of the consequences of Gandhi's power enables us to let him act on our behalf for the time being but to resume our own control afterwards.

The strategy is set down here in astonishingly stark terms. Yet it is the product of a complex, even if contradictory, understanding of history and society, continually seeking a rational legitimation of its single-minded pursuit of political power. From its own understanding of Indian society, this emerging state leadership recognized the historical limits of its powers of direct intervention. It was a 'progressive' leadership, with its own conception of the sort of changes that were necessary if Indian society was to progress. It identified the chief obstacle to these changes in the existence of a colonial state power, and looked towards its replacement by a national state power as the central agency of change. But it also knew that a successful movement to create a new national state would require the incorporation of the vast mass of the peasantry into the political nation. And here its own understanding of society had made it conscious of the great inconsistencies that existed between the real objective interests of the peasants and their unreasonable subjective beliefs. It also knew, and this is what distinguished them as an emerging *state* leadership, that given its historical circumstances, it could not realistically hope for a transformation of the social and cultural conditions of Indian agrarian society before the political objective was reached. The colonial state was an insurmountable impediment to all such attempts at a transformation. Hence, rather than wasting one's energies in futile projects like 'constructive work in the villages', it was necessary first of all to concentrate on the immediate political task of winning self-government. The task of transforming the countryside could be taken up *afterwards*.

And yet the colonial state itself could not be overthrown unless the peasantry was mobilized into the national movement. How could this be done if the peasantry did not see that it was in its objective interest to join in the struggle for an independent and united national state? To accomplish this historical task, it was necessary, first of all, to be 'sympathetic' towards the conditions of the peasantry, to 'gain their trust'. If the political leadership was prepared to adopt this sympathetic attitude, it would immediately become apparent that the peasants were capable of heroic resistance 'in their own way'. There were, of course, major limitations to these forms of resistance: they were guided by irrational emotions, they were localized and sporadic and prone to violence, they could easily be misdirected by unscrupulous and irresponsible leaders. But that precisely was the task of a responsible national leadership: to organize, coordinate and keep under control a whole series of local movements of this kind.

But this would still leave unresolved the problem of releasing in the first place these more or less spontaneous forces of resistance within the peasantry. How were they to be moved into political action? This could be done by 'reaching into their hearts', by speaking a language which they understood. One must have a 'knack' for this, because it was not a language that would emerge out of a rational understanding of objective interests. It would have to be a very special 'knack', and only a great and unique man like Gandhi would have it.

And so the split between two domains of politics — one, a politics of the elite, and the other, a politics of the subaltern classes — was replicated in the sphere of mature nationalist thought by an explicit recognition of the split between a domain of rationality and a domain of unreason, a domain of science and a domain of faith, a domain of organization and a domain of spontaneity. But it was a rational understanding which, by the very act of its recognition of the Other, also effaced the Other.

If the consciousness of the peasantry lay in the domain of unreason, it could never be understood in rational terms. Thus by the very recognition of its Otherness, the possibility was denied that it could be rationally comprehended in its specific subjectivity. It could only be reached by a political 'genius', a 'unique' man with a 'knack' for 'spellbinding' the masses. And thus, once again, by the very recognition of his power as unique, and therefore not subject to normal criteria of judgment, the specific historical subjectivity of the 'genius' was consigned to the zone of incomprehensibility.

But the *consequences* of his intervention were capable of being appropriated. They could become part of the rational progression of history, because they were capable of being understood rationally. In fact, these excursions into the other domain had to be judged by a criterion of functionality — whether or not they fitted in with the rational (the scientific/the desired) progression of history, defined, of course, in the rational domain — and approved or disapproved of accordingly. Thus, the Gandhian intervention, though its fundamental nature was incomprehensible, was worthy of approval because it was functional in its consequences. 'Communalist' interventions, equally incomprehensible in their powers of mobilization, were to be disapproved of because they were divisive, and hence dysfunctional in their consequences. It was with this notion of functionality, then, that the recognition of the split between the two domains of politics, and of the interventions from one domain into the other, could be reconstituted into the monistic unity of a linear progression of *real* history, both rational and progressive.

The notion of functionality also served to break up this linear progression into distinct, tactically manageable, historical *stages*. There is first a stage where conditions are created in the 'real' domain of politics for a sympathetic approach into the other domain. Then comes the second stage when a 'blank cheque' is given to the great and 'unique' leader to reach out into that other domain: the result is a mobilization of the peasantry. The third stage is when the consequences of the mobilization are appropriated within the 'real' domain of politics and direct control over the now reconstituted political process is resumed.

We have seen in the previous chapter how the thought of Gandhi, beginning as it did from a critique of the very idea of civil society, proceeded to make itself relevant as an effective intervention in the domain of elite-nationalist politics by coming to terms with the problematic and thematic of nationalism. It was, to be sure, a profoundly ambiguous agreement. But by agreeing to recognize the practicality of the problematic, and by implication the validity of the thematic, it connived in the transference of its fundamental moral critique from the domain of the political to that of the utopian. Now Nehru could say, without desecrating the moral sanctity of Gandhi's 'utter sincerity', that he was merely 'a peasant', albeit a great one, 'with a peasant's blindness to some aspects of life'. He could say that Gandhi's project was 'impossible of achievement'. Once Gandhism had acknowledged that the sinfulness of political life might finally force it to save its morality by withdrawing from politics, the path was opened for a new state leadership to appropriate the political consequences of the Gandhian intervention at the same time as it rejected its Truth. The critical point of Gandhism's ideological intervention was now pushed back into the zone of the 'purely religious' or the metaphysical; only its political consequences were 'real'. Thus, it now became possible for Jawaharlal Nehru, Prime Minister of India, to inaugurate on Gandhi's birthday a new factory for making railway coaches and say, 'I am quite sure that if it had been our good fortune to have Gandhiji with us today he would have been glad at the opening of this factory.'[80] For now, Gandhi's Truth had surrendered the specificity of its moral critique: it had been cleansed of its religious idiom and subsumed under the rational monism of historical progress. Was it not true, after all, that Gandhi's 'real' objective was the welfare of the masses? Was it not possible, then, to interpret Gandhi's opposition to machinery in its proper rational context? 'People think that he was against machinery. I don't think he was against it. He did not want machinery except in the context of the well-being of the mass of our people.'[81] Indeed, once the Truth of Gandhism had been retrieved from the irrational trappings of its 'language', the possibilities were endless: it could justify everything that was 'progressive'. Thus the Congress 'formulated a policy of land reform and social justice, and took some steps towards the formulation of a public sector. The whole philosophy of Gandhiji, although he did not talk perhaps in a modern language, was not only one of social justice, but of social reform and land reform. All these concepts were his.'[82]

It is possible, of course, to argue that this is what his political successors had made of Gandhi; it had nothing to do with the Gandhian ideology itself. To take this position would, I think, involve the danger of overlooking the very real effectivity of the new nationalist state ideology. It would imply our having to characterize that ideology as a massive and cynical fraud perpetrated on the Indian people. That in turn would confound the very problem of isolating the justificatory structures of the ideology. If instead we look at the specific unity of the process of development of a mature nationalist ideology constructed around the contemporary Indian state, we would see that the Gandhian intervention was a *necessary* stage in that process, the stage in the passive revolution where the possibility emerged for 'the thesis to incorporate a part of the antithesis'. Paradoxical as it is, the fact still remains that Gandhism, originally the product of an anarchist philosophy of resistance to state oppression, itself becomes a participant in its imbrication with a nationalist state ideology.

Let us briefly glance through Nehru's own representation of the history of the Gandhian intervention in the politics of the nation, and the nature of this imbrication will emerge more clearly. The Gandhian intervention 'forced India to think of the poor peasant in human terms', it bridged the gap betwen 'the English-educated class' and the 'mass of the population' and 'forced [the former] to turn their heads and look towards their own people'.[83] At this stage, the 'India' which was forced to think of the poor peasant is identical with the 'English-educated class' which was forced to look towards their own people, for that indeed was the political nation. 'And then Gandhi came . . . suddenly, as it were, that black pall of fear was lifted from the people's shoulders.'[84] As Gandhi began to perform his 'spellbinding' on the masses, the whole character of the organized national movement changed completely. 'Now the peasants rolled in, and in its new garb it began to assume the look of a vast agrarian organization with a strong sprinkling of the middle classes.'[85] Gandhi transformed 'the Indian habit of mind' which was 'essentially one of quietism'.[86] He, indeed, 'effected a vast psychological revolution'.[87] He came to 'represent the peasant masses of India'. In fact, he was more than a mere representative:

> he is the quintessence of the conscious and subconscious will of those millions . . . he is the idealised personification of those vast millions . . . withal he is the great peasant, with a peasant's outlook on affairs, and with a peasant's blindness to some aspects of life. But India is peasant India, and so he knows his India well and reacts to her slightest tremors, and gauges a situation accurately and almost instinctively, and has a knack of acting at the psychological moment.

What a problem and a puzzle he has been not only to the British Government, but to his own people and his closest associates![88]

His ideas on history and society were, of course, all wrong. They were guided by 'metaphysical and mystical reasons'.[89] He had a 'pure religious attitude to life and its problems'.[90] The ideas of *Hind Swaraj* represented an 'utterly wrong and harmful doctrine, and impossible of achievement'.[91] He was always 'thinking in terms of personal salvation and of sin, while most of us have society's welfare uppermost in our minds'.[92]

But despite all this, 'with all his greatness and his contradictions and power of moving masses, he is above the usual standards. One cannot measure him or judge him as we would others.'[93] He was a genius, a man with unique and incomprehensible powers. 'He was obviously not of the world's ordinary coinage; he was minted of a different and rare variety, and often the unknown stared at us through his eyes.'[94]

His power to move people was incomprehensible, but the consequences were not. Many who joined him

> did not agree with his philosophy of life, or even with many of his ideals. Often they did not understand him. But the action that he proposed was something tangible which could be understood and appreciated intellectually . . . Step by step he convinced us of the rightness of the action, and we went with him, although we did not accept his philosophy. To divorce action from the thought underlying it was not perhaps a proper procedure and was bound to lead to mental conflict and trouble later . . . [But] the road he was following was the right one thus far, and if the future meant a parting it would be folly to anticipate it . . .
>
> Always we had the feeling that while we might be more logical, Gandhi knew India far better than we did, and a man who could command such tremendous devotion and loyalty must have something in him that corresponded to the needs and aspirations of the masses.[95]

But in the final analysis, it was the logical, the rational, the scientific, which had to be the basis for one's understanding of the *real* progression of history. The resort to an incomprehensible power which could rouse the masses was only a functional loop, a necessary detour into the domain of the irrational and the unknown. Soon the rational path of real history would have to be resumed in order to move on to the next historical stage. The detour had meant 'solid gain for the country'. But 'the real thing is the attainment of the goal and every step that we take must be taken from the viewpoint of the very early attainment of this goal'. It had to be consciously borne in mind that the detour was indeed a detour. Or else, one would 'relapse into a dreary round of activity, good in itself, but feeble and ineffective and wholly uninspiring from the larger viewpoint. There are some people who perhaps imagine that the goal is really a distant one and that immediately we must aim at something else. This cannot be the Congress viewpoint and can be ignored.'[96] The goal now was definitely set before the emerging state leadership: 'What then are we aiming at? We have definitely put before us the attainment of a revolutionary, that is root and branch, change in our national political structure.'[97] The perspective was that of the creation of a new national *state*. And this could only be undertaken in the domain of rational politics. And it was obvious, therefore, that Gandhi could no longer be the appropriate guide at this stage of the journey. The disjuncture between the philosophy and the politics could be successfully handled only as long as the detour was recognised as a detour, a move into a 'special field'. When the time came to resume the real course of history, that philosophy could only act as a source of confusion and had to be firmly rejected.

> I came to the conclusion that Gandhiji's difficulties had been caused because he was moving in an unfamiliar medium. He was superb in his special field of Satyagrahic direct action, and his instinct unerringly led him to take the right steps. He was also very good in working himself and making others work quietly for social reform among the masses. He could understand absolute war or absolute peace. Anything in between he did not appreciate.[98]

Gandhian politics was not guided by 'clearly conceived ends', by a conception of historical objectives. 'In spite of the closest association with him for many years I am not clear in my own mind about his objective. I doubt if he is clear himself. One step enough for me, he says, and he does not try to peep into the future or to have a clearly conceived end before him.'[99] He was 'more or less of a philosophical anarchist'[100] and however functional such a philosophy might be in the stage of rousing the masses to political resistance, it could hardly be a reliable guide when the immediate task was to create a new state.

And so the final stage of the nationalist project was defined. No matter how imperfect the preparation, how difficult the circumstances, or even how incomplete and fragmented the final result, the struggle was now one of building the new national state.

> It is a race between the forces of peaceful progress and construction and those of disruption and disaster ... We can view this prospect as optimists or as pessimists, according to our predilections and mental make-up. Those who have faith in a moral ordering of the universe and in the ultimate triumph of virtue can, fortunately for them, function as lookers on or as helpers, and cast the burden on God. Others will have to carry that burden on their own weak shoulders, hoping for the best and preparing for the worst.[101]

This was the epitaph, wondrous and yet condescending, put up on the grave of Gandhian politics by the new nationalist state leadership. The relentless thrust of its rationalist thematic turned the Gandhian intervention into a mere interlude in the unfolding of the real history of the nation. And thus it was that the political consequences of that intervention were fully appropriated within the monistic progression of real history.

V

'Socialism is more than mere logic', Nehru had said when criticizing Communists for being overly dogmatic and theoretical and not paying enough attention to the cultural peculiarities of India. But talking about the socialism which he envisaged for a free India, he was equally forthright: 'The emotional appeal to socialism is not enough. This must be supplemented by an intellectual and reasoned appeal based on facts and arguments and detailed criticism . . . We want experts in the job who study and prepare detailed plans.'[102]

The emphasis on expertise was a distinctive, and central, element in the reconstitution of nationalism as a state ideology. The principal architect in the construction of a modern nation would be a scientific consciousness, knowledgeable and wise, with a broad and subtle understanding of the course of world history, marshalling the latest knowledge made available by science and technology, collecting the widest possible range of information on the precise empirical state of the economy, registering the particular interests and demands of each separate group in society, and then taking a finely balanced view to propose the most efficient as well as the most widely acceptable course for the progress of the economy. The necessary political focus would, of course, be provided by the state. For the state would represent the balanced aggregate interest of the people as a whole. It would not be dominated by any particular group or class; it would not even be the site for the struggle, always potentially violent, between classes. It would stand above these conflicts and provide an autonomous political will to control and direct the economy in the interest of the people as a whole.

A primary object of this scientifically planned development would, of course, be the rapid industrialization of the economy. This was an object which had been globally determined by the inexorable logic of universal history, and there were no grounds left for a moral choice on its desirability or otherwise. Indeed, this objective had now attained a historical status that was quite independent of social ideologies and political programmes.

> We are trying to catch up, as far as we can, with the Industrial Revolution that occurred long ago in Western countries . . . The Revolution ultimately branched off in two directions which are, at present, represented by the high degree of technological development in the United States of America on the one hand and by the Soviet Union on the other. These two types of development, even though they might be in conflict, are branches of the same tree.[103]

It was now a demonstrated truth of history that only an industrialized economy could provide sufficient resources for the balanced satisfaction of wants of all sections of society. The alternative was simply a balanced distribution of poverty. Unless the productive processes of society were revitalized by industrialization, there would be nothing to distribute. It was also a demonstrated truth that an advanced industrial society required a considerable degree of state control and coordination. Things could not be left to the mythical balancing mechanism of the 'hidden hand'. That was yet another economic dogma that had been falsified by history. *Laissez faire*

> is a bullock-cart variety of economic talk, which has no relation with the present. If one wants to live in this modern age of technology, one must also think in terms of modern thought.[104]
> . . . practically nobody now believes in *laissez faire* . . . Everywhere, even in the most highly developed countries of the capitalist economy, the State functions in a way which possibly a socialist fifty years ago did not dream of.[105]

The question of state control, too, had nothing to do with socialism *per se*; its validity derived simply from its being a constituent part of modernity.

Where socialism did come in was on the question of equality. 'Scientific planning enables us to increase our production, and socialism comes in when we plan to distribute production evenly.'[106] But what justified the adoption of equality as a goal of planned development? Was it simply a recognition of the empirical fact that a lot of people wanted equality? That would be a very uncertain justification, for it was not at all clear that everyone meant the same thing by equality or that everyone wanted the same degree of equality. The principle of equality could not be left to be determined on such a contentious field. No, equality was justified by a much more universal logic:

> The spirit of the age is in favour of equality, though practice denies it almost everywhere . . . Yet the spirit of the age will triumph. In India, at any rate, we must aim at equality. That does not and cannot mean that everybody is physically or intellectually or spiritually equal or can be made so. But it does mean equal opportunities for all and no political, economic, or social barrier in the way of any individual or group. It means a faith in humanity and a belief that there is no race or group that cannot advance and make good in its own way, given the chance to do so. It means a realization of the fact that the backwardness or degradation of any group is not due to inherent failings in it but principally to lack of opportunities and long suppression by other groups . . . Any such attempt to open the doors of opportunity to all in India will release enormous energy and ability and transform the country with amazing speed.[107]

Thus, the need for equality was entailed in the very logic of progress: progress meant industrialization, industrialization required the removal of barriers which prevented particular groups from fully participating in the entire range of new economic activities, hence industrialization required equality of opportunity. It did not necessarily mean a fundamental reallocation of rights in society, or a revolution in the nature of property. It did not mean an equalization of incomes either. Only a 'progressive tendency' towards equalization of incomes would result from the fact that every person had the freedom to choose his occupation. 'In any event, the vast differences that exist today will disappear completely, and class distinctions, which are essentially based on differences in income, will begin to fade out.'[108]

Thus, neither industrialization nor equality were innately political questions to be resolved in the battlefield of politics. The universal principle and the world standards had been already set by history; there was no room for choice on those matters. Only the specific national path remained to be determined. But this was now a *technical* problem, a problem of balancing and optimisation. It was a job for experts. 'Planning,' Nehru would later say in 1957, 'essentially consists in balancing: the balancing between industry and agriculture, the balancing between heavy industry and light industry, the balancing between cottage industry and other industry. If one of them goes wrong then the whole economy is upset.'[109] The question was one of collecting detailed information on as many aspects of the economy as possible, of working out the complex interdependence of each of those aspects. There was no merit in imposing one's preconceived theoretical ideas on what was essentially a technical problem. Already in 1938-9, when the National Planning Committee set up by the Congress began its work, Nehru realized that the fact that the need to achieve a broad-based consensus meant the abandonment_ of abstract theories and definite guidelines was not necessarily a drawback; on the contrary, there were distinct advantages in the situation. 'We decided to consider the general problem of planning as well as each individual problem concretely and not in the abstract, and allow principles to develop out of such considerations.'[110] Help was also taken of a very large number of experts, from universities, chambers of commerce, trade unions, research institutes and public bodies. In the end, Nehru

> was greatly surprised at the large measure of unanimity achieved by us in spite of the incongruous elements in our committee. The big-business element was the biggest single group, and its outlook on many matters, especially financial and commercial, was definitely conservative. Yet the urge for rapid progress, and the conviction that only thus could we solve our problems of poverty and unemployment, were so great that all of us were forced out of our grooves and compelled to think on new lines. We had avoided a theoretical approach, and as each practical problem was viewed in its larger context, it led us inevitably in a particular direction. To me the spirit of co-operation of the members of the Planning Committee was particularly soothing and gratifying, for I found it a pleasant contrast to the squabbles and conflicts of politics.[111]

This now became the new utopia, a realist's utopia, a utopia here and now. It was a utopia supremely statist, where the function of government was wholly abstracted out of the messy business of politics and established in its pristine purity as rational decision-making conducted through the most advanced operational techniques provided by the sciences of economic management. Indeed it was a systems-theorist's utopia, where government was the perfect black box, receiving inputs from all parts of society, processing them, and finally allocating the optimal values for the common satisfaction and preservation of society as a whole. No squabbles, no struggles for power, no politics. Place all your prayers at the feet of the *sarkar*, the omnipotent and supremely enlightened state, and they will be duly passed on to the body of experts who are planning for the overall progress of the country. If your requests are consistent with the requirements of progress, they will be granted.

Socialism, Nehru would now repeatedly warn, should not be looked at in purely political terms. A constant emphasis on politics and class struggle 'distorts' the vision of socialism. 'Socialism should . . . be considered apart from these political elements or the inevitability of violence.' All that socialism taught us was that 'the general character of social, political and intellectual life in a society is governed by its productive resources'.[112] Socialism, therefore, was a business of rational management of productive resources. It should also not be defined in *a priori* theoretical terms. 'I do not see why I should be asked to define socialism in precise, rigid terms.'[113] It was something that must evolve from the concrete, the particular: 'We cannot bind the future. We can only deal with facts as they are.'[114] And it is not surprising that an attempt now to morally unify such an infinitely regressive technicism would lead to that most metaphysical of all conceptions, which a younger Jawaharlal would have regarded as wholly imprecise and vague, where everything is related to everything else. Now he would appeal to 'the old Vedantic conception that everything, whether sentient or insentient, finds a place in the organic whole: that everything has a spark of what might be called the divine impulse or the basic energy or life force which pervades the Universe'.[115]

The world of the concrete, the world of differences, of conflict, of the struggle between classes, of history and politics, now finds its unity in the life of the state. The aim was ultimately to achieve equality, a classless society, indeed a lot more:

> Our final aim can only be a classless society with equal economic justice and opportunity for all, a society organised on a planned basis for the raising of mankind to higher material and cultured levels, to a cultivation of spiritual values, of cooperation, unselfishness, the spirit of service, the desire to do right, goodwill and love — ultimately a world order.[116]

This might seem 'fanciful and Utopian', but it was not. It could be realized here and now, in the rational life of the state. The mistaken path, fruitless and destructive, was in fact to try to achieve that final aim by means of politics, through the violent struggle between classes. Nothing would be achieved by the clash of particular interests.

> India is not only a big country but a country with a good deal of variety; and if any one takes to the sword, he will inevitably be faced with the sword of someone else. This clash between swords will degenerate into fruitless violence and, in the process, the limited energies of the nation will be dissipated or, at any rate, greatly undermined.[117]

So was there no violence in the life of the state? Was it not in itself an institution which exercised power over the various parts of society? What if there were impediments in the path of progress? Would not the state, acting on behalf of society as a whole, be required to exercise power to remove those impediments?

> Everything that comes in the way will have to be removed, gently if possible, forcibly if necessary. And there seems to be little doubt that coercion will often be necessary. But [and this is a significant 'but'] . . . if force is used it should not be in the spirit of hatred or cruelty, but with the dispassionate desire to remove an obstruction.[118]

The coercion of the state was itself a rational instrument for the achievement of progress by the nation. It was to be used by the state with surgical dispassion, and would be justified by the rationality of its own ends.

Nationalism has arrived; it has now constituted itself into a state ideology; it has appropriated the life of the nation into the life of the state. It is rational and progressive, a particular manifestation of the universal march of Reason; it has accepted the global realities of power, accepted the fact that World History resides Elsewhere. Only it has now found its place within that universal scheme of things.

Has the history of nationalism then exhausted itself? Such a conclusion will be unwarranted. For hardly anywhere in the post-colonial world has it been possible for the nation-state to fully appropriate the life of the nation into its own. Everywhere the intellectual-moral leadership of the ruling classes is based on a spurious ideological unity. The fissures are clearly marked on its surface.

Where then will the critique emerge of nationalism? How will nationalism supersede itself? A historical discourse, unfortunately, can only struggle with its own terms. Its evolution will be determined by history itself.

Notes

1. Jawaharlal Nehru, *An Autobiography* (London: Bodley Head, 1936) [hereafter *A*], p.370.
2. *A*, pp.383-4.
3. Jawaharlal Nehru, *The Discovery of India* (New York: John Day, 1946) [hereafter *DI*].
4. *DI*, pp.133-4.
5. *DI*, pp.141-2.
6. *DI*, p.142.
7. *DI*, p.143.
8. *DI*, p.143.
9. *DI*, p.217.
10. *DI*, p.220.
11. *DI*, p.221.
12. *DI*, pp.221-2.
13. *DI*, p.222.
14. *DI*, p.256.
15. *DI*, p.256.
16. *DI*, p.261.
17. *DI*, pp.261-2.
18. *DI*, p.261.
19. *DI*, p.518.
20. *DI*, p.516.
21. *DI*, p.578.
22. *DI*, pp.570-1.
23. *DI*, pp.517-8.
24. *DI*, p.522.
25. *DI*, p.522.
26. *DI*, p.523.
27. *DI*, p.526. It is also interesting to note that the most conclusive evidence of the greatness of Indian civilization is found when 'the better type of the modern mind', can be shown to be appreciative of its intrinsic worth. The sections of *The Discovery of India* dealing with the achievements of the classical Indian civilization are replete with dozens of quotations from Schopenhauer, von Humboldt, Max Müller, Sylvain Lévi, Romain Rolland, even H.G. Wells, and one from 'M.

Foucher, the French savant' on the charms of Kashmir. *DI*, p.568.

28. *A*, p.544. In 1934, criticizing communalist politicians for their ignorance of economic matters, Nehru said

> It is notorious that the era of politics has passed away and we live in an age when economics dominate national and international affairs. What have the communal organizations to say in regard to these economic matters? . . . whether socialism or communism is the right answer or some other, one thing is certain — that the answer must be in terms of economics and not merely politics. For India and the world are oppressed by economic problems and there is no escaping them.

Statement to the press, Allahabad, 5 January 1934. *Selected Works of Jawaharlal Nehru* (New Delhi: Orient Longman, 1972-82) [hereafter *SW*], vol.6, pp.184-5.

29. *A*, pp.362-3.

30. *DI*, p.387.

31. *DI*, p.387. There are innumerable places in Nehru's works where he says quite categorically that communalism has nothing to do with religion, that its causes are partly economic and partly political, and that if the economic problems are solved and the foreign power removed, there would be no communalism any more. For example:

> The communal problem is not a religious problem, it has nothing to do with religion. It is partly an economic problem, and partly a middle class problem in a largely political sense . . . I do not think it is a very difficult problem to solve. If social and economic issues come to the front the communal problem falls into the background.

Interview to the press in London, 27 January 1936. *SW*, vol.7, p.82.

> Fundamentally this communal problem is a problem of the conflict between the members of the upper middle-class Hindus and Moslems for jobs and power under the new constitution. It does not affect the masses at all. Not a single communal demand has the least reference to any economic issues in India or has the least reference to the masses.

Discussion with the India Conciliation Group in London, 4 February 1936. *SW*, vol.7, pp.96-7.

> Communalism is essentially a hunt for favours from a third party — the ruling power. The communalist can only think in terms of a continuation of foreign domination and he tries to make the best of it for his own particular group. Delete the foreign power and the communal arguments and demands fall to the ground.

Statement to the press, Allahabad, 5 January 1934. *SW*, vol.6, p.182.

32. *A*, p.137.

33. *A*, pp.137-8.

34. *DI*, p.387.

35. *A*, p.138.

36. *A*, p.462.

37. *A*, p.465.

38. *A*, p.466.

39. *A*, pp.466-7.

40. *A*, pp.467-8.
41. *DI*, p.413.
42. *DI*, p.414.
43. *DI*, p.413.
44. *DI*, p.414.
45. *DI*, p.416.
46. For an interesting argument on this point, see Carmen Claudin-Urondo, *Lenin and the Cultural Revolution*, tr. Brian Pearce (Brighton: Harvester Press, 1977). Returning from his first visit to the Soviet Union in 1928, Nehru made the intriguing comment: 'The Soviet system has become so much identified with Bolshevism and Russia that it is difficult to think of it apart from them. Yet it is conceivable that it may exist, or rather that its outward structure may exist, without communism.' 'The Soviet System', *SW*, vol.2, p.390.
47. *DI*, pp.286-7.
48. *DI*, p.300.
49. *DI*, p.515.
50. *DI*, pp.48-9.
51. In 1908, a young Jawaharlal had written to his mother from Trinity College, Cambridge: 'You have written to me that you are going to read *Anand Math*. Do read it. Although I have not read the book myself, I think it is a good book.' *SW*, vol.1, p.63.
52. For a discussion of the symbolisms of this phase of middle-class nationalism, see in particular Sumit Sarkar, *The Swadeshi Movement in Bengal 1903-08* (New Delhi: People's Publishing House, 1973), esp. pp.252-335.
53. *DI*, p.38.
54. *A*, p.49.
55. For the historical details, see Gyan Pandey, 'Peasant Revolt and Indian Nationalism: The Peasant Movement in Awadh, 1919-1922' in Ranajit Guha, ed., *Subaltern Studies I: Writings on South Asian History and Society* (Delhi: Oxford University Press, 1982), pp.143-97; and Majid Hayat Siddiqi, *Agrarian Unrest in North India: The United Provinces, 1918-22* (New Delhi: Vikas, 1978).
56. *A*, p.52.
57. *A*, p.63.
58. *A*, p.51.
59. *A*, p.52.
60. *A*, p.62.
61. *A*, p.53.
62. *A*, p.78.
63. *A*, p.60.
64. *A*, pp.297-312.
65. *A*, p.305.
66. *A*, pp.61-2.
67. *A*, p.54.
68. *A*, p.59.
69. *A*, p.366.
70. *A*, p.368.
71. It is instructive to note for the sake of comparison what Nehru wrote on Lenin after a visit to the Soviet Union in 1927:

It is difficult for most of us to think of our ideals and our theories in terms of reality . . . In Russia also the revolutionaries of an older generation lived in a world of theory, and hardly believed in the realisation of their ideals. But Lenin came with his directness and realism and shook the fabric of old time orthodox socialism and revolution. He taught people to think that the ideal they had dreamed of and worked for was not mere theory but something to be realised then and there. By amazing force of will he hypnotised a nation and filled a disunited and demoralised people with energy and determination and the strength to endure and suffer for a cause.

'Lenin', *SW*, vol.2, p.408.

    72. *A*, p.505.

    73. *A*, p.506.

    74. *A*, p.406.

    75. *DI*, p.362.

    76. *A*, p.372.

    77. *A*, pp.129-30.

    78. *A*, p.72.

    79. *A*, pp.72-3.

    80. Speech at the inauguration of production at the Integral Coach Factory, Perambur, Madras, 2 October 1955. *Jawaharlal Nehru's Speeches* (New Delhi: Publications Division, 1954-1968) [hereafter *S*], vol.3, p.23.

    81. Speech at a Seminar on Social Welfare in a Developing Economy, New Delhi, 22 September 1963. *S*, vol.5, p.104.

    82. Speech on the No-Confidence Motion in Parliament, 22 August 1963. *S*, vol.5, p.80.

    83. *DI*, pp.412-3.

    84. *DI*, p.361.

    85. *DI*, pp.363.

    86. *DI*, p.364.

    87. *DI*, p.367.

    88. *A*, p.253.

    89. *A*, p.506.

    90. *A*, p.536.

    91. *A*, p.510.

    92. *A*, p.511.

    93. *A*, p.548.

    94. *A*, p.254.

    95. *A*, pp.254-5.

    96. Note written in Naini Central Jail, *SW*, vol.4, pp.444-51.

    97. Ibid.

    98. *A*, pp.127-8.

    99. *A*, p.509.

    100. *A*, p.515.

    101. *DI*, p.520.

    102. *A*, pp.588-9.

    103. Speech in Parliament, 15 December 1952. *S*, vol.2, p.93.

    104. Address to the Associated Chambers of Commerce, Calcutta, 14 December 1953. *S*, vol.3, p.59.

    105. Speech in Parliament, 21 December 1953. *S*, vol.3, p.13.

    106. Speech at a public meeting, Bangalore, 6 February 1962. *S*, vol.4, p.151.

    107. *DI*, pp.532-3.

108. *DI*, p.534.

109. Speech to All-India Congress Committee, Indore, 4 January 1957. *S*, vol.3, p.51.

110. *DI*, p.401.

111. *DI*, p.405.

112. 'The Basic Approach', *S*, vol.4, p.121.

113. Speech to All-India Congress Committee, Indore, 4 January 1957. *S*, vol.3, p.52.

114. Speech in Parliament, 15 December 1952. *S*, vol.2, p.96.

115. 'The Basic Approach', *S*, vol.4, p.119.

116. *A*, p.552.

117. Speech in Parliament, 15 December 1952. *S*, vol.2, p.95.

118. *A*, p.552. In 1935, he wrote:

State violence is preferable to private violence in many ways, for one major violence is far better than numerous petty private violences. State violence is also likely to be a more or less ordered violence and thus preferable to the disorderly violence of private groups and individuals, for even in violence order is better than disorder . . . But when a state goes off the rails completely and begins to indulge in disorderly violence, then indeed it is a terrible thing.

'The Mind of a Judge', *SW*, vol.6, pp.487-8.

6. The Cunning of Reason

> Thus God knows the world, because He conceived it in
> His mind, as if from the outside, before it was created,
> and we do not know its rule, because we live inside it,
> having found it already made.
>
> Umberto Eco, *The Name of the Rose*

There is a scene in Dinabandhu Mitra's play *Sadhabār Ekādaśī* (1866) in which the leading character, Nimchand Datta, a product of the 19th century 'renaissance' in Bengal and, quite typically, alienated from the rest of his society by his own enlightenment, roams drunkenly at night through the streets of Calcutta giving vent to his feelings of irreverent, anarchic anguish, at which point an English police sergeant, dutifully performing his task of preserving the public order, appears.

[Enter Sergeant with two native sentries]

Nimchand.   [looking at the lamp in the Sergeant's hand]
         Hail, holy light, offspring of Heaven first-born,
         Or of th' Eternal co-eternal beam,
         May I express thee unblamed?

Sergeant.   What is this?

Sentry 1.   A drunkard, sir.

Sergeant.   What is the matter with you?

Nimchand.   Thou canst not say I did it: never shake
         Thy gory locks at me.

Sergeant.   Ah, you're scared? You know what'll happen to you, don't you?

Nimchand.   Dear aunt, hold out your arms, save me! I am Ahalyā, turned into stone!

Sergeant.   You'll have to come to the police station. Get up!

Nimchand.   Man but a rush against Othello's breast,
         And he retires.

Sergeant.   Who are you?

Nimchand.   I am Maināka, son of the mountain, now cooling my wings in the bosom of the ocean.

Sergeant.   I will drown you in the Hooghly.

Nimchand.   . . . drown cats and blind puppies.

167

Sergeant.	Pick him up, quick!
Sentry 2.	Get up, you bastard! [ties his hands and drags him]
Sergeant.	Every drunkard should be treated thus.
Nimchand.	And made a son-in-law . . . Yes, let us go to the nuptial chamber. [Exit][1]

That is the story of Enlightenment in the colonies: it comes in the hands of the policeman, and the marriage is consummated in the station-house. And when those who have seen the light try to assert the sovereignty of the admittedly 'particular' ethical values of their nation, including its 'vices, deceptions, and the like', can we then conclude that the Cunning of Reason has met its match? Unfortunately not. Reason is, indeed, far more cunning than the liberal conscience will care to acknowledge. It sets 'the passions to work in its service': it keeps Itself 'in the background, untouched and unharmed', while it 'sends forth the particular interests of passion to fight and wear themselves out in its stead'.[2] No, the universality — the sovereign, tyrannical universality — of Reason remains unscathed.

Nationalist thought has not emerged as the antagonist of universal Reason in the arena of world history. To attain this position, it will need to supersede itself. For ever since the Age of Enlightenment, Reason in its universalizing mission has been parasitic upon a much less lofty, much more mundane, palpably material and singularly invidious force, namely the universalist urge of capital. From at least the middle of the 18th century, for two hundred years, Reason has travelled the world piggyback, carried across oceans and continents by colonial powers eager to find new grounds for trade, extraction and the productive expansion of capital. To the extent that nationalism opposed colonial rule, it administered a check on a specific political form of metropolitan capitalist dominance. In the process, it dealt a death blow (or so at least one hopes) to such blatantly ethnic slogans of dominance as the civilizing mission of the West, the white man's burden, etc. That must be counted as one of the major achievements in world history of nationalist movements in colonial countries.

But this was achieved in the very name of Reason. Nowhere in the world has nationalism qua nationalism challenged the legitimacy of the marriage between Reason and capital. Nationalist thought, as we have tried to show above, does not possess the ideological means to make this challenge. The conflict between metropolitan capital and the people–nation it resolves by absorbing the political life of the nation into the body of the state. Conservatory of the passive revolution, the national state now proceeds to find for 'the nation' a place in the global order of capital, while striving to keep the contradictions between capital and the people in perpetual suspension. All politics is now sought to be subsumed under the overwhelming requirements of the state-representing-the-nation. The state now acts as the rational allocator and arbitrator for the nation. Any movement which questions this presumed identity between the people–nation and the state-representing-the-nation is denied the status of legitimate politics. Protected by the cultural–ideological sway of this identity between the nation and the state, capital continues its passive revolution by assiduously exploring the possibilities of marginal development, using the state as the

principal mobiliser, planner, guarantor and legitimator of productive investment.

By now, of course, the historical identity between Reason and capital has
taken on the form of an epistemic privilege, namely, 'development' as dictated
by the advances of modern science and technology. Notwithstanding the
occasional recognition of problems of 'appropriateness' or 'absorption' of
modern technology, the sovereignty of science itself in its given, historically
evolved form is presumed to lie outside the pale of national or other
particularities of cultural formations. This sovereignty nationalist thought can
hardly question. It can only submit to it and adapt its own path of development
to those requirements. But like all relations of subordination, this one too
remains fraught with tension, for even in submitting to the dominance of a world
order it is powerless to change, nationalism remains reluctant, complaining,
demanding, sometimes angry, at other times just shamefaced. The political
success of nationalism in ending colonial rule does not signify a true resolution
of the contradictions between the problematic and thematic of nationalist
thought. Rather, there is a forced closure of possibilities, a 'blocked dialectic'; in
other words, a false resolution which carries the marks of its own fragility.

The incompleteness of the ideological resolution accomplished by nationalist
thought in its fully developed form can be identified in the very process by which
it reaches its moment of arrival. It is a characteristic of the passive revolution
that it 'incorporates in the thesis a part of the antithesis'. We have shown above
how in its journey nationalist thought necessarily passes through its moment of
manoeuvre. The political appropriation of the Gandhian intervention in
nationalist politics in India is only a particular and rather intricate example of
this process. There could be other ways in which the conflict between capital
and the people–nation can be posed and the political consequences appropriated by the passive revolution of capital: Mexico and Algeria readily appear
as two dramatic examples. What is historically decisive in this process is
precisely the asymmetry between the contending 'subjective forces'. The
victorious side enjoys the crucial advantage of affiliation with a 'world
consciousness', thus having access to vastly superior ideological resources for
running the machineries of a 'modern' state. In this it can, as we have seen, even
mobilize for purely nationalist purposes the 'economic' slogans of a socialist
ideology.

But no matter how skilfully employed, modern statecraft and the application
of technology cannot effectively suppress the very real tensions which remain
unresolved. They are apparent in the political life of every post-colonial
nationalist regime in the world. In numerous cases they appear as separatist
movements based on ethnic identities, proofs of the incomplete resolution of
'the national question'. More significantly, they often appear as fervently
anti-modern, anti-Western strands of politics, rejecting capitalism too for its
association with modernism and the West and preaching either a fundamentalist
cultural revival or a utopian millennialism. There too the fragility of the forced
resolution by nationalism of the contradiction between capital and the people–
nation is shown up.

But to the extent that these antagonisms remain bound by ideological forms such as ethnic separatism or peasant populism, they are in principle capable of being appropriated by the passive revolution by means of yet another manoeuvre. The asymmetry between the 'subjective forces' can be removed only when the antithesis acquires the political–ideological resources to match the 'universal' consciousness of capital. This is no simple task. For a large part of this century it was believed that the association of national liberation movements with the ideology of socialism could achieve not only the completion of the democratic tasks of the national revolution but also the world-wide consolidation of the struggle against capital and the establishment of a socialist internationalism. The experience of the last three decades has shown that the task is far more difficult than what the founding fathers of socialism had visualized. In fact, many of the problems faced by socialist countries today show to what extent the identity between Reason and capital, in its contemporary form of the unchallenged prerogative of 'modern' technology, still remains a reality. Reason, as we said before, has not exhausted its cunning.

Inasmuch as he was a child of the Enlightenment, Marx retained his faith in Reason. But in his life-long critique of Hegel, he also pleaded that Reason be rescued from the clutches of capital. In the process, he provided the fundamental theoretical means to examine and criticize the historical relation between capital and Reason. And this relationship, as he repeatedly pointed out in the final, mature phase of his work, was no simple process of unilineal development. Correcting many of his earlier formulations, Marx in his last years saw little regenerative value in the depredations of colonialism in Asian countries. And it was in Russia that he saw in 1881 'the finest chance' in history for a country to pass into a phase of socialist development without first submitting to capital and thus 'committing suicide'. Marx was convinced that capital in its global form had reached a stage where it was definitely 'against science and enlightened reason' and he saw even in the 'archaic' resistance of the popular masses in countries still not enslaved by capital the possibility of a new beginning.[3]

Thus, much that has been suppressed in the historical creation of post-colonial nation-states, much that has been erased or glossed over when nationalist discourse has set down its own life history, bear the marks of the people–nation struggling in an inchoate, undirected and wholly unequal battle against forces that have sought to dominate it. The critique of nationalist discourse must find for itself the ideological means to connect the popular strength of those struggles with the consciousness of a new universality, to subvert the ideological sway of a state which falsely claims to speak on behalf of the nation and to challenge the presumed sovereignty of a science which puts itself at the service of capital, to replace, in other words, the old problematic and thematic with new ones.

Notes

1. Act II, Scene 2.
2. G.F.W. Hegel, *Lectures on the Philosophy of World History: Introduction,* tr. H.B. Nisbet (Cambridge: Cambridge University Press, 1975), p.89.
3. See in particular the drafts of Marx's letter to Vera Zasulich, now available in English translation in Teodor Shanin, *Late Marx and the Russian Road* (London: Routledge and Kegan Paul, 1983).

Bibliography

Major Texts

Bankimchandra Chattopadhyay
1. *Bankim Racanābalī* (ed.) Jogesh Chandra Bagal, 2 vols. (Calcutta: Sahitya Samsad, 1965).
2. *Bankim Racanābali (English works)* (ed). Jogesh Chandra Bagal (Calcutta: Sahitya Samsad, 1969).

Mohandas Karamchand Gandhi
1. *The Collected Works of Mahatma Gandhi*, 87 vols. (New Delhi: Publications Division, 1958-   ).

Jawaharlal Nehru
1. *Selected Works of Jawaharlal Nehru*, 15 vols. (New Delhi: Orient Longman, 1972-82).
2. *Jawaharlal Nehru's Speeches*, 5 vols. (New Delhi: Publications Division, 1954-68).
3. *An Autobiography* (London: Bodley Head, 1936).
4. *The Discovery of India* (New York: John Day, 1946).

Others

Abdel-Malek, Anouar, 'Orientalism in Crisis', *Diogenes* 44 (Winter, 1963) pp.102-40.

Althusser, Louis, *For Marx*, tr. Ben Brewster (London: Allen Lane, 1969).

Althusser, Louis and Balibar, Étienne, *Reading Capital*, tr. Ben Brewster (London: New Left Books, 1970).

Amin, Shahid, 'Gandhi as Mahatma: Gorakhpur District, Eastern U.P., 1921-1922' in Ranajit Guha (ed.) *Subaltern Studies III* (Delhi: Oxford University Press, 1985), pp.1-61.

Anderson, Benedict, *Imagined Communities: Reflections on the Origin and Spread of Nationalism* (London: Verso, 1983).

Apter, David E., *The Politics of Modernization* (Chicago: University of Chicago Press, 1965).

Bandyopadhyay, Brajendranath and Das, Sajanikanta, *Sāhitya Sādhak Caritmālā*, vol.2 (Calcutta: Bangiya Sahitya Parishad, 1945).

Bhattacharya, Pradyumna, 'Rammohun Roy and Bengali Prose' in V.C. Joshi (ed.) *Rammohun Roy and the Process of Modernization in India* (Delhi: Vikas, 1975).

Breuilly, John, *Nationalism and the State* (Manchester: Manchester University Press, 1982).

Buci-Glucksmann, Christine, 'State, Transition and Passive Revolution' in Chantal Mouffe (ed.) *Gramsci and Social Theory* (London: Routledge and Kegan Paul, 1979) pp.113-67.

————— *Gramsci and the State*, tr. David Fernbach (London: Lawrence and Wishart, 1980).

Carpenter, Edward, *Civilisation: Its Cause and Cure and Other Essays* (London: George Allen and Unwin, 1921).

Chandra, Bipan, *The Rise and Growth of Economic Nationalism in India* (New Delhi: People's Publishing House, 1966).

Claudin-Urondo, Carmen, *Lenin and the Cultural Revolution*, tr. Brian Pearce (Brighton: Harvester Press, 1977).

Collingwood, R.G., *Ruskin's Philosophy* (Chichester, Sussex: Quentin Nelson, 1971).

Das, Sisir Kumar, *The Artist in Chains: The Life of Bankimchandra Chatterji* (New Delhi: New Statesman, 1984).

Davidson, Donald, 'On the very idea of a conceptual scheme', *Proceedings of the American Philosophical Association*, 17 (1973-74) pp.5-20.

Davis, Horace B., *Toward a Marxist Theory of Nationalism* (New York: Monthly Review Press, 1978).

De Barun, 'A Biographical Perspective on the Political and Economic Ideas of Rammohun Roy' in V.C. Joshi (ed.) *Rammohun Roy and the Process of Modernization in India* (Delhi: Vikas, 1975).

————— 'A Historiographical Critique of Renaissance Analogues for Nineteenth-century India' in Barun De (ed.) *Perspectives in the Social Sciences I: Historical Dimensions* (Calcutta: Oxford University Press, 1977) pp.178-218.

Desai, A.R., *Social Background of Indian Nationalism* (Bombay: Popular Book Depot, 1948).

Desai, Mahadev, *The Gospel of Selfless Action or the Gita According to Gandhi* (Ahmedabad: Navajivan, 1946).

Deutsch, Karl W., *Nationalism and Social Communication* (Cambridge, Mass: MIT Press, 1966).

Dunn, John, *Western Political Theory in the Face of the Future* (Cambridge: Cambridge University Press, 1979).

————— 'The Identity of the History of Ideas' in P. Laslett, W.G. Runciman and Q. Skinner (eds.) *Philosophy, Politics and Science*, Series IV (Oxford: Oxford University Press, 1972).

————— 'Practising History and Social Science on "Realist" Assumptions' in C. Hookway and P. Pettit (eds.) *Action and Interpretation: Studies in the Philosophy of the Social Sciences* (Cambridge: Cambridge University Press, 1978).

Dutt, R.P., *India Today* (Bombay: People's Publishing House, 1949).

Fleisher, Martin, *Radical Reform and Political Persuasion in the Life and Writings of Thomas More* (Geneva: Librairie Droz, 1973).

Gellner, Ernest, *Thought and Change* (London: Weidenfeld and Nicolson, 1964).

————— *Nations and Nationalism* (Oxford: Basil Blackwell, 1983).

Gramsci, Antonio, *Selections from the Prison Notebooks*, tr. Q. Hoare and G. Nowell Smith (New York: International Publishers, 1971).

Guha, Ranajit, 'Neel Darpan: The Image of the Peasant Revolt in a Liberal Mirror',

Journal of Peasant Studies, 2 (October 1974) pp.1-46.

    Elementary Aspects of Peasant Insurgency in Colonial India (Delhi: Oxford University Press, 1983).

Hayes, Carlton J.H., *The Historical Evolution of Modern Nationalism* (New York: R.R. Smith, 1931).

    Nationalism: A Religion (New York: Macmillan, 1960).

Hegel, G.F.W., *Lectures on the Philosophy of World History: Introduction*, tr. H.B. Nisbet (Cambridge: Cambridge University Press, 1975).

Hollis, Martin, 'Reason and Ritual', *Philosophy*, 43 (1967), 165, pp.231-47.

Huntington, Samuel P., *Political Order in Changing Societies* (New Haven, Conn: Yale University Press, 1969).

Iyer, Raghavan N., *The Moral and Political Thought of Mahatma Gandhi* (New York: Oxford University Press, 1973).

Joshi, V.C. (ed.) *Rammohun Roy and the Process of Modernization in India* (Delhi: Vikas, 1975).

Kautsky, Karl, *Thomas More and his Utopia*, tr. H.J. Stenning (London: Lawrence and Wishart, 1979).

Kedourie, Elie, *Nationalism* (London: Hutchinson, 1960).

    (ed.) *Nationalism in Asia and Africa* (London: Weidenfeld and Nicolson, 1970).

Kemiläinen, Aira, *Nationalism* (Jyväskylä: Jyväskylä Kasvatusopillinen Korkea-koulu, 1964).

Kohn, Hans, *The Idea of Nationalism* (New York: Macmillan, 1944).

    Nationalism, Its Meaning and History (Princeton: N.J.: Van Nostrand, 1955).

    The Age of Nationalism (New York: Harper, 1962).

Lenin, V.I., 'What the "Friends of the People" Are and How They Fight the Social-Democrats', *Collected Works* (Moscow: Progress Publishers, 1964), vol.1, pp.129-332.

    'A Characterisation of Economic Romanticism', *Collected Works*, vol.2, pp.129-265.

    'Critical Remarks on the National Question', *Collected Works*, vol.20, pp.17-54.

    'The Right of Nations to Self-determination', *Collected Works*, vol.20, pp.393-454.

    'The Socialist Revolution and the Right of Nations to Self-determination', *Collected Works*, vol.22, pp.143-56.

    'The Discussion on Self-determination Summed Up', *Collected Works*, vol.22, pp.320-60.

Lowy, Michael, 'Marxists and the National Question', *New Left Review*, 96 (March-April 1976) pp.81-100.

MacIntyre, Alasdair, 'Is Understanding Religion Compatible with Believing?' in Bryan R. Wilson (ed.) *Rationality* (Oxford: Basil Blackwell, 1970).

Marx, Karl, 'The British Rule in India' in K. Marx and F. Engels, *The First Indian War of Independence 1857-1859* (Moscow: Foreign Languages Publishing House, 1959).

    'Preface to *A Contribution to the Critique of Political Economy*' in K. Marx and F. Engels, *Selected Works*, vol.1 (Moscow: Progress Publishers, 1969).

Mill, John Stuart, *Nature, The Utility of Religion, and Theism* (London: Watts, 1904).

Paggi, Leonardo, 'Gramsci's General Theory of Marxism' in Chantal Mouffe (ed.) *Gramsci and Marxist Theory* (London: Routledge and Kegan Paul, 1979) pp.113-67.

Pandey, Gyan, 'Peasant Revolt and Indian Nationalism: The Peasant Movement in Awadh, 1919-1922' in Ranajit Guha (ed.) *Subaltern Studies I: Writings on South Asian History and Society* (Delhi: Oxford University Press, 1982) pp.143-97.

Plamenatz, John, 'Two Types of Nationalism' in Eugene Kamenka (ed.) *Nationalism: The Nature and Evolution of an Idea* (London: Edward Arnold, 1976) pp.23-36.

Poddar, Arabinda, *Baṅkim-mānas* (Calcutta: Indiana, 1960).
　　　Renaissance in Bengal: Search for Identity (Simla: Indian Institute of Advanced Study, 1977).

Porshnev, Boris, 'Historical Interest of Marx in his last years of Life: The Chronological Notes' in E.A. Zelubovskaya, L.I. Golman, V.M. Dalin and B.F. Porshnev (eds.) *Marks Istorik* (Moscow: Institute of History, Academy of Sciences, 1968) pp.404-43.

Rolland, Romain, *Mahatma Gandhi: A Study in Indian Nationalism*, tr. L.V. Ramaswami Aiyar (Madras: S. Ganesan, 1923).

Rorty, Richard, *Philosophy and the Mirror of Nature* (Oxford: Basil Blackwell, 1980).

Rosdolsky, Roman, 'Worker and Fatherland: A Note on a Passage in the *Communist Manifesto*', *Science and Society*, 29 (1965) pp.330-7.

Ruskin, John, *Unto this Last* (London: W.B. Clive, 1931).

Said, Edward W., *Orientalism* (London: Routledge and Kegan Paul, 1978).

Sarkar, S.C., *Bengal Renaissance and Other Essays* (New Delhi: People's Publishing House, 1970).

Sarkar, Sumit, *The Swadeshi Movement in Bengal 1903-08* (New Delhi: People's Publishing House, 1973).
　　　'Rammohun Roy and the Break with the Past', in V.C. Joshi (ed.) *Rammohun Roy and the Process of Modernization in India* (Delhi: Vikas, 1975).

Sassoon, Anne Showstack, 'Passive Revolution and the Politics of Reform' in Sassoon (ed.) *Approaches to Gramsci* (London: Writers and Readers, 1982) p.127-48.

Sen, Asok, 'The Bengal Economy and Rammohun Roy' in V.C. Joshi (ed.) *Rammohun Roy and the Process of Modernization in India* (Delhi: Vikas, 1975).
　　　Iswar Chandra Vidyasagar and his Elusive Milestones (Calcutta: Riddhi-India, 1977).

Seton-Watson, Hugh, *Nations and States: An Enquiry into the Origins of Nations and the Politics of Nationalism* (London: Methuen, 1977).

Shanin, Teodor (ed.) *Late Marx and the Russian Road* (London: Routledge and Kegan Paul, 1983).

Siddiqi, Majid Hayat, *Agrarian Unrest in North India: The United Provinces, 1918-22* (New Delhi: Vikas, 1978).

Skinner, Quentin, 'Meaning and Understanding in the History of Ideas', *History and Theory*, 8 (1969) pp.3-53.
　　　'Some Problems in the Analysis of Political Thought and Action', *Political Theory*, 2 (1974) pp.277-303.

Smith, Anthony D., *Theories of Nationalism* (London: Duckworth, 1971).

Stalin, J.V., 'Marxism and the National Question', *Works*, vol.2 (Calcutta: Gana-Sahitya Prakash, 1974) pp.194-215.

Tolstoy, Leo, 'The Kingdom of God is Within You', in *The Kingdom of God and Other Essays*, tr. Aylmer Maude (London: Oxford University Press, 1936).
    The Slavery of Our Times, tr. Aylmer Maude (London: John Lawrence, 1972).

Van Dijk, Teun A., *Text and Context: Explorations in the Semantics and Pragmatics of Discourse* (London: Longman, 1977).

Walicki, Andrzej, *The Controversy Over Capitalism: Studies in the Social Philosophy of the Russian Populists* (Oxford: Clarendon Press, 1969).
    The Slavophile Controversy: History of a Conservative Utopia in Nineteenth Century Russian Thought, tr. Hilda Andrews-Rusiecka (Oxford: Clarendon Press, 1975).

Wilson, Bryan R. (ed.) *Rationality* (Oxford: Basil Blackwell, 1970).

Winch, Peter, 'Understanding a Primitive Society', *American Philosophical Quarterly*, 1 (1964) pp.307-24.

Wolf, Ken, 'Hans Kohn's Liberal Nationalism: The Historian as Prophet', *Journal of the History of Ideas*, 37, 4 (October-December 1976) pp.651-72.

Index

THE NATION
AND
ITS FRAGMENTS
Colonial and Postcolonial Histories

Contents

BY NOW knowledgeable people all over the world have become familiar with the charges leveled against the subject-centered rationality characteristic of post-Enlightenment modernity. This subject-centered reason, we have now been told, claims for itself a singular universality by asserting its epistemic privilege over all other local, plural, and often incommensurable knowledges; it proclaims its own unity and homogeneity by declaring all other subjectivities as inadequate, fragmentary, and subordinate; it declares for the rational subject an epistemic as well as moral sovereignty that is meant to be self-determined, unconditioned, and self-transparent. Against this arrogant, intolerant, self-aggrandizing rational subject of modernity, critics in recent years have been trying to resurrect the virtues of the fragmentary, the local, and the subjugated in order to unmask the will to power that lies at the very heart of modern rationality and to decenter its epistemological and moral subject. In this effort at criticism, materials from colonial and postcolonial situations have figured quite prominently.

However, a persistent difficulty has been that by asserting an inseparable complicity between knowledge and power, this critique has been unable adequately to vindicate its own normative preferences and thus to provide valid grounds for claiming agency on behalf of persons, groups, or movements. I do not propose to offer in this book a general solution to this problem. What I attempt instead is a series of interventions in different disciplinary fields, localized and bound by their own historically produced rules of formation, but thematically connected to one another by their convergence upon the one most untheorized concept of the modern world—the nation.

In this project, the present work carries forward an argument begun in my *Nationalist Thought and the Colonial World* (1986). All my illustrations come from colonial and postcolonial India, and even more particularly from Bengal. But it must also be remembered that the very form of imagining nations is such that even as one talks about a particular historically formed nation, one is left free to implicate in one's discourse others that have not been so formed or whose forms remain suppressed, and perhaps even some whose forms have still not been imagined.

I thought about and wrote various parts of this book over the past four years but put it together in its present form in an inspired two-week spell in April 1992. Not surprisingly, I have a long list of acknowledgments.

PREFACE AND ACKNOWLEDGMENTS

My colleagues at the Centre for Studies in Social Sciences, Calcutta—
Pradip Bose, Amitav Ghosh, Anjan Ghosh, Tapati Guha-Thakurta,
Debes Roy, Tapti Roy, Ranabir Samaddar and Asok Sen, in particular—
have been a constant source of ideas, criticisms, and encouragement. My
colleagues in the Editorial Group of Subaltern Studies—Shahid Amin,
David Arnold, Gautam Bhadra, Dipesh Chakrabarty, Ranajit Guha,
David Hardiman, Gyan Pandey, and Sumit Sarkar—have been the most
active and faithful partners in my intellectual life for more than a decade;
they have a share in the production of most of the ideas that have gone
into this book. I am also deeply indebted to Raghab Chattopadhyay, Ajit
Chaudhuri, Sushil Khanna, Rudrangshu Mukherjee, Bhaskar Mukhopadhyay, Kalyan Sanyal, and Anup Sinha (besides, of course, the shad-
owy presence of Arup Mallik), with whom I participated in that remarkable reading circle which went by the name of the Kankurgachhi Hegel
Club and which met every week for three years to make the texts of Hegel
the pretext for intense debates on many of the subjects discussed here.
Two semesters of teaching at the New School for Social Research, New
York, in 1990 and 1991 gave me the respite from my routine obligations
to allow me to get on with my writing; I thank Talal Asad, Debbie Poole,
Rayna Rapp, Bill Roseberry, and Kamala Visweswaran for reading and
commenting on several parts of this book.

I have presented much of the material discussed here in conferences or
talks at Calcutta, Shimla, Istanbul, Moscow, Berlin, Tübingen, London,
and Sussex, and at universities in the following places in the United
States: New York, New Haven, Princeton, Rochester, Philadelphia,
Charlottesville, Pittsburgh, Chicago, Madison, Minneapolis, Berkeley,
Stanford, Santa Cruz, and Los Angeles. These discussions have all contributed to the present form of this text. I must also express my thanks to
the participants of those invigorating meetings in Chicago in 1990 and
1991 of the Forum on Social Theory organized by Benjamin Lee and the
Center for Psychosocial Studies.

I am particularly grateful to Craig Calhoun, Nicholas Dirks, Prabha-
kara Jha, and Gyan Prakash for their generous and detailed comments,
appreciative as well as critical, on the entire manuscript.

I take this opportunity to thank my students in the last few years in
Calcutta and New York who were forced to tackle many of the themes
dealt with here in their early, half-formed stages.

The research on this book was carried out in Calcutta at the Centre for
Studies in Social Sciences and at the National Library. Four or five short
spells of work at the India Office Library, London, allowed me to find
from its Vernacular Tracts collection much material from little-known
nineteenth-century Bengali sources. When I was in New York, the School
of International and Public Affairs at Columbia University was kind

enough to grant me the status of a Visiting Scholar, which allowed me to use the Butler Library at Columbia. The first draft manuscript of this book was produced during my short stay in April 1992 as Visiting Fellow at the A. E. Havens Center in the Department of Sociology at the University of Wisconsin at Madison: I thank Allen Hunter and Polly Ericksen for their generous help.

In the matter of finding books, I have to express my deep indebtedness to Nirmalya Acharya, whose native knowledge of the labyrinthine world of College Street publishing continues to be of invaluable help to me. And to Susanta Ghosh I remain indebted for his encouragement as well as criticism, well meant if not always well deserved.

I am grateful to the publishers of the following journals for allowing me to use in this book sections from my previously published articles: "Whose Imagined Community?" *Millennium: Journal of International Studies* 20, no. 3 (Winter 1991): 521–26; "History and the Nationalization of Hinduism," *Social Research* 59, no. 1 (Spring 1992): 111–49; "Colonialism, Nationalism, and Colonialized Women: The Contest in India," *American Ethnologist* 16, no. 4 (November 1989): 622–33; "For an Indian History of Peasant Struggle," *Social Scientist* 16, no. 11 (November 1988): 3–17; "A Response to Taylor's Modes of Civil Society," *Public Culture* 3, no. 1 (Fall 1990): 119–32. I am also grateful to Blackwell Publishers for permission to use parts of my article "Their Own Words? An Essay for Edward Said," in Michael Sprinker, ed., *Edward Said: A Critical Reader* (Oxford: Blackwell, 1992), pp. 194–220; and to the School for American Research for permission to use my article "Alternative Histories/Alternative Nations," to be published in the forthcoming conference volume "Making Alternative History," edited by Peter A. Schmidt and Tom Patterson.

Except when otherwise stated, all translations in this book from Bengali sources are my own.

My thanks to Mary Murrell, Beth Gianfagna, and Cindy Crumrine of Princeton University Press for their enthusiasm about this book and the care they have taken over its production.

And finally, as always, my thanks to Gouri.

Calcutta
10 November 1992

CHAPTER ONE

Whose Imagined Community?

NATIONALISM has once more appeared on the agenda of world affairs. Almost every day, state leaders and political analysts in Western countries declare that with "the collapse of communism" (that is the term they use; what they mean is presumably the collapse of Soviet socialism), the principal danger to world peace is now posed by the resurgence of nationalism in different parts of the world. Since in this day and age a phenomenon has first to be recognized as a "problem" before it can claim the attention of people whose business it is to decide what should concern the public, nationalism seems to have regained sufficient notoriety for it to be liberated from the arcane practices of "area specialists" and been made once more a subject of general debate.

However, this very mode of its return to the agenda of world politics has, it seems to me, hopelessly prejudiced the discussion on the subject. In the 1950s and 1960s, nationalism was still regarded as a feature of the victorious anticolonial struggles in Asia and Africa. But simultaneously, as the new institutional practices of economy and polity in the postcolonial states were disciplined and normalized under the conceptual rubrics of "development" and "modernization," nationalism was already being relegated to the domain of the particular histories of this or that colonial empire. And in those specialized histories defined by the unprepossessing contents of colonial archives, the emancipatory aspects of nationalism were undermined by countless revelations of secret deals, manipulations, and the cynical pursuit of private interests. By the 1970s, nationalism had become a matter of ethnic politics, the reason why people in the Third World killed each other—sometimes in wars between regular armies, sometimes, more distressingly, in cruel and often protracted civil wars, and increasingly, it seemed, by technologically sophisticated and virtually unstoppable acts of terrorism. The leaders of the African struggles against colonialism and racism had spoiled their records by becoming heads of corrupt, fractious, and often brutal regimes; Gandhi had been appropriated by such marginal cults as pacifism and vegetarianism; and even Ho Chi Minh in his moment of glory was caught in the unyielding polarities of the Cold War. Nothing, it would seem, was left in the legacy of nationalism to make people in the Western world feel good about it.

This recent genealogy of the idea explains why nationalism is now viewed as a dark, elemental, unpredictable force of primordial nature threatening the orderly calm of civilized life. What had once been successfully relegated to the outer peripheries of the earth is now seen picking its way back toward Europe, through the long-forgotten provinces of the Habsburg, the czarist, and the Ottoman empires. Like drugs, terrorism, and illegal immigration, it is one more product of the Third World that the West dislikes but is powerless to prohibit.

In light of the current discussions on the subject in the media, it is surprising to recall that not many years ago nationalism was generally considered one of Europe's most magnificent gifts to the rest of the world. It is also not often remembered today that the two greatest wars of the twentieth century, engulfing as they did virtually every part of the globe, were brought about by Europe's failure to manage its own ethnic nationalisms. Whether of the "good" variety or the "bad," nationalism was entirely a product of the political history of Europe. Notwithstanding the celebration of the various unifying tendencies in Europe today and of the political consensus in the West as a whole, there may be in the recent amnesia on the origins of nationalism more than a hint of anxiety about whether it has quite been tamed in the land of its birth.

In all this time, the "area specialists," the historians of the colonial world, working their way cheerlessly through musty files of administrative reports and official correspondence in colonial archives in London or Paris or Amsterdam, had of course never forgotten how nationalism arrived in the colonies. Everyone agreed that it was a European import; the debates in the 1960s and 1970s in the historiographies of Africa or India or Indonesia were about what had become of the idea and who was responsible for it. These debates between a new generation of nationalist historians and those whom they dubbed "colonialists" were vigorous and often acrimonious, but they were largely confined to the specialized territories of "area studies"; no one else took much notice of them.

Ten years ago, it was one such area specialist who managed to raise once more the question of the origin and spread of nationalism in the framework of a universal history. Benedict Anderson demonstrated with much subtlety and originality that nations were not the determinate products of given sociological conditions such as language or race or religion; they had been, in Europe and everywhere else in the world, imagined into existence.[1] He also described some of the major institutional forms through which this imagined community came to acquire concrete shape, especially the institutions of what he so ingeniously called "print-capitalism." He then argued that the historical experience of nationalism in Western Europe, in the Americas, and in Russia had supplied for all subsequent nationalisms a set of modular forms from which nationalist elites in Asia and Africa had chosen the ones they liked.

Anderson's book has been, I think, the most influential in the last few years in generating new theoretical ideas on nationalism, an influence that of course, it is needless to add, is confined almost exclusively to academic writings. Contrary to the largely uninformed exoticization of nationalism in the popular media in the West, the theoretical tendency represented by Anderson certainly attempts to treat the phenomenon as part of the universal history of the modern world.

I have one central objection to Anderson's argument. If nationalisms in the rest of the world have to choose their imagined community from certain "modular" forms already made available to them by Europe and the Americas, what do they have left to imagine? History, it would seem, has decreed that we in the postcolonial world shall only be perpetual consumers of modernity. Europe and the Americas, the only true subjects of history, have thought out on our behalf not only the script of colonial enlightenment and exploitation, but also that of our anticolonial resistance and postcolonial misery. Even our imaginations must remain forever colonized.

I object to this argument not for any sentimental reason. I object because I cannot reconcile it with the evidence on anticolonial nationalism. The most powerful as well as the most creative results of the nationalist imagination in Asia and Africa are posited not on an identity but rather on a *difference* with the "modular" forms of the national society propagated by the modern West. How can we ignore this without reducing the experience of anticolonial nationalism to a caricature of itself?

To be fair to Anderson, it must be said that he is not alone to blame. The difficulty, I am now convinced, arises because we have all taken the claims of nationalism to be a *political* movement much too literally and much too seriously.

In India, for instance, any standard nationalist history will tell us that nationalism proper began in 1885 with the formation of the Indian National Congress. It might also tell us that the decade preceding this was a period of preparation, when several provincial political associations were formed. Prior to that, from the 1820s to the 1870s, was the period of "social reform," when colonial enlightenment was beginning to "modernize" the customs and institutions of a traditional society and the political spirit was still very much that of collaboration with the colonial regime: nationalism had still not emerged.

This history, when submitted to a sophisticated sociological analysis, cannot but converge with Anderson's formulations. In fact, since it seeks to replicate in its own history the history of the modern state in Europe, nationalism's self-representation will inevitably corroborate Anderson's decoding of the nationalist myth. I think, however, that as history, nationalism's autobiography is fundamentally flawed.

By my reading, anticolonial nationalism creates its own domain of sovereignty within colonial society well before it begins its political battle with the imperial power. It does this by dividing the world of social institutions and practices into two domains—the material and the spiritual. The material is the domain of the "outside," of the economy and of statecraft, of science and technology, a domain where the West had proved its superiority and the East had succumbed. In this domain, then, Western superiority had to be acknowledged and its accomplishments carefully studied and replicated. The spiritual, on the other hand, is an "inner" domain bearing the "essential" marks of cultural identity. The greater one's success in imitating Western skills in the material domain, therefore, the greater the need to preserve the distinctness of one's spiritual culture. This formula is, I think, a fundamental feature of anticolonial nationalisms in Asia and Africa.[2]

There are several implications. First, nationalism declares the domain of the spiritual its sovereign territory and refuses to allow the colonial power to intervene in that domain. If I may return to the Indian example, the period of "social reform" was actually made up of two distinct phases. In the earlier phase, Indian reformers looked to the colonial authorities to bring about by state action the reform of traditional institutions and customs. In the latter phase, although the need for change was not disputed, there was a strong resistance to allowing the colonial state to intervene in matters affecting "national culture." The second phase, in my argument, was already the period of nationalism.

The colonial state, in other words, is kept out of the "inner" domain of national culture; but it is not as though this so-called spiritual domain is left unchanged. In fact, here nationalism launches its most powerful, creative, and historically significant project: to fashion a "modern" national culture that is nevertheless not Western. If the nation is an imagined community, then this is where it is brought into being. In this, its true and essential domain, the nation is already sovereign, even when the state is in the hands of the colonial power. The dynamics of this historical project is completely missed in conventional histories in which the story of nationalism begins with the contest for political power.

In order to define the main argument of this book, let me anticipate a few points that will be discussed more elaborately later. I wish to highlight here several areas within the so-called spiritual domain that nationalism transforms in the course of its journey. I will confine my illustrations to Bengal, with whose history I am most familiar.

The first such area is that of language. Anderson is entirely correct in his suggestion that it is "print-capitalism" which provides the new institutional space for the development of the modern "national" language.[3] However, the specificities of the colonial situation do not allow a simple transposition of European patterns of development. In Bengal, for instance, it is at the initiative of the East India Company and the European missionaries that the first printed books are produced in Bengali at the end of the eighteenth century and the first narrative prose compositions commissioned at the beginning of the nineteenth. At the same time, the first half of the nineteenth century is when English completely displaces Persian as the language of bureaucracy and emerges as the most powerful vehicle of intellectual influence on a new Bengali elite. The crucial moment in the development of the modern Bengali language comes, however, in midcentury, when this bilingual elite makes it a cultural project to provide its mother tongue with the necessary linguistic equipment to enable it to become an adequate language for "modern" culture. An entire institutional network of printing presses, publishing houses, newspapers, magazines, and literary societies is created around this time, *outside* the purview of the state and the European missionaries, through which the new language, modern and standardized, is given shape. The bilingual intelligentsia came to think of its own language as belonging to that inner domain of cultural identity, from which the colonial intruder had to be kept out; language therefore became a zone over which the nation first had to declare its sovereignty and then had to transform in order to make it adequate for the modern world.

Here the modular influences of modern European languages and literatures did not necessarily produce similar consequences. In the case of the new literary genres and aesthetic conventions, for instance, whereas European influences undoubtedly shaped explicit critical discourse, it was also widely believed that European conventions were inappropriate and misleading in judging literary productions in modern Bengali. To this day there is a clear hiatus in this area between the terms of academic criticism and those of literary practice. To give an example, let me briefly discuss Bengali drama.

Drama is the one modern literary genre that is the least commended on aesthetic grounds by critics of Bengali literature. Yet it is the form in which the bilingual elite has found its largest audience. When it appeared in its modern form in the middle of the nineteenth century, the new Bengali drama had two models available to it: one, the modern European drama as it had developed since Shakespeare and Molière, and two, the virtually forgotten corpus of Sanskrit drama, now restored to a reputation of classical excellence because of the praises showered on it by Orientalist scholars from Europe. The literary criteria that would presumably direct the new drama into the privileged domain of a modern national culture were therefore clearly set by modular forms provided by Europe. But the performative practices of the new institution of the public theater made it impossible for those criteria to be applied to plays written for the theater. The conventions that would enable a play to succeed on the Calcutta stage were very different from the conventions approved by critics schooled in the traditions of European drama. The tensions have not been resolved to this day. What thrives as mainstream public theater in West Bengal or Bangladesh today is modern urban theater, national and clearly distinguishable from "folk theater." It is produced and largely patronized by the literate urban middle classes. Yet their aesthetic conventions fail to meet the standards set by the modular literary forms adopted from Europe.

Even in the case of the novel, that celebrated artifice of the nationalist imagination in which the community is made to live and love in "homogeneous time,"[4] the modular forms do not necessarily have an easy passage. The novel was a principal form through which the bilingual elite in Bengal fashioned a new narrative prose. In the devising of this prose, the influence of the two available models—modern English and classical Sanskrit—was obvious. And yet, as the practice of the form gained greater popularity, it was remarkable how frequently in the course of their narrative Bengali novelists shifted from the disciplined forms of authorial prose to the direct recording of living speech. Looking at the pages of some of the most popular novels in Bengali, it is often difficult to tell whether one is reading a novel or a play. Having created a modern prose language in the fashion of the approved modular forms, the literati, in its search for artistic truthfulness, apparently found it necessary to escape as often as possible the rigidities of that prose.

The desire to construct an aesthetic form that was modern and national, and yet recognizably different from the Western, was shown in perhaps its most exaggerated shape in the efforts in the early twentieth century of the so-called Bengal school of art. It was through these efforts that, on the one hand, an institutional space was created for the modern professional artist in India, as distinct from the traditional craftsman, for the dissemination through exhibition and print of the products of art and for the creation of a public schooled in the new aesthetic norms. Yet this agenda for the construction of a modernized artistic space was accompanied, on the other hand, by a fervent ideological program for an art that was distinctly "Indian," that is, different from the "Western."[5] Although the specific style developed by the Bengal school for a new Indian art failed to hold its ground for very long, the fundamental agenda posed by its efforts continues to be pursued to this day, namely, to develop an art that would be modern and at the same time recognizably Indian.

Alongside the institutions of print-capitalism was created a new network of secondary schools. Once again, nationalism sought to bring this area under its jurisdiction long before the domain of the state had become a matter of contention. In Bengal, from the second half of the nineteenth century, it was the new elite that took the lead in mobilizing a "national" effort to start schools in every part of the province and then to produce a suitable educational literature. Coupled with print-capitalism, the institutions of secondary education provided the space where the new language and literature were both generalized and normalized—outside the domain of the state. It was only when this space was opened up, outside the influence of both the colonial state and the European missionaries, that it became legitimate for women, for instance, to be sent to school. It was also in this period, from around the turn of the century, that the University of Calcutta was turned from an institution of colonial education to a distinctly national institution, in its curriculum, its faculty, and its sources of funding.[6]

Another area in that inner domain of national culture was the family. The assertion here of autonomy and difference was perhaps the most dramatic. The European criticism of Indian "tradition" as barbaric had focused to a large extent on religious beliefs and practices, especially those relating to the treatment of women. The early phase of "social reform" through the agency of the colonial power had also concentrated on the same issues. In that early phase, therefore, this area had been identified as essential to "Indian tradition." The nationalist move began by disputing the choice of agency. Unlike the early reformers, nationalists were not prepared to allow the colonial state to legislate the reform of "traditional" society. They asserted that only the nation itself could have the right to intervene in such an essential aspect of its cultural identity.

As it happened, the domain of the family and the position of women underwent considerable change in the world of the nationalist middle class. It was undoubtedly a new patriarchy that was brought into existence, different from the "traditional" order but also explicitly claiming to be different from the "Western" family. The "new woman" was to be modern, but she would also have to display the signs of national tradition and therefore would be essentially different from the "Western" woman.

The history of nationalism as a political movement tends to focus primarily on its contest with the colonial power in the domain of the outside, that is, the material domain of the state. This is a different history from the one I have outlined. It is also a history in which nationalism has no option but to choose its forms from the gallery of "models" offered by European and American nation-states: "difference" is not a viable criterion in the domain of the material.

In this outer domain, nationalism begins its journey (after, let us remember, it has already proclaimed its sovereignty in the inner domain) by inserting itself into a new public sphere constituted by the processes and forms of the modern (in this case, colonial) state. In the beginning, nationalism's task is to overcome the subordination of the colonized middle class, that is, to challenge the "rule of colonial difference" in the domain of the state. The colonial state, we must remember, was not just the agency that brought the modular forms of the modern state to the colonies; it was also an agency that was destined never to fulfill the normalizing mission of the modern state because the premise of its power was a rule of colonial difference, namely, the preservation of the alienness of the ruling group.

As the institutions of the modern state were elaborated in the colony, especially in the second half of the nineteenth century, the ruling European groups found it necessary to lay down—in lawmaking, in the bureaucracy, in the administration of justice, and in the recognition by the state of a legitimate domain of public opinion—the precise difference between the rulers and the ruled. If Indians had to be admitted into the judiciary, could they be allowed to try Europeans? Was it right that Indians should enter the civil service by taking the same examinations as British graduates? If European newspapers in India were given the right of free speech, could the same apply to native newspapers? Ironically, it became the historical task of nationalism, which insisted on its own marks of cultural difference with the West, to demand that there be no rule of difference in the domain of the state.

In time, with the growing strength of nationalist politics, this domain became more extensive and internally differentiated and finally took on the form of the national, that is, postcolonial, state. The dominant elements of its self-definition, at least in postcolonial India, were drawn from the ideology of the modern liberal-democratic state.

In accordance with liberal ideology, the public was now distinguished from the domain of the private. The state was required to protect the inviolability of the private self in relation to other private selves. The legitimacy of the state in carrying out this function was to be guaranteed by its indifference to concrete differences between private selves—differences, that is, of race, language, religion, class, caste, and so forth.

The trouble was that the moral-intellectual leadership of the nationalist elite operated in a field constituted by a very different set of distinctions—those between the spiritual and the material, the inner and the outer, the essential and the inessential. That contested field over which nationalism had proclaimed its sovereignty and where it had imagined its true community was neither coextensive with nor coincidental to the field constituted by the public/private distinction. In the former field, the hegemonic project of nationalism could hardly make the distinctions of language, religion, caste, or class a matter of indifference to itself. The project was that of cultural "normalization," like, as Anderson suggests, bourgeois hegemonic projects everywhere, but with the all-important difference that it had to choose its site of autonomy from a position of subordination to a colonial regime that had on its side the most universalist justificatory resources produced by post-Enlightenment social thought.

The result is that autonomous forms of imagination of the community were, and continue to be, overwhelmed and swamped by the history of the postcolonial state. Here lies the root of our postcolonial misery: not in our inability to think out new forms of the modern community but in our surrender to the old forms of the modern state. If the nation is an imagined community and if nations must also take the form of states, then our theoretical language must allow us to talk about community and state at the same time. I do not think our present theoretical language allows us to do this.

Writing just before his death, Bipinchandra Pal (1858–1932), the fiery leader of the Swadeshi movement in Bengal and a principal figure in the pre-Gandhian Congress, described the boardinghouses in which students lived in the Calcutta of his youth:

> Students' messes in Calcutta, in my college days, fifty-six years ago, were like small republics and were managed on strictly democratic lines. Everything was decided by the voice of the majority of the members of the mess. At the end of every month a manager was elected by the whole "House," so to say, and he was charged with the collection of the dues of the members, and the general supervision of the food and establishment of the mess. . . . A successful manager was frequently begged to accept re-election; while the more careless and lazy members, who had often to pay out of their own pockets for their mismanagement, tried to avoid this honour.
>
> . . . Disputes between one member and another were settled by a "Court" of the whole "House"; and we sat night after night, I remember, in examining these cases; and never was the decision of this "Court" questioned or disobeyed by any member. Nor were the members of the mess at all helpless in the matter of duly enforcing their verdict upon an offending colleague. For they could always threaten the recalcitrant member either with expulsion from the mess, or if he refused to go, with the entire responsibility of the rent being thrown on him. . . . And such was the force of public opinion in these small republics that I have known of cases of this punishment on offending members, which so worked upon him that after a week of their expulsion from a mess, they looked as if they had just come out of some prolonged or serious spell of sickness. . . .

The composition of our mess called for some sort of a compromise be-tween the so-called orthodox and the Brahmo and other heterodox members of our republic. So a rule was passed by the unanimous vote of the whole "House," that no member should bring any food to the house . . . which outraged the feelings of Hindu orthodoxy. It was however clearly under-stood that the members of the mess, as a body and even individually, would not interfere with what any one took outside the house. So we were free to go and have all sorts of forbidden food either at the Great Eastern Hotel, which some of us commenced to occasionally patronise later on, or any-where else.[7]

The interesting point in this description is not so much the exaggerated and obviously romanticized portrayal in miniature of the imagined politi-cal form of the self-governing nation, but rather the repeated use of the institutional terms of modern European civic and political life (republic, democracy, majority, unanimity, election, House, Court, and so on) to describe a set of activities that had to be performed on material utterly incongruous with that civil society. The question of a "compromise" on the food habits of members is really settled not on a principle of demar-cating the "private" from the "public" but of separating the domains of the "inside" and the "outside," the inside being a space where "unanim-ity" had to prevail, while the outside was a realm of individual freedom. Notwithstanding the "unanimous vote of the whole House," the force that determined the unanimity in the inner domain was not the voting procedure decided upon by individual members coming together in a body but rather the consensus of a community—institutionally novel (be-cause, after all, the Calcutta boardinghouse was unprecedented in "tradi-tion"), internally differentiated, but nevertheless a community whose claims preceded those of its individual members.

But Bipinchandra's use of the terms of parliamentary procedure to de-scribe the "communitarian" activities of a boardinghouse standing in place of the nation must not be dismissed as a mere anomaly. His lan-guage is indicative of the very real imbrication of two discourses, and correspondingly of two domains, of politics. The attempt has been made in recent Indian historiography to talk of these as the domains of "elite" and "subaltern" politics.[8] But one of the important results of this histori-ographical approach has been precisely the demonstration that each do-main has not only acted in opposition to and as a limit upon the other but, through this process of struggle, has also shaped the emergent form of the other. Thus, the presence of populist or communitarian elements in the liberal constitutional order of the postcolonial state ought not to be read as a sign of the inauthenticity or disingenuousness of elite politics; it is rather a recognition in the elite domain of the very real presence of an arena of subaltern politics over which it must dominate and yet which also had to be negotiated on its own terms for the purposes of producing consent. On the other hand, the domain of subaltern politics has increasingly become familiar with, and even adapted itself to, the institutional forms characteristic of the elite domain. The point, therefore, is no longer one of simply demarcating and identifying the two domains in their separateness, which is what was required in order first to break down the totalizing claims of a nationalist historiography. Now the task is to trace in their mutually conditioned historicities the specific forms that have appeared, on the one hand, in the domain defined by the hegemonic project of nationalist modernity, and on the other, in the numerous fragmented resistances to that normalizing project.

This is the exercise I wish to carry out in this book. Since the problem will be directly posed of the limits to the supposed universality of the modern regime of power and with it of the post-Enlightenment disciplines of knowledge, it might appear as though the exercise is meant to emphasize once more an "Indian" (or an "Oriental") exceptionalism. In fact, however, the objective of my exercise is rather more complicated, and considerably more ambitious. It includes not only an identification of the discursive conditions that make such theories of Indian exceptionalism possible, but also a demonstration that the alleged exceptions actually inhere as forcibly suppressed elements even in the supposedly universal forms of the modern regime of power.

The latter demonstration enables us to make the argument that the universalist claims of modern Western social philosophy are themselves limited by the contingencies of global power. In other words, "Western universalism" no less than "Oriental exceptionalism" can be shown to be only a particular form of a richer, more diverse, and differentiated conceptualization of a new universal idea. This might allow us the possibility not only to think of new forms of the modern community, which, as I argue, the nationalist experience in Asia and Africa has done from its birth, but, much more decisively, to think of new forms of the modern state.

The project then is to claim for us, the once-colonized, our freedom of imagination. Claims, we know only too well, can be made only as contestations in a field of power. The studies in this book will necessarily bear, for each specific disciplinary field, the imprint of an unresolved contest. To make a claim on behalf of the fragment is also, not surprisingly, to produce a discourse that is itself fragmentary. It is redundant to make apologies for this.

CHAPTER TWO

The Colonial State

THE COLONIAL STATE AS A MODERN REGIME OF POWER

I will begin by asking the following question: Does it serve any useful analytical purpose to make a distinction between the colonial state and the forms of the modern state? Or should we regard the colonial state as simply another specific form in which the modern state has generalized itself across the globe? If the latter is the case, then of course the specifically colonial form of the emergence of the institutions of the modern state would be of only incidental, or at best episodic, interest; it would not be a necessary part of the larger, and more important, historical narrative of modernity.

The idea that colonialism was only incidental to the history of the development of the modern institutions and technologies of power in the countries of Asia and Africa is now very much with us. In some ways, this is not surprising, because we now tend to think of the period of colonialism as something we have managed to put behind us, whereas the progress of modernity is a project in which we are all, albeit with varying degrees of enthusiasm, still deeply implicated.

Curiously though, the notion that colonial rule was not really about colonial rule but something else was a persistent theme in the rhetoric of colonial rule itself. As late as ten years before Indian independence, a British historian of the development of state institutions in colonial India began his book with the following words: "It was the aim of the greatest among the early British administrators in India to train the people of India to govern and protect themselves . . . rather than to establish the rule of a British bureaucracy."[1] And at about the same time, Edward Thompson and G. T. Garratt, two liberal British historians sympathetic toward the aspirations of Indian nationalism, closed their book with the following assessment:

> Whatever the future may hold, the direct influence of the West upon India is likely to decrease. But it would be absurd to imagine that the British connection will not leave a permanent mark upon Indian life. On the merely material side the new Federal Government [the Government of India reorganized under the 1935 constitutional arrangements] will take over the largest irrigation system in the world, with thousands of miles of canals and water-cuts

fertilising between thirty and forty million acres; some 60,000 miles of metalled roads; over 42,000 miles of railway, of which three-quarters are State-owned; 230,000 scholastic institutions with over twelve million scholars; and a great number of buildings, including government offices, inspection bungalows, provincial and central legislatures. The vast area of India has been completely surveyed, most of its lands assessed, and a regular census taken of its population and its productivity. An effective defensive system has been built up on its vulnerable North-East frontier, it has an Indian army with century-old traditions, and a police force which compares favourably with any outside a few Western countries. The postal department handles nearly 1500 million articles yearly, the Forestry Department not only prevents the denudation of immense areas, but makes a net profit of between two and three crores. These great State activities are managed by a trained bureaucracy, which is to-day almost entirely Indian.[2]

Having read our Michel Foucault, we can now recognize in this account a fairly accurate description of the advance of the modern regime of power, a regime in which power is meant not to prohibit but to facilitate, to produce. It is not without significance, therefore, that Thompson and Garratt should mention this as the "permanent mark" left by the colonial presence in India. It is also significant that they entitle their history the *Rise and Fulfilment of British Rule in India*.

Indian nationalists are not, of course, quite so generous in attributing benevolent intentions to the colonial mission. But their judgment on the historical value of the state institutions created under British rule is not fundamentally different. The postcolonial state in India has after all only expanded and not transformed the basic institutional arrangements of colonial law and administration, of the courts, the bureaucracy, the police, the army, and the various technical services of government. M. V. Pylee, the constitutional historian, describes the discursive constraints with disarming simplicity. "India," he says, "inherited the British system of government and administration in its original form. The framers of the new Constitution *could not think* of an altogether new system."[3]

As a matter of fact, the criticism Indian nationalists have made in the postcolonial period is that the colonial institutions of power were not modern enough, that the conditions of colonial rule necessarily limited and corrupted the application of the true principles of a modern administration. B. B. Misra, the nationalist historian of colonial bureaucracy, identified these limits as proceeding

from two premises. The first was the Indian social system which was governed by irrational and prescriptive customs rather than a well-regulated rational system of law and a common code of morality. The second . . . was the British Imperial interest, which bred discrimination in the Services on racial grounds as well as differentiation in respect of social status and conditions of service.

Yet, despite these limits, "the degree of administrative rationalization during this period of bureaucratic despotism was far ahead of the country's Brahmanic social order, which knew of no rule of law in the contractual sense."[4]

Whether imperialist or colonialist, all seem to share a belief in the self-evident legitimacy of the principles that are supposed universally to govern the modern regime of power. It is something of a surprise, therefore, to discover that a persistent theme in colonial discourse until the earlier half of this century was the steadfast refusal to admit the universality of those principles.

THE RULE OF COLONIAL DIFFERENCE

Although Vincent Smith was not the most distinguished imperial historian of India, he was probably the most widely known in India because of the success of his textbooks on Indian history. In 1919, Smith published a rejoinder to the Montagu-Chelmsford constitutional proposals seeking to placate nationalist demands by conceding a certain measure of "responsible government" to Indians. The proposals, Smith said, were based on two propositions: "(1) that a policy, assumed to have been successful in Western communities, *can* be applied to India; and (2) that such a policy *ought* to be applied to India, even at the request of an admittedly small body of Indians, because Englishmen believe it to be intrinsically the best."[5] His argument was that both propositions were false.

The policy of responsible and democratic government, "supposed to be of universal application," could not be applied to India because it went against "a deep stream of Indian tradition which has been flowing for thousands of years. . . . The ordinary men and women of India do not understand impersonal government. . . . They crave for government by a person to whom they can render loyal homage." The reason for the legitimacy of British rule in India lay in the fact that the King-Emperor was regarded by the Indian people as "the successor of Rama, Asoka and Akbar. Their heartfelt loyalty should not be quenched by the cold water of democratic theory."[6] In terms of social divisions, "India has been the battle-ground of races and religions from time immemorial," and the anticipation of a common political identity was "not justified either by the facts of history or by observation of present conditions." The fundamental principle of social organization in India was caste, which was incompatible with any form of democratic government. More importantly, the spread of modern institutions or technologies had not weakened the hold of caste in any way.

> The necessities of cheap railway travelling compel people to crowd into car- riages and touch one another closely for many hours. . . . The immense prac- tical advantages of a copious supply of good water from stand-pipes in the larger towns are permitted to outweigh the ceremonial pollution which un- doubtedly takes place. . . . But such merely superficial modifications of caste regulations . . . do not touch the essence of the institution. . . . The Brahman who rides in a third-class carriage or drinks pipe-water does not think any better of his low-caste neighbour than when he travelled on foot and drank from a dirty well. . . . So long as Hindus continue to be Hindus, caste cannot be destroyed or even materially modified.[7]

Smith then went on to argue that contrary to the plea of the reformers, the policy of promoting responsible government in India was bad even as a practical strategy of power. It would produce not consent for authority but its very opposite.

> Contentment, so far as it exists, is to be deliberately disturbed by the rulers ·of India in order to promote the ideal of Indian nationhood, the formation of a genuine electorate, and the development of the faculty of self-help. Do the high officials charged with the government of India, who propose delib- erately to disturb the contentment of three hundred millions of Asiatic peo- ple, mostly ignorant, superstitious, fanatical, and intensely suspicious, real- ize what they are doing? Have they counted the cost? Once the disturbance of content has been fairly started among the untutored masses, no man can tell how far the fire may spread. Discontent will not be directed to the polit- ical objects so dear to Mr. Montagu and Mr. Curtis. It will be turned fiercely upon the casteless, impure foreigner, and, inflamed by the cry of "religion in danger," will attract every disorderly element and renew the horrors of 1857 or the great anarchy of the eighteenth century. The lesson of history cannot be mistaken.[8]

Our reaction today would be to dismiss these arguments as coming from a diehard conservative imperialist putting up what was even then a quixotic defense of old-style paternalistic colonialism. Yet Smith's rejec- tion of the claims to universality of the modern institutions of self-govern- ment raises, I think, an important question.

Let me put this plainly, even at the risk of oversimplification. If the principal justification for the modern regime of power is that by making social regulations an aspect of the self-disciplining of normalized individ- uals, power is made more productive, effective, and humane, then there are three possible positions with regard to the universality of this argument. One is that this must apply in principle to all societies irrespective of historical or cultural specificities. The second is that the principle is inescapably tied to the specific history and culture of Western societies and cannot be exported elsewhere; this implies a rejection of the universality of the principle. The third is that the historical and cultural differences, although an impediment in the beginning, can be eventually overcome by a suitable process of training and education. The third position, therefore, while admitting the objection raised by the second, nevertheless seeks to restore the universality of the principle.

While these three positions have been associated with distinct ideological formations, they are produced, however, in the same discursive field. My argument is, first, that all three remain available today; second, that it is possible easily to slide from one to the other, because, third, all three adopt the same tactic of employing what I will call the rule of colonial difference. The implication of this argument is that if a rule of colonial difference is part of a common strategy for the deployment of the modern forms of disciplinary power, then the history of the colonial state, far from being incidental, is of crucial interest to the study of the past, present, and future of the modern state.

I will first demonstrate the application of this rule in two well-known colonial debates over bureaucratic rationality, rule of law, and freedom of speech. I will then show that the same rule is effective in contemporary debates over colonial history.

RACE AND RATIONAL BUREAUCRACY

It is in the fitness of things that it took an event such as the suppression of a rebellion of the scale and intensity of the Great Revolt of 1857 for the various pieces of the colonial order properly to fall into place. The rebels ripped the veil off the face of the colonial power and, for the first time, it was visible in its true form: a modern regime of power destined never to fulfill its normalizing mission because the premise of its power was the preservation of the alienness of the ruling group.

The debates over colonial policy in the decades following the revolt are instructive. Historians generally characterize this period as an era of conservatism. Metcalf's well-known study traces this shift to a decline in the enthusiasm for Benthamism and evangelism in Britain. Strengthening this reluctance to embark upon any further reform in India was the suspicion that the earlier attack upon "immoral" native customs might have had something to do with the rebellion. Official opinion was now virtually unanimous in thinking that local customs were best left to themselves. "Radical reform," says Metcalf, "was not just dangerous, it had ceased to be fashionable."[9]

In keeping with this move away from liberal reform was the hardening of a certain intellectual opinion in Britain that was particularly influential in the making of colonial policy. Distressed by the extension of suffrage and of the politics of Gladstonian liberalism at home, this school of opinion sought to reestablish the precepts of property and order upon unashamedly authoritarian foundations and increasingly turned to British India as the ground where these theories could be demonstrated. James Fitzjames Stephen and Henry Maine were two leading figures in this campaign to unmask the "sentimentality" of all reformist postures in matters of colonial policy. The Indian people, Stephen reminded his countrymen, were "ignorant to the last degree" and "steeped in idolatrous superstition." The British were under no obligation to fit such people for representative institutions. All they were expected to do was administer the country and look after the welfare of the people. The empire, he said,

> is essentially an absolute Government, founded, not on consent, but on conquest. It does not represent the native principles of life or of government, and it can never do so until it represents heathenism and barbarism. It represents a belligerent civilization, and no anomaly can be so striking or so dangerous as its administration by men who, being at the head of a Government . . . having no justification for its existence except [the] superiority [of the conquering race], shrink from the open, uncompromising, straightforward assertion of it, seek to apologize for their own position, and refuse, from whatever cause, to uphold and support it.[10]

The merit of hard-nosed arguments such as this was to point unambiguously to the one factor that united the ruling bloc and separated it from those over whom it ruled. Marking this difference was race. As officials in India attempted, under directions from London, to install the processes of an orderly government, the question of race gave rise to the most acerbic debates. Indeed, the more the logic of a modern regime of power pushed the processes of government in the direction of a rationalization of administration and the normalization of the objects of its rule, the more insistently did the issue of race come up to emphasize the specifically colonial character of British dominance in India.

It seems something of a paradox that the racial difference between ruler and ruled should become most prominent precisely in that period in the last quarter of the nineteenth century when the technologies of disciplinary power were being put in place by the colonial state. Recent historians have shown that during this period there was a concerted attempt to create the institutional procedures for systematically objectifying and normalizing the colonized terrain, that is, the land and the people of India. Not only was the law codified and the bureaucracy rationalized, but a whole apparatus of specialized technical services was instituted in order to scientifically survey, classify, and enumerate the geographical, geological, botanical, zoological, and meteorological properties of the natural environment and the archaeological, historical, anthropological, linguistic, economic, demographic, and epidemiological characteristics of the people. Yet, a social historian of the period notes that "racial feeling among the British became more explicit and more aggressive in the course of the nineteenth century and reached its peak during Lord Curzon's viceroyalty, between 1899 and 1905."[11]

There is, however, no paradox in this development if we remember that to the extent this complex of power and knowledge was colonial, the forms of objectification and normalization of the colonized had to reproduce, within the framework of a universal knowledge, the truth of the colonial difference. The difference could be marked by many signs, and varying with the context, one could displace another as the most practicable application of the rule. But of all these signs, race was perhaps the most obvious mark of colonial difference.

In the case of bureaucratic rationalization, for instance, which had proceeded through the middle decades of the century, the most difficult political problem arose when it became apparent that the system of nonarbitrary recruitment through competitive academic examinations would mean the entry of Indians into the civil service. Several attempts were made in the 1870s to tamper with recruitment and service regulations in order first to keep out Indians, and then to split the bureaucracy into an elite corps primarily reserved for the British and a subordinate service for Indians.[12]

But it was the so-called Ilbert Bill Affair that brought up most dramatically the question of whether a central claim of the modern state could be allowed to transgress the line of racial division. The claim was that of administering an impersonal, nonarbitrary system of rule of law. In 1882 Behari Lal Gupta, an Indian member of the civil service, pointed out the anomaly that under the existing regulations, Indian judicial officers did not have the same right as their British counterparts to try cases in which Europeans were involved. Gupta's note was forwarded to the Government of India with a comment from the Bengal government that there was "no sufficient reason why Covenanted Native Civilians, with the position and training of District Magistrate or Sessions Judge, should not exercise the same jurisdiction over Europeans as is exercised by other members of the service."[13] The viceroy at this time was Ripon, a liberal, appointed by Gladstone's Liberal government. But it did not require much liberalism to see that the anomaly was indeed an anomaly, and after more or less routine consultations, Ilbert, the law member, introduced in 1883 a bill to straighten out the regulations.

Some historians have suggested that if Ripon had had even an inkling of the storm that was to break out, he would not have allowed such a minor issue to jeopardize the entire liberal project in India.[14] As it happened, it was the force of public opinion of the dominant race that organized itself to remind the government what colonial rule was all about. The nonofficial Europeans—planters, traders, and lawyers in particular, and in Bengal more than anywhere else—rose in "almost mutinous opposition."[15] The agitation reached a fever pitch in Calcutta. Meetings were held to denounce the bill that sought to take away "a much-valued and prized and time-honoured privilege of European British subjects" and aroused "a feeling of insecurity as to the liberties and safety of the European British subjects employed in the *mufassal* and also of their wives and daughters."[16] The British Indian press, with the *Englishman* of Calcutta at its head, declared a call to arms by claiming that the Europeans were "fighting against their own ruin and the destruction of British rule in India."[17] A European and Anglo-Indian Defence Association was formed, functions at Government House were boycotted, and there was even a conspiracy "to overpower the sentries at Government House, put the Viceroy on board a steamer at Chandpal *ghat*, and send him to England *via* the Cape."[18]

Gladstone, surveying the fracas from the vantage point of the metropolitan capital, was in a better position than most to see how this episode fitted into a longer story. "There is a question," he said,

> to be answered: where, in a country like India, lies the ultimate power, and if it lies for the present on one side but for the future on the other, a problem has to be solved as to preparation for that future, and it may become right and needful to chasten the saucy pride so apt to grow in the English mind toward foreigners, and especially toward foreigners whose position has been subordinate.[19]

Ripon, on the other hand, chose to see his move as "an error in tactics" and decided to beat a retreat. The provisions of the bill were so watered down that the earlier anomalies were not only reinstated but made even more cumbrous.

The question was not, as some historians have supposed, whether Ripon was "too weak a man" to carry out the liberal mission of making Indians fit for modern government. What his "failure" signaled was the inherent impossibility of completing the project of the modern state without superseding the conditions of colonial rule. When George Couper, lieutenant governor of the Northwestern Provinces, said in 1878 that the time had come to stop "shouting that black is white," he was not being metaphorical. "We all know that in point of fact black is *not* white. . . . That there should be one law alike for the European and Native is an excellent thing in theory, but if it could really be introduced in practice we should have no business in the country."[20]

The argument, in other words, was not that the "theory" of responsible government was false, nor that its truth was merely relative and contingent. Rather, the point was to lay down in "practice" a rule of colonial difference, to mark the points and the instances where the colony had to become an exception precisely to vindicate the universal truth of the theory.

RACE AND PUBLIC OPINION

Another question on which the Ilbert Bill Affair threw light was the relation between the state and those relatively autonomous institutions of public life that are supposed to constitute the domain of civil society. The interesting feature of this relation as it developed in colonial Calcutta, for instance, in the nineteenth century was that the "public" which was seen to deserve the recognition due from a properly constituted state was formed exclusively by the European residents of the country. Their opinion counted as public opinion, and the question of the appropriate relationship between government and the public came to be defined primarily around the freedoms of the British Indian press.

English-language newspapers began to be published in Calcutta from the 1780s. In those early days of empire, when power was restrained by little more than brute force and intrigue and commerce was driven by the lust for a quick fortune, the press not unexpectedly provided yet another means for carrying out personal and factional feuds within the small European community in Bengal. Governors-general were quick to use legal means to "tranquilize" newspaper editors and even deport those who refused to be subdued. By the 1820s a more stable relation had been established and the censorship laws were lifted. But the events of 1857, when the very future of British rule seemed to be at stake, forced the issue once more into the open. "Public opinion" was now defined explicitly as the opinion of the "nonofficial" European community, and the English-language press of Calcutta, crazed by panic, directed its wrath at a government that, in its eyes, seemed too soft and indecisive in punishing the "d——d niggers." Canning, the governor-general, was a special target of vituperation, and in June 1857 he imposed the censorship laws once again, for a period of one year.[21]

The contours of state-civil society relations in the new context of the Raj were revealed in interesting ways in the so-called Nil Durpan Affair. The origin of the case lay, curiously enough, in an effort by officials in Bengal to find out a little more about "native" public opinion. In 1861, when the agitations in the Bengal countryside over the cultivation of indigo had begun to subside, John Peter Grant, the governor, came to hear about Dinabandhu Mitra's (1830–73) play. Thinking this would be a good way "of knowing how natives spoke of the indigo question among themselves when they had no European to please or to displease by opening their minds," he asked for a translation to be prepared of *Nīldarpaṇ.* Grant's intentions were laudable.

> I have always been of opinion that, considering our state of more than semi-isolation from all classes of native society, public functionaries in India have been habitually too regardless of those depths of native feeling which do not show upon the surface, and too habitually careless of all means of information which are available to us for ascertaining them. Popular songs everywhere, and, in Bengal, popular native plays, are amongst the most potent, and most neglected, of those means.[22]

Seton-Karr, the secretary to the Government of Bengal, arranged for James Long, an Irish missionary later to become a pioneering historian of Calcutta, to supervise the translation "by a native" of the play. He then had it printed and circulated, along with a preface by Dinabandhu and an introduction by Long, to several persons "to whom copies of official documents about the indigo crisis had been sent."[23]

The planters were immediately up in arms. They charged the government with having circulated "a foul and malicious libel on indigo planters." When it was clarified that circulation of the play did not mean the government's approval of its contents and that in any case the circulation had not been expressly authorized by the governor, the planters' association went to court. An "extraordinary" summing up by the judge, which is said "not to have erred on the side of impartiality," influenced the jury at the Supreme Court into pronouncing James Long guilty of libel. He was sentenced to a fine and a month's imprisonment. Long became a cause célèbre among the Indian literati of Calcutta: his fine, for instance, was paid by Kaliprasanna Sinha (1840–70), and a public meeting presided over by Radhakanta Deb (1783–1867) demanded the recall of the judge for his "frequent and indiscriminate attacks on the characters of the natives of the country with an intemperance . . . not compatible with the impartial administration of justice." But, more interestingly, Long also attracted a good deal of sympathy from Europeans, particularly officials and missionaries. They felt he had been punished for no offense at all. The bishop of Calcutta remarked that the passages "which the Judge described as foul and disgusting, are in no way more gross than many an English story or play turning on the ruin of a simple hunted rustic which people read and talk about without scruple."[24] At the same time, Canning, the viceroy, rebuked Grant for having allowed things to go this far and Seton-Karr, despite an apology, was removed from his posts both in the Bengal government and in the legislative council. The planters, it would seem, won an unqualified victory.

Nevertheless, it is worth considering what really was on trial in this curious case. It was to all intents and purposes a conflict between government and the public, the "public" being constituted by "nonofficial"

Europeans. The charge against the government was that by circulating the play, it had libeled an important section of this public. Long was a scapegoat; in fact, neither he nor the play was on trial. Or rather, to put it more precisely, although Long was an ostensible culprit in the circulation of a libelous tract, the play itself and the body of opinion it represented were not recognized elements in this discourse about free speech. Such in fact was the confusion about where this principle of freedom of expression was supposed to apply that when one of Long's supporters remarked that his punishment was "exactly as if the French clergy had prosecuted Molière,"[25] it did not strike him that Dinabandhu Mitra, the author of the play, had not even been deemed worthy of being named in a suit of libel and that Long was neither the author nor even the translator of the impugned material. Within these assumptions, of course, there really was no confusion. The real target of attack was clearly the government itself, and Canning, in trying to appease "public opinion," recognized this when he moved against Grant and Seton-Karr.

The original intent of the Bengal officials, however, had been to familiarize themselves and members of the European community with the state of "native" public opinion—a perfectly reasonable tactic for a modern administrative apparatus to adopt. What incensed the planters was the implicit suggestion that the government could treat "native" public opinion on the same footing as European opinion. A native play, circulated under a government imprint, seemed to give it the same status of "information" as other official papers. This the planters were not prepared to countenance. The only civil society that the government could recognize was theirs; colonized subjects could never be its equal members. Freedom of opinion, which even they accepted as an essential element of responsible government, could apply only to the organs of this civil society; Indians, needless to add, were not fit subjects of responsible government.

LANGUAGE AND FREEDOM OF SPEECH

The question of native public opinion came up once again in the 1870s. In 1878, when the government felt it necessary to devise legal means to curb "seditious" writings in the native press, the law made an explicit distinction between the English-language and the vernacular press. An official pointed out that this would be "class legislation of the most striking and invidious description, at variance with the whole tenour of our policy,"[26] but the objection was overruled on the ground that in this instance the exception to the general rule was palpable. The presumed difficulty, said Ashley Eden, the Bengal governor, was "imaginary rather than real." That is to say, the notion of an undifferentiated body of public opinion that the government was supposed to treat impartially was only a theoretical idea; in practice, it was the duty of a colonial government to differentiate, and language was a simple and practical sign of difference.

> The papers published in this country in the English language are written by a class of writers for a class of readers whose education and interests would make them naturally intolerant of sedition; they are written under a sense of responsibility and under a restraint of public opinion which do not and cannot exist in the case of the ordinary Native newspapers. It is quite easy and practicable to draw a distinction between papers published in English and papers published in the vernacular, and it is a distinction which really meets all the requirements of the case, and should not be disregarded merely because some evil-disposed persons may choose to say that the Government has desired to show undue favour to papers written in the language of the ruling power.
>
> . . . On the whole the English Press of India, whether conducted by Europeans or Natives, bears evidence of being influenced by a proper sense of responsibility and by a general desire to discuss public events in a moderate and reasonable spirit. There is no occasion to subject that Press to restraint, and therefore, naturally enough, it is exempted. It would be a sign of great weakness on the part of Government to bring it within the scope of this measure merely to meet a possible charge of partiality.[27]

The Vernacular Press Act of 1878 was enacted in great haste so as to forestall long debates over principles, especially in Britain. Lytton, the viceroy, himself described it as "a sort of coup d'état to pass a very stringent gagging Bill."[28] The provisions were indeed stringent, since local officers were given the power to demand bonds and deposits of money from printers and publishers, and the printing of objectionable material could lead to confiscation of the deposit as well as the machinery of the press, with no right of appeal in the courts. Four years later, Ripon in his liberalism repealed the act, and "a bitter feeling obtained among officials that they were denied proper and reasonable protection against immoderate Press criticism."[29] In the 1890s, when the question of "sedition" acquired a new gravity, provisions were included in the regular penal law to allow the government to move against statements "conducing to public mischief" and "promoting enmity between classes." The distinction by language had by then ceased to be a practical index of difference because native publications in English could no longer be said to be confined in their influence to a class "naturally intolerant of sedition." Other, more practical, means emerged to distinguish between proper members of civil society and those whom the state could recognize only as subjects, not citizens. And in any case, a contrary movement of nationalism was then well on its way to constituting its own domain of sovereignty, rejecting the dubious promise of being granted membership of a second-rate "civil society of subjects."

NATIONALISM AND COLONIAL DIFFERENCE

This domain of sovereignty, which nationalism thought of as the "spiritual" or "inner" aspects of culture, such as language or religion or the elements of personal and family life, was of course premised upon a difference between the cultures of the colonizer and the colonized. The more nationalism engaged in its contest with the colonial power in the outer domain of politics, the more it insisted on displaying the marks of "essential" cultural difference so as to keep out the colonizer from that inner domain of national life and to proclaim its sovereignty over it.

But in the outer domain of the state, the supposedly "material" domain of law, administration, economy, and statecraft, nationalism fought relentlessly to erase the marks of colonial difference. Difference could not be justified in that domain. In this, it seemed to be reasserting precisely the claims to universality of the modern regime of power. And in the end, by successfully terminating the life of the colonial state, nationalism demonstrated that the project of that modern regime could be carried forward only by superseding the conditions of colonial rule.

Nevertheless, the insistence on difference, begun in the so-called spiritual domain of culture, has continued, especially in the matter of claiming agency in history.[30] Rival conceptions of collective identity have become implicated in rival claims to autonomous subjectivity. Many of these are a part of contemporary postcolonial politics and have to do with the fact that the consolidation of the power of the national state has meant the marking of a new set of differences within postcolonial society. But the origin of the project of modernity in the workings of the colonial state has meant that every such historical claim has had to negotiate its relationship with the history of colonialism. The writing of the history of British India continues to this day to be a matter of political struggle.

In this contemporary battle, the case for a history of subordinated groups has often been stated by pointing out the continuities between the colonial and the postcolonial phases of the imposition of the institutions of the modern state and by asserting the autonomous subjectivity of the oppressed.[31] But since the modern discourse of power always has available a position for the colonizer, the case on behalf of the colonizing mission can now also be stated in these new terms. To show the continued relevance of the question of the universality of the modern regime of power and of the rule of colonial difference, I will end this chapter by reviewing a recent attempt to revise the history of colonialism in India.

"IT NEVER HAPPENED!"

This revisionist history begins by challenging the assumption, shared by both colonialist and nationalist historiographies, that colonial rule represented a fundamental break in Indian history. There are two parts to this argument.

The first part of the argument has been advanced by Burton Stein.[32] He disputes the assumption in both imperialist and nationalist historiographies that the British regime in India was "completely different from all prior states." The recent work of Christopher Bayly, David Washbrook, and Frank Perlin shows, he says, that "early colonial regimes" were "continuations of prior indigenous regimes," that the eighteenth century was a time of "economic vigour, even development," and not of chaos and decline and that the period from 1750 to 1850 was a "period of transition" from extant old regimes to the colonial regimes. The continuations were marked in two ways.

One "structural contradiction" in pre-British state formations was between "centralizing, militaristic regimes" and numerous local lordships. The British inserted themselves into these formations, "not as outsiders with new procedural principles and purposes (as yet), but, contingently, as part of the political system of the subcontinent, but possessed of substantially more resources to deploy for conquest than others." The colonial state resolved the contradiction in favor of the centralizing tendency of "military-fiscalism" inherited from previous regimes. Here lay the continuity of the colonial state with its predecessors.

The other contradiction was between "sultanism" (Max Weber's term), which implied a patrimonial order based on personal loyalty of subordination to the ruler, and the existence of ideological discontinuities between ruler and local lordships, which made such patrimonial loyalties hard to sustain. Patrimonial sultanism was incompatible with the economic tendencies inherent in military-fiscalism. After initial hesitations, the colonial state in the second half of the nineteenth century broke entirely with the sultanist forms and founded a regime based not on patrimonial loyalties but on modern European principles, different both from the old regimes and the early colonial regimes. Here lay the discontinuity of the later colonial state with its predecessors.

Although Stein appeals, inter alia, to the work of Perlin,[33] the latter actually makes a much more qualified argument,[34] a qualification important for the revisionist position as well as for our judgment on it. Perlin argues that the process of centralization that characterized colonial rule "possessed roots in the earlier period." But in accelerating this process, colonial rule gave it "a new, more powerful form deriving from its location in the agency of a conquest regime possessing sources of fiat external to the subcontinent, from its radical concentration of decision making, and from the surplus of new knowledge in the instruments of rule." This produced "a substantial break" between the early colonial polity and its predecessors, despite the colonial use of "old-order institutions and its social underpinnings." Moreover, whereas in the indigenous regimes of the eighteenth century the attempt to centralize produced large areas of "quasi-autonomy," where contrary forces and contrary principles of rights and social organization could emerge to resist the larger order, colonial rule up to the early nineteenth century was marked by a substantial loss of this "intermediary ground." "Beneath the carapace of old terms and institutional shells, there has occurred a fundamental alteration of both State and state. This is bound up with the European origins and international character of the new colonial polity."

Notwithstanding Perlin's qualification, the idea of continuity from the precolonial to the early colonial period dominates this part of the revisionist argument. Since the later phase of colonialism is specifically distinguished from its early phase, one is justified in wondering if the revision is merely a matter of dates. Is the question one of identifying *when* the decisive break of colonialism took place? Earlier historians, whether imperialist or nationalist, with their simple faith in the proclamations of political rulers, had assumed that this occurred in the middle of the eighteenth century; are the revisionist historians, more skeptical of legal fictions and more sensitive to underlying social processes, now telling us that the date must be pushed forward by a hundred years?

If this is all there is to the debate, the matter is easily settled. For if the period from the middle of the eighteenth century to the middle of the nineteenth is to be seen as a period of "transition," then it must reveal not only the traces of continuity from the earlier period, as claimed by our recent historians, but surely also the signs of emergence of all of those elements that would make the late colonial period structurally different from the precolonial. In terms of periodization, then, the hundred years of transition must be seen as constituting the "moment" of break, the "event" that marks the separation of the precolonial from the colonial. The apparent conundrum of continuity and discontinuity then becomes one more example of the familiar historiographical problem of combining, and at the same time separating, structure and process. One might then react to the revisionist argument in the manner of the student radical in a Calcutta university in the early 1970s who, when asked in a history test whether Rammohan Roy was born in 1772 or 1774, replied, "I don't know. But I do know that he grew up to be a comprador."

But it would be unfair to our revisionist historians to judge them on what is only one part of their argument. In its stronger version, the revisionist argument contains another part in which the continuity from the precolonial to the early colonial period is given a new construction. Not only was it the case, the argument runs, that the Europeans in the late eighteenth and early nineteenth centuries achieved "on a larger and more ominous scale what Indian local rulers had been doing for the last century," but in responding to this conquering thrust Indians too "became active agents and not simply passive bystanders and victims in the creation of colonial India." This, says Chris Bayly in a recent book-length survey of the early colonial period, gives us a "more enduring perspective" on modern Indian history than do the earlier debates about the success or failure of the "progressive" impact of colonialism.[35]

This perspective reveals, first of all, the economic history of India from the eighteenth century to the present as a history of "Indian capitalism," born prior to the colonial incursion and growing to its present form by responding to the forces generated by the European world economy. Most of the economic institutions of capitalism in India today, such as commodity production, trading and banking capital, methods of accounting, a stock of educated expertise and of mercantile groups that would ultimately become industrial entrepreneurs, emerged in the precolonial period. So did many of the political and cultural movements, including the rise of intermediary groups between townsmen and the countryside, the formation of regional cultures, movements for cultural reform and self-respect among disprivileged groups, and even the politics of "communalism."[36]

Second, such a perspective on Indian history also shows the resilience of both townspeople and country people in resisting the onslaughts on their means of survival and ways of life, especially in the period of colonialism. Indigenous propertied groups frustrated the "more grandiose economic plans" of both the colonial state and European businessmen to extract Indian wealth, while peasants overcame the pressures of war, taxation, and repression "to adapt in a creative way to their environment." By recovering these connections, Bayly says, the new perspective enables one to construct a narrative running from the precolonial past to the postcolonial present in which the Indian people are the subjects of history.

What, then, of colonialism? Surprisingly, there is no clear answer to this question. Nevertheless, it is not difficult to read the implication of the argument. At the time of their entry, the European trading companies were merely so many indigenous players in the struggle for economic and political power in eighteenth-century India, striving for the same goals and playing by the same rules. In the latter half of the nineteenth century, when the British appear to have achieved complete dominance at the apex of the formal structure of power, their ability to reach into the depths of

Indian social life was still severely restricted. By the early twentieth century, even this hold at the top was seriously challenged, and of course by the middle of the century the colonial power was forced to leave. Looked at from the "more enduring" perspective of Indian history, then, colonialism appears as a rather brief interlude, merging with the longer narrative only when its protagonists manage to disguise themselves as Indian characters but falling hopelessly out of place and dooming itself to failure when it aspires to carry out projects that have not already taken root in the native soil.

We have a more detailed presentation of this stronger version of the revisionist argument in Washbrook. Once again, the claim is made that by tracing the continuities from precolonial to early colonial processes, one can restore the "Indianness" of this historical narrative and "recover the subject from European history." Further, and this is Washbrook's contribution to the argument, "historical theory" "is put on a rather more objective, or at least less ethnocentric, footing." It is on this high ground of "historical theory," then, that the revisionist flag is finally hoisted.[37]

What is this theory? It is the familiar theme of capitalist development, which in one form or another has framed all discussions of modern history. The new twist on this theme has as its vortex the claim that not all forms of development of capital necessarily lead to modern industrialism. The development of industrial capital in England, or in Western Europe and North America, was the result of a very specific history. It is the perversity of Eurocentric historical theories that has led to the search for similar developments everywhere else in the world; whenever that search has proved fruitless, the society has been declared incapable of producing a true historical dynamic. Instead of tracing the particular course of the indigenous history, therefore, the practice has been to see the history of "backward" countries as a history of "lack," a history that always falls short of true history.

The perspective can be reversed, says Washbrook, by taking more seriously the similarities rather than the differences between the development of capitalism in Europe and, in this case, in India. We will then see that the similarities are indeed striking. Contrary to the earlier judgment of imperialist, nationalist, and even Marxist historians, recent researches show that the economic and social institutions of precolonial India, far from impeding the growth of capitalism, actually accommodated and encouraged most of the forms associated with early modern capital. Not only did trading and banking capital grow as a result of long-distance trade, but large-scale exchange took place even in the subsistence sector. The legal-political institutions too acquired the characteristic early modern forms of military fiscalism, centralization of state authority, destruction of community practices, and the conversion of privileged entitlements into personal rights over property. Despite the cultural differences with Europe in the early capitalist era, India too produced institutions that were "capable of supplying broadly similar economic functions." The East India Company entered the scene as one more player capable of pursuing the same functions: "rather than representing a set of governing principles imported from a foreign and 'more advanced' culture, the early East India Company state might be seen as a logical extension of processes with distinctively 'indigenous' origins." And if one is not to disregard the "preponderant evidence" of early capitalist groups in India subverting indigenous regimes in order to seek support from the Company, one must accept the conclusion that "colonialism was the logical outcome of South Asia's own history of capitalist development."[38]

The tables have been turned! Once colonialism as an economic and political formation is shown to have been produced by an indigenous history of capitalist development, everything that followed from colonial rule becomes, by the ineluctable logic of "historical theory," an integral part of that same indigenous history. Thus, the restructuring of the Indian economy in the period between 1820 and 1850, when all of the principal features of colonial underdevelopment emerged to preclude once and for all the possibilities of transition to modern industrialization, must be seen not as a process carried out by an external extractive force but as one integral to the peculiar history of Indian capitalism. The colonial state, responding as it did to the historical demands of Indian capital, offered the necessary legal and political protection to the propertied classes and their attempts to enrich themselves: "rarely in history," says Washbrook, "can capital and property have secured such rewards and such prestige for so little risk and so little responsibility as in the society crystallizing in South Asia in the Victorian Age." The result was a process in which not only the British but all owners of property—"capital in general"—secured the benefits of colonial rule. The specific conditions of capitalism in India had, of course, already defined a path in which the forms of extractive relations between capital and labor did not favor a transition to industrialism. The late colonial regime, by upholding the privileges of capital, destroying the viability of petty manufacturers, pulling down the remnants of already decrepit community institutions, and consolidating the formation of a mass of overexploited peasants constantly reduced to lower and lower levels of subsistence, made the transition more or less impossible. On the cultural side, the colonial regime instituted a "traditionalization" of Indian society by its rigid codification of "custom" and "tradition," its freezing of the categories of social classification such as caste, and its privileging of "scriptural" interpretations of social law at the expense of the fluidity of local community practices. The result was the creation by colonial rule of a social order that bore a striking resemblance to its own caricature of "traditional India": late colonial society was "nearer to the ideal-type of Asiatic Despotism than anything South Asia had seen before." All this can now be seen as India's own history, a history made by Indian peoples, Indian classes, and Indian powers.

COLONIAL DIFFERENCE AS POSTCOLONIAL DIFFERENCE

There is something magical about a "historical theory" that can with such ease spirit away the violent intrusion of colonialism and make all of its features the innate property of an indigenous history. Indeed, the argument seems to run in a direction so utterly contrary to all received ideas that one might be tempted to grant that the revisionist historians have turned the tables on both imperialist and nationalist histories and struck out on a radically new path.

Like all feats of magic, however, this achievement of "historical theory" is also an illusion. If the revisionist account of Indian history makes one suspicious that this is one more attempt to take the sting out of anticolonial politics, this time by appropriating the nationalist argument about colonialism's role in producing underdevelopment in India and then turning the argument around to situate the origins of colonialism in India's own precolonial history, then one's suspicion would not be unjustified. There is much in this new historiographic strategy that is reminiscent of the debates I cited at the beginning of this chapter between conservative and liberal imperialists and their nationalist opponents. Like those earlier debates, this account shows a continued effort to produce a rule of colonial difference within a universal theory of the modern regime of power.

Washbrook argues, for instance, that Eurocentrism and the denial of subjectivity to Indians were the result of the emphasis on difference; emphasizing similarity restores to Indian history its authenticity. It is obvious, of course, though not always noticed, that the difference which produces India (or the Orient) as the "other" of Europe also requires as its condition an identity of Europe and India; otherwise they would be mutually unintelligible. By "emphasizing" either identity or difference, however, it is possible to produce varied meanings; in this case, the effects noticed by Washbrook are those of Indian authenticity on the one hand and Eurocentrism on the other. What he does not recognize is that the two histories are produced within the same discursive conditions. All that Washbrook is doing by emphasizing "similarity" is restating the condition of discursive unity.

This condition is nothing other than the assumption that the history of Europe and the history of India are united within the same framework of universal history, the assumption that made possible the incorporation of the history of India into the history of Britain in the nineteenth century: Europe became the active subject of Indian history because Indian history was now a part of "world history." The same assumption has characterized the "modern" historiography of India for at least the last hundred years, although the principal task of this nationalist historiography has been to claim for Indians the privilege of making their own history.

There have been many ways of conceptualizing this universal history. Washbrook chooses the one most favored in the rational, scientific discussions of academic social theory, namely, the universality of the analytical categories of the modern disciplines of the social sciences. In his version, this takes the form of assuming the universality of the categories of political economy. Thus, although the history of Indian capitalism, in his argument, is different from that of European capitalism, it is nonetheless a history of "capitalism." The distinctness, and hence the authenticity, of Indian capitalism is produced at the level of Indian history by first asserting the universality of capitalism at the level of world history. Instead of saying, as do his predecessors in the discipline of political economy, that India was so different that it was incapable of capitalism and therefore required British colonialism to bring it into the orbit of world history, Washbrook has simply inverted the order of similarity and difference within the same discursive framework. In the process, he has also managed to erase colonialism out of existence.

What he has produced instead is a way of talking about postcolonial backwardness as the consequence entirely of an indigenous history. Indian capitalism today, his argument seems to say, looks so backward because it has been, from its birth, *different* from Western capitalism. It was ridiculous for anyone to have believed that it could be made to look like Western capitalism; if it ever did, it would stop being itself. Fitzjames Stephen or Vincent Smith would have understood the argument perfectly.

It is possible to give many instances of how the rule of colonial difference—of representing the "other" as inferior and radically different, and hence incorrigibly inferior—can be employed in situations that are not, in the strict terms of political history, colonial.[39] These instances come up not only in relations between countries or nations, but even within populations that the modern institutions of power presume to have normalized into a body of citizens endowed with equal and nonarbitrary rights. Indeed, invoking such differences are, we might say, commonplaces in the politics of discrimination, and hence also in the many contemporary struggles for identity. This reason makes it necessary to study the specific history of the colonial state, because it reveals what is only hidden in the universal history of the modern regime of power.

Having said this, we need to move on to the next, and more substantial, part of our agenda, which is to look at the ways in which nationalism responded to the colonial intervention. That will be my task in the rest of this book. This, then, will be the last time that we will talk about Gladstone and Curzon, Lytton and Ripon, and pretend that the history of India can be written as a footnote to the history of Britain. Leaving such exiguous projects behind us, let us move on to a consideration of the history of India as a nation.

CHAPTER THREE

The Nationalist Elite

THE TERMS *middle class, literati,* and *intelligentsia* all have been used to describe it. Marxists have called it a petty bourgeoisie, the English rendering of *petit* marking its character with the unmistakable taint of historical insufficiency. A favorite target of the colonizer's ridicule, it was once famously described as "an oligarchy of caste tempered by matriculation." More recently, historians inspired by the well-meaning dogmas of American cultural anthropology called it by the name the class had given to itself—the *bhadralok,* "respectable folk"; the latter interpreted the attempt as a sinister plot to malign its character. Whichever the name, the object of description has, however, rarely been misunderstood: in the curious context of colonial Bengal, all of these terms meant more or less the same thing.

Needless to say, much has been written about the sociological characteristics of the new middle class in colonial Bengal.[1] I do not wish to intervene in that discussion. My concern in this book is with social agency. In this particular chapter, my problem is that of mediation, in the sense of the action of a subject who stands "in the middle," working upon and transforming one term of a relation into the other. It is more than simply a problem of "leadership," for I will be talking about social agents who are preoccupied not only with leading their followers but who are also conscious of doing so as a "middle term" in a social relationship. In fact, it is this "middleness" and the consciousness of middleness that I wish to problematize. Of all its appellations, therefore, I will mostly use the term *middle class* to describe the principal agents of nationalism in colonial Bengal.

THE "MIDDLENESS" OF THE CALCUTTA MIDDLE CLASS

Like middle classes elsewhere in their relation to the rise of nationalist ideologies and politics, the Calcutta middle class too has been generally acknowledged as having played a pre-eminent role in the last century and a half in creating the dominant forms of nationalist culture and social institutions in Bengal. It was this class that constructed through a modern vernacular the new forms of public discourse, laid down new criteria of social respectability, set new aesthetic and moral standards of judgment, and, suffused with its spirit of nationalism, fashioned the new forms of political mobilization that were to have such a decisive impact on the political history of the province in the twentieth century.

All this has also been written about at length. But this literature adopts, albeit necessarily, a standpoint external to the object of its inquiry. It does not let us into that vital zone of belief and practice that straddles the domains of the individual and the collective, the private and the public, the home and the world, where the new disciplinary culture of a modernizing elite has to turn itself into an exercise in self-discipline. This, however, is the investigation we need to make.

I propose to do this by taking up the question of middle-class religion.[2] As a point of entry, I will consider the phenomenon of Sri Ramakrishna (1836–86), which will afford us an access into a discursive domain where "middleness" can be talked about, explored, problematized, lived out, and, in keeping with the role of cultural leadership that the middle class gave to itself, normalized.

The colonial middle class, in Calcutta no less than in other centers of colonial power, was simultaneously placed in a position of subordination in one relation and a position of dominance in another. The construction of hegemonic ideologies typically involves the cultural efforts of classes placed precisely in such situations. To identify the possibilities and limits of nationalism as a hegemonic movement, therefore, we need to look into this specific process of ideological construction and disentangle the web in which the experiences of simultaneous subordination and domination are apparently reconciled.

For the Calcutta middle class of the late nineteenth century, political and economic domination by a British colonial elite was a fact. The class was created in a relation of subordination. But its contestation of this relation was to be premised upon its cultural leadership of the indigenous colonized people. The nationalist project was in principle a hegemonic project. Our task is to probe into the history of this project, to assess its historical possibility or impossibility, to identify its origins, extent, and limits. The method, in other words, is the method of critique.

I will concentrate on a single text, the *Rāmkṛṣṇa kathāmṛta*,[3] and look specifically at the construction there of a new religion for urban domestic life. The biographical question of Ramakrishna in relation to the middle class of Bengal has been studied from new historiographical premises by Sumit Sarkar:[4] I will not address this question. Rather, I will read the *Kathāmṛta* not so much as a text that tells us about Ramakrishna as one that tells us a great deal about the Bengali middle class. The *Kathāmṛta*, it seems to me, is a document of the fears and anxieties of a class aspiring to hegemony. It is, if I may put this in a somewhat paradoxical form, a text that reveals to us the subalternity of an elite.

But before we turn to the *Kathāmṛta*, it will be useful to recount the story of how Ramakrishna quite suddenly entered the spiritual life of the Calcutta middle class. It is an interesting episode in the secret history of nationalism and modernity.

DOUBTS

At the time, Belgharia was little more than a village five miles north of Calcutta. Today it is an indistinguishable part of the northern industrial belt of the city, gloomy and dilapidated, its days of vigor well behind it. But in 1875, it was beginning to enter the industrial age as British entrepreneurs, many of them from the Scottish town of Dundee, set up jute factories along the banks of the Hooghly.[5] Nevertheless, Belgharia, like the other townships of northern 24-Parganas, still retained a largely rural character. However, since it was close to Calcutta and not far from the riverside, it contained, besides the large houses of the local landed families, several garden houses owned by wealthy residents of Calcutta who used them as holiday retreats and pleasure spots.

It was one such house that Keshabchandra Sen (1838–84), the Brahmo leader, had converted into his *sādhan kānan*, a place where he often retired with his followers to engage in spiritual exercises. Sibnath Sastri (1847–1919), once a close associate of Keshab but now becoming increasingly critical of the new turn in his leader's spiritual views, later described the place as one given to asceticism, where everyone cooked his own food, sat under trees on tiger hides in imitation of Hindu mendicants, and spent long hours in meditation.[6] Keshab had begun to come here only a few months before, and the move marked both his own inner turmoil regarding the course of the religious reformation in which he had engaged since his youth and the trouble he was having with his critics within the Brahmo movement in Calcutta.

Keshab had, however, made up his mind about the general direction in which he and his movement needed to go. In his youth he had been a fiery reformer, working tirelessly within the Brahmo Samaj as the younger associate of Debendranath Tagore (1817–1905) and becoming perhaps the most charismatic figure among the college-going young men of Calcutta in the 1860s. Grandson of Ramkamal Sen (1783–1844), who was a senior official of the Calcutta Mint and treasurer of the Bank of Bengal, Keshab had been born into one of the leading families of the new Bengali elite of Calcutta. Ramkamal had not only become wealthy; he was also a leading figure in the Asiatic Society, one of the founders of Hindu College,

Sanskrit College, and the Horticultural Society, and the author of a Bengali-English dictionary. But he belonged to what later historians would call the "conservative" faction among the Bengali notables of the city, and his home was run according to the canons of Vaishnav orthodoxy.

The grandson, however, went to Hindu College, took to Western learning, joined the followers of Rammohan Roy, and wrote and lectured exclusively in English. In 1865 he led the campaign in the Brahmo Samaj against Debendranath Tagore, accusing the old guard of compromising with Hindu ritualism and custom. He traveled extensively through India, organizing the Brahmo Samaj principally among the middle-class Bengali diaspora that had fanned out into the cities and towns of British India and performed its role as loyal underlings of the colonial power. In 1870 he made a trip to England that his followers regarded as triumphant. He addressed numerous meetings, had breakfast with Prime Minister Gladstone and an audience with Queen Victoria, and was noticed in all the major newspapers. His visit even elicited the following doggerel in *Punch*:

> Who on earth of living men,
> Is BABOO KESHUB CHUNDER SEN?
> I doubt if even one in ten
> Knows BABOO KESHUB CHUNDER SEN?
>
> Let's beard this "lion" in his den—
> This BABOO KESHUB CHUNDER SEN.
> So come to tea and muffins, then,
> With BABOO KESHUB CHUNDER SEN.[7]

Keshab was a man of too keen an intelligence to look at everything he saw in England with starry-eyed admiration; he was also sufficiently self-assured not to hide his feelings. In his farewell address in London he expressed his surprise at the "vast amount of poverty and pauperism" in the streets of the city and at "so much moral and spiritual dissolution and physical suffering, caused by intemperance." He had been astonished to discover in England an institution he "certainly did not expect to find in this country—I mean caste. Your rich people are really Brahmins, and your poor people are Sudras."[8]

He also realized that he had taken too literally the claims made on behalf of modern Christian civilization. Of course, the representatives of colonial power in India did not usually measure up to the models of Christian humility. Four years ago, in an electrifying lecture in Calcutta, he had said:

I regard every European settler in India as a missionary of Christ, and I have a right to demand that he should always remember and act up to his high responsibilities. (*Applause*) But alas! owing to the reckless conduct of a number of pseudo-Christians, Christianity has failed to produce any wholesome moral influence on my countrymen. (*"Hear! hear!" "They are only nominal Christians!"*) Yes, their muscular Christianity has led many a Native to identify the religion of Jesus with the power and privilege of inflicting blows and kicks with impunity. (*Deafening cheers*) And thus has Jesus been dishonoured in India.[9]

But now in England he saw that the defect lay in European Christianity itself. "English Christianity appears too muscular and hard," he told his English audience.

It is not soft enough for the purposes of the human heart. . . . Christian life in England is more materialistic and outward than spiritual and inward. . . . In England there is hardly anything like meditation and solitary contemplation. Englishmen seek their God in society; why do they not, now and then, go up to the heights of the mountains in order to realize the sweetness of solitary communion with God?[10]

Returning to India, Keshab began to introduce changes in the organizational practices of the Brahmo Samaj. Many of his Brahmo followers were puzzled and dismayed, some outraged. On the one hand, he opened a communal boarding house called the Bharat Asram, "a modern apostolic organization," as Keshab himself described it, in which "a number of Brahmo families were invited to live together, boarding together in the fashion of a joint family, each bearing its portion of the expenses and sharing in common the spiritual and educational advantages of the institution."[11] The idea was to train a group of Brahmo families who were most active in the organization "to ideas of neatness, order, punctuality and domestic devotions, which form such striking features in a well-regulated middle-class English home." On the other hand, Keshab experimented with new, or rather newly revived, methods of popular communication. He introduced into Brahmo worship the Vaishnav forms of collective singing and processions through the streets, accompanied by instruments such as the *khol* and the *kartāl*, typical symbols of popular *boṣṭam* religion regarded with much scorn by urban people of enlightened sensibilities. Even in his personal life, Keshab began to cultivate a certain asceticism: he replaced the metal drinking cups he used with earthen cups and cooked his own food in a little thatched room on the terrace of his house. More significantly, as Sibnath Sastri notes, "Mr Sen no longer spoke in English, except once a year on the occasion of the anniversary festival."[12]

Keshab was certain that a new direction was needed, and he was keen to find it. Half a century after Rammohan Roy's campaigns to change a tradition steeped in what he saw as superstition, degeneracy, and unthinking allegiance to religious ritual, Keshab had come face-to-face with the limits of rationalist reform. The Brahmo religion, influential as it had been in the social life of urban Bengal, was undoubtedly restricted in its appeal to a very small section of the new middle class. In the 1870s there were scarcely more than a hundred Brahmo families in Calcutta; fewer than a thousand persons in the city declared themselves as Brahmos in the 1881 census.[13] Keshab was beginning to feel that there was something inherently limiting in the strict rationalism of the new faith. In his writings and speeches of the mid-1870s, Keshab talked frequently of the importance of a faith that was not shackled by the debilitating doubts of cold reason. Indeed, he was pleading for a little madness.

> By madness I mean heavenly enthusiasm, the highest and most intense spirituality of character, in which faith rules supreme over all sentiments and faculties of the mind. . . . The difference between philosophy and madness is the difference between science and faith, between cold dialectics and fiery earnestness, between the logical deductions of the human understanding and the living force of inspiration, such as that which cometh direct from heaven. . . . Philosophy is divine, and madness too is divine. . . . The question naturally suggests itself—why should not men be equally mad for God?[14]

Of course, Keshab was too much of a modernist not to anticipate the obvious objection to his plea and was quick to make the necessary qualification.

> I admit that both Hinduism and Buddhism, whose chief principle was meditation, have done incalculable mischief by teaching their votaries to forsake the world and become dreamy devotees and hermits. But there is no reason why if the mischief has been once perpetrated it must be wrought again. In these days of scientific thought, and within the citadel of true philosophy, there is no possibility of the reign of quietism being revived. Gentlemen, we are going to combine meditation and science, madness and philosophy, and there is no fear of India relapsing into ancient mysticism.[15]

There was something else in Keshab's search for a new path. He was deeply concerned that the rationalist ideal which he and his predecessors had pursued was alien to the traditions of his country and its people. When in England, he had remarked: "Truth is not European, and it would be a mistake to force European institutions upon the Hindus, who would resist any attempt to denationalize them."[16] He seemed to suggest that the ideals of reason and rational religion that may have been suitable for Europe were not so for India. Something else, something different, was needed for an authentic Indian religion of modernity. Indeed, far more than the strength of British arms, it was this alien moral force which British rule had brought with it which was holding India in subjection.

Who rules India? . . . You are mistaken if you think that it is the ability of
Lord Lytton in the Cabinet, or the military genius of Sir Frederick Haines in
the field that rules India. It is not politics, it is not diplomacy that has laid a
firm hold of the Indian heart. It is not the glittering bayonet, nor the fiery
cannon of the British army that can make our people loyal. No, none of these
can hold India in subjection. . . . That power—need I tell you?—is Christ. It
is Christ who rules British India, and not the British Government. England
has sent out a tremendous moral force, in the life and character of that
mighty prophet, to conquer and hold this vast empire.

And it was the very alienness of this moral power, its lack of conformity
with the beliefs and practices of the people of India, that made it inadequate for its purpose.

It is true that the people of India have been satisfied in some measure with
what they have read and heard of Jesus, but they have been disappointed in
a far greater measure. For England has sent unto us, after all, a Western
Christ. This is indeed to be regretted. Our countrymen find that in this
Christ, sent by England, there is something that is not quite congenial to the
native mind, not quite acceptable to the genius of the nation. It seems that
the Christ that has come to us is an Englishman, with English manners and
customs about him. Hence is it that the Hindu people shrink back and say—
who is this revolutionary reformer who is trying to sap the very foundations
of native society, and establish here an outlandish faith and civilization quite
incompatible with oriental instincts and ideas? Why must we submit to one
who is of a different nationality? Why must we bow before a foreign product? . . . Hundreds upon hundreds, thousands upon thousands, even among
the most intelligent in the land, stand back in moral recoil from this picture
of a foreign Christianity trying to invade and subvert Hindu society; and this
repugnance unquestionably hinders the progress of the true spirit of Christianity in this country.

But there was no reason why this "true spirit of Christianity" should
remain hidden under an English, or even a European, mask. After all,
was not Christianity itself born in the East? "Why should you Hindus go
to England to learn Jesus Christ? Is not his native land nearer to India
than to England? Is he not, and are not his apostles and immediate followers, more akin to Indian nationality than Englishmen?" Why could
not one, then, recover Christ for India? To Europeans, he had this to say:
"if you wish to regenerate us Hindus, present Christ to us in his Hindu
character. When you bring Christ to us, bring him to us, not as a civilized
European, but as an Asiatic ascetic, whose wealth is communion, and
whose riches prayers."[17]
It is also significant that in his search for a path of reform in conso-
nance with Eastern spirituality, Keshab was looking for an inspired mes-

senger through whom God makes his appearance in human history. The idea was repugnant to many enlightened Brahmos, for it smacked of the age-old Hindu belief in the *avatāra* (divine incarnation); Debendranath Tagore is said to have remarked that in a country where even fish and turtles were regarded as incarnations of God, he found it strange that Keshab should aspire to be one.[18] But Keshab's doubts were of a different sort: he had become skeptical about the powers of the human intellect and will. The soul, he said,

> wants godly life, and this can never be had by the most rigid tension of mental discipline, or the highest effort of human will. . . . It is God's free gift, not man's acquisition. It comes not through our calculation or reasoning, not through industry or struggle, but through prayerful reliance upon God's mercy. . . . It keeps man in a state of holy excitement. . . . He is then seized with the frenzy of devotion, and is not only above sin, but also above temptation; for nothing is then attractive to him except holiness.[19]

This was roughly Keshab Sen's frame of mind when, one day in the middle of March 1875, he retired as usual to the quiet of the garden house in Belgharia and had a visitor.

THE MEETING

Ramakrishna, it is said, had seen Keshabchandra once, in 1864.[20] Led by his insatiable curiosity about every variety of religious experience, the saint of Dakshineswar, then a relatively young man of twenty-eight, had gone to watch a prayer meeting in the Brahmo Samaj in Calcutta. Keshab and Ramakrishna did not speak to each other on that occasion, although Ramakrishna later said that of all the people assembled on the stage, he thought Keshab was the one most advanced in spiritual qualities. But Ramakrishna maintained his interest in the activities of the Brahmos. Once he had been to see Debendranath Tagore, in the company of Mathuranath Biswas, son-in-law of his patron Rani Rasmani (1793–1861). The social distance between Debendranath and Ramakrishna was virtually unbridgeable, but Mathuranath had been to Hindu College with Debendranath and, seeing Ramakrishna's eagerness to visit the eminent religious leader, had agreed to take him to the Tagore house in Jorasanko. The meeting apparently passed unremarkably and ended with Debendranath inviting Ramakrishna to the anniversary ceremony at the Brahmo Samaj. Ramakrishna pointed to his clothes and expressed doubts about whether he would be entirely presentable at such a gentlemanly gathering. Debendranath laughed off the objection, but the next morning wrote to Mathuranath withdrawing the invitation.

Ramakrishna was at this time entirely unknown among the Calcutta middle class. True, he had been patronized by Rani Rasmani of Janbazar, and she along with several members of her family regarded Ramakrishna with much veneration. But Rasmani's family, largely because of its lower-caste background, was not a part of the culturally dominant elite of Calcutta, although she herself was well known as a spirited and philanthropic woman. The only other prominent person close to Ramakrishna before 1875 was Sambhucharan Mallik, a wealthy and generous landlord and trader—and he died in 1876. And there was also Captain Viswanath Upadhyay, a businessman from Nepal who did not belong to Calcutta.

On this particular day in the middle of March 1875, Ramakrishna was in Calcutta when he had a great urge to meet Keshabchandra. Accompanied by his nephew Hriday and Captain Viswanath, he went to Keshab's house in Kolutola only to be told that Keshab was in Belgharia. Ramakrishna declared that he had to go there straightaway. There was, of course, the small matter of finding the fare for the long carriage ride, but Captain Viswanath agreed to pay it.

Thus it was that in order to meet Keshab, Ramakrishna had to take a carriage all the way from Calcutta past Dakshineswar to a garden house in Belgharia. For it is a fact of history that when Ramakrishna went looking for him in Calcutta, Keshab Sen had already made his way to his spiritual retreat somewhere in the vicinity of Dakshineswar.

Hriday got off the carriage and went looking for Keshabchandra. He found the leader sitting with his companions on the steps of a pool in front of the house. Hriday walked up to him and said that his uncle, who was sitting outside in the carriage, would like to see him. When asked who his uncle was, he explained that he was the Paramahamsa of Dakshineswar. Keshabchandra immediately asked Hriday to bring him in.

Pratap Mozoomdar (1840–1905), a childhood friend and close associate of Keshab who was present on the occasion, later described the scene:

> There came one morning in a ricketty *ticca gari*, a disorderly-looking young man, insufficiently clad, and with manners less than insufficient. . . . His appearance was so unpretending and simple, and he spoke so little at his introduction, that we did not take much notice of him at first.[21]

Mozoomdar, of course, gives the date of this meeting as March 1876, although all later historians agree that it took place in March 1875. It is also curious that twelve years after the incident he remembered Ramakrishna as a "young man," although the latter was then thirty-nine years old, two years older than Keshab Sen and four years older than Mozoomdar himself.

What might be called the official biography of Ramakrishna, the *Rāmkṛṣṇa līlāprasaṅga*, describes Ramakrishna on this day as clothed in "a dhoti with a red border, one end thrown across the left shoulder." On being introduced, he said, "Babu, I am told that you people have seen God. I have come to hear what you have seen." This is how the conversation began. After some time, Ramakrishna began to sing one of his favorite songs—a composition by Ramprasad Sen—"Who Knows What Kālī Is Like?" As he sang, he swooned and went into a trance. Hriday began to whisper in his ears, "Hari Om! Hari Om!" Slowly, Ramakrishna recovered consciousness.[22]

The same incident is described by Pratap Mozoomdar from the point of view of Keshab's followers. "Soon he began to discourse in a sort of half-delirious state, becoming now and then quite unconscious. What he said, however, was so profound and beautiful that we soon perceived he was no ordinary man."[23]

Ramakrishna was talking about the nature of God, telling his half-skeptical audience some of the stories that two decades later would be familiar to all of literate Bengal.

> A man who had seen a chameleon under a tree returned and said, "I have seen a beautiful red chameleon under the tree." Another said, "I was there before you. The chameleon is not red, but green. I have seen it with my own eyes." A third said, "I too know it well. I saw it before either of you, and it was neither red nor green, but—and I saw with my own eyes—it was blue." Others declared it was yellow, or grey, and so on. Soon they began to quarrel among themselves as to who was correct. A man passing by asked what the trouble was. When he was told he said, "I live under that very tree, and I know the chameleon well. All of you are right, every one. The chameleon is sometimes green, sometimes blue, it is all colours by turn, and sometimes it is absolutely colourless."[24]

Ramakrishna was beginning to enjoy himself. "When a strange animal comes into a herd of cattle," he said, "the cows go after it with their horns. But when they see another cow, they lick its hide. That's what has happened to me here." Suddenly, he turned to Keshab and said, "Yes, your tail has dropped off." Undoubtedly Keshab and his followers were taken aback by this remark. Ramakrishna quickly explained himself, however. "You must have seen tadpoles. As long as they have tails, they must live in water; but when the tail falls away they can live on land as well as in water. . . . Your mind, Keshab, is in such a state now. You can live in the world, and enjoy divine bliss as well."[25]

THE DISCOVERY

Keshab Sen ran two newspapers. The English paper, the *Indian Mirror*, began as a weekly and in 1871 became a daily. The Bengali weekly, *Sulabh samācār*, was started in November 1870 and in three months reached a peak circulation of twenty-seven thousand. Even in 1877 when its circulation had dropped somewhat because of competition from other publications it was still the most widely circulated paper in Bengali.[26]

Two weeks after the meeting between Keshab Sen and Ramakrishna, the *Indian Mirror* published an article entitled "A Hindu Saint." After describing the great Hindu devotees talked about in the religious literature of India and still revered in popular memory, it continued:

> We met one not long ago, and were charmed by the depth, penetration and simplicity of his spirit. The never-ceasing metaphors and analogies in which he indulged are, most of them, as apt as they are beautiful. The characteristics of the mind are the very opposite of those of Pandit Dayanand Saraswati, the former being gentle, tender and contemplative as the latter is sturdy, masculine and polemical. Hinduism must have in it a deep source of beauty, truth and goodness to inspire such men as these.[27]

It is more than likely that the article was written by Keshab himself and a few weeks later something along the same lines appeared in *Sulabh samācār*, the first of several articles on Ramakrishna published in that paper.

Suddenly Ramakrishna became an object of great curiosity among the educated young men of Calcutta. Ramchandra Datta, a doctor at the Calcutta Medical College, and his cousin Manomohan Mitra, a businessman, read about Ramakrishna in *Sulabh samācār* and came to Dakshineswar in 1879 to see him.[28] Surendranath Mitra, a friend of Ramchandra and a fairly wealthy man with a job in a British firm, was troubled by his incurable weakness for liquor and women and began visiting Dakshineswar. Ramakrishna told him, "But, Suren, when you drink, why do you think of it as ordinary wine? Offer it first to the Mother and drink it as her *prasād* [sanctified food]. Then you will never get drunk." Henceforth, before Surendranath drank, he offered some wine to Kālī. This action filled him with devotion, and he began to cry like a child. He never became intoxicated again.[29]

Balaram Bose, who came from a wealthy family of landlords and was one of Ramakrishna's principal patrons in the last years of his life, first read about him in Keshab Sen's newspapers.[30] So did Girishchandra Ghosh, the foremost personality in the Calcutta theater at this time.[31] By the early years of the 1880s, when most of the men who would form the closest circle of disciples around Ramakrishna had gathered in Dakshineswar,[32] he was a frequently discussed personality in the schools, colleges, and newspapers of Calcutta.

Remarkably, the enormous legend that would be built around Ramakrishna's name in the words and thoughts of the Calcutta middle class was the result of a fairly short acquaintance, beginning only eleven years

before his death. Only in those last years of his life did he cast his spel'
over so many distinguished men, who would make his name a household
word among educated Bengalis.

The followers of Keshabchandra and Ramakrishna have, of course,
never managed to agree on which of the two great leaders influenced the
other. The hagiographers of Ramakrishna write as though Keshab, a determined seeker after truth who roamed aimlessly for the greater part of
his life, finally found salvation at the feet of the Master. Saradananda, for
instance, writes of Keshab's break with the Brahmo Samaj and his founding of a new order: "As this faith came into existence shortly after Kesav's
acquaintance with the Master, it is probable that it was a partial acceptance and propagation of the Master's final conclusion." Saradananda
nevertheless remains skeptical about Keshab's ability to accept Ramakrishna in the true spirit of the devotee: "Although he was dearly loved by
the Master and had many opportunities to see and hear him, it is doubtful
whether Kesav, inspired with Western ideas and ideals as he was, understood him perfectly" (GM, p. 314). A biographer of Keshab, on the other
hand, complains: "It is sad to contemplate that such friendship should be
misunderstood, misinterpreted. It has even been suggested that Keshub
borrowed his religion of Harmony, the New Dispensation, from
Ramakrishna."[33]

With the advantage of a hundred years of hindsight, we have no need
to take sides in this quarrel. But for precisely that reason—the fact that we
are prisoners of an incorrigibly historical vision of our selves and the
world—we had to begin our story with the meeting in Belgharia on a
spring afternoon in 1875.

DIVINE PLAY

This, however, is not how the story is supposed to begin. Those who tell
the story of Ramakrishna remind us that the Master's life was not the life
of any ordinary man, not even that of an extraordinary man. The Absolute Being, in one of his inscrutable, playful decisions, appears on earth
from time to time in the guise of a human being to act out an exemplary
life for the edification of the world. According to the authorized version,
therefore, the story of Ramakrishna's life must be told as one more episode in an eternal līlā.

The story, in fact, is supposed to begin with a dream. In the winter of
1835, Kshudiram Chattopadhyay of Kamarpukur in Hugli, then already
a man of sixty, went to Gaya to offer worship to his forefathers. There he
dreamed of himself in the temple, surrounded by his forefathers, who
appeared before him "in luminous celestial bodies," accepting the pinda

he offered to them. He then saw the temple fill "with divine light," and there in front of him was "a wonderful divine being"—Viṣṇu himself in the form of Gadādhar—"seated happily on a beautiful throne." Then the divine being spoke to him. "I bless you and will be born as your son and will receive your loving care" (GM, pp. 31–32).

Soon after this, Kshudiram's wife, Chandra, then forty-five years old, conceived. Saradananda, Ramakrishna's biographer, tells us that "one peculiar characteristic of divine and subtle origin was shared by every one of Kshudiram's pious household": they all had a predilection for unusual spiritual experiences (GM, p. 29). Chandra's visions became more numerous after she had conceived (GM, p. 37). The birth of the son was again followed by something of a miracle, because the child disappeared from the place where Dhani, the midwife, had kept it. Looking around in panic, she found it lying in a hollow fireplace "with its body adorned with ashes, and still not crying." Everyone marveled at the beauty and size of the child, for it was as large as a six-month-old infant. The astrologers agreed that Kshudiram's son had been born at an especially auspicious moment (GM, p. 40).

In the Līlāprasaṅga, Saradananda takes great pains to explain to what he presumes will be a skeptical readership the significance of these extraordinary and miraculous happenings surrounding Ramakrishna's birth.[34] He argues, for instance, that such events are common to the life stories of all great souls "who sanctify the earth by their birth," stories that "are recorded in the religious books of all races." Similar events portray "the unique spiritual experiences and visions" of the parents of Rama, Krishna, the Buddha, Jesus, Śaṅkara and Caitanya (GM, p. 33). Again, he suggests that there must be some significance to the fact that with the exceptions of Rama and the Buddha, "all the great souls who are to this day worshipped as the incarnations of the Divine," such as Krishna, Jesus, Śaṅkara, Caitanya or Muhammad, were born "in poverty and hardship" (L 1:24; GM, p. 17). Miraculousness, it would seem, is the aura that surrounds the life histories of those who are the incarnations of God and marks out their lives as different from history itself.

But Saradananda also has other arguments to offer. India, he thinks, has been particularly blessed by the Almighty Being in the matter of incarnations. This explains the spirituality of Indian culture.

> When we make a comparative study of the spiritual beliefs and ideals of India and of other countries, we notice a vast difference between them. From very ancient times India has taken entities beyond the senses, namely, God, the self, the next world, etc., to be real, and has employed all its efforts towards their direct realization. . . . All its activities have accordingly been coloured by intense spirituality throughout the ages. . . . The source of this

absorbing interest in things beyond the senses is due to the frequent birth in India of men possessing a direct knowledge of these things and endowed with divine qualities. (*GM*, p. 5)

Knowledge of a similar kind, Saradananda is sure, is denied to the West, for the procedures of Western knowledge are "attracted only by external objects."

> Although capable of achieving great progress in physical science, the [Western] procedure . . . could not lead men to the knowledge of the Atman. For the only way to attain that knowledge is through self-control, selflessness and introspection, and the only instrument for attaining it is the mind, with all its functions brought under absolute control.

Western knowledge could not accomplish this. Consequently, Western people "missed the path to Self-knowledge and became materialists, identifying themselves with the body" (*GM*, p. 13).

We have here the familiar nationalist problematic of the material and the spiritual, the identification of an incompleteness in the claims of the modern West to a superior culture and asserting the sovereignty of the nation over the domain of spirituality. In itself, this is not surprising because Saradananda himself was very much a part of the middle-class culture of Bengal that had, by the turn of the century, come to accept these criteria as fundamental in the framing of questions of cultural choice. What is curious is that instead of "cleaning up" the layers of myth and legend from the life story of someone like Ramakrishna and presenting it as the rational history of human exemplariness, as in Bankim's *Kṛṣṇacaritra*, for instance, Saradananda seeks to do the very opposite: he authenticates the myth by declaring that the life of Ramakrishna is not to be read as human history but as divine play.[35]

Indeed, Saradananda is forthright in stating his purpose. Why does he feel called upon to write the story of Ramakrishna's life for his educated readership? The reason has to do with "the occupation of India by the West."

> Coming more and more under the spell of the West, India rejected the ideal of renunciation and self-control and began to run after worldly pleasures. This attitude brought with it the decay of the ancient system of education and training, and there arose atheism, love of imitation and lack of self-confidence. Thus the nation lost its backbone. People came to believe that their long-cherished beliefs and practices were erroneous, and they felt that perhaps their traditions were crude and semi-civilized, as the West with its wonderful knowledge of science said them to be. . . . Finding that, even for worldly enjoyment, she had to depend upon others, India was overcome with a sense of frustration. Having thus lost the way both to enjoyment and

to liberation, and yet being bent on imitating others, the nation was now buffeted by waves of desires, like a boat drifting without a helmsman. . . . Prostrate India was made to listen to lectures—delivered at public meetings held in the Western manner—on politics, sociology, the freedom of women and widow-marriage. But the feeling of frustration and despair, instead of lessening, grew stronger. . . . The influence of the West had brought about its fall. Would it not be futile, then, to look to the atheistic West for its resurrection? Being itself imperfect, how could the West make another part of the world perfect? (GM, p. 15)

The conditions of the problem were clear. The assertion of spirituality would have to rest on an essential difference between East and West, and the domain of autonomy thus defined would have to be ordered on one's own terms, not on those set by the conqueror in the material world. If myth is the form in which the truth is miraculously revealed in the domain of Eastern spirituality, then it is myth that must be affirmed and the quibbles of a skeptical rationalism declared out of bounds.

Saradananda thus goes on to talk about many extraordinary events from Ramakrishna's childhood, all of which showed him, even at an early age, as a person with a touch of divinity in him. Thus, there are stories about his "remarkable memory and intelligence" and about his "remarkable courage" (GM, pp. 44, 47). There is also the story about how young Gadadhar, at the age of nine, resolved a scriptural dispute at a scholarly gathering (GM, p. 55). Of course, there were spiritual experiences too—meditation, ecstasy, and visions.

Ramakrishna's marriage at the age of twenty-two puts Saradananda into something of a quandary. Ramakrishna never consummated the marriage, and although he had his wife Sarada come and live in Dakshineswar, it could never have been his intention to lead the life of a family man. Why then did Ramakrishna agree to marry? Saradananda finds an answer.

At the present time we have almost forgotten that, besides the satisfaction of the senses, there is a very sacred and high purpose of marriage and this is why we are reducing ourselves to being worse than beasts. It is only in order to destroy this beastliness of men and women of modern India that the Master, the teacher of his people, was married. Like all the other acts of his life the act of marriage also was performed for the good of all. (GM, p. 409)

The youth of Ramakrishna is recounted by Saradananda as a narrative of the great soul in his "attitude of the devotee" (sādhaka-bhāva). During this time Ramakrishna goes through a series of spiritual exercises: in Tantra with the Bhairavi, in the forms of nondualistic Vedantic sādhanā (spiritual exercise) with Totapuri, and in certain forms of Sufi meditation with

Govinda Ray, besides his meetings with various religious personalities during his trip to Varanasi and Vrindavan. Ramakrishna is said to have attained mastery (*siddhi*) in each of these forms of religious practice. Saradananda even has a short section on "the extraordinary way in which the Master attained proficiency in the religion founded by Śrī Śrī Īśā" (*L* 2:370–73). The method was a mystical encounter with Christ himself. During one of his conversations with his disciples many years later, Ramakrishna asked them what the Bible said about Christ's physical appearance. The disciples reasoned that being Jewish, he must have been "very fair, with long eyes and an aquiline nose."

> The Master said, "But I saw that the tip of his nose was a little flat. I don't know why I saw him like that." . . .
>
> But we came to know, shortly after the Master passed away, that there were three different descriptions of Jesus' physical features; and according to one of them the tip of his nose was a little flat. (*GM*, p. 297)

All this time, until Ramakrishna took up "the attitude of the teacher" (*guru-bhāva*), he lived his life "free from the influence of Western ideas and ideals" (*GM*, p. 707). Only when he came into contact with Keshabchandra and the Brahmos did he become aware of the spiritual state of the educated sections of society. What he saw was a state of crisis.

> He saw that, although [the Brahmos] were making efforts to realize God, they had deviated from the ancient national ideal of renunciation. His mind, therefore, engaged itself in finding out its cause. It was thus that he became acquainted for the first time with the mass of exotic ideas entering the lives of the people of India because of Western education and training. (*GM*, p. 708)

Ramakrishna decided that behind all this lay some shrewd purpose of the divine will.

> The Master, therefore, perfectly comprehended that it was only owing to the Divine Mother's will that Western ideas and ideals had entered India and that by Her will alone had the Brahmos and other educated communities become mere toys in their hands. . . . The Master said, "Let them accept as much of the immediate knowledge of the seers as is possible for them; the Mother of the universe will bring forward in future such persons as will fully accept that knowledge." (*GM*, p. 709)

Thus it was that Ramakrishna decided to gather around him a circle of young disciples and to initiate them into his religion. In each case, the Master had a yogic vision of the disciple before he actually arrived in Dakshineswar (*GM*, p. 811). From the beginning of 1881, "the all-renouncing devotees, the eternal playmates of the Master in his Lila, began coming to him one by one" (*GM*, p. 711). By 1884, they had all arrived. It was only then that Ramakrishna finally took up his *divya-bhāva*, "the attitude of the divine."

The purpose of all this is clear to Saradananda. Had not the Divine Lord promised in the *Gītā* that whenever religion declines, he would assume a human body and manifest his powers? (*GM*, p. 16). Now, when the nation lay enslaved and its brightest minds confused and frustrated, had not such a time arrived?

> Did India, shorn of its glory and reduced to an object of contempt to foreigners, once again arouse the compassion of the Lord to incarnate Himself? That this did happen will become clear on a perusal of the life-story of the great soul, possessed of an infinite urge to do good, which is here recorded. India was once more blessed by the coming, in response to the need of the age, of One who, incarnating Himself as Sri Rama, Sri Krishna and others, renewed the eternal religion again and again. (*GM*, pp. 9–10)

To explain this "purpose of his advent" (*GM*, p. 3), Saradananda recounts the story of Ramakrishna's life as an episode in an eternal play—a story that begins with a dream.

But although the *Līlāprasaṅga* claims to be something like an official biography, it is not the text that is most familiar to generations of avid readers of Ramakrishna literature. That honor is reserved for the *Rāmkṛṣṇa kathāmṛta*. Circulated now in several editions and virtually annual reprints, it is a collection of the Master's "sayings." Ever since its publication in the early years of this century, its five volumes have acted as the principal sourcebook on Ramakrishna.

LANGUAGE

Sumit Sarkar has noted the stylistic peculiarity of the *Kathāmṛta* in the way it combines two radically different linguistic idioms—one, the rustic colloquial idiom spoken by Ramakrishna, and the other, the chaste formality of the new written prose of nineteenth-century Calcutta.[36] The former, for all its rusticity (a "rusticity," we must remember, itself produced by the difference created in the nineteenth century between the new high culture of urban sophistication and everything else that became marked as coarse, rustic, or merely local), was by no means a language that any villager in nineteenth-century Bengal would have spoken, for its use by Ramakrishna shows great conceptual richness, metaphoric power, and dialectical skill. It was the language of preachers and poets in precolonial Bengal, and even when used by someone without much formal learning (such as Ramakrishna), it was able to draw upon the conceptual and rhetorical resources of a vast body of literate tradition. By contrast, the new written prose of late nineteenth-century Calcutta, in what may be called its post-Bankim phase, was distinct not so much as a "development" of earlier narrative forms but fundamentally by virtue of its adoption of a wholly different, that is, modern European, discursive framework. Recent studies have identified the ways in which grammatical models borrowed from the modern European languages shaped the "standard" syntactic forms of modern Bengali prose; other studies have shown similar "modular" influences of rhetorical forms borrowed from English in particular.[37]

The appearance of these formal differences between the two idioms was of course intricately tied to another difference—a difference in the very conceptual and logical apparatus articulated in language. The users of the new Bengali prose not only said things in a new way, they also had new things to say. This was the principal intellectual impetus that led to the rapid flourishing of the modern Bengali prose literature; by the 1880s, when Mahendranath Gupta (1854–1932) was recording his diary entries of Ramakrishna's sayings for what was to become the Kathāmṛta, a considerable printing and publishing industry operated in Calcutta (in fact, one of the more important industrial activities in the city), testifying to the creation of both a modern "high culture" and a "print-capitalism," the two sociological conditions that are supposed to activate the nationalist imagination.[38] What is nevertheless intriguing is the quite rapid "standardization" of this prose. The 1850s was still a time when a "standard" form had not appeared; by the 1880s, the "standard" form had come to stay. It is worth speculating whether the sheer proximity of European discursive models—available, palpable, already standardized by more momentous historical processes and hence unquestionably worthy of emulation—had something to do with the astonishing speed with which the entirely new form of narrative prose came to be accepted as "normal" by the English-educated Bengali middle class.

The modular influence was strongest when written prose was employed to discuss subjects that were explicitly theoretical or philosophical. The Kathāmṛta is marked not only by the divergence between the "rustic" and the "urban" idioms in Bengali; it is an even more explicitly bilingual text in its repeated employment of English terms, phrases, and quotations. It is remarkable how often Mahendranath introduces with a heading in English sections in which Ramakrishna discusses questions of a philosophical nature: there must be some fifty sections with titles such as "Reconciliation of Free Will and God's Will—of Liberty and Necessity" or "Identity of the Absolute or Universal Ego and the Phenomenal World" or "Problems of Evil and the Immortality of the Soul" or "Philosophy and Scepticism," and so on. Each heading of this kind is followed by a recording of Ramakrishna's own words or a conversation, directly reported, between him and his disciples. Mahendranath, in his self-appointed role of narrator, does not attempt to explicate the sayings of his preceptor, and yet this form of introducing sections serves to create the impression that Ramakrishna is dealing with the same questions that are discussed in European philosophy. Mahendranath also repeatedly translates various philosophical concepts used by Ramakrishna with English terms and inserts them into the text in parentheses or in footnotes. Thus, for instance, when Ramakrishna describes his state of trance as one in which he is unable to count things—*ek duier pār* (literally, "beyond ones and twos")—Mahendranath adds a footnote in English: "The absolute as distinguished from the relative." He explains *Kālī* as "God in His relations with the conditioned" or *Brahma* as "the Unconditioned, the Absolute." When Ramakrishna says *pratyakṣa*, Mahendranath adds in parentheses "perception"; when Ramakrishna says that in a trance *īśvara* does not appear as a *vyakti*, Mahendranath adds "person." A section entitled "Perception of the Infinite" has a footnote saying, "Compare discussion about the order of perception of the Infinite and of the Finite in Max Müller's Hibbert Lectures and Gifford Lectures."

This bilingual dialogue runs through the text, translating the terms of an Indian philosophical discourse into those of nineteenth-century European logic and metaphysics. It is as though the wisdom of an ancient speculative tradition of the East, sustained for centuries not only in philosophical texts composed by the learned but through debates and disquisitions among preachers and mystics, is being made available to minds shaped by the modes of European speculative philosophy. (The invocation of Max Müller is significant.) This dialogue also expresses the desire to assert that the "common" philosophy of "rustic" Indian preachers is no less sophisticated, no less "classical" in its intellectual heritage, than the learned speculations of modern European philosophers: in fact, the former is shown as providing different, and perhaps better, answers to the same philosophical problems posed in European philosophy.[39] (Mahendranath also embellishes some of Ramakrishna's words with quotations in Sanskrit from texts such as the Upaniṣads and the *Gītā*; Ramakrishna himself almost never used Sanskrit aphorisms in his conversations.) But for both narrator and reader of the *Kathāmṛta*, the terrain of European thought is familiar ground—familiar, yet foreign—from which they set out to discover (or perhaps, rediscover) the terrain of the indigenous and the popular, a home from which they have been wrenched. The bilingu.

discourse takes place within the same consciousness, where both lord and bondsman reside. Contestation and mediation have taken root within the new middle-class mind, a mind split in two.

NARRATIVE TIME

The internal arrangement of each volume of the *Kathāmṛta* is strictly chronological. The book was not originally planned to run into five volumes. The first volume consequently is composed of selections from Mahendranath's diaries in the period from 26 February 1882 to 27 December 1885, beginning with an account of his first meeting with Ramakrishna. The later volumes contain other selections, but covering roughly the same period (vol. 2, 17 October 1882 to 24 April 1886; vol. 3, 5 August 1882 to 13 April 1886; vol. 4, 1 April 1883 to 21 April 1886; vol. 5, 11 March 1882 to 24 September 1885). Each volume has appendixes; those added to volume 5 record some events of 1881 while those in the other volumes deal with conversations between Ramakrishna's disciples after the Master's death in August 1886.

Mahendranath is scrupulous not only in maintaining a chronological order within each volume but also in meticulously recording the date, time, and place of each conversation. He also adds wherever possible a description of the physical surroundings and invariably notes the names of those present at the time. Mahendranath is clearly conscious of the requirements of authentic documentation. And yet, as soon as he passes to the reporting of the Master's sayings, he not only abandons the formal structure of a rational narrative prose, he surrenders himself completely in his journey with Ramakrishna through the fluid space of mythic time, from Rāma, Hanumāna, Bhīṣma, and Yudhiṣṭhira to the ancient sages Nārada, Vaśiṣṭha, or Viśvāmitra, to the apocryphal stories of folklore to Ramakrishna's own spiritual mentors Totāpurī or the Bhairavi to contemporary figures like Keshab Sen or Vidyasagar or Bankimchandra, jumping from one to another, equating, contrasting, connecting, with complete disregard for historical specifics. Mahendranath's careful construction of a narrative grid was designed to authenticate the historical truth of his master's sayings; yet the truth is seized only after it has escaped the grid of historical time.

It is possible, of course, to use the narrative arrangement of materials in the *Kathāmṛta* for a historical-biographical study of Ramakrishna. But as far as the "message" of the *Kathāmṛta* is concerned, the arrangement of the materials does not matter in the least. The chronological arrangement completely defeats any attempt at indicating a progression or thematization. What it produces instead is a repetitiousness: the same arguments, the same stories, even the same jokes, repeated over and over again. Redundancy is, of course, a characteristic element of the structure of self-evidence of mythic truth.

THE PRISONHOUSE OF REASON

For the colonized middle-class mind, caught in its "middleness," the discourse of Reason was not unequivocally liberating. The invariable implication it carried of the historical necessity of colonial rule and its condemnation of indigenous culture as the storehouse of unreason, or (in a stage-of-civilization argument) of reason yet unborn, which only colonial rule would bring to birth (as father, mother, or midwife—which?), made the discourse of Reason oppressive. It was an oppression that the middle-class mind often sought to escape. Bankimchandra Chattopadhyay (1838–94), unquestionably the most brilliant rationalist essayist of the time, escaped into the world not of mythic time but of imaginary history, sliding imperceptibly from the past-as-it-might-have-been to the past-as-it-should-have-been to an invocation of the past-as-it-will-be.[40] So did the most brilliant rationalist defender of "orthodox" tradition—Bhudeb Mukhopadhyay (1827–94), in that remarkable piece of utopian history *Svapnalabdha bhāratbarṣer itihās* (The history of India as revealed in a dream). More common was the escape from the oppressive rigidities of the new discursive prose into the semantic richness and polyphony of ordinary, uncolonized speech. It would be an interesting project to study the ways in which Bengali prose writers have found it so compelling to adopt the device of shifting from an authorial narrative prose to the dramatic forms of direct dialogue. Even more striking is the communicative power of the modern Bengali drama, the least commended on aesthetic grounds by the critics of modern Bengali literature (certainly so in comparison with the novel or the short story or poetry) and yet arguably the most effective cultural form through which the English-educated literati of Calcutta commanded a popular audience (and the one cultural form subjected to the most rigorous and sustained police censorship by the colonial government). Reborn in the middle of the nineteenth century in the shapes prescribed by European theater, the modern Bengali drama found its strength not so much in the carefully structured directedness of dramatic action and conflict as in the rhetorical power of speech. Where written prose marked a domain already surrendered to the colonizer, common speech thrived within its zealously guarded zone of autonomy and freedom.

FEAR

It is important to note that the subordination of the Bengali middle class to the colonial power was based on much more than a mental construct. Hegemonic power is always a combination of force and the persuasive self-evidence of ideology. To the extent that the persuasive apparatus of colonial ideology necessarily and invariably fails to match the requirements of justifying direct political domination, colonial rule is always marked by the palpable, indeed openly demonstrated, presence of physical force.

For the middle-class Bengali babu of late nineteenth-century Calcutta, the figures of the white boss in a mercantile office or a jute mill, the magistrate in court, the officer in the district, the police sergeant or uniformed soldiers and sailors roaming the streets of Calcutta (invariably, it seems, in a state of drunkenness) were not objects of respect and emulation: they were objects of fear.

Consider the following episode from a skit written by Girishchandra Ghosh (1844–1912), the most eminent playwright and producer on the nineteenth-century Calcutta stage and a close disciple of Ramakrishna. This minor farce, *Bellik-bājār*, was first performed at the Star Theater on Christmas Eve of 1886, only a few months after Ramakrishna's death.[41]

The opening scene is set, not without reason, in the Death Registration office at the Nimtala cremation ground in Calcutta. We meet first a doctor and then a lawyer inquiring from a *murdāpharās* (whose business it is to burn dead bodies) about recent cremations. They are practitioners of the new arts of commercialization of death: the first works upon bodies in a state of sickness, prolonging the disease while holding death at bay; the second begins his work after death, entangling surviving relatives in an endless chain of litigation. The colonial city is where people come to make money out of death. The sole official representative here—the registration clerk (who, when we meet him, is, suitably enough, asleep)—has the job of putting into the official accounts the details of every death.

Enter Dokari, himself a recent and lowly entrant into the world of the Calcutta babus, learning to survive by his wits in a city of worldly opportunities. He tells the two gentlemen about the death of a wealthy trader whose only son, Lalit, would be an easy prey for all of them. The three strike a deal and proceed to lure the moneyed young man into the path of expensive living, dubious property deals, and lawsuits. In time, Dokari is predictably outmaneuvered by his more accomplished partners and, thrown out by his wealthy patron, finds himself back on the street. It is

Christmas Eve, and the lawyer and doctor have arranged a lavish party, at Lalit's expense, of course, where they are to deliver upon their unsuspecting victim the coup de grâce. Dokari, roaming the streets, suddenly comes upon three Englishmen and, instinctively, turns around and runs. (The italicized words in the following extracts are in English in the original.)

ENG 1: *Not so fast, not so fast* . . .

They catch hold of Dokari.

DOKARI: Please, saheb! *Poor man!* . . . *License have, thief not.*
ENG 1: *Hold the ankle, Dick. Darkee wants a swing* . . .

They lift him up and swing him in the air.

DOKARI: My bones *all another place*, my insides *up down, head making thus thus.* [Falls]

ENG 2: *Grog-shop?*
DOKARI: Curse in English as much as you please. I don't understand it, so it doesn't touch me.
ENG 2: *A good ale house?*
DOKARI: Let me give it back to you in Bengali. My great-grandson is married to your sister, I'm married to your sister, I'm her bastard. . . .
ENG 3: *Wine shop* . . . sharab ghar . . .

Dokari now realizes what the Englishmen want and remembers the party in Lalit's gardenhouse.

DOKARI: *Yes, sir, your servant, sir. Wine shop here not. Master eat wine? Come garden, very near. . . . Brandy, whiskey, champagne, all, all, fowl, cutlet . . . free, free, come garden, come my back, back me, not beat, come from my back.*

The party is a travesty of "enlightened" sociability, with a couple of hired dancing girls posing as the liberated wives of our friends the lawyer and the doctor. A social reformer delivers an impassioned speech on the ignorance and irrationality of his countrymen. As he ends his speech with the words *"Oh! Poor India, where art thou, come to your own country,"* Dokari enters with the three Englishmen. The sight of the white men causes immediate panic, the party breaks up in confusion, and the Englishmen settle down to a hearty meal.

A mortal fear of the Englishman and of the world over which he dominated was a constituent element in the consciousness of the Calcutta middle class—in its obsequious homages in pidgin English and foul-mouthed

denunciations in Bengali no less than in the measured rhetoric of enlightened social reformers. But fear can also be the source of new strategies of
survival and resistance.

WITHDRAWAL FROM KARMA

MASTER (to Keshab and other Brahmo admirers): You people speak of
doing good to the world. Is the world such a small thing? And who are you,
pray, to do good to the world? First realize God, see Him by means of spiritual discipline. If He imparts power, then you can do good to others; otherwise not.

A BRAHMO DEVOTEE: Then must we give up our activities [*karma*] until
we realize God?

MASTER: No. Why should you? You must engage in such activities as
contemplation, singing His praises, and other daily devotions.

BRAHMO: But what about our worldly duties—duties associated with our
earning money, and so on?

MASTER: Yes, you can perform them too, but only as much as you need for
your livelihood. At the same time, you must pray to God in solitude with
tears in your eyes, that you may be able to perform those duties in an unselfish manner. You should say to Him: "O God, make my worldly duties
fewer and fewer; otherwise, O Lord, I find that I forget Thee when I am
involved in too many activities. I may think I am doing unselfish work
[*niṣkāma karma*], but it turns out to be selfish." . . . Sambhu Mallik once
talked about establishing hospitals, dispensaries, and schools, making
roads, digging public reservoirs, and so forth. I said to him: "Don't go out of
your way to look for such works. Undertake only those works that present
themselves to you and are of pressing necessity—and those also in a spirit of
detachment." It is not good to become involved in too many activities. That
makes one forget God. . . . Therefore I said to Sambhu, "Suppose God appears before you; then will you ask Him to build hospitals and dispensaries
for you?" (*Laughter*) A lover of God never says that. He will rather say: "O
Lord, give me a place at Thy Lotus Feet. Keep me always in Thy company.
Give me sincere and pure love [*bhakti*] for Thee."

Karmayoga is very hard indeed. In the Kaliyuga it is extremely difficult to
perform the rites enjoined in the scriptures. . . . In the Kaliyuga the best way
is bhaktiyoga, the path of devotion—singing the praises of the Lord, and
prayer. The path of devotion is the religion [*dharma*] of this age. (*K*, pp.
41–42)[42]

This recurrent message runs through the *Kathāmṛta*. Worldly pursuits
occupy a domain of selfish and particular interests. It is a domain of
conflict, of domination and submission, of social norms, legal regula-

tions, disciplinary rules enforced by the institutions of power. It is a domain of constant flux, ups and downs of fortune, a domain of greed and of humiliation. It is a domain that the worldly householder cannot do without, but it is one he has to enter because of the force of circumstances over which he has no control. But he can always escape into his own world of consciousness, where worldly pursuits are forgotten, where they have no essential existence. This is the inner world of devotion, a personal relation of *bhakti* (devotion) with the Supreme Being.

The strategy of survival in a world that is dominated by the rich and the powerful is withdrawal. Do not attempt to intervene in the world, do not engage in futile conflict, do not try to reform the world. Those who involve themselves in such activities do so not because they wish to change the world for the better but because they too pursue their particular interests—fame, popularity, power. This is a strong element operating in that part of the middle-class consciousness in which it is submissive, weak, afraid of its fate in the world.

WITHDRAWAL FROM JÑĀNA

Ramakrishna asks Narendranath (later Swami Vivekananda, 1863–1902) and Girish Ghosh to do *vicāra* (debate) in English. The debate starts, not quite in English, but in Bengali interspersed with English words. Narendra talks about the infinite form of God and the incapacity of thought to conceive of that form. Girish suggests that God might also appear in a finite, phenomenal, form. Narendra disagrees.

> Gradually Narendra and Girish become involved in a heated discussion. If God is Infinity, how can He have parts? What did Hamilton say? What were the views of Herbert Spencer, of Tyndall, of Huxley? And so forth and so on.
> MASTER (to M.): I don't enjoy these discussions. Why should I argue at all? I clearly see that God is everything; He Himself has become all. I see that whatever is, is God. He is everything; again, He is beyond everything. (*K*, pp. 160–61; *G*, p. 733)

Later, calling Narendra aside, Ramakrishna says,

> As long as a man argues about God, he has not realized Him. You two were arguing. I didn't like it. . . .
> The nearer you approach God, the less you reason and argue. When you attain Him, then all sounds—all reasoning and disputing—come to an end. (*K*, p. 163; *G*, p. 735)

Ramakrishna is heard repeating the argument several times in the *Kathāmṛta*. Learning is futile: it produces no true knowledge, only the pride of the learned. While acknowledging the pursuit of knowledge by the Vedantic scholar, he pronounces this an impossible project for the ordinary man in the present age. He is curious about the forms of logical argument in European philosophy and often inquires from his learned disciples about this (including staging the absurd theater of European-style *vicāra* mentioned above), but his impatience soon gets the better of his curiosity.

This attitude strikes a sympathetic chord in his disciples. They are convinced of the limits of science and rational knowledge, of their failure to grasp the truth in its eternal, unchanging essence. Trained in the new schools of colonialism—some, like Narendranath, are in fact highly proficient in several branches of modern European knowledge—they feel oppressed in the prisonhouse of Reason and clamor to escape into the vicāra-less freedom of bhakti.

Mahendranath closes the first volume of the *Kathāmṛta* with a long section on the disputations between Dr. Mahendralal Sarkar (1833–1904) and Ramakrishna's disciples. Dr. Sarkar, the most eminent practitioner in his time of Western medicine in Calcutta and founder of the first Indian institution for modern scientific research, was the only one of those close to Ramakrishna to openly voice his skepticism about Ramakrishna's preaching. (The italicized words in the following extract are in English in the original.)

DOCTOR: Just because some fisherman [the reference is to Mathuranath Biswas, Ramakrishna's erstwhile patron, who came from a caste of fishermen] accepted all that you say, do you think I will accept you too? Yes, I respect you, I have *regard* for you, as I have *regard* for human beings. . . .

MASTER: Have I asked you to accept?

GIRISH: Has he asked you to accept?

DOCTOR (to the Master): So, you say it's all God's will?

MASTER: That is all that I say. . . .

DOCTOR: If it is God's will, why do you talk so much? Why do you try to preach so much?

MASTER: I talk because He makes me talk. I am the instrument, He is the player.

DOCTOR: Then say you are only an instrument, or else keep quiet. Let God speak.

GIRISH: Think what you will. He makes me do what I do. Can one take *a single step against the Almighty Will*?

DOCTOR: He has given me *free will*. I can contemplate God if I so decide. I can also forget him if I feel like it. . . . I don't say it is completely *free*. It is like a cow tied to a leash. It is free as far as the rope will let it go.

MASTER: Jadu Mallik gave me the same analogy. Is it an English analogy? . . .

GIRISH: How do you know it is *free will*?

DOCTOR: Not by *reason. I feel it.*

GIRISH: *Then I and others feel it to be the reverse.*

. . . The Master and another devotee ask the doctor, "Will you listen to some songs?"

DOCTOR: But then you will start to jump about. You have to keep your bhāva under control. . . .

The doctor tells Mahendranath, "*It is dangerous to him.*" . . .

MASTER: . . . If someone eats the flesh of pigs and still retains bhakti for God, he is a worthy man, and if someone eats the purest food but remains attached to the world . . .

DOCTOR: He is unworthy! But let me say this. The Buddha used to eat pork. Pork causes colic pain, for which the Buddha took opium. Do you know what nirvāṇa is? Drugged by opium, drugged senseless—that's nirvāṇa. . . . (to Girish) Do what you wish, *but do not worship him* [Ramakrishna] *as God.* Why are you spoiling this good man?

GIRISH: What else can we do? He has helped us cross the oceans of worldly living and scepticism. . . .

NARENDRA (to the doctor): We regard him as god. . . . There is a zone between the *man-world* and the *god-world*, where it is difficult to say whether a person is man or god. . . .

DOCTOR: One has to control these feelings. It is not proper to express them in public. No one understands my feelings. *My best friends* think I am devoid of compassion. . . . My son, my wife, even they think I am *hardhearted,* because my fault is that I don't express my feelings to anyone. . . . My *feelings* get *worked up* even more than yours do. *I shed tears in solitude.* . . .

NARENDRA: Think of this. You have *devoted* your *life* to the cause of *scientific discovery.* You risk your health. The knowledge of God is *the grandest of all sciences.* Why should he [Ramakrishna] not *risk* his *health* for it?

DOCTOR: All religious reformers—Jesus, Chaitanya, Buddha, Muhammad—each one in the end comes out as self-opinionated: "This I have said, this is the final truth!" What sort of attitude is that?

GIRISH: Sir, you are guilty of the same crime. When you say they are self-opinionated, you make the same error.

The DOCTOR stays silent.

NARENDRA: *We offer him worship bordering on divine worship.*

The MASTER laughs like a child. (*K*, pp. 193–205)[43]

Skeptical rationalism, which had strayed into the hostile territory of "feelings" and unquestioning devotion, has been tamed and conquered. Mahendranath can now close his book.

OF WOMAN AND GOLD

What is it that stands between the family man and his quest for God? It is a double impediment, fused into one. *Kāminī-kāñcan,* "woman and gold," "woman-gold": one stands for the other. Together they represent *māyā,* man's attachment to and greed for things particular and transient, the fickle pursuit of immediate worldly interest. Together they stand as figures of the bondage of man.

MASTER: It is woman-and-gold that binds man [*jīva*] and robs him of his freedom. It is woman that creates the need for gold. For woman one man becomes the slave of another, and so loses his freedom. Then he cannot act as he likes. . . . You can see for yourself the condition in which you live, working for others. All these learned men who have learnt English, passed so many examinations, all they do now is serve their masters who kick them with their boots everyday. The one cause of all this is woman. You marry and settle down in the marketplace; now you cannot get out of the market. You suffer humiliation, the pain of bondage. (*K,* pp. 58–59; *G,* pp. 166–67)[44]

MASTER: How can a man living in the midst of woman-and-gold realize God? It is very hard for him to lead an unattached life. First, he is the slave of his wife, second, of money, and third, of the master whom he serves. (*K,* p. 374; *G,* p. 710)

This woman who stands as a sign of man's bondage in the world is the woman of flesh and blood, woman in the immediacy of everyday life, with a fearsome sexuality that lures, ensnares, and imprisons the true self of man. It binds him to a pursuit of worldly interests that can only destroy him. The figure of this woman is typically that of the seductress.

MASTER: Just see the bewitching power of women! I mean women who are the embodiment of *avidyā,* the power of delusion. They fool men. They reduce their men into stupid useless creatures. When I see a man and woman sitting together, I say to myself, "There, they are done for!" (*Looking at M.*) Haru, such a nice boy, is possessed by a witch [*petni, pretinī* = a female malignant spirit, presumed in popular demonology to live in trees]. People ask: "Where is Haru? Where is he?" But where do you expect him to be?

They all go to the banyan and find him sitting quietly under it. He no longer has his beauty, power or joy. Ah! He is possessed by the witch that lives in the banyan!

If a woman says to her husband, "Go there," he at once stands up, ready to go. If she says, "Sit down here," immediately he sits down.

A job-seeker got tired of visiting the manager [head babu] in an office. He couldn't get the job. The manager said to him, "There is no vacancy now, but come and see me now and then." This went on for a long time, and the candidate lost all hope. One day he told his tale of woe to a friend. The friend said, "How stupid you are! Why are you wearing away the soles of your feet going to that fellow? Go to Golap. You will get the job tomorrow." "Is that so?" said the candidate. "I am going right away." Golap was the manager's mistress. The candidate called on her and said: "Mother, I am in great distress. You must help me out. I am the son of a poor brahmin. Where else shall I go for help? Mother, I have been out of work for many days. My children are about to starve to death. I can get a job if you but say the word." Golap said to him, "Child, whom should I speak to?" And she said to herself, "Ah! this poor brahmin boy! He has been suffering so much." The candidate said to her, "I am sure to get the job if you just put in a word about it to the manager." Golap said, "I shall speak to him today and settle the matter." The very next morning a man called on the candidate and said, "You are to work in the manager's office, beginning today." The manager said to his English boss: "This man is very competent. I have appointed him. He will do credit to the firm."

All are deluded by woman-and-gold. (*K*, pp. 524–25; *G*, p. 748)

MASTER: Haripada has fallen into the clutches of a woman of the Ghoshpara sect. He can't get rid of her. He says that she takes him on her lap and feeds him. She claims that she looks on him as the Baby Krishna. I have warned him a great many times. She says that she thinks of him as a child. But this maternal affection soon degenerates into something dangerous.

You see, you should keep far away from woman; then you may realize God. It is extremely harmful to have anything to do with women who have bad motives, or to eat food from their hands. They rob a man of his true being [*sattā*] . . .

You must be extremely careful about women. *Gopāla bhāva*! Pay no attention to such things. The proverb says: "Woman devours the three worlds." Many women, when they see handsome and healthy young men, lay snares for them. That's *gopāla bhāva*! (*K*, pp. 334–35; *G*, p. 603)

The female body is here a representation of the prison of worldly interests, in which the family man is trapped and led to a daily existence of subordination, anxiety, pain, and humiliation, whose only culmination is decay and destruction. The female body hides with the allurements of *māyā* its true nature, which is nothing but dirt and filth.

MASTER: What is there in the body of a woman? Blood, flesh, fat, gut, worms, urine, shit, all this. Why do you feel attracted to a body like this? (*K*, p. 426, my translation; *G*, p. 113)

The only path for survival for the householder is to reduce one's attachments in the world, to sever oneself and withdraw from the ties of worldly interest, escape into the freedom of a personal relationship of devotion to an absolute power that stands above all temporal and transient powers.

> MASTER: The "I" that makes one a worldly person and attaches one to woman-and-gold is the "wicked I." There is a separation between *jīva* and *ātman* because this "I" stands in between. . . .
> Who is this "wicked I"? The "I" which says, "Don't you know who I am? I have so much money! Who is richer than me?" If a thief steals ten rupees, he first snatches the money back, then beats up the thief, then he calls the police and has the thief arrested, sent to prison. The "wicked I" says, "What? Steal ten rupees from me? What insolence!"
> . . . if the "I" must remain, let the rascal remain as the "servant I." As long as you live, you should say, "O God, you are the master and I am your servant." Let it stay that way. (*K*, p. 62; *G*, p. 170)

The "wicked I" that works, schemes, oppresses, does violence to others in order to gain a fragmented, transitory power in the world is an "I" that also subjects a part of itself. For every act of domination, there is a corresponding subjection, within the same consciousness. The "servant I," paradoxically, becomes the figure of the free householder, who stoically reduces his subjection in the world to an inessential part of his life.

> MASTER: . . . you must practise discrimination. Woman-and-gold is impermanent. God is the only eternal substance. What does a man get with money? Food, clothes, a dwelling-place—nothing more. It does not get you God. Therefore money can never be the goal of life. This is discrimination. Do you understand?
> M.: Yes. I have just read a Sanskrit play called *Probodhacandrodaya*. There it is called discrimination among things [*vastuvicāra*].
> MASTER: Yes, discrimination among things. Consider—what is there in money, or in a beautiful body? Discriminate and you will find that even the body of a beautiful woman consists of bones, flesh, fat, and other disagreeable things. Why should men set their minds on such things and forget God? (*K*, p. 19; *G*, p. 82)

The creation of this autonomous domain of freedom in consciousness impels the family man to an everyday routine of nonattached performance of worldly activities, guided by duty (*kartavya*) and compassion (*dayā*), not by the sensual pursuit of *kāma* (desire) or the interested pursuit of *artha* (wealth).

> TRAILOKYA: Where do they have the time? They have to serve the English.
> MASTER: Give God your power of attorney. If you place your trust in a good man, does he do you harm? Give Him the responsibility and stop worrying. Do what He has asked you to do. . . .

Of course you have duties. Bring up your children, support your wife, make arrangements for her maintenance in your absence. If you don't do all this, you have no compassion. . . . He who has no compassion is no man.

SUB-JUDGE: How long is one to look after one's children?

MASTER: Until they become self-sufficient. . . .

SUB-JUDGE: What is one's duty towards one's wife?

MASTER: Give her advice on dharma, support her while you are alive. If she is chaste, you will have to provide for her after your death. (*K*, p. 123; *G*, p. 628)

M.: Is it right to make efforts to earn more money?

MASTER: It is alright in a home where there is truth. Earn more money but by proper means. The aim is not to earn, the aim is to serve god. If money can be used to serve god, then there is nothing wrong in that money. (*K*, p. 427; *G*, p. 114)

MASTER: When one has true love for God [*rāgabhakti*], there are no ties of attachment with one's wife or child or kin. There is only compassion. The world becomes a foreign land, a land where one comes to work. Just as one's home is in the village, Calcutta is only a place where one works. (*K*, pp. 64–65; *G*, p. 173)

Absolute freedom in spirit while accepting bondage in a transient world: the strategy is explained through the analogy of the servant-woman.

MASTER: I tell people that there is nothing wrong in the life of the world. But they must live in the world as a maidservant lives in her master's house. Referring to her master's house, she says, "That is our house." But her real home is perhaps in a far-away village. Pointing out her master's house to others, she says, no doubt, "This is our house," but in her heart she knows very well that it doesn't belong to her and that her own home is in a far-away village. She brings up her master's son and says, "My Hari has grown very naughty," or "My Hari doesn't like sweets." Though she repeats "My Hari" with her lips, yet she knows in her heart that Hari doesn't belong to her, that he is her master's son.

So I say to those who visit me: "Live in the world by all means. There is no harm in that. But always keep your mind on God. Know for certain that this house, family and property are not yours. They are God's. Your real home is beside God." (*K*, pp. 104–5; *G*, pp. 456–57)

In fact, with an attitude of nonattachment, the family man can turn his home into a haven for his spiritual pursuits.

MASTER: When you have to fight a war, it is best to fight it from your own fort. You have to fight a war against your senses [*indriya*] and against hunger and thirst. It is best to do all this while remaining in the world. Again, in this age, life depends on food. Suppose you have no food. Then all your thoughts of God will go haywire. . . .

Why should you leave the world? In fact, there are advantages at home. You don't have to worry about food. Live with your wife—nothing wrong in that. Whatever you need for your physical comforts, you have them at home. If you are ill, you have people to look after you. (*K*, p. 122; *G*, p. 627)

But if others in the family deliberately create obstacles in the way of one's spiritual quest, those obstacles would have to be removed.

A DEVOTEE: Suppose someone's mother says to him, "Don't go to Dakshineswar." Suppose she curses him and says, "If you do, you will drink my blood." What then?

MASTER: A mother who says that is no mother. She is the embodiment of *avidyā*. It is not wrong to disobey such a mother. She obstructs the way to God. (*K*, p. 510; *G*, p. 722)

M.: What should one do if one's wife says: "You are neglecting me. I shall commit suicide." What does one do?

MASTER (*in a grave voice*): Give up such a wife. She is an obstacle in the path to God. Let her commit suicide or anything else she likes. A woman who puts obstacles in the way of God is a woman of *avidyā*.

M. moves to one side of the room and stands, leaning against the wall, deep in thought. NARENDRA and the other devotees remain speechless for a while. (*K*, p. 215; *G*, p. 126)

This, however, is extreme. For the most part, the life of a householder can be ordered by means of a suitable *aśramadharma*.

MASTER: The renunciation of woman-and-gold is meant for the sannyasi. . . . [It] is not meant for householders like you. . . . As for you, live with woman in an unattached way, as far as possible. From time to time, go away to a quiet place and think of God. Women must not be present there. If you acquire faith and devotion in God, you can remain unattached. After the birth of one or two children, husband and wife must live like brother and sister, and constantly think of God, so that their minds do not turn to sensual pleasure, so that they do not have any more children. (*K*, p. 177; *G*, p. 866)

For a domestic life of true nonattachment, the figure of woman as temptress, with a threatening sexuality, is turned into the safe, comforting figure of the mother, erased of sexuality.

MASTER: He who has found God does not look upon woman with lust; so he is not afraid of her. He looks at women as so many aspects of the Divine Mother. He worships all women as the Mother herself. (*K*, p. 59; *G*, p. 168)

MASTER: Man forgets God if he is entangled in the world of *māyā* through woman. It is the Mother of the Universe who has assumed the form of *māyā*, the form of woman. One who knows this rightly does not feel like leading the life of *māyā* in the world. But he who realizes that all women are manifestations of the Divine Mother may lead a spiritual life in the world. Without realizing God one cannot truly know what woman is. (*K*, p. 400; *G*, p. 965)

Indeed, this true knowledge of the essence of womanhood would transcend all the distinctions between women in the immediate world and bring out that which is universally true in them. It would enable man to relate to woman without either lust and attachment or fear and disgust.

MASTER: Do I feel disgust for them? No. I appeal to the Knowledge of Brahman. He has become everything; all is Narayana. All *yoni* is *yoni* of the Mother. Then I see no distinctions between a whore and a chaste woman. (*K*, p. 374; *G*, p. 710)

With this knowledge, the family man can live up to a new ideal of masculinity.

The Master is very anxious about Bhabanath who has just got married. Bhabanath is about twenty-three or twenty-four years old.

MASTER (*to Narendra*): Give him a lot of courage.

Narendra and Bhabanath look at the Master and smile. Sri Ramakrishna says to Bhabanath, "Be a hero. Don't forget yourself when you see her weeping behind her veil. Oh, women cry so much—even when they blow their noses! (*Narendra, Bhabanath and M. laugh.*)

"Keep your mind firm on God. He who is a hero lives with woman [*ramaṇī*] but does not engage in sexual relations [*raman*]." (*K*, p. 401; *G*, pp. 965–66)

There is, in fact, another figure whom Ramakrishna often invokes to describe this state beyond sexuality—the androgynous figure of the female-in-the-male—a transcendence of sexuality achieved by the mystical (or magical) transposition of the attributes of femininity in the male.

MASTER (*to the young man*): A man can change his nature by imitating another's character. By transposing on to yourself the attributes of woman, you gradually destroy lust and the other sensual drives. You begin to behave like women. I have noticed that men who play female parts in the theater speak like women or brush their teeth while bathing—exactly like women. (*K*, p. 623; *G*, p. 176)

MASTER: How can a man conquer the senses? He should assume the attitude of a woman. I spent many days as the handmaid of God. I dressed myself in women's clothes, put on ornaments. . . . Otherwise, how could I have kept my wife with me for eight months? Both of us behaved as if we were the handmaids of the Divine Mother.

I could not call myself "*pu*" [male]. One day I was in an ecstatic mood. My wife asked me, "Who am I to you?" I said, "The Blissful Mother." (*K*, p. 335; *G*, p. 603)

THE ASSERTION OF MASCULINITY

The figure of woman often acts as a sign in discursive formations, standing for concepts or entities that have little to do with women in actuality. Each signification of this kind also implies a corresponding sign in which the figure of man is made to stand for other concepts or entities, opposed to and contrasted with the first. However, signs can be operated upon—connected to, transposed with, differentiated from other signs in a semantic field where new meanings are produced.

The figure of woman as *kāminī* and the identification of this figure with *kāñcan* (gold) produced a combination that signified a social world of everyday transactions in which the family man was held in bondage. In terms of genealogy, the specific semantic content of this idea in Ramakrishna's sayings could well be traced to a very influential lineage in popular religious beliefs in Bengal, in which the female, in her essence of *prakṛti*, the principle of motion or change, is conceived of as unleashing the forces of *pravṛtti*, or desire, to bring about degeneration and death in the male, whose essence of *puruṣa* represents the principle of stasis or rest.[45] (One must, however, be careful, first, not to attribute to this any essentialist meaning characteristic of "Hindu tradition" or "Indian tradition" or even "popular tradition," for it is only one strand in precolonial religious and philosophical thought. Second, we must bear in mind that even this idea of the male and female principles operated within a rich semantic field and was capable of producing in religious doctrines and literary traditions a wide variety of specific meanings.)

But in the particular context of the *Kathāmṛta* in relation to middle-class culture, the figure of woman-and-gold could acquire the status of a much more specific sign: the sign of the economic and political subordination of the respectable male householder in colonial Calcutta. It connoted humiliation and fear, the constant troubles and anxieties of maintaining a life of respectability and dignity, the sense of intellectual confusion and spiritual crisis in which neither the traditional prescriptions of ritual practice nor the unconcretized principles of enlightened rationality could provide adequate guidance in regulating one's daily life in a situation that, after all, was unprecedented in "tradition." The sign, therefore, was loaded with negative meanings: greed, venality, deception, immorality, aggression, violence—the qualifications of success in the worlds both of commerce and of statecraft. The signification, in other words, could work toward a moral condemnation of the wealthy and the powerful. It would also produce a searing condemnation in nationalist mythography of the British imperialist—the unscrupulous trader turned ruthless conqueror.

The figure of woman-and-gold also signified the enemy within: that part of one's own self which was susceptible to the temptations of an ever-unreliable worldly success. From this signification stemmed a strategy of survival, of the stoical defense of the autonomy of the weak encountered in the "message" of Ramakrishna. It involved, as we have seen, an essentialization of the "inner" self of the man-in-the-world and an essentialization of womanhood in the protective and nurturing figure of the mother. This inner sanctum was to be valorized as a haven of mental peace, spiritual security, and emotional comfort: woman as mother, safe, comforting, indulgent, playful, and man as child, innocent, vulnerable, ever in need of care and protection.

But we are dealing here with a middle class whose "middleness" would never let its consciousness rest in stoical passivity. The "hypermasculinity" of imperialist ideology made the figure of the weak, irresolute, effeminate babu a special target of contempt and ridicule.[46] The colonized literati reacted with rage and indignation, inflicting upon itself a fierce assault of self-ridicule and self-irony. No one was more unsparing in this than Bankimchandra.[47]

By the grace of the Almighty, an extraordinary species of animal has been found on earth in the nineteenth century: it is known as the modern Bengali. After careful investigation, zoologists have concluded that this species displays all the external features of *homo sapiens*. It has five fingers on its hands and feet; it has no tail, and its bones and cranial structure are identical with those of bimanous mammals. As yet, there is no comparable certainty about its inner nature. Some believe that in its inner nature too it resembles humans; others hold that it is only externally human, in its inner nature it is closer to beasts. . . .

Which side do we support in this controversy? We believe in the theory which asserts the bestiality of Bengalis. We have learnt this theory from writers in English newspapers. According to some of these copper-bearded savants, just as the creator took grains of beauty from all of the world's beautiful women to create Tilottama, in exactly the same way, by taking grains of bestiality from all animals, he has created the extraordinary character of the modern Bengali. Slyness from the fox, sycophancy and supplication from the dog, cowardliness from sheep, imitativeness from the ape and volubility from the ass—by a combination of these qualities he has caused the modern Bengali to shine in the firmament of society, lighting up the horizon, kindling the future hopes of India and attracting the particular affection of the sage Max Müller.[48]

And if this passage strikes one as being too indecisive in choosing between the babu and his European critics as its target of irony, then consider the following, purportedly a prediction by the sage Vaiśampāyana, the all-seeing reciter of the *Mahābhārata*:

The word "babu" will have many meanings. Those who will rule India in the Kali age and be known as Englishmen will understand by the word a common clerk or superintendent of provisions; to the poor it will mean those wealthier than themselves, to servants the master. . . . Like Viṣṇu the babu will always lie on an eternal bed. Like Viṣṇu again, he will have ten incarnations: clerk, teacher, Brahmo, broker, doctor, lawyer, judge, landlord, newspaper editor and idler. Like Viṣṇu, in every incarnation, he will destroy fearful demons. In his incarnation as clerk, he will destroy his attendant, as teacher he will destroy the student, as station master the ticketless traveller, as Brahmo the poor priest, as broker the English merchant, as doctor his patient, as lawyer his client, as judge the litigant, as landlord his tenants, as editor the innocent gentleman, as idler the fish in the pond. . . . He who has one word in his mind, which becomes ten when he speaks, hundred when he writes and thousands when he quarrels is a babu. He whose strength is one-time in his hands, ten-times in his mouth, a hundred times behind the back and absent at the time of action is a babu. He whose deity is the Englishman, preceptor the Brahmo preacher, scriptures the newspapers and pilgrimage the National Theater is a babu. He who declares himself a Christian to missionaries, a Brahmo to Keshabchandra, a Hindu to his father and an atheist to the Brahman beggar is a babu. One who drinks water at home, alcohol at his friend's, receives abuse from the prostitute and kicks from his boss is a babu. He who hates oil when he bathes, his own fingers when he eats and his mother tongue when he speaks is indeed a babu. . . .

O King, the people whose virtues I have recited to you will come to believe that by chewing *pān*, lying prone on the bed, making bilingual conversation and smoking tobacco, they will reconquer India. (*BR* 2:11–12)

The mode of self-ridicule became a major literary form of expressing the bhadralok's view of himself. And once the moral premises of the auto-critique had been stated publicly—the valorization, that is to say, of courage, achievement, control, and just power as the essence of true manliness—the critique of babu effeminacy could be legitimately voiced even by the babu's indigenous "others," that is, by the women in their families and by both men and women of the lower classes. Fiction and drama in late nineteenth-century Bengal are replete with instances of women, from "respectable" families as well as from the urban poor, showing up the pretentiousness, cowardice, and effeminacy of the educated male.

We have then, simultaneously with the enchantment of the middle class with Ramakrishna's mystical play upon the theme of the feminization of the male, an invocation of physical strength as the true history of the nation, an exhortation to educated men to live up to their responsibilities as leaders of the nation, as courageous sons of a mother humiliated by a foreign intruder. Narendranath transformed into Swami Vivekananda is the most dramatic example of this switching of signs, converting Ramakrishna's message of inner devotion into a passionate plea for moral action in the world, turning the attitude of defensive stoicism into a call for vanguardist social and, by implication, political activism. Bankim too used the inherently polysemic possibilities of the construction of social entities as gendered categories by classicizing, in an entirely "modern" way, the ideal of masculinity as standing for the virtues of self-respect, justice, ethical conduct, responsibility, and enlightened leadership and of femininity as courage, sacrifice, inspiration, and source of strength.

Ramakrishna was hardly appreciative of these exhortations of hypermasculinity in the male or of the supposed activization of the masculine-in-the-female. The *Kathāmṛta* has a reference to a meeting between Ramakrishna and Bankim. Ramakrishna had asked Bankim what he thought were the true duties of human beings. Feigning a crass materialism, Bankim replied, "To eat, sleep and have sex." Ramakrishna was scandalized. He said, "What kind of talk is this? You are a real rogue! That's all you think of day and night, and that's what comes out of your mouth" (*K*, p. 191; *G*, p. 891). More interesting is a report on Mahendranath's reading passages from Bankim's novel *Debī Caudhurāṇī* to Ramakrishna.

> M. said: "A young girl—the heroine—fell into the hands of a robber named Bhabani Pathak. Her name had been Praphulla, but the robber changed it to Devi Choudhurani. At heart Bhabani was a good man. He made Praphulla go through many spiritual disciplines; he also taught her how to perform selfless action. He robbed wicked people and with that money fed the poor and helpless. He said to Praphulla, 'I put down the wicked and protect the virtuous.'"
>
> MASTER: But that is the duty of the king!

Mahendranath then read from the novel the section on Praphulla's education, on how she read grammar, poetry, Sāṅkhya, Vedānta, logic.

MASTER: Do you know what this means? That you cannot have knowledge without learning. This writer and people like him think, "Learning first, God later. To find God you must first have knowledge of books!"

Ramakrishna was thoroughly unconvinced by the emerging middle-class ideal of the "new" woman who would fulfill her vocation as daughter, wife, or mother in respectable urban homes precisely by means of an education that had been denied to "traditional" women or to women of the lower classes.

M. continued to read: "To provide for all, one has to organize a great deal of labour. One needs a little display, an imposing appearance, a graciousness of living. Therefore Bhabani said, 'A little shopkeeping is necessary.'"

MASTER (*sharply*): Shopkeeping! One speaks as one thinks. Nothing but worldly thoughts, deceiving people—even their words become like that! If one eats radish, one belches radish. Instead of saying "shopkeeping," he could have said, "Act as subject while knowing one is not the subject." (*K*, pp. 362–66; *G*, pp. 683–86)

What is rational and realistic to Bankim becomes immoral worldliness to Ramakrishna; what is true devotion to Ramakrishna becomes hypocrisy to Bankim. Both attitudes were, however, parts of the same consciousness. They came to be reconciled in curious ways, most importantly by an ingenious and not always comfortable separation between, on one plane, the outer and the inner selves, and on another plane, the public and the private selves. The public self of the intelligentsia was its political self—rationalist, modern, expressing itself within the hegemonic discursive domain of enlightened nationalism. The private self was where it retreated from the humiliation of a failed hegemony. Dr. Mahendralal Sarkar was not untypical: the story of his encounter with Ramakrishna tells us a great deal about why, in the public postures of the Bengali intelligentsia to this day, its relationship to Ramakrishna has been both uneasy and shamefaced.

TO RETURN TO MEDIATION

There are three themes in this reading of the *Kathāmrta* that I will pursue in the rest of this book. All of them have to do with nationalism as a project of mediation.

First is the appropriation of the popular. Mahendranath's favorite description of Ramakrishna is that of the child—laughing, innocent, mischievous, playful. This innocence is not quite pre-adult, but an innocence that has passed through the anxieties and misfortunes of adulthood to return to itself. It is an innocence that contains within itself a wisdom far richer and more resilient than the worldly cunning of worldly adults.

We know this to be the preferred form in which middle-class consciousness desires to appropriate the popular. The popular becomes the repository of natural truth, naturally self-sustaining and therefore timeless. It has to be approached not by the calculating analytic of rational reasoning but by "feelings of the heart," by lyrical compassion. The popular is also the timeless truth of the national culture, uncontaminated by colonial reason. In poetry, music, drama, painting, and now in film and the commercial arts of decorative design, this is the form in which a middle-class culture, constantly seeking to "nationalize" itself, finds nourishment in the popular.

The popular is also appropriated in a sanitized form, carefully erased of all marks of vulgarity, coarseness, localism, and sectarian identity. The very timelessness of its "structure" opens itself to normalization.

The popular enters hegemonic national discourse as a gendered category. In its immediate being, it is made to carry the negative marks of concrete sexualized femininity. Immediately, therefore, what is popular is unthinking, ignorant, superstitious, scheming, quarrelsome, and also potentially dangerous and uncontrollable. But with the mediation of enlightened leadership, its true essence is made to shine forth in its natural strength and beauty: its capacity for resolute endurance and sacrifice and its ability to protect and nourish.

The second theme is that of the classicization of tradition. A nation, or so at least the nationalist believes, must have a past. If nineteenth-century Englishmen could claim, with scant regard for the particularities of geography or anthropology, a cultural ancestry in classical Greece, there was no reason why nineteenth-century Bengalis could not claim one in the Vedic age. All that was necessary was a classicization of tradition. Orientalist scholarship had already done the groundwork for this. A classicization of modern Bengali high culture—its language, literature, aesthetics, religion, philosophy—preceded the birth of political nationalism and worked alongside it well into the present century.

A mode of classicization could comfortably incorporate as particulars the diverse identities in "Indian tradition," including such overtly anti-Brahmanical movements as Buddhism, Jainism, and the various deviant popular sects. A classicization of tradition was, in any case, a prior requirement for the vertical appropriation of sanitized popular traditions.

The real difficulty was with Islam in India, which could claim, within the same classicizing mode, an alternative classical tradition. The national past had been constructed by the early generation of the Bengali intelligentsia as a "Hindu" past, regardless of the fact that the appellation itself was of recent vintage and that the revivalism chose to define itself by

a name given to it by "others." This history of the nation could accommodate Islam only as a foreign element, domesticated by shearing its own
lineages of a classical past. Popular Islam could then be incorporated in
the national culture in the doubly sanitized form of syncretism.

The middle-class culture we have spoken of here was, and still is, in its
overwhelming cultural content, "Hindu." Its ability and willingness to
extend its hegemonic boundaries to include what was distinctly Islamic
became a matter of much contention in nineteenth- and twentieth-century
Bengal, giving rise to alternative hegemonic efforts at both the classicization of the Islamic tradition and the appropriation of a sanitized popular
Islam.

The third theme concerns the structure of the hegemonic domain of
nationalism. Nationalism inserted itself into a new public sphere where it
sought to overcome the subordination of the colonized middle class. In
that sphere, nationalism insisted on eradicating all signs of colonial difference by which the colonized people had been marked as incorrigibly
inferior and therefore undeserving of the status of self-governing citizens
of a modern society. Thus, the legal-institutional forms of political authority that nationalists subscribed to were entirely in conformity with
the principles of a modern regime of power and were often modeled on
specific examples supplied by Western Europe and North America. In this
public sphere created by the political processes of the colonial state,
therefore, the nationalist criticism was not that colonial rule was imposing alien institutions of state on indigenous society but rather that it was
restricting and even violating the true principles of modern government.
Through the nineteenth century and into the twentieth, accompanied by
the spread of the institutions of capitalist production and exchange, these
legal and administrative institutions of the modern state penetrated
deeper and deeper into colonial society and touched upon the lives of
greater and greater sections of the people. In this aspect of the political
domain, therefore, the project of nationalist hegemony was, and in its
postcolonial phase, continues to be, to institute and ramify the characteristically modern forms of disciplinary power.

But there was another aspect of the new political domain in which this
hegemonic project involved an entirely contrary movement. Here, unlike
in Europe in the eighteenth and nineteenth centuries, the public sphere in
the political domain, and its literary precursors in the debating societies
and learned bodies, did not emerge out of the discursive construction of
a social world peopled by "individuals." Nor was there an "audience-
oriented subjectivity," by which the new conjugal family's intimate domain became publicly transparent and thus consistent with and amenable
to the discursive controls of the public sphere in the political domain.[49] In
Europe, even as the distinction was drawn between the spheres of the

private and the public, of "man" and "bourgeois" and later of "man" and "citizen," the two spheres were nevertheless united within a single political domain and made entirely consistent with its universalist discourse. In colonial society, the political domain was under alien control and the colonized excluded from its decisive zones by a rule of colonial difference. Here for the colonized to allow the intimate domain of the family to become amenable to the discursive regulations of the political domain inevitably meant a surrender of autonomy. The nationalist response was to constitute a new sphere of the private in a domain marked by cultural difference: the domain of the "national" was defined as one that was different from the "Western." The new subjectivity that was constructed here was premised not on a conception of universal humanity, but rather on particularity and difference: the identity of the "national" community as against other communities.[50] In this aspect of the political domain, then, the hegemonic movement of nationalism was not to promote but rather, in a quite fundamental sense, to resist the sway of the modern institutions of disciplinary power.

The contradictory implications of these two movements in the hegemonic domain of nationalism have been active right through its career and continue to affect the course of postcolonial politics. The process could be described, in Gramscian terms, as "passive revolution" and contains, I think, a demonstration of both the relevance and the insurmountable limits of a Foucauldian notion of the modern regime of disciplinary power.[51] The search for a postcolonial modernity has been tied, from its very birth, with its struggle against modernity.

I will, in the rest of this book, follow these three themes, beginning with the theme of classicization and the imagining of the nation as endowed with a past.

CHAPTER FOUR

The Nation and Its Pasts

"WE MUST HAVE A HISTORY!"

In a series of lectures delivered in Calcutta in 1988, Ranajit Guha discussed the conditions and limits of the agenda developed in the second half of the nineteenth century for "an Indian historiography of India."[1] It was an agenda for self-representation, for setting out to claim for the nation a past that was not distorted by foreign interpreters. Reviewing the development of historiography in Bengal in the nineteenth century, Guha shows how the call sent out by Bankimchandra—"We have no history! We must have a history!"—implied in effect an exhortation to launch the struggle for power, because in this mode of recalling the past, the power to represent oneself is nothing other than political power itself.[2]

Of course, Bankim's observation that "Bengalis have no history" was, strictly speaking, incorrect. In 1880, when he began to write his essays on the history of Bengal,[3] there was a fair amount of historical writing in Bengali. Even Bankim refers, in the book review in which he first sets out his agenda, to "the books in the Bengali language which are being written everyday for the instruction of schoolboys. . . ." His objection was, of course, that these books did not contain the true history of Bengal. What he meant by true history was also clear: it was the memory of the glorious deeds of one's ancestors. "There are a few godforsaken jāti in this world who are unaware of the glorious deeds of their forefathers. The foremost among them is the Bengali." And to emphasize the depth of this shame, Bankim adds, "Even the Oriyas have their history." It is hardly necessary to remind ourselves of the pretensions to cultural superiority of the English-educated intelligentsia of Bengal to realize that for Bankim's readers this would have been a stinging condemnation.

His reason for this reproach was that there was no history of Bengal written by Bengalis themselves. "In our judgment, there is not a single English book which contains the true history of Bengal." Why? Because the English had based their histories of Bengal on the testimonies of foreign Muslim chroniclers; there was no Bengali testimony reflected in those histories. Consequently, Bengalis could not accept them as their own history. "Anyone who uncritically accepts as history the testimony of these lying, Hindu-hating Musalman zealots is not a Bengali."

It is, needless to say, a primary sign of the nationalist consciousness that it will not find its own voice in histories written by foreign rulers and that it will set out to write for itself the account of its own past. What is noteworthy in Bankim's nationalist call to history writing is, first, that whereas he identifies his subject nation sometimes as "Bengali" and at other times as "Indian" (bhāratavarṣīya), in both cases he names the foreign ruler and aggressor as the Muslim.[4] Second, the historical consciousness he is seeking to invoke is in no way an "indigenous" consciousness, because the preferred discursive form of his historiography is modern European. Third, in 1880, when Bankim was making his exhortation—"Bengal must have a history, or else there is no hope for it. Who will write it? You will write it, I will write it, all of us will write it. Every Bengali will have to write it"—the numerous books that were being written in Bengali on the history of Bengal and of India, although dismissed by Bankim as "adolescent literature," were actually informed by a historiographic practice that was in no way different from his own. When compared with many other, admittedly less talented, Bengali writers of history of his time, Bankim's views on history were not exceptional.[5]

Some of these writings are contained mainly in school textbooks.[6] None of these books was written by major historians, and none claimed any great originality in historical interpretation. But for that very reason, they are good indicators of the main features of a commonly shared discursive formation within which Indian nationalist historiography made its appearance.

But before I present this material from the middle and late nineteenth century, let me begin with a text from the very early years of the century that demonstrates how a radical transformation was effected in the forms of recounting the political events of the past.

A PURANIC HISTORY

The first three books of narrative prose in Bengali commissioned by the Fort William College in Calcutta for use by young Company officials learning the local vernacular were books of history. Of these, Rājābali (1808) by Mrityunjay Vidyalankar was a history of India—the first history of India in the Bengali language that we have in print.[7] Mrityunjay (ca. 1762–1819) taught Sanskrit at Fort William College and was the author of some of the first printed books in Bengali. When he decided to set down in writing the story of "the Rajas and Badshahs and Nawabs who have occupied the throne in Delhi and Bengal," he did not need to undertake any fresh "research" into the subject; he was only writing down an account that was in circulation at the time among the Brahman literati and their landowning patrons.[8] His book was, we might say, a good example of the historical memory of elite Bengali society as exemplified in contemporary scholarship.

The book starts with a precise reckoning of the time at which it is being written.

> In course of the circular motion of time, like the hands of a clock, passing through the thirty *kalpa* such as Pitṛkalpa etc., we are now situated in the Śvetavarāha kalpa. Each kalpa consists of fourteen *manu*; accordingly, we are now in the seventh manu of Śvetavarāha kalpa called Vaivasvata. Each manu consists of 284 *yuga*; we are now passing through the one hundred and twelfth yuga of Vaivasvata manu called Kaliyuga. This yuga consists of 432,000 years. Of these, up to the present year 1726 of the Śaka era, 4,905 years have passed; 427,095 years are left. (R, pp. 3–4)

The calendrical system is also precisely noted. For the first 3,044 years of Kaliyuga, the prevailing era (*śaka*) was that of King Yudhiṣṭhira. The next 135 years comprised the era of King Vikramāditya. These two eras are now past.

> Now we are passing through the era of the King called Śālivāhana who lived on the southern banks of the river Narmadā. This śaka will last for 18,000 years after the end of the Vikramāditya era. After this there will be a king called Vijayābhinandana who will rule in the region of the Citrakūṭa mountains. His śaka will last for 10,000 years after the end of the Śālivāhana era.
>
> After this there will be a king called Parināgārjuna whose era will last until 821 years are left in the Kaliyuga, at which time will be born in the family of Gautabrāhmaṇa in the Sambhala country an *avatāra* of Kalkideva. Accordingly, of the six eras named after six kings, two are past, one is present and three are in the future. (R, p. 8)

Whatever one might say of this system of chronology, lack of certitude is not one of its faults.

Mrityunjay is equally certain about identifying the geographical space where the historical events in his narrative take place.

> Of the five elements—space [*ākāśa*], air, fire, water and earth—the earth occupies eight *ānā* [half] while the other four occupy two *ānā* [one-eighth] each. . . . Half of the earth is taken up by the seas, north of which is Jambudvipa. . . . There are seven islands on earth of which ours is called Jambudvipa. Jambudvipa is divided into nine *varṣa* of which Bhāratavarṣa is one. Bhāratavarṣa in turn is divided into nine parts [*khaṇḍa*] which are called Aindra, Kaseru, Tāmraparṇa, Gavastimata, Nāga, Saumya, Vāruṇa, Gandharva and Kumārikā. Of these, the part in which the *varṇāśrama* [caste] system exists is the Kumārikākhaṇḍa.

The other parts [of Bhāratavarṣa] are inhabited by the *antyaja* people [those outside caste]. (*R*, pp. 4–6)

Thus *Rājābali* is the history of those who ruled over the earth, in which there are seven islands, of which the one called Jambudvipa has nine parts, of which Bhāratavarṣa is one, and so forth, and so on. Where does this history begin?

In the Satyayuga, the Supreme Lord [*parameśvara*] had planted in the form of an Aśvathva tree a king called Ikṣāku to rule over the earth. The two main branches of this tree became the Sūrya and the Candra *vaṃśa*. The kings born in these two lineages have ruled the earth in the four yuga. Of these, some were able to acquire the greatest powers of dharma and thus ruled over the entire earth consisting of the seven islands. Others had lesser powers and thus ruled over only Jambudvipa or only Bhāratavarṣa or, in some cases, only the Kumārikākhaṇḍa. If a king from one lineage became the emperor [*samrāṭa*], then the king of the other lineage would become the lord of a *maṇḍala*. The accounts of these kings are recorded in the branches of knowledge [*śāstra*] called the Purāṇa and the Itihāsa. (*R*, pp. 6–7)

A few things may be clarified at this point. In Mrityunjay's scheme of history, the rulers on earth are, as it were, appointed by divine will. They enjoy that position to the extent, and as long as, they acquire and retain the powers of dharma. By attaining the highest levels of dharma, one could even become the ruler of the entire earth. In order to distinguish this variety of history writing from that we are more familiar with today, Mrityunjay's narrative can be called a Puranic history. Mrityunjay would not have quarreled with this description, not because he was aware of the distinction, but because *purāṇetihāsa* was for him the valid form of retelling the political history of Bhāratavarṣa.

The discipline of Puranic history cannot be accused of being sloppy in its counting of dynasties and kings. "In the 4,267 years since the beginning of the Kaliyuga, there have been 119 Hindus of different jāti who have become *samrāṭ* on the throne of Delhi" (*R*, p. 10). The count begins with King Yudhiṣṭhira of the *Mahābhārata*, who heads a list of twenty-eight Kṣatriya kings who ruled for a total of 1,812 years. "After this the actual reign of the Kṣatriya jāti ended." Then came fourteen kings of the Nanda dynasty, starting with "one called Mahānanda born of a Kṣatriya father and a Śūdra mother," who ruled for a total of 500 years. "The Rājput jāti started with this Nanda."

After this came the Buddhist kings: "Fifteen kings of the Nāstika faith, from Vīravāhu to Āditya, all of the Gautama lineage, ruled for four hundred years. At this time the Nāstika views enjoyed such currency that the Vaidika religion was almost eradicated."

We then have a curious list of dynasties—nine rulers of the Mayūra dynasty, sixteen of the Yogi dynasty, four of the Bairāgi dynasty, and so on. Of course, there are "the Vikramādityas, father and son, who ruled for ninety-three years." We are also told of "thirteen kings, from Dhī Sena to Dāmodara Sena, of the Vaidya jāti of Bengal who ruled for 137 years and one month"—from, let us remember, "the throne in Delhi"! The rule of the "Chohān Rājput jāti" ends with

> Prthorāy who ruled for fourteen years and seven months. . . . This is as far as the empire [sāmrājya] of the Hindu kings lasted.
>
> After this began the sāmrājya of the Musalman. From the beginning of the empire of the Yavanas to the present year 1726 of the Śaka era, fifty-one kings have ruled for 651 years three months and twenty-eight days. (R, pp. 12–13)

What is interesting about this chronology is the way in which its dynastic sequence passes ever so smoothly from the kings of the Mahābhārata to the kings of Magadha and ends with the Mughal Emperor Shah Alam II, "of the lineage of Amir Taimur," occupying the throne in Delhi at the time of Mrityunjay's writing. Myth, history, and the contemporary—all become part of the same chronological sequence; one is not distinguished from another; the passage from one to another, consequently, is entirely unproblematical.[9] There is not even an inkling in Mrityunjay's prose of any of the knotty questions about the value of Puranic accounts in constructing a "proper" historical chronology of Indian dynasties, which would so exercise Indian historians a few decades later. Although Mrityunjay wrote at the behest of his colonial masters, his historiographic allegiances are entirely precolonial.

It would therefore be of some interest to us to discover how a Brahman scholar such as Mrityunjay describes the end of "the Hindu dynasties" and the accession to the throne at Delhi of "the Yavana emperors." Curiously, the story of the defeat of Prithviraj Chauhan at the hands of Shihabuddin Muhammad Ghuri takes the form of a Puranic tale.

Prithviraj's father had two wives, one of whom was a demoness (rākṣasī) who ate human flesh. She had also introduced her husband into this evil practice. One day the rākṣasī ate the son of the other queen who, taken by fright, ran away to her brother. There she gave birth to a son who was called Prthu. On growing up, Prthu met his father. At his request, Prthu cut off his father's head and fed the flesh to twenty-one women belonging to his jāti. Later, when Prthu became king, the sons of those twenty-one women became his feudatories (sāmanta). "Because Prthu had killed his father, the story of his infamy spread far and wide. Kings who paid tribute to him stopped doing so." In other words, Prithviraj was not a ruler who enjoyed much respect among his subjects.

It was at this time that Shihabuddin Ghuri threatened to attack Prithviraj.

When the King heard of the threatening moves of the Yavanas, he called a number of scholars learned in the Vedas and said, "Oh learned men! Arrange a sacrifice which will dissipate the prowess and the threats of the Yavanas." The learned men said, "Oh King! There is such a sacrifice and we can perform it. And if the sacrificial block [yūpa] can be laid at the prescribed moment, then the Yavanas can never enter this land." The King was greatly reassured by these words and arranged for the sacrifice to be performed with much pomp. When the learned men declared that the time had come to lay the block, much efforts were made but no one could move the sacrificial block to its assigned place. Then the learned men said, "Oh King! What Īsvara desires, happens. Men cannot override his wishes, but can only act in accordance with them. So, desist in your efforts. It seems this throne will be attacked by the Yavanas."

Hearing these words, Prithviraj was greatly disheartened and "slackened his efforts at war." His armies were defeated by Shihabuddin, who arrived triumphantly at Delhi. Then Prithviraj

emerged from his quarters and engaged Śāhābuddīn in a ferocious battle. But by the grace of Īsvara, the Yavana Śāhābuddīn made a prisoner of Prthurājā. On being reminded that Prthurājā was son-in-law of King Jayacandra [Jaichand, ruler of a neighboring kingdom], had already collaborated with Muhammad Ghuri], he did not execute him but sent him as a prisoner to his own country of Ghaznin. (R, pp. 109–10)

Let us remember that in Mrityunjay's scheme of history, dynasties are founded by the grace of the divine power, and kingdoms are retained only as long as the ruler is true to dharma. The Chauhan dynasty was guilty of such heinous offenses as cannibalism and patricide. That Prithviraj had lost divine favor was already revealed at the sacrificial ceremony. His defeat and the establishment of "Yavana rule" by Muhammad Ghuri were, therefore, acts of divine will.

Half a century later, when Puranic history would be abandoned in favor of rational historiography, this account of the battle of Thanesar would undergo a complete transformation. English-educated Brahman scholars would not accept with such equanimity the dictates of a divine will.

Mrityunjay has a few more things to say about the reasons for the downfall of the Chauhan dynasty. These remarks are prefaced by the following statement: "I will now write what the Yavanas say about the capture of the throne of Delhi by the Yavana Śāhābuddīn"

(R, pp. 112–13). Mrityunjay then goes back to the earlier raids into various Indian kingdoms by Nasruddin Sabuktagin, father of Mahmud Ghaznavi.

> When Nāsruddīn came to Hindustan, there was no harmony among the kings of Hindustan. Each thought of himself as the emperor [bādśah]; none owed fealty to anyone else and none was strong enough to subjugate the others. On discovering this, the Yavanas entered Hindustan. The main reason for the fall of kingdoms and the success of the enemy is mutual disunity and the tendency of each to regard itself as supreme. When Sekandar Shah [Alexander] had become emperor in the land of the Yavanas, he had once come to Hindustan, but seeing the religiosity and learning of the Brahmans, he had declared that a land whose kings had such advisers [hākim] could never be conquered by others. Saying this, he had returned to his country and had never come back to Hindustan. Now there were no more such Brahmans and, bereft of their advice, the kings of this country lost divine grace and were all defeated by the Yavanas. (R, pp. 121–22)

Mrityunjay's accounts of the Sultanate and the Mughal periods were very likely based on the Persian histories in circulation among the literati in late eighteenth-century Bengal. It is possible that some of these texts contained comments on the disunity among Indian kings and perhaps even the statement attributed to Alexander. But the argument that it was because of the failings of the Brahmans that the kings strayed from the path of dharma and thus lost the blessings of god was undoubtedly one formulated by Mrityunjay the Brahman scholar. It was the duty of the Brahmans to guide the king along the path of dharma. They had failed in that duty and had brought about the divine wrath which ended the rule of the Hindu kings and established the rule of the Yavanas. Later, as the role of divine intervention in history becomes less credible, this story of the fall acquires in the modern writings the form of a general decay of society and polity.

But this is anticipating. Note, for purposes of comparison, Mrityunjay's account of the destruction by Mahmud Ghaznavi of the temple at Somnath. The main details of the story are the same as those which would appear in later histories, for they all come from Persian sources such as the Tārīkh-i-Firishta. But Mrityunjay mentions one "fact" about the idol at Somnath that is never to be mentioned again. "There was a very large sacred idol called Somnath which was once in Mecca. Four thousand years after the time when the Yavanas say the human race was born, this idol was brought by a king of Hindustan from Mecca to its present place" (R, p. 129). Mrityunjay's source for this information is uncertain, but it is never to be mentioned again by any Bengali historian.

Two Mughal emperors are subjects of much controversy in nationalist historiography, and Mrityunjay has written about them both. On Akbar, Mrityunjay is effusive. "Since Śrī Vikramāditya, there has never been in Hindustan an emperor with merits equal to those of Akbar Shah" (R, p. 195). Apart from having a deep sense of righteousness and performing all his duties in protecting his subjects, Akbar also had, according to Mrityunjay, an additional merit:

> Because of his knowledge of many śāstra, his spiritual views were skeptical of the doctrines of Muhammad and were closer to those of the Hindus. The kings of Iran and Turan often complained about this. . . . He did not eat beef and forbid the slaughter of cows within his fort. To this day, cow-slaughter is prohibited in his fort. (R, pp. 191, 194)

On Aurangzeb, on the other hand, Mrityunjay has this to say:

> He became very active in spreading the Muhammadī faith. And he destroyed many great temples. Many ceremonies of the Hindus such as the worship of the sun and of Gaṇeśa had been performed in the fort of the Badshah since the time of Akbar; [Aurangzeb] discontinued these practices and issued new rules invented by himself.

He then adds:

> Although he destroyed many great temples, he was favored by the divine powers at Jvālāmukhī and Lachmanbālā and made sizable grants of land for the maintenance of those temples. He later lived at Aurangabad for twelve years and, on being cursed by a Brahman, died uttering horrible cries of pain. (R, p. 221)

Where kings acquire kingdoms and hold power by divine grace, the business of arriving at a verdict on the character of rulers has to be negotiated between kings and gods. The only role that the ordinary *prajā* (subject) has in all this is in bearing the consequences of the actions of these superior entities. Of course, the prajā knows the difference between a good king and a bad one, which is why he praises a ruler such as Akbar. And when Aurangzeb dies "uttering horrible cries of pain," perhaps the prajā shudders a little at the ferocity of divine retribution, but is reassured in the end by the victory of dharma. In all this, however, the prajā never implicates himself in the business of ruling; he never puts himself in the place of the ruler. In recalling the history of kingdoms, he does not look for a history of himself.

If it was ever suggested to Mrityunjay that in the story of the deeds and fortunes of the kings of Delhi might lie the history of a nation, it is doubtful that he would have understood. His own position in relation to his narrative is fixed—it is the position of the prajā, the ordinary subject, who is most often only the sufferer and sometimes the beneficiary of acts of government. It is from that position that he tells the story of Prithviraj's misdeeds or of Akbar's righteousness. But the thought would never have occurred to him that because of the associations of "nationality," he, Mrityunjay Vidyalankar, a Brahman scholar in the employment of the East India Company in Calcutta in the early nineteenth century, might in some way become responsible for the acts of Prithviraj or Akbar. *Rājābali* is not a national history because its protagonists are gods and kings, not peoples. The bonds of "nation-ness" have not yet been imagined that would justify the identification of the historian with the consciousness of a solidarity that is supposed to act itself out in history.

THE PRESENT AS PURANIC HISTORY

It is in his telling of the recent history of Bengal that Mrityunjay's position becomes the clearest. Mrityunjay was born only a few years after the battle of Plassey. The history of those times must have been fresh in popular memory in the years of his boyhood and youth. His condemnation of the misrule of Siraj-ud-daulah is severe: "The violations of dharma multiplied when [the Nawab] abducted the wives, daughters-in-law and daughters of prominent people, or amused himself by cutting open the stomachs of pregnant women or by overturning boats full of passengers" (R, pp. 268–69).

When Siraj "attempted to destroy the clan" of Raja Rajballabh, the Raja sought the protection of the English in Calcutta. The English refused to hand him over to the nawab. "Then Nawab Siraj-ud-daulah sowed the seeds of his own destruction by plundering the *kuṭhi* of the Company Bahadur and the town of Calcutta" (R, p. 270). The English were forced temporarily to leave Calcutta. After some time,

> [the sahibs] returned to Calcutta and, accepting without a question the estimates of damages suffered in the raid by traders, shopkeepers and residents, compensated all of them. Then, after consulting through Khwaja Petrus the Armenian with leading men such as Maharaj Durlabhram, Bakshi Jafarali Khan, Jagat Seth Mahatabray and his brother Maharaj Swarupchandra, and collecting money and some soldiers, [the English], intending to defend their protégé and holding aloft the flag of dharma, marched to battle at Palasi. (R, p. 271)

What happened in the battle is common knowledge. Siraj tried to flee, but was captured.

> Then Miran Sahib, son of Jafarali Khan, without informing Maharaj Durlabhram or anyone else and ignoring the pleas of mercy from a terrified

Siraj-ud-daulah, carved up the body of the Nawab with his own hands, and putting the dismembered body on top of an elephant, displayed it around the town. Thus, by the will of god, was demonstrated the consequences of such misdeeds as . . . the treacherous murder of Nawab Sarfraz Khan and the secret executions of Alibhaskar and other Maharashtrian sardars and the raping of women by Siraj-ud-daulah. (R, p. 276)

Thus, Miran acted in accordance with the divine will and Siraj faced the consequences of his misdeeds. But what happened to Miran in the end? "Thereafter, Nawab Miran was once coming from Azimabad to Murshidabad when at Rajmahal, as a consequence of his having betrayed Nawab Siraj-ud-daulah, he was struck by lightning. Even after his death, lightning struck twice on Nawab Miran's grave." And Mir Jafar? "Nawab Jafarali Khan, on resuming his *subahdari* for two years, died of leprosy after much suffering" (R, pp. 281, 289).

It is the force of divine will that acts in history, and in the end it is dharma that is vindicated. This belief frames Mrityunjay's description of the most recent events in the history of Bengal. At the conclusion of his story, he locates himself unhesitatingly as someone seeking the protection of the Company—the same Company that, flying the flag of dharma, had gone to battle with the promise to defend those under its protection.

When, because of the evil deeds of certain emperors and kings and nawabs, from Viśārad of the Nanda dynasty to Shah Alam and from Nawab Munaim Khan to Nawab Kasemali Khan, this land of Hindustan was facing utter destruction, the Supreme Lord willed that the rule of the Company Bahadur be established. Thus ends this book called Rājataraṅga composed in the Gauḍīya language by Śrī Mṛtyuñjay Śarmā, pandit in the school established by the *baḍa sāheb* [governor-general] who is like the flower and the fruit of the tree which is the Company Bahadur. (R, pp. 294–95)

Let us remember, the Company rules by divine will in order to protect its subjects. It remains a constant implication that if that object is not fulfilled and if the subjects are oppressed, then, by divine intervention, the kingdom would pass to someone else and the truth of dharma would be vindicated once again.

MORE MYTHIC HISTORY

This was the form of historical memory before the modern European modes were implanted in the mind of the educated Bengali. In Mrityunjay, the specific form of this memory was one that was prevalent among the Brahman literati in eighteenth-century Bengal. What, then, was the form followed by Bengali Muslim writers? The court chronicles of the Afghan or the Mughal nobility are not of concern here because these were never written in Bengali. The examples of dynastic history written by Bengali Muslim writers show that notions of divine intervention, punishment for misdeeds, and the victory of righteousness are as prominent in them as they were in Mrityunjay. The following text is from 1875, a much later date than those of the Fort William College histories. But it is so prominently marked by the features of the *puthi* literature of the village poets of eastern Bengal and so completely devoid of the influence of modern historical education that we should have no difficulty in assuming that this poet from Barisal was in fact following a form that had been conventional for some time.[10] The dynastic history begins thus:

> How the name of Delhi became Hindustan
> Can be learnt from its kings, from beginning to end.

However, Hindu writers cannot tell the full story.

> The Hindus believe in the four yuga;
> They cannot grasp the full significance.
> Satya, Tretā, Dvāpar and Kali: these are the four yuga
> In which the Hindus ruled with pleasure.

That, presumably, is the story that Hindu writers are best qualified to tell. This poet then gives his list of fifty-nine Muslim kings of Delhi ending with "Shah Alam Bahadur," the last Mughal emperor. It is only a list, composed in verse, with no descriptions of events and no comments on the rulers. Then comes a miraculous event.

> Suddenly by a miracle [*daiva*], the English came to this land
> And defeated the Nawab in battle.
> The English occupied most of the kingdom:
> Since then there is the rule of Maharani Victoria.
> Putting to death Kumar Singh, the Company
> Abolished all *ijārā* and made the land *khās* of the Maharani.

It is curious that the only event of the Revolt of 1857 that is mentioned is the suppression of Kunwar Singh's rebellion. Then there is a panegyric to Queen Victoria and a list of the marvels of modern technology.

> The people are governed with full justice.
> In her reign, the prajā have no complaints.
> Cowries have been abolished; now
> People buy what they need with coins.
> People exchange news through the mail.
> The towns are now lit with gaslights.

> The steamer has vanquished the pinnace and the sailboat.
> The railway has reduced a week's journey to hours.
> In Calcutta they can find out what's happening in England
> In a matter of moments—with the help of the wire.
> If in court an injustice is done,
> Then it is corrected in another court.

But even such a well-ruled kingdom as the Maharani's cannot last forever.

> The prajā is fortunate that the Maharani rules now.
> What happens after this, I do not know.

In particular, if the British occupy Turkey, then all hell will break loose.

> If the Queen comes to rule over Rūm [Turkey],
> Then only Mecca and Medina will be left.
> There will be despair and anarchy in the land,
> And all will lose jāt and become one jāt.

And then, after a series of cataclysmic events, the day of judgment will arrive.

> The Prophet Isā [Jesus] will come down from the sky,
> And again the Musalmani faith will appear.
> From the east to the west, and from north to south,
> The world will be shattered by a terrible storm.
> This is how it has been written in the Ayat Kudria
> And explained clearly in the Hadis.
> When the sun rises in the west,
> All the doors of tauba will be closed thereafter.
> The sun will rise only a few cubits
> And will set soon after, and the night will be long.
> Each night will stretch for six or seven nights,
> And the people will rise only to sleep again. . . .
> From the year 1300 Hijri,
> And before 1400 is past, let it be known,
> Those who are still alive
> Will see many unnatural things in this world.

We might compare this with Mrityunjay's prediction: "After this there will be a king called Parināgārjuna whose era will last until 821 years are left in the Kaliyuga, at which time there will be born in the family of Gautabrāhmaṇa in the Sambhala country an avatāra of Kalkideva" (R, p. 8). There does not seem to be much difference in the mode of historical thinking.

HISTORY AS THE PLAY OF POWER

This framework changed radically as the Bengali literati was schooled in the new colonial education. Now Indians were taught the principles of European history, statecraft, and social philosophy. They were also taught the history of India as it came to be written from the standpoint of modern European scholarship. The Orientalists had, from the last years of the eighteenth century, begun to "recover" and reconstruct for modern historical consciousness the materials for an understanding of Indian history and society. The English-educated class in Bengal, from its birth in the early decades of the nineteenth century, became deeply interested in this new discipline of Indology.

But, curiously enough, the new Indian literati, while it enthusiastically embraced the modern rational principles of European historiography, did not accept the history of India as it was written by British historians. The political loyalty of the early generation of English-educated Bengalis toward the East India Company was unquestioned, and in 1857, when most of northern India was in revolt, they were especially demonstrative in their protestations of loyalty. And yet, by the next decade, they were engaged in open contestation with the colonialist interpretation of Indian history. By the 1870s, the principal elements were already in place for the writing of a nationalist history of India. It is interesting to trace the genealogy of this new history of "the nation."

In 1857–58, with the inauguration of the University of Calcutta, a set of translations was produced in Bengali, for use in schools, of histories of India and of Bengal written by British historians. By then, fifty years had passed after the publication of *Rājābali*, written in Bengali for the instruction of English officers in the history of India. The new translations were meant for the instruction of Bengali students in the history of their country as written by the colonizer.

One volume of J. C. Marshman's *History of Bengal* was translated by Iswarchandra Vidyasagar (1820–91).[11] The other volume was translated at Vidyasagar's request by Ramgati Nyayaratna (1831–94).[12] The latter contains sentences like "Sultan Suja arrived as the *gabharṇar* of Bengal" or "Murshid sent his son-in-law to Orissa as his *deputi*," betraying in its use of administrative terminology its source in an English history of Bengal. And at the point where the book ends with the Maratha raids on Bengal in the period of Alivardi Khan, Ramgati feels it necessary to indicate the miraculous transformation that was about to take place.

> At that time the influence of the Marathas was so strong that everyone thought they would become the rulers of the country. But how ineffable is

the greatness of the divine will! Those who had come to this country only as ordinary traders, those who were often on the verge of leaving this country for ever, those who had never even dreamed of becoming rulers of this country—they, the English, ousted Siraj-ud-daulah from the throne of Alivardi and have now become the virtual sovereign of all of India.[13]

Only ten years later, however, in 1869, a book of questions and answers based on the same English textbooks had the following entry:

Q: How did Clive win?
A: If the treacherous Mir Jafar had not tricked the Nawab [Siraj-ud-daulah], Clive could not have won so easily.

Or, the following question about the ethics of English officials:

Q: Was Nandakumar's execution carried out in accordance with justice?
A: His offenses did not in any way deserve the death sentence. It was at the request of the unscrupulous Hastings that Chief Justice Elijah Impey conducted this gross misdeed.[14]

A Bengali textbook of 1872 tells the story of the betrayal of Nawab Siraj-ud-daulah in much greater detail. Siraj, says Kshetranath Bandyopadhyay, was a tyrant, but, contrary to the canard spread by the English, he was not responsible for the "black hole of Calcutta." Yet it was against him that the English conspired. Siraj was suspicious of the loyalties of his general Mir Jafar and made him swear on the Koran. But Mir Jafar betrayed him at Plassey, although his other generals fought valiantly. "If this battle had continued for some time, then Clive would surely have lost. But fortune favored the English, and weakened by the betrayal of Mir Jafar, the Nawab was defeated and Clive was victorious." Kshetranath's hatred is directed particularly against Mir Jafar and Miran. "Mir Jafar was cruel, stupid, greedy and indolent. On becoming the Nawab, he sought to plunder the wealth of prominent Hindus." "Miran was stupid and cruel, a beast among men. He was such an evil character that his oppressions made people forget all the misdeeds of Siraj."[15]

Nawab Mir Kasim too was a victim of betrayal:

[Mir Kasim] scrapped the duties on all goods. Thus all traders, English or Bengali, were treated on an equal footing, and unlike before, when all except the English were discriminated against, now others began to prosper. This angered the English. They began to prepare for war. . . . Mir Kasim's army was undoubtedly the best in Bengal, and yet it never won a single battle. There was a hidden reason for this, which was the treachery of Gargin [Mir Kasim's Armenian general].[16]

Kshetranath also describes the condition of the emperor in Delhi:

The emperor at this time was in a pitiable condition. Even his capital was under the control of others. He had no throne to sit on. The table at which the English dined became his throne, from which the emperor of all of India offered to the English the *diwani* of three provinces and thirty million subjects. The Emperor of Delhi, whose pomp was once without limit and at whose power the whole of India trembled, was now reduced to a condition that was truly sad.[17]

Not only in gaining an empire, but even in administering one, the English resorted to conspiracy and force. In the period before and after Clive, says Kshetranath, "the English committed such atrocities on the people of this country that all Bengalis hated the name of the English." Because of his intrigues, Hastings "is despised by all and is condemned in history." In 1857, just as the soldiers committed atrocities, so did the English: "At the time of the suppression of the revolt, the English who are so proud of their Christian religion wreaked vengeance upon their enemies by cutting out the livers from the bodies of hanged rebels and throwing them into the fire." Even the end of the mutiny did not bring peace.

In no age do the poor and the weak have anyone to protect them. When the disorder died down at other places, a huge commotion began in Bengal. In the areas of Bengal where indigo is grown, the English planters became truculent. The cruelties they perpetrated on the poor tenants will prevent them for all time from being counted among human beings.[18]

It was in fact in the course of writing the history of British rule in India that English-educated Bengalis abandoned the criteria of divine intervention, religious value, and the norms of right conduct in judging the rise and fall of kingdoms. The recent history of Bengal demonstrated that kingdoms could be won and, what was more, held by resorting to the grossest acts of immorality. The modern historiography seemed to validate a view of political history as simply the amoral pursuit of *raison d'état*.

The popular textbook of Krishnachandra Ray portrayed the political success of the British in India as the result of a cynical pursuit of power devoid of all moral principles. On Clive's intrigues, he said, "Most people criticize Clive for these heinous acts, but according to him there is nothing wrong in committing villainy when dealing with villains." The new revenue arrangements of 1772 are described as follows:

"The land belongs to him who has force on his side." It is from this time that the Company stopped being a revenue collector and really became the ruler. If the Emperor [in Delhi] had been strong, there would have been a huge incident over this. But there was nothing left [to the Empire]. Whatever Hastings decided, happened.

The deep hatred we saw in Mrityunjay of Siraj's misrule has disappeared completely in Krishnachandra. In its place, there is a political explanation of his actions. For instance, when the English strengthened their fortifications in Calcutta, Siraj ordered the new constructions demolished. "Which ruler can allow foreigners to build forts within his territory? . . . [Siraj] could not accept any longer that this bunch of traders should suddenly arrive in his kingdom and defy his commands. Humiliated, his anger was now boiling over." Or his role in the so-called black hole incident is explained as follows:

> It must have been an inauspicious moment when Siraj-ud-daulah entered Calcutta. He knew nothing of the black hole deaths and did not order the imprisonment of the English captives. Yet, that became the source of his downfall. Intoxicated by power, he had stepped on a tiger thinking it was only a cat. In the end, it was this error of judgment which led to the loss of his kingdom, his death and the endless misery of his family. Indeed, it was the black hole deaths which created the opportunity for the rise of the English power in India.

The downfall of Siraj is not seen any more as the consequence of immoral acts. It is now the result of an error of judgment: mistaking a tiger for a cat.[19]

History was no longer the play of divine will or the fight of right against wrong; it had become merely the struggle for power. The advent of British rule was no longer a blessing of Providence. English-educated Bengalis were now speculating on the political conditions that might have made the British success impossible.

> If this country had been under the dominion of one powerful ruler, or if the different rulers had been united and friendly towards one another, then the English would never have become so powerful here and this country would have remained under the Musalman kings. Perhaps no one in this country would have ever heard of the English.

The book ends with a list of the benefits of British rule. And yet it is clearly implied that this does not establish its claims to legitimacy: "In any case, whatever be the means by which the English have come to acquire this sprawling kingdom, it must be admitted that infinite benefits have been effected by them to this country."[20] We have almost reached the threshold of nationalist history.

Kshirodchandra Raychaudhuri's book, published in 1876, had this announcement by its author in the preface: "I have written this book for those who have been misled by translations of histories written in English." The extent to which European historiography had made inroadsd into the consciousness of the Bengali literati can be judged from the following comment on relations between the European colonial powers:

> The English and the French have always been hostile towards each other. Just as the conflict between the Mughals and the Pathans is proverbial in India, so is the hostility between the English and the French in Europe. Thus it was beyond belief that in India they would not attack each other and instead drink from the same water.

The book ends with the following sentences:

> Having come to India as a mere trader, the East India Company became through the tide of events the overlord of two hundred million subjects, and the shareholders of the Company, having become millionaires and billionaires, began to institute the laws and customs of foreign peoples. In no other country of the world has such an unnatural event taken place.[21]

ELEMENTS OF A NATIONALIST HISTORY

Earlier I spoke of Mrityunjay's position with respect to the political events he was describing as that of an ordinary subject. The same could be said of the authors of the textbooks I have just mentioned. But these "subjects" were very different entities. In the seventy years that had passed, the creature known as the educated Bengali had been transmuted. Now he had grown used to referring to himself, like the educated European, as a member of "the middle class." Not only was he in the middle in terms of income, but he had also assumed, in the sphere of social authority, the role of a mediator. On the one hand, he was claiming that those who had wealth and property were unfit to wield the power they had traditionally enjoyed. On the other hand, he was taking upon himself the responsibility of speaking on behalf of those who were poor and oppressed. To be in the middle now meant to oppose the rulers and to lead the subjects. Our textbook historians, while they may have thought of themselves as ordinary subjects, had acquired a consciousness in which they were already exercising the arts of politics and statecraft.

Simultaneously, the modern European principles of social and political organization were now deeply implanted in their minds. The English-educated middle class of Bengal was by the 1870s unanimous in its belief that the old institutions and practices of society needed to be fundamentally changed. It is useful to remind ourselves of this fact, because we often tend to forget that those who are called "conservative" or "traditionalist" and who are associated with the movements of Hindu revivalism were also vigorous advocates of the reform and modernization of

Hindu society. Whatever the differences between "progressives" and "conservatives" among the new intellectuals in the nineteenth century, they were all convinced that the old society had to be reformed in order to make it adequate for coping with the modern world.

This becomes clear from reading the most commonplace writings of minor writers in the second half of the nineteenth century. A completely new criterion of political judgment employed in these writings is, for instance, the notion of "impartiality." An 1866 text by an author who is undoubtedly a "traditionalist Hindu" recommends in a chapter titled "The Treatment of Young Women" that "whether indoors or out, no young woman should at any time be left alone and unwatched." Yet, he is opposed to polygamy and the practice of dowry. In another chapter, "The Subject of Political Loyalty," this traditionalist, Tarakrishna Haldar, writes:

> In the days when this country was under the rule of the Hindu jāti, the arbitrariness of kings led to the complete domination by a particular jāti over all the others. That jāti wielded the power to send others to heaven or hell. . . . When the kingdom was in the hands of the Yavanas, they treated all Hindus as infidels. In all respects they favored subjects belonging to their own jāti and oppressed those who were Hindu. . . . The principles of government followed by the British jāti do not have any of these defects. When administering justice, they treat a priest of their own jāti as equal to someone of the lowest occupation in this country, such as a sweeper. . . . No praise is too great for the quality of impartiality of this jāti.[22]

One step further and we get the next argument in nationalist history: the reason Hindu society was corrupt and decadent was the long period of Muslim rule. The following is an extract from a lecture by a certain Bholanath Chakravarti at an Adi Brahmo Samaj meeting in 1876:

> The misfortunes and decline of this country began on the day the Yavana flag entered the territory of Bengal. The cruelty of Yavana rule turned this land to waste. Just as a storm wreaks destruction and disorder to a garden, so did the unscrupulous and tyrannical Yavana jāti destroy the happiness and good fortune of Bengal, this land of our birth. Ravaged by endless waves of oppression, the people of Bengal became disabled and timid. Their religion took distorted forms. The education of women was completely stopped. In order to protect women from the attacks of Yavanas, they were locked up inside their homes. The country was reduced to such a state that the wealth of the prosperous, the honor of the genteel and the chastity of the virtuous were in grave peril.[23]

Half of nationalist history has been already thought out here. In the beginning, the history of the nation was glorious; in wealth, power, learning, and religion, it had reached the pinnacle of civilization. This nation was sometimes called Bengali, sometimes Hindu, sometimes Arya, sometimes Indian, but the form of the history remained the same. After this came the age of decline. The cause of the decline was Muslim rule, that is to say, the subjection of the nation. We do not get the rest of nationalist history in this lecture I have just cited, because although Bholanath Chakravarti talks about the need for the regeneration of national society, he also thinks that its possibility lies entirely in the existence of British rule.

> There are limits to everything. When the oppressions of the Musalman became intolerable, the Lord of the Universe provided a means of escape. . . . The resumption of good fortune was initiated on the day the British flag was first planted on this land. Tell me, if Yavana rule had continued, what would the condition of this country have been today? It must be loudly declared that it is to bless us that īsvara has brought the English to this country. British rule has ended the atrocities of the Yavanas. . . . There can be no comparison between Yavana rule and British rule: the difference seems greater than that between darkness and light or between misery and bliss.[24]

However, even if Bholanath Chakravarti did not subscribe to it, the remainder of the argument of nationalist history was already fairly current. Take, for example, the eighteenth edition, published in 1878, of "The History of India," by Tarinicharan Chattopadhyay.[25] Tarinicharan (1833–97) was a product of colonial education, a professor at Sanskrit College, and a social reformer. His textbooks on history and geography were extremely popular and were the basis for many other lesser-known textbooks. His *History of India* was probably the most influential textbook read in Bengali schools in the second half of the nineteenth century.

In the next chapter, I will recount some of the stories from Tarinicharan's history in order to point out how the materials of Hindu-extremist political rhetoric current in postcolonial India were fashioned from the very birth of nationalist historiography.

CHAPTER FIVE

Histories and Nations

THE CONSTRUCTION OF A CLASSICAL PAST

The first sentence of *Bhāratbarṣer itihās* is striking: "India [*bhāratavarṣa*] has been ruled in turn by Hindus, Muslims and Christians. Accordingly, the history of this country [*deś*] is divided into the periods of Hindu, Muslim and Christian rule [*rājatva*]" (*BI*, p. 1).

This sentence marks the passage from the "history of kings" to the "history of this country." Never again will *Rājābali* be written; from now on, everything will be the "history of this *deś*." This history, now, is periodized according to the distinctive character of rule, and this character, in turn, is determined by the religion of the rulers. The identification here of country (deś) and realm (rājatva) is permanent and indivisible. This means that although there may be at times several kingdoms and kings, there is in truth always only one realm which is coextensive with the country and which is symbolized by the capital or the throne. The rājatva, in other words, constitutes the generic sovereignty of the country, whereas the capital or the throne represents the center of sovereign statehood. Since the country is *bhāratavarṣa*, there can be only one true sovereignty that is coextensive with it, represented by a single capital or throne as its center. Otherwise, why should the defeat of Prithviraj and the capture of Delhi by Muhammad Ghuri signal the end of a whole period of Indian history and the beginning of a new one? Or why should the battle of Plassey mark the end of Muslim rule and the beginning of Christian rule? The identification in European historiography between the notions of country or people, sovereignty, and statehood is now lodged firmly in the mind of the English-educated Bengali.

On the next page follows another example of the modernity of this historiographic practice. "All Sanskrit sources that are now available are full of legends and fabulous tales; apart from the *Rājataraṅginī* there is not a single true historical account" (*BI*, p. 2). The criteria of the "true historical account" had been, of course, set by then by European historical scholarship. That India has no true historical account was a singular discovery of European Indology. The thought had never occurred to Mrityunjay. But to Tarinicharan, it seems self-evident.

We then have a description of the inhabitants of India:

In very ancient times, there lived in India two very distinct communities [*sampradāy*] of people. Of them, one resembled us in height and other aspects of physical appearance. The descendants of this community are now called Hindu. The people of the other community were short, dark and extremely uncivilized. Their descendants are now known as Khas, Bhilla, Pulinda, Sāoṅtāl and other primitive [*jaṅglā*, "of the bush"] jāti. (*BI*, p. 2)

There were others who were the products of the mixing of sampradāy. Thus, the first three varṇa among the Hindus are said to be twice-born, but the Śūdra are not entitled to that status. "This shows that in the beginning the former were a separate *sampradāy* from the latter. The latter were subsequently included in the former community, but were given the status of the most inferior class" (*BI*, p. 4).

The notion of the gradual spread of "the Hindu religion" from the north of the country to the south is also introduced. This spread is the result of the expansion of the realm.

> The south of the country was in the beginning covered by forests and inhabited by non-Hindu and uncivilized jāti. Rāmacandra was the first to hoist the Hindu flag in that part of India. . . . To this day there are many popular tales of the ancient colonization of the south by the Hindus. (*BI*, p. 27)

The image of the hero of the *Rāmāyaṇa* holding aloft the modern symbol of national sovereignty came easily to the mind of this English-educated Bengali Brahman a hundred years ago, although the votaries of political Hinduism today would probably be embarrassed by the suggestion that Rama had subdued the inhabitants of southern India and established a colonial rule.

Since there is a lack of authentic sources, the narrative of ancient Indian history is necessarily fragmentary. Gone is the certitude of Mrityunjay's dynastic lists; Tarinicharan states quite clearly the limits to a rational reconstruction of the ancient past.

> European historians have proved by various arguments that the battle of Kurukṣetra took place before the fourteenth century B.C. For a long period after the battle of Kurukṣetra, the historical accounts of India are so uncertain, partial and contradictory that it is impossible to construct from them a narrative. (*BI*, pp. 16–17)

The narrative he does construct is not particularly remarkable, because he follows without much amendment the history of ancient India as current among British writers on the subject. The only interesting comment in these chapters of Tarinicharan's book is the one he makes on Buddhism:

> [The Buddha] became a great enemy of the Hindu religion, which is why Hindus describe him as an atheist and the destroyer of dharma. Nevertheless, the religion founded by him contains much advice of the highest spiri-

tual value. He did not admit anything that was devoid of reason [*yukti*]. No matter how ancient the customs of a jāti, if stronger reasons can be presented against the traditional views, then the opinions of at least some people are likely to change. (*BI*, p. 17)

The reasonableness of the religious views of Buddhism is not denied. On the contrary, Buddhism is presented as a rationalist critique from within "the Hindu religion." Otherwise, in accordance with the criterion of periodization, the period of the Buddhist rulers would have had to be classified as a separate period of ancient Indian history. Now it is given a place within the "Hindu period."

Although the historical sources for the ancient period are said to be fragmentary and unreliable, on one subject there seems to be no dearth of evidence: "the civilization and learning of the ancient Indians." This is the title of chapter 6 of Tarinicharan's book. The main argument is as follows:

What distinguishes the giant from the dwarf or the mighty from the frail is nothing compared to the difference between the ancient and the modern Hindu. In earlier times, foreign travellers in India marvelled at the courage, truthfulness and modesty of the people of the Arya *vaṃśa*; now they remark mainly on the absence of those qualities. In those days Hindus would set out on conquest and hoist their flags in Tatar, China and other countries; now a few soldiers from a tiny island far away are lording it over the land of India. In those days Hindus would regard all except their own jāti as *mleccha* and treat them with contempt; now those same *mleccha* shower contempt on the descendants of Aryans. Then the Hindus would sail to Sumatra and other islands, evidence of which is still available in plenty in the adjacent island of Bali. Now the thought of a sea voyage strikes terror in the heart of a Hindu, and if anyone manages to go, he is immediately ostracized from society. (*BI*, p. 32)

Ancient glory, present misery: the subject of this entire story is "us." The mighty heroes of ancient India were "our" ancestors, and the feeble inhabitants of India today are "ourselves." That ancient Indians conquered other countries or traded across the seas or treated other people "with contempt" is a matter of pride for "us." And it is "our" shame that "the descendants of Aryans" are today subordinated to others and are the objects of the latter's contempt. There is a certain scale of power among the different peoples of the world; earlier, the people of India were high on that scale, while today they are near the bottom.

Not only physical prowess but the achievements of ancient Indians in the field of learning were also universally recognized.

In ancient times, when virtually the whole world was shrouded in the darkness of ignorance, the pure light of learning shone brightly in India. The discoveries in philosophy which emanated from the keen intellects of ancient Hindus are arousing the enthusiasm of European scholars even today. (*BI*, p. 33)

Note that the opinion of European scholars in this matter is extremely important to Tarinicharan. In fact, all the examples he cites on the excellence of ancient Indian learning—in the fields of astronomy, mathematics, logic, and linguistics—were discoveries of nineteenth-century Orientalists. By bringing forward this evidence, Tarinicharan seems to be suggesting that although Europeans today treat Indians with contempt because of their degraded condition, Indians were not always like this, because even European scholars admit that the arts and sciences of ancient India were of the highest standard. This evidence from Orientalist scholarship was extremely important for the construction of the full narrative of nationalist history.

That Tarinicharan's history is nationalist is signified by something else. His story of ancient glory and subsequent decline has a moral at the end: reform society, remove all of these superstitions that are the marks of decadence, and revive the true ideals of the past. These false beliefs and practices for which Indians are today the objects of contempt did not exist in the past because even Europeans admit that in ancient times "we" were highly civilized.

Today we find Hindu women treated like slaves, enclosed like prisoners and as ignorant as beasts. But if we look a millennium and a quarter earlier, we will find that women were respected, educated and largely unconstrained. Where was child marriage then? No one married before the age of twenty-four. (*BI*, p. 33)

Ancient India became for the nationalist the classical age, while the period between the ancient and the contemporary was the dark age of medievalism. Needless to say, this pattern was heartily approved by European historiography. If the nineteenth-century Englishman could claim ancient Greece as his classical heritage, why should not the English-educated Bengali feel proud of the achievements of the so-called Vedic civilization?

NARRATIVE BREAK

The chapter "The Civilization and Learning of the Ancient Indians" closes Tarinicharan's history of ancient India. He then takes the reader outside India—to Arabia in the seventh century. Why should it be necessary, in discussing a change of historical periods in twelfth-century India, to begin the description from seventh-century Arabia? The answer to this question is, of course, obvious. But implicit in that answer is an entire ensemble of assumptions and prejudices of nineteenth-century European historiography.

> Muhammad gave to his followers the name *musalman*, that is, the faithful, and to all other humans the name *kafir* or infidel. . . . Directing his followers to take the sword in order to destroy the *kafir*, he said that God had ordained that those Muslims who die in the war against false religion will go to paradise and live in eternal pleasure in the company of doe-eyed nymphs. But if they run away from battle, they will burn in hell. The Arab jāti is by nature fearless and warlike. Now, aroused by the lust for plunder in this world and for eternal pleasure in the next, their swords became irresistible everywhere. All of Arabia came under Muhammad's control and only a few years after his death the Muslim flag was flying in every country between Kabul and Spain. Never before in history had one kingdom after another, one land after another, fallen to a conqueror with the speed at which they fell to the Muslims. It was impossible that such people, always delirious at the prospect of conquest, would not covet the riches of India. (*BI*, pp. 36–37)

The ground is being prepared here for the next episode that will result from the clash of this distinct history of the Muslims with the history of Indians. This distinct history originates in, and acquires its identity from, the life of Muhammad. In other words, the dynasty that will be founded in Delhi at the beginning of the thirteenth century and the many political changes that will take place in the subsequent five centuries are not to be described merely as the periods of Turko-Afghan or Mughal rule in India; they are integral parts of the political history of Islam.

The actors in this history are also given certain behavioral characteristics. They are warlike and believe that it is their religious duty to kill infidels. Driven by the lust for plunder and the visions of cohabiting with the nymphs of paradise, they are even prepared to die in battle. They are not merely conquerors, but "delirious at the prospect of conquest" (*digvijayonmatta*), and consequently are by their innate nature covetous of the riches of India.

It is important for us at this point to note the complex relation of this new nationalist historiography to the histories of India produced by British writers in the nineteenth century. While James Mill's *History of British India*, completed in 1817, may have been "the hegemonic textbook of Indian history" for European Indology,[1] for the first nationalist historians of India it represented precisely what they had to fight against. Mill did not share any of the enthusiasm of Orientalists such as William Jones for the philosophical and literary achievements of ancient India. His condemnation of the despotism and immorality of Indian civilization was total, and even his recognition of "the comparative superiority of Islamic civilisation" did not in any significant way affect his judgment that until the arrival of British rule, India had always been "condemned to semi-barbarism and the miseries of despotic power."[2] Nationalist history in India could be born only by challenging such an absolute and comprehensive denial of all claims to historical subjectivity.[3]

Far more directly influential for the nationalist school texts we are looking at was Elphinstone's *History of India* (1841). This standard textbook in Indian universities was the most widely read British history of India until Vincent Smith's books were published in the early twentieth century. The reason why nationalist readers found Elphinstone more palatable than Mill is not far to seek. As E. B. Cowell, who taught in Calcutta and added notes to the later editions of Elphinstone's *History*, explained in a preface in 1866, a "charm of the book is the spirit of genuine hearty sympathy with and appreciation of the native character which runs though the whole, and the absence of which is one of the main blemishes in Mr. Mill's eloquent work."[4] In this spirit of sympathy, Elphinstone wrote entire chapters in his volume called "Hindús" on "Philosophy," "Astronomy and Mathematical Science," "Medicine," "Language," "Literature," "Fine Arts," and "Commerce." He also began his volume on "Mahometans" with a chapter called "Arab Conquests A.D. 632, A.H. 11–A.D. 753, A.H. 136," whose first section was "Rise of the Mahometan Religion."

Another source often acknowledged in the Bengali textbooks is the series called *The History of India as Told by Its Own Historians*.[5] Compiled by Henry Elliot, and edited and published after his death by John Dowson between 1867 and 1877, these eight volumes comprise translated extracts from over 150 works, principally in Persian, covering a period from the ninth to the eighteenth centuries. It was a gigantic example of the privilege claimed by modern European scholarship to process the writings of a people supposedly devoid of historical consciousness and render into useful sources of history what otherwise could "scarcely claim to rank higher than Annals." The technical qualities of the scholarship of Elliot and Dowson were to be questioned in subsequent decades,[6] but with the substitution of English for Persian as the language of the state, it was through their mediation that the Persian sources of Indian history would now become available to the modern literati in Bengal.

The assumptions which regulated the selection and translation of these sources were quite explicitly stated by Elliot:[7]

In Indian Histories there is little which enables us to penetrate below the glittering surface, and observe the practical operation of a despotic Government. . . . If, however, we turn our eyes to the present Muhammadan kingdoms of India, and examine the character of the princes, . . . we may fairly draw a parallel between ancient and modern times. . . . We behold kings, even of our own creation, slunk in sloth and debauchery, and emulating the vices of a Caligula or a Commodus. . . . Had the authors whom we are compelled to consult, pourtrayed their Caesars with the fidelity of Suetonius, instead of the more congenial sycophancy of Paterculus, we should not, as now, have to extort from unwilling witnesses, testimony to the truth of these assertions. . . . The few glimpses we have, even among the short Extracts in this single volume, of Hindús slain for disputing with Muhammadans, of general prohibitions against processions, worship, and ablutions, and of other intolerant measures, of idols mutilated, of temples razed, of forcible conversions and marriages, of proscriptions and confiscations, of murders and massacres, and of the sensuality and drunkenness of the tyrants who enjoined them, show us that this picture is not overcharged, and it is much to be regretted that we are left to draw it for ourselves from out of the mass of ordinary occurrences.

The fact that even Hindu writers wrote "to flatter the vanity of an imperious Muhammadan patron" was, Elliot thought, "lamentable": "there is not one of this slavish crew who treats the history of his native country subjectively, or presents us with the thoughts, emotions and raptures which a long oppressed race might be supposed to give vent to." Elliot also drew for his readers the conclusions from his presentation of these extracts:

They will make our native subjects more sensible of the immense advantages accruing to them under the mildness and equity of our rule. . . . We should no longer hear bombastic Bábús, enjoying under our Government the highest degree of personal liberty, and many more political privileges than were ever conceded to a conquered nation, rant about patriotism, and the degradation of their present position. If they would dive into any of the volumes mentioned herein, it would take these young Brutuses and Phocions a very short time to learn, that in the days of that dark period for whose return they sigh, even the bare utterance of their ridiculous fantasies would have been attended, not with silence and contempt, but with the severer discipline of molten lead or empalement.

Ironically, when the young Brutuses and Phocions did learn Elliot's lessons on Muhammadan rule, their newly acquired consciousness of being "a long oppressed race" did not stop with a condemnation of Islamic despotism; it also turned against British rule itself.

In the second half of the nineteenth century, European Indological scholarship seemed to have agreed that the history of Hinduism was one of a classical age—for some the Vedic civilization, for others the so-called Gupta revival in the fourth to the seventh centuries—followed by a medieval decline from the eighth to the eighteenth centuries.[8] For some, this decline was itself the reason why the country fell so quickly to the Muslim invaders. In any case, the theory of medieval decline fitted in nicely with the overall judgment of nineteenth-century British historians that "Muslim rule in India" was a period of despotism, misrule, and anarchy[9]—this, needless to say, being the historical justification for colonial intervention.

For Indian nationalists in the late nineteenth century, the pattern of classical glory, medieval decline, and modern renaissance appeared as one that was not only proclaimed by the modern historiography of Europe but also approved for India by at least some sections of European scholarship. What was needed was to claim for the Indian nation the historical agency for completing the project of modernity. To make that claim, ancient India had to become the classical source of Indian modernity, while "the Muslim period" would become the night of medieval darkness. Contributing to that description would be all the prejudices of the European Enlightenment about Islam. Dominating the chapters from the twelfth century onward in the new nationalist history of India would be a stereotypical figure of "the Muslim," endowed with a "national character": fanatical, bigoted, warlike, dissolute, and cruel.

MUSLIM TYRANNY, HINDU RESISTANCE

The story that begins with the birth of Islam in Arabia does, of course, shift to India, but this happens in stages. Tarinicharan gives long descriptions of the Arab invasions of Sind and the successive raids by Mahmud Ghaznavi into different Indian kingdoms, all of which take place well before the establishment of the so-called Slave dynasty in Delhi in the early thirteenth century. These descriptions trace a common pattern that can be clarified by looking at three examples: Tarinicharan's accounts of the invasion of Sind by Muhammad Ibn Kasim, of Mahmud Ghaznavi's attack on Punjab, and of the victory of Muhammad Ghuri at Thanesar.

Muhammad Kasim began his war on Dahir, the king of Sind, in 712.

> Fortune favored him. A ball of fire thrown by his soldiers struck King Dahir's elephant which panicked and fled from the battlefield. Dahir's troops, thinking that their king had given up the battle, fell into disarray. Later it will be seen that even when Indians had every chance of victory, similar misfortunes often led to their defeat at the hands of the Muslims. (*BI*, p. 38)[10]

It must be noted that what Tarinicharan calls "fortune" (*daiva*) and "misfortune" (*durddaiva*) are not the same as the daiva that was divine intervention in Mrityunjay's narrative. Misfortune here is mere accident, a matter of chance. There is no suggestion at all of retribution for immoral conduct. It is the misfortune not of kings, but of "Indians" that despite deserving to win, they have repeatedly lost because of accidents.

> Finally, after displaying much heroism, [King Dahir] was killed at the hands of the enemy. His capital was besieged, but Dahir's wife, displaying a courage similar to her husband's, continued to defend the city. In the end, food supplies ran out. Deciding that it was preferable to die rather than submit to the enemy, she instructed the inhabitants of the city to make necessary arrangements. Everyone agreed; everywhere, pyres were lit. After the immolations [of the women], the men, completing their ablutions, went out sword in hand and were soon killed by the Muslims. (*BI*, p. 38)[11]

Similar stories of defeat in battle appear later. Two features are worth notice: one, the courage of Hindu women in resisting aggression, and the other, the death in battle of Hindu men as a ritualized form of self-sacrifice. Thus appear such narrative indexes as "everywhere, pyres were lit" and "completing their ablutions . . . killed by the Muslims." The corresponding index for Muslim soldiers is "driven by the prospect of cohabiting with doe-eyed nymphs . . . etc." The contrast is significant.

Tarinicharan tells another story about Kasim that is part of the same narrative structure.

> On completing his conquest of Sind, Kasim was preparing to drive further into India when the resourcefulness of a woman became his undoing. Among the women who were captured in war in Sind were two daughters of King Dahir. They were not only of high birth but were also outstandingly beautiful. Kasim thought they would make appropriate presents for the Khalifa and accordingly sent them to his master. The ruler of the Muslims was bewitched by the beauty of the elder daughter and began to look upon her with desire. At this, she burst into tears and said, "It is a pity that I am not worthy of receiving the affections of someone like you, because Kasim has already sullied my dharma." Hearing of this act of his servant, the Khalifa was enraged and ordered that Kasim be sown in hide and brought before him. When this order was carried out, the Khalifa showed Kasim's corpse to the princess. Eyes sparkling with delight, she said, "Kasim was entirely innocent. I had made the allegation only in order to avenge the deaths of my parents and the humiliation of their subjects." (*BI*, p. 39)[12]

To the courage of Hindu women is added another element: intelligence. And parallel to the story of self-sacrifice is created another story: vengeance on the enemy for the death of one's kin.

Let us move to the beginning of the eleventh century and the period of Mahmud of Ghazna. "Of all Muslims, it was his aggressions which first brought devastation and disarray to India, and from that time the freedom of the Hindus has diminished and faded like the phases of the moon" (*BI*, p. 41). Tarinicharan mentions some of Mahmud's qualities such as courage, foresight, strategic skill, and perseverance, but ignores the fact, discussed in Elphinstone, that Mahmud was also a great patron of arts and letters. "Although he was endowed with these qualities, he was also a great adherent, at least in public, of the Musalman religion, a bitter opponent of the worship of idols and an unyielding pursuer of wealth and fame" (*BI*, p. 42). This was another alleged trait of the Muslim character: where faith in Islam was a reason for war, it was not true faith but only an apparent adherence to religion.

Mahmud moved against King Anandapal of the Shahiya dynasty.

> "The Muslims are determined to destroy the independence of all of India and to eradicate the Hindu religion. If they conquer Lahore, they will attack other parts of the country. It is therefore a grave necessity for all to unite in suppressing the *mleccha* forces." Saying this, the King [Elphinstone writes the name as Anang Pál, as does Tarinicharan] sent emissaries to all the principal Hindu kings. His appeal did not go unheeded. The kings of Delhi, Kanauj, Ujjain, Gwalior, Kalinjar and other places joined with Anangapal. Masses of troops arrived in Punjab. Worried by this sudden increase in the strength of the opposition, Mahmud decided, for reasons of safety, to halt near Peshawar. The Hindu forces increased daily. Hindu women from far away sold their diamonds, melted down their gold ornaments and sent supplies for war. (*BI*, pp. 43–44)[13]

King Anandapal is unlikely to have had the historical foresight to anticipate that the fall of Lahore to Mahmud would lead to "the destruction of the independence of all of India." Needless to say, these are Tarinicharan's words. But by putting them on the lips of the ruler of Punjab, he turns this story into a war of the Hindu jāti: "the kings joined with Anangapal," "the Hindu forces increased daily," "Hindu women from far away sent supplies," and so forth. But then came the inevitable stroke of misfortune. "A fire-ball or a sharp arrow flung from the Musalman camp struck the elephant of the Hindu commander Anangapal. The elephant, with the king on its back, fled from the field of battle. At this, the Hindu soldiers fell into disarray" (*BI*, p. 44).

This episode too ends with a story of vengeance, but this time of another variety: "The king of Kanauj, who had collaborated with Mahmud, became an object of hatred and contempt in the community of Hindu kings. Hearing this, the ruler of Ghazni entered India for the tenth time to help his protégé. But well before his arrival, the king of Kalinjar performed the execution of the king of Kanauj" (*BI*, p. 46). Needless to say, this too was a ritual; hence, it was not just an execution, but the "performance of an execution."

On Muhammad Ghuri, Tarinicharan says that his soldiers were

> inhabitants of the hills, hardy and skilled in warfare. By comparison, the
> Hindu kings were disunited and their soldiers relatively docile and undisci-
> plined. Consequently, it was only to be expected that Muhammad would
> win easily. But that is not what happened. Virtually no Hindu ruler surren-
> dered his freedom without a mighty struggle. In particular, the Rajahpūta
> were never defeated. The rise, consolidation and collapse of Muslim rule
> have been completed, but the Rajahpūta remain free to this day. (BI, p. 53)

Not only did the Hindu kings not submit without resistance, but after the
first attack by Muhammad, they even "chased the Muslims away for
twenty *kroś* [forty miles]" (BI, p. 54). On his second attack, the treachery
of Jaichand and the unscrupulousness of Muhammad led to the defeat of
Prithviraj. This account by Tarinicharan bears no resemblance at all to
the narratives of Mrityunjay. There is also a story of revenge at the end.
A hill tribe Tarinicharan calls "Gokṣur" (Elphinstone calls them "a band
of Gakkars") had been defeated by Muhammad; one night, some of them
managed to enter his tent and kill the Sultan in revenge.

With the establishment of the Sultanate, the story of the oppression of
Hindus by intolerant rulers will be repeated a number of times. For instance, Sikandar Lodi:

> Sekendar prohibited pilgrimage and ritual bathing in the Ganga and other
> sacred rivers. He also destroyed temples at many places. A Brahman who
> had declared that "The Lord recognizes every religion if followed sincerely"
> was called before Sekendar, and when he refused to discard his tolerant
> views was executed by the cruel ruler. When a Musalman holy man criti-
> cized the ban on pilgrimage, the king was enraged and shouted, "Rascal! So
> you support the idolaters?" The holy man replied, "No, that is not what I am
> doing. All I am saying is that the oppression by rulers of their subjects is
> unjust." (BI, p. 83)[14]

Tarinicharan's barbs are the sharpest when they are directed against
Aurangzeb. "Arāñjib was deceitful, murderous and plundered the wealth
of others" (BI, p. 220). "His declaration of faith in the Musalman religion only facilitated the securing of his interests. . . . In truth, Arāñjib
would never forsake his interests for reasons of religion or justice" (BI, p.
173). On the other hand, Tarinicharan has praise for Akbar, although his
reasons are interesting.

> Akbar attempted to eradicate some irrational practices prescribed in the Mu-
> salman religion. He also tried to stop several irrational practices of the Hin-
> dus. He prohibited the ordeal by fire, the burning of widows against their
> wishes and child-marriage. He also allowed the remarriage of widows. . . .

Orthodox Muslims were strongly opposed to him because of his liberal views on religion. Many called him an atheist. (*BI*, p. 141)

Thus, it was not his impartiality in matters of religion but his use of the powers of the state to reform both the Hindu and the Muslim religions that makes Akbar worthy of praise.

The issue of the alliance of certain Hindu kings with Muslim rulers comes up again in the context of Akbar's policy. Thus, on the subject of the marriages of Rajput princesses with Mughals:

> The Rajahpūta who consented to such marriages became particular favorites of the emperor. Far from regarding such marriages as humiliating and destructive of jāti, all Rajahpūta kings, with the exception of the ruler of Udaipur, felt themselves gratified and honored by them. But the king of Udaipur broke off all ties with these Yavana-loving kings. For this reason, the lineage of Udaipur is today honored as the purest in caste among the Rajahpūta. Other kings consider it a great privilege to have social transactions with him. (*BI*, pp. 125–26)

OTHER CLAIMS TO A NATIONAL PAST

Not only was Tarinicharan's book reprinted every year, it also served as a model for many other textbooks.[15] One such is called "Questions and Answers on the History of India." Written by Saiyad Abdul Rahim of Barisal, it follows Tarinicharan very closely, but with a few significant amendments.

First, Abdul Rahim writes the story of the Aryans differently: "The Hindus are not the original inhabitants of India. They came from the west of the river Sindhu and became inhabitants of India by the force of arms."[16] Where Tarinicharan had written "the non-Aryans were included in the Arya *sampradāy*," or "the Aryans established colonies" or "planted the Hindu flag," the description is now changed to "became inhabitants of India by the force of arms."

In the remaining part of the historical narrative, Abdul Rahim does not deviate from Tarinicharan. Thus: "Between Muhammad Ghaznavi and Muhammad Ghori, the latter caused greater harm to the Hindus, because whereas Muhammad Ghaznavi only looted and plundered, Muhammad Ghori robbed the Hindus of the precious treasure of independence." Or, "The benevolent [*mahātmā*] Akbar had scrapped the *jiziya* tax; the wicked [*durātmā*] Arañjib reinstated it." Indeed, in answer to a question, there is even an explanation, echoing Tarinicharan, that "the reason for the collapse of the Mughal empire was the bigotry and oppression of Arañjib."[17]

The change comes with the very last question in the book.

TEACHER: What lesson have you drawn from your reading of the history of Musalman rule?

STUDENT: Arya! This is what I have learnt for certain by reading the history of Musalman rule. To rule a kingdom is to destroy one's life both in this world and in the next. To rule, one must give up for all time the god-given gifts of forgiveness and mercy. How lamentable it is that one must, for the sake of a kingdom, redden the earth with the blood of one's own brother in whose company one has spent so many years of one's childhood. Oh kingdom! I have learnt well from the history of Musalman rule how you turn the human heart into stone. For your sake, to kill one's parents or one's brothers and sisters, or even to sacrifice the great treasure of religion, seems a matter of little concern. Oh kingdom, how bewitching are your powers of seduction![18]

In spite of having plowed through his book, this student of Tarinicharan has clearly developed little appreciation for the charms of *raison d'état*. Where Saiyad Abdul Rahim writes in his own words, we can still hear the voice of Mrityunjay's *prajā*.

But we will not hear it for much longer. If there is no place for Islam in the classical heritage of Indian culture, then, in the new mode of historiography, it is going to be thought of as constituting an alternative and different classical tradition. Writing a biography of the Prophet in 1886, Sheikh Abdar Rahim cites, like Tarinicharan, the authority of European scholars to make his claim: "Islam has been far more beneficial to the human *jāti* than the Christian religion. Philosophy and science were first taken to the European continent from the Musalman of Asia and the Moors of Spain. . . . The Musalman of Spain were the founders of philosophy in Europe." He also refutes the false accusations against Islam by Europeans:

All the biographies of the Prophet Muhammad which hitherto have been written in the Bengali language are incomplete. Especially since they have followed English books on the subject, they are in many respects unsuitable for Musalman readers. People of other religions have falsely accused Muhammad of spreading his religion by the sword; a perusal of this book will show how little truth there is in that charge.

Further, the assessment made by Hindu authors on the history of Muslim rule in India is denied: "Although some Musalman rulers have oppressed people on grounds of religion, these were acts contrary to religion and must not lead to a charge against Islam itself."[19]

In the last decade of the nineteenth century, the journal *Mihir o sudhākar*, edited by the same Abdar Rahim, would call for, using almost the same rhetoric as Bankim's *Bangadarśan* in the previous decade, the writing of "a national history appropriate for the Musalman of Bengal." Responding to that call, Abdul Karim (1863–1943) would write the history of Muslim rule in India,[20] and Ismail Husain Siraji (1880–1931) the historical ballad *Anal prabāha*.[21] These writers were clearly imbued with the ideas of a modern English-educated middle class. They were highly conscious of their role as leaders of the people, in this case of the Muslim prajā of Bengal. They would not end their books with the lament "Oh kingdom, how bewitching are your powers of seduction!"

On the contrary, Abdul Karim chose to write his history of Muslim rule in India in the belief that a true account of the glorious achievements of the Muslims in India would produce a better appreciation of their heroism, generosity, and love of learning and create greater amity between Hindus and Muslims (*BMRI*, preface). The narrative structure he adopts is, however, exactly the same as that used by the British historians he condemns. The story of Muslim rule in India begins with the birth of Muhammad, the conversion of Arabs to the new monotheistic religion, their "abandonment of false beliefs, false customs and superstition" and their "acceptance of true religion and morality," and the new feelings among them of fraternity and unity. All this enabled the Arabs to become "a jāti of unprecedented power" (*BMRI*, p. 11).

However, beginning with the accounts of the early Arab incursions into Sind, Abdul Karim takes great care to point out that the Arab military commanders were punctilious in following the codes of honor and justice in warfare.

> [Muhammad Kasim] captured the fort and killed all men bearing arms, but spared all merchants, artisans and ordinary people. . . . Muhammad then wrote to Hejaz to ask whether the Hindus should be allowed to follow their own religion. Hejaz wrote back to say: "Now that they have accepted our suzerainty and agreed to pay taxes to the Khalifa, they must be protected by us and their life and property secured. They are hereby allowed to worship their own gods." (*BMRI*, pp. 40-41)

On the account of Mahmud Ghaznavi's destruction of the Somnath idol, Abdul Karim comments: "Modern historians think that this account is completely fictitious. . . . Since Mahmud adopted the honorific title of 'The Destroyer of Idols,' the Persian historians decided to turn Mahmud's raid of the Somnath temple into a story of his religious fervor" (*BMRI*, p. 59).

Abdul Karim is scrupulous in distinguishing between just and honorable conduct of the affairs of state, as approved by Islam, and religious bigotry, to be condemned at all times. Thus Sikandar Lodi, he says, had an extremely narrow and intolerant view of religion and was oppressive toward Hindus (*BMRI*, p. 151). In all this, his concern clearly was to repudiate the slander that it was a characteristic of Islam as a religion and of Muslims as rulers to be violent, intolerant, and oppressive toward others. This, he suggests, is a calumny spread by European historians; if one were only to listen to Muslim historians telling the story of their own past, it would promote the self-esteem of Muslims as a people and elicit the respect of others toward Islamic civilization and tradition. The structure of this historiographic response was, of course, no different from what Bankim had suggested for the nationalist past.

HISTORY AS THE SOURCE OF NATIONHOOD

Discussing the identification in Bankim's agenda of the national past with a Hindu past, Ranajit Guha has suggested that there is an inconsistency here.[22] Although Bankim urged that one must reclaim one's own history which, moreover, was a history of power (*bāhubal*), he confined the memory of that struggle for power entirely to the pre-British past. In spite of enumerating the conditions for the historical liberation of a subject nation from colonial rule, he refrained from announcing that the struggle for power be launched against British colonialism. All he tells his readers are stories of the struggle of the Hindu jāti against its Muslim rulers. "The excision of colonial rule from the history of *bahubol*, hence the exclusion of *bahubol* from the history of colonial rule, prevented the agenda for an alternative historiography from being put into effect even as it was formulated and urged with such fervour."[23]

If we read Bankim alongside the other less notable history writers of his time, we find, first, that although much less sophisticated, the other writers held more or less the same views on historiography. Second, their writings are also marked by the same inconsistency referred to by Guha. Third, to explain this inconsistency, even if we say in the case of Bankim that the real struggle for power had already been posed against the British although it could not be declared openly,[24] we cannot say the same for the other writers. Because in the 1880s, a number of Bengali writers were announcing quite openly that the struggle for an independent historiography and the struggle for independent nationhood were both to be waged against colonialism. The difficulty is that by colonial rule, they meant both British rule and Muslim rule. In both cases, the object of national freedom was the end of colonial rule; in both cases, the means was a struggle for power. There was no inconsistency in their agenda.

It is remarkable how pervasive this framework of nationalist history became in the consciousness of the English-educated Hindu middle class in Bengal in the late nineteenth century. In their literary and dramatic productions as well as in their schools and colleges, this narrative of national history went virtually unchallenged until the early decades of the twentieth century.

The idea that "Indian nationalism" is synonymous with "Hindu nationalism" is not the vestige of some premodern religious conception. It is an entirely modern, rationalist, and historicist idea. Like other modern ideologies, it allows for a central role of the state in the modernization of society and strongly defends the state's unity and sovereignty. Its appeal is not religious but political. In this sense, the framework of its reasoning is entirely secular. A little examination will show that compared to Mrityunjay's historiography, which revolved around the forces of the divine and sacred, Tarinicharan's is a wholly secular historiography.

In fact, the notion of "Hindu-ness" in this historical conception cannot be, and does not need to be, defined by any religious criteria at all. There are no specific beliefs or practices that characterize this "Hindu," and the many doctrinal and sectarian differences among Hindus are irrelevant to its concept. Indeed, even such anti-Vedic and anti-Brahmanical religions as Buddhism and Jainism count here as Hindu. Similarly, people outside the Brahmanical religion and outside caste society are also claimed as part of the Hindu jāti. But clearly excluded from this jāti are religions like Christianity and Islam.

What then is the criterion for inclusion or exclusion? It is one of historical origin. Buddhism or Jainism are Hindu because they originate in India, out of debates and critiques that are internal to Hinduism. Islam or Christianity come from outside and are therefore foreign. And "India" here is the generic entity, with fixed territorial definitions, that acts as the permanent arena for the history of the jāti.

What, we may ask, is the place of those inhabitants of India who are excluded from this nation? There are several answers suggested in this historiography. One, which assumes the centrality of the modern state in the life of the nation, is frankly majoritarian. The majority "community" is Hindu; the others are minorities. State policy must therefore reflect this preponderance, and the minorities must accept the leadership and protection of the majority. This view, which today is being propagated with such vehemence in postcolonial India by Hindu-extremist politics, actually originated more than a hundred years ago, at the same time Indian nationalism was born.

Consider the utopian history of Bhudeb Mukhopadhyay, written in 1876.[25] The army of Ahmad Shah Abdali is engaged in battle with the Maratha forces in the fields of Panipat. A messenger from the Maratha commander comes to Ahmad Shah and says that although the Muslims had always mistreated the Hindus, the Hindus were prepared to forgive. "'You may return home unhindered with all your troops. If any Musalman living in India wishes to go with you, he may do so, but he may not return within five years.'"

This is, of course, "the history of India as revealed in a dream": Ahmad Shah therefore says:

> "Go to the Maharashtrian commander and tell him that . . . I will never attack India again."
>
> Hearing this, the messenger saluted [Ahmad Shah] and said, ". . . I have been instructed to deliver another message. All Musalman nawabs, subahdars, zamindars, jagirdars, etc. of this country who choose not to accompany you may return immediately to their own estates and residences. The Maharashtrian commander has declared, 'All previous offenses of these people have been condoned.'"

There is then held a grand council of all the kings of India in which the following proposal is made:

> Although India is the true motherland only of those who belong to the Hindu jāti and although only they have been born from her womb, the Muslims are not unrelated to her any longer. She has held them at her breast and reared them. The Muslims are therefore her adopted children.
>
> Can there be no bonds of fraternity between two children of the same mother, one a natural child and the other adopted? There certainly can; the laws of every religion admit this. There has now been born a bond of brotherhood between Hindus and Muslims living in India. . . .
>
> Now all will have to unite in taking care of our Mother. But without a head, no union can function. Who among us will be our leader? By divine grace, there is no room left for debate in this matter. This throne which has been prepared for Raja Ramchandra . . . will never be destroyed. There, behold the wise Badshah Shah Alam coming forward to hand over of his own accord his crown, and with it the responsibility of ruling over his empire, to Raja Ramchandra.

Thus, the Mughal emperor hands over his throne to the Maratha ruler Ramchandra. "As soon as the assembly was dissolved and everyone rose from their seats, no one was able to see Shah Alam again. Seated on the throne of Delhi was Raja Ramchandra of the dynasty of Shivaji, on his head the crown given to him by Shah Alam."

It may be mentioned that in this imaginary council a constitution is then promulgated more or less along the lines of the German Reich, with strongly protectionist economic policies that succeed, in this anticolonial utopia, in keeping the European economic powers firmly in check.

The second answer, which also made the distinction between majority and minority "communities," is associated with what is called the politics of "secularism" in India. This view holds that in order to prevent the oppression of minorities by the majority, the state must enact legal measures to protect the rights and the separate identities of the minorities. The difficulty is that the formal institutions of the state, based on an undifferentiated concept of citizenship, cannot allow for the separate representation of minorities. Consequently, the question of who represents minorities necessarily remains problematic, and constantly threatens the tenuous identity of nation and state.

There was a third answer in this early nationalist historiography. This denied the centrality of the state in the life of the nation and instead pointed to the many institutions and practices in the everyday lives of the people through which they had evolved a way of living with their differences. The writings of Rabindranath Tagore in his post-Swadeshi phase are particularly significant in this respect. The argument here is that the true history of India lay not in the battles of kings and the rise and fall of empires but in this everyday world of popular life whose innate flexibility, untouched by conflicts in the domain of the state, allowed for the coexistence of all religious beliefs.

The principal difficulty with this view, which has many affinities with the later politics of Gandhism, is its inherent vulnerability to the overwhelming sway of the modern state. Its only defense against the historicist conception of the nation is to claim for the everyday life of the people an essential and transhistorical truth. But such a defense remains vulnerable even within the grounds laid by its own premises, as is shown rather interestingly in Rabindranath's hesitation in this matter. Reviewing Abdul Karim's history of Muslim rule in India, Rabindranath remarks on the reluctance of Hindus to aspire to an achievement of power and glory which would lead them to intervene in the lives of other people and on their inability to cope with those who do.[26] The political history of Islam and, more recently, the history of European conquests in the rest of the world show, he says, that people who have world-conquering ambitions hide under the edifice of civilized life a secret dungeon of ferocious beastliness and unbridled greed. Compared to this, it often seems preferable to lie in peace in a stagnant pool, free from the restlessness of adventure and ambition.

> But the fortifications put up by the *śāstra* have failed to protect India and conflicts with other peoples have become inevitable. We are now obliged to defend our interests against the greed of others and our lives against the violence of others. It would seem to be advisable then to feed a few pieces of flesh to the beast which lies within us and to have it stand guard outside our doors. At the very least, that would arouse the respect of people who are powerful.[27]

None of these answers, however, can admit that the Indian nation as a whole might have a claim on the historical legacy of Islam. The idea of the singularity of national history has inevitably led to a single source of Indian tradition, namely, ancient Hindu civilization. Islam here is either the history of foreign conquest or a domesticated element of everyday popular life. The classical heritage of Islam remains external to Indian history.

The curious fact is, of course, that this historicist conception of Hindu nationalism has had few qualms in claiming for itself the modern heritage of Europe. It is as rightful participants in that globalized domain of the modern state that today's contestants in postcolonial India fight each other in the name of history.

SUPPRESSED HISTORIES

There was a fourth answer, so unclear and fragmented that it is better to call it only the possibility of an answer. It raises doubts about the singularity of a history of India and also renders uncertain the question of classical origins. This history does not necessarily assume the sovereignty of a single state; it is more confederal in its political assumptions.

Surprisingly, there is a hint of this answer in Bankim's own writings.[28] "Just because the ruler is of a different jāti does not mean that a country is under subjection." Indeed, it was Bengal under the independent sultans that Bankim regarded as the birthplace of the renaissance in Bengali culture.

> History tells us that a principal consequence of subjection is that the intellectual creativity of a subject jāti is extinguished. Yet the intellect of the Bengali shone more brightly during the reign of the Pathans. . . . Never before and never after has the face of Bengal lit up more brightly than in these two hundred years. (BR, p. 332)

> How did we come upon this *renaissance*? Where did this sudden enlightenment in the intellectual life of the jāti come from?. . . How was this light extinguished? (BR, p. 339)[29]

> It was Emperor Akbar, upon whom we shower praises, who became Bengal's nemesis. He was the first to make Bengal a truly subject country. . . . The Mughal is our enemy, the Pathan our ally. (BR, p. 332)

There is a great disjuncture here between the history of India and the history of Bengal. The putative center of a generically sovereign state, coextensive with the nation, also becomes uncertainly located. Bankim notes that the Aryans appeared in Bengal at a much later date; does this weaken the claims of the Bengali upon the classical heritage of the Aryans?

Many will think that the claims of Bengal and Bengalis have now become less formidable, and that we have been slandered as a jāti of recent origin. We who flaunt our ancient origins before the modern English have now been reduced to a modern jāti.

But it is hard to see why there should be anything dishonorable in all this. We still remain descendants of the ancient Arya jāti: no matter when we may have come to Bengal, our ancestors are still the glorious Aryans. (*BR*, p. 326)

But, on the other hand, the question is raised: who of the Bengalis are Aryans? What is the origin of the Bengali jāti? Bankim looked for answers to these questions in a long essay, "The Origins of the Bengalis." The "scientific" evidence he accumulated in support of his arguments will now seem extremely dubious, and this is now one of his least remembered essays. But its conclusion was not very comfortable for the writing of a singular history of the Indian nation.

The English are one jāti, the Bengalis are many jāti. In fact, among those whom we now call Bengali can be found four kinds of Bengalis: one, Aryan; two, non-Aryan Hindu; three, Hindu of mixed Aryan and non-Aryan origin; and four, Bengali Musalman. The four live separately from one another. At the bottom of Bengali society are the Bengali non-Aryans, mixed Aryans and Bengali Muslims; the top is almost exclusively Aryan. It is for this reason that, looked from the outside, the Bengali jāti seems a pure Aryan jāti and the history of Bengal is written as the history of an Aryan jāti. (*BR*, p. 363)

Elements of this alternative history can be found not only in Bankim but in other writers as well. Rajkrishna Mukhopadhyay, whose book provided the occasion for Bankim's first comments on the history of Bengal, observed that unlike in other parts of India, Islam did not spread in Bengal by the sword.[30] Krishnachandra Ray compares the British period with that of Sultani or Nawabi rule and notes that in the latter "there was no hindrance to the employment in high office of people of this country."[31] And the process of "nationalization" of the last nawab of Bengal, which reached its culmination in Akshaykumar Maitreya's *Sirājuddaulā* (1898), has already been noted.

The question is whether these two alternative forms of "national" history—one, a history of the *bhāratavarṣīya*, assuming a classical Aryan past and centered in northern India, and the other of Bengalis of many jāti, derived from uncertain origins—contained in the divergences in their trajectories and rhythms the possibility of a different imagining of nationhood. It is difficult now to explore this possibility in positive terms, because the second alternative in the pair has been submerged in the last hundred years by the tidal wave of historical memory about Arya-Hindu-Bhāratavarṣa. But the few examples considered here show that it would be impossible, according to this line of thinking, to club Pathan and

Mughal rule together and call it the Muslim period, or to begin the story of the spread of Islam in Bengal with "Muhammad instructed his followers to take up the sword and destroy the infidels."

It might be speculated that if there were many such alternative histories for the different regions of India, then the center of Indian history would not need to remain confined to Aryavarta or, more specifically, to "the throne of Delhi." Indeed, the very centrality of Indian history would then become largely uncertain. The question would no longer be one of "national" and "regional" histories: the very relation between parts and the whole would be open for negotiation. If there is any unity in these alternative histories, it is not national but confederal.

But we do not yet have the wherewithal to write these other histories. Until such time that we accept that it is the very singularity of the idea of a national history of India which divides Indians from one another, we will not create the conditions for writing these alternative histories.

The Nation and Its Women

THE PARADOX OF THE WOMEN'S QUESTION

The "women's question" was a central issue in the most controversial debates over social reform in early and mid-nineteenth-century Bengal—the period of its so-called renaissance. Rammohan Roy's historical fame is largely built around his campaign against the practice of the immolation of widows, Vidyasagar's around his efforts to legalize widow remarriage and abolish Kulin polygamy; the Brahmo Samaj was split twice in the 1870s over questions of marriage laws and the "age of consent." What has perplexed historians is the rather sudden disappearance of such issues from the agenda of public debate toward the close of the century. From then onward, questions regarding the position of women in society do not arouse the same degree of public passion and acrimony as they did only a few decades before. The overwhelming issues now are directly political ones—concerning the politics of nationalism.

How are we to interpret this change? Ghulam Murshid states the problem in its most obvious, straightforward form.[1] If one takes seriously, that is to say, in their liberal, rationalist and egalitarian content, the mid-nineteenth-century attempts in Bengal to "modernize" the condition of women, then what follows in the period of nationalism must be regarded as a clear retrogression. Modernization began in the first half of the nineteenth century because of the penetration of Western ideas. After some limited success, there was a perceptible decline in the reform movements as popular attitudes toward them hardened. The new politics of nationalism "glorified India's past and tended to defend everything traditional"; all attempts to change customs and life-styles began to be seen as the aping of Western manners and were thereby regarded with suspicion. Consequently, nationalism fostered a distinctly conservative attitude toward social beliefs and practices. The movement toward modernization was stalled by nationalist politics.

This critique of the social implications of nationalism follows from rather simple and linear historicist assumptions. Murshid not only accepts that the early attempts at social reform were impelled by the new nationalist and progressive ideas imported from Europe, he also presumes that the necessary historical culmination of such reforms in India ought to have been, as in the West, the full articulation of liberal values in social institutions and practices. From these assumptions, a critique of nationalist ideology and practices is inevitable, the same sort of critique as that of the colonialist historians who argue that Indian nationalism was nothing but a scramble for sharing political power with the colonial rulers; its mass following only the successful activization of traditional patron-client relationships; its internal debates the squabbles of parochial factions; and its ideology a garb for xenophobia and racial exclusiveness.

Clearly, the problem of the diminished importance of the women's question in the period of nationalism deserves a different answer from the one given by Murshid. Sumit Sarkar has argued that the limitations of nationalist ideology in pushing forward a campaign for liberal and egalitarian social change cannot be seen as a retrogression from an earlier radical reformist phase.[2] Those limitations were in fact present in the earlier phase as well. The renaissance reformers, he shows, were highly selective in their acceptance of liberal ideas from Europe. Fundamental elements of social conservatism such as the maintenance of caste distinctions and patriarchal forms of authority in the family, acceptance of the sanctity of the *śāstra* (scriptures), preference for symbolic rather than substantive changes in social practices—all these were conspicuous in the reform movements of the early and mid-nineteenth century.

Following from this, we could ask: How did the reformers select what they wanted? What, in other words, was the ideological sieve through which they put the newly imported ideas from Europe? If we can reconstruct this framework of the nationalist ideology, we will be in a far better position to locate where exactly the women's question fitted in with the claims of nationalism. We will find, if I may anticipate my argument in this chapter, that nationalism did in fact provide an answer to the new social and cultural problems concerning the position of women in "modern" society, and that this answer was posited not on an identity but on a difference with the perceived forms of cultural modernity in the West. I will argue, therefore, that the relative unimportance of the women's question in the last decades of the nineteenth century is to be explained not by the fact that it had been censored out of the reform agenda or overtaken by the more pressing and emotive issues of political struggle. The reason lies in nationalism's success in situating the "women's question" in an inner domain of sovereignty, far removed from the arena of political contest with the colonial state. This inner domain of national culture was constituted in the light of the discovery of "tradition."

THE WOMEN'S QUESTION IN "TRADITION"

Apart from the characterization of the political condition of India preceding the British conquest as a state of anarchy, lawlessness, and arbitrary despotism, a central element in the ideological justification of British co-

lonial rule was the criticism of the "degenerate and barbaric" social customs of the Indian people, sanctioned, or so it was believed, by the religious tradition. Alongside the project of instituting orderly, lawful, and
rational procedures of governance, therefore, colonialism also saw itself
as performing a "civilizing mission." In identifying this tradition as "degenerate and barbaric," colonialist critics invariably repeated a long list
of atrocities perpetrated on Indian women, not so much by men or certain
classes of men, but by an entire body of scriptural canons and ritual practices that, they said, by rationalizing such atrocities within a complete
framework of religious doctrine, made them appear to perpetrators and
sufferers alike as the necessary marks of right conduct. By assuming a
position of sympathy with the unfree and oppressed womanhood of
India, the colonial mind was able to transform this figure of the Indian
woman into a sign of the inherently oppressive and unfree nature of the
entire cultural tradition of a country.

Take, for example, the following account by an early nineteenth-
century British traveler in India:

at no period of life, in no condition of society, should a woman do any thing
at her mere pleasure. Their fathers, their husbands, their sons, are verily
called her protectors; but it is such protection! Day and night must women
be held by their protectors in a state of absolute dependence. A woman, it is
affirmed, is never fit for independence, or to be trusted with liberty . . . their
deity has allotted to women a love of their bed, of their seat, and of ornaments, impure appetites, wrath, flexibility, desire of mischief and bad conduct. Though her husband be devoid of all good qualities, yet, such is the
estimate they form of her moral discrimination and sensibilities, that they
bind the wife to revere him as a god, and to submit to his corporeal chastise-
ments, whenever he chooses to inflict them, by a cane or a rope, on the back
parts. . . . A state of dependence more strict, contemptuous, and humiliating, than that which is ordained for the weaker sex among the Hindoos,
cannot easily be conceived; and to consummate the stigma, to fill up the cup
of bitter waters assigned to woman, as if she deserved to be excluded from
immortality as well as from justice, from hope as well as from enjoyment, it
is ruled that a female has no business with the texts of the Veda—that having
no knowledge of expiatory texts, and no evidence of law, sinful woman must
be foul as falsehood itself, and incompetent to bear witness. To them the
fountain of wisdom is sealed, the streams of knowledge are dried up; the
springs of individual consolation, as promised in their religion, are guarded
and barred against women in their hour of desolate sorrow and parching
anguish; and cast out, as she is, upon the wilderness of bereavement and
affliction, with her impoverished resources, her water may well be spent in
the bottle; and, left as she is, will it be a matter of wonder that, in the mo-

ment of despair, she will embrace the burning pile and its scorching flames, instead of lengthening solitude and degradation, of dark and humiliating suffering and sorrow?[3]

An effervescent sympathy for the oppressed is combined in this breathless prose with a total moral condemnation of a tradition that was seen to produce and sanctify these barbarous customs. And of course it was suttee that came to provide the most clinching example in this rhetoric of condemnation—"the first and most criminal of their customs," as William Bentinck, the governor-general who legislated its abolition, described it. Indeed, the practical implication of the criticism of Indian tradition was necessarily a project of "civilizing" the Indian people: the entire edifice of colonialist discourse was fundamentally constituted around this project.

Of course, within the discourse thus constituted, there was much debate and controversy about the specific ways in which to carry out this project. The options ranged from proselytization by Christian missionaries to legislative and administrative action by the colonial state to a gradual spread of enlightened Western knowledge. Underlying each option was the liberal colonial idea that in the end, Indians themselves must come to believe in the unworthiness of their traditional customs and embrace the new forms of civilized and rational social order.

I spoke, in chapter 2, of some of the political strategies of this civilizing mission. What must be noted here is that the so-called women's question in the agenda of Indian social reform in the early nineteenth century was not so much about the specific condition of women within a specific set of social relations as it was about the political encounter between a colonial state and the supposed "tradition" of a conquered people—a tradition that, as Lata Mani has shown in her study of the abolition of *satīdāha* (immolation of widows),[4] was itself produced by colonialist discourse. It was colonialist discourse that, by assuming the hegemony of Brahmanical religious texts and the complete submission of all Hindus to the dictates of those texts, defined the tradition that was to be criticized and reformed. Indian nationalism, in demarcating a political position opposed to colonial rule, took up the women's question as a problem already constituted for it: namely, as a problem of Indian tradition.

THE WOMEN'S QUESTION IN NATIONALISM

I described earlier the way nationalism separated the domain of culture into two spheres—the material and the spiritual. The claims of Western civilization were the most powerful in the material sphere. Science, technology, rational forms of economic organization, modern methods of statecraft—these had given the European countries the strength to subjugate the non-European people and to impose their dominance over the whole world. To overcome this domination, the colonized people had to learn those superior techniques of organizing material life and incorporate them within their own cultures. This was one aspect of the nationalist project of rationalizing and reforming the traditional culture of their people. But this could not mean the imitation of the West in every aspect of life, for then the very distinction between the West and the East would vanish—the self-identity of national culture would itself be threatened. In fact, as Indian nationalists in the late nineteenth century argued, not only was it undesirable to imitate the West in anything other than the material aspects of life, it was even unnecessary to do so, because in the spiritual domain, the East was superior to the West. What was necessary was to cultivate the material techniques of modern Western civilization while retaining and strengthening the distinctive spiritual essence of the national culture. This completed the formulation of the nationalist project, and as an ideological justification for the selective appropriation of Western modernity, it continues to hold sway to this day.

The discourse of nationalism shows that the material/spiritual distinction was condensed into an analogous, but ideologically far more powerful, dichotomy: that between the outer and the inner. The material domain, argued nationalist writers, lies outside us—a mere external that influences us, conditions us, and forces us to adjust to it. Ultimately, it is unimportant. The spiritual, which lies within, is our true self; it is that which is genuinely essential. It followed that as long as India took care to retain the spiritual distinctiveness of its culture, it could make all the compromises and adjustments necessary to adapt itself to the requirements of a modern material world without losing its true identity. This was the key that nationalism supplied for resolving the ticklish problems posed by issues of social reform in the nineteenth century.

Applying the inner/outer distinction to the matter of concrete day-to-day living separates the social space into *ghar* and *bāhir*, the home and the world. The world is the external, the domain of the material; the home represents one's inner spiritual self, one's true identity. The world is a treacherous terrain of the pursuit of material interests, where practical considerations reign supreme. It is also typically the domain of the male. The home in its essence must remain unaffected by the profane activities of the material world—and woman is its representation. And so one gets an identification of social roles by gender to correspond with the separation of the social space into ghar and bāhir.

Thus far we have not obtained anything that is different from the typical conception of gender roles in traditional patriarchy. If we now find continuities in these social attitudes in the phase of social reform in the nineteenth century, we are tempted to label this, as indeed the liberal historiography of India has done, as "conservatism," a mere defense of traditional norms. But this would be a mistake. The colonial situation, and the ideological response of nationalism to the critique of Indian tradition, introduced an entirely new substance to these terms and effected their transformation. The material/spiritual dichotomy, to which the terms *world* and *home* corresponded, had acquired, as noted before, a very special significance in the nationalist mind. The world was where the European power had challenged the non-European peoples and, by virtue of its superior material culture, had subjugated them. But, the nationalists asserted, it had failed to colonize the inner, essential, identity of the East, which lay in its distinctive, and superior, spiritual culture. Here the East was undominated, sovereign, master of its own fate. For a colonized people, the world was a distressing constraint, forced upon it by the fact of its material weakness. It was a place of oppression and daily humiliation, a place where the norms of the colonizer had perforce to be accepted. It was also the place, as nationalists were soon to argue, where the battle would be waged for national independence. The subjugated must learn the modern sciences and arts of the material world from the West in order to match their strengths and ultimately overthrow the colonizer. But in the entire phase of the national struggle, the crucial need was to protect, preserve, and strengthen the inner core of the national culture, its spiritual essence. No encroachments by the colonizer must be allowed in that inner sanctum. In the world, imitation of and adaptation to Western norms was a necessity; at home, they were tantamount to annihilation of one's very identity.

Once we match this new meaning of the home/world dichotomy with the identification of social roles by gender, we get the ideological framework within which nationalism answered the women's question. It would be a grave error to see in this, as liberals are apt to in their despair at the many marks of social conservatism in nationalist practice, a total rejection of the West. Quite the contrary: the nationalist paradigm in fact supplied an ideological principle of *selection*. It was not a dismissal of modernity but an attempt to make modernity consistent with the nationalist project.

DIFFERENCE AS A PRINCIPLE OF SELECTION

It is striking how much of the literature on women in the nineteenth century concerns the threatened Westernization of Bengali women. This theme was taken up in virtually every form of written, oral, and visual communication—from the ponderous essays of nineteenth-century moralists, to novels, farces, skits and jingles, to the paintings of the *paṭuā* (scroll painters). Social parody was the most popular and effective medium of this ideological propagation. From Iswarchandra Gupta (1812–59) and the *kabiyāl* (songsters) of the early nineteenth century to the celebrated pioneers of modern Bengali theater—Michael Madhusudan Dutt (1824–73), Dinabandhu Mitra, Jyotirindranath Tagore (1849–1925), Upendranath Das (1848–95), Amritalal Bose (1853–1929)—everyone picked up the theme. To ridicule the idea of a Bengali woman trying to imitate the ways of a *memsāheb* (and it was very much an idea, for it is hard to find historical evidence that even in the most Westernized families of Calcutta in the mid-nineteenth century there were actually any women who even remotely resembled these gross caricatures) was a sure recipe calculated to evoke raucous laughter and moral condemnation in both male and female audiences. It was, of course, a criticism of manners, of new items of clothing such as the blouse, the petticoat, and shoes (all, curiously, considered vulgar, although they clothed the body far better than the single length of sari that was customary for Bengali women, irrespective of wealth and social status, until the middle of the nineteenth century), of the use of Western cosmetics and jewelry, of the reading of novels, of needlework (considered a useless and expensive pastime), of riding in open carriages. What made the ridicule stronger was the constant suggestion that the Westernized woman was fond of useless luxury and cared little for the well-being of the home. One can hardly miss in all this a criticism—reproach mixed with envy—of the wealth and luxury of the new social elite emerging around the institutions of colonial administration and trade.

Take, for example, a character called "Mister Dhurandhar Pakrashi," whose educated wife constantly calls him a "fool" and a "rascal" (in English) and wants to become a "lady novelist" like Mary Correlli. This is how their daughter, Phulkumari, makes her entrance:

PHULKUMARI: Papa! Papa! I want to go to the races, please take me with you.

DHURANDHAR: Finished with your tennis?

PHULKUMARI: Yes, now I want to go to the races. And you have to get me a new bicycle. I won't ride the one you got me last year. And my football is torn: you have to get me another one. And Papa, please buy me a self-driving car. And also a nice pony. And please fix an electric lamp in my drawing-room; I can't see very well in the gaslight.

DHURANDHAR: Nothing else? How about asking the Banerjee Company to rebuild this house upside down, ceiling at the bottom and floor on top?

PHULKAMARI: How can that be, Papa? You can't give me an education and then expect me to have low tastes?[5]

Or take the following scene, which combines a parody of the pretensions to Westernized manners of the reformists with a comment on their utter impotence against the violence and contempt of the British. A group of enlightened men, accompanied by their educated wives, are meeting to discuss plans for "female emancipation" when they are interrupted by three English soldiers called—yes!—James, Frederick, and Peter. (Most of the scene is in English in the original.)

JAMES: What is the matter? my dear—something cheering seems to take place here?

UNNATA BABU: Cheering indeed, as ninety against twenty—a meeting for the Hindu female liberty.

JAMES: A meeting for the Hindu female liberty? A nice thing indeed amidst poverty.

FREDERICK: Who sit there, both males and females together?

PETER: These seem to be the Hindu Heroes, met to unveil their wives' veiled nose.

FREDERICK: Nose alone won't do—if eyes and head be set to full liberty, Hindu ladies are sure to be the objects of curiosity.

PETER: Curiosity, nicety, and charity too.

UNNATA BABU: This is offensive—this is offensive.

JAMES: Nothing offensive—nothing offensive.

UNNATA BABU: Go hence, ye foreigners. Why come here, ye vain intruders?

JAMES: To dance, to sing and to feast—
        With our rising cousins of the East.

He takes Unnata Babu's wife by her hand, sings and dances with her, and then kisses her.

UNNATA BABU [Catches JAMES by the hand]: Leave her, leave her. She is my wife, my married wife.

JAMES [Throws UNNATA to the ground]:
        O! thou nigger of butter and wax made,
        Dared come, my hand to shake!
        If Jupiter himself with his thunder-bolt in hand,
        Comes to fight us, we will here him withstand.
        [Takes out his sword]
        Look, look, here is my sword.
        Come, please, stain it with your blood.
        [FREDERICK and PETER also take out their swords]
        Strike him, strike the devil right and left,
        We both better strike the rest.

The English soldiers make their exit with the following words to Unnata's wife:

JAMES: , . . O! pretty poor lady! We good-bye,
Pray you—go, go forward—
Wait upon, and guard your husband,
A treacherous, bloody coward.[6]

The literature of parody and satire in the first half of the nineteenth century clearly contained much that was prompted by a straightforward defense of existing practices and outright rejection of the new. The nationalist paradigm had still not emerged in clear outline. In hindsight, this period—from Rammohan to Vidyasagar—appears as one of great social turmoil and ideological confusion among the literati. And then a new discourse, drawing from various sources, began to form in the second half of the century—the discourse of nationalism.

In 1851, for instance, a prize essay on "Hindu female education" marshalled evidence that women's education was encouraged in ancient India and that it was not only not harmful but positively beneficial for women to be educated.[7] It went into numerous practical considerations on how women from respectable families could learn to read and write without any harm to their caste or their honor. In 1870, however, a tract on the duties of wives was declaring that the old prejudices about women's education had virtually disappeared. "Now the times are such that most people believe that . . . by educating women the condition of the country will improve and that there will be happiness, welfare and civilized manners in social life."[8]

The point of the new discussions was to define the social and moral principles for locating the position of women in the "modern" world of the nation. Take, for example one of the most clearly formulated tracts on the subject: Bhudeb Mukhopadhyay's *Pāribārik prabandha* (Essays on the family), published in 1882. Bhudeb states the problem in his characteristic matter-of-fact style:

> Because of the hankering for the external glitter and ostentation of the English way of life . . . an upheaval is under way within our homes. The men learn English and become *sahibs*. The women do not learn English but nevertheless try to become *bibis*. In households which manage an income of a hundred rupees, the women no longer cook, sweep or make the bed . . . everything is done by servants and maids; [the women] only read books, sew carpets and play cards. What is the result? The house and furniture get untidy, the meals poor, the health of every member of the family is ruined; children are born weak and rickety, constantly plagued by illness—they die early.
>
> Many reform movements are being conducted today; the education of women, in particular, is constantly talked about. But we rarely hear of those great arts in which women were once trained—a training which if it had still

been in vogue would have enabled us to tide over this crisis caused by injudi-
cious imitation. I suppose we will never hear of this training again.[9]

The problem is put here in the empirical terms of a positive sociology,
a genre much favored by serious Bengali writers of Bhudeb's time. But the
sense of crisis he expresses was very much a reality. Bhudeb is voicing the
feelings of large sections of the newly emergent middle class of Bengal
when he says that the very institutions of home and family were threatened under the peculiar conditions of colonial rule. A quite unprecedented external condition had been thrust upon us; we were forced to
adjust to those conditions, for which a certain degree of imitation of alien
ways was unavoidable. But could this wave of imitation be allowed to
enter our homes? Would that not destroy our inner identity? Yet it was
clear that a mere restatement of the old norms of family life would not
suffice; they were breaking down because of the inexorable force of circumstance. New norms were needed, which would be more appropriate
to the external conditions of the modern world and yet not a mere imitation of the West. What were the principles by which these new norms
could be constructed?

Bhudeb supplies the characteristic nationalist answer. In an essay
entitled "Modesty," he talks of the natural and social principles that
provide the basis for the feminine virtues.[10] Modesty, or decorum in manner and conduct, he says, is a specifically human trait; it does not exist
in animal nature. It is human aversion to the purely animal traits that
gives rise to virtues such as modesty. In this aspect, human beings seek to
cultivate in themselves, and in their civilization, spiritual or godlike qualities wholly opposed to the forms of behavior which prevail in animal nature. Further, within the human species, women cultivate and cherish these godlike qualities far more than men. Protected to a certain
extent from the purely material pursuits of securing a livelihood in the
external world, women express in their appearance and behavior the
spiritual qualities that are characteristic of civilized and refined human
society.

The relevant dichotomies and analogies are all here. The material/spir-
itual dichotomy corresponds to animal/godlike qualities, which in turn
corresponds to masculine/feminine virtues. Bhudeb then invests this ideological form with its specifically nationalist content:

In a society where men and women meet together, converse together at all
times, eat and drink together, travel together, the manners of women are
likely to be somewhat coarse, devoid of spiritual qualities and relatively
prominent in animal traits. For this reason, I do not think the customs of
such a society are free from all defect. Some argue that because of such close
association with women, the characters of men acquire certain tender and
spiritual qualities. Let me concede the point. But can the loss caused by

coarseness and degeneration in the female character be compensated by the acquisition of a certain degree of tenderness in the male?

The point is then hammered home:

> Those who laid down our religious codes discovered the inner spiritual quality which resides within even the most animal pursuits which humans must perform, and thus removed the animal qualities from those actions. This has not happened in Europe. Religion there is completely divorced from [material] life. Europeans do not feel inclined to regulate all aspects of their life by the norms of religion; they condemn it as clericalism. . . . In the Arya system there is a preponderance of spiritualism, in the European system a preponderance of material pleasure. In the Arya system, the wife is a goddess. In the European system, she is a partner and companion.[11]

The new norm for organizing family life and determining the right conduct for women in the conditions of the modern world could now be deduced with ease. Adjustments would have to be made in the external world of material activity, and men would bear the brunt of this task. To the extent that the family was itself entangled in wider social relations, it too could not be insulated from the influence of changes in the outside world. Consequently, the organization and ways of life at home would also have to be changed. But the crucial requirement was to retain the inner spirituality of indigenous social life. The home was the principal site for expressing the spiritual quality of the national culture, and women must take the main responsibility for protecting and nurturing this quality. No matter what the changes in the external conditions of life for women, they must not lose their essentially spiritual (that is, feminine) virtues; they must not, in other words, become essentially Westernized. It followed, as a simple criterion for judging the desirability of reform, that the essential distinction between the social roles of men and women in terms of material and spiritual virtues must at all times be maintained. There would have to be a marked *difference* in the degree and manner of Westernization of women, as distinct from men, in the modern world of the nation.

A GENEALOGY OF THE RESOLUTION

This was the central principle by which nationalism resolved the women's question in terms of its own historical project. The details were not, of course, worked out immediately. In fact, from the middle of the nineteenth century right up to the present day, there have been many controversies about the precise application of the home/world, spiritual/material, feminine/masculine dichotomies in various matters concerning the everyday life of the "modern" woman—her dress, food, manners, education, her role in organizing life at home, her role outside the home. The concrete problems arose out of the rapidly changing situation, both external and internal, in which the new middle-class family found itself; the specific solutions were drawn from a variety of sources—a reconstructed "classical" tradition, modernized folk forms, the utilitarian logic of bureaucratic and industrial practices, the legal idea of equality in a liberal democratic state. The content of the resolution was neither predetermined nor unchanging, but its form had to be consistent with the system of dichotomies that shaped and contained the nationalist project.

The new woman defined in this way was subjected to a *new* patriarchy. In fact, the social order connecting the home and the world in which nationalists placed the new woman was contrasted not only with that of modern Western society; it was explicitly distinguished from the patriarchy of indigenous tradition, the same tradition that had been put on the dock by colonial interrogators. Sure enough, nationalism adopted several elements from tradition as marks of its native cultural identity, but this was now a "classicized" tradition—reformed, reconstructed, fortified against charges of barbarism and irrationality.

The new patriarchy was also sharply distinguished from the immediate social and cultural condition in which the majority of the people lived, for the "new" woman was quite the reverse of the "common" woman, who was coarse, vulgar, loud, quarrelsome, devoid of superior moral sense, sexually promiscuous, subjected to brutal physical oppression by males. Alongside the parody of the Westernized woman, this other construct is repeatedly emphasized in the literature of the nineteenth century through a host of lower-class female characters who make their appearance in the social milieu of the new middle class—maidservants, washer women, barbers, peddlers, procuresses, prostitutes. It was precisely this degenerate condition of women that nationalism claimed it would reform, and it was through these contrasts that the new woman of nationalist ideology was accorded a status of cultural superiority to the Westernized women of the wealthy parvenu families spawned by the colonial connection as well as to common women of the lower classes. Attainment by her own efforts of a superior national culture was the mark of woman's newly acquired freedom. This was the central ideological strength of the nationalist resolution of the women's question.

We can follow the form of this resolution in several specific aspects in which the life and condition of middle-class women have changed over the last one hundred years or so. Take the case of female education, that contentious subject that engaged so much of the attention of social reformers in the nineteenth century.[12] Some of the early opposition to the opening of schools for women was backed by an appeal to tradition, which supposedly prohibited women from being introduced to bookish learning, but this argument hardly gained much support. The real threat was seen to lie in the fact that the early schools, and arrangements for teaching women at home, were organized by Christian missionaries; there was thus the fear of both proselytization and the exposure of women to harmful Western influences.[13] The threat was removed when in the 1850s Indians themselves began to open schools for girls. The spread of formal education among middle-class women in Bengal in the second half of the nineteenth century was remarkable. From 95 girls' schools with a total attendance of 2,500 in 1863, the figures went up to 2,238 schools in 1890 with a total of more than 80,000 students.[14] In the area of higher education, Chandramukhi Bose (1860–1944) and Kadambini Ganguli (1861–1923) were celebrated as examples of what Bengali women could achieve in formal learning: they took their bachelor of arts degrees from the University of Calcutta in 1883, before most British universities agreed to accept women on their examination rolls. Kadambini then went on to medical college and became the first professionally schooled woman doctor.

The development of an educative literature and teaching materials in the Bengali language undoubtedly made possible the quite general acceptance of formal education among middle-class women. The long debates of the nineteenth century on a proper "feminine curriculum" now seem to us somewhat quaint, but it is not difficult to identify the real point of concern. Much of the content of the modern school education was seen as important for the "new" woman, but to administer it in the English language was difficult in practical terms, irrelevant because the central place of the educated woman was still at home, and threatening because it might devalue and displace that central site where the social position of women was located. The problem was resolved through the efforts of the intelligentsia, which made it a fundamental task of the national project to create a modern language and literature suitable for a widening readership that would include newly educated women. Through textbooks, periodicals, and creative works, an important force that shaped the new literature of Bengal was the urge to make it accessible to women who could read only one language—their mother tongue.

Formal education became not only acceptable but, in fact, a requirement for the new *bhadramahilā* (respectable woman) when it was demonstrated that it was possible for a woman to acquire the cultural refinements afforded by modern education without jeopardizing her place at home, that is, without becoming a memsāheb. Indeed, the nationalist construct of the new woman derived its ideological strength from making the goal of cultural refinement through education a personal challenge for every woman, thus opening up a domain where woman was an autonomous subject. This explains to a large extent the remarkable degree of enthusiasm among middle-class women themselves to acquire and use for themselves the benefits of formal learning. They set this goal for themselves in their personal lives and as the objects of their will: to achieve it was to achieve freedom.[15] Indeed, the achievement was marked by claims of cultural superiority in several different aspects: superiority over the Western woman for whom, it was believed, education meant only the acquisition of material skills to compete with men in the outside world and hence a loss of feminine (spiritual) virtues; superiority over the preceding generation of women in their own homes who had been denied the opportunity of freedom by an oppressive and degenerate social tradition; and superiority over women of the lower classes who were culturally incapable of appreciating the virtues of freedom.

It is this particular nationalist construction of reform as a project of both emancipation and self-emancipation of women (and hence a project in which both men and women had to participate) that also explains why the early generation of educated women themselves so keenly propagated the nationalist idea of the "new woman." Recent historians of a liberal persuasion have often been somewhat embarrassed by the profuse evidence of women writers of the nineteenth century, including those at the forefront of the reform movements in middle-class homes, justifying the importance of the so-called feminine virtues. Radharani Lahiri, for instance, wrote in 1875: "Of all the subjects that women might learn, housework is the most important. . . . Whatever knowledge she may acquire, she cannot claim any reputation unless she is proficient in housework."[16] Others spoke of the need for an educated woman to develop such womanly virtues as chastity, self-sacrifice, submission, devotion, kindness, patience, and the labors of love. The ideological point of view from which such protestations of "femininity" (and hence the acceptance of a new patriarchal order) were made inevitable was given precisely by the nationalist resolution of the problem, and Kundamala Debi, writing in 1870, expressed this well when she advised other women

> If you have acquired real knowledge, then give no place in your heart to *memsāheb*-like behavior. That is not becoming in a Bengali housewife. See how an educated woman can do housework thoughtfully and systematically in a way unknown to an ignorant, uneducated woman. And see how if God had not appointed us to this place in the home, how unhappy a place the world would be.[17]

Education then was meant to inculcate in women the virtues—the typically bourgeois virtues characteristic of the new social forms of "disciplining"—of orderliness, thrift, cleanliness, and a personal sense of responsibility, the practical skills of literacy, accounting, hygiene, and the ability to run the household according to the new physical and economic conditions set by the outside world. For this, she would also need to have some idea of the world outside the home, into which she could even venture as long as it did not threaten her femininity. It is this latter criterion, now invested with a characteristically nationalist content, that made possible the displacement of the boundaries of the home from the physical confines earlier defined by the rules of purdah to a more flexible, but nonetheless culturally determinate, domain set by the *differences* between socially approved male and female conduct. Once the essential femininity of women was fixed in terms of certain culturally visible spiritual qualities, they could go to schools, travel in public conveyances, watch public entertainment programs, and in time even take up employment outside the home. But the "spiritual" signs of her femininity were now clearly marked—in her dress, her eating habits, her social demeanor, her religiosity.

The specific markers were obtained from diverse sources, and in terms of their origins, each had its specific history. The dress of the bhadramahilā, for instance, went through a whole phase of experimentation before what was known as the brāhmikā sari (a form of wearing the sari in combination with blouse, petticoat, and shoes made fashionable in Brahmo households) became accepted as standard for middle-class women.[18] Here too the necessary differences were signified in terms of national identity, social emancipation, and cultural refinement—differences, that is to say, with the memsāheb, with women of earlier generations, and with women of the lower classes. Further, in this as in other aspects of her life, the spirituality of her character had also to be stressed in contrast with the innumerable ways men had to surrender to the pressures of the material world. The need to adjust to the new conditions outside the home had forced upon men a whole series of changes in their dress, food habits, religious observances, and social relations. Each of these capitulations now had to be compensated for by an assertion of spiritual purity on the part of women. They must not eat, drink, or smoke in the same way as men; they must continue the observance of religious rituals that men were finding difficult to carry out; they must maintain the cohesiveness of family life and solidarity with the kin to which men could not now devote much attention. The new patriarchy advocated by nationalism conferred upon women the honor of a new social responsibility, and by associating the task of female emancipation with the historical goal of sovereign nationhood, bound them to a new, and yet entirely legitimate, subordination.

As with all hegemonic forms of exercising dominance, this patriarchy combined coercive authority with the subtle force of persuasion. This was expressed most generally in the inverted ideological form of the relation of power between the sexes: the adulation of woman as goddess or as mother. Whatever its sources in the classical religions of India or in medieval religious practices, the specific ideological form in which we know the "Indian woman" construct in the modern literature and arts of India today is wholly and undeniably a product of the development of a dominant middle-class culture coeval with the era of nationalism. It served to emphasize with all the force of mythological inspiration what had in any case become a dominant characteristic of femininity in the new construct of "woman" standing as a sign for "nation," namely, the spiritual qualities of self-sacrifice, benevolence, devotion, religiosity, and so on. This spirituality did not, as we have seen, impede the chances of the woman moving out of the physical confines of the home; on the contrary, it facilitated it, making it possible for her to go into the world under conditions that would not threaten her femininity. In fact, the image of woman as goddess or mother served to erase her sexuality in the world outside the home.

There are many important implications of this construct. To take one example, consider an observation often made: the relative absence of gender discrimination in middle-class occupations in India, an area that has been at the center of demands for women's rights in the capitalist West. Without denying the possibility that there are many complexities that lie behind this rather superficial observation, it is certainly paradoxical that, whereas middle-class employment has been an area of bitter competition between cultural groups distinguished by caste, religion, language, and so on, in the entire period of nationalist and postcolonial politics in India, gender has never been an issue of public contention. Similarly, the new constitution of independent India gave women the vote without any major debate on the question and without there ever having been a movement for women's suffrage at any period of nationalist politics in India. The fact that everyone assumed that women would naturally have the vote indicates a complete transposition of the terms in which the old patriarchy of tradition was constituted. The fixing by nationalist ideology of masculine/feminine qualities in terms of the material/spiritual dichotomy does not make women who have entered professional occupations competitors to male job seekers, because in this construct there are no specific cultural signs that distinguish women from men in the material world.

In fact, the distinctions that often become significant are those that operate *between* women in the world outside the home. They can mark out women by their dress, eating habits (drinking/smoking), adherence to religious marks of feminine status, behavior toward men, and so on, and classify them as Westernized, traditional, low-class (or subtler variations on those distinctions)—all signifying a deviation from the acceptable norm. A woman identified as Westernized, for instance, would invite the ascription of all that the "normal" woman (mother/sister/wife/daughter) is not—brazen, avaricious, irreligious, sexually promiscuous—and this not only from males but also from women who see themselves as conforming to the legitimate norm, which is precisely an indicator of the hegemonic status of the ideological construct. An analogous set of distinctions would mark out the low-class or common woman from the normal. (Perhaps the most extreme object of contempt for the nationalist is the stereotype of the Anglo-Indian *mῡyāś*—Westernized and common at the same time.) Not surprisingly, deviation from the norm also carries with it the possibility of a variety of ambiguous meanings—signs of illegitimacy become the sanction for behavior not permitted for those who are "normal"—and these are the sorts of meaning exploited to the full by, for instance, the commercial media of film, advertising, and fashion. Here is one more instance of the displacement in nationalist ideology of the construct of woman as a sex object in Western patriarchy: the nationalist male thinks of his own wife/sister/daughter as "normal" precisely because she is not a "sex object," while those who could be "sex objects" are not "normal."

ELEMENTS OF A CRITIQUE OF THE RESOLUTION

I end this chapter by pointing out another significant feature of the way in which nationalism sought to resolve the women's question in accordance with its historical project. This has to do with the one aspect of the question that was directly political, concerning relations with the state. Nationalism, as we have noticed before, located its own subjectivity in the spiritual domain of culture, where it considered itself superior to the West and hence undominated and sovereign. It could not permit an encroachment by the colonial power in that domain. This determined the characteristically nationalist response to proposals for effecting social reform through the legislative enactments of the colonial state. Unlike the early reformers from Rammohan to Vidyasagar, nationalists of the late nineteenth century were in general opposed to such proposals, for such a method of reform seemed to deny the ability of the nation to act for itself even in a domain where it was sovereign. In the specific case of reforming the lives of women, consequently, the nationalist position was firmly based on the premise that this was an area where the nation was acting on its own, outside the purview of the guidance and intervention of the colonial state.

We now get the full answer to the historical problem I raised at the beginning of this chapter. The reason why the issue of "female emancipation" seems to disappear from the public agenda of nationalist agitation in the late nineteenth century is not because it was overtaken by the more emotive issues concerning political power. Rather, the reason lies in the refusal of nationalism to make the women's question an issue of political negotiation with the colonial state. The simple historical fact is that the lives of middle-class women, coming from that demographic section that effectively constituted the "nation" in late colonial India, changed most rapidly precisely during the period of the nationalist movement—indeed, so rapidly that women from each generation in the last hundred years could say quite truthfully that their lives were strikingly different from those led by the preceding generation. These changes took place in the colonial period mostly outside the arena of political agitation, in a domain where the nation thought of itself as already free. It was after independence, when the nation had acquired political sovereignty, that it became legitimate to embody the idea of reform in legislative enactments about marriage rules, property rights, suffrage, equal pay, equality of opportunity, and so on. Now, of course, the women's question has once again become a political issue in the life of the nation-state.

Another problem on which we can now obtain a clearer perspective is that of the seeming absence of any autonomous struggle by women themselves for equality and freedom. We would be mistaken to look for evidence of such struggle in the public archives of political affairs, for unlike the women's movement in nineteenth- and twentieth-century Europe or America, the battle for the new idea of womanhood in the era of nationalism was waged in the home. We know from the evidence left behind in autobiographies, family histories, religious tracts, literature, theater, songs, paintings, and such other cultural artifacts, that it was the home that became the principal site of the struggle through which the hegemonic construct of the new nationalist patriarchy had to be normalized. This is the real history of the women's question whose terrain our genealogical investigation into the nationalist idea of "woman" has identified. The nationalist discourse we have heard so far is a discourse *about* women; women do not speak here. In the next chapter, we will explore the problem of enabling women in recent Indian history to speak for themselves.

The location of the state in the nationalist resolution of the women's question in the colonial period has yet another implication. For sections of the middle class that felt themselves culturally excluded from the formation of the nation and that then organized themselves as politically distinct groups, their relative exclusion from the new nation-state would act as a further means of displacement of the legitimate agency of reform. In the case of Muslims in Bengal, for instance, the formation of a new middle class was delayed, for reasons we need not go into here. Exactly the same sorts of ideological concerns typical of a nationalist response to issues of social reform in a colonial situation can be seen to operate among Muslims as well, with a difference in chronological time.[19] Nationalist reforms do not, however, reach political fruition in the case of the Muslims in independent India, because to the extent that the dominant cultural formation among them considers the community excluded from the state, a new colonial relation is brought into being. The system of dichotomies of inner/outer, home/world, feminine/masculine are once again activated. Reforms that touch upon what is considered the inner essence of the identity of the community can be legitimately carried out only by the community itself, not by the state. It is instructive to note how little institutional change has been allowed in the civil life of Indian Muslims since independence and to compare the degree of change with that in Muslim countries where nationalist cultural reform was a part of the successful formation of an independent nation-state. The contrast is striking if one compares the position of middle-class Muslim women in West Bengal today with that of neighboring Bangladesh.

The continuance of a distinct cultural "problem" of the minorities is an index of the failure of the Indian nation to effectively include within its body the whole of the demographic mass that it claims to represent. The failure becomes evident when we note that the formation of a hegemonic "national culture" was *necessarily* built upon the privileging of an "essential tradition," which in turn was defined by a system of exclusions. Ideals of freedom, equality, and cultural refinement went hand in hand with a set of dichotomies that systematically excluded from the new life of the nation the vast masses of people whom the dominant elite would represent and lead, but who could never be culturally integrated with their leaders. Both colonial rulers and their nationalist opponents conspired to displace in the colonial world the original structure of meanings associated with Western liberal notions of right, freedom, equality, and so on. The inauguration of the national state in India could not mean a universalization of the bourgeois notion of "man."

Indeed, in setting up its new patriarchy as a hegemonic construct, nationalist discourse not only demarcated its cultural essence as distinct from that of the West but also from that of the mass of the people. It has generalized itself among the new middle class, admittedly a widening class and large enough in absolute numbers to be self-reproducing, but is situated at a great distance from the large mass of subordinate classes. My analysis of the nationalist construction of woman once again shows how, in the confrontation between colonialist and nationalist discourses, the dichotomies of spiritual/material, home/world, feminine/masculine, while enabling the production of a nationalist discourse which is different from that of colonialism, nonetheless remains trapped within its framework of false essentialisms.

CHAPTER SEVEN

Women and the Nation

THE TROUBLE WITH THEIR VOICES

If there is one theme that dominates the new literature which emerged in Bengal in the nineteenth century, it is the theme of change. Everything was changing; nothing was likely to remain the same. Prolonged and bitter debates ensued about how best to cope with all this change. But at bottom the assumption was shared that the force working to alter the very foundations of society was both overwhelming and alien: the source of change itself lay outside and beyond control. It is important to remember this when considering the emergence of a "modern" consciousness of the self under colonial conditions.

The question of the "new woman" was, like other contemporary social issues, formulated, as we have just seen, as a question of coping with change. But who was to do the coping? Bankimchandra, the most eminent literary figure in Bengal in the late nineteenth century, wrote in the early 1870s an essay comparing the virtues and faults of women of an older age with those of women of modern times.[1] Bankim began the essay by declaring that in all societies it was men who always laid down the ways in which women must behave. "Self-interested men are mindful of the improvement of women only to the extent that it furthers their self-interest; not for any other reason." There was, consequently, no confusion in Bankim's mind about the social agency in question when considering the character of women. If the modern woman differed from her predecessors, she did so as the result of social policies pursued by men; men's attitudes and actions were on trial here.

Bankim then goes on to list the virtues and defects of the "new" woman compared with those of the "traditional." It is a familiar list, reproduced, embellished, and canonized in succeeding decades in the prodigious nationalist literature on women. In the past, women were uneducated, and therefore coarse, vulgar, and quarrelsome. By comparison, modern women have more refined tastes. On the other hand, whereas women were once hardworking and strong, they were now lazy and fond of luxury, unmindful of housework, and prone to all sorts of illnesses. Further, in the olden days women were religious. They were faithful to their husbands, hospitable to guests, and charitable to the needy. They genuinely believed in the norms of right conduct. Today, if women do these things, they do so more because of fear of criticism than because they have faith in dharma.

Bankim may have felt that despite his initial remarks about the responsibility of men as lawmakers of society, the essay was likely to be read as a criticism of women themselves, whether traditional or modern. In the subsequent issue of the journal in which the essay appeared, Bankim appended three letters, supposedly written by women in response to the article. All three complained that women had been treated unfairly by the author. The first retaliated with a list of accusations against the educated male.

> Alright, we are lazy. But what about you? . . . You work only because the English have tied you to the millstone. . . . We have no bonds of religion, you say. And you? You are ever fearful of religion because it is like a noose around your neck: one end of the rope is held by the owner of the liquor-store and the other by the prostitute.

The second argued that the defects of the modern woman had been produced only by the "virtues" of the modern man.

> Yes, by your virtues, not by your faults. If only you had not loved us so much, we would not have had so many defects. We are lazy because you have made us so contented. . . . We are unmindful of guests because we are so mindful of our husbands and children. . . . And, finally, are we not afraid of religion? In truth, it is only because we are afraid of religion that we dare not tell you what we should. You are our only religion. We are so afraid of you that we have no fear of any other religion. . . . If this is a crime against religion, then it is both your fault and your virtue. And if you do not mind being asked a question by this prattling female—"You are our teachers, we are your disciples: what religion do you teach us?" . . . Oh shame! Don't spread tales about your slaves!

The third correspondent offered to exchange places with the modern male. "Come indoors and take charge of the house. Let us go out to work. Slaves for seven hundred years, and still you pride yourselves on your masculinity! Aren't you ashamed?"[2]

I mention this essay by Bankim at the very beginning of my discussion of women's writings about themselves not only to remind us that the hegemonic discourse which framed these writings—the discourse of anti-colonial nationalism—was in its core a male discourse, but also to point out the capacity of this discourse to appropriate discordant, marginal, and critical voices. In Bankim's case, the device was self-irony. The strand of nationalist thinking Bankim represented sought to create a national leadership in the image of ideal masculinity—strong, proud, just, wise, a protector of the righteous, and a terror to the mischievous. Relentlessly, he poured scorn and ridicule on an educated elite that, he thought, was failing to live up to this ideal. Self-irony was the mode by which he could, as a member of this inadequate elite, expose to itself its own weaknesses, even by assuming the voices of its "others"—those of the illiterate, the poor and the "mad," and also those of women.[3] The form was used widely. Indeed, fiction and drama in late nineteenth-century Bengal are full of instances of women, from "respectable" families as well as from the urban poor, using the rhetorical skills of "common" speech and the moral precepts of "common" sense to show up the pretentiousness and hypocrisy of the educated male. We must not overlook the hegemonic possibilities of this internalized critique: it could, up to a point, retain its own legitimacy and appropriate both feminine and popular ridicule simply by owning up to them.[4]

The question is: Up to what point? Or rather, in which discursive field? Within what sort of boundaries? We cannot find a historically nuanced answer to this question unless we think of the field of discourse as one of contention, peopled by several subjects, several consciousnesses. We must think of discourse as situated within fields of power, not only constituting that field but also constituted by it. Dominance here cannot exhaust the claims to subjectivity, for even the dominated must always retain an aspect of autonomy. Otherwise, power would cease to be a relation; it would no longer be constituted by struggle.

If nationalist ideology in late nineteenth-century Bengal legitimized the subjection of women under a new patriarchy, its history must be a history of struggle. The difficulty which faces historians here is that by working from the conventional archives of political history, women appear in the history of nationalism only in a "contributive" role.[5] All one can assert here is that women *also* took an active part in nationalist struggle, but one cannot identify any autonomous subjectivity of women and from that standpoint question the manner in which the hegemonic claims of nationalist culture were themselves fashioned.

My argument is that because of the specific conditions of colonial society, this history is to be found less in the external domain of political conflict and more in the "inner" space of the middle-class home. Fortunately, there exists something of an archive for us to delve into: a series of autobiographies by educated women who wrote about their lives and their struggles in this eventful period of modern Indian history. I propose to present here a reading of five such autobiographies, beginning with a woman who was born in the first decade of the nineteenth century and ending with one who reached middle age in the first decade of the twentieth.

The autobiography would seem to be obvious material for studying the emergence of "modern" forms of self-representation. Unfortunately, here too the colonial condition works to displace the points of application of the usual critical apparatus. Historians of Bengali literature conventionally agree that the modern forms of the biography and the autobiography made their appearance in Bengal sometime in the middle of the nineteenth century because of the emergence of a new concept of the "individual" among the English-educated elite.[6] Yet, despite the continued popularity of the genre, it is difficult to explain why the facts of social history and the development of new cultural norms for the collective life of the nation, rather than the exploration of individuality and the inner workings of the personality, constitute the overwhelming bulk of the material of these life stories. The first comprehensive social history of nineteenth-century Bengal was written in the form of a biography of a social reformer,[7] while the foremost political leader of Bengal at the turn of the century entitled his autobiography A Nation in Making.[8] The "new individual," it would seem, could represent the history of his life only by inscribing it in the narrative of the nation.

Not unexpectedly, autobiographies of women have characteristics rather different from those of men. It is not simply that women's life stories are concerned more with the domestic than with the public sphere, a feature often noticed in women's autobiographies of the modern period in all countries. Nor is it a particular characteristic that the self-discovery of female identity acknowledges "the real presence and recognition of another consciousness" and that "the disclosure of female self is linked to the identification of some 'other.'"[9] In a fundamental sense, all identity has to be disclosed by establishing an alterity.[10] Men's autobiographies, it seems to me, do the same: the difference lies in the textual strategies employed. In the case of the women's autobiographies discussed here, the most striking feature is the way in which the very theme of disclosure of self remains suppressed under a narrative of changing times, changing manners, and customs, and changing values.

When the first autobiographies came to be written in the second half of the nineteenth century by men who had achieved eminence in the new public life of colonial Bengal, the most common title given to these works was the ātmacarit. While this was meant to stand as a literal translation of the English word autobiography, it also carried, more significantly, an allusion to the entire body of carita literature of the classical and medieval eras in which the lives of kings and saints were recorded. Buddhacarita by Aśvaghoṣa and Harṣacarita by Bāṇa are perhaps the most well known examples of a whole genre of religious and secular hagiographic writings in Sanskrit, whereas the Caitanyacaritāmṛta (1615) is the most distinguished of numerous carit writings in Bengali in the two centuries preceding the colonial age. While the more obvious hagiographic conventions were quickly abandoned in the new biographical literature of the nineteenth century, the idea of the carit as the life of an illustrious man, told either by himself or by others, clearly persisted even in its modern sense. Women's life stories were not given the status of carit. Of some twenty or so autobiographies I have seen of nineteenth-century Bengali women, not one is called an *ātmacarit*.[11] This, in fact, gives us a clue to the nature of women's autobiographical writings in this period: these were not simply variants on men's autobiographical writings but constituted a distinct literary genre. The most common name by which they were described was the *smṛtikathā*: "memoirs," or more accurately, "stories from memory." What held these stories together into a single narrative was not the life history of the narrator or the development of her "self" but rather the social history of the "times." The most commonly employed narrative device was the contrast: "In those days . . ."/"Nowadays . . ." The stories told were those of everyday life in the "inner" part of the house inhabited by women, of rituals and celebrations, of births, deaths, and marriages, of the sudden interruptions of everyday routine by calamitous events, and, of course, of how everything was so different "nowadays." It is not surprising that the first systematic surveys of women's autobiographical writings have treated this material principally as a source for reconstructing the social history of nineteenth-century Bengal,[12] and a recent book-length study of women's autobiographies has carried out this exercise much more elaborately.[13]

What made the narrative history of domestic life particularly suitable as a "feminine" literary genre was the belief, inculcated, needless to say, by male guardians of literary conventions, that this required little more than the retelling from memory of impressions left by direct personal experience. One did not have to have the imaginative power or stylistic flair of the poet or the novelist in order to tell one's smṛtikathā: anyone could do it. The immediacy, directness, and indeed the very artlessness of the form was seen to make it appropriate for an authentic "feminine" literary voice. When Charulata, the heroine of Rabindranath Tagore's story "The Broken Nest" (made into a film by Satyajit Ray), first tried her hand at writing, she began with an essay called "The August Clouds" but soon discovered that it read too much like another essay called "The July Moon," written by her brother-in-law Amal. She then proceeded to write about the Kālī temple in the village in which she had lived as a child. Tagore approved of this change in Charu's style: "Although in the early part her writing was cluttered by the excessively ornamental style of Amal, it soon acquired a simplicity and charm of its own, filled as it now was with the richness of a rural idiom."[14]

The genre, in short, did not require the author to express her "self" or examine the development of her personality. It was not the telling of an exemplary life, not even of a life of any importance: to this day, it is useful to remember, there are fewer biographies of Bengali women written by others than there are autobiographies. The genre required the writer only to tell her readers, mainly women from a younger generation, how the everyday lives of women had changed. This allowed the questions to be raised: How are we to cope with this change? In what ways must we change ourselves? These were, of course, the central questions of nationalist discourse. However, in this particular case, the discourse enabled a more specific question to be asked—and answered: How must women behave in these changing times?

To discover how educated women of the nineteenth century answered this question, we will now look at some of their own writings. We will listen to their own words, but we will also do well to remember that sovereignty over language, a tricky business under the best of circumstances, is doubly vitiated for those who were subordinated, at one and the same time, to colonialism as well as to a nationalist patriarchy.

BEFORE ENLIGHTENMENT

Shanta Nag, who came from a generation of middle-class women whose mothers were already educated, tells the story of how she learned to read the alphabet. It was sometime around the turn of the century. Her mother would sit across the table teaching her elder brother and she would stand beside her, silently watching the proceedings. In a few months, without anybody suspecting it, she had learned to read the first two books of the Bengali primer. The only difficulty was that in order to read, she had to hold the book upside down.[15] Of course, by her time the education of women had become normal practice in middle-class homes in Bengal, and she herself would have learned the alphabet and gone to school as a matter of routine. But the sense of acquiring a skill that was really meant for somebody else seems to have stayed with these early generations of educated women.

Nowhere is this more poignant than in the story of Rassundari Debi (1809–1900). For her, learning to read and write was nothing less than a lifelong struggle. She had been born in a wealthy, landed family and the village school was located in one of the buildings on the estate. When she was eight, her uncle sent her to this school, where, for the next two years, she sat everyday on the floor, the only girl in a roomful of boys, and was taught the Bengali alphabet, some arithmetic, and some Persian (which had still not been replaced by English as the language of bureaucracy). The teacher was an Englishwoman.[16] Rassundari does not tell us this, but we know from other sources that during this brief spell in the early nineteenth century, Christian missionary women attempted to educate Indian girls, first in schools and then in their homes.[17] The attempt had to be given up rather quickly because the idea of women being exposed to Christian influences seemed far too threatening to the men of their families, and it was only in the latter half of the century, when Indians themselves began to open schools for women and to produce what was considered a suitable modern educational literature in Bengali, that the practice of middle-class girls going to school would become legitimate.

In the meantime, Rassundari's education came to an abrupt halt when she was ten because the building in which her school was housed was destroyed in a fire.[18] It is doubtful how far her education would have progressed in any case, because at the age of twelve, in accordance with the prevailing custom, she was given in marriage.

From then on, her life was enclosed by the daily performance of her household duties. After the death of her mother-in-law a few years later, she had to take on the entire burden of running the house. She cooked three times a day for about thirty members of the household. She gave birth to twelve children, of whom seven died in her lifetime. Her responsibilities in the family would not allow her to go anywhere. Even when she did, to visit her husband's relatives on weddings and other ritual occasions, she would be accompanied on the boat by two guards, two maids, and ten or fifteen other people, and, "like a prisoner on parole," would have to return in a couple of days. Rassundari particularly lamented her failure to visit her mother before she died.

> I tried in so many ways to go and see my mother, but I was not fated to do so. This is not a matter of small regret to me. Oh Lord, why did you give birth to me as a human being? Compared to all the birds and beasts and other inferior creatures in this world, it is a rare privilege to be granted a human birth. And yet, despite this privilege, I have failed grievously in my duty. Why was I born a woman? Shame on my life! . . . If I had been my mother's son and known of her imminent death, no matter where I happened to be, I would have flown to her side like a bird. Alas, I am only a bird in a cage.[19]

Had this been all there was to Rassundari's life, it would have been no different from those of thousands of other women in upper-caste landed families in early nineteenth-century Bengal, and we would have had no opportunity to read about it in her own words. Fortunately, she nursed a secret dream. She was always a devout woman, and sometime in her late youth she had a longing to read the religious epics and the lives of the great saints. She did not so much as dare look at even a piece of paper that had been written on, for fear of adverse comments, but every day, she tells us, she would pray to her god: "Oh Lord, give me learning, so that I can read books. . . . If you do not teach me, who will?"[20] And yet, she did not know how this impossible feat would be accomplished.

The way was shown to her in a dream.

> One day, in my sleep, I dreamt I had opened a copy of the *Caitanya-bhāgavat* and was reading it. As soon as I woke up, my body and mind were filled with delight. I closed my eyes and again thought of the dream, and realized what a precious gift I had received. . . . I said to myself, "How remarkable! I have never seen a copy of the *Caitanya-bhāgavat* and would not recognize it even if I saw one. And yet, there I was reading it in my dream." . . . Every day I had asked the Almighty, "Teach me to read. I want to read books." The Almighty had not taught me to read, but had now given me the power to read books in my dream. I was delighted and thanked the Almighty.[21]

Rassundari, however, was to be blessed even more generously. That very day, while she was busy in the kitchen, her husband came in looking for their eldest son and said to him, "This is my *Caitanya-bhāgavat*. Keep it here somewhere. I'll send for it later." Rassundari waited until no one was around, removed a page of the unbound manuscript, and hid it in her room. Later, she tried to read it and discovered that so many years after her brief period of schooling, she could not recognize most of the letters. She then stole a page on which her son had practiced his alphabets, and for months thereafter, whenever she was alone, she would compare the two pieces of paper and, painfully and in absolute secrecy, teach herself to read.

Over the next couple of years, she worked her way through the *Caitanya-bhāgavat*. No one in the household, except a few trusted maids, knew of her accomplishment. But Rassundari had perceived the existence of a whole new world that still seemed out of her reach.

> My mind seemed to have acquired six hands. With two of them, it wanted to do all the work of the household so that no one, young or old, could find fault with me. With two others, it sought to draw my children close to my heart. And with the last two, it reached out for the moon. . . . Has anyone held the moon in her hands? . . . And yet, my mind would not be convinced; it yearned to read the *purāna*.[22]

Rassundari gathered up courage and shared her secret with her widowed sisters-in-law. To her surprise, not only did they not reprimand her, but in fact eagerly conspired to start a secret reading circle, arranging to procure books from the outer quarters of the house and setting up an elaborate warning system to prevent discovery.[23]

In time, when her sons were grown, it was no longer necessary to keep up the secrecy. In any case, the times had also changed, and men of her son's generation looked upon the education of women as a virtue. It was with the assistance of her sons that Rassundari learned to read the printed book and later on to write.[24]

Rassundari thought of her achievement as a divine gift. In fact, her testimony is quite unique in the collection we are looking at for the utterly sincere way in which it tells the story of a life shaped entirely by the inscrutable whims and fancies of a divine power, including the dreams and miraculous coincidences in which that power revealed its presence. It could well be a fragment, paraphrased in the prose of the nineteenth century, from the devotional literature of an earlier era. All subjectivity is attributed here to a divine agency, and Rassundari recounts her toil and sorrow—"the burden of three lives thrust into one"—only as the story of a fate assigned to her. I should also mention that she notes with great satisfaction the good fortune of women younger than her, for "the Lord of the Universe has now made new rules for everything. Women today do not have to suffer. . . . Nowadays parents take great care to educate their daughters. I feel very pleased when I see this."[25]

Before we leave Rassundari to move on to the life histories of women whose beliefs were shaped more directly by the sensibilities of this "modern" world, we must note the way in which her story was given a place in the autobiographical literature of Bengal. When her book was published in the early decades of this century, it was introduced with two forewords—one by the dramatist Jyotirindranath Tagore and the other by the pioneering historian of Bengali literature Dineshchandra Sen (1866–1939). Jyotirindranath saw in her writing "a simple and unselfconscious charm" and noted in particular the fact that "it was her thirst for religious knowledge which drove her to learn to read and write."[26]

Dineshchandra saw in it "a true portrait of the traditional Hindu woman," "the original picture of the long-suffering, compassionate Bengali woman." He remarked on the tendency in modern literature to focus on woman exclusively as the subject of romantic love, which produced, he says, a very incomplete picture of the Hindu woman who was, after all, also a mother, daughter, sister, sister-in-law, daughter-in-law, and mistress of the household and "had to earn credit in all of these roles before she would be praised by society." Rassundari's life was a model of such traditional virtues.[27] Of course, the social norms within which she led her life were often oppressive, but those were the undesirable aspects of tradition which had to be reformed.

Nationalists of the twentieth century saw in Rassundari's story only a confirmation of their construction of the true essence of Indian womanhood: self-sacrificing, compassionate, spiritual, and possessing great resources of emotional strength drawn from personal faith and devotion. This essence, they thought, needed to be recovered from the morass of bigotry and superstition into which tradition had fallen, and reform and education could accomplish this. What they did not recognize was that Rassundari's struggle emanated from a consciousness that was yet uncolonized by the Enlightenment. She submitted to as well as resisted a patriarchy that was premodern; her strategies of resistance also sprang out of traditions that far predated the advent of "women's education" as an agenda of nationalist reform. Above all, the intervention of nationalist male reformers was not required to set Rassundari's consciousness into motion.[28] Indeed, in her time, the nationalist project had not even begun. Only later did nationalism appropriate her story into its own prehistory.

If I might stay with this transitional period a little longer, I would like to bring in here the story of Saradasundari Debi (1819–1907). Saradasundari was married at the age of nine into one of the most prominent families of colonial Calcutta. Ramkamal Sen, her father-in-law, was, as I mentioned before in another context, a close associate of English traders and officials and although very much an advocate of Western education, he was also concerned with the preservation of religious orthodoxy. Saradasundari's husband had been educated into the new world, and every night, in the secrecy of their bedroom, he would teach her to read and rite.[29] She, however, became a widow when she was still a young woman, and later in her life, while she could still read, she had lost her ability to write. The account we are reading was dictated by her to a younger male relative.

The story she tells us is one of suffering—the suffering of a widow with small children surrounded by male relatives intent on defrauding her of her property. Her main responsibility in the world was toward her children—giving her sons a good education and arranging for the marriage of her daughters. Whenever she could, she sought to escape the sufferings of the world by going on pilgrimage. She too was a devout woman, and the happiest episodes in the story that she tells occur in her journeys away from home.

Once again, this is a life that might have been led by numerous other upper-caste women of her time. What prompted her amanuensis to record Saradasundari's story was the fact that her son Keshabchandra Sen was one of the most charismatic leaders of the religious reform movement in Bengal in the second half of the nineteenth century. It is as the life history of Keshab's mother that Saradasundari's autobiography found a place in the archives of Bengali literature.[30]

And it is in this respect that her account reveals traces of the struggle inside urban homes caught in the vortex of cultural reform. Unlike Rassundari, Saradasundari is much more self-conscious about her religiosity. She talks about her joy and fulfillment in the many pilgrimages she made in her life, and yet she also expresses a sense of guilt.

I felt then that I was being virtuous. I would not feel the same way now. I was a little childish then. Even now, I go on pilgrimages, but not to earn religious merit. I go only out of love, in the same way that I have love for my children and those who are my own. But I do not believe that I will gain salvation by going on pilgrimages. . . . I had this obsession for religion and a strong urge to see the holy places. Even now I perform many kinds of worship, but all from the same feeling [of love]. I believe in my heart that there is only one God and unless I worship Him I will never find salvation. I cannot say with certainty that people never achieve salvation if they worship the deities with form [*sākār*], but I do know that they achieve it if they worship the formless God [*nirākār*] and that my own salvation depends upon His grace.

Those who know the social history of Bengal in this period will immediately hear in these words resonances of that contentious debate between monotheistic Brahmo reformers and the defenders of Hindu orthodoxy. Living in an orthodox family, and yet the proud mother of a son celebrated for his radical religious views, Saradasundari was clearly caught in a conflict that was not of her own making. She had, therefore, to speak in two voices—one recalling with gratitude and joy her visits to the great Vaishnav temples of India and her miraculous visions of the deity, and the other asserting her role as Keshab Sen's mother. It would be presumptuous on our part to declare one of the two as her true voice; what was true was her struggle to make both voices her own.

I had to suffer a great deal because [Keshab] became a Brahmo. I had to bear with much insult . . . and ill treatment. There was not a day when I did not cry. . . . There were times when even I thought that Keshab was doing wrong. I do not think so anymore. . . . I sought advice from my *guru*. He told me, "If your son accepts this new religion, he will become a great man. People will flock to him. Don't worry about this anymore." I was calmed by his words.[31]

It should not be surprising to notice that for this early generation of women from the new middle class of Bengal, the presence of society and religion as a set of regulatory practices appeared in the immediacy of family and kin relations converging upon the home. So did the presence of new currents in the outside world, including the presence of the West itself, appear in the person of a male member of the family, usually the husband or a son. The great conflicts over social reform in a public domain peopled exclusively by males were thus transmitted into the lives of women inside their homes. Women, consequently, had to devise strategies to cope with the new demands made upon their loyalties and their desires. If Saradasundari seems painfully torn between a conventional devotion which gave her solace in an oppressive world and a rational religion preached by her radical son, we have another testimony which suggests a resolution of this dilemma. Significantly, this occurs in the case of a woman who was able to escape the daily surveillance of the extended family and live a life with her modernist husband, as it were, outside the reaches of "society."

THE NEW WOMEN

Kailasbasini Debi (1830–95) was the wife of Kishorichand Mitra (1822–73), a prominent figure among the social reformers of the mid-nineteenth century.[32] Kishorichand was an employee of the East India Company and held important administrative positions in the district towns of Bengal and Bihar. For several years of her married life, therefore, Kailasbasini lived alone with her husband, away from home, in company bungalows and houseboats. Her husband taught her to read and write Bengali and some English as well. Later, when he settled down in Calcutta, Kishorichand built a garden house in the outskirts of the city, where Kailasbasini would often live with her husband and daughter.

In marked contrast to the other stories we have heard so far, Kailasbasini talks of her married life as one of happiness. She looked from a critical distance at the traditional life of the family she had left behind but that was always waiting for her out there. She was horrified by the unhygienic and degrading conditions in which women in traditional homes were confined at childbirth and regretted that other women she knew did not have the benefits of enlightened teaching which her husband had given her.[33] She was quite conscious of the way in which her husband had assiduously molded her thoughts and beliefs, and was grateful for it. Most of these views were rationalist, in the way in which rationalist arguments were used in the nineteenth century to supply instrumental justifications for traditional beliefs and customs. Thus, Kailasbasini says, echoing her husband, widows are traditionally restricted to a hard life devoid of luxury in order to make them unattractive to men, so that they do not become objects of their lust. Meat eating is regarded as polluting because India is a warm country in which meat is bad for the health. Idolatry meets the need to provide a practical religion for ignorant people who find it difficult to conceive of an abstract, formless God.[34]

There is no question that Kailasbasini saw herself as both more fortunate than and superior to other women around her. She was happy in the formative company of her enlightened husband. When he was away on tour, she tells us with a stunning simile, she spent her time "like Robinson Crusoe, eating, sleeping, reading, sewing, teaching my daughter and writing this journal."[35]

And yet, even for someone so free from the rigors of customary regulation and so happily enveloped by an entirely new conjugal tutelage, Kailasbasini required strategies to protect herself against the consequences of her husband's reformist projects.

> I do not believe in the rituals of Hindu orthodoxy, but I follow all of them. For I know that if I relax my hold, my husband will give up the Hindu religion altogether. My closest relatives are Hindus and I can never abandon them. For this reason, I scrupulously follow all the rules of the Hindu religion.
>
> I have this great fear that no one will accept food from my hands. That would be a shame worse than death. As it is, my husband eats out [without observing ritual regulations]; if I too join him, it would be a calamity.
>
> . . . Since I follow the Hindu rules, I have no problems, no matter what my husband does. That is the religion of the Bengalis, which is why those who are clever do not believe in it. But I never say this to my husband, although I know it would please him to no end if he heard it from me.[36]

I wish to suggest that we have here a moment where a strategy worked out within the space of the emergent nationalist middle-class home anticipated the form of a more general strategy which political nationalism would later attempt to use in order to make the solidarity of cultural communities compatible with the requirements of the modern state. A neat separation between a private sphere of diverse individuals residing in bourgeois patriarchal families and a public sphere inhabited by homogeneous citizens was not available to Indian nationalism. The rational-bureaucratic form of the modern state brought to India by the colonial power was premised precisely upon the denial of citizenship to colonized Indians. The strategy, therefore, had to use another distinction—between the spiritual or the inner, on the one hand, and the material or the outer, on the other. The latter was a ground surrendered to the colonial power; the former was where nationalism began to fashion its claims to hegemony. Kailasbasini, speaking from within this emergent middle-class home, is not telling us that religious beliefs and practices are private matters and that what is important for the life of the nation is the public behavior of its citizens. On the contrary, she has discovered that the practices of the outside world which men have to get used to are in the end inconsequential, since what truly matters in the life of the nation are practices in the inner space of community life. Here it is the duty of women to hold fast to the religious practices of the community: even "private" beliefs are of no consequence. Her strategy mirrors a crucial move in the cultural politics of nationalism.

The home, I suggest, was not a complementary but rather the original site on which the hegemonic project of nationalism was launched.

Women from the new middle class in nineteenth-century India thus became active agents in the nationalist project—complicit in the framing of its hegemonic strategies as much as they were resistant to them because of their subordination under the new forms of patriarchy.

To return to Kailasbasini: the apparent stability of the manner in which she chose to reconcile the conflicting demands on her loyalty was undoubtedly made possible by the fortuitous distance between her conjugal home and the effective center of her social life. The situation was to be repeated in the cases of many middle-class families of the Bengali diaspora that spread out into the cities and towns of northern India with the expansion of colonial administration in the second half of the nineteenth century. But in her case at least, the fragility of an individual solution worked out in the peripheries of society was exposed rather tragically. In 1873, when Kailasbasini was in her early forties, her husband died.

> I took the name "widow." When I hear that name, it is as though lightning strikes my heart. Oh Lord, why have you given me this name? How long am I to live with it? I will not be able to bear the suffering. I hope this name soon vanishes into dust. What a terrible name! My heart trembles at its very sound.[37]

Those are the last words in Kailasbasini's diary. As far as we know, she never wrote again.[38]

The project of cultural reform which nationalist ideology placed on the agenda in the second half of the nineteenth century did, however, provide the resources for women to turn personal misfortune into a new social identity. This becomes clear in the story of Prasannamayi Debi (1857–1939). Born in an upper-caste landed family, Prasannamayi was married at the age of ten to a husband who turned out to be mentally deranged. After she had made two brief visits to her in-laws, her father refused to send her back, and from the age of fourteen Prasannamayi lived for the rest of her life with her parents and brothers. Her father was committed to the cause of reform and arranged not only to give the best possible education to his sons, many of whom were later to reach positions of eminence in their respective professions, but also to educate his daughter at home.

From a very young age, Prasannamayi showed signs of literary talent. Because of her father's literary and musical interests, the family was part of a cultural circle that included some of the most prominent literary figures of the time. Prasannamayi was not only allowed to listen to these discussions but encouraged to take an active part in them. Often she would read aloud her own poetry in these distinguished gatherings. Even as a young woman, her writings began to be published regularly in major literary magazines, and she soon came out with her own books of poems.

Indeed, she became quite a celebrity as a woman who had overcome a personal tragedy caused by the retrograde custom of child marriage and gone on to make a name for herself as a writer. Protected and encouraged by a circle of male relatives and friends that, in the late nineteenth century, was now far more self-assured about its cultural project, Prasannamayi became an exemplary figure, standing for all the virtues claimed on behalf of the "new woman."

We know about the tragedy of Prasannamayi's marriage from other sources;[39] she herself tells us absolutely nothing about it. In ninety-one pages of detailed description of domestic life in her childhood and youth and of dozens of relatives and acquaintances, she does not once mention her husband. All that she says about her experience of married life is that when she first arrived at her in-laws, dressed in the new fashion with petticoat and jacket and surrounded by rumors about her ability to read and write, she was regarded with great curiosity as "the English bride" (*mem bau*), and when she innocently made a display of her accomplishments, including a demonstration on the concertina, she was rebuked by her mother-in-law (*PK*, p. 44). She allows herself only one comment on the custom of hypergamous *kulīn* marriage, of which she was a victim: "avaricious *kulīn* parents," she says, "in their desire to preserve the reputation of their lineages, did not consider the uncertain consequences of giving their daughters in marriages of this sort, although many of these incompatible marriages led to much unhappiness. But it was difficult suddenly to break with a social custom" (*PK*, p. 37). She mentions the fact that several other women in her family had suffered because of such marriages, but then adds: "It is best that this unfortunate history remains unknown to the public [*janasamāj*]" (*PK*, p. 89).

Thus, even as the new form of the conjugal family was being institutionalized within the middle class in Bengal, and its normative ideals produced discursively in the social reform debates and imaginatively in the new fictional and poetical literature, a whole set of differentiations of the inside/outside was also being put in place in order to demarcate those aspects of family life which could be spoken of and those which could not. It is not the case, therefore, that a sphere of the intimate was created, peopled by privatized individuals with subjectivities "oriented toward an audience."[40] Rather, the sphere of the intimate, even when it was subjected to a reformist critique on ethical or aesthetic grounds, was nevertheless declared a subject that could not be spoken of "in public." It was a fiercely guarded zone lodged deep inside the precincts of community life; even its memory could not be revealed in the open arena of the janasamāj.

There is only one place where Prasannamayi slips from her objective narrative of social history to allow us a glimpse into the domain where women in her situation had to wage the struggle for identity and recognition. This occurs when she talks of Indumati, the widowed daughter of the reformer Ramtanu Lahiri (1813–98). "This remarkable woman," she says, "was born only to teach the world the duty of love, to demonstrate that the purpose of human life is not indulgence, but sacrifice—the sacrifice of the pleasures and desires of youth to the cause of service to others." But she also knew Indumati as a friend, and in their friendship, both found the means to forget the immediate world.

> I cannot explain now how wonderful it was to forget ourselves completely. From morning to evening and then late into the night, we would talk, and time would fly past us. This was no political conspiracy, nor was it a discussion on some scientific problem. It was only the dream-like imagination and the pain of unfulfilled desire of two people inexperienced in the ways of the world. All the feelings and scenes that went into the making of this imagined world were products of our minds, bearing no relationship at all to the world of phenomenal things. (PK, p. 55)

Apart from this brief slippage, the rest of Prasannamayi's story is a model of nationalist social history written from the standpoint of the "new woman." She is critical of the irrationality and superstitiousness of many religious beliefs and customs.[41] She is horrified by the excesses of caste discrimination and is hopeful that the extreme rigidities of the system will be gradually weakened. "All must join in bringing about the welfare of the nation. We cannot live separately anymore. All must join in worshipping the Mother" (PK, p. 71). She is grateful to her father, her brothers, and their circle of friends for the guidance and encouragement they gave her in fashioning a completely new role as a woman with an identity in public life. Her view on contemporary history is entirely one of the legitimacy of reform and national progress. On the other hand, she bemoans the fact that English education was leading to so much superficial aping of Western manners and the negligence of what was good in tradition: "Young people today can recite by heart the names of [Admiral] Nelson's ancestors but do not know the names of their own grandparents" (PK, p. 51). And she affirms without question the essential identity of woman as faithful wife and exemplary mother:

> My mother, Srimati Magnamayi Debi, was very patriotic. Her love for her country was without comparison. Every grain of Indian sand was to her like a speck of gold. . . . Her immediate deity was her husband. Always abiding by the commands of her husband, she built her life according to an ideal and taught her children to follow that ideal. (PK, p. 14)

If we are to take a linear view of history as progress, then our journey that began with Rassundari in the early decades of the nineteenth century has reached its fulfillment with Prasannamayi at the close of the century. For in Prasannamayi, the nationalist idea of the "new woman" as a hegemonic construct would seem to have been actualized; her struggle has been completely encapsulated in the project to produce the nation—everything else is erased from public memory.

THE WOMEN LEFT OUT

If I stop my culling of these archives at this point, the principal course of the narrative will have thus described a linear movement. Needless to say, this is not an accident. I have deliberately chosen and arranged the four texts in such a way as to produce exactly that effect. My object was to trace through these supposedly self-revelatory texts the genealogy of the nationalist construct of the "new woman." I could, of course, have read the same texts in the opposite direction, against the grain, as texts that show the marks of resistance to a hegemonizing discourse; I have, even in this account, pointed out several of these marks. But I wish to retain up to this point the smooth linearity of my story, if only to emphasize once more the powers of a hegemonizing nationalism to take in its stride a whole range of dissenting voices.

We have therefore a linear narrative. The nationalist will read this as a movement from bondage to emancipation; the feminist critic of nationalism will read it as a movement from one kind of bondage to another. In order now to mess up the picture and forestall both of these closures, I will continue my story a little further and bring in the autobiography of Binodini.[42]

Binodini (1863–1941) was perhaps the most celebrated actress on the Calcutta stage in the last decades of the nineteenth century. This position of the professional actress was itself a creation of the new educated middle-class culture, supplying a need produced by the requirements of the new public theater modeled on European lines. Yet it was a need that was difficult to fulfill within the norms of respectability laid down for women. The solution devised by the early generation of theater producers was to recruit young women from among the city's prostitutes and train them in the modern techniques of the dramatic arts. It became a remarkable educative project in itself, producing women schooled in the language and sensibilities of a modernist literati who learned to think of themselves as professional career artists and yet were excluded from respectable social life by the stigma of immoral living. Binodini's life as a professional actress was produced by these contradictions of the new world of middle-class cultural production.

She was brought into the theater at the age of ten; when she was eighteen, she was at the peak of her career; at twenty-three, she decided to leave the stage. The autobiography she wrote and published when she was forty-nine describes the thirteen years of her professional life as a historical sequence of events, but everything before and after exists as though in a zone of timelessness. As a child, she was brought up in a Calcutta slum, in a household characterized by the absence of adult males. In her autobiography, she talks about the environment of the slum with considerable distaste, and remembers herself as a child looking upon her neighbors "with fear and surprise" and hoping she would never have to face such contempt.[43] She had been told of her marriage at the age of five or six, and there was a boy in the neighborhood whom others referred to as her husband.[44] Whether this might have become a significant event in her life can only be speculated upon, because everything changed when her mother agreed to give her to the theater as a child actress on a monthly salary.

For a girl eleven or twelve years old, training to become a professional actress was hard work. But then again, being in the theater was also like living in a large family. Binodini saw her identity as an actress entirely in terms of her place within this family of artistes. She submitted to its rules, did all that was required of her with dedication, and brought fame and popularity to the theaters she worked for. It is only when we locate this collective site where she grounded her identity and into which she poured out her feelings of loyalty—the extended family transposed on to the artificially constructed world of the middle-class professional theater, which to her was the very real surrogate for society itself—that we begin to see the significance of the central theme of Binodini's autobiography: betrayal.

Binodini had been driven by the belief that the shame of being a woman of ill repute would be removed by her dedication and accomplishments as an artist. Indeed, her acceptance of a position of concubinage to various wealthy patrons seemed to her to be justified by the greater cause of art. She desperately needed to believe in the solidarity and well-being of her surrogate family, for it was only there that she could lead a life of worth and dignity. When her theater company faced a crisis, she even agreed, at considerable personal risk, to become the mistress of a wealthy businessman who was prepared to finance the founding of a new theater only if he could have in exchange the famous Miss Binodini. She was led to believe that her "brothers and sisters" in the company would express their gratitude to her by naming their new theater after her. When this did not happen, she felt betrayed.[45] This was the first of a series of betrayals with which Binodini marks out for us the story of her life.

Trained in the language and sensibilities of the new middle-class culture, Binodini, we can well imagine, felt an intense desire to believe in the emancipatory claims made on behalf of the "new woman." Her life in the theater had introduced her to Greek tragedy and Shakespeare, to the new humanism of Michael Madhusudan Dutt, Bankimchandra, and Dinabandhu Mitra, and to the fervently nationalist representations by Girishchandra Ghosh of Hindu mythology and religious history. When she realized that she could be transformed only to fulfill the cultural needs of a class claiming to represent the nation but would not be given the place of respectability that the class had set aside for its own women, she learned not to believe anymore.

> Ever since I was thrust into the affairs of the world in my adolescence, I have learnt not to trust. The responsibility for this lies with my teachers, my social position and myself. But what is the use of apportioning blame? The distrust remains. . . . How deeply rooted it is in my heart will become clear from the events of my life. . . . And it is impossible to uproot it! I realize that faith is the basis of peace, but where is that faith?[46]

Something, Binodini felt, had been promised to her in return for her dedication to the ideals and disciplines she had been taught. If the enlightened virtues of respectable womanhood meant conformity to a new set of disciplinary rules, she was prepared to conform. Yet respectability was denied to her. She had a daughter whom she wanted to send to school; no school would have her. When the daughter died, she felt she had been betrayed once more.[47]

In late middle age, when she decided to write down the story of her life "to blacken white sheets of paper with the stigma of my heart,"[48] she asked her teacher, Girishchandra Ghosh, to write a foreword to her book. Girish did, but Binodini did not like what her teacher wrote. Girish in fact sought to apply the classic appropriating strategy, pointing out "the great moral lesson in the insignificant life of an ordinary prostitute. . . . On reading this autobiography, the pride of the pious will be curbed, the self-righteous will feel humble, and the sinner will find peace." He went on to comment on "the aspersions" cast by Binodini on the guardians of society. "Rather than emphasizing the didactic aspects of her art, she has tried to tell her own story. The concealing of the personal which is the essence of the technique of writing an autobiography has been compromised." Girish recognized that Binodini had her reasons to feel bitter, "but such bitter words are best left out of one's own life-story. For the reader whose sympathy [Binodini] must expect will refuse to give it when he encounters such harshness."[49]

Binodini, as I said, was not satisfied with this foreword and insisted that her teacher and the greatest actor on the Calcutta stage write "a true account" of all that had happened. The revised version never came, because a few months later Girish Ghosh died. To Binodini, this was another betrayal. "My teacher had told me, 'I will write the foreword before

I die.' . . . But it was not in my fate. . . . By leaving the foreword unfinished, my teacher taught me once more that all that one wishes in life is not fulfilled."[50]

The most heartbreaking betrayal, however, came in Binodini's attempt to build a life of her own outside the theater. For thirty years, from about the time she left the stage, she lived with a gentleman from one of the wealthiest and most respected families in the city. She put into this relationship all her feelings of loyalty and devotion and felt free, loved, respected, and cared for. What she did not realize was the inevitable fragility of the arrangement, because individual patronage, no matter how sincere, could hardly overcome the boundaries of a newly constructed world of the dominant that could only claim to speak on her behalf but never recognize her as its constituent part. Lying on his deathbed, the worthy gentleman made her a promise: "If I have devotion and faith in God, if I have been born in a virtuous family, you will never have to beg for protection." Death, however, rendered him powerless to fulfill his promise. His family, one can guess, did not feel in the least bit obliged to recognize an embarrassing relationship. Binodini was betrayed once more.

Ignoring the advice and admonitions of all her teachers, therefore, Binodini in turn felt that she was under no obligation to hide her deep-rooted skepticism about the verities of customary belief and convention. Determined to tell "her own story," she violated every canon of the feminine smṛtikathā and wrote down what amounted to her indictment of respectable society in the form of a series of letters addressed to her deceased lover. Perhaps her very marginality enabled her to assert this autonomy over her own words. With bitter irony, she wrote in her preface to the book:

> Hindu men and women, I take it, believe with complete sincerity in heaven and hell, in birth and rebirth. . . . Although he [her lover] is no longer on earth, he must be in heaven, from where he can see all that has happened to me and can feel the pain in my heart—if, that is, the Hindu religion is true and the gods are true; if, that is, birth and rebirth are true.[51]

Before we close our narrative of the nationalist transition, therefore, we need to remind ourselves of Binodini's story. For it tells us once more that the story of nationalist emancipation is necessarily a story of betrayal. Because it could confer freedom only by imposing at the same time a whole set of new controls, it could define a cultural identity for the nation only by excluding many from its fold; and it could grant the dignity of citizenship to some only because the others always needed to be represented and could not be allowed to speak for themselves. Binodini reminds us once more that the relations between the people and the nation, the nation and the state, relations which nationalism claims to have resolved once and for all, are relations which continue to be contested and are therefore open to negotiation all over again.

A PESSIMISTIC AFTERWORD

Having written this nicely inconclusive last sentence, I am struck by doubt. The sentence promises further episodes in the story of women and nationalism, and I feel I have succeeded in avoiding a closure. Have I?

In a recent article, Edward Said has spoken of "an incipient and unresolved tension" in the contest "between stable identity as it is rendered by such affirmative agencies as nationality, education, tradition, language and religion, on the one hand, and all sorts of marginal, alienated or . . . anti-systemic forces on the other." This tension, he says, "produces a frightening consolidation of patriotism, assertions of cultural superiority, mechanisms of control, whose power and ineluctability reinforce . . . the logic of identity."[52]

Said is thinking of "the cruel, insensate, shameful violence" that has taken place so often in the name of patriotic affirmation of identity in the Middle East. I am thinking of the equally shameful violence that has become virtually endemic in India in the matter of political relations between religious or linguistic communities. I therefore find myself in agreement with Said when he says, "it must be incumbent upon even those of us who support nationalist struggle in an age of unrestrained nationalist expression to have at our disposal some decent measure of intellectual refusal, negation and skepticism."

But then he says: "It is at precisely that nexus of committed participation and intellectual commitment that we should situate ourselves to ask *how much* identity, *how much* positive consolidation, *how much* administered approbation we are willing to tolerate in the name of our cause, our culture, our state." And here I begin once again to have doubts. Are we still trying to sort out that old liberal problem of "good nationalism" versus "bad nationalism"? Must it be our argument that a little bit of identity and positive consolidation and administered approbation is all for the good, but beyond a point they are intolerable? It is hard for me to accept this, because I have long argued against the posing of this kind of liberal paradox.[53]

One of the ways of avoiding the paradox is to question and reproblematize the all-too-easy identification, claimed by every nationalist state ideology, of the state with the nation and the nation with the people. As an act of intellectual skepticism, this might well involve risks that are more than intellectual. But speaking now only of effects in the intellectual domain, one important effect will be, I think, the somewhat startling discovery that the most powerful and authentic historical achievements of anticolonial nationalism were often won outside the political battlefield and well before the actual contest for political power was settled. This discovery will open up once more the question of who led and who followed, and of when it all began. It will introduce, in short, an agenda to rewrite the history of nationalism with different actors and a different chronology. It will also demonstrate that the culturally creative forms of anticolonial nationalism seeking to establish a zone of hegemony outside the intervention of the colonial state cannot be covered by the "modular" forms of nationalism produced in Europe or the Americas.

What is crucial, however, is for us to be able to show the many risky moments in this narrative of anticolonial nationalism, the alternative sequences that were suppressed, the marks of resistance that were sought to be erased. Much intellectual work of dissent in postcolonial countries is today performing precisely this task. It is arguing that the history of the transition from colonial to postcolonial regimes is highly problematical, that the promise of national emancipation was fulfilled, if not fraudulently, then certainly by the forcible marginalization of many who were supposed to have shared in the fruits of liberation. Indeed, the opening up of the whole problematic of the national project within and outside the domain of the state makes it possible for us now to make the radical suggestion that the cultural history of nationalism, shaped through its struggle with colonialism, contained many possibilities of authentic, creative, and plural development of social identities that were violently disrupted by the political history of the postcolonial state seeking to replicate the modular forms of the modern nation-state. We too, like Binodini, have a story to tell of betrayal.

My doubts are about the effectiveness of this critique. Having to survive in a world pulverized by the concentrated violence of the Gulf War, I cannot, I am afraid, share Said's easy optimism in "scholarship and politics from a world viewpoint, past domination, toward community."[54] It is the very biculturalism of intellectuals in postcolonial countries—a necessary biculturalism that they must work hard to acquire—which enables them to see through the sham and hypocrisy of today's myths of global cooperation. For us, it is hard to imagine a plausible state of the world in which our relation to the dominant structures of scholarship and politics will be anything other than adversarial.

It would be dishonest, therefore, to claim that the critique of nationalism is easy. Rather, the more realistic tactic is not to underestimate nationalism's capacity to appropriate, with varying degrees of risk and varying degrees of success, dissenting and marginal voices. I must, for the sake of truthfulness, note here that Binodini today is an honored name in the public history of the theater in Bengal. Her life as a story of struggle and betrayal is a popular subject for plays and films, and the official liberality of the new domain of the postcolonial state does not allow any judgment of sexual morality to affect the esteem accorded to her as an artist.

In the public sphere within the new domain of the state? Yes. In the ethical domain of the community? Doubtful. Only a few months ago, I came across in a Calcutta daily a brief letter. A leading actress of yesteryear, now in her seventies and honored with several state awards, was complaining about an article in the newspaper on a deceased actor in which she had been mentioned as his "close friend and companion." "At the age of 78, do I have to prove by a letter in a newspaper," she asked, "that Nirmalendu Lahiri was my husband and that I bore four of his children? Yes, there was certainly friendship between me and Mr Lahiri, just as there was a relationship of disciple to master. But this is my first and last word: I was his first wife and the mother of his children."[55]

The ethical domain of nationalism remains very much a contested terrain.

CHAPTER EIGHT

The Nation and Its Peasants

THE MODERN STATE AND THE PEASANTRY

The relationship between the modern state and a peasantry is ambiguous and shot through with tension. In Western Europe, the institutionalization of a modern regime of power coincides with or follows a process of the extinction of the peasantry. Even in France, where it survived as a significantly large mass of the population in the second half of the nineteenth century, the peasantry was associated with such supposedly aberrant political phenomena as Bonapartism and had to be systematically disciplined and transformed into "Frenchmen."[1] Hegel, we know, assigned to the class of peasants—the "substantial class"—an ambiguous position in civil society: it was a part of the class structure produced by the "system of needs" but had an ethical life that was only immediate. Even when agriculture was conducted "on methods devised by reflective thinking, i.e. like a factory," Hegel would allow a member of this class only to accept "unreflectively what is given to him." The agricultural class had "little occasion to think of itself" and was "inclined to subservience."[2] Further east, the peasantry figured for more than half a century as the hub of a fierce debate between populists and Marxists over its role in a revolutionary Russia. This debate also highlighted the controversy, known in one form or the other everywhere in Europe, between modernizers who thought of peasants as embodying all that was backward and premodern and those modern critics of modernity, especially romantics, who saw in a peasantry the rapidly vanishing virtues of simplicity, naturalness, and cultural authenticity. In the end, the matter was settled in Russia by the elimination of the peasantry under the collectivization program of the 1930s.

In the agrarian societies of the colonial East, peasants of course became the repositories of all of those cultural presuppositions that allegedly made those societies incapable of modern self-government and hence justified the paternal authoritarianism of Western colonial rule. In India, the colonial mind thought of Indian peasants as simple, ignorant, exploited by landlords, traders, and moneylenders, respectful of authority, grateful to those in power who cared for and protected them, but also volatile in temperament, superstitious and often fanatical, easily aroused by agitators and troublemakers from among the Indian elite who wanted to use them for their narrow political designs. Indian nationalists, not surprisingly, shared similar assumptions. For them, too, the peasants were simple and ignorant, unaware of the fact that their poverty was the result of the exploitative nature of colonial rule and therefore in need of being woken up to a new consciousness, of being guided and led into effective political action by a nationalist organization. This was a necessary task if the opposition to colonial rule was to acquire the form of a mass movement, but it was also a difficult and dangerous task because the ignorance and volatility of the peasantry could easily lead it astray. In thus proceeding toward their opposed political objectives—located, however, within the same historical career of the modern state—both colonial and nationalist politics thought of the peasantry as an object of their strategies, to be acted upon, controlled, and appropriated within their respective structures of state power.

What does the history of anticolonial struggles in India tell us about the relation between the nation and the peasantry? It is now reasonably clear that contrary to the claims of both colonialist and nationalist historiographies, neither the competitive factional interests of Indian elite groups nor the efforts of the Congress leadership to arouse an all-embracing nationalist consciousness among the entire people can explain the dynamics of the involvement of the peasantry in anticolonial movements. Indeed, several studies published in the 1970s and the early 1980s on the course of the Congress movement among peasants in different parts of India have shown, some explicitly and others implicitly, the existence of a structure of duality in the nationalist mass movement.[3] A coming together of two domains of politics seems to have occurred. On the one hand was the domain of the formally organized political parties and associations, moving within the institutional processes of the bourgeois state forms introduced by colonial rule and seeking to use their representative power over the mass of the people to replace the colonial state by a bourgeois nation-state. On the other hand was the domain of peasant politics where beliefs and actions did not fit into the grid of "interests" and "aggregation of interests" that constituted the world of bourgeois representative politics. Seen from the former domain, the latter could appear only as the realm of spontaneity, which was of course nothing more than the acknowledgment that the specific determinants of the domain of peasant political activity remained incomprehensible from the standpoint of bourgeois politics.

Specifically, two major aspects of the mass movement of nationalism were brought out by these studies. First, the meeting of these two domains of politics was marked by an unresolved contradiction. There was undoubtedly a coming together of the two domains, so that the organization, ideology, and programs of the formally constituted political domain underwent considerable transformation with the entry of a mass peasant element, just as the peasantry too became aware of an entirely new world of political issues, languages, leaders, and forms of action. And yet the very union of these two domains was of a form which required that they be kept apart. While the nationalist leadership sought to mobilize the peasantry as an anticolonial force in its project of establishing a nation-state, it was ever distrustful of the consequences of agitational politics among the peasants, suspicious of their supposed ignorance and backward consciousness, careful to keep their participation limited to the forms of bourgeois representative politics in which peasants would be regarded as a part of the nation but distanced from the institutions of the state. On the other hand, while peasants became aware of the hitherto unknown world of nationalist agitation, they made sense of it not in terms of the discursive forms of modern bourgeois politics but rather by translating it into their own codes, so that the language of nationalism underwent a quite radical transformation of meaning in the peasant domain of politics.[4] The meeting of the two domains did not therefore mean that the first domain was able to absorb and appropriate its other within a single homogeneous unity; the unity itself remained fragmented and fraught with tension.

The second aspect of the meeting of the two domains was that it did not bring about a linear development of the consciousness of the peasantry into a new sense of nationhood. While peasants in different parts of India became aware, albeit in varying degrees, of the realities of nationalist politics, their participation in it seemed to be marked by radical breaks and often reversals, for spells of militant anticolonial action by peasants were often followed by bitter sectarian strife, sometimes in the course of a single movement, and at other times by spells of apparently inexplicable quiescence. Both of these aspects of peasant participation in nationalist politics seemed to point in the same direction: the need for a critique of both colonialist and nationalist historiographies by bringing in the peasantry as a subject of history, endowed with its own distinctive forms of consciousness and making sense of and acting upon the world on its own terms.

PEASANT INSURGENTS OF COLONIAL INDIA

The problem was formulated specifically by Ranajit Guha, using the material on peasant insurgency in the period immediately preceding that of nationalist mass movements.[5] From the series of peasant revolts in colonial India between 1783 and 1900, Guha undertook to isolate the ideological invariants of peasant consciousness and their relational unity—that is to say, its paradigmatic form. He began by assuming that the domination and exploitation under which the peasant lived and worked existed within a relation of power. There was thus an opposed pair: on the one side, the dominators (the state or the landlords or moneylenders), and on the other, the peasants. A relational opposition of power necessarily meant that the dominated had to be granted their own domain of subjectivity, where they were autonomous, undominated. If it were not so, the dominators would, in the exercise of their domination, wholly consume and obliterate the dominated. Dominance then would no longer exist within a social relation of power with its own conditions of reproduction. In this specific case, therefore, the peasantry had to be granted its autonomous domain.

Where was one to locate this domain? If domination is one aspect of this relation of power, its opposed aspect must be resistance. The dialectical opposition of the two gives this relation its unity. This opposition also creates the possibility for a movement within that relation, and thus makes it possible for there to be a history of the relation of dominance and subordination. In searching for the characteristic form of the autonomous domain of peasant consciousness, Guha was led to a study of the aspect of resistance. This did not mean that resistance was more important, or more true, than domination. On the contrary, by placing the forms of peasant consciousness within a dialectical relation of power, peasant consciousness would be assigned its proper theoretical value: its significance was to be established only in relation to its other, namely, the consciousness of the dominator.

If resistance was the aspect of the power relation through which the peasantry expressed its distinct and autonomous identity, as opposed to that of its dominators, where were we to find it in the historical material available to us? Precisely in the material on peasant insurgency, where the insurgent consciousness left its imprint on that of its dominator, and where the dominator was forced expressly to "recognize" its other. Thus the inquiry into the characteristic forms of peasant consciousness became in Guha a study of the elementary aspects of peasant insurgency. The study of peasant insurgency was, in other words, a methodological procedure by which one obtained an access into peasant consciousness, expressed through its resistance at the point of insurgency and recognized as an antagonistic force in the historical records prepared by the dominant classes. The instituted knowledge of society, as it exists in recorded history, is the knowledge obtained by the dominant classes in their exercise of power. The dominated, by virtue of their very powerlessness, have no means of recording their knowledge within those instituted processes, except as an object of the exercise of power. Thus, Guha used the colonial discourse of counterinsurgency to read, as a mirror image, the discourse of insurgency.

He identified six "elementary aspects," as he called them, of the insurgent peasant consciousness: negation, ambiguity, modality, solidarity, transmission, and territoriality. The insurgent consciousness was, first of all, a "negative consciousness," in the sense that its identity was expressed solely through an opposition, namely, its difference from and antagonism to its dominators. It was an identity whose limits were fixed by the very conditions of subordination under which the peasantry lived and worked; only the relations were inverted. The signs of domination, such as the imposition of taxes or rent or of the power to punish, now became the targets of resistance. A characteristic feature of peasant rebellions was the urge of the oppressed to assert his resistance to authority "not in terms of his own culture but his enemy's." Second, the forms of resistance involved a high degree of ambiguity. Precisely because relations of domination were inverted at the moment of insurgency, the signs of rebellion were liable to be misread by the rulers who would fail to distinguish them from such "normal" signs of aberrant behavior as crime. But unlike crime, "rebellions are necessarily and invariably public and communal events"; "crime and insurgency derive from two very different codes of violence." Third, insurgent peasant movements had their characteristic modalities or forms. On the one hand, the political and yet innately negative character of inverting the dominant relations of power took the form of destroying the signs of authority, such as the police station or the landlord's rent-collection office or the moneylender's house. Specifically for the case of colonial India, Guha identified four forms of destruction: wrecking, burning, eating, and looting. On the other hand, the negativity of the insurgent consciousness of the peasant was also expressed in the setting up of a rebel authority, in the inverted image of the authority that it replaced, equally public in character and with its own powers to impose sanctions and levies on the community. Fourth, the self-definition of the insurgent peasant, his awareness of belonging to a collectivity that was separate from and opposed to his enemies, lay in the aspect of solidarity. Its specific expression varied from rebellion to rebellion, sometimes even from one phase to another within the same rebellion. Often it was expressed in terms of ethnicity or kinship or some such affinal category. Sometimes one can read in it the awareness of a class. But solidarity was the total expression of the communal character of an insurgency. Fifth, within the solidarity thus defined, the message of insurgency was transmitted with an ease and rapidity that the ruling classes often found bewildering, but this too had its characteristic channels. Rumor, for instance, was one such channel, in which the source of a message was anonymous and unknown and which involved no distinction between the communicator and his audience. Absolutely transitive, rumor, as distinct from news, was "an autonomous type of popular discourse." Finally, the solidarity of an insurgent peasantry also occupied a specific geographical space. The limits of this geographical space were determined, on the one hand, negatively by the rebel's perception of the geographical spread of the enemy's authority, that is to say, by a principle of exclusion, and on the other, positively by a notion of the ethnic space occupied by the insurgent community, that is, by the principle of solidarity. The intersection of these two spaces defined the territoriality of the insurgency.

THE NOTION OF COMMUNITY

In all these aspects that Guha identified, there is a single unifying idea that gives to peasant insurgency its fundamental social character: the notion of community. Every aspect expresses itself in its specific political forms through the principle of community. Whether through the negatively constituted character of the forms and targets of insurgent action, defined by applying the criterion of "we" and "they," or whether through the rebel's self-definition of the territorial space of insurgency, a principle of community gives to all these specific aspects their fundamental constitutive character as the purposive political acts of a collective consciousness. This principle, again, enables us to read from the actions of a rebellious peasantry at the moment of insurgency the total constitutive character of a peasant consciousness, to relate those actions to the forms of everyday social existence of the peasantry.

It is important to stress this point, because what the principle of community as the characteristic unifying feature of peasant consciousness does is directly place it at the opposite pole to a bourgeois consciousness. The latter operates from the premise of the individual and a notion of his interests (or, in more fashionable vocabulary, his preferences). Solidarities in bourgeois politics are built up through an aggregative process by which individuals come together into alliances on the basis of common interests (or shared preferences). The process is quite the opposite in the consciousness of a rebellious peasantry. There solidarities do not grow because individuals feel they can come together with others on the basis of their common individual interests: on the contrary, individuals are enjoined to act within a collectivity because, it is believed, bonds of solidarity that tie them together already exist. Collective action does not flow from a contract among individuals; rather, individual identities themselves are derived from membership in a community.

The implication is that peasant consciousness cannot be understood in its own constitutive aspects if we continue to reduce it to the paradigm of bourgeois rationality. We must grant that peasant consciousness has its own paradigmatic form, which is not only different from that of bourgeois consciousness but in fact its very other. This central theoretical proposition is brought out by Guha's book, and it poses a basic challenge to the methodological procedures followed not only by bourgeois economists and sociologists (including those of the Chayanovian and "moral economy" varieties) searching for the "rational peasant" (however defined), but also by many Marxist scholars writing on the agrarian question.

This notion of community cannot be immediately assigned a single determinate value based on a determinate social institution such as totemism or caste or religious denomination. The boundaries or forms of solidarity in peasant rebellions have no single determinate character that can be directly deduced either from its immediate socioeconomic context or from its cultural world. On the contrary, the cultural apparatus of signs and meanings—the language, in the broadest sense—available to a peasant consciousness, far from being narrow and inflexible, is capable of a vast range of transformations to enable it to understand, and to act within, varying contexts, both of subordination and of resistance. It is precisely this ability that makes insurgency the purposeful political work of a deliberate and active insurgent consciousness. Without it, this consciousness could in fact be "objectivized" easily, by reducing it to its determinate institutional form—tribe, caste, religious denomination, locality, whatever. Such a reductionism grossly underestimates, and in fact misunderstands, the ideological resilience and innovativeness of peasant consciousness.

THE CONCRETE FORMS OF COMMUNITY

Guha, therefore, has proposed a paradigmatic form of the insurgent peasant consciousness. Its contours are drawn from a reading of the material on peasant revolts in colonial India from the point of view of the peasant as an active and conscious subject of history. But because of his objective of isolating an invariant structural form, in line with the structuralism inherent in his method, he has not attempted to give us a *history* of this consciousness as a movement of self-transformation. Rather, having found an access into the structural form of this consciousness in its aspect of autonomy, he has given us a basis to ask the appropriate questions about its history.

The first area where this interrogation can begin is precisely that which binds together the structure of peasant consciousness as described by Guha, namely, the community. We have seen that Guha, quite correctly, does not give to this community any immediately determinate content; or rather, to put it more accurately, while he describes the community in the historical context of a particular peasant rebellion in the relevant terms of clan, tribe, caste, village, and so forth, he leaves the theoretical conceptualization of the community in peasant consciousness as a formal construct, abstract and empty. It is necessary now to attempt to give to this crucial concept its proper theoretical content. We already have something to go on. We know, for instance, that the identification of the enemy in peasant revolts, the separation of the "they" from the "we," occurs within a framework where distinct communities are seen as being in antagonistic relation with each other. The same framework of communities provides room for the establishment of solidarities and alliances on the side of the rebels (and, for that matter, on the side of the enemy), and even of collaboration and treachery. The alliances are not seen as the result of contracts based on common interests; rather, they are believed to be the necessary duty of groups bound together by mutual bonds of kinship: "You are our brothers. Do join with all expedition." This invitation of the first group of rebels in the Rangpur uprising of 1783 to the peasants of neighboring villages was, in fact, the standard form of insurgent alliance in peasant rebellions all over India. It applied even in the case of a perceived breach of mutual duty; this was no breach of contract. When the villagers of Kallas wrote to those of Akola blaming them for breaking the solidarity of the movement during the Deccan Revolt of 1875, they did not appeal to a mutuality of interest. Rather, they said, "It is wrong of you people to keep communication with persons who are deemed as excluded from the community of the village. . . . As we consider Kallas and Akola as one village, we have made the above suggestions to you."

We also know that the boundaries of solidarity, the line separating the "we" from the "they," can shift according to changing contexts of struggle. Pandey has given us an account of how a strife between Rajput landlords and Muslim weavers in a small town in Uttar Pradesh in the middle of the nineteenth century quickly changed into the solidarity of the entire town in its defense against outside attack and back again to internal strife, all within the space of a few weeks, without any apparent sign that the people of the town saw anything anomalous in these rapid changes in the boundaries of solidarity. Hardiman, Sarkar, and Chatterjee have also considered this problem of shifting boundaries of solidarity in terms of the changing context of struggle.[6] What is necessary now is to formulate the concept of community within a set of systematic relationships signifying the mutual identity and difference of social groups.

In the Indian context, the system of castes seems to represent an obvious paradigmatic form for signifying identity and difference. On the one hand, castes are mutually separate as though they were distinct species of natural beings, and on the other, they are mutually bound together as parts, arranged hierarchically, within a social whole. In traditional social anthropology, to the extent that these relations were seen as constituting a system, the dominant view has been that it provides a framework for harmonizing the mutual interdependence of separate groups through the inculcation of a set of shared values about the unity of the system as a whole.[7] What is not recognized is the equally systematic nature of the rejection of the supposedly "shared" values by groups that are inferior in caste ranking. There seems to be ample evidence to enable us to ground the system of castes within the totality of power relations, because the changing relations between castes and the periodic attempts to redefine the content of ethical conduct in the Indian religions bear the signs of a continuing struggle, and its temporary resolutions, within social relations of domination and subordination. In short, we have here the possibility of linking a history of peasant struggle with a *history* of the caste system, and through it, with a history of religious beliefs and practices. I will consider this issue at length in the next chapter.

There are strong reasons to suspect that the system of castes operates as a paradigmatic form not merely in the domain of relations between jātis within the fold of the Brahmanical religion; it is probably the case that it is the general cultural form of conceptualizing and ordering the relations of identity and difference between several kinds of social groupings. Significantly, the word *jāti* in most Indian languages can be used to designate not merely caste, but caste agglomerations, tribes, race, linguistic groups, religious groups, nationalities, nations. Anthropologists have, of course, often noted the existence of caste or caste-like forms not only among religious groups such as Buddhists, Jains, or the medieval devotional sects that emerged in opposition to the Brahmanical religion, but also among Indian Muslims and Christians. But this point is of a more general significance: the extent to which a caste-like system provides the cultural form for conceptualizing relations of domination, as well as of resistance, between social groups needs to be examined in its concreteness.

Apart from this question of identifying the boundaries of the community in varying contexts of struggle, there is the other aspect of the internal structure of the community in peasant consciousness. It is clear that the notion of community, especially among the nontribal agrarian population, is not egalitarian, even in the matter of rights in the basic means of production, namely, land. For most parts of India, in the sector of settled peasant cultivation, something like a fifth or more of the population, belonging to the lowest castes, have never had any recognized rights in land. But the unity of a community was nevertheless established by recognizing the rights of subsistence of all sections of the population, albeit a differential right entailing differential duties and privileges. The point then is that the notion of community as itself a differentiated unity operates not merely between peasants as a community and their dominators, but between peasants themselves. The full range of possibilities of alliances and oppositions, with the boundaries of community shifting with changing contexts of struggle, may then be said to operate in relations between sections of the peasantry. The point goes against a populist idealization of the peasantry as an egalitarian and harmonious community, free from internal dissention and struggle.

AN INDIAN HISTORY OF PEASANT STRUGGLE

Following Guha, the argument of the *Subaltern Studies* group of historians has been that by studying the history of peasant rebellions from the point of view of the peasant as an active and conscious subject of history, one obtains an access into that aspect of his consciousness where he is autonomous, undominated. One thereby has the means to conceptualize the unity of that consciousness as grounded in a relationship of power, namely, of domination and subordination. Peasant consciousness, then, is a contradictory unity of two aspects: in one, the peasant is subordinate, where he accepts the immediate reality of power relations that dominate and exploit him; in the other, he denies those conditions of subordination and asserts his autonomy. It has also been argued that the community is the space where this contradictory unity of peasant consciousness makes its appearance. So far, the community has been characterized only in the abstract and formal sense. But there is sufficient historical material to begin a more concrete conceptualization of the community, itself differentiated, as the *site* of peasant struggle, where respective rights and duties are established and contested.

Already this gives us a path of investigation that is likely to deviate from the conventional ways of studying peasant revolts in Europe. In fact, I will argue that what the recent debates about the role of the peasantry in the nationalist movement lead to is a project to write an Indian history of peasant struggle.[8] In principle, this is a different project from that of a history of peasant struggles in India. The semantic difference signifies a quite radical difference in the approach to historiography. The latter stands for an arrangement of the historical material on peasant struggles in India according to a framework in which the fundamental concepts and analytical relations are taken as given, established in their generality by the forms of a universal history (for example, the theory of transition from feudalism to capitalism, or modernization theory, or the theory of world systems, or the theory of the moral economy of the peasant, and so on). The former seeks to discover in that material the forms of an immanent historical development, fractured, distorted, and forced into the grid of "world history" only by the violence of colonialism. The framework of this other history does not take as given its appointed place within the order of a universal history, but rather submits the supposedly universal categories to a constant process of interrogation and contestation, modifying, transforming, and enriching them. The object is not to resume the course of a precolonial history by erasing from historical memory and present reality the experience of colonialism: this would be not only archaic and utopian, it would in fact be reactionary even to pretend that this is possible. Rather, the task is to ground one's historical consciousness in the immanent forms of social development that run through Indian history and from that standpoint to engage our colonial experience in a process of struggle—negating and superseding that experience by appropriating it on one's own terms.

This agenda implies the relegation of the universal categories of social formations into a temporary state of suspension, or rather a state of unresolved tension. But this again is a task fundamental to the historian's practice. The relation between history and the theoretical disciplines of the social sciences is necessarily one where the structural neatness of the latter is constantly disturbed and refashioned by the intransigent material of the former. The plea for an Indian history of peasant politics, then, is also one that calls for the historian to take up his or her proper role as agent provocateur among social scientists.

A calumny was spread by European writers on India in the eighteenth and nineteenth centuries to the effect that because of the lack of a historical consciousness among Indians, there existed next to no material on Indian history, save a few court chronicles, hagiographies, and genealogical tables of questionable veracity. This misrepresentation ought not to be attributed solely to the malicious intentions of the colonial mind to tarnish the character of a conquered people. There were more profound difficulties with the very conception of history as a form of knowledge in post-Enlightenment Europe. Judged from the European standpoint, the overwhelming mass of material out of which the institutions and practices of social relations among the Indian people were fashioned, and which survived as palpable evidence of a living past, was simply not recognized as valid historical material. All evidence that did not fit into the linear order of progression of state forms defined by principalities, kingdoms, and empires was relegated to the exotic, timeless domain of Indian ethnology, where history played only a marginal role.

We now know that the situation is quite the opposite. The variety of structural forms of social relations in India, the intricacy of their interconnections, the multiple layers and degrees of differentiation, the ideological forms of identity and difference, and the long course of the historical evolution of these forms through social struggle are stamped on the living beliefs and practices of the people. In its sheer vastness and intricacy, this material is incomparably richer than what is contained in the received histories of Europe, a fact that the efflorescence of modern anthropology in the period after World War II has brought home to the European consciousness. In fact, the recent attempts to exhume a "popular history" of Europe from the rubble of a dead past have been provoked precisely by this challenge thrown by the new sciences of anthropology and linguistics, working on the material of non-European societies, to the accepted dogmas of post-Enlightenment European knowledge.

Now that there is a much greater eagerness to face up to this evidence as historical material, its very richness forces us to throw up our hands and declare that it is much too complex. Every practicing social scientist of India will confess to this feeling of inadequacy and helplessness. For colonial ethnographers, this was evidence of the orderless mélange that was the mysterious Orient, and for colonial administrators, additional proof of the historical necessity to impose linearity and order on an ungovernable society. For Indian nationalists, this was evidence of the greatness of the indigenous tradition which was capable, they said, of absorbing diverse social forms into a single unity without destroying the marks of difference. Needless to say, the colonial view tended to emphasize the inherent disorderliness of Indian society and its lack of a united consciousness, while the nationalists glorified the absorptive capacity without taking notice of the considerable internal struggles that marked the process of absorption.

For those of us who face up to this problem today, the feeling of unmanageable complexity is, if we care to think of it, nothing other than the result of the inadequacy of the theoretical apparatus with which we work. Those analytical instruments were fashioned primarily out of the process of understanding historical developments in Europe. When those instruments now meet with the resistance of an intractably complex material, the fault surely is not of the Indian material but of the imported instruments. If the day comes when the vast storehouse of Indian social history will become comprehensible to the scientific consciousness, we will have achieved along the way a fundamental restructuring of the edifice of European social philosophy as it exists today.

The second point of strength of the Indian material on peasant struggle arises, curiously enough, from an apparent weakness. There is a common tendency to regard the evidence of open revolts of the peasantry in India as insignificant when compared to the historical experience of medieval Europe or to that of neighboring China. One must, however, be careful in judging the nature of this insufficiency. It has sometimes been suggested, for instance, that a history of peasant insurgency in India is a nonstarter because there has never been a peasant revolt in India which was anything more than local and brief. The fact is, first of all, that the number of such "local" revolts is quite considerable, and from about the seventeenth century, through the period of British rule and right up to the contemporary period of the postcolonial state, the accounts of several hundred peasant revolts from all over the country exist in the historical records. Second, what appears to be only "localized" in the context of a vast country like India may often be found to involve a territory and a rebel population larger than those in even the most famous peasant revolts in European history. The crucial difference lies elsewhere. It is undoubtedly true that peasant revolts in India do not seem to have the same political impact on the evolution of state forms or on legal-proprietary relations as they do in Europe or China.[9] An important reason for this is that dominance in Indian society was not exercised exclusively, or even primarily, through the legal forms of sovereign power embodied in the institutions of the state or of feudal estates. Consequently, resistance was not restricted only to the domain of legal-political relations. The study of peasant struggles in India must therefore encompass a field of social relations far wider than what is conventionally regarded as appropriate in European history. Once again, therefore, what the Indian material calls for is an opening up and restructuring of the received disciplinary boundaries for the study of peasant movements.

THE MOVEMENT OF CONSCIOUSNESS

The immediate implications for the project of an Indian history of peasant politics is, first, that the domain of legal-political relations constituted by the state cannot be regarded as the exclusive, perhaps not even the principal, site of peasant struggle. Second, the domain of community will appear as intricately differentiated and layered, with a structural form that affords far greater flexibility, and hence strategic opportunities for both peasants and the dominant classes, in the making of alliances and oppositions than in the "peasant community" in feudal Europe. Third, in the long intervals between open, armed rebellions by peasants or the spread of the great heterodox religious movements, one is likely to notice, if one looks for it, a continuing and pervasive struggle between peasants and the dominant classes in everyday life. The forms of such struggle will range from absenteeism, desertion, selective disobedience, sabotage, and strikes to verbal forms such as slander, feigned ignorance, satire, and abuse—the "Brechtian forms of class struggle," as James Scott has described them.[10] The storehouse of popular culture in India has preserved an enormously rich collection of the material and ideological artifacts of such everyday forms of peasant protest, which have never been incorporated into the study of the processes of subordination and resistance within which Indian peasants have lived and struggled.

This brings us to our final, and crucial, question. If our objective is to write the history of peasant struggle in the form of a history of peasants as active and conscious agents, then their consciousness must also have a history. Their experience of varying forms of subordination, and of resistance, their attempts to cope with changing forms of material and ideological life both in their everyday existence and in those flashes of open rebellion, must leave their imprint on consciousness as a process of learning and development. Some like Scott have sought to privilege the everyday forms of resistance over those of open rebellion because the former are supposedly more enduring and, in the long run, more effective in their slow and almost imperceptible transformation of the conditions of subordination. It may be premature to dismiss this argument on a priori grounds, but the fact remains that the domain of the quotidian, which is also the domain of the seeming perpetuity of subordination, is circumscribed by a limit beyond which lies the extraordinary, apocalyptic, timeless moment of a world turned upside down. It is the historical record of those brief moments of open rebellion which gives us a glimpse of that undominated region in peasant consciousness and enables us to see the everyday and the extraordinary as parts of a single unity in historical time.

To push the point a little further, we could argue that it is always the specter of an open rebellion by the peasantry which haunts the consciousness of the dominant classes in agrarian societies and shapes and modifies their forms of exercise of domination. This was true of the colonial state in the period of British rule in India, just as it is true today, notwithstanding the establishment of universal adult franchise. Of course, the nature and forms of domination of peasants have changed quite fundamentally in the last hundred years or so. The older forms of feudal extraction and ties of bondage have been replaced to a large extent by new forms of extraction mediated through the mechanisms of the market and of fiscal policies. These changes themselves have not come about solely through reforms at the top; a whole series of peasant struggles from the days of colonial rule have acted upon the structures of domination in order to change and modify them. Even the new political institutions of representative government, struggling to give political form to the material of social relations of a large agrarian country, are themselves being shaped into figures that would be unrecognizable in the liberal democracies of the West. To give one example, the phenomenon of massive and uniform swings in the vote across large regions, which has been a characteristic of several recent elections in India, is of a magnitude and geographical spread unknown in Western liberal democracies and inexplicable in terms of the normal criteria of voting behavior. Do we see in this the form of an insurgent peasant consciousness which, having learned in its own way the mechanisms of the new system of power, is now expressing itself through entirely novel methods of political action?

An Indian history of peasant struggle will tell us a great deal more than simply the story of medieval peasant rebellions. For it is a history that constitutes our living and active present. It is a history that will tell us why when peasants identified the colonial state as their enemy, as they did in 1857 or 1942, they could be so much more radical and thoroughgoing in their opposition than their more enlightened compatriots. It is a history that will educate those of us who claim to be their educators. Indeed, an Indian history of peasant struggle is a fundamental part of the real history of our people; the task is for the Indian historian to perceive in this a consciousness of his or her own self.

CHAPTER NINE

The Nation and Its Outcasts

THE SYNTHETIC THEORY OF CASTE

If there was one social institution that, to the colonial mind, centrally and essentially characterized Indian society as radically different from Western society, it was the institution of caste. All arguments about the rule of colonial difference, and hence about the inherent incapacity of Indian society to acquire the virtues of modernity and nationhood, tended to converge upon this supposedly unique Indian institution.

In responding to this charge, Indian nationalists have adopted, broadly speaking, one of two strategies. The first is to deny the suggestion that caste is essential to the characterization of Indian society. This position has been especially favored by the nationalist left as well as by Marxists. Caste, according to this argument, is a feature of the superstructure of Indian society; its existence and efficacy are to be understood as the ideological products of the specific precapitalist social formations that have made their appearance in Indian history. With the supersession of these precapitalist formations, caste too would disappear. One implication of this argument is that by its refusal to ascribe to caste any fundamental significance, it is able to uphold without qualification the legal-political principles of the modern state, to dispute the rule of colonial difference in the public sphere, and to boldly advocate the cultural project of modernity.

Its difficulty as a nationalist argument, however, is that by wholeheartedly embracing all of the claims made on behalf of Western modernity and advocating them for modern India, it leaves little room for disputing on empirical grounds the colonialist criticism of India as a degenerate, caste-ridden society. By explaining the innumerable instances of caste practices as ideological manifestations of a premodern social formation, it seems to condemn virtually the entire corpus of traditional cultural institutions in India, both elite and popular. Such undifferentiated advocacy of the "modern" does not sit too well on claims about the identity of the "national." The case is made worse by a growing evidence that the spread of capitalist economic activities or of modern education does not necessarily bring about an end to caste practices. Even such a historically perspicuous observer as D. D. Kosambi, after noting in 1944 that "it is not necessarily true that caste will disappear with modern means of production any more than the feudal ideology disappeared from Japanese society with modern machinery," was driven to add:

> With the development of the country as a whole [in the period following the decline of Buddhism], and the foundation of its basic economy on the village unit with the family as a sub-unit, the progressive function of caste may be said to have ended, so that caste itself must thereafter attempt to be static. . . . Thus it is that so much of Indian philosophy and literature, which went on developing, had to take the religious path. This "opium of the people" was needed if life were to be worth living. . . . Without thinking of the consequences of their action, our philosophers followed this pattern, which will have to be discarded when the productive system of the country reaches a stage of maturity.[1]

The second strategy seeks to avoid these difficulties by retaining caste as an essential element of Indian society. The presence of a caste system, the assertion goes, makes Indian society essentially different from the Western. What is denied, however, in this nationalist argument is the charge that caste is necessarily contradictory to, and incompatible with, a modern and just society. This is achieved by distinguishing between the empirical-historical reality of caste and its ideality. Ideally, the caste system seeks to harmonize within the whole of a social system the mutual distinctness of its parts. This is a requirement for any stable and harmonious social order; the caste system is the way this is achieved in India.

This enormously influential nationalist argument has been addressed at different levels. Gandhi used to argue that the empirical reality of caste discrimination and even its sanction in the religious texts had "nothing to do with religion."[2] The ideal fourfold *varna* scheme was meant to be a noncompetitive functional division of labor and did not imply a hierarchy of privilege. This idealism found a metaphysical exposition in Sarvepalli Radhakrishnan, who asserted that the varna scheme was a universal form of the organic solidarity of the individual and the social order.[3] Since then, successive generations of Indian sociologists, working with increasingly detailed and sophisticated ethnographic materials, have propounded the idea that there is a systematic form to the institutionalized practices of caste, that this system is in some sense fundamental to a characterization of Indian society, and that it represents a way of reconciling differences within a harmonious unity of the social order.[4]

Of the two strategies, one contains a critique of the other. Both, however, accept the premise of modernity, the former espousing it to condemn caste as an oppressive and antiquated institution inconsistent with a modern society, the latter asserting that caste in its ideal form is not oppressive and not inconsistent with the aspirations of individuality within the harmony of a unified social order. The former could be said to represent the pure theory of universal modernity; the latter, its genealogy running deep into the traditions of Orientalist scholarship, upholds a theory of Oriental exceptionalism. As nationalist arguments, both adopt the externally given standpoint of bourgeois equality to criticize the empirical reality of caste practices and to advocate modernist reform. As for their overall framing devices, the former argument, of course, has available to it the entire Western discourse on modernity; the latter, on the other hand, has to construct a special theory, in this case the synthetic theory of caste, which however has the same form as any synthetic theory of "the unity of Indian society."

REQUIREMENTS OF AN IMMANENT CRITIQUE OF CASTE

I wish to state here the requirements for a critique of the synthetic theory of caste that does not rely on an external standpoint.[5] These, in other words, will be the requirements for an immanent critique of caste. By implication, these will also give us the general form for an immanent critique of all synthetic theories about "the unity of Indian society."

1. The starting point is the *immediate* reality of caste, namely the diversity of particular jātis with specific characteristics. Each jāti can be shown to have its particular quality: on the one hand a definition-by-self that is the positive characteristic which identifies the jāti as itself, and on the other a definition-for-another by which other jātis are distinguished from it. Any particular qualitative criterion that is supposed to identify a jāti will imply both the positive and the negative definitions. Thus, if the Chamar is identified as a caste that disposes of dead cattle, this definition-by-self immediately implies a definition-for-another, namely that other castes (at least, some other castes) do not have this occupation. It is thus that distinctions and classifications by quality can be made among jātis.

Now, these distinctive qualities of particular castes are finite and hence alterable. We have innumerable examples of the qualitative marks of particular jātis varying both regionally and over time. We also know that there is a multiplicity of qualitative criteria which can serve to distinguish jāti from jāti. The finiteness of quality is negated by a definition-for-self of caste that shows the diverse individual castes to be many particular forms, distinguished by quantity, of one universal measure of caste. To give an example from another scientific field, particular commodities are immediately distinguishable from one another by a variety of finite qualities, but a definition-for-self of commodity, namely value, enables us to order by quantity, that is, exchange value, the entire range of particular commodities. Similarly, we can make determinate distinctions by quantity between all castes if we have a similar definition-for-self of caste. The most powerful candidate in sociological literature for this definition of "casteness" is hierarchy. According to this argument, hierarchy fixes a universal measure of "casteness" so that, at any given time and place, the immediate qualitative diversity of jātis can be ordered as a quantitative ranking in a scale of hierarchy. The universal measure appears for each particular caste as a determinate position, quantitatively fixed (higher/lower) and hence comparable, in the hierarchy of all castes. Thus the move is made from the unintelligibility of immediate diversity to an identification of the *being-for-self* of caste. Now it is possible to identify *determinate* castes, here and now, as an ordered set, unambiguous and non-contradictory, at least in principle. In fact, like the Maître de Philosophie telling M. Jourdain that he had been speaking prose all his life without knowing it, this is precisely what Louis Dumont tells us in chapter 2 of *Homo Hierarchicus*: he uses the substantive material of caste ethnology to fix the determinate being of castes.[6]

2. Dumont does something more, which also happens to be the next step in our immanent critique of caste. The being-for-self of caste, namely hierarchy, can be shown to imply a contradictory *essence*. As soon as we try to arrange the determinate, here-and-now evidence of the ethnological material in a sequence of change, we will discover in place of the immediacy of being the reflected or mediated self-identity of caste on the one hand and a self-repulsion or difference on the other. Dumont identifies from within the immediacy of caste practices a contradictory essence, mediated by ideology (or religion), namely, the opposition between purity and pollution. While the need to maintain purity implies that the castes must be kept separate (thus, Brahmans cannot engage in the polluting occupations of menial castes), it also necessarily brings the castes together (since Brahmans cannot do without the menial castes if their economic services are to be provided). The unity of identity and difference—in this case, vide Dumont, the unity of purity and pollution—gives us the *ground* of caste as a totality or system. The being of caste is here shown as mediated; its existence is now relative in terms of its interconnections with other existents within the totality of the ground. Dumont devotes the greater part of his book to defending his case that the unity of the opposites purity and pollution provides adequate ground for defining the totality of caste relations as a system.

Once grounded, the immediate relation in the system of castes will appear as the relation between the whole and the parts. Only the parts have independent being, but the relations between the parts themselves are the result of the contradictory unity of identity and difference. The parts can be held together only if they are mediated into self-relation within the whole of the system by *force*. In Dumont's treatment, the force that holds together the different castes within the whole of the caste system is the ideological force of *dharma*. The construct of dharma assigns to each jāti its place within the system and defines the relations between jātis as the simultaneous unity of mutual separateness and mutual dependence.

The movement of force must make apparent the process of uniting the essence of a system with its existence. Here, Dumont's claim is categorical. The central argument of his work is that the ideological force of dharma does in fact unite the mediated being of caste with its ideality. Thus the ideal construct of dharma is actualized in the immediacy of social institutions and practices. This claim is central not merely in Dumont; it must in fact be central to all synthetic constructions of the theory of caste, for all such theories must claim that the conflicting relations between the differentiated parts of the system (namely, jātis) are effectively united by the force of dharma so that the caste system as a whole can continue to reproduce itself. I have chosen to use Dumont's book as the most influential and theoretically sophisticated construction of the synthetic theory of caste.

3. In order to make a critique of the ideology of caste, then, we must show that this process of actualization necessarily contains a contradiction. We must show, in other words, that the unification of the essence of caste with its existence through the movement of the force of dharma is inadequate and one-sided; it is a resolution that reveals its falsity by concealing the contradiction within it. This is the crucial step in the critique of caste. By locating our critique at this level, where the claim that the mediated being of caste (that is to say, its ideality) has been actualized in immediate social reality is brought under critical examination, we look at caste neither as base nor as superstructure but precisely as the level of social reality that claims to unite the two. If this claim can be shown to be false, that is, if the idea of caste can be shown to be *necessarily* at variance with its actuality, we will have the elementary means for an immanent critique of caste.

Dumont traverses the first two stages of this dialectic without attempting to move to the third. It is at the third stage that this critique of Dumont must be grounded. There may of course be several inaccuracies or incorrect statements in Dumont's delineation of the movement in the first two stages. To point these out is undoubtedly justified, and many commentators in the last two decades have done so, but these do not amount to a critique of Dumont, for it is theoretically possible to modify the actual contents of *Homo Hierarchicus* to yield a more correctly constituted Dumont-type construction. The critique must consist in showing the inherent plausibility and justification of the transition from the second to the third stage—and that move will destroy the central claim of

Dumont (or of any synthetic construction of that type) that ideality lies united with actuality in the immediate reality of caste.

Interestingly, Dumont seems to be aware of this line of attack, and in his 1979 preface has attempted to fortify his position against it by declaring that the anthropologist's construction of a global ideology can never hope to "cover without contradiction the entire field of its application" and must, at every stage, leave a certain irreducible residue in the observed object. The demand for an ideology that is "identical in its breadth and content to the reality as lived" is the demand of idealism, "and it is surprising to see it formulated by the same critics who have reproached us in the name of empiricism for granting too much importance to ideas and values." He then states his own position, now suitably modified: "At the most general level, what our conclusion means is that hierarchical ideology, like egalitarian ideology, is not perfectly realized in actuality, or, in other terms does not allow direct consciousness of all that it implies."[7] One could, of course, say to Dumont that he cannot have it both ways. But let us refrain from raising this obvious objection and point out instead that the matter is not simply one of the *empirical* residue of unexplained observations. Our objection will be that any Dumont-like construction of the ideology of caste will be necessarily at variance with its actuality because the unification is contested *within* the "observed object," that is to say, within the immediate system of castes.

We may also note here that Dumont himself acknowledges that he has confined himself to the first two stages of the movement I have delineated above: his object, he says, is to "understand" the caste system, not to criticize it. Speaking—necessarily—from within the system of castes, I cannot, unfortunately, afford this anthropologist's luxury, notwithstanding the fact that many Indian anthropologists, in the mistaken belief that this is the only proper scientific attitude to culture, have presumed to share the same observational position with their European teachers. Dumont further says that his is a study of "structure," not of "dialectic." The oppositions within his structure do not "produce" anything; they are static and not surpassed through a "development"; the global setting of the structure is given once and for all.[8] I am, of course, looking for contradictions that are dialectical, where oppositions are surpassed through negation, producing a developed unity and, once again, a new set of contradictions. I do not, however, agree with Dumont that the dialectical method is necessarily "synthetic." It is rather the Dumont-type method of "structure," where the whole is a "structural" rather than a "dialectical" whole, which, when applied to immediate phenomena bearing the unexamined content of history, becomes profoundly "synthetic" in its assertion that all oppositions are necessarily contained within a global unity "given once and for all."

DUMONT DISINTERRED

It would be redundant here to attempt a review of the contents of such a well-known work as *Homo Hierarchicus*. I propose instead to rearrange the materials of a criticism of Dumont by Dipankar Gupta in terms of the framework outlined above and then assess what remains to be done for an adequate critique to emerge.[9]

Gupta's central criticism of Dumont consists in questioning the latter's claim that the essence of caste lies in a continuous hierarchy along which castes can be ordered in terms of relative purity. Gupta's counterargument is that the essence of caste lies in differentiation into separate and discrete endogamous jātis; the attribute of hierarchy is a property that does not belong to the essence of caste, and in any case, where hierarchy exists it is not purity/pollution that is the necessary criterion.

A little reflection will show that, put in this form, the criticism cannot be sustained. The discreteness of separate endogamous jātis is of course the most obvious aspect of the immediate phenomenon of caste. When this separateness is seen as based on qualitative differences, we necessarily have for each jāti its being-by-self and being-for-another, involving, in this case, the ascription of the natural differences of biological species on an order of cultural differentiation. Every recognized qualitative attribute of a jāti serves to establish its *natural* difference from other jātis, and this difference is upheld above all in the rule of endogamy, which lays down that the natural order of species must not be disturbed. Kane notes the agreement of all medieval *dharmaśāstra* texts on this point and cites the *Sūtasaṃhitā*, which states explicitly that the "several castes are like the species of animals and that caste attaches to the body and not to the soul."[10] The point, however, is that as soon as these discrete jātis are recognized as particular forms belonging to the same class of entities, that is to say, they are all recognized as *castes*, the finiteness of discrete qualities will be negated by a being-for-self of caste embodying the universal measure of "casteness." Dumont identifies this universal measure as one of having a place in the hierarchy of castes. In relation to this being-for-self, particular castes can only be distinguished from one another by quantity, namely their relative place in that hierarchy. An ordering among determinate castes will then be necessarily implied. (Continuity is not, strictly speaking, necessary, even in Dumont's scheme: an unambiguous and transitive ranking by quantity is all that is required.) Gupta's criticism here is misplaced, for the critique of Dumont's method cannot be sustained at the level of the determinate being of caste.

Gupta, however, makes another set of criticisms that is far more promising. There is not one caste ideology, he says, but several, sharing some principles in common but articulated at variance and even in opposition to one another. Now, this criticism is leveled at the essence of caste as identified by Dumont. We have seen already that Dumont locates the essence of caste on the religious ground defined by the opposition purity/pollution and claims that the force of dharma unites the determinate parts (the separate jātis) into a whole. To establish this claim, however, Dumont has first to dispose of a rather serious problem that arises in establishing the unity of the actuality of the institutions and practices of caste with its ideality. This problem has to do with the fact that the actual rankings of caste take variable forms in space (regional caste systems) and in time (caste mobility) and, further, that these specific orderings are not necessarily consistent with an ideal ordering in terms of purity/pollution. Dumont attempts to solve this problem, first, by positing an absolute separation between *dharma* and *artha*, and then asserting the absolute superiority of the former, the domain of ideology, to the latter, the domain of power. This enables him to allow power (economic, political) to play a residual role in the actual ranking of castes; specifically, the quantitative criterion of hierarchical ordering becomes a weighted numeraire where purity/pollution is the only variable allowed to fix the two extreme poles of the scale of ranking, while power variables are allowed to affect the ordering in the middle.

There is something inelegant in this solution offered by Dumont, and a large number of his critics have produced both textual and practical evidence to show that his assertion here is doubtful.[11] But Gupta's criticism that there is not one caste ideology (dharma) but several has the potential, if adequately theorized, for a more serious critique of Dumont. If substantiated, it would amount to the assertion that the very universality of dharma as the ideality of caste is not generally acknowledged by every part of the system of castes. This criticism would hold even if Dumont's specific characterization of dharma is modified to take care of the factual inaccuracies; in other words, the criticism would hold for any synthetic theory of caste.

To develop these criticisms into a theoretical critique of Dumont one would need to show: (1) that the immediate reality of castes represents the appearance not of one universal ideality of caste, but of several which are not only at variance but often in opposition; (2) that the universal dharma which claims to be the force binding the parts of the system into a whole is a one-sided construction; (3) that this one-sided ideality succeeds in its assertion of universality not because of the self-conscious unity of subject and object in each individual part but because of the effectiveness of a relation of domination and subordination; and (4) that the fragmented and contradictory consciousnesses represent an actuality that can be unified only by negating the one-sided ideality of the dominant construction of dharma.

Let me state the implications of this project. I am suggesting, first, that there is in popular beliefs and practices of caste an implicit critique which questions the claim of the dominant dharma to unify the particular jātis into a harmonious whole and which puts forward contrary claims.[12] Second, just as the effectiveness of the claims of the one dharma is contingent upon the conditions of power, so also are the possibilities and forms of the contrary claims conditioned by those relations of power. Third, in their deviance from the dominant dharma, the popular beliefs draw upon the ideological resources of given cultural traditions, selecting, transforming, and developing them to cope with new conditions of subordination but remaining limited by those conditions. Finally, the negativity of these contrary claims is an index of their failure to construct an alternative universal to the dominant dharma and is thus the mark of subalternity; the object of our project must be to develop, make explicit, and unify these fragmented oppositions in order to construct a critique of Indian tradition that is at the same time a critique of bourgeois equality.

What I have identified here are therefore the requirements for an immanent critique of caste ideology. The critique itself cannot be sustained unless one can address the corpus of caste ethnology right up to our contemporary times from this standpoint. I cannot claim any such expertise for myself. All I can attempt here is a brief illustrative exercise to show some of the possibilities of this approach. The interested reader may wish to compare my approach with Dumont's treatment of the same problem in his essay "World Renunciation in Indian Religions."[13] Whereas Dumont treats the series of oppositions—life in the world/life of the renouncer, group religion/disciplines of salvation, caste/individual—as having been unified within the "whole" of Hinduism by integration at the level of doctrinal Brahmanism and by toleration at the level of the sects, I will offer a different interpretation that treats these oppositions as fundamentally unresolved—unified, if at all, not at the level of the self-consciousness of "the Hindu" but only within the historical contingencies of the social relations of power.

THE DHARMA OF THE MINOR SECTS

The so-called minor religious sects of Bengal commanded, at various points of time between the seventeenth and nineteenth centuries, the following of quite a major section of the population of Bengal. Ramakanta Chakrabarty has compiled a list of fifty-six heterodox sects of this kind, many of which survive to this day.[14] Of these, the Bāul, the Jaganmohinī, the Kartābhajā, the Kiśorībhajā, the Sāhebdhanī, and a few others are relatively well known, the Kartābhajā in particular attracting much attention for its easy syncretism from the Calcutta intelligentsia in the nine-

teenth century, and the Bāul, of course, having been granted the status of
an export item in the Festival of India circuit. Most of these sects are
broadly classified as Vaiṣṇava or semi-Vaiṣṇava, but it is heterodoxy that
is the hallmark of their status as "minor sects." Besides the general presence of what is loosely described as Sahajiyā Vaiṣṇavism, observers have
variously noted the strong doctrinal and ritual influence on these sects of
Buddhist Sahajiyā ideas, of "left" Tantric practices, of the religion of the
Nāth cults, of Sufi doctrines, and of the Dharma cult of lower Bengal. The
other crucial characteristic is that their following was predominantly,
though not always exclusively, among the lower castes.

If one situates the rise of these cults in relation to the history of
Vaiṣṇavism in Bengal, the crucial development that has to be noticed is
the systematic introduction of caste practices in the religious and social
life of orthodox Vaiṣṇavas. Ramakanta Chakrabarty suggests that caste
rules began to be strictly applied after the historic festival held in Kheturi
(Rajshahi) sometime between 1576 and 1582, which was attended by
representatives of nearly a hundred Vaiṣṇava groups from all over Bengal.[15] The Kheturi council laid down the doctrinal and ritual framework
of what was to become the dominant orthodoxy of Gauḍīya Vaiṣṇavism,
based on canons prescribed by the gosvāmīs of Vrindavan.[16] The attempt,
as Hitesranjan Sanyal suggests, may have been on the one hand to provide doctrinal respectability to a relatively unsophisticated popular religious movement by engaging in the discourse of Puranic Brahmanism and
the great systems of Vaiṣṇava religious thought, and on the other to create
the forms of practical religion that would integrate the diverse Sahajiyā
Vaiṣṇava cults into the main trend of the bhakti movement.[17]

But soon enough, the differentiated forms of social identity and distinction appeared in the body of the Vaiṣṇava sampradāy. In contrast with
the earlier phase of the movement, when several prominent non-Brahman
Vaiṣṇava gurus such as Narahari Sarkar, Narottam Datta, and Rasika-
nanda had Brahman disciples, or unlike the "neo-Brahman" phase, when
some Vaiṣṇavas such as the followers of Shyamananda Pal in Midnapore
began to wear the sacred thread irrespective of caste, the new orthodoxy
that grew up frowned upon such practices. Indeed, the emphasis now was
against indiscriminate proselytization, and the highest status was accorded among Vaiṣṇavas to the Brahman kulaguru, who acted as initia-
tor and spiritual guide to a small number of respectable upper-caste families. Gradually, a clearly recognized social distinction emerged between
high-caste Gauḍīya Vaiṣṇava householders and the low-caste jāt baiṣnab
(that is, Vaiṣṇava by caste), who were for all practical purposes regarded
by the former as outcastes. Indeed, a whole series of stereotypes of the jāt
baiṣnab, combining the familiar prejudices of caste impurity with aspersions on their sexual morality, emerged to condemn the low-caste converts beyond the pale of the orthodox Gauḍīya Vaiṣṇava sampradāy. The

sexual aspersions, in particular, derived from the simplicity of the marriage ceremony practiced by the followers of most minor sects, which explicitly rejected the ritual injunctions of the *smṛti*; upper-caste Vaiṣṇavas refused to regard these as proper weddings. Further, the sects were looked down upon for the refuge they often provided to widows and abandoned women; it was believed that the women were engaged in illicit liaisons with cult followers and used in orgiastic rituals, and the ranks of the sect were swelled by the children of such unsanctified unions.[18]

Seen from the standpoint of the history of Vaiṣṇavism in Bengal, this imposition of more or less orthodox caste practices on the Vaiṣṇava movement was part of the same process that gave rise to the deviant sects. As historians have pointed out, it was a situation where, after a spell of substantial mobility and readjustment of positions mostly in the middle rungs of the caste hierarchy in Bengal, and a significant process of incorporation of tribal populations in the peripheral regions into some form of Puranic religious practice,[19] the dominant ideological need was to reproduce a stable structure of social divisions within a harmonious whole. A universalizing religion such as Vaiṣṇavism could justify itself only by accommodating those differences within itself. The points of historical interest for us, therefore, are first the doctrinal and practical means by which this was attempted, and second the marks of unresolved and continuing conflict that this process of unification bears.

"The assertion of Brahmanical dominance," says Ramakanta Chakrabarty, "in a religious movement which was rooted in mysticism, and which was anti-caste and anti-intellectual, inevitably led to the growth of deviant orders."[20] He then gives an account of the origins, mostly in the eighteenth century, of some of these orders that were usually founded by Vaiṣṇavas from the "untouchable" Śūdra castes and that usually had a following among the trading and artisanal castes, the untouchables, and sometimes tribals converted to the new faith.

In talking about the doctrinal beliefs and ritual practices of these sects, the usual description offered is "eclecticism." Thus: "The spread of Vaiṣṇavism among the low castes strengthened eclectic tendencies. Eclecticism was produced by a combination of circumstances."[21] Chakrabarty lists some of these: the secret practice by Vaiṣṇava gurus of Tantric worship while openly professing Vaiṣṇavism; the continued respect for folk gods and goddesses among Vaiṣṇava converts; the obeisance paid to Kṛṣṇa, Rādhā, and Caitanya by non-Vaiṣṇava medieval poets, even Muslim poets, and in non-Vaiṣṇava temple art; and the participation of non-sectarians, including Muslims, in Vaiṣṇava festivals. But to characterize these faiths as eclectic is, of course, nothing more than to acknowledge that they cannot be classified under one or the other of the well-known and dominant theological systems. It is, as a matter of fact, merely to recognize that the existence of these sects is itself evidence of an unstable layering in popular consciousness of material drawn from diverse dominant as well as subordinate traditions, the only principle of unity being the contradictory one of simultaneous acceptance and rejection of domination. To characterize the particular structure of this consciousness, we must identify in the particular historical conjuncture the specific form of this contradictory unity.

What were the doctrinal means used by Vaiṣṇavism to construct the unity of an internally divided community? In the post-Caitanya phase, the fundamental devotional attitude of bhakti was itself explicated along two lines. On the one hand, the more orthodox strand following upon the canonical strictures of the Vrindavan gosvāmīs insisted on the performance by ordinary devotees of *vaidhi*, or ritually sanctioned, bhakti. The *Haribhaktivilāsa* of Gopala Bhaṭṭa Gosvāmin became the authoritative text for this form of Vaiṣṇava devotion, and it went a long way in reconciling the ideal of Vaiṣṇava love with the ritual norms of Brahmanical caste practices. On the other hand, Gauḍīya Vaiṣṇavas also granted doctrinal sanction to what was called *rāgānuga* bhakti, which had a more mystical form and which was said to originate in an unbearable desire or thirst for God in the being of the devotee. Although the forms of rāgānuga devotion soon acquired their own disciplinary modes of practice, and the orthodox school insisted that they could be open only to a select few, the important point was that these forms were not required to conform to scriptural injunctions or institutional arrangements. This was the first mode of doctrinal differentiation by which the religion of Vaiṣṇavism in Bengal would try to unify its fold of believers. It provided a means by which Vaiṣṇava householders could retain their allegiance to the faith while participating in the ritual procedures of social and personal life as laid down in the śāstra, whereas the deviant orders of the *sahajiyā sādhak* could also proclaim to their followers the esoteric connection between their pursuit of ecstatic bhakti and the doctrinal principles of the main body of the movement.

The second mode of differentiation was provided in the forms and methods of Vaiṣṇava worship. It took some time, and a fair amount of debate, for the idea of Caitanya as an incarnation of Kṛṣṇa to be firmly fixed, and even then much controversy followed about a suitable hagiology that would replicate the divine deeds at Vrindavan with those at Nabadwip, a matter complicated further by the Gauḍīya doctrine of Caitanya as the dual incarnation of Kṛṣṇa as well as Rādhā. But the crucial concept that gained predominance within the Bengal school of Vaiṣṇavism and that enabled a wide variety of forms of devotional worship to be doctrinally unified was the theory of *parakīyā* love. Sashibhusan Das Gupta has shown how the celebration in Vaiṣṇava thought of the extramarital love of Kṛṣṇa and Rādhā was appropriated into the forms of an earlier tradition in Bengal of yogic practices leading to the state of *mahāsukha* or *sahaja* as conceived in Tantric Buddhism.[22] But the important point for us is that even in this process of transformation, the doctrine of parakīyā love became internally differentiated. While it was generally acknowledged that the *līlā* of Kṛṣṇa and Rādhā was the means by which Kṛṣṇa in his active, worldly, quality-infused form of *bhagavāna* realized the unity of his ultimate nature, or *svarūpa-śakti*, in the form of an infinite state of love or bliss, the attitude of the Vaiṣṇava devotees to this sport of the gods came to be structured in a differentiated form.

The Gauḍīya orthodoxy (or at least that section of it which subscribed to the superiority of parakīyā over svakīyā love) insisted that the *rādhābhāva*, or the attitude of worship of Kṛṣṇa as a married woman for her lover, was proper only to Śrī Caitanya himself. For his devotees, the prescribed attitude of worship was that of the *sakhī* or the *mañjarī*, who comprised a differentiated circle of female companions of the divine couple and whose task it was to act as reverential accomplices, attendants, and voyeurs to the sacred union. In time, especially in the post-Kheturi phase, the orthodox prescription to devotees was to adopt the mañjarī mode of worship, for only by choosing to serve as the humble attendant could one eliminate from one's person all traces of *puruṣābhimāna*, which was proper only to Kṛṣṇa and not to a true Vaiṣṇava devotee. For the latter, the eternal sport of *nityavṛndāvana* was only a memory to be cherished, contemplated, and ritually remembered in daily life.[23] This prescription seems to have opened a way for personal peace and harmony through a devout religiosity but only at the cost of an all-suffering social quiescence.

The deviant Sahajiyā orders, however, turned their affiliation to parakīyā worship in a wholly contrary direction. They subscribed to the doctrine of eternal love as represented in the *līlā* of Kṛṣṇa and Rādhā in nityavṛndāvana and called it the state of *sahaja*, or supreme bliss, but argued that it was possible for mortal men and women living in a gross material world to make the transition to the state of supreme love through a disciplined process of spiritual culture, or *sādhan*. The Sahajiyā supplemented the orthodox doctrine of bhakti with a theory of *āropa*, that is, the attribution of divinity to mortal men and women, and thus effected its transformation into a fundamentally different doctrine. The argument now was that the *svarūpa*, or true spiritual self, resided within the physical form (*rūpa*) of every human being and had to be realized in its developed and perfect state without denying or annihilating his or her physical existence. Indeed, it is human love, moving from the gross forms of carnal desire through successive stages of spiritual development, that finally attains the perfect and infinite forms of divine love while retaining and subsuming within it the earlier forms. Through such a process of sādhan, it is possible for men and women to realize the svarūpa of Kṛṣṇa and Rādhā in their own selves.

As a doctrine this was heretical, and the actual procedures of parakīyā love practiced by the various Sahajiyā sects were looked upon by "respectable" Vaiṣṇava householders as unclean and disreputable. Sometimes there were fairly violent attempts at suppression, such as in the *pāṣaṇḍīdalan* diatribes launched by the defenders of Brahmanical orthodoxy and in the unrelenting campaigns by the Islamic orthodoxy to suppress the various *marfati* sects, particularly the Bāul. At other times they were allowed to exist, but as degraded orders on the peripheries of normal social life. Nevertheless, the possibility of a doctrinal attachment between the domain of the regular and orthodox on the one hand and that of the degraded and deviant on the other, through an appropriation of one or the other meaning of the inherently polysemic concepts which sought to unify the field of dogma and ritual, meant that on either side the unity, however tenuous, of the whole could be emphasized when required, just as the irreconcilability of differences could also be asserted if necessary.

The question of identity or difference, one dharma or many, then becomes not so much a matter of judging the inherent strength of the synthetic unification proclaimed by a dominant religion. Any universalist religion will bear in its essence the contradictory marks of identity and difference, the parts being held together in a whole by an ideological force that proclaims, with varying degrees of effectiveness, its unity.[24] The question, rather, becomes a historical one of identifying the determinants that make this unity a matter of *contingency*.

It will be apparent from the histories of the minor sects that the varying intensities of their affiliation with the larger unity, the degree of "eclecticism," the varying measures and subtleties in emphasizing their difference and their self-identity reveal not so much the desire to create a new universalist system but rather varying strategies of survival, and of self-assertion. The Bāuls openly proclaim their unconventionality and rejection of scriptural injunctions, both Brahmanical and Islamic, but live as mendicants outside society. They talk of love and the divine power that resides in all men and women and thus engage philosophically in the discourses both of Vaiṣṇavism and Sufism, yet are marked out as unorthodox and deviant, not a proper part of the congregation. They enthrall their audiences by singing, with much lyricism, subtlety, and wit, of the "man of the heart" and the "unknown bird" that flies in and out of the cage which is the human body, but practice their own disciplines of *sādhan* and worship in secret, under the guidance of the *murshid*.[25] Of sects that live on among a lay following of ordinary householders, most do not display any distinct sect-marks on the person of the devotee, so that in their daily lives the sectarians are largely indistinguishable from others. What they offer to their followers, as in the case of the Kartābhajā or the Sāhebdhanī, is a congregational space defined outside the boundaries of the dominant religious life, outside caste society or the injunctions of the *shari'ah*, but a space brought into active existence only periodically, at thinly attended weekly meetings with the *mahāśay* or the *fakir* and at the three or four large annual festivals where sectarians perform the prescribed duties of allegiance to their preceptor and their faith, while numerous others come just as they would to any religious fair—to eat and drink, listen to the music, pick up a few magic cures for illnesses and disabilities, and generally to collect one's share of virtue that is supposed to accrue from such visits. The sect leaders preach, often in language that conceals under its surface imagery an esoteric meaning open only to initiates, doctrines that talk of their rejection of the Vedas and of caste, of idolatry and sastric or *shariati* ritual, but the greater their sect's reach across the caste hierarchy, the less strident is their critical tone and the more vapid their sentiments about the sameness of all faiths. The Kartābhajā, for instance, originated in the eighteenth century from a founder who was probably Muslim, but the sect was organized in its present form in the early nineteenth century by a prosperous Sadgop family. It has retained its following among the middle and lower castes, and in particular draws a very large number of women, especially widows, to its festivals, but a fair number of upper-caste people have also been initiated into the faith. Not surprisingly, a distinction has been innovated between the *vyavahārik*, the practical social aspect of the life of the devotee, and the *pāramārthik*, the supreme spiritual aspect, the former virtually becoming marked as a ground of inevitable compromise and surrender to the dominant norms of society and the latter the secret preserve of autonomy and self-assertion.[26]

All of these, then, are strategies devised within a relationship of dominance and subordination, and they take on doctrinal or ritual attributes and acquire different values according to the changing contingencies of power. But in all their determinate manifestations in particular historical circumstances, they are shaped by the condition of subalternity. I now propose to discuss the case of a minor sect whose historical effectiveness in propagating a deviant religion for the lowest castes seems to have been particularly unsuccessful: let us see if even this rather extreme case of "failure" tells us something about the strategies of resistance and assertion.

A TEACHER AMONG THE HĀDI

Along with the Ḍom, the Hāḍi is an archetypal *antaja* caste of Bengal. It is not particularly numerous in Nadia district, where in 1931 it constituted only about 0.02 percent of all untouchable castes and was considerably fewer in number than the Bāgdi, Muchi, Namaśūdra, or Mālo, which comprised the bulk of the 30 percent or so of the Hindu population of that district which was classifiable as untouchable.[27] But it stands as a cultural stereotype of the lowest among the low; thus, for instance, when a Chittagong saying ridicules the proclivity among low castes to assert mutual superiority in ranking, it illustrates the fact precisely by picking out the Hāḍi and the Ḍom: "The Ḍom thinks he is purer than the HāḌi, the HāḌi thinks he is purer than the Ḍom."[28] Risley classifies the Hāḍi as "a menial and scavenger class of Bengal Proper," with whom no one will eat and from whom no one will accept water.[29] The Hāḍis have priests of their own and are forbidden from entering the courtyards of the great temples. In the nineteenth century, they sometimes had tenancy rights in land as occupancy or nonoccupancy *raiyats*, but were mostly day laborers in agriculture, their traditional occupations the tapping of date-palm trees, making bamboo implements, playing musical instruments at weddings and festivals, carrying palanquins, serving as syces, and scavenging. The removal of nightsoil was confined exclusively to the Methar subcaste. Risley reports that the Hāḍis also preferred infant marriage and permitted both divorce and the remarriage of widows, although the synonymous caste of Bhuiṅmāli in Dacca did not at that time allow the latter.

James Wise tells a story about the Dacca Bhuiṅmāli.[30] They were, they say, Śūdras originally and were once invited along with all other castes to a feast given by the goddess Pārvatī. On seeing the goddess, a guileless Bhuiṅmāli remarked: "If I had such a beautiful woman in my house, I would cheerfully perform the most menial offices for her." Śiva overheard the remark, took the Bhuiṅmāli up on his word, gave him a beautiful wife, and made him her sweeper for life. A Dacca proverb makes the comment that the Bhuiṅmāli is the only Hindu ever to be degraded for love of garbage.

Balarām Hāḍi, founder of the Balarāmī sect, was born in Meherpur in Nadia sometime around 1780.[31] In his youth he was employed as a watchman at the house of the Malliks, the Vaidya zamindars of Meherpur.[32] It is said that among the employees of the Malliks, a number of Bhojpuri Brahmans worked as guards and servants, with whom Balaram spent a lot of his time, listening to recitations from Tulsidas's *Rāmāyaṇa* and other devotional compositions. At this time there occurred one night a theft of some valuable jewelry with which the family deity of the Malliks was adorned. Balaram was suspected to have been involved in the crime and, by the order of his employer, was tied to a tree and severely beaten. Mortified by this, Balaram left Meherpur and did not return to his village for the next twenty years or more. He is said to have wandered about in the company of religious men, and when he came back to Meherpur to found his sect, he was fifty years old and a mendicant.

Balaram was illiterate but was credited with a quick wit and an unusual flair for the use of words. The Hāḍis, he used to say, did not have any of the taints with which the Brahmans had stigmatized them; just as the Gharāmi was one who built houses (*ghar*), so was the Hāḍi one who had created *hāḍ*—the bones with which all living beings are made. Akshaykumar Datta relates an apocryphal story that illustrates rather well Balaram's reputed facility with argumentation:

> Balaram had gone to bathe in the river, when he saw some Brahmans offering *tarpaṇ* to their ancestors. Imitating their actions, he too began to throw water on the river-bank. One of the Brahmans asked him, "Balai, what do you think you are doing?" Balaram answered, "I am watering my field of spinach." The Brahman asked, "Your field of spinach? Here?" Balaram replied, "Well, your ancestors aren't here either. If you think that the water you pick up and throw back into the river reaches your ancestors, then why shouldn't the water I throw on the river-bank reach my fields?"[33]

Balaram emerged as a religious leader sometime in the 1830s. Writing in the 1890s, some three decades after Balaram's death, Jogendra Nath Bhattacharya reported that the sect had a following of about twenty thousand people.[34] Collective memory within the sect has it that at some point in his life as a preacher, Balaram was invited by one of his disciples to Nischintapur in the Tehatta area of Nadia (not far from the infamous fields of Plassey), where he set up another center of activity. Sudhir Chakrabarti gives a list of twelve of his direct disciples, all of whom were low-caste (Muchi, Namaśūdra, Jugi, Hāḍi, Māhiṣya, and Muslim), and three were women described as "earning their livelihood by begging."[35] Balaram also had a female companion, described variously as his wife or his *sevikā* (attendant),[36] who later came to be known as Brahmamātā. She was Mālo by caste and ran the Meherpur center after Balaram's death, while the Nischintapur center was run by a Māhiṣya disciple called Tinu Mandal. Unlike the Sahajiyā Vaiṣṇava sects, the Balarāmīs do not have a guru-disciple structure in their order: the various centers are run by leaders called *sarkār*, but the post is not necessarily hereditary. Until a few decades ago, there were about a dozen active centers in various villages in Nadia. At present, most are in a decrepit state, although a few centers survive in Burdwan, Bankura, and Purulia, where two or three large festivals are held every year.

Like many other religious leaders who have been invested with the attributes of divinity, Balaram too has been the subject of myths that give to the story of his birth an aura of extraordinariness. It is said that at the time of his father's wedding the astrologers had predicted that the son born of this marriage would be the last in the lineage. When the wife became pregnant she concealed the fact from everyone else. One afternoon a small child with a full growth of hair and beard suddenly dropped from the ceiling and, miraculously, the woman found her womb empty. She wrapped the child in a piece of cloth and quietly left it in the jungle. But she had a sister who lived in the next village. Balaram visited her in her dream. The next morning she came to the jungle and found the child lying under a tree, protected by two tigers. She took him away with her. The foster mother found work in the house of a landlord, and when Balaram grew up to be a young boy, he was employed to tend the landlord's cattle.

The birth was miraculous, and the story has a certain resemblance with that of the cowherd Kṛṣṇa, brought up by his aunt in Vrindavan. One day the landlord Jiban Mukherjee was visited by his family guru and the boy Balaram was asked to accompany him to the river Bhairav, where the guru was to bathe. It was here that the aforementioned conversation between Balaram and the Brahmans supposedly took place, and the story goes on to assert that Balaram did in fact perform the miracle of sending the river water to a distant field. Greatly impressed by this feat, the Brahman guru came back and reprimanded his landlord disciple for employing a person with such miraculous powers as a mere servant. Balaram then asked that he be allowed to go back to the jungle from where he had come. Jiban Mukherjee donated a small piece of forest land to Balaram, and it was there that he set up his *ākhḍā*.[37]

Not all Brahmans, however, were quite so generous in acknowledging Balaram's spiritual merits. The Brahman landlord of Nischintapur, for instance, greatly resented Balaram's growing influence over his tenants. One afternoon, while Balaram was away, the landlord arranged to set fire to the Nischintapur ākhḍā. When Balaram was told of this he remarked, "He who sets fire to my house destroys his own." Saying this, he left Nischintapur and in three long steps was ten miles away in Meherpur. Apparently, it began to rain from that moment, and it did not let up for the next nine days. Huge cracks appeared on the land surrounding the zamindar's barnhouse, and by the time the rain stopped, the entire barn had been swallowed by an enormous crater. The place is now called the "barnhouse lake."

Balaram's teachings, not surprisingly, were directed against the Vedas, the ritual injunctions of the śāstra, and the practices of caste. J. N. Bhattacharya, in his brief account of Balaram's sect, makes the remark: "The most important feature of his cult was the hatred that he taught his followers to entertain towards Brahmans."[38] He also forbade them to display any distinctive marks of their sect or, significantly, to utter the name of any deity when asking for alms. The mantras they were asked to chant were in plain Bengali, devoid even of the ornamental semblance of an *oṃ* or a Tantric *hrīṃ klīṃ ślīṃ*, and without the hint of an esoteric subtext. When Balaram died, his body was neither cremated nor buried nor thrown in the water; on his instructions, it was simply left in the forest to be fed to other living creatures. For a few generations after Balaram, the sect leaders were buried after death or their bodies thrown into the river, but now the śāstric procedure of cremation is generally followed.

The sectarian ideology of the Balāhāḍis pitted itself not only against the dominant Brahmanical religion, it also demarcated itself from the religion of the Vaiṣṇavas. Their songs refer with much derision to the practices of the Sahajiyā—their fondness for food, drink, sex, and intoxicants, their obsession with counting the rosary, indeed their very existence as vagabonds without habitation or kin. They laugh at the Gauḍīya dogma of complete servility of the devotee and retort: "Why should I stoop so low when Hāḍirām is within me?" Ridiculing the concept of Caitanya as the dual incarnation of Kṛṣṇa and Rādhā, they ask, "If Caitanya is Kṛṣṇa, then why does he cry for him? If it is the Rādhā in him that cries, then Caitanya is only half a being. Who is the complete being? Hāḍirām, of course. It is for him that Caitanya cries, for Caitanya can never find him. The perfect being appeared not in Nabadwip but in Meherpur."[39]

The songs of the Balarāmī breathe the air of sectarianism. Boastful, aggressive, often vain, they produce the impression of an open battle waged on many fronts. There is little that is secretive about the ways of the sect. Although its following consisted overwhelmingly of low-caste and poor laboring people, there are none of the esoteric practices associated with the Sahajiyā cults. Perhaps the absence of prosperous householders among them made it unnecessary for the Balarāmīs to conceal their defiance of the dominant norms—after all, who cared what a few Hāḍis or Mālos proclaimed in their own little circles? As far as "respectable" people were concerned, these untouchables were not particularly good religionists anyway—indeed, in a certain sense, incapable of good religion. It was their very marginality that may have taken the sting out of their revolt against subordination, and by asserting the unrelenting negativity and exclusiveness of their rebellious faith, they condemned themselves to eternal marginality.

THE GENEALOGY OF INSUBORDINATION

But the defiance was not without conceit. It would be worth our while to delve into some of the mythic material with which the Balarāmīs constructed their faith in order to address the question raised before: How do the contingencies of power determine the form and the outcome of rebellions against the dominance of a dharma that proclaims its universality?

Among the myths is a very curious and distinctive account of the origin of the species, which the Balarāmīs call their *jātitattva*. It seems that in the earliest age, the *ādiyug*, there was nothing: this was, so to speak, time before creation. In the next, the *anādi yug*, were created plants. In the third age, the *divya yug*, there was only Hāḍirām—and no one else. From his *hāi* (yawn) was created Haimabatī, the first female, and from her the first gods, Brahmā, Viṣṇu, and Śiva, who would direct the course of the sacred and profane histories in the *satya*, *tretā*, *dvāpar*, and *kali* ages spoken of in the Purāṇas. This historical time of the four ages is described in the Balarāmī songs as a trap, a vicious snare that binds people to Vedic and Puranic injunctions. The quest for Hāḍirām is to find in one's mortal life the path of escape into that mythic time before history when the Hāḍi was noble, pure, and worthy of respect.

The form of this creation myth is the same as that which occurs in most of the popular cult literature of Bengal, the archetypal form of which is to be found in the *Śūnyapurāṇa*.[40] There too we find an age before all ages, when there was nothing and the supreme lord moved about in a vacuum. The lord then creates out of his compassion another personality called Nirañjana, out of whose yawn is born the bird Uluka. From the lord's sweat is born Ādyāśakti, primordial energy in the form of a woman. From Ādyāśakti are born the three gods Brahmā, Viṣṇu, and Śiva. In the Balarāmī cosmogony, not only does Hāḍirām take the place of Nirañjana, but he seems to usurp the powers of the supreme lord as well.

Specifically, however, there is in the story of Haimabati's birth a more direct and yet curiously unacknowledged element of borrowing. The literature of the Nāth cults of northern and eastern Bengal tells the legend of how at the time of creation Śiva came out of the mouth of the primordial lord, while out of the lord's *hāḍ*, or bone, was born Hāḍipā.[41] When Śiva decided to take Gaurī, the mother of the earth, as his wife and come down to earth, Hāḍipā, along with the other siddha Mīnanāth, accompanied them as their attendants. Hāḍipā, however, expressed his willingness to accept even the occupation of a sweeper if he could have as wife a woman as beautiful as Gaurī, and Śiva ordained that he live on earth as a Hāḍi in the company of the queen Maynāmatī.[42] Hāḍipā was later to be celebrated in the Nāth literature as the preceptor of the great *siddha* Gopīcandra.

The similarity between this creation myth, hallowed in a much more well-known tradition in Bengal's folk literature, and the one held by the Balarāmīs, strongly suggests that Balarām in fact picked it up in order to assert a sacred origin of the Hāḍi. It is not surprising that a further transposition should be introduced into the Nāth legend in order to give Hāḍirām himself the status of the originator of the human species. What is remarkable, however, is that this source of the myth in a fairly well-established strand of popular religious tradition is entirely unacknowl-

edged. There is nothing in the Balarāmī beliefs that claims any affiliation with the Nāth religion or with any other tradition of Śaiva religious
thought.

All that is conceded is a somewhat desultory recognition that of the
three sons of Haimabatī, Śiva went a little farther than his brothers
Brahmā and Viṣṇu along the path of worship that led to Hāḍirām: he
counted all of the 108 bones created by the latter and still wanders about,
wearing a necklace of bones around his neck and singing the praises of
Hāḍirām.[43] Of the other two sons of Haimabatī, we get, in the third generation in the line of Brahmā's eldest daughter Ghāmkāñcanī,[44] two
brothers called Ājir Methar and Bhusi Ghoṣ, the Methar being a subcaste
of the Hāḍi but the most degraded among them, while Ghoṣ is probably
the Goālā caste, which is a "touchable" Śūdra caste, higher in status than
both the Methar and the Hāḍi. Viṣṇu's section is more colorful, for in the
line of his second daughter, Muchundarī Kālī, we get Hāoyā and Ādam,
of whom are born two sons, Hābel and Kābel. Undoubtedly, we have
here the Old Testament story of the genesis as related in the Koran—that
is, Haw'wa (Eve) and Adam and their sons Habil (Abel) and Qabil
(Cain)—slotted in the fourth and fifth generations of the human species.
In Hābel's line, we then get four jātis—Sheikh, Saiyad, Mughal, and Pathan, the four traditional classificatory groups among Indian Muslims—
and in Kābel's line we get Nikiri, Jolā (low-status Muslim fishermen and
weaver castes), and, believe it or not, Rajput.[45] Of Viṣṇu's third child,
Musuk Kali, are born three sons. The eldest, Parāśar, is a sage and he
fathers eleven children, namely, goat, tiger, snake, vulture, mouse, mos-
quito, elephant, horse, cat, camel, and monkey! The youngest son,
Ṛṣabh, is also a *muṇi* (sage) and from his grandsons originate thirteen
Brahman groups, whose names are Dobe, Cobe, Pāṭhak, Pāṇḍe, Teoyāri,·
Miśir, and so forth—the most recognizable names here are those of Bihar
and Uttar Pradesh Brahmans, and none is a Bengali name. (Perhaps we
ought to recall Balarām's early association with Bhojpuri Brahmans in
the house of his landlord employer.) The Bengali Brahmans originate in
a particularly degraded section, for Pāṭhak had two children, Vṛṣa (bull)
and Meṣa (sheep), one born of an untouchable Bede woman and the other
of an untouchable Bāgdi woman. From them originate all of the Brahman
lineages of Bengal, such as Bhāṭije, Bāḍije, Mukhuje, Gaṅgāl, Ghuṣāl,
Bāgji, Lahaḍī, Bhādariyā, and so forth.

There is much more in this extraordinary genealogical tree whose
meanings are not transparent to the uninitiated; even the present-day
leaders of the cult cannot explain many of the references. The ramifica-
tions of Balarām's jātitattva, inasmuch as it attempts to define a new set
of relations between various existent social groups, are for the most part
unclear. What is clear, however, is first that the scheme continues to un-

dertake the classification of social groups in terms of the natural division into species, and it does this to a great extent by transforming the relations between elements within a popularly inherited mythic code; and second that by overturning the hierarchical order of the Puranic creation myths, it pushes the very ideality of the dominant scheme of caste to a limit where it merges with its opposite. Balarām's jātitattva does not assert that there are no jātis or differences between social groups akin to the differences between natural species. Rather, by raising the Hāḍi to the position of the purest of the pure, the self-determining originator of differentiations within the genus, and by reducing the Brahman to a particularly impure and degenerate lineage, it subverts the very claim of the dominant dharma that the actual social relations of caste are in perfect conformity with its universal ideality.

Without, of course, asserting a new universal. That mark is imprinted on the consciousness of the yet unsurpassed limit of the condition of subalternity. The conceit shown in the construction of Balarām's jātitattva is a sign of conscious insubordination. But there is no trace in it of a self-conscious contest for an alternative social order.

Or are we being too hasty in our judgment?

THE BODY AS THE SITE OF APPROPRIATION

Caste attaches to the body, not to the soul. It is the biological reproduction of the human species through procreation within endogamous caste groups that ensures the permanence of ascribed marks of caste purity or pollution. It is also the physical contact of the body with defiling substances or defiled bodies that mark it with the temporary conditions of pollution, which can be removed by observing the prescribed procedures of physical cleansing. Further, if we have grasped the essence of caste, the necessity to protect the purity of his body is what forbids the Brahman from engaging in acts of labor that involve contact with polluting material and, reciprocally, requires the unclean castes to perform those services for the Brahman. The essence of caste, we may then say, requires that the laboring bodies of the impure castes be reproduced in order that they can be subordinated to the need to maintain the bodies of the pure castes in their state of purity. All the injunctions of dharma must work to this end.

When popular religious cults deviate from the dogma of the dominant religion, when they announce the rejection of the Vedas, the śāstric rituals or caste, they declare a revolt of the spirit. But the conditions of power which make such revolts possible are not necessarily the same as those that would permit a practical insubordination of laboring bodies. To question the ideality of caste is not directly to defy its immediate reality.

It is not as though this other battle has not been waged. Let us leave aside those high points of popular protest which take the explicit political forms of insurgency: these have received a fair amount of attention from historians, their general features have been examined, and their historical limits broadly delineated. We are also not considering here those particular or individual instances of disobedience, whether demonstrative or covert, which undoubtedly occur in the daily life of every village in India. Instead, let us turn our eyes to the practical aspects of the religious life of the deviant cults we have been talking about. All of these are fundamentally concerned with the body. The Sahajiyā cults practice the forms of bodily worship that do not respect the dictums of either the śāstra or the sharī'ah. But they can be conducted only in secret, under the guidance of the guru, and their principles can be propagated only in the language of enigma. Where they seek an open congregation, it takes the antistructural form of the *communitas* of periodic and momentary religious festivals. And yet there is, underlying it all, the attempt to define a claim of proprietorship over one's own body, to negate the daily submission of one's body and its labor to the demands made by the dominant dharma and to assert a domain of bodily activity where it can, with the full force of ethical conviction, disregard those demands. Notice, therefore, the repeated depiction of the body in the songs of dehatattva not simply as a material entity but as an artifact—not a natural being at all but a physical construct. The body is a house, or a boat, or a cart, or a weaver's loom, or a potter's wheel, or any of countless other instruments or products of labor that remain at the disposal and use of one who possesses them. But the very secretiveness of those cult practices, the fact that they can be engaged in only, as it were, outside the boundaries of the social structure, sets the limit to the practical effectiveness of the claim of possession; not surprisingly, it draws upon itself the charge of licentiousness.

The practical religion of the Balāhāḍis takes a different form. Their sectarianism is not, as we have seen, secretive, nor is it primarily conceived as a set of practices engaged in beyond the margins of social life. Rather, their forms of worship involve a self-disciplining of the body in the course of one's daily social living. Here too the body is an artifact, but it can be used by its owner with skill and wisdom or wasted and destroyed by profligacy. The specific forms of self-discipline, as far as one can gather from the material supplied by Sudhir Chakrabarti, again seem to bear close resemblance with the *haṭhayoga* practices of the Nāth cults. The main principle is that of *ulṭasādhanā*, which involves yogic exercises that produce a regressive or upward movement in the bodily processes. It is believed that in the normal course, the force of *pravṛtti* or activity and change moves in a downward direction, taking the body along the path of decay and destruction. The aim of self-discipline is to reverse this process by moving it in the upward direction of *nivṛtti*, or rest. More specifically, the bodily practices involve the retention of the *bindu* or *śukra* (semen) and prevention of its waste. The Balāhāḍi literature does not, of course, prescribe the full range of haṭhayoga practices, which can be performed only in strict celibacy, with a view to reaching the perfect *siddha* state of immortality.[46] What it does, however, is lay down a sort of new *āśramadharma* for its adherents—a graded series of states of bodily discipline that can be attempted in the course of a mortal, and social, life.

The lowest state is that of *bodhitan*, where the body is completely a prisoner of impulses and base desires. It is a state where one does not even will an escape from the debilitating demands of the "four ages"—that snare of historical time in which all the forces of activity and change work toward the bondage and annihilation of free life. To us, this appears to be a state characterized by the mindless pursuit of instant pleasure, although the Balarāmī would put this as its opposite. The body, he would say, is here completely under the sway of *man*, that is, of mind that is the repository of impulse and desire. In bodhitan, the body is not its own; it is the state of alienation of the body from itself. Indeed, this bodily state becomes the representation of that condition of the laboring classes which provokes such remarks as "The Hāḍi's Lakṣmī finds her way into the Śuṇḍi's [liquor seller's] house."[47] The passage of the body from this state to that of eyotan is the crucial transition for a Balarāmī householder. In *eyotan*, the bodily processes are under the control of its owner. The semen is preserved and spent only for procreation.[48] This, in this world of representations where the body stands as microcosm for the universe, is the daily affirmation of a proprietorship constantly threatened. If the purity and perfection of the body can be controlled from within itself, nothing external can pollute it. For most lay followers of the sect, this is as far as their sādhan is expected to go. For the fortunate few, a successful life in eyotan is followed by the state of *nityan*, where there is complete unconcern for the world. This is a stage of life spent outside the bonds of family and kin. The final and most perfect state of sādhan is that of *khāstan*. It is a state of complete freedom and hence of unconditioned proprietorship over one's bodily existence, for, as the Balarāmīs say, the prajā of khāstan are entities such as light, air, sky, fire, or water, which do not pay a rent to anyone for their earthly existence. This is a state that only Balarām was able to attain.

What are we to say of this? There are unmistakable signs here of a consciousness alienated from the dominant dharma but apparently bound to nothing else than its spirit of resolute negativity. Its practical defeat too is borne out by the facts of social history. Yet, is there not here an implicit, barely stated, search for a recognition whose signs lie not outside but within one's own self? Can one see here the trace of an identity that is defined not by others but by oneself? Perhaps we have allowed ourselves to be taken in too easily by the general presence of an abstract negativity in the autonomous domain of subaltern beliefs and practices and have missed those marks, faint as they are, of an immanent process of criticism and learning, of selective appropriation, of making sense of and using on one's own terms the elements of a more powerful cultural order. We must, after all, remind ourselves that subaltern consciousness is not merely structure, characterized solely by negativity; it is also history, shaped and developed through a changing process of interaction between the dominant and the subordinate. Surely it would be wholly contrary to our project to go about as though only the dominant culture has a life in history and subaltern consciousness is eternally frozen in its structure of negation.

THE IMPLICIT AND THE EXPLICIT

We must, however, be careful to avoid the easy, mechanical transposition of the specifics of European history. The specific forms of immanent development necessarily work with a definite cultural content. It seems quite farfetched to identify in the criticisms of caste among the deviant religions the embryo of a Protestant ethic or an incipient urge for bourgeois freedom. What we have is a desire for a structure of community in which the opposite tendencies of mutual separateness and mutual dependence are united by a force that has a greater universal moral actuality than the given forms of the dominant dharma. For want of a more concrete concept of praxis, we may call this desire, in an admittedly abstract and undifferentiated sense, a desire for *democratization*, where rights and the application of the norms of justice are open to a broader basis of consultation, disputation, and resolution.

Every social form of the community, in the formal sense, must achieve the unity of mutual separateness and mutual dependence of its parts. The system of castes, we have seen, makes this claim, but its actuality is necessarily in disjunction with its ideality. The external critique of caste, drawn from the liberal ideology of Europe, suggests that a legal framework of bourgeois freedom and equality provides an alternative and, in principle, more democratic basis for this unification. This has been the formal basis of the constitutional structure of the postcolonial state in India. And yet the practical construction of this new edifice out of the given cultural material has been forced into an abandonment of its principles from the very start—notice, for instance, the provisions of special reservations on grounds of caste.[49] The new political processes have, it would seem, managed to effect a displacement of the unifying force of dharma but have replaced it with the unifying concept of "nation" as concretely embodied in the state. What has resulted is not the actualization of bourgeois equality at all but rather the conflicting claims of caste groups (to confine ourselves to this particular domain of social conflict), not on the religious basis of dharma but on the purely secular demands of claims upon the state. The force of dharma, it appears, has been ousted from its position of superiority, to be replaced with a vengeance by the pursuit of artha, but, pace Dumont, on the basis again of caste divisions. On the one hand, we have the establishment of capitalist relations in agricultural production in which the new forms of wage labor fit snugly into the old grid of caste divisions.[50] On the other hand, we have the supremely paradoxical phenomenon of low-caste groups asserting their very backwardness in the caste hierarchy to claim discriminatory privileges from the state, and upper-caste groups proclaiming the sanctity of bourgeois equality and freedom (the criterion of equal opportunity mediated by skill and merit) in order to beat back the threat to their existing privileges. This was evidenced most blatantly in the violent demonstrations over the adoption of so-called Mandal Commission recommendations by the government of India in 1990. What are we to make of these conflicting desires for democratization?

There is no alternative for us but to undertake a search, both theoretical and practical, for the concrete forms of democratic community that are based neither on the principle of hierarchy nor on those of bourgeois equality. Dumont's posing of the principles of *homo hierarchicus* against those of *homo equalis* is a false, essentialist, positing of an unresolvable antinomy. We must assert that there is a more developed universal form of the unity of separateness and dependence that subsumes hierarchy and equality as lower historical moments.

The point is to explicate the principles and to construct the concrete forms of this universal. In Indian politics the problem of unifying the opposed requirements of separateness and dependence has been concretely addressed only at the level of the structure of federalism, a level where the problem is seen as permitting a territorial resolution. The attempt has had dubious success. In other domains, of which caste is a prime example, politics has drifted from one contentious principle to another (bourgeois equality, caste-class correlation, discriminatory privileges for low castes through state intervention, etc.) without finding adequate ground on which it can be superseded by a new universal form of community.

But, and this has been my somewhat Gramscian argument in this chapter, there does exist a level of social life where laboring people in their practical activity have constantly sought in their "common sense" the forms, mediated by culture, of such community. The problem of politics is to develop and make explicit what is only implicit in popular activity, to give to its process of mediation the conditions of sufficiency. The point, in other words, is to undertake a criticism of "common sense" on the basis of "common sense";[51] not to inject into popular life a "scientific" form of thought springing from somewhere else, but to develop and make critical an activity that already exists in popular life.

CHAPTER TEN

The National State

PLANNING FOR PLANNING

In August 1937, the Congress Working Committee at its meeting in Wardha adopted a resolution recommending "to the Congress Ministries the appointment of a Committee of Experts to consider urgent and vital problems the solution of which is necessary to any scheme of national reconstruction and social planning. Such solution will require extensive survey and the collection of data, as well as a clearly defined social objective."[1] The immediate background to this resolution was the formation by the Congress, under the new constitutional arrangements, of ministries in six (later eight) provinces of India and the questions raised, especially by the Gandhians (including Gandhi himself) about the responsibility of the Congress in regulating (more precisely, restricting) the growth of modern industries. The Left within the Congress sought to put aside this nagging ideological debate by arguing that the whole question of Congress policy toward industries must be resolved within the framework of an "all-India industrial plan," which this committee of experts would be asked to draw up. Accordingly, Subhas Chandra Bose in his presidential speech at the Haripura Congress in February 1938 declared that the national state "on the advice of a Planning Commission" would adopt "a comprehensive scheme for gradually socializing our entire agricultural and industrial system in the sphere of both production and appropriation." In October that year, Bose summoned a conference of the Ministers of Industries in the Congress ministries and soon after announced the formation of a National Planning Committee (NPC) with Jawaharlal Nehru as chairman. Of the fifteen members of the committee, four (Purushottamdas Thakurdas, A. D. Shroff, Ambalal Sarabhai, and Walchand Hirachand) were leading merchants and industrialists, five were scientists (Meghnad Saha, A. K. Saha, Nazir Ahmed, V. S. Dubey, and J. C. Ghosh), two were economists (K. T. Shah and Radhakamal Mukherjee)—three, if we include M. Visvesvaraya, who had just written a book on planning—and three had been invited on their political credentials (J. C. Kumarappa the Gandhian, N. M. Joshi the labor leader, and Nehru himself). The Committee began work in December 1938.

The National Planning Committee, whose actual work virtually ceased after about a year and a half, following the outbreak of the war, the resignation of the Congress ministries, and finally Nehru's arrest in October 1940, was nevertheless the first real experience the emerging state leadership of the Congress, and Nehru in particular, had with working out the idea of "national planning." Before making a brief mention of the actual contents of the discussions in that committee, let us take note of the most significant aspects of the *form* of this exercise.

First, planning appeared as a form of determining *state* policy, initially the economic policies of the provincial Congress ministries, but almost immediately afterward the overall framework of a coordinated and consistent set of policies of a national state that was already being envisioned as a concrete idea. In this respect, planning was not only a part of the anticipation of power by the state leadership of the Congress, it was also an anticipation of the concrete forms in which that power would be exercised within a national state. Second, planning as an exercise in state policy already incorporated its most distinctive element: its constitution as a body of *experts* and its activity as one of the technical evaluation of alternative policies and the determination of choices on "scientific" grounds. Nehru, writing in 1944–45, mentioned this as a memorable part of his experience with the NPC: "We had avoided a theoretical approach, and as each particular problem was viewed in its larger context, it led us inevitably in a particular direction. To me the spirit of cooperation of the members of the Planning Committee was particularly soothing and gratifying, for I found it a pleasant contrast to the squabbles and conflicts of politics."[2]

Third, the appeal to a "committee of experts" was in itself an important instrument in resolving a political debate that, much to the irritation of the emerging state leadership of the Congress, still refused to go away. This leadership, along with the vast majority of the professional intelligentsia of India, had little doubt about the central importance of industrialization for the development of a modern and prosperous nation. Yet the very political strategy of building up a mass movement against colonial rule had required the Congress to espouse Gandhi's idea of machinery, commercialization, and centralized state power as the curses of modern civilization, thrust upon the Indian people by European colonialism. It was industrialism itself, Gandhi argued, rather than the inability to industrialize, that was the root cause of Indian poverty. This was, until the 1940s, a characteristic part of the Congress rhetoric of nationalist mobilization. But now that the new national state was ready to be conceptualized in concrete terms, this archaic ideological baggage had to be jettisoned. J. C. Kumarappa brought the very first session of the NPC to an impasse by questioning its authority to discuss plans for industrialization. The national priority as adopted by the Congress, he said, was to restrict and eliminate modern industrialism. Nehru had to intervene and declare that most members of the Committee felt that large-scale industry ought to be promoted as long as it did not "come into conflict with the cottage industries." Emphasizing the changed political context in which the Congress was working, Nehru added significantly: "Now that the Congress is, to some extent, identifying itself with the State it cannot ignore the question of establishing and encouraging large-scale industries. There can be no planning if such planning does not include big industries . . . [and] it is not only within the scope of the Committee to consider large-scale industries, but it is incumbent upon it to consider them." Kumarappa kept up his futile effort for a while after virtually every other member disagreed with his views and finally dropped out. Gandhi himself did not appreciate the efforts of the NPC, or perhaps he appreciated them only too well. "I do not know," he wrote to Nehru, "that it is working within the four corners of the resolution creating the Committee. I do not know that the Working Committee is being kept informed of its doings. . . . It has appeared to me that much money and labour are being wasted on an effort which will bring forth little or no fruit."[3] Nehru in turn did not conceal his impatience with such "visionary" and "unscientific" talk and grounded his own position quite firmly on the universal principles of historical progress: "We are trying to catch up, as far as we can, with the Industrial Revolution that occurred long ago in Western countries."[4]

The point here is not so much whether the Gandhian position had already been rendered politically inviable, so that we can declare the overwhelming consensus on industrialization within the NPC as the "reflection" of an assignment of priorities already determined in the political arena outside. Rather, the very institution of a process of planning became a means for the determination of priorities on behalf of the "nation." The debate on the need for industrialization, it might be said, was politically resolved by successfully constituting planning as a domain outside "the squabbles and conflicts of politics." As early as the 1940s, planning had emerged as a crucial institutional modality by which the state would determine the material allocation of productive resources within the nation: a modality of political power constituted outside the immediate political process itself.

THE RATIONALITY OF THE NEW STATE

Why was it necessary to devise such a modality of power that could operate both inside and outside the political structure constructed by the new postcolonial state? An answer begins to appear as soon as we discover the logic by which the new state related itself to the "nation." For the emerging state leadership (and as the bearer of a fundamental ideological orientation, this group was much larger than simply a section of the leaders of the Congress, and in identifying it, the usual classification of Left and Right is irrelevant), this relation was expressed in a quite distinctive way. By the 1940s, the dominant argument of nationalism against colonial rule was that the latter was impeding the further development of India: colonial rule had become a historical fetter that had to be removed before the nation could proceed to develop. Within this framework, therefore, the economic critique of colonialism as an exploitative force creating and perpetuating a backward economy came to occupy a central place. One might ask what would happen to this late nationalist position if (let us say, for the sake of argument) it turned out from historical investigation that by every agreed criterion foreign rule had indeed promoted economic development in the colony. Would that have made colonialism any more legitimate or the demand for national self-government any less justified? Our nationalist would not have accepted a purely negative critique of colonial rule as sufficient and would have been embarrassed if the demand for self-rule was sought to be filled in by some primordial content such as race or religion. Colonial rule, he would have said, was illegitimate not because it represented the political domination by an alien people over the indigens: alienness had acquired the stamp of illegitimacy because it stood for a form of *exploitation* of the nation (the drain of national wealth, the destruction of its productive system, the creation of a backward economy, etc.). Self-government consequently was legitimate because it represented the historically necessary form of national development. The economic critique of colonialism then was the foundation from which a positive content was supplied for the independent national state: the new state represented the only legitimate form of exercise of power because it was a necessary condition for the development of the nation.

A developmental ideology then was a constituent part of the self-definition of the postcolonial state. The state was connected to the people-nation not simply through the procedural forms of representative government; it also acquired its representativeness by directing a program of economic development on behalf of the nation. The former connected, as in any liberal form of government, the legal-political sovereignty of the state with the sovereignty of the people. The latter connected the sovereign powers of the state directly with the economic well-being of the people. The two connections did not necessarily have the same implications for a state trying to determine how to use its sovereign powers. What the people were able to express through the representative mechanisms of the political process as their will was not necessarily what was good for their economic well-being; what the state thought important for the economic development of the nation was not necessarily what would be ratified through the representative mechanisms. The two criteria of representativeness, and hence of legitimacy, could well produce contradictory implications for state policy.

The contradiction stemmed from the very manner in which a developmental ideology needed to cling to the state as the principal vehicle for its historical mission. "Development" implied a linear path, directed toward a goal, or a series of goals separated by stages. It implied the fixing of priorities between long-run and short-run goals and conscious choice between alternative paths. It was premised, in other words, upon a *rational* consciousness and will, and insofar as "development" was thought of as a process affecting the whole of society, it was also premised upon *one* consciousness and will—that of the whole. Particular interests needed to be subsumed within the whole and made consistent with the general interest. The mechanisms of civil society, working through contracts and the market, and hence defining a domain for the play of the particular and the accidental, were already known to be imperfect instruments for expressing the general. The one consciousness, both general and rational, could not simply be assumed to exist as an abstract and formless force, working implicitly and invisibly through the particular interests of civil society. It had to, as Hegel would have said, "shine forth," appear as an existent, concretely expressing the general and the rational.

Hegel has shown us that this universal rationality of the state can be concretely expressed at two institutional levels—the bureaucracy as the universal class and the monarch as the immediately existent will of the state. The logical requirement of the latter was taken care of, even under the republican constitutional form adopted in India, by the usual provisions of embodying the sovereign will of the state in the person of the Head of State. In meeting the former requirement, however, the postcolonial state in India faced a problem that was produced specifically by the form of the transition from colonial rule. For various reasons that were attributed to political contingency (whose historical roots we need not explore here), the new state chose to retain in a virtually unaltered form the basic structure of the civil service, the police administration, the judicial system, including the codes of civil and criminal law, and the armed forces as they existed in the colonial period. As far as the normal executive functions of the state were concerned, the new state operated within a framework of rational universality, whose principles were seen as having been contained (even if they were misapplied) in the preceding state structure. In the case of the armed forces, the assertion of unbroken continuity was rather more paradoxical, so that even today one is forced to witness such unlovely ironies as regiments of the Indian Army proudly displaying the trophies of colonial conquest and counterinsurgency in their barrack rooms or the Presidential Guards celebrating their birth two hundred years ago under the governor-generalship of Lord Cornwallis! But if the ordinary functions of civil and criminal administration were to continue within forms of rationality that the new state had not given to itself, how was it to claim its legitimacy as an authority that was specifically different from the old regime? This legitimacy, as we have mentioned before, had to flow from the nationalist criticism of colonialism as an alien and unrepresentative power that was exploitative in character and from the historical necessity of an independent state that would promote national development. It was in the universal function of "development" of national society as a whole that the postcolonial state would find its distinctive content. This was to be concretized by the embodiment within itself of a new mechanism of developmental administration, something the colonial state, because of its alien and extractive character, had never possessed. It was in the administration of development that the bureaucracy of the postcolonial state was to assert itself as the universal class, satisfying in the service of the state its private interests by working for the universal goals of the nation.

Planning therefore was the domain of the rational determination and pursuit of those universal goals. It was a bureaucratic function, to be operated at a level above the particular interests of civil society, and institutionalized as such as a domain of policy-making outside the normal processes of representative politics and of execution through a developmental administration. But as a concrete bureaucratic function, it was in planning above all that the postcolonial state would claim its legitimacy as a single will and consciousness—the will of the nation—pursuing a task that was both universal and rational: the well-being of the people as a whole.

In its legitimizing role, therefore, planning, constituted as a domain outside politics, was to become an instrument of politics. If we then look at the process of politics itself, we will discover the specific ways in which planning would also become implicated in the modalities of power.

PLANNING AND IMPLEMENTING

We could first describe the political process in its own terms and then look for the connections with the process of planning. But this would take us into a lengthy excursion into a wholly different field. Let us instead start with the received understanding of the planning experience in India and see how the political process comes to impinge upon it.

Chakravarty has given us a summary account of this experience from within the theoretical boundaries of development planning.[5] From this perspective, the political process appears as a determinate and changing existent when the question arises of "plan implementation." Chakravarty discusses the problems of plan implementation by treating the "planning authorities" as the central directing agency, firmly situated outside the political process itself and embodying, one might justifiably say, the single, universal, and rational consciousness of a state that is promoting the development of the nation as a whole.[6] An implementational failure, Chakravarty says, occurs when (a) the planning authorities are inefficient in gathering the relevant information; (b) they take so much time to respond that the underlying situation has by then changed, and (c) the public agencies through which the plans are to be implemented do not have the capacities to carry them out and the private agencies combine in "strategic" ways to disrupt the expectations about their behavior that the planners had taken as "parametric." Chakravarty adds that the last possibility—that of strategic action by private actors—has greatly increased in recent years in the Indian economy.

Let us look a little more closely at this analysis. What does it mean to say that plans may fail because of the inadequacy of the information planners use? The premise here is that of a separation between the planner on the one hand and the objects of planning on the other, the latter consisting of both physical resources and human economic agents. "Information" is precisely the means through which the objects of planning are constituted for the planner: they exist "out there," independently of his consciousness, and can appear before it only in the shape of "information." The "adequacy" of this information then concerns the question of whether those objects have been constituted "correctly," that is to say, constituted in the planner's consciousness in the same form as they exist outside it, in themselves. It is obvious that on these terms an entirely faultless planning would require in the planner nothing less than omniscience. But one should not use the patent impossibility of this project to turn planning into a caricature of itself. While the epistemological stance of apprehending the external objects of consciousness in their intrinsic and independent truth continues, as is well known, to inform the expressly declared philosophical foundations of the positive sciences, including economics, the actual practice of debates about planning are more concerned with those objects as they have been constituted by the planning exercise itself. Thus, if it is alleged that planners have incorrectly estimated the demand for electricity because they did not take into account the unorganized sector, the charge really is that whereas the "unorganized sector" was already an object of planning since it was *known* that it too was a consumer of electricity, it had not been explicitly and specifically constituted as an object since its demand had not been estimated.

The point about all questions of "inadequate information" is not whether one knows what the objects of planning are: if they are not known, the problem of information cannot arise. The question is whether they have been explicitly specified as objects of planning.

It is here that the issues of the modalities of knowledge and implementation become central to the planning exercise. All three conditions that Chakravarty mentions as leading to faulty implementation concern the ways in which the planner, representing the rational consciousness of the state, can produce a knowledge of the objects of planning. In this sense, even the so-called implementing agencies are the objects of planning, for they represent not the will of the planner but determinate "capacities": a plan that does not correctly estimate the capacities of the implementing agencies cannot be a good plan. Consequently, these agencies—bureaucrats or managers of public enterprises—become entities that act in determinate ways according to specific kinds of "signals," and the planner must know these in order to formulate his plan. The planner even needs to know how long his own machinery will take to implement a plan, or else the information on the basis of which he plans may become obsolete.

If one is not to assume omniscience on behalf of the planner, how is this information ever expected to be "adequate"? Here the rationality of planning can be seen to practice a self-deception—a necessary self-deception, for without it, planning could not constitute itself. Planning, as the concrete embodiment of the rational consciousness of a state promoting economic development, can proceed only by constituting the objects of planning as objects of knowledge. It must *know* the physical resources whose allocation is to be planned, it must *know* the economic agents who act upon those resources, *know* their needs, capacities, and propensities, *know* what constitutes the signals according to which they act, *know* how they respond to those signals. When the agents relate to each other in terms of power, that is, in relations of domination and subordination, the planner must *know* the relevant signals and capacities. This knowledge would enable him to work upon the total configuration of power itself, use the legal powers of the state to produce signals and thereby affect the actions of agents, play off one power against another to produce a general result in which everybody would be better off. The state as a planning authority can promote the universal goal of development by harnessing within a single interconnected whole the discrete subjects of power in society. It does this by turning those subjects of power into the objects of a single body of knowledge.

Here the self-deception occurs. For the rational consciousness of the state embodied in the planning authority does not exhaust the determinate being of the state. The state is also an existent as a site at which the subjects of power in society interact, ally, and contend with one another in the political process. The specific configuration of power that is constituted within the state is the result of this process. Seen from this perspective, the planning authorities themselves are objects for a configuration of power in which others are subjects. Indeed, and this is the paradox that a "science" of planning can never unravel from within its own disciplinary boundaries, the very subjects of social power which the rational consciousness of the planner seeks to convert into objects of its knowledge by attributing to them discrete capacities and propensities can turn the planning authority itself into an object of their power. Subject and object, inside and outside—the relations are reversed as soon as we move from the domain of rational planning, situated outside the political process, to the domain of social power exercised and contested within that process. When we talk of the state, we must talk of both of these domains as its constituent field, and situate one in relation to the other. Seen from the domain of planning, the political process is only an external constraint, whose strategic possibilities must be known and objectified as parameters for the planning exercise. And yet even the best efforts to secure "adequate information" leave behind an unestimated residue, which works imperceptibly and often perversely to upset the implementation of plans. This residue, as the irreducible, negative, and ever-present "beyond" of planning, is what we may call, in its most general sense, politics.

THE POLITICS OF PLANNING: PART ONE

Let us return to history, this time of more recent vintage. Chakravarty says that in the early 1950s, when the planning process was initiated in India, there was a general consensus on a "commodity-centered" approach.[7] That is to say, everyone agreed that more goods were preferable to less goods and a higher level of capital stock per worker was necessary for an improved standard of living. Obviously, the central emphasis of development was meant to be placed on accumulation. But this was not all; in the specific context in which planning was taken up in India, accumulation had to be reconciled with legitimation. "Adoption of a representative form of government based on universal adult suffrage did have an effect on the exercise of political power, and so did the whole legacy of the national movement with its specifically articulated set of economic objectives." These two objectives—accumulation and legitimation—produced two implications for planning in India. On the one hand, planning had to be "a way of avoiding the *unnecessary rigours* of an industrial transition in so far as it affected the masses resident in India's villages." On the other hand, planning was to become "a positive instrument for *resolving conflict* in a large and heterogeneous subcontinent."[8] What did these objectives mean in terms of the relation between the state and the planning process?

In the classical forms of capitalist industrialization, the originary accumulation required the use of a variety of coercive methods to separate a large mass of direct producers from their means of production. This was the "secret" of the so-called primitive accumulation, which was not the result of the capitalist mode of production but its starting point; in a concrete historical process, it meant "the expropriation of the agricultural producer, of the peasant, from the soil."[9] The possibility and limits of originary accumulation were set by the specific configuration in each country of the political struggle between classes in the precapitalist social formation,[10] but in each case a successful transition to capitalist industrialization required that subsistence producers be "robbed of all their means of production and of all the guarantees of existence afforded by the old feudal arrangements." Whatever the political means adopted to effect this expropriation of direct producers, and with it the destruction of precapitalist forms of community concretely embodying the unity of producers with the means of production, they could not have been legitimized by any active principle of universal representative democracy. (It is curious that in the one country of Europe where a "bourgeois" political revolution was carried out under the slogan of liberty, equality, and fraternity, the protection of small-peasant property after the Revolution meant the virtual postponement of industrialization by some five or six decades.)

Once in place, accumulation under capitalist production proper could be made legitimate by the equal right of property and the universal freedom of contract on the basis of property rights over commodities. Originary accumulation having already effected the separation of the direct producer from the means of production, labor-power was now available as a commodity owned by the laborer, who was entitled to sell it according to the terms of a free contract with the owner of the means of production. As a political ideology of legitimation of capitalist accumulation, this strictly liberal doctrine of "freedom," however, enjoyed a surprisingly short life. By the third and fourth decades of the nineteenth century, when the first phase of the Industrial Revolution had been completed in Britain, the new context of political conflict made it necessary to qualify "freedom" by such notions as the rights to subsistence, to proper conditions of work, and to a decent livelihood. In time, this meant the use of the legal powers of the state to impose conditions on the freedom of contract (on hours of work, on minimum wage, on physical conditions of work and living) and to curtail the free enjoyment of returns from the productive use of property (most importantly by the taxation on higher incomes to finance public provisions for hygiene, health, education, etc.). While this may be seen as consistent with the long-term objectives of capitalist accumulation, on the ground that it facilitated the continued reproduction of labor-power of a suitable concretized quality, it must also be recognized as a political response to growing oppositional movements and social conflict. As a political doctrine of legitimation this meant, first, the creation of a general content for social good that combined capitalist property ownership with the production of consent through representative political processes and, second, the determination of this content not mediately through the particular acts of economic agents in civil society but directly through the activities of the state. The course of this journey from the strictly liberal concept of "freedom" to that of "welfare" is, of course, coincidental with the political history of capitalist democracy in the last century and a half. What we need to note here is the fact that as a universal conception of the social whole under capitalist democracy, the elements of a concept of "welfare" had already superseded those of pure freedom and were available to the political leadership in India when it began the task of constructing a state ideology.

The "unnecessary rigors" of an industrial transition, consequently, meant those forms of expropriation of subsistence producers associated with originary accumulation which could not be legitimized through the representative processes of politics. This was, our planner would say, a parametric condition set by the political process at the time when planning began its journey in India. Yet, accumulation was the prime task if industrialization was to take place. Accumulation necessarily implied the use of the powers of the state, whether directly through its legal and administrative institutions or mediately through the acts of some agents with social power over others, to effect the required degree of dissociation of direct producers from their means of production. As Chakravarty himself says, the development model first adopted in India was a variant of the Lewis model, with a "modern" sector breaking down and superseding the "traditional" sector, the two significant variations being that the modern sector itself was disaggregated into a capital goods and a consumer goods sector and that the major role in the modern sector was assigned to a development bureaucracy instead of to capitalists.[11] Despite these variations, the chosen path of development still meant conflicts between social groups and the use of power to attain the required form and rate of accumulation. Since the "necessary" policies of the state that would ensure accumulation could not be left to be determined solely through the political process, it devolved upon the institution of planning, that embodiment of the universal rationality of the social whole standing above all particular interests, to lay down what in fact were the "necessary rigors" of industrialization. Given its location outside the political process, planning could then become "a positive instrument for resolving conflict" by determining, within a universal framework of the social good, the "necessary costs" to be borne by each particular group and the "necessary benefits" to accrue to each. But who was to use it in this way as a "positive instrument"? We have still to address this question.

The specific form in which this twin problem of planning—accumulation with legitimation—was initially resolved, especially in the Second and Third Five-Year Plans, is well known. There was to be a capital-intensive industrial sector under public ownership, a private industrial sector in light consumer goods, and a private agricultural sector. The first two were the "modern" sectors, which were to be financed by foreign aid, low-interest loans, and taxation of private incomes mainly in the second sector. The third sector was seen as being mainly one of petty production, and it was there that a major flaw of this development strategy was to appear. It has been said that the Second and Third Plans did not have an agricultural strategy at all, or even if they did, there was gross overoptimism about the long-term ability of traditional agriculture to contribute to industrialization by providing cheap labor and cheap food.[12] The problem is often posed as one of alternative planning strategies, with the suggestion that if suitable land reforms had been carried out soon after independence, a quite different development path might have been discovered that would have avoided the "crisis" in which the planning process found itself in the middle of the 1960s. The difficulty with this suggestion, if we are to look at it from a political standpoint, is precisely the confusion it entails regarding the effective relation between the whole and the parts, the universal and the particulars, in the acts of a state promoting and supervising a program of planned capitalist development. To discover the nature of this relation, we need to look upon planned industrialization as part of a process of what may be called the "passive revolution of capital."

PASSIVE REVOLUTION

Antonio Gramsci has talked of the "passive revolution" as one in which the new claimants to power, lacking the social strength to launch a full-scale assault on the old dominant classes, opt for a path in which the demands of a new society are "satisfied in small doses, legally, in a reformist manner"—in such a way that the political and economic position of the old feudal classes is not destroyed, agrarian reform is avoided, and the popular masses especially are prevented from going through the political experience of a fundamental social transformation.[13] Gramsci, of course, treats this as a "blocked dialectic," an exception to the paradigmatic form of bourgeois revolution he takes to be Jacobinism. It now seems more useful to argue, however, that as a historical model, passive revolution is in fact the general framework of capitalist transition in societies where bourgeois hegemony has not been accomplished in the classical way.[14] In "passive revolution," the historical shifts in the strategic relations of forces between capital, precapitalist dominant groups, and the popular masses can be seen as a series of contingent, conjunctural moments. The dialectic here cannot be assumed to be blocked in any fundamental sense. Rather, the new forms of dominance of capital become understandable, not as the immanent supersession of earlier contradictions, but as parts of a constructed hegemony, effective because of the successful exercise of both coercive and persuasive power, but incomplete and fragmented at the same time because the hegemonic claims are fundamentally contested within the constructed whole.[15] The distinction between "bourgeois hegemony" and "passive revolution" then becomes one in which, for the latter, the persuasive power of bourgeois rule cannot be constructed around the universal idea of "freedom"; some other universal idea has to be substituted for it.[16]

In the Indian case, we can look upon "passive revolution" as a process involving a political-ideological program by which the largest possible nationalist alliance is built up against the colonial power. The aim is to form a politically independent nation-state. The means involve the creation of a series of alliances—within the organizational structure of the national movement, between the bourgeoisie and other dominant classes—and the mobilization, under this leadership, of mass support from the subordinate classes. The project is a reorganization of the political order, but it is moderated in two quite fundamental ways. On the one hand, it does not attempt to break up or transform in any radical way the institutional structures of "rational" authority set up in the period of colonial rule. On the other hand, it also does not undertake a full-scale assault on all precapitalist dominant classes; rather, it seeks to limit their former power, neutralize them where necessary, attack them only selectively, and in general bring them round to a position of subsidiary allies within a reformed state structure. The dominance of capital does not emanate from its hegemonic sway over "civil society." On the contrary, it seeks to construct a synthetic hegemony over the domains of both civil society and the precapitalist community. The reification of the "nation" in the body of the state becomes the means for constructing this hegemonic structure, and the extent of control over the new state apparatus becomes a precondition for further capitalist development. It is by means of an interventionist state, directly entering the domain of production as mobilizer and manager of investable "national" resources, that the foundations are laid for industrialization and the expansion of capital. Yet the dominance of capital over the national state remains constrained in several ways. Its function of representing the "national-popular" has to be shared with other governing groups and its transformative role restricted to reformist and "molecular" changes. The institution of planning, as we have seen, emerges in this process as the means by which the "necessity" of these changes is rationalized at the level not of this or that particular group but of the social whole.

For the development model adopted in India, the modern sector is clearly the dynamic element. Industrialization as a project emanated from the particular will of the modern sector; the "general consensus" Chakravarty refers to was in fact the consensus within this modern sector. But this will for transformation had to be expressed as a general project for the "nation," and this could be done by subsuming within the cohesive body of a single plan for the nation all of those elements which appeared as "constraints" on the particular will of the modern sector. If land reform was not attempted in the 1950s, it was not a "fault" of planning, nor was it the lapse of a squeamish "political will" of the rulers. It was because at this stage of its journey the ideological construct of the "passive revolution of capital" consciously sought to incorporate within the framework of its rule not a representative mechanism solely operated by individual agents in civil society but entire structures of precapitalist community taken in their existent forms. In the political field, this was expressed in the form of the so-called vote banks, a much-talked-about feature of Indian elections in the 1950s and 1960s, by which forms of social power based on landed proprietorship or caste loyalty or religious authority were translated into "representative" forms of electoral support. In the economic field, the form preferred was that of "community development," in which the benefits of plan projects meant for the countryside were supposed to be shared collectively by the whole community. That the concrete structures of existent communities were by no means homogeneous or egalitarian but were in fact built around precapitalist forms of social power was not so much ignored or forgotten as tacitly acknowledged, for these were precisely the structures through which the "modernizing" state secured legitimation for itself in the representative processes of elections. It is therefore misleading to suggest as a criticism of this phase of the planning strategy that the planners "did not realize the nature and dimension of political mobilization that would be necessary to bring about the necessary institutional changes" to make agriculture more productive.[17] Seen in terms of the political logic of passive revolution, what the strategy called for precisely was promoting industrialization without taking the risk of agrarian political mobilization. This was an essential aspect of the hegemonic construct of the postcolonial state: combining accumulation with legitimation while avoiding the "unnecessary rigors" of social conflict.

Rational strategies pursued in a political field, however, have the unpleasant habit of producing unintended consequences. Although the objective of the Indian state in the 1950s was to lay the foundations for rapid industrialization without radically disturbing the local structures of power in the countryside, the logic of accumulation in the "modern" sector could not be prevented from seeping into the interstices of agrarian property, trade, pattèrns of consumption, and even production. It did not mean a general and radical shift all over the country to capitalist farming, but there were clear signs that agrarian property had become far more "commoditized" than before, that even subsistence peasant production was deeply implicated in large-scale market transactions, that the forms of extraction of agricultural surplus now combined a wide variety and changing mix of "economic" and "extra-economic" power, and that a steady erosion of the viability of small-peasant agriculture was increasing the ranks of marginal and landless cultivators. Perhaps there were conjunctural reasons why the "food crisis" should have hit the economic, and immediately afterward the political, life of the country with such severity in the mid-1960s. But it would not be unwarranted to point out a certain inevitability of the logic of accumulation breaking into an agrarian social structure that the politics of the state was unwilling to transform.

Other consequences of this phase of planned industrialization under state auspices were to be of considerable political significance.

THE POLITICS OF PLANNING: PART TWO

The object of the strategy of passive revolution was to *contain* class conflicts within manageable dimensions, to control and manipulate the many dispersed power relations in society to further as best as possible the thrust toward accumulation. But conflicts surely could not be avoided altogether. And if particular interests collided, mobilizations based on interests were only to be expected, specially within a political process of representative democracy. In fact, the very form of legitimacy by electoral representation, insofar as it involves a *relation* between the state and the people, implies a mutual recognition by each of the organized and articulate existence of the other, the general on the one hand and the particular on the other. Mobilizations, consequently, did take place, principally as oppositional movements and in both the electoral and nonelectoral domains. The response of the state was to subsume these organized demands of particular interests within the generality of a rational strategy.

The form of this strategy is for the state to insist that all conflicts between particular interests admit of an "economic" solution—"economic" in the sense of allocations to each part that are consistent with the overall constraints of the whole. Thus, a particular interest, whether expressed in terms of class, language, region, caste, tribe, or community, is to be recognized and given a place within the framework of the general by being assigned a priority and an allocation relative to all the other parts. This, as we have seen before, is the form that the single rational consciousness of the developmental state must take—the form of planning. It is also the form that the political process conducted by the state will seek to impose on all mobilizations of particular interests: the demands therefore will be for a reallocation or a reassignment of priorities relative to other particular interests.

It is curious to what extent a large variety of social mobilizations in the last two decades have taken both this "economic" form and the form of demands upon the state. Mobilizations that admit of demographic solidarities defined over territorial regions can usually make this claim within the framework of the federal distribution of powers. This claim could be for greater shares of the federating units from out of the central economic pool, or for a reallocation of the relative shares of different federating units, or even for a redefinition of the territorial boundaries of the units or the creation of new units out of old ones. On the one hand, we therefore have a continuous process of bargaining between the union and the states over the distribution of revenues, which such statutory bodies as the Finance Commissions seek to give an orderly and rational form, but which inevitably spills over into the disorderly immediacy of contingent political considerations, such as the compulsions of party politics, electoral advantage, or the pressures of influential interest lobbies, and which takes the form of an ever-growing series of ad hoc allocations that defy rational and consistent justification. On the other hand, we also have many examples of demands for the creation of new states within the federal union. While the solidarities over which these demands are defined are cultural, such as language or ethnic identity, the justification for statehood inevitably carries with it a charge of economic discrimination within the existing federal arrangements and is thus open to political strategies operating within the "economic" framework of distribution of resources between the center and the states.

For mobilizations of demographic sections that cannot claim representative status of territorial regions, the demands made upon the state are nevertheless also of an "economic" form. These include not only the demands made by the organizations of economic classes but also by social segments such as castes or tribes or religious communities. Examples of the management of class demands of this kind are, of course, innumerable and form the staple of the political economy literature. They affect virtually all aspects of economic policy-making and include taxation, pricing, subsidies, licensing, wages, and the like. But for the economic demands of "ethnic" sections too, the state itself has legitimized the framework by qualifying the notion of citizenship with a set of special protections for culturally underprivileged and backward groups (lower castes, tribes) or minority religious communities. The framework has virtually transformed, to repeat a point made in the previous chapter, the nature of caste movements in India over the last fifty years from movements of lower castes claiming higher ritual status within a religiously sanctified cultural hierarchy to the same castes now proclaiming their ritually degraded status in order to demand protective economic privileges in the fields of employment or educational opportunities. In response, the higher castes, whose superiority has historically rested upon the denial of any notion of ritual equality with lower castes, are now defending their economic privileges precisely by appealing to the liberal notion of equality and by pointing out the economic inefficiencies of special protection.

The point could therefore be made here that the centrality which the state assumes in the management of economic demands in India is not simply the result of the large weight of the public sector or the existence of state monopolies, as is often argued.[18] Even otherwise, a developmental state operating within the framework of representative politics would necessarily require the state to assume the role of the central allocator if it has to legitimize its authority in the political domain.

THE AMBIGUITIES OF LEGITIMATION

There is no doubt that the fundamental problematic of the postcolonial state—furthering accumulation in the modern sector through a political strategy of passive revolution—has given rise to numerous ambiguities in the legitimation process. In the field of economic planning, these ambiguities have surfaced in the debates over the relative importance of market signals and state commands, over the efficiency of the private sector and the inefficiency of the state sector, over the growth potential of a relatively "open" economy and the technological backwardness of the strategy of "self-reliance," and over the dynamic productive potential of a relaxation of state controls compared with the entrenchment of organized privileges within the present structure of state dominance. It is not surprising that in these debates, the proponents of the former argument in each opposed pair have emphasized the dynamic of accumulation while those defending the latter position have stressed the importance of legitimation (although there have been arguments, increasingly less forceful over recent years, that defend the latter on the grounds of accumulation as well). We need not go into the details of these debates here, for they have now become the staple of political discussion in India with the adoption by the government of the "open market" policy prescriptions of international financial agencies. What should be pointed out, however, is, first, that these ambiguities are *necessary* consequences of the specific relation of the postcolonial developmental state with the people-nation; second, that it is these ambiguities which create room for maneuver through which the passive revolution of capital can proceed; and third, that these ambiguities cannot be removed or resolved within the present constitution of the state.

Let me briefly illustrate this point. Given the political process defined by the Indian state, the ambiguities of legitimacy are expressed most clearly in the mechanisms of representation. As far as the modern sector is concerned, particular interests are organized and represented in the well-known forms of interest groups: the variety of permanent associations of industrialists, merchants, professionals, and workers as well as temporary agitational mobilizations based on specific issues. Demands compete in this sector, and the state may use both coercive and persuasive powers to allocate relative priorities in satisfying these demands. But the overall constraint here is to maintain the unity of the modern sector as a whole, for that, as we have seen before, stands forth within the body of the state as the overwhelmingly dominant element of the nation. The unity of the modern sector is specified in terms of a variety of criteria encompassing the domains of industrial production, the professional, educational, and service sectors connected with industrial production, and agricultural production outside the subsistence sector, and also embracing the effective demographic boundaries of the market for the products of the modern sector. The identification of this sector cannot be made in any specific regional terms, nor does it coincide with a simple rural/urban dichotomy. But because of its unique standing as a particular interest that can claim to represent the dynamic aspect of the nation itself, the entire political process conducted by the state, including the political parties that stake their claims to run the central organs of the state, must work toward producing a consensus on protecting the unity of the modern sector. Any appearance of a fundamental lack of consensus here will resonate as a crisis of national unity itself. Thus the political management of economic demands requires that a certain internal balance—an acceptable parity—be maintained between the several fractions within the modern sector. Seen from this angle, the analysis of the "political economy" of Indian planning as a competitive game between privileged pressure groups within a self-perpetuating modern sector will appear one-sided,[19] for it misses the fundamental ambiguity of a state process that must further accumulation while legitimizing the modern sector itself as representative of the nation as a whole.

Indeed, more profound ambiguities appear in the relations between the modern sector and the rest of the people-nation. On the one hand, there is the system of electoral representation on a territorial basis in the form of single-member constituencies. On the other hand, competing demands may be voiced not only on the basis of permanent interest-group organizations but also as mobilizations building upon pre-existing cultural solidarities such as locality, caste, tribe, religious community, or ethnic identity. It would be wrong to assume that no representative process works here. Rather, the most interesting aspect of contemporary Indian politics is precisely the way in which solidarities and forms of authority deriving from the precapitalist community insert themselves into the representational processes of a liberal electoral democracy. This allows, on the one hand, for organizations and leaders to appear in the domain of the state process claiming to represent this or that "community," and for groups of people threatened with the loss of their means of livelihood or suffering from the consequences of such loss to use those representatives to seek the protection, or at least the indulgence, of the state. On the other hand, the state itself can manipulate these "premodern" forms of relations between the community and the state to secure legitimacy for its developmental role.

An instance of the latter is the shift from the earlier strategy of "community development" to that of distributing "poverty removal" packages directly to selected target groups among the underprivileged sections. This strategy, developed during Indira Gandhi's regime in the 1970s, allows for the state to use a political rhetoric in which intermediate rungs of both the social hierarchy (local power barons, dominant landed groups) and the governmental hierarchy (local officials and even elected political representatives) can be condemned as obstacles in the way of the state trying to extend the benefits of development to the poor and to directly present the package of benefits to groups of the latter as a gift from the highest political leadership.[20] From the standpoint of a rational doctrine of political authority, these forms of legitimation doubtless appear as premodern, harking back to what sociologists would call "traditional" or "charismatic" authority. But the paradox is that the existence, the unity, and indeed the representative character of the modern sector as the leading element within the nation has to be legitimized precisely through these means.

There is the other side to this relation of legitimation: the ambiguous image of the state in popular consciousness. If, as we have seen in chapter 8, it is true that the state appears in popular consciousness as an external and distant entity, then, depending upon the immediate perception of local antagonisms, the state could be seen either as an oppressive intruder in the affairs of the local community or as a benevolent protector of the people against local oppressors. The particular image in which the state appears is determined contextually. But this again opens up the possibility for the play of a variety of political strategies of which the story of modern Indian politics offers a vast range of examples.

Such ambiguities show up the narrow and one-sided manner in which the "science" of planning defines itself—a necessary one-sidedness, for without it, the singular rationality of its practice would not be comprehensible to itself. From its own standpoint, planning will address the inefficiency and wastage of the public sector, the irrationality of choosing or locating projects purely on grounds of electoral expediency, the granting of state subsidies in response to agitational pressure. The configuration of social powers in the political process, on the other hand, will produce these inefficient and irrational results that will go down in the planning literature as examples of implementational failures. Yet, in the process of projecting the efficiency of productive growth as a rational path of development for the nation as a whole, the particular interests in the modern sector must shift on to the state the burden of defraying the costs of producing a general consent for their particular project. The state sector, identified as the embodiment of the general, must bear these social costs of constructing the framework of legitimacy for the passive revolution of capital.

What I have tried to show is that the two processes—one of "rational" planning and the other of "irrational" politics—are inseparable parts of the very logic of this state that is conducting the passive revolution. The paradox in fact is that it is the very "irrationality" of the political process which continually works to produce legitimacy for the rational exercise of the planner. While the planner thinks of his own practice as an instrument for resolving conflict, the political process uses planning itself as an instrument for producing consent for capital's passive revolution.

It is not surprising then to discover that the rational form of the planning exercise itself supplies to the political process a rhetoric for conducting its political debates. *Growth* and *equity*—both terms are loaded with potent rhetorical ammunition which can serve to justify as well as to contest state policies that seek to use coercive legal powers to protect or alter the existent relations between social groups. I have shown how the very form of an institution of rational planning located outside the political process is crucial for the self-definition of a developmental state embodying the single universal consciousness of the social whole. I have also shown how the wielders of power can constrain, mold, and distort the strategies of planning in order to produce political consent for their rule. What is science in the one domain becomes rhetoric in the other; what is the rational will of the whole in the one becomes the contingent agglomeration of particular wills in the other. The two together—this contradictory, perennially quarrelsome, and yet ironically well-matched couple—constitute the identity of the developmental state in India today.

Communities and the Nation

KAMALAKANTA had been called in as a witness in court in a case of petty theft. Both magistrate and counsel were eager to get on to his testimony, but the preliminaries were proving to be difficult, since Kamalakanta, with the extreme analytical skills found only among the mad, had raised a series of unanswerable objections to the oath he was required to take. Finally, those difficulties had somehow been overcome and the identity of the witness was being recorded.

The lawyer then asked him, "What jāti are you?"

K: Am I a jāti?

LAWYER: What jāti do you belong to?

K: To the Hindu jāti.

LAWYER: Oh, come now! What varṇa?

K: A very very dark varṇa.

LAWYER: What the hell is going on here! Why did I have to call a witness like this? I say, do you have *jāt*?

K: Who can take it from me?

The magistrate saw that the lawyer was getting nowhere. He said, "You know there are many kinds of jāti among the Hindus, such as Brahman, Kayastha, Kaibarta. Which one of these jāti do you belong to?"

K: My lord! All this is the lawyer's fault! He can see I have the sacred thread around my neck. I have said my name is Chakravarti. How am I to know that he will still not be able to deduce that I am a Brahman?

The magistrate wrote, "Caste: Brahman."[1]

Those who know Kamalakanta will recall how, in Bankim's trenchant narration, he shows up, with his madman's logic, the utter madness of all the claims to rationality made on behalf of colonial reason.[2] In this particular piece, Bankim uses Kamalakanta's uncolonizable voice to mock the trappings of colonial justice, including the way in which it required an unambiguous classification of caste to locate and fix the identity of the colonial subject. Kamalakanta here does not dwell very long on the ambiguities that the "modern" forms of social knowledge face when confronted with a term such as *jāti*. But we can already guess that those ambiguities will, in fact, be literally endless.

THE MANIFOLD USES OF JĀTI

Consider the ways in which the word *jāti* can be used in any modern Indian language. I take as an example the word as used in Bengali. Pick up any standard Bengali dictionary and look through the entries under *jāti*. (It would be useful to remember that these dictionaries themselves have been compiled according to European models so as to conform to the requirements of "modern" forms of knowledge.) It will first give the Sanskrit etymology of the word: √*jan* (to originate, to be born) + *ti*, a noun that literally means "birth," "origin." This will be followed typically by at least a dozen different senses in which the word can be used. Jnanendramohan Das, for instance, lists, among others, the following:

1. *jāti* as origin, such as Musalman by birth, Vaiṣṇav by birth, a beggar by birth [*jātite musalmān, jātbhikhārī*]
2. classes of living species, such as human *jāti*, animal *jāti*, bird *jāti*, etc.
3. *varṇa* following from classifications according to *gūṇa* and *karma*, such as Brahman, etc.
4. *vaṃśa, gotra, kula* [lineage, clan], such as Arya *jāti*, Semitic *jāti*
5. human collectivities bound by loyalty to a state or organized around the natural and cultural characteristics of a country or province [Jnanendramohan adds in English "nation; race"], such as English, French, Bengali, Punjabi, Japanese, Gujarati, etc.[3]

Let us pass over the other, technical, uses of the word in logic, grammar, music, rhetoric, and the like, and concentrate on these—its uses as a category of social classification. Haricharan Bandyopadhyay lists most of the above uses but adds, curiously, to (3)—the sense in which *jāti* is used to denote "caste" in Indian sociology—a derivation from the Persian *zat*.[4] Jnanendramohan too takes note of this alternative derivation but restricts it to the non-Sanskritic word *jāt*, presumed to be a corruption of *jāti* and used in Bengali in all of the first three senses. Finally, in order to clarify our criteria for translation (since, in this particular case, we are discussing the terms of political discourse in India in the English language), let us note that a Sanskrit-Bengali-English trilingual dictionary gives as the English equivalents of *jāti* the following: "species, caste, birth, family, universals."[5]

Between (1) and (5) above, the range of meanings available to the word *jāti* is immense. It is not surprising that Kamalakanta in court should have found it so easy to play around with the word. Indeed, he could have gone on endlessly, describing himself as belonging to the human jāti, the Indian jāti, the Bengali jāti, the jāti of madmen, even (one suspects, with some degree of pride) the jāti of opium addicts. One could, obviously and without any contradiction, belong to several jāti, not simultaneously but contextually, invoking in each context a collectivity in which membership is not a matter of self-interested individual choice or contractual agreement but an immediate inclusion, originary, as it is by birth. We should not be surprised therefore when political discourse permits the imagining of collective solidarities to slide from one particular form to another, each activated contextually but proclaiming each time a bond of kinship, a natural bond that unites all who share the same origin and who therefore must share the same destiny.

Consider the form of imaginative construction of large political solidarities through the union of several jāti. Let us recall a text we have already discussed in an earlier chapter. Bhudeb Mukhopadhyay is giving us his picture of the nationalist utopia emerging out of a counterfactual past.[6] In the grand council that meets after the new emperor of India has been crowned, the following proposal is made:

> Although India is the true motherland only of those who belong to the Hindu jāti and although only they have been born from her womb, the Musalmans are not unrelated to her any longer. She has held them at her breast and reared them. Musalmans are therefore her adopted children.
>
> Can there be no bonds of fraternity between two children of the same mother, one a natural child and the other adopted? There certainly can; the laws of every religion admits this. There has now been born a bond of brotherhood between Hindus and Musalmans living in India.

Remember that for Bhudeb Indian nationalism is synonymous with Hindu nationalism. But he is also a nationalist of a perfectly modern kind, because in this imaginary council a constitution is promulgated more or less along the lines of the German Reich, with strongly protectionist economic policies which succeed, in this anticolonial utopia, in keeping the European economic powers at bay. Yet in order to think of a nation that includes both Hindu and Musalman jāti, albeit under the leadership of Hindus, Bhudeb has to use the language of kinship.

Nevertheless, this imputation of kinship is clearly contextual. Bhudeb would have been horrified if, for instance, someone had appealed to these imputed affinal ties to make a case, let us say, for marriage between Hindus and Muslims or, for that matter, for eating the same food. Identities and solidarities within the language of jāti are contextually defined. The language affords the possibility of imagining new bonds of affinity, but it does this precisely by imposing restrictions on their free flow. There are no substantive affinities that define identity regardless of context.

It is political discourse of the "modern" kind which insists that these collectivities have a fixed, determinate, form, and, if there are several to which an individual can belong, that there be a priority among them, so that it becomes imperative to ask: "Are you a Muslim first or a Bengali first?" "Are you a Bengali first or an Indian first?" Since these are questions that recur constantly in contemporary political discourse in India, we must ask what it is that seeks to erase the contextuality of a concept such as jāti and give it the fixity that was demanded of Kamalakanta in court.

COMMUNITIES: FUZZY AND ENUMERATED

Sudipta Kaviraj has recently argued that a fundamental change effected in the discursive domain of modern politics in the colonial period was the impoverishment of the earlier "fuzzy" sense of the community and an insistence upon the identification of community in the "enumerable" sense.[7] Earlier, communities were fuzzy, in the sense that, first, a community did not claim to represent or exhaust all the layers of selfhood of its members, and second, the community, though definable with precision for all practical purposes of social interaction, did not require its members to ask how many of them there were in the world. The colonial regime, once firmly in place in the second half of the nineteenth century, sought to fashion the conceptual instruments of its control over an alien population precisely by enumerating the diverse communities that, in the colonial imagination, constituted the society over which it had been destined by History to rule. Bernard Cohn, in a well-known piece, has shown how caste and religion became established both conceptually and instrumentally as the "sociological keys" to the numerical description of Indian society.[8] That this classificatory scheme did not reside exclusively in the colonial imagination is also documented by Cohn, because it shaped in turn the subsequent forms of mobilization seeking representation in the state domain—representation, that is, by caste or religion.

To us, situated on this side of the divide represented by postcolonial politics and poststructuralist theory, the move by a colonial power toward the enumeration of Indian society by ethnic communities seems almost natural. One of the fundamental elements in the colonial conceptualization of India as a "different" society was the fixed belief that the population was a mélange of communities. As discussed in an earlier chapter, the conservative opinion said to have dominated imperial policy in the post-Mutiny decades considered this an irredeemable racial characteristic: it was foolish to think that Western education would somehow improve the moral quality of a colonized people and turn them into individuals fit to inhabit a liberal-democratic society. If the colonial state was to seek legitimacy, it had to do so by picking out and bringing over to its side the "natural leaders" of the various communities. This theory of representation informed even the constitutional reforms of the late colonial period.

Mature colonial thought adopted this fairly obvious position because, after all, it could not countenance the idea that subject peoples might constitute, in the same way that advanced people did, a singular and true political community such as the nation. At the same time, if "communities" rather than "nation" were what characterized this society, those communities had to be singular and substantive entities in themselves, with determinate and impermeable boundaries, so insular in their differences with one another as to be incapable of being merged into larger, more modern political identities.

Nationalists, of course, rejected this presumptuous postulate that India could never become a nation. What is curious is the way in which, despite the establishment of a postcolonial regime, an underlying current of thinking about the sociological bases of Indian politics continues to run along channels excavated by colonial discourse. The most obvious example of this is the notion of majority and minority communities defined in terms of criteria such as religion, language, or tribe and applied over a variety of territorial units ranging from a part of a district to the country itself. The other example is the continued preoccupation with precise calculations of proportionality in demands both for and against "reservations," not only for the statutorily designated Scheduled Castes and Tribes but also for that contentious category of "backward castes." And finally, although caste enumerations have been banished from the schedules of the census in independent India, it is remarkable how tenaciously political discourse clings on to the idea of representation by enumerable communities: virtually every discussion on Indian elections looks for supportive evidence in the complicated political arithmetic of caste and communal alliances, calculations taken seriously into account even in the electoral strategies of parties and candidates. Therefore, even if we dismiss the sociological view that declares India to be a mere collection of discrete communities as a peculiarly colonial construct, we are apparently still left with a brand of postcolonial politics whose discursive forms are by no means free of that construct.

"COMMUNITY" IN POSTCOLONIAL POLITICS

I think, however, that there has been a transformation in the terms of political discourse. It would be too facile to make the criticism that all our forms of modern politics are merely the unfortunate legacy of colonialism. It is true, of course, that the fuzziness which enabled a wide variety of solidarities ranging from subcaste to gender to nation to be encompassed under the single rubric of jāti has come under great strain when those solidarities have been forcibly inserted into the grid of the modern regime of power. On the other hand, it is also true that the modern disciplinary regime in India is itself limited and conditioned by the numerous resistances to its hegemonic sway. The result has been an unresolved tension through which the twin constituents of political discourse within the modern domain—one, the categories of the liberal-democratic state produced theoretically in the West, and the other, the categories that made up the Orientalist construction of India—are continuously being re-created in ever more unrecognizable forms.

In the days when the nation was being produced imaginatively without the actual shape of a state, many possibilities of communities that colonial knowledge would have declared as radically distinct came together into large political solidarities. The period of the Khilafat-Noncooperation movement (1919–22) is an obvious instance. Conventional historiography often explains this solidarity as the result of a conscious policy of "alliance" pursued especially by Gandhi and the Ali brothers. However, as our example from Bhudeb's utopian history showed, the idiom of love and kinship in which the nationalist imagination sought to cast the relation between the Hindu jāti and the Muslim jāti can hardly be said to belong to a discourse of group interests and alliances, even when, as in Bhudeb's case, the partnership between different jātis was not on the basis of equality.

More interesting are the instances of sanctions imposed by such political collectivities upon those suspected of deviating from community norms. Ranajit Guha has recently discussed the significance of the "social boycott" that was a widespread phenomenon at the time of the Swadeshi movement in Bengal in 1905–9.[9] The forms of punishment traditionally imposed for violation of caste rules were at this time imposed on those accused of violating the injunctions of the "nation"—offenses such as trading in foreign goods or collaborating with government officials, for instance. Even in the rhetoric of the topmost leaders of the movement, the slide from one sense of jāti to another seemed fairly unproblematical. Hitesranjan Sanyal's researches among participants of the Noncooperation or the Civil Disobedience movements in Midnapore showed how persuasively, almost with the transparency of the self-evident, the concept of the nation, be it jāti, or dés, "the country," was made tangible in the concreteness of an imagined network of kinship extending outward from the local structures of community.[10]

I do not believe that the imaginative possibilities afforded by the fuzziness of the community have disappeared from the domain of popular political discourse. On the contrary, I suspect that with the greater reach of the institutions and processes of the state into the interiors of social life, the state itself is being made sense of in the terms of that other discourse, far removed from the conceptual terms of liberal political theory. The notions of representation and the legitimation of authority, for instance, have taken on a set of meanings in the popular domain of contemporary

Indian politics that would be impossible to describe, let alone justify, in the terms of a theory of interest aggregation or of the rationalization of authority. Our helplessness in understanding processes such as the elections since 1977 or the sudden rise and demise of "ethnic" movements or the inexplicable fluctuations in the authority of particular political leaders seems largely due to the fact that we lack a theoretical language to talk about this domain of popular political discourse.

That this lack is critical is shown by the responses in the domain of "high" discourse to this process of increasing interpenetration of the two domains of politics. There have been, it seems to me, two principal responses, both enabled by the play between the "pure" theory of the modern state and the theory of Oriental exceptionalism. One response involves the reassertion of the universal truth of the pure theory. Thus, claims are being made all over again on behalf of the citizen as a rational individual, transacting public business in accordance with calculations of rational interest and keeping "culture" tucked away within the confines of private belief. There are similar claims about the need to separate politics and ethnicity, politics and religion.

In one sense, these claims are paradoxical. Thus, when the "secular" historian asserts that although medieval rulers may often have acted to inflict damage upon the institutions or followers of a rival religion, there was nothing "religious" about this—it was all "politics"—the claim also empties the domain of politics of that culturally rooted sense of moral solidarity that the same historian would need to uphold when talking, for instance, of the struggle of the "nation" against colonial rule. On the other hand, this same "modernist" discourse would allow the argument to be made that the policy of "reservations" by caste is divisive because it is prompted only by sectional political interests and is harmful for such general national concerns as merit and efficiency. Our modern discourse, it would seem, has to insist that although "politics" may at times be good for the nation, at other times it is best abjured.

There is a further irony. The assertion of a zone of pure politics, while rejecting the colonialist dogma that Indian society is unfit to have a modern state, acknowledges at the same time that the cultural realities in the domain of mass politics can only pollute and corrupt the rational processes of the state. Whether it is communalism or casteism, nepotism or power brokerage, thoughtless populism or the absence of a work ethic, the impact of the popular domain is seen as bearing the mark of an impurity.

Take as an example a recent collection of essays on the politics of caste.[11] The list of writers is a fairly representative sample of the strands of thinking among social scientists writing in Bengali today. (Let me add, since I do not wish to suggest a false standpoint of distance, that this list includes my name as well.) The title of the volume is significant, for it announces itself as a book on the politics of *jātpāt*, not just caste but "casteism," and not only casteism but the entire gamut of divisive politics based on religion, language, or ethnicity. *Jātpāt* is a curious word. A very recent entrant into the vocabulary of politics, it cannot be found in any standard Bengali dictionary. It has probably made its way into the lexicon of Bengali journalism and social science from Hindi,[12] and in its use within this sophisticated discourse of rationality and progress, it carries a double imprint of corruption. *Jāt* itself, according to our lexicographers, is a corruption of *jāti* (or else it is derived from the Persian); *jātpāt* pushes it even further into the dark recesses of the "cow belt" or the "deep south," where they practice a politics so arcane and medieval that progressive Bengalis can only throw up their hands in despair.

The word *jātpāt* also enables one to hierarchize the many senses of *jāti*. *Jāti* can now be given a proper place within the modern discursive formation by reserving its use to the "good" community, namely, the nation. The other senses will then connote undesirable forms of community, evidence of the cultural backwardness of the people and describable as the politics of jātpāt.

The other response in the domain of "high" discourse involves the assertion that all the forms of the modern state in India today represent the unwelcome intrusion of the West and that "traditional" institutions, if allowed to function freely, are still capable of devising adequate instruments for the harmonious functioning of large collectivities.[13] This is the theory of Oriental exceptionalism turned around, for it argues, first, that the Orient can create its own brand of modernity and, second, that the Orient could not care less if its modernity qualifies as modern or not by the criteria of the West. What the argument overlooks is the depth to which the processes of the modern state have taken root in the contemporary history of India. It is not the origins but the process of domestication of the modern state in India that is at issue; one does not, unfortunately, have the option of sending this state back to its origins.

THE MODERN STATE AND CIVIL SOCIETY

We can see then that to sort out these problems of correspondence between the terms of discourse in the domains of elite and popular politics, we need to confront the central question of the modern state and its mechanisms of normalization that seek to obliterate the fuzziness of communities. I will end by raising this rather large question, which we have encountered several times, in one form or another, during the course of this book.

The crux of the matter concerns the presumed emergence in Western Europe of a domain of civil society and its continued autonomous existence, sometimes in opposition to and at other times supportive of the state. What is this civil society? In a recent essay, Charles Taylor has distinguished between three different senses in which civil society can be identified in the European political tradition:[14]

1. In a minimal sense, civil society exists where there are free associations, not under the tutelage of state power.

2. In a stronger sense, civil society only exists where society as a whole can structure itself and coordinate its actions through such associations which are free of state tutelage.

3. As an alternative or supplement to the second sense, we can speak of civil society wherever the ensemble of associations can significantly determine or inflect the course of state policy.

He then spells out five distinct ideas that historically contributed to the production in Europe of a concept of civil society separate from the idea of the state:

A. The medieval idea that society is not identical with its political organization and that political authority is only one organ among others.

B. The Christian idea of the Church as an independent society.

C. The development within feudalism of a legal notion of subjective rights.

D. The growth in medieval Europe of relatively independent, self-governing cities.

E. The secular dualism of the medieval polity in which a monarch ruled with the intermittent and uncertain support of a body of Estates.

Taylor then describes how these ideas were brought together in two quite distinct ways by Locke and Montesquieu, respectively, to produce two different conceptualizations of the state-civil society relation.

In Locke, (A) is interpreted to mean that society is created before government, through a first contract by which individuals in the state of nature give themselves a society. This society then sets up government as a trust. The implication is that if government should violate its trust, society would recover its freedom against government. (B) is given the meaning of a prepolitical community constituted by a natural law received from God. This now becomes the foundation for subjective rights in (C): no positive law can be valid if it contravenes these rights. This particular combination of (A), (B), and (C) produces in Locke the notion of a civil society distinguished from political authority, in which much that is valuable and creative in social life, especially in the sphere of social production, is seen as belonging to the domain of civil society, outside the direction or intervention of the political authority. We can immediately notice the centrality of this notion in the ideological self-representation of English capitalism.

Montesquieu, on the other hand, since he does not presume a prepolitical natural community, does not need to appeal to either (A) or (B). For him, society and political authority are coeval. In order to establish his antiabsolutist doctrine, he brings together (C), (D), and (E) in a form that enables him to distinguish between central political authority on the one hand and a set of entrenched rights, defended by citizens who have a republican sense of patriotic virtue, on the other. His view of society then is that of a balance between two elements, neither prior to the other, which remain as it were in perpetual but creative tension, seeking always to achieve that equilibrium in which both retain their identities without destroying each other.

What is significant in this distinction drawn by Taylor between the two streams of thinking leading to the state/civil society opposition, represented by Locke and Montesquieu, respectively, is the element they share in common. Element (C)—the notion of subjective rights—plays the crucial role in establishing both the distinction between as well as the unity of state and civil society in both these antiabsolutist doctrines. I think this commonality is important especially because of the way in which the history of these two streams of political thinking in Europe becomes implicated in another history: the history of capital. I will return to this point later.

In the meantime, let us note another curious feature shared by both streams. Both Locke and Montesquieu defend subjective rights by appealing to a notion of community. In Locke, this is straightforward. Subjective rights have their source in the prepolitical natural community God creates for mankind: (C) is grounded in (B). People in the state of nature are already constituted as "subjects" by the community of natural law, even before the emergence of society. They can, therefore, proceed, as already constituted "individuals," to create through mutual contracts first society and then government, and thereby establish the institutions for the defense of their subjective rights. In Montesquieu, although (C) is related in institutional terms to the equilibrating forces contained in (D) and (E), the ultimate defense of subjective rights is *vertu*, the patriotic spirit of citizens who "feel shame in obeying any order which derogates from their code" and who "defend the laws to the death against internal and external threats." One would be justified, it seems to me, to think of *vertu* as that sense of community, which is not prior to the establishment of political authority but coeval with it, which nevertheless regards itself as having an identity distinct from that of the political authority.

Why else would the defense of subjective rights against royal encroachment be "patriotic"?

Subjective rights and the grounding of those rights in community—these are the two features that are common to the otherwise different arguments made by Locke and Montesquieu. The problems that appear in the subsequent history of the state-civil society relation in Europe are, I think, fundamentally shaped by divergences in conceptualizing the relation between rights and community. These divergences are framed within two extreme positions: on the one hand, abolishing community altogether and thinking of rights as grounded solely in the self-determining individual will, and on the other, attributing to community a single determinate form, delegitimizing all other forms of community. This subsequent history, I will argue, is intricately tied with the history of capital.

CIVIL SOCIETY AND COMMUNITY

The two streams represented by Locke and Montesquieu were brought together in its most celebrated form by Hegel. Yet, as Taylor notes, the two "sit uneasily together" in Hegel's new concept of civil society. Let me explore the source of this tension in Hegel.

Hegel, as we know, strenuously resisted the line of argument that preferred to think of the state as having been founded by contract. Contracts follow from the accidental, and entirely contingent, agreements among individual wills. They properly belong to the domain of the "system of needs" but are too fickle to be the basis of Right itself. Hegel also would not admit that the family, that first elementary moment of social life, was founded on contract. To admit this would mean having to recognize that members of a family, whether adults or children, might have rights against each other and even the right to dissociate from or dissolve the family at will. That would make the primary elements of social life subject to the transient and utterly chaotic accidents of contingent agreements. Contracts, for Hegel, belong neither to the domain of the state nor to that of the family; their place is in civil society.

How, then, is the family formed? Hegel, as we know, begins the *Philosophy of Right* by first establishing subjective will in abstract right. But when he moves to the actualizing of subjective will in the concreteness of "ethical life," he grounds the first moment—the family—in "love," which is precisely the free surrender of will and personality. The family is ethical mind "in its natural or immediate phase," where it "is specifically characterized by love, which is mind's feeling of its own unity. . . . One is in it not as an independent person but as a member."[15] I quote some of the other things Hegel has to say about this "natural or immediate phase" of ethical life because I prefer to read these passages as a suppressed narrative of community, flowing through the substratum of liberal capitalist society, which those who celebrate the absolute and natural sovereignty of the individual will refuse to recognize. Hegel says:

> Love means in general terms the consciousness of my unity with another, so that I am not in selfish isolation but win my self-consciousness only as the renunciation of my independence and through knowing myself as the unity of myself with another and of the other with me. Love, however, is feeling, i.e. ethical life in the form of something natural. . . . The first moment in love is that I do not wish to be a self-subsistent and independent person and that, if I were, then I would feel defective and incomplete. The second moment is that I find myself in another person, that I count for something in me. Love, therefore, is the most tremendous contradiction; the Understanding cannot resolve it since there is nothing more stubborn than this point of self-consciousness which is negated and which nevertheless I ought to possess as affirmative. Love is at once the propounding and the resolving of this contradiction. As the resolving of it, love is unity of an ethical type.

> The right of the family properly consists in the fact that its substantiality should have determinate existence. Thus it is a right against externality and against secessions from the family unity. On the other hand, to repeat, love is a feeling, something subjective, against which unity cannot make itself effective. The demand for unity can be sustained, then, only in relation to such things as are by nature external and not conditioned by feeling.[16]

Hegel, of course, restricts this substantial unity to the nuclear family, in which it finds its determinate existence as a right against externality and secession in, first, the family property, and second, the male head of the family—husband and father. In doing this, Hegel leads himself into a precarious position, for no matter how hard he tries to resist the idea of the family as based on a contractual agreement in which the members retain their individual rights against each other, he cannot prevent the tide of individualism from seeping into the representations of marriage and inheritance even in the positive law of modern Western societies. Reading these passages today, Hegel's arguments on marriage, gender relations, and inheritance seem to us either quaint, if one takes a charitable view, or outrageously conservative.

I wish to argue, however, that there is another narrative in which Hegel's eloquence on the subject of love will not seem so outmoded. This is the narrative not of the bourgeois family but of community. Think of the rhetoric in which, even in this age of the triumph of individualism, all movements that appeal to the "natural" solidarity of community speak. They claim precisely the right against externality and secession, they seek determinate existence precisely in "property" and "representation" through collectively recognized heads, they speak in the language of love and of self-recognition through the free surrender of individual will to others in the community. One might object that this idea of "natural" affiliation to a community (or an indeterminate set of communities) does violence to the freedom of choice inherent in the subjective will. It is this objection that becomes the basis for the identification in European sociological theory—fed, let us remember, on large doses of Orientalist literature and colonial anthropology—of all precapitalist gemeinschaften as the domain of ascription, and hence unfreedom, and of modern associations as the field where freedom and choice can blossom. Hegel's arguments on the family remind us, it seems to me, of the irreducible immediacy in which human beings are born in society: not as pure unattached individuals free to choose their social affiliations (whether gender, ethnicity, or class) but as already ascribed members of society. Liberal individualism seeks to erase this level of immediacy where people are not free to choose the social locus of their birth. Indeed, liberalism seeks to forget that the question of choice here is itself fallacious, for human beings cannot exist as "individuals" before they are born, and when they are born, they are already ascribed as particular members of society. Liberal theory then can only deal with this phenomenon as accidents of "natural inequality," which social policies of welfare or equal opportunity must mitigate. It can, in other words, deal with it only in bad faith.

If I am allowed the conceit of reading Hegel against the grain, I will choose to read this subsection of "Ethical Life" as a narrative of community where subjective rights must be negotiated within the "ascribed" field of the ethical life of the community. I will also recall here that Hegel makes the family the site for that other great process by which "individual" subjectivities could be negotiated in society, namely, the education of children,[17] which site too he would not be able to defend against the relentless sway of the modern disciplinary regime of power constantly striving to produce the "normalized" individual. Against the grain of liberal sociology, I prefer to read Hegel as saying that education properly belongs to the field of the ethical life of the community, and not to the compulsory discipline of the school, the prison, the hospital, and the psychiatrist's clinic. I will not describe this field of community ethical life as one devoid of choice, nor will I give it a place at some early stage in the sequence of development of the bourgeois nuclear family. Rather, I will read this as a narrative that continues to unfold to this day *against the grain* of that other narrative of bourgeois individualism.

To return to Hegel and civil society: families, united within themselves against the externality constituted by other families and each represented by its head—the burgher, the bourgeois—comprise the domain of civil society. This is the domain of particular interests, based on particular needs and the mutual satisfaction of the needs of all through contractually mediated exchange of the products of labor. This is also the domain where the property of each family is mutually protected through the administration of justice. Civil society, in other words, is the well-known domain of the market economy and civil law.

Hegel, however, also includes within civil society a residual category, providing for "contingencies still lurking" in the system of needs and the administration of justice and for the "care of particular interests as a common interest." This residual category includes the police and the corporation. Curiously, in demarcating the limits of public surveillance organized by civil society (Hegel is clearly thinking here of the administrative functions of what was known in eighteenth-century Germany and Italy as "the police" and which had become the subject of an entire discipline called *Polizeiwissenschaft*),[18] Hegel admits that "no objective line can be drawn." In other words, at this interface between family and civil society, no objective line separates the private from the public. The separation can be made only contextually, taking into view specific contingencies. "These details," Hegel says, "are determined by custom, the spirit of the rest of the constitution, contemporary conditions, the crisis of the hour, and so forth."[19] How is one to read this lack of objective separation between the civil and the familial, the public and the private? What is it that produces this zone of contingency and indeterminacy where "everything is subjective"? Can one read this as one more instance where a suppressed narrative of community is seeping through the interstices of the objectively constructed, contractually regulated structure of civil society?

A final illustration, and I will stop this strenuous reading of Hegel. Still on the subject of civil society and its residual function of taking care of particular interests as a common interest, Hegel writes:

> In its character as a universal family, civil society has the right and duty of superintending and influencing education, inasmuch as education bears upon the child's capacity to become a member of society. Society's right here is paramount over the arbitrary and contingent preferences of parents. . . . Parents usually suppose that in the matter of education they have complete freedom and may arrange everything as they like. . . . None the less, society has a right . . . to compel parents to send their children to school, to have them vaccinated, and so forth. The disputes that have arisen in France between the advocates of state supervision and those who demand that education shall be free, i.e. at the option of the parents, are relevant here.[20]

Once again, I wish to suggest, that suppressed narrative is raising its irrepressible head. How else can Hegel suddenly slip in the idea of civil society as "a universal family"? How can civil society represent itself as a family that, according to Hegel himself, is born not out of contract but out of love, the free surrender of individual wills? By reducing family to the single determinate form of the bourgeois nuclear family, Hegel has narrowed and impoverished its scope. The gap has to be filled in by civil society arrogating the role of a "universal family." Ironically, by admitting this, Hegel immediately opens himself to appropriation by that powerful strand of thinking which claims that this role of the universal family can be properly played by the only legitimate community in modern society—the nation—a role that must then be enforced by the disciplinary mechanisms of the nation-state. Hegel becomes complicit in this act of appropriation, not innocently but as an inevitable consequence of his own construction of the system of Right: the contingent contractual domain of civil society must, after all, be unified at the higher, universal level of the absolute idea of Right, embodied in the state as *the* political community.

CAPITAL AND COMMUNITY

I am suggesting, therefore, that this suppression in modern European social theory of an independent narrative of community makes possible both the posing of the distinction between state and civil society and the erasure of that distinction. At one extreme, then, we have arguments proclaiming the sovereignty of the individual will, insisting that the state has no business to interfere in the domain of individual freedom of choice and contractual arrangements. At the other extreme are the arguments that would have the *one* political community, given the single, determinate, demographically enumerable form of the nation-state, assume the directing role in all regulatory functions of society, usurping the domain of civil society and family, and blurring the distinctions between the public and the private. It is to this range of arguments that people must refer when they say that the state-civil society relation in Western thought is not one of simple opposition. I will argue that the possibilities of opposition as well as encapsulation arise because the concepts of the individual and the nation-state both become embedded in a new grand narrative: the narrative of capital. This narrative of capital seeks to suppress that other narrative of community and produce in the course of its journey both the normalized individual and the modern regime of disciplinary power.

The historical specificity of European social thought cannot be described simply by Taylor's conditions (A) to (E). It would not be surprising at all if one finds in the premodern histories of other, non-European, countries similar features in state-society relations. It is also difficult to explain why, if European thought is indeed conditioned by these specifics, people from Poland to the Philippines to Nicaragua should appeal to these philosophers from Britain, France, or Germany to think out and justify what they do to their own societies and states. If there is one great moment that turns the provincial thought of Europe to universal philosophy, the parochial history of Europe to universal history, it is the moment of capital—capital that is global in its territorial reach and universal in its conceptual domain. It is the narrative of capital that can turn the violence of mercantilist trade, war, genocide, conquest and colonialism into a story of universal progress, development, modernization, and freedom.

For this narrative to take shape, the destruction of community is fundamental. Marx saw this clearly when he identified as the necessary condition for capitalist production the separation of the mass of laborers from their means of labor. This so-called primitive accumulation is nothing else but the destruction of precapitalist community, which, in various forms, had regulated the social unity of laborers with their means of production. Thus community, in the narrative of capital, becomes relegated to the latter's prehistory, a natural, prepolitical, primordial stage in social evolution that must be superseded for the journey of freedom and progress to begin. And since the story of capital is universal, community too becomes the universal prehistory of progress, identified with medievalism in Europe and the stagnant, backward, undeveloped present in the rest of the world.

It could not, however, be entirely suppressed. The domain of civil society, ruled by "liberty, equality, property and Bentham," could not produce an adequate justification for the lack of freedom and equality within the industrial labor process itself and the continued division of society into the opposed classes of capital and labor. What Marx did not see too well was the ability of capitalist society to ideologically reunite capital and labor at the level of the political community of the nation, borrowing from another narrative the rhetoric of love, duty, welfare, and the like. Notwithstanding its universalist scope, capital remained parasitic upon the reconstructed particularism of the nation. (It would be an interesting exercise to identify in Marx's *Capital* the places where this other narrative makes a surreptitious appearance: for instance, money, the universal equivalent, which nevertheless retains the form of a national currency assigned a particular exchange-value by the national state; or the value of labor-power, homogeneous and normalized, which is nevertheless determined by specific historical and cultural particularities.)

We must remember that the rise of a public sphere in Europe, which is said to be a space outside the supervision of political authority where "opinion could present itself as that of society," was also crucial in connecting a reconstructed cultural identity of the people with the legitimate jurisdiction of the state. It was principally in this public space where, through the medium of print-capitalism, the homogenized forms of a national culture were forged—through the standardization of language, aesthetic norms, and consumer tastes. The public sphere, then, was not only a domain that marked the distinction of state and civil society; by creating the cultural standards through which "public opinion" could claim to speak on behalf of the nation, it also united state and civil society. Civil society now became the space for the diverse life of individuals in the nation; the state became the nation's singular representative embodiment, the only legitimate form of community.

But community is not easily appropriated within the narrative of capital. Community, from the latter's standpoint, belongs to the domain of the natural, the primordial. Only in its sanitized, domesticated form can it become a shared subjective feeling that protects and nurtures (good nationalism). But it always carries with it the threatening possibility of becoming violent, divisive, fearsome, irrational (bad nationalism). It is not so much the state/civil society opposition but rather the capital/community opposition that seems to me to be the great unsurpassed contradiction in Western social philosophy. Both state and civil-social institutions have assigned places within the narrative of capital. Community, which ideally should have been banished from the kingdom of capital, continues to lead a subterranean, potentially subversive, life within it because it refuses to go away.

Recent attempts in social philosophy to produce arguments from a "communitarian" standpoint against the dominant orthodoxy of liberal or bureaucratic individualism have sought either to rediscover premodern forms of the political community, lost under the rubble left behind by the onward march of modernity, or to find them among suppressed groups or deviant cults surviving on the margins of normalized society. Alasdair MacIntyre, for instance, sets up his argument against the Enlightenment project of modernity, and by implication against the Nietzschean critique of modernity, by vindicating a classical Aristotelian concept of virtue.[21] In doing this, he has to conjure up the vision of the polis, a determinate political community institutionalizing the practices, goals, and tradition of a moral community. Recent theorists of anarchism have looked for support in the ethnographic evidence on stateless tribal communities or in the practices of marginal utopian communities. And Michel Foucault, seeking in the last years of his life to find the ground for resistance to the all-conquering sway of disciplinary power, located it in the possibility of "an insurrection of subjugated knowledges," a localized but autonomous and noncentralized kind of theoretical production "whose validity is not dependent on the approval of the established régimes of thought."[22]

I am pointing out a different possibility. Looking at the relatively untheorized idea of "the nation" in Western social philosophy, one notices an inelegant braiding of an idea of community with the concept of capital. This is not an archaic idea buried in the recesses of history, nor is it part of a marginal subculture, nor can it be dismissed as a premodern remnant that an absentminded Enlightenment has somehow forgotten to erase. It is very much a part of the here-and-now of modernity, and yet it is an idea that remains impoverished and limited to the singular form of the nation-state because it is denied a legitimate life in the world of the modern knowledges of human society. This denial, in turn, is related to the fact that by its very nature, the idea of the community marks a limit to the realm of disciplinary power. My hypothesis, then, is that an investigation into the idea of the nation, by uncovering a necessary contradiction between capital and community, is likely to lead us to a fundamental critique of modernity from within itself.

But beyond the intellectual history of Europe, our inquiry into the colonial and postcolonial histories of other parts of the world is more likely to enable us to make this critique.[23] The contradictions between the two narratives of capital and community can be seen quite clearly in the histories of anticolonial nationalist movements. The forms of the modern state were imported into these countries through the agency of colonial rule. The institutions of civil society, in the forms in which they had arisen in Europe, also made their appearance in the colonies precisely to create a public domain for the legitimation of colonial rule. This process was, however, fundamentally limited by the fact that the colonial state could confer only subjecthood on the colonized; it could not grant them citizenship. The crucial break in the history of anticolonial nationalism comes when the colonized refuse to accept membership of this civil society of subjects. They construct their national identities within a different narrative, that of the community. They do not have the option of doing this within the domain of bourgeois civil-social institutions. They create, consequently, a very different domain—a cultural domain—marked by the distinctions of the material and the spiritual, the outer and the inner. This inner domain of culture is declared the sovereign territory of the nation, where the colonial state is not allowed entry, even as the outer domain remains surrendered to the colonial power. The rhetoric here (Gandhi is a particularly good example)[24] is of love, kinship, austerity, sacrifice. The rhetoric is in fact antimodernist, antiindividualist, even anticapitalist. The attempt is, if I may stay with Gandhi for a while, to find, against the grand narrative of history itself, the cultural resources to negotiate the terms

through which people, living in different, contextually defined, communities, can coexist peacefully, productively, and creatively within large political units.

The irony is, of course, that this other narrative is again violently interrupted once the postcolonial national state attempts to resume its journey
along the trajectory of world-historical development. The modern state,
embedded as it is within the universal narrative of capital, cannot recognize within its jurisdiction any form of community except the single,
determinate, demographically enumerable form of the nation. It must
therefore subjugate, if necessary by the use of state violence, all such aspirations of community identity. These other aspirations, in turn, can give
to themselves a historically valid justification only by claiming an alternative nationhood with rights to an alternative state.

One can see how a conception of the state-society relation, born within
the parochial history of Western Europe but made universal by the global
sway of capital, dogs the contemporary history of the world. I do not
think that the invocation of the state/civil society opposition in the struggle against socialist-bureaucratic regimes in Eastern Europe or in the former Soviet republics or, for that matter, in China, will produce anything
other than strategies seeking to replicate the history of Western Europe.
The result has been demonstrated a hundred times. The provincialism of
the European experience will be taken as the universal history of progress; by comparison, the history of the rest of the world will appear as the
history of lack, of inadequacy—an inferior history. Appeals will be made
all over again to philosophies produced in Britain, France, and Germany.
The fact that these doctrines were produced in complete ignorance of the
histories of other parts of the world will not matter: they will be found
useful and enlightening.[25] It would indeed be a supreme irony of history
if socialist industrialization gets written into the narrative of capital as the
phase when socialist-bureaucratic regimes had to step in to undertake
"primitive accumulation" and clear the way for the journey of capital to
be resumed along its "normal" course.

In the meantime, the struggle between community and capital, irreconcilable within this grand narrative, will continue. The forms of the modern state will be forced into the grid of determinate national identities.
This will mean a substantialization of cultural differences, necessarily excluding as "minorities" those who would not conform to the chosen
marks of nationality. The struggle between "good" and "bad" nationalism will be played out all over again.

What, then, are the true categories of universal history? State and civil
society? public and private? social regulation and individual rights?—all
made significant within the grand narrative of capital as the history of
freedom, modernity and progress? Or the narrative of community—

untheorized, relegated to the primordial zone of the natural, denied any subjectivity that is not domesticated to the requirements of the modern state, and yet persistent in its invocation of the rhetoric of love and kinship against the homogenizing sway of the normalized individual?

It is this unresolved struggle between the narratives of capital and community within the discursive space of the modern state that is reflected in our embarrassment at the many uses of *jāti*. Kamalakanta, if he is still around, is now, I suspect, laughing at us.

Notes

The following abbreviations have been used in the notes:

BI Tarinicharan Chattopadhyay. *Bhāratbarṣer itihās*. Vol. 1. 1858. Reprint. Calcutta, 1878.

BMRI Abdul Karim. *Bhāratbarṣe musalmān rājatver itibṛtta*. Vol 1. Calcutta: Sanskrit Press Depository, 1898.

BR Bankimchandra Chattopadhyay. *Baṅkim racanābalī*. Edited by Jogeshchandra Bagal. Vol. 2. Calcutta: Sahitya Samsad, 1965.

G [Mahendranath Gupta]. *The Gospel of Sri Ramakrishna*. Translated by Swami Nikhilananda. New York: Ramakrishna-Vivekananda Center, 1942.

GM Swami Saradananda. *Sri Ramakrishna the Great Master*. Translated by Swami Jagadananda. Madras: Sri Ramakrishna Math, 1952.

K Ma [Mahendranath Gupta]. *Śrīśrīrāmkṛṣṇa kathāmṛta*. 1902–32. Reprint. Calcutta: Ananda, 1983.

L Swami Saradananda. *Śrīśrīrāmakṛṣṇalīlāprasaṅga*. 2 vols. Calcutta: Udbodhan, 1965.

PK Prasannamayi Debi. *Pūrbba kathā*. 1917. Reprint. Calcutta: Subarnarekha, 1982.

R Mrityunjay Vidyalankar. *Rājābali*. Serampore: Baptist Mission Press, 1808.

Chapter One
Whose Imagined Community?

1. Benedict Anderson, *Imagined Communities: Reflections on the Origin and Spread of Nationalism* (London: Verso, 1983).

2. This is a central argument of my book *Nationalist Thought and the Colonial World: A Derivative Discourse?* (London: Zed Books, 1986).

3. Anderson, *Imagined Communities*, pp. 17–49.

4. Ibid., pp. 28–40.

5. The history of this artistic movement has been recently studied in detail by Tapati Guha-Thakurta, *The Making of a New "Indian" Art: Artists, Aesthetics and Nationalism in Bengal, 1850–1920* (Cambridge: Cambridge University Press, 1992).

6. See Anilchandra Banerjee, "Years of Consolidation: 1883–1904"; Tripurari Chakravarti, "The University and the Government: 1904–24"; and Pramathanath Banerjee, "Reform and Reorganization: 1904–24," in Niharranjan Ray and Pratulchandra Gupta, eds., *Hundred Years of the University of Calcutta* (Calcutta: University of Calcutta, 1957), pp. 129–78, 179–210, and 211–318.

7. Bipinchandra Pal, *Memories of My Life and Times* (1932; reprint, Calcutta: Bipinchandra Pal Institute, 1973), pp. 157–60.

8. Represented by the various essays in Ranajit Guha, ed., *Subaltern Studies*, vols. 1–6 (Delhi: Oxford University Press, 1982–90). The programatic statement of this approach is in Ranajit Guha, "On Some Aspects of the Historiography of Colonial India," in Guha, ed., *Subaltern Studies I* (Delhi: Oxford University Press, 1982), pp. 1–8.

Chapter Two
The Colonial State

1. Arthur Berriedale Keith, *A Constitutional History of India, 1600–1935* (1937; reprint, New York: Barnes and Noble, 1969), p. vii.

2. Edward Thompson and G. T. Garratt, *Rise and Fulfilment of British Rule in India* (1934; reprint, Allahabad: Central Book Depot, 1962), p. 654.

3. M. V. Pylee, *Constitutional History of India, 1600–1950* (Bombay: Asia, 1967), p. v. Emphasis mine. It is also not a coincidence that the title of Pylee's book replicates that of Keith's; it only extends the time period by fifteen years.

4. B. B. Misra, *The Bureaucracy in India: An Historical Analysis of Development up to 1947* (Delhi: Oxford University Press, 1977), pp. x, 157.

5. Vincent A. Smith, *Indian Constitutional Reform Viewed in the Light of History* (London: Humphrey Milford, 1919), p. 78. Emphasis in original.

6. Ibid., pp. 21, 22.

7. Ibid., p. 41.

8. Ibid., pp. 50–51.

9. T. R. Metcalf, *The Aftermath of Revolt* (Princeton: Princeton University Press, 1964), p. 96.

10. Stephen in *The Times*, 1 March 1883, cited in Metcalf, *The Aftermath of Revolt*, p. 318.

11. Kenneth Ballhatchet, *Race, Sex and Class under the Raj: Imperial Attitudes and Policies and Their Critics, 1793–1905* (London: Weidenfeld and Nicolson, 1980), p. 6.

12. See Misra, *Bureaucracy in India*, pp. 91–210.

13. C. E. Buckland, *Bengal under the Lieutenant Governors* (1901; reprint, New Delhi: Deep, 1976), 2:769.

14. S. Gopal, *British Policy in India, 1858–1905* (Cambridge: Cambridge University Press, 1965), p. 149; Anil Seal, *The Emergence of Indian Nationalism* (Cambridge: Cambridge University Press, 1971), p. 163.

15. Gopal, *British Policy*, p. 150.

16. Resolutions adopted at a public meeting of the European community at the Town Hall, Calcutta, 28 February 1883. Buckland, *Bengal* 2:775–76.

17. Seal, *Emergence*, p. 166.

18. Buckland, *Bengal* 2:787.

19. Cited in Gopal, *British Policy*, p. 151.

20. Seal, *Emergence*, pp. 170, 144.

21. For a brief account of this history, see H. E. A. Cotton, *Calcutta Old and New* (1909; reprint, Calcutta: General Printers, 1980), pp. 163–70.

22. Grant's minute, 19 June 1861, in Buckland, *Bengal* 1:198.

23. W. H. Seton-Karr's letter to the government of Bengal, 29 July 1861, ibid., p. 200.

24. Cotton, *Calcutta*, pp. 175–76.

25. Ibid, p. 176.

26. Note of Arthur Hobhouse, cited in Gopal, *British Policy*, p. 118.

27. Buckland, *Bengal* 2:716–17.

28. Letter by Lytton, 15 March 1878, cited in Gopal, *British Policy*, p. 118.

29. Buckland, *Bengal* 2:719. For an account of the making of the Vernacular Press Act and its impact, see Uma Dasgupta, *Rise of an Indian Public: Impact of Official Policy, 1870–1880* (Calcutta: Rddhi India, 1977), pp. 269–300.

30. For a review of some of these debates on recent Indian historiography, see Gyan Prakash, "Writing Post-Orientalist Histories of the Third World: Perspectives from Indian Historiography," *Comparative Studies in Society and History* 32, no. 2 (April 1990): 383–408; Dipesh Chakrabarty, "Postcoloniality and the Artifice of History: Who Speaks for 'Indian' Pasts?" *Representations* 37 (Winter 1992): 1–26.

31. Some of the methodological problems of autonomy and subjectivity involved in this project are discussed in Gayatri Chakravorty Spivak, "Can the Subaltern Speak?" in Cary Nelson and Lawrence Grossberg, eds., *Marxism and the Interpretation of Culture* (Urbana: University of Illinois Press, 1988); and Spivak, "Subaltern Studies: Deconstructing Historiography," in Ranajit Guha, ed., *Subaltern Studies IV* (Delhi: Oxford University Press, 1985), pp. 330–63.

32. Burton Stein, "State Formation and Economy Reconsidered," *Modern Asian Studies* 19, no. 3 (1985): 387–413.

33. Frank Perlin, "Of White Whale and Countrymen in the Eighteenth-Century Maratha Deccan," *Journal of Peasant Studies* 5, no. 2 (January 1978): 172–237; "Proto-Industrialization and Pre-Colonial South Asia," *Past and Present* 98 (February 1983): 30–95.

34. Frank Perlin, "State Formation Reconsidered," *Modern Asian Studies* 19, no. 3 (1985): 415–80.

35. C. A. Bayly, *Indian Society and the Making of the British Empire*, The New Cambridge History of India, pt. 2, vol. 1 (Cambridge: Cambridge University Press, 1988).

36. The last point is argued in C. A. Bayly, "The Pre-History of 'Communalism'? Religious Conflict in India, 1700–1860," *Modern Asian Studies* 19, no. 2 (1985): 177–203.

37. D. A. Washbrook, "Progress and Problems: South Asian Economic and Social History, c. 1720–1860," *Modern Asian Studies* 22, no. 1 (1988): 57–96.

38. Ibid., pp. 68, 76.

39. For a remarkable analysis of the general rhetorical patterns involved in what I have called the rule of colonial difference, see François Hartog, *The Mirror of Herodotus: The Representation of the Other in the Writing of History*, trans. Janet Lloyd (Berkeley and Los Angeles: University of California Press, 1988).

Chapter Three
The Nationalist Elite

1. To mention only a few of the more notable works: J. H. Broomfield, *Elite Conflict in a Plural Society: Twentieth-Century Bengal* (Berkeley: University of California Press, 1968); Anil Seal, *Emergence of Indian Nationalism* (Cambridge:

Cambridge University Press, 1971); Pradip Sinha, *Calcutta in Urban History* (Calcutta: Firma KLM, 1978); Sumit Sarkar, *The Swadeshi Movement in Bengal* (New Delhi: People's Publishing House, 1973); Rajat K. Ray, *Social Conflict and Political Unrest in Bengal, 1875–1914* (Delhi: Oxford University Press, 1984).

2. A recent work that raises this question is Tapan Raychaudhuri, *Europe Reconsidered: Perceptions of the West in Nineteenth-Century Bengal* (Delhi: Oxford University Press, 1988).

3. Ma [Mahendranath Gupta], *Śrīśrīrāmkṛṣṇa kathāmṛta*, 5 vols. (Calcutta: 1902–1932). For this study, I have used the single-volume complete edition (Calcutta: Ananda, 1983) (hereafter references are cited parenthetically in text as *K*).

4. Sumit Sarkar, " 'Kaliyuga,' 'Chakri' and 'Bhakti': Ramkrishna and His Times," *Economic and Political Weekly* 27, 29 (18 July 1992): 1543–66.

5. Dipesh Chakrabarty, *Rethinking Working-Class History: Bengal, 1890–1940* (Princeton: Princeton University Press, 1989), pp. 15–32.

6. Sivanath Sastri, *History of the Brahmo Samaj* (1911–12; reprint, Calcutta: Sadharan Brahmo Samaj, 1974), p. 171.

7. *Punch*, 16 March 1870, cited in Meredith Borthwick, *Keshub Chunder Sen: A Search for Cultural Synthesis* (Calcutta: Minerva Associates, 1977), p. 108.

8. "Farewell Soirèe," address in London, 12 September 1870, in *Keshub Chunder Sen in England: Diaries, Sermons, Addresses and Epistles* (1871; reprint, Calcutta: Writers Workshop, 1980), p. 450.

9. "Jesus Christ: Europe and Asia," lecture in Calcutta, 5 May 1866, in David C. Scott, ed., *Keshub Chunder Sen* (Madras: Christian Literature Society, 1979), pp. 62–63.

10. *Keshub Chunder Sen in England*, pp. 454–55.

11. Borthwick, *Keshub Chunder Sen*, pp. 148–49.

12. Sastri, *History of the Brahmo Samaj*, pp. 160, 170–71, 172.

13. In 1931, there were a total of 1,554 Brahmos in Calcutta, nearly two-thirds of them concentrated in the single municipal ward of Sukea's Street. *Census of India, 1931*, vol. 6 (Calcutta), pts. 1 and 2 (Calcutta: Central Publication Branch, 1933), imperial table 13, pp. 169–71.

14. "Philosophy and Madness in Religion," lecture delivered in Calcutta, 3 March 1877, in T. E. Slater, *Keshab Chandra Sen and the Brahma Samàj* (Madras: Society for Promoting Christian Knowledge, 1884), app., pp. 85–86.

15. Ibid., pp. 86–87.

16. *Keshub Chunder Sen in England*, p. 271.

17. "India Asks—Who is Christ?" lecture delivered in Calcutta, 9 April 1879, in Slater, *Keshab and the Brahma Samàj*, app., pp. 91–92, 92–93, 93, 102.

18. Rajnarayan Basu, *Ātmacarit* (1909), in Nareschandra Jana, Manu Jana, and Kamalkumar Sanyal, eds., *Ātmakathā* (Calcutta: Ananya, 1981), 1:72.

19. "Great Men," lecture in Calcutta, 28 September 1866, in Scott, *Keshub Chunder Sen*, pp. 99–100.

20. Keshab's mother recounts this incident in talking about Ramakrishna and her son. Saradasundari Debi, *Keśabjananī debī sāradāsundarīr ātmakathā*, ed. Jogendralal Khastagir (Dhaka, 1913); reprint, *Ekṣaṇ* (Autumn 1983): 1–52.

21. P. C. Mozoomdar, *The Life and Teachings of Keshub Chunder Sen* (1887; reprint, Calcutta: Nababidhan Trust, 1931), p. 227.

22. Swami Saradananda, *Śrīśrīrāmakṛṣṇalīlāprasaṅga* (1908–20; reprint, Cal-

cutta: Udbodhan, 1965), 2:398–99 (hereafter references will be cited parenthetically in text as *L*).

23. Mozoomdar, *Life and Teachings*, p. 227.

24. *Life of Ramakrishna Compiled from Various Authentic Sources* (1924; reprint, Calcutta: Advaita Ashrama, 1964), pp. 269–70.

25. Ibid., p. 270.

26. Borthwick, *Keshub Chunder Sen*, pp. 140–41. Anil Seal, quoting Grierson, gives much lower figures: in 1882–83 there were, according to this government source, only two Bengali papers, the *Baṅgabāsī* and *Sulabh samācār*, with circulations of four thousand. Seal, *Emergence*, p. 366.

27. Nanda Mookerjee, ed., *Sri Ramakrishna in the Eyes of Brahma and Christian Admirers* (Calcutta: Firma KLM, 1976), p. 2.

28. Swami Saradananda, *Sri Ramakrishna the Great Master*, trans. Swami Jagadananda (Madras: Sri Ramakrishna Math, 1952), p. 710 (hereafter references will be cited parenthetically in text as *GM*); Christopher Isherwood, *Ramakrishna and His Disciples* (New York: Simon and Schuster, 1965), pp. 168–72.

29. Isherwood, *Disciples*, pp. 172–74.

30. Ibid., p. 240.

31. Ibid., p. 248.

32. The closest devotees all arrived between 1879 and 1884. *GM*, p. 811. A recent study of Ramakrishna's disciples is Swami Chetanananda, *They Lived with God: Life Stories of Some Devotees of Sri Ramakrishna* (St. Louis, Mo.: Vedanta Society of St. Louis, 1989).

33. Prosanto Kumar Sen, *Keshub Chunder Sen* (Calcutta: Keshub Sen Birth Centenary Committee, 1938), p. 119.

34. Saratchandra Chakrabarti (1865–1927), who with the founding of the monastic order after Ramakrishna's death adopted the name Swami Saradananda, was the secretary of the Ramakrishna Math and Mission from 1898 to his death. Between 1908 and 1920 he wrote the series of articles that were later compiled to form the *Līlāprasaṅga*, the authorized account of the Master's life, of which *GM* is a translation.

35. See Partha Chatterjee, *Nationalist Thought and the Colonial World: A Derivative Discourse?* (London: Zed Books, 1986), pp. 58–60.

36. Sarkar, "'Kaliyuga,' 'Chakri' and 'Bhakti.'"

37. I have in mind the researches of Sisirkumar Das, Tarapada Mukhopadhyay, Anisuzzaman, Pradyumna Bhattacharya, Debes Ray, and Prabal Dasgupta. For a recent survey of the questions surrounding the development of the new Bengali prose, see Pradyumna Bhattacharya, "Rāmmohan rāy ebaṃ bāṅlā gadya," *Bāromās* 11, no. 2 (April 1990): 1–22.

38. Ernest Gellner, *Nations and Nationalism* (Oxford: Basil Blackwell, 1983); Benedict Anderson, *Imagined Communities: Reflections on the Origin and Spread of Nationalism* (London: Verso, 1983).

39. There have been many attempts in the last hundred years to place Ramakrishna in the tradition of classical Indian philosophy. One of the most erudite of these is Satis Chandra Chatterjee, *Classical Indian Philosophies: Their Synthesis in the Philosophy of Sri Ramakrishna* (Calcutta: University of Calcutta, 1963).

40. Sudipta Kaviraj, "Bankimchandra and the Making of Nationalist Consciousness. IV: Imaginary History," manuscript.

41. Girishchandra Ghosh, *Giriś racanābalī*, vol. 1, ed. Rathindranath Ray and Debipada Bhattacharya (Calcutta: Sahitya Samsad, 1969), pp. 113–28.

42. *K*, pp. 41–42; [Mahendranath Gupta], *The Gospel of Sri Ramakrishna*, trans. Swami Nikhilananda (New York: Ramakrishna-Vivekananda Center, 1942), pp. 142–43 (references hereafter cited parenthetically in text as *G*). Unless otherwise specified, I will quote from this translation of the *Kathāmṛta*. I must, however, point out that there is a quite deliberate attempt in the *Gospel* to "Christianize" Ramakrishna's language: the translation into English provides the opportunity to put yet another gloss on the language of the *Kathāmṛta*.

43. My translation: the *Gospel* here glosses over the words and phrases that appear in the English in the original.

44. I have changed the translation somewhat.

45. A useful account of these religious ideas will be found in Sashibhusan Das Gupta, *Obscure Religious Cults* (Calcutta: Firma KLM, 1969).

46. Ashis Nandy, *The Intimate Enemy: Loss and Recovery of Self under Colonialism* (Delhi: Oxford University Press, 1983).

47. See Sudipta Kaviraj, "Bankimchandra and the Making of Nationalist Consciousness: I. Signs of Madness; II. The Self-Ironical Tradition; III. A Critique of Colonial Reason," Occasional Papers 108, 109 and 110 (Calcutta: Centre for Studies in Social Sciences, 1989).

48. "Anukaraṇ," in Bankimchandra Chattopadhyay, *Bankim racanābalī* (Calcutta: Sahitya Samsad, 1965), 2:200–201 (hereafter cited parenthetically in text as *BR*). I have in the main followed Sudipta Kaviraj's translation in "Bankimchandra and the Making of Nationalist Consciousness."

49. The classic analysis of this process in Western Europe is in Jürgen Habermas, *The Structural Transformation of the Public Sphere: An Inquiry into a Category of Bourgeois Society*, trans. Thomas Burger (Cambridge: MIT Press, 1991).

50. Homi Bhabha points out an interesting distinction in nationalist narratives between the people as "a pedagogical object" and the people "constructed in the performance of the narrative." The former produces a self-generating tradition for the nation, while the latter "intervenes in the sovereignty of the nation's *self-generation* by casting a shadow between the people as 'image' and its signification as a differential sign of Self, distinct from the Other or the Outside." "DisseminaNation: Time, Narrative, and the Margins of the Modern Nation," in Bhabha, ed., *Nation and Narration* (London: Routledge, 1990), pp. 291–322. I am trying to explore a similar disjunctive process in anticolonial nationalist encounters with the narrative of modernity.

51. I have attempted to trace the course of anticolonial nationalist politics in India in these terms in *Nationalist Thought and the Colonial World*.

Chapter Four
The Nation and Its Pasts

1. Ranajit Guha, *An Indian Historiography of India: A Nineteenth-Century Agenda and Its Implications* (Calcutta: K. P. Bagchi, 1988).

2. Although Bankim himself wrote very little that could be designated as his-

tory, his essays on historiography are widely regarded as a landmark in the growth of modern historical research and writing in Bengal. Prabodhchandra Sen makes them the canonical texts for Bengali historiography: *Bāṅgālār itihās sādhanā* (Calcutta: Visvabharati, 1953). A. R. Mallick calls them "the great force" that transformed history writing in Bengal: "Modern Historical Writing in Bengali," in C. H. Philips, ed., *Historians of India, Pakistan and Ceylon* (London: Oxford University Press, 1961), pp. 446–60. It is worth pointing out that although only six of the thirty-five essays in this volume edited by Philips deal with modern Indian historians, one of them is devoted exclusively to Bankimchandra: "The Role of Bankimchandra in the Development of Nationalism." For brief surveys of history writing in nineteenth-century Bengal, see Shyamali Sur, "Bāṅgālir itihāscarcār kayekṭi dik, 1835–1874," *Aitihāsik* 1 (1976): 17–35; and Subodh Kumar Mukhopadhyay, "Evolution of Historiography in Bengali (1800–1947): A Study of the Pattern of Growth," in Tarasankar Banerjee, ed., *Historiography in Modern Indian Languages, 1800–1947* (Calcutta: Naya Prokash, 1987), pp. 29–42.

3. These were included in vol. 2 of his "Bibidha prabandha" and are now published in *BR*.

4. There is some ambiguity in Bankim's writings about the status of the independent sultans of Bengal; I will discuss this point in the last section of chapter 5.

5. I have used in this section quotations from two of Bankim's essays: "Bāṅgālār itihās," in *BR*, pp. 330–33; and "Bāṅgālār itihās sambandhe kayekṭi kathā," in *BR*, pp. 336–40.

6. I have discussed these sources in my essay "Itihāser uttarādhikār," *Bāromās* 12, no. 2 (April 1991): 1–24.

7. Mṛtyuñjaya Śarmaṇah, *Rājābali* (Scrampore: Baptist Mission Press, 1808) (hereafter references will be cited parenthetically in text as *R*).

8. R. C. Majumdar has discussed some of the dynastic lists in circulation among prominent landed families in eighteenth-century Bengal in Rameschandra Majumdar, "Saṃskṛta rājābalī grantha," *Sāhitya pariṣat patrikā* 46, no. 4 (1953): 232–39. I am grateful to Gautam Bhadra for this reference.

9. I cannot agree with Ranajit Guha that there is an "irresolvable contradiction" in Mrityunjay's introduction of "clockwork into the mythic time of the Kalpas" or of the authorial present into aeonic space. Guha, *An Indian Historiography*, pp. 35–36. The "traditional" form of recounting genealogical lists of ruling dynasties had no problems in combining "mythic matter" with the historical present. Indeed, the distinction between Puranic and historical time is not one that belongs to Mrityunjay's discourse; it has to be made outside that discourse for his text to be read as one informed by "a sense of the past still partially bound to tradition."

10. Munshi Alimaddin, *Dīllir rājādir nām* (Barisal, 1875).

11. Iswarchandra Vidyasagar, *Bāṅgālār itihās, dvitīya bhāg, sirāj uddaulār siṃhāsanārohaṇ abadhi lārḍ uiliām beṇṭiker adhikār paryyanta* (Calcutta, 1858).

12. Ramgati Nyayaratna, *Bāṅgālār itihās, pratham bhāg, hindu rājādiger caramābasthā abadhi nabāb ālībarddi khāṇr adhikār kāl paryyanta* (1859; revised and reprinted, Hooghly, 1867).

13. Ibid., pp. 179–80.

14. Ramsaday Bhattacharya, *Bāṅgālā itihāser praśnottar* (Calcutta, 1869), pp. 110–11, 126–27.

15. Kshetranath Bandyopadhyay, *Śiśupāṭh bāṅgālār itihās, bargīr hāṅgām haite lārḍ narthbruker āgaman paryyanta* (Calcutta, 1872), pp. 22, 27, 31.

16. Ibid., pp. 34–35.

17. Ibid., p. 41.

18. Ibid., pp. 39, 59, 98, 100.

19. Krishnachandra Ray, *Bhāratbarṣer itihās, imrejdiger adhikārkāl* (1859; reprint, Calcutta: J. C. Chatterjee, 1870), pp. 43–44, 70, 38, 40.

20. Ibid., pp. 214, 238.

21. Kshirodchandra Raychaudhuri, *Samagra bhārater saṃkṣipta itihās* (Calcutta, 1876), preface, and pp. 115, 211.

22. Tarakrishna Haldar, *Camatkār svapnadarśan* (Calcutta, 1868), pp. 134–36.

23. Bholanath Chakravarti, *Sei ek din ār ei ek din, arthāt baṅger pūrbba o barttamān abasthā* (Calcutta: Adi Brahmo Samaj, 1876), p. 10.

24. Ibid., pp. 11–12.

25. Tarinicharan Chattopadhyay, *Bhāratbarṣer itihās*, vol. 1 (1858; reprint, Calcutta, 1878) (hereafter references will be cited parenthetically in text as *BI*).

Chapter Five
Histories and Nations

1. Ronald Inden has recently made this point with much force. *Imagining India* (Oxford: Basil Blackwell, 1990), pp. 45–46.

2. For a discussion of Mill's comparative treatment of the Hindu and Muslim periods in Indian history, see J. S. Grewal, *Muslim Rule in India: The Assessments of British Historians* (Calcutta: Oxford University Press, 1970), pp. 64–97.

3. Romila Thapar has argued that Mill's *History* nevertheless remained influential for Indian writers because "it laid the foundation for a communal interpretation of Indian history and thus provided the historical justification for the two-nation theory." His severe condemnations "led to a section of the Orientalists and later to Indian historians having to defend 'Hindu civilisation' even if it meant overglorifying the ancient past." "Communalism and the Writing of Ancient Indian History," in Romila Thapar, Harbans Mukhia, and Bipan Chandra, *Communalism and the Writing of Indian History* (Delhi: People's Publishing House, 1969), p. 4.

4. "Advertisement to the Fifth Edition," in Mountstuart Elphinstone, *The History of India: The Hindu and Mahometan Periods*, 9th ed. (London: John Murray, 1905), p. vii.

5. H. M. Elliot, *The History of India as Told by Its Own Historians: The Muhammadan Period*, ed. John Dowson, 8 vols. (London: Trübner, 1867–77).

6. The most detailed criticism was in Shahpurshah Hormasji Hodivala, *Studies in Indo-Muslim History: A Critical Commentary on Elliot and Dowson's "History of India as Told by Its Own Historians,"* 2 vols. (1939; reprint, Lahore: Islamic Book Service, 1979). But far more trenchant and politically significant is the criticism made in 1931 by Muhammad Habib: "An Introduction to the Study

of Medieval India (A.D. 1000–1400)," in K. A. Nizami, ed., *Politics and Society during the Early Medieval Period: Collected Works of Professor Muhammad Habib* (New Delhi: People's Publishing House, 1974), pp. 3–32. In it, Habib makes the following comment on the effects of this form of historical memory: "The Hindu feels it his duty to dislike those whom he has been taught to consider the enemies of his religion and his ancestors; the Mussalman, lured into the false belief that he was once a member of a ruling race, feels insufferably wronged by being relegated to the status of a minority community. Fools both! Even if the Mussalman eight centuries ago were as bad as they were painted, would there be any sense in holding the present generation responsible for their deeds? It is but an imaginative tie that joins the modern Hindu with Harshavardhana or Asoka, or the modern Mussalman with Shihabuddin or Mahmud" (p. 12).

7. "Sir Henry Elliot's Original Preface," in Elliot and Dowson, *Own Historians*, 1:xv–xxvii.

8. The point is discussed in Inden, *Imagining India*, pp. 117–22.

9. On this, see Grewal, *Muslim Rule*.

10. The same description occurs in Elphinstone, *History*, pp. 300–301, minus the last comment.

11. These details also appear in Elphinstone, *History*, p. 301, where the source mentioned is Tod's *Rajasthan*. James Tod, *Annals and Antiquities of Rajasthan, or the Central and Western Rajput States of India*, ed. William Crooke (1829–32; reprint, London: Oxford University Press, 1920). What is a story from Rajput folklore in Tod, having entered modern historiography in Elphinstone as the slaughter of a "Rájpút tribe by the Mahometans," becomes in Tarinicharan an episode in the history of the resistance by "Indians" to Muslim conquest.

12. The story occurs in Elphinstone, *History*, pp. 303–4, which is undoubtedly the source for Tarinicharan. There is a much more detailed account in an extract from "Chach-náma, or Taríkh-i Hind wa Sind," in Elliot and Dowson, *Own Historians* 1: 209–11, in which in the end the princess rebukes the Khalifa for passing such peremptory orders against an innocent man.

13. *BI*, pp. 43–44. All of these details, once again, are in Elphinstone, *History*, pp. 320–21, where the authority cited is David Price, *Chronological Retrospect, or Memoirs of the Principal Events of Mahommedan History*, vol. 2 (London, 1821).

14. These stories appear in Elphinstone, *History*, pp. 409–10.

15. I have seen one book that is little more than an abridged edition of Tarinicharan; entire paragraphs are plagiarized. Jibankrishna Chattopadhyay, *Bhāratbarṣer purābṛtta*, 5th ed. (Calcutta, 1875).

16. Saiyad Abdul Rahim, *Bhāratbarṣer itihāser praśnottar* (Dhaka, 1870), p. 2.

17. Ibid., pp. 16, 78.

18. Ibid., pp. 100–101.

19. Sheikh Abdar Rahim, *Hajrat mahammader jīban carit o dharmmanīti* (Calcutta, 1886), pp. 173, preface, 178.

20. Abdul Karim, *Bhāratbarṣe musalmān rājatver itibṛtta*, vol. 1 (Calcutta: Sanskrit Press Depository, 1898) (references hereafter cited parenthetically in text as *BMRI*).

21. For a discussion of these literary trends, see Rafiuddin Ahmed, *The Bengal*

Muslims, 1871–1906: A Quest for Identity (Delhi: Oxford University Press, 1981), pp. 93–97.

22. Ranajit Guha, *An Indian Historiography of India: A Nineteenth-Century Agenda and Its Implications* (Calcutta: K. P. Bagchi, 1988), pp. 55–67.

23. Ibid., p. 63.

24. As Guha does: ibid., pp. 66–67.

25. Bhudeb Mukhopadhyay, "Svapnalabdha bhāratbarṣer itihās," in *Bhūdeb racanā sambhār*, ed. Pramathanath Bisi (Calcutta: Mitra and Ghosh, 1969), pp. 341–74.

26. Rabindranath Thakur, "Grantha-samālocanā," in *Rabīndra racanābalī* (Calcutta: Government of West Bengal, 1961), 13:484–87.

27. Ibid., p. 487.

28. I quote here from the following essays in *Bibidha prabandha*: "Bañge brāhmaṇādhikār"; "Bāñgālār itihās"; "Bāñgālār itihās sambandhe kayekṭi kathā"; "Bāñgālīr utpatti." *BR* 2:319–27, 330–33, 336–40, 344–63.

29. The word *renaissance* is in the original.

30. Rajkrishna Mukhopadhyay, *Pratham śikṣā bāñgālār itihās* (Calcutta, 1875), pp. 61–62.

31. Krishnachandra Ray, *Bhāratbarṣer itihās, iṃrājdiger adhikārkāl*, 14th ed. (Calcutta: Sanskrit Press Depository, 1875), p. 245.

Chapter Six
The Nation and Its Women

1. Ghulam Murshid, *Reluctant Debutante: Response of Bengali Women to Modernization, 1849–1905* (Rajshahi: Rajshahi University Press, 1983).

2. Sumit Sarkar, *A Critique of Colonial Reason* (Calcutta: Papyrus, 1985), pp. 71–76.

3. J. W. Massie, *Continental India* (London: Thomas Ward, 1839), 2:153–54.

4. Lata Mani, "The Production of an Official Discourse on *Sati* in Early Nineteenth-Century Bengal," *Economic and Political Weekly: Review of Women's Studies* 21 (April 1986): WS 32–40; "Contentious Traditions: The Debate on *Sati* in Colonial India," in Kumkum Sangari and Sudesh Vaid, eds., *Recasting Women: Essays in Colonial History* (New Delhi: Kali for Women, 1989), pp. 88–126.

5. Amarendranath Datta, *Majā* (Calcutta, 1900), pp. 7–8.

6. *Meye manṣṭār miṭim* (Calcutta: Girish Vidyaratna, 1874), pp. 28–31.

7. Tarasankar Sharma, *Strīgaṇer bidyā śikṣā* (Calcutta, 1851).

8. Sibchandra Jana, *Pātibratya-dharma-śikṣa* (Calcutta: Gupta Press, 1870).

9. Bhudeb Mukhopadhyay, "Gṛhakāryer byabasthā," in *Bhūdeb racanāsambhār*, ed. Pramathanath Bisi (Calcutta: Mitra and Ghosh, 1969), p. 480.

10. "Lajjāśīlatā," ibid., pp. 445–48.

11. Ibid., pp. 446, 447.

12. See the survey of these debates in Murshid, *Reluctant Debutante*, pp. 19–62; Meredith Borthwick, *The Changing Role of Women in Bengal, 1849–1905* (Princeton: Princeton University Press, 1984), pp. 60–108; and Malavika Kar-

lekar, "Kadambini and the Bhadralok: Early Debates over Women's Education in Bengal," *Economic and Political Weekly: Review of Women's Studies* 21 (April 1986): WS25–31.

13. M. A. Laird, *Missionaries and Education in Bengal, 1793–1837* (Oxford: Clarendon Press, 1972).

14. Murshid, *Reluctant Debutante*, p. 43.

15. The autobiographies of the early generation of educated middle-class women are infused with this spirit of achievement. For a recent study, see Malavika Karlekar, *Voices from Within: Early Personal Narratives of Bengali Women* (Delhi: Oxford University Press, 1991).

16. Cited in Murshid, *Reluctant Debutante*, p. 60.

17. Cited in Borthwick, *Changing Role of Women*, p. 105.

18. See ibid., pp. 245–56.

19. See Murshid, *Reluctant Debutante.*

Chapter Seven
Women and the Nation

1. "Prācīnā ebaṃ nabīnā," in *BR*, pp. 249–56.

2. "Tin rakam," in *RR*, pp. 254–56.

3. Sudipta Kaviraj has analyzed the use of self-irony in Bankim's writings. "Bankimchandra: I. Signs of Madness; II. The Self-Ironical Tradition," Occasional Papers 108 and 109 (Calcutta: Centre for Studies in Social Sciences, 1989).

4. That every such critique and its subsequent appropriation also sows the seeds of instability in the field of discourse goes without saying. Bankim, for instance, as Sibaji Bandyopadhyaya has reminded me has to cover the risk of his statement about universal male dominance by asserting the ethical truth, independent of male actions, of the virtue of wifely devotion. The contradiction is only barely concealed.

5. "This generally signifies an addition of women into the framework of conventional history. . . . In this sense, with a few exceptions, the women worked within boundaries laid down by men. The history uncovered in this way is a 'contributive' history." Kumari Jayawardena, *Feminism and Nationalism in the Third World* (London: Zed Books, 1986), pp. 260–61.

6. This is the central argument of the most systematic study of the biographical genre in Bengali literature: Debipada Bhattacharya, *Bāṃlā carit sāhitya* (Calcutta: Dey's, 1982).

7. Sibnath Sastri, *Rāmtanu lāhiḍī o tatkālīn baṅgasamāj* (1904), in *Sibnāth racanāsaṃgraha* (Calcutta: Saksharata Prakashan, 1979).

8. Surendranath Banerjea, *A Nation in Making: Being the Reminiscences of Fifty Years of Public Life* (1925; reprint, Bombay: Oxford University Press, 1966).

9. This is how Mary Mason identifies the difference between women's autobiographies and those of men. Mary G. Mason, "The Other Voice: Autobiographies of Women Writers," in James Olney, ed., *Autobiography: Essays Theoretical and Critical* (Princeton: Princeton University Press, 1980), pp. 207–35.

10. The point is made—famously—in Georges Gusdorf, "Conditions and

Limits of Autobiography," trans. James Olney, in Olney, *Autobiography*, pp. 28–48. Also, more recently, Philippe Lejeune, *On Autobiography*, trans. Katherine Leary (Minneapolis: University of Minnesota Press, 1989).

11. I should qualify this statement a bit. There are no women's autobiographies that are called *ātmacarit*, but I have seen two nineteenth-century biographies of women that are called *carit*. Of these, *Kumudinī-carit* (1868) is the life of a Brahmo woman presented as a devout and exemplary, almost saintly, figure. The other, *Lakṣīmaṇīcarit* (1877), is an account by a husband of his deceased wife.

12. Chitra Deb, *Antahpurer ātmakathā* (Calcutta: Ananda, 1984); Srabashi Ghosh, "'Birds in a Cage': Changes in Bengali Social Life as Recorded in Autobiographies by Women," *Economic and Political Weekly: Review of Women's Studies* 21 (October 1986): WS88–96; Meenakshi Mukherjee, "The Unperceived Self: A Study of Five Nineteenth-Century Autobiographies," in Karuna Chanana, ed., *Socialisation, Education and Women: Explorations in Gender Identity* (New Delhi: Orient Longman, 1988).

13. Karlekar, *Voices from Within*. The publication of this recent work makes it unnecessary for me to talk at length about the social-historical location of these autobiographical texts.

14. Rabindranath Thakur, "Naṣṭanīḍ," in *Rabīndra racanābalī* (Calcutta: Government of West Bengal, 1962), 7:433–74.

15. Shanta Nag, *Pūrbasmṛti* (1970; reprint, Calcutta: Papyrus, 1983), p. 16.

16. Rassundari Dasi, *Āmār jīban* (1876; reprint, Calcutta: De Book Store, 1987), pp. 5–6.

17. See Ghulam Murshid, *Reluctant Debutante: Response of Bengali Women to Modernization, 1849–1905* (Rajshahi: Rajshahi University Press, 1983); and Meredith Borthwick, *The Changing Role of Women in Bengal, 1849–1905* (Princeton: Princeton University Press, 1984).

18. Rassundari, *Amār jīban*, p. 14.

19. Ibid., pp. 38–39.

20. Ibid., pp. 32, 41.

21. Ibid., p. 41.

22. Ibid., p. 56.

23. Ibid., pp. 57–58.

24. Ibid., pp. 63–66.

25. Ibid., pp. 97, 109.

26. Jyotirindranath Thakur, "Bhūmikā," ibid., p. v.

27. Dineshchandra Sen, "Grantha paricay," ibid., pp. vii–xiii.

28. Conventional history has it that Bengali women in general were illiterate before the period of social reform in the middle of the nineteenth century. We have some evidence, however, that this was not necessarily the case. See, for instance, Paramesh Acharya, *Bāṃlār deśaja śikṣādhārā*, vol. 1 (Calcutta: Anushtup, 1989). Even upper-caste women, for whom the prohibitions on reading and writing were likely to have been the most stringent, sometimes managed to escape them. Prasannamayi Debi, whose autobiography I discuss later in this chapter, mentions that several women from an earlier generation in her village were literate and one even ran a school, where she taught both male and female children.

Prasannamayi Debi, *Pūrbba kathā*, ed. Nirmalya Acharya (1917; reprint, Calcutta: Subarnarekha, 1982) (references hereafter cited parenthetically in text as *PK*).

29. Saradasundari Debi, *Keśabjananī debī sāradāsundarīr ātmakathā*, ed. Jogendralal Khastagir (Dhaka, 1913); reprint, *Ekṣaṇ* 17 (Autumn 1983): 4.

30. Being an "as-told-to" account, this is not, strictly speaking, an autobiography, although that is how it is titled. It is clearly directed toward satisfying the curiosity of Keshab Sen's followers and admirers. Saradasundari herself seems quite conscious of the role she is expected to play, but she also resists it. I am grateful to Kamala Visweswaran for alerting me to the need to point this out.

31. Saradasundari, *Sāradāsundarīr ātmakathā*, pp. 17, 33–34.

32. Kailasbasini Debi, *Janaikā gṛhabadhūr ḍāyerī* (1952); reprint, *Ekṣaṇ* 15, nos. 3–4 (Autumn 1981): 7–48. Page references are to reprint.

33. Ibid., pp. 11, 44.

34. Ibid., pp. 42–43.

35. Ibid., p. 21.

36. Ibid., p. 32.

37. Ibid., p. 45.

38. This Kailasbasini is not to be confused with the Kailasbasini Debi (Gupta) who wrote the well-known early tracts on women's education, *Hindu mahilādiger hīnābasthā* (1863) and *Hindu abalākuler bidyābhyās o tāhār samunnati* (1865).

39. Nirmalya Acharya, "Grantha-pariciti," in *PK*, pp. 99–104.

40. As described for Western Europe by Jürgen Habermas, *Structural Transformation of the Public Sphere: An Inquiry into a Category of Bourgeois Society*, trans. Thomas Burger (Cambridge: MIT Press, 1991), pp. 43–51.

41. For instance, the annual pilgrimage for a bath in the Ganga, which often led to numerous deaths in boat disasters. *PK*, p. 34.

42. Binodini Dasi, *Āmār kathā o anyānya racanā*, ed. Soumitra Chattopadhyay and Nirmalya Acharya (1912; reprint, Calcutta: Subarnarekha, 1987).

43. Ibid., pp. 17–18.

44. Ibid., pp. 16, 78.

45. Ibid., pp. 38–45.

46. Ibid., p. 13.

47. Ibid., p. 62.

48. Ibid., p. 64.

49. Girishchandra Ghosh, "Baṅga-raṅgālaye Śrīmatī binodinī," ibid., pp. 135–44.

50. Binodini Dasi, *Āmār kathā*, p. 8.

51. Ibid., p. 3.

52. Edward W. Said, "Identity, Negation and Violence," *NLR* 171 (1988): 46–60.

53. Partha Chatterjee, *Nationalist Thought and the Colonial World: A Derivative Discourse?* (London: Zed Books, 1986), pp. 1–35.

54. Edward W. Said, "Third World Intellectuals and Metropolitan Culture," *Raritan Quarterly* 9, no. 3 (Winter 1990): 27–50. For the same reason, I am not persuaded by Habermas's invitation to an "unconstrained consensus formation in

a communication community standing under cooperative constraints." See, especially, Jürgen Habermas, *The Philosophical Discourse of Modernity*, trans. Frederick Lawrence (Cambridge: MIT Press, 1987).

55. Sarajubala Debi, letter to the editor, *Ānandabājār patrikā*, 6 April 1991.

Chapter Eight
The Nation and Its Peasants

1. A well-known account of this process is Eugen Weber, *Peasants into Frenchmen: The Modernization of Rural France, 1870–1914* (London: Chatto and Windus, 1979).

2. G. W. F. Hegel, *Philosophy of Right*, trans. T. M. Knox (1952; reprint, London: Oxford University Press, 1967), par. 203 and additions 128–29, pp. 131–32 and 270–74.

3. For instance, David Hardiman, *Peasant Nationalists of Gujarat* (Delhi: Oxford University Press, 1984); Gyanendra Pandey, *The Ascendancy of the Congress in Uttar Pradesh, 1926–1934* (Delhi: Oxford University Press, 1978); Majid Hayat Siddiqi, *Agrarian Unrest in North India: The United Provinces, 1918–1922* (New Delhi: Vikas, 1978); Arvind Narayan Das, *Agrarian Unrest and Socio-economic Change, 1900–1980* (Delhi: Manohar, 1983); Atlury Murali, "Civil Disobedience Movement in Andhra, 1920–1922: The Nature of Peasant Protest and the Methods of Congress Political Mobilization," in Kapil Kumar, ed., *Congress and Classes: Nationalism, Workers and Peasants* (New Delhi: Manohar, 1988), pp. 152–216.

4. A telling example of this can be found in Shahid Amin, "Gandhi as Mahatma: Gorakhpur District, Eastern UP, 1921–1922," in Ranajit Guha, ed., *Subaltern Studies III* (Delhi: Oxford University Press, 1984), pp. 1–61.

5. Ranajit Guha, *Elementary Aspects of Peasant Insurgency in Colonial India* (Delhi: Oxford University Press, 1983).

6. Gyanendra Pandey, "Encounters and Calamities: The History of a North Indian Qasba in the Nineteenth Century," in Guha, *Subaltern Studies III*, pp. 231–70; David Hardiman, "The Bhils and Shahukars in Eastern Gujarat," in Ranajit Guha, ed., *Subaltern Studies V* (Delhi: Oxford University Press, 1987), pp. 1–54; Tanika Sarkar, "Jitu Santal's Movement in Malda, 1924–1932: A Study in Tribal Protest," in Ranajit Guha, ed., *Subaltern Studies IV* (Delhi: Oxford University Press, 1985), pp. 136–64; Partha Chatterjee, *Bengal 1920–1947: The Land Question* (Calcutta: K. P. Bagchi, 1984).

7. Argued most powerfully by Louis Dumont, *Homo Hierarchicus*, trans. Mark Sainsbury (London: Paladin, 1970).

8. For two recent surveys of these debates, see Rosalind O'Hanlon, "Recovering the Subject: *Subaltern Studies* and Histories of Resistance in Colonial South Asia," *Modern Asian Studies* 22, no. 1 (1988): 189–224; and Mridula Mukherjee, "Peasant Resistance and Peasant Consciousness in Colonial India: 'Subaltern' and Beyond," *Economic and Political Weekly* 23, nos. 41 and 42 (8 and 15 October 1988): 2109–20 and 2174–85.

9. A point made by Irfan Habib, "The Peasant in Indian History," *Social Scientist* 11, no. 3 (March 1983): 21–64.

10. James Scott, *Weapons of the Weak: Everyday Forms of Peasant Resistance* (New Haven, Conn.: Yale University Press, 1985).

Chapter Nine
The Nation and Its Outcasts

1. "Caste and Class in India," in A. J. Syed, ed., *D. D. Kosambi on History and Society: Problems of Interpretation* (Bombay: University of Bombay, 1985), p. 132.

2. M. K. Gandhi, "Dr. Ambedkar's Indictment II," in *Collected Works* (New Delhi: Publications Division, 1976), 63:153.

3. S. Radhakrishnan, *Eastern Religions and Western Thought* (1939; reprint, New York: Oxford University Press, 1959).

4. Some of the most distinguished examples being Nirmal Kumar Bose, *Hindu samājer gaḍan* (Calcutta: Visvabharati, 1949), later translated into English by André Beteille as *The Structure of Hindu Society* (New Delhi: Orient Longman, 1975); G. S. Ghurye, *Caste and Class in India* (Bombay: Popular Prakashan, 1957); Irawati Karve, *Hindu Society: An Interpretation* (Poona: Deccan College, 1961); M. N. Srinivas, *Caste in Modern India and Other Essays* (Bombay: Asia, 1962); and *Social Change in Modern India* (Bombay: Allied, 1966).

5. The reader will notice that this "dialectical" exercise closely follows the form laid out in Hegel's "Little Logic." G. W. F. Hegel, *Encyclopaedia of the Philosophical Sciences*, pt. 1, trans. William Wallace (Oxford: Clarendon Press, 1975).

6. Louis Dumont, *Homo Hierarchicus*, trans. Mark Sainsbury (London: Paladin, 1970).

7. Louis Dumont, *Homo Hierarchicus*, rev. English ed. (Delhi: Oxford University Press, 1988), p. xxx.

8. Ibid., pp. 242–43.

9. Dipankar Gupta, "Continuous Hierarchies and Discrete Castes," *Economic and Political Weekly* 19, nos. 46–48 (17 and 24 November and 1 December 1984): 1955–58, 2003–5, 2049–53.

10. P. V. Kane, *History of Dharmasastra*, vol. 2, pt. 1 (Poona: Bhandarkar Oriental Research Institute, 1974), p. 52. It is thus that when the exception to endogamy is allowed, it is only in the case of *anuloma*, which literally means "with the hair," that is, in the natural order, and never in the case of *pratiloma*, which would be against the natural order.

11. A recent work which argues that the domain of power, specifically represented by the institution of kingship, may actually influence the ideology and practice of caste is Nicholas B. Dirks, *The Hollow Crown: Ethnohistory of an Indian Kingdom* (Cambridge: Cambridge University Press, 1987). Dirks, however, retains the scheme of separation between the domains of ideology and power; in criticizing Dumont, he reverses the relation between the two domains.

12. In empirical terms, this is now well recognized in recent ethnographic literature. See, for example, Pauline Mahar Kolenda, "Religious Anxiety and Hindu Fate," *Journal of Asian Studies* 23 (1964): 71–82; Owen Lynch, *The Politics of Untouchability: Social Mobility and Social Change in a City of India* (New York: Columbia University Press, 1969); Mark Juergensmeyer, *Religion as Social Vi-*

sion: The Movement against Untouchability in Twentieth-Century Punjab (Berkeley and Los Angeles: University of California Press, 1982); R. S. Khare, *The Untouchable as Himself: Ideology and Pragmatism among the Lucknow Chamars* (Cambridge: Cambridge University Press, 1983); Rosalind O'Hanlon, *Caste, Conflict and Ideology: Mahatma Jotirao Phule and Low Caste Protest in Nineteenth-Century Western India* (Cambridge: Cambridge University Press, 1985).

13. Louis Dumont, "World Renunciation in Indian Religions," in *Homo Hierarchicus*, rev. English ed., app. B, pp. 267–86.

14. Ramakanta Chakrabarty, *Vaiṣṇavism in Bengal* (Calcutta: Sanskrit Pustak Bhandar, 1985), p. 349.

15. Ibid., p. 321.

16. Five of this celebrated circle of six *gosvāmīs* were Brahmans. The intellectual leaders of the circle—the brothers Rūpa and Sanātana and their nephew Jīva—were Karnataka Brahmans settled in Bengal and came from a family of senior ministers to the Bengal Sultan. They are said to have considered themselves somewhat impure because of their close contact with the Muslim ruling elite, but were all highly learned in the philosophical and literary disciplines. Gopāla Bhaṭṭa is also said to have been a Karnataka Brahman. Raghunātha Bhaṭṭa was a Brahman settled in Varanasi and may have been of Bengali origin, while Raghunātha Dāsa was from a Kayastha landlord family of Hooghly. The last two, however, made virtually no significant contribution to the doctrinal development of Gauḍīya Vaiṣṇavism. See Sushil Kumar De, *Early History of the Vaisnava Faith and Movement in Bengal* (Calcutta: Firma KLM, 1961), pp. 111–65.

17. Hitesranjan Sanyal, "Trends of Change in the Bhakti Movement in Bengal," Occasional Paper 76 (Calcutta: Centre for Studies in Social Sciences, 1985).

18. The slurs on the sexual reputation of the women followers of Vaiṣṇava sects are legion. A popular saying has a Vaiṣṇava woman declaring: "I was a prostitute first, a maid-servant later, and a procuress in between; now at last I am a Vaiṣṇavī." ("Āge beśye, pare dāsye, madhye madhye kuṭnī, sarba karma parityājya ekhan boṣṭamī.") Sushilkumar De, *Bāmlā prabād* (1946; reprint, Calcutta: A. Mukherjee, 1986), p. 9.

19. For an account of these processes in the period of Caitanya and after, see Hitesranjan Sanyal, *Social Mobility in Bengal* (Calcutta: Papyrus, 1981), pp. 33–64.

20. Chakrabarty, *Vaiṣṇavism in Bengal*, p. 324.

21. Ibid., p. 342.

22. Sashibhusan Das Gupta, *Obscure Religious Cults* (Calcutta: Firma KLM, 1969), pp. 113–46.

23. The activity of "remembrance" of the *līlā* was ritually formalized in the eighteenth century. See Chakrabarty, *Vaiṣṇavism in Bengal*, pp. 309–18.

24. Antonio Gramsci comments on this phenomenon with great insight, especially in the context of Catholicism ("in reality a multiplicity of distinct and often contradictory religions"). See especially *Selections from the Prison Notebooks*, trans. Quintin Hoare and Geoffrey Nowell Smith (New York: International Publishers, 1971), pp. 325–43. I have discussed Gramsci's ideas on popular religion,

and particularly what he calls "common sense," in my essay "Caste and Subaltern Consciousness," in Ranajit Guha, ed., *Subaltern Studies VI* (Delhi: Oxford University Press, 1989), pp. 169–209.

25. On the Bāul, see Upendranath Bhattacharya, *Bāṃlār bāul o bāul gān* (Calcutta: Orient Book Company, 1957). On the relationship between the Bāul and the Sufi doctrines, also see Muhammad Enamul Haq, *A History of Sufi-ism in Bengal* (Dhaka: Asiatic Society of Bangladesh, 1975), pp. 260–367.

26. On the Sāhebdhanī, see Sudhir Chakrabarti, *Sāhebdhanī sampradāy: Tāder gān* (Calcutta: Pustak Bipani, 1988); on the Kartābhajā, see the brief account in Chakrabarty, *Vaiṣṇavism in Bengal*, pp. 346–84.

27. Computed from imperial table 18, *Census of India, 1931*, vol. 5 (Bengal and Sikkim), pt. 2, pp. 226–42. The Hāḍi is in fact more numerous in the western districts of Bengal such as Burdwan, Birbhum, and Midnapore.

28. "Hāḍittun ḍom kulīn, ḍomattun hāḍi kulīn." Mohammad Hanif Pathan, ed., *Bāṃlā prabād pariciti*, vol. 2, pt. 1 (Dhaka: Bangla Academy, 1982), p. 86.

29. H. H. Risley, *The Tribes and Castes of Bengal* (1891; reprint, Calcutta: Firma KLM, 1981), 1:314–16.

30. James Wise, *Notices on the Races, Castes and Tribes of Eastern Bengal* (London, 1883), cited in Risley, *Tribes and Castes* 1:314–16.

31. Meherpur is now an *upajilā* (subdistrict) in Bangladesh.

32. This account is based on the biographical details collected by Sudhir Chakrabarti, *Balāhāḍi sampradāy ār tāder gān* (Calcutta: Pustak Bipani, 1986). Unless otherwise indicated, all information on the sect and its songs are also from the same source. Dr Chakrabarti, of course, is not to be blamed for my interpretation of his material.

33. Akshaykumar Datta, *Bhāratbarṣīya upāsak-sampradāy*, ed. Benoy Ghosh (1870; reprint, Calcutta: Pathabhavan, 1969), pp. 137–39. Balaram's argument here resembles a much older form of *nāstika* argumentation found in the so-called Cārvāka philosophy. "If those living in heaven can be nourished by the offerings of those living on earth, then why should not those living on the upper floor of a building be nourished by the offerings made on the lower floor?" See Sāyaṇamādhava, *Cārvāka-darśanam*, trans. (from Sanskrit to Bengali) Panchanan Sastri (Agarpara: Samyabrata Chakravarti, 1987), p. 87.

34. J. N. Bhattacharya, *Hindu Castes and Sects* (1896; reprint, Calcutta: Editions Indian, 1973), pp. 388–89.

35. Chakrabarti, *Balāhāḍi sampradāy*, pp. 27–28.

36. Sudhir Chakrabarti thinks the latter is more probable, and that version is certainly accepted by the sectarians. Ibid., p. 20.

37. This, according to Sudhir Chakrabarti, is confirmed by the land records at Meherpur, where a gift of 0.35 acres of land from the landlord Jiban Mukherjee to Balaram Hāḍi is recorded. Ibid., p. 31.

38. The meeting of this English-educated Brahman scholar with Brahmamātā was not without a touch of irony. "I met her in the year 1872. Her first question to me was about my caste. I knew well about the hatred of the sect towards Brahmans, and instead of mentioning that I was a Brahman, I used a pun to say that I was a human being. She was very much pleased, and after offering me a seat

she went on propounding the tenets of her sect. The greater part of her utterances was meaningless jargon, but she talked fluently and with the dignity of a person accustomed to command. Though a Hari by caste, she did not hesitate to offer me her hospitality. I declined it as politely as I could but considering the courtesy that she showed to me, I could not but feel some regret that the barrier of caste rendered it quite impossible for me to comply with her request." Bhattacharya, *Hindu Castes and Sects*, p. 389.

39. Chakrabarti, *Balāhāḍi sampradāy*, pp. 44–45.

40. See Das Gupta, *Obscure Religious Cults*, pp. 311–37.

41. Ibid., pp. 211–55, 367–98. For a detailed account of the religion of the Nāth sect, see Kalyani Mallik, *Nāth-sampradāyer itihās, darśan o sādhan praṇālī* (Calcutta: University of Calcutta, 1950).

42. This is undoubtedly the source of the story picked up by James Wise about the origin of the Bhuiṅmālī.

43. Here again is an element of commonality with the *Śūnyapurāṇa* cosmogony, for there too it is Śiva alone of the three sons of Ādyāśakti who is able to recognize the supreme lord in disguise.

44. *Ghām* = sweat. In the *Śūnyapurāṇa* myths, the first female Ādyāśakti is born from the sweat of the lord, but the relation here has been transposed to the progeny of Brahmā.

45. Actually, the classification of jātis in Hābel's line is elaborated still further and includes divisions such as Shia and Sunni among the Mughals, or Sur, Surani, Lodi, and Lohani among Pathans. Hābel's line seems to comprise groups that claim an aristocratic Muslim lineage, while Kābel's is definitely of inferior social status, although the inclusion of Rajputs in the latter line remains a complete mystery.

46. This may be a good reason why it does not claim any allegiance to the religion of the Nāth siddhas. However, the stories about Balarām's own miraculous powers of transportation indicate a claim of considerable facility in haṭhayoga skills.

47. "Hāḍir lakṣmī śuṅḍir ghare yāy." Sushilkumar De, *Bāṃlā prabād*, p. 224.

48. Once a month, before sunrise on the fourth day after the end of the wife's menstrual cycle. It will also be evident that the attempt to claim proprietorship over one's own body is an exclusively male enterprise. Woman is in fact the embodiment of external pravṛtti, which tempts, subjugates, and destroys the male body. This raises a crucial question about the relationship of subaltern consciousness to gender, a matter that is only beginning to receive serious attention.

49. For an account of the legal muddle on this question, see Marc Galanter, *Competing Equalities: Law and the Backward Classes in India* (Delhi: Oxford University Press, 1984).

50. Numerous studies have shown this. See, for example, John Harriss, *Capitalism and Peasant Farming: Agrarian Structure and Ideology in Northern Tamil Nadu* (Delhi: Oxford University Press, 1982).

51. Antonio Gramsci: "A philosophy of praxis . . . must be a criticism of 'common sense', basing itself initially, however, on common sense in order to demonstrate that 'everyone' is a philosopher and that it is not a question of introducing

from scratch a scientific form of thought into everyone's individual life, but of renovating and making 'critical' an already existing activity." *Prison Notebooks,* pp. 330–31.

Chapter Ten
The National State

1. This section is largely based on Raghabendra Chattopadhyay, "The Idea of Planning in India, 1930–1951" (Ph.D. diss., Australian National University, Canberra, 1985).

2. Jawaharlal Nehru, *The Discovery of India* (New York: John Day, 1946), p. 405.

3. M. K. Gandhi, *Collected Works of Mahatma Gandhi,* 90 vols. (New Delhi: Publications Division, 1978), 70:56.

4. Jawaharlal Nehru, *Jawaharlal Nehru's Speeches* (New Delhi: Publications Division, 1954), 2: 93.

5. Sukhamoy Chakravarty, *Development Planning: The Indian Experience* (Oxford: Clarendon Press, 1987).

6. Ibid., pp. 40–42.

7. Ibid., p. 7.

8. Ibid., pp. 2–3. Emphases mine.

9. Karl Marx, *Capital,* vol. 1, trans. Samuel Moore and Edward Aveling (Moscow: Progress Publishers, 1971), pp. 667–70.

10. See T. H. Aston and C. H. E. Philpin, eds., *The Brenner Debate: Agrarian Class Structure and Economic Development in Pre-Industrial Europe* (Cambridge: Cambridge University Press, 1987).

11. Chakravarty, *Development Planning,* p. 14.

12. Ibid., p. 21.

13. Antonio Gramsci, *Selections from the Prison Notebooks,* trans. Quintin Hoare and Geoffrey Nowell Smith (New York: International Publishers, 1971), pp. 44–120.

14. Asok Sen, "The Frontiers of the *Prison Notebooks,*" *Economic and Political Weekly: Review of Political Economy* 23, no. 5 (1988): PE31–36.

15. On this point, see the discussion in Ajit Chaudhuri, "From Hegemony to Counter-hegemony," and Partha Chatterjee, "On Gramsci's 'Fundamental Mistake,'" *Economic and Political Weekly: Review of Political Economy,* 23, no. 5 (1988): PE19–23 and 24–26.

16. I am grateful to Kalyan Sanyal for suggesting this point.

17. Chakravarty, *Development Planning,* p. 21.

18. For instance, in Pranab Bardhan, *The Political Economy of Development in India* (Oxford: Basil Blackwell, 1984); or Lloyd H. Rudolph and Susanne Hoeber Rudolph, *In Search of Lakshmi: The Political Economy of the Indian State* (Chicago: University of Chicago Press, 1987).

19. For instance, once again, Bardhan, *Political Economy*; and Rudolph and Rudolph, *In Search of Lakshmi.*

20. See Arun Patnaik, "Gramsci's Concept of Hegemony: The Case of Devel-

opment Administration in India," *Economic and Political Weekly: Review of Political Economy* 23, no. 5 (1988): PE12–18; Atul Kohli, *The State and Poverty in India: The Politics of Reform* (Cambridge: Cambridge University Press, 1987).

Chapter Eleven
Communities and the Nation

1. "Kamalākānter jobānbandī," in *BR*, pp. 101–8.
2. For an analysis of the Kamalakanta writings, see Sudipta Kaviraj, "Signs of Madness: The Figure of Kamalakanta in the Work of Bankimchandra Chattopadhyay," *Journal of Arts and Ideas* 17–18 (June 1989): 9–32.
3. Jnanendramohan Das, *Bāṅgālā bhāṣār abhidhān*, 2d ed. (1937; reprint, Calcutta: Sahitya Samsad, 1988), 1:848–49.
4. Haricharan Bandyopadhyay, *Baṅgīya śabdakoṣ* (New Delhi: Sahitya Akademi, 1966), 1:936.
5. Govindagopal Mukhopadhyay and Gopikamohan Bhattacharya, *A Tri-lingual Dictionary*, Calcutta Sanskrit College Research Series 47, lexicon no. 1 (Calcutta: Sanskrit College, 1966).
6. Bhudeb Mukhopadhyay, "Svapnalabdha bhāratbarṣer itihās," in *Bhūdeb racanāsambhār*, pp. 341–74.
7. Sudipta Kaviraj, "The Imaginary Institution of India," in Partha Chatterjee and Gyanendra Pandey, eds., *Subaltern Studies VII* (Delhi: Oxford University Press, 1992), pp. 1–39.
8. Bernard S. Cohn, "The Census, Social Structure and Objectification in South Asia," in Cohn, *An Anthropologist among the Historians and Other Essays* (Delhi: Oxford University Press, 1987), pp. 224–54.
9. Ranajit Guha, "Discipline and Mobilize," in Chatterjee and Pandey, *Subaltern Studies VII*, pp. 69–120.
10. Hitesranjan Sanyal, "Abhayer kathā," *Bāromās* 7, no. 2 (Autumn 1984): 97–128.
11. Sujit Sen, ed., *Jātpāter rājnīti* (Calcutta: Pustak Bipani, 1989).
12. Hindi dictionaries list the word *jātpānt* under the entry for *jāt*, the corrupt form of *jāti*, and give as its meaning *birādarī*, "the collective 'brotherhood' of a subcaste." There is also a listing for *jātipāntī*, once again a non-Sanskritic Hindi word, which could mean *varṇa*, "caste" or "tribe." Kalika Prasad, Rajballabh Sahay, and Mukundilal Srivastava, *Bṛhat hindī koś* (Banaras: Gyanmandal, 1970).
13. While I do not wish to reduce the importance of the immensely suggestive writings of Ashis Nandy, it nevertheless seems to me that they often lend themselves to this kind of interpretation.
14. Charles Taylor, "Modes of Civil Society," *Public Culture* 3, no. 1 (Fall 1990): 102–19.
15. G. W. F. Hegel, *Philosophy of Right*, trans. T. M. Knox (London: Oxford University Press, 1967), par. 158, p. 110.
16. Ibid., addition 101, pp. 261–62; addition 102, p. 262.
17. Ibid., par. 175, pp. 117–18.
18. Foucault, of course, makes much of these "police functions" of the early

modern state. See, in particular, his Tanner Lectures at Stanford University, reprinted as "Politics and Reason," in Michel Foucault, *Politics, Philosophy, Culture: Interviews and Other Writings, 1977–1984*, trans. Alan Sheridan et al. (New York: Routledge, 1988), pp. 58–85.

19. Hegel, *Philosophy of Right*, par. 234, p. 146.

20. Ibid., par. 239, p. 148, and addition 147, p. 277.

21. Alasdaire MacIntyre, *After Virtue: A Study in Moral Theory* (London: Duckworth, 1981).

22. Michel Foucault, *Power/Knowledge: Selected Interviews and Other Writings, 1972–1977*, ed. Colin Gordon (New York: Pantheon, 1980), pp. 78–92.

23. Foucault was well aware of the fact that contemporary non-Western cultures contained powerful resources for resisting disciplinary power. This was shown quite dramatically, if rather embarrassingly for many of Foucault's admirers, in his enthusiasm for the Iranian revolt against the shah. Those events, he wrote, "did not represent a withdrawal of the most outmoded groups before a modernization that is too brutal. It was, rather, the rejection by an entire culture, an entire people, of a modernization that is an archaism in itself." In their will for an "Islamic government," he added, the Iranian people were seeking, "even at the price of their own lives, something that we have forgotten, even as a possibility, since the Renaissance and the great crises of Christianity: a political spirituality. I can already hear the French laughing. But I know they are wrong." See Didier Eribon, *Michel Foucault*, trans. Betsy Wing (Cambridge: Harvard University Press, 1991), pp. 281–91; Foucault, "Iran: The Spirit of a World without Spirit," in *Politics, Philosophy, Culture*, pp. 211–24. Foucault's so-called Iran mistake tells us a great deal about both the possibilities as well as the difficulties of an "antistrategic" theoretical practice: "be respectful when singularity rises up, and intransigent when power infringes on the universal."

24. I have discussed this aspect of Gandhi in *Nationalist Thought*, pp. 85–130.

25. I am grateful to Dipesh Chakrabarty for pointing out to me the implications of this formulation. Chakrabarty has argued this point in his *Rethinking Working-Class History* and in "Postcoloniality and the Artifice of History."

Bibliography

Bengali Sources

Abdar Rahim, Sheikh. *Hajrat mahammader jīban carit o dharmmanīti.* Calcutta, 1886.

Abdul Karim. *Bhāratbarṣe musalmān rājatver itibṛtta.* Vol. 1. Calcutta: Sanskrit Press Depository, 1898.

Abdul Rahim, Saiyad. *Bhāratbarṣer itihāser praśnottar.* Dhaka, 1870.

Akshaykumar Datta. *Bhāratbarṣīya upāsak-sampradāy.* Edited by Benoy Ghosh. 1870. Reprint. Calcutta: Pathabhavan, 1969.

Alimaddin, Munshi. *Dillir rājādir nām.* Barisal, 1875.

Amarendranath Datta. *Majā.* Calcutta, 1900.

Bankimchandra Chattopadhyay. *Baṅkim racanābalī.* Edited by Jogeshchandra Bagal. Vol. 2. Calcutta: Sahitya Samsad, 1965.

Binodini Dasi. *Āmār kathā o anyānya racanā.* 1912. Edited by Soumitra Chattopadhyay and Nirmalya Acharya. Reprint. Calcutta: Subarnarekha, 1987.

Bholanath Chakravarti. *Sei ek din ār ei ek din, arthāt baṅger pūrbba o barttamān abasthā.* Calcutta: Adi Brahmo Samaj, 1876.

Bhudeb Mukhopadhyay. *Bhūdeb racanāsambhār.* Edited by Pramathanath Bisi. Calcutta: Mitra and Ghosh, 1969.

Chitra Deb. *Antahpurer ātmakathā.* Calcutta: Ananda, 1984.

Debipada Bhattacharya. *Bāṃlā carit sāhitya.* Calcutta: Dey's, 1982.

Girishchandra Ghosh. *Giriś racanābalī.* Edited by Rathindranath Ray and Debipada Bhattacharya. Vol. 1, Calcutta: Sahitya Samsad, 1969.

Haricharan Bandyopadhyay. *Baṅgīya śabdakoṣ.* Vol. 1. New Delhi: Sahitya Akademi, 1966.

Hitesranjan Sanyal. "Abhayer kathā." *Bāromās* 7, no. 2 (Autumn 1984): 97–128.

Iswarchandra Vidyasagar. *Baṅgālār itihās, dvitīya bhāg, sirāj uddaulār siṃhāsanārohaṇ abadhi lārḍ uiliām beṇṭiker adhikār paryyanta.* Calcutta, 1858.

Jibankrishna Chattopadhyay. *Bhāratbarṣer purābṛtta.* 5th ed. Calcutta, 1875.

Jnanendramohan Das. *Bāṅgālā bhāṣār abhidhān.* Vol. 1. 1937. Reprint. Calcutta: Sahitya Samsad, 1988.

Kailasbasini Debi. *Janaikā gṛhabadhur ḍāyerī.* 1952. Reprint. *Ekṣaṇ* 15, nos. 3 and 4 (Autumn 1981): 7–48.

Kalyani Mallik. *Nāth-sampradāyer itihās, darśan o sādhan praṇālī.* Calcutta: University of Calcutta, 1950.

Krishnachandra Ray. *Bhāratbarṣer itihās, iṃrejdiger adhikārkāl.* 9th ed. Calcutta: J. C. Chatterjee, 1870; 14th ed. Calcutta: Sanskrit Press Depository, 1875.

Kshetranath Bandyopadhyay. *Śiśupāṭh baṅgālār itihās, bargīr haṅgām haite lārḍ narthbruker āgaman paryyanta.* Calcutta, 1872.

Kshirodchandra Raychaudhuri. *Samagra bhārater saṃkṣipta itihās.* Calcutta, 1876.

Ma [Mahendranath Gupta]. *Śrīśrīrāmkṛṣṇa kathāmṛta.* 1902–32. Reprint. Calcutta: Ananda, 1983.

Meye manṣṭār miṭiṃ. Calcutta: Girish Vidyaratna, 1874.

Mohammad Hanif Pathan, ed. *Bāṃlā prabād pariciti.* Vol. 2. Pt. 1. Dhaka: Bangla Academy, 1982.

Mrityunjay Vidyalankar. *Rājābali.* Serampore: Baptist Mission Press, 1808.

Nirmalkumar Basu. *Hindu samājer gaḍan.* Calcutta: Visvabharati, 1949.

Paramesh Acharya. *Bāṃlār deśaja śikṣādhārā.* Vol. 1. Calcutta: Anushtup, 1989.

Partha Chattopadhyay. "Itihāser uttarādhikār." *Bāromās* 12, no. 2 (April 1991): 1–24.

Prabodhchandra Sen. *Bāṅgālār itihās sādhanā.* Calcutta: Visvabharati, 1953.

Pradyumna Bhattacharya. "Rāmmohan rāy ebaṃ bāṅlā gadya." *Bāromās* 11, no. 2 (April 1990): 1–22.

Prasannamayi Debi. *Pūrbba kathā.* Edited by Nirmalya Acharya. 1917. Reprint. Calcutta: Subarnarekha, 1982.

Rabindranath Thakur. "Naṣṭanīḍ." In *Rabīndra racanābalī,* 7: 433–74. Calcutta: Government of West Bengal, 1961.

———. "Grantha-samālocanā." In *Rabīndra racanābalī,* 13:484–87. Calcutta: Government of West Bengal, 1961.

Rajkrishna Mukhopadhyay. *Pratham śikṣā bāṅgālār itihās.* Calcutta, 1875.

Rajnarayan Basu. *Ātmacarit* (1909). In Nareschandra Jana, Manu Jana, and Kamalkumar Sanyal, eds., *Ātmakathā,* vol. 1. Calcutta: Ananya, 1981.

Rameschandra Majumdar. "Saṃskṛta rājābalī grantha." *Sāhitya pariṣat patrikā* 46, no. 4 (1953): 232–39.

Ramgati Nyayaratna. *Bāṅgālār itihās, pratham bhāg, hindu rājādiger caramābasthā abadhi nabāb ālībarddi khāṇr adhikār kāl paryyanta.* 1859. Revised and reprinted. Hooghly, 1867.

Ramsaday Bhattacharya. *Bāṅgālā itihāser praśnottar.* Calcutta, 1869.

Rassundari Dasi. *Āmār jīban.* 1876. Reprint. Calcutta: De Book Store, 1987.

Saradananda, Swami. *Śrīśrīrāmakṛṣṇalīlāprasaṅga.* Vol. 2. Reprint. Calcutta: Udbodhan, 1965.

Saradasundari Debi. *Keśabjananī debī sāradāsundarīr ātmakathā.* Edited by Jogendralal Khastagir. Dhaka, 1913. Reprint. *Ekṣaṇ* 17 (Autumn 1983): 1–52.

Sāyaṇamādhava. *Cārvāka-darśanam.* In *Sarvadarśana-saṃgraha.* Translated from Sanskrit to Bengali by Panchanan Shastri. (Agarpara: Samyabrata Chakravarti, 1987).

Shanta Nag. *Pūrbasmṛti.* 1970. Reprint. Calcutta: Papyrus, 1983.

Shyamali Sur. "Bāṅgālir itihāscarcār kayekṭi dik, 1835–1874." *Aitihāsik* 1 (1976): 17–35.

Sibchandra Jana. *Pātibratya-dharma-śikṣa.* Calcutta: Gupta Press, 1870.

Sibnath Sastri. *Rāmtanu lāhiḍī o tatkālīn baṅgasamāj.* 1904. In *Śibnāth racanāsaṃgraha.* Calcutta: Saksharata Prakashan, 1979.

Sudhir Chakrabarti. *Balāhāḍi sampradāy ār tāder gān.* Calcutta: Pustak Bipani, 1986.

———. *Sāhebdhanī sampradāy: Tāder gān.* Calcutta: Pustak Bipani, 1988.

Sujit Sen, ed. *Jātpāter rājnīti.* Calcutta: Pustak Bipani. 1989.

Sushilkumar De. *Bāṃlā prabād.* 1946. Reprint. Calcutta: A. Mukherjee, 1986.

Tarakrishna Haldar. *Camatkār svapnadarśan.* Calcutta, 1868.

Tarasankar Sharma. *Strīgaṇer bidyā śikṣā.* Calcutta, 1851.

Tarinicharan Chattopadhyay. *Bhāratbarṣer itihās.* Vol. 1. 1858. Reprint. Calcutta, 1878.

Upendranath Bhattacharya. *Bāṃlār bāul o bāul gān.* Calcutta: Orient Book Company, 1957.

Hindi Source

Kalika Prasad, Rajballabh Sahay, and Mukundilal Srivastava. *Bṛhat hindī kos.* Banaras: Gyanmandal, 1970.

European-Language Sources

Ahmed, Rafiuddin. *The Bengal Muslims, 1871–1906: A Quest for Identity.* Delhi: Oxford University Press, 1981.

Amin, Shahid. "Gandhi as Mahatma: Gorakhpur District, Eastern UP, 1921–1922." In Ranajit Guha, ed., *Subaltern Studies III,* pp. 1–61. Delhi: Oxford University Press, 1984.

Anderson, Benedict. *Imagined Communities: Reflections on the Origin and Spread of Nationalism.* London: Verso, 1983.

Aston, T. H., and C. H. E. Philpin, eds. *The Brenner Debate: Agrarian Class Structure and Economic Development in Pre-Industrial Europe.* Cambridge: Cambridge University Press, 1987.

Ballhatchet, Kenneth. *Race, Sex and Class under the Raj: Imperial Attitudes and Policies and Their Critics, 1793–1905.* London: Weidenfeld and Nicolson, 1980.

Banerjea, Surendranath. *A Nation in Making: Being the Reminiscences of Fifty Years of Public Life.* 1925. Reprint. Bombay: Oxford University Press, 1966.

Banerjee, Anilchandra. "Years of Consolidation: 1883–1904." In Niharranjan Ray and Pratulchandra Gupta, eds., *Hundred Years of the University of Calcutta,* pp. 129–78. Calcutta: University of Calcutta, 1957.

Banerjee, Pramathanath. "Reform and Reorganization: 1904–24." In Niharranjan Ray and Pratulchandra Gupta, eds., *Hundred Years of the University of Calcutta,* pp. 211–318. Calcutta: University of Calcutta, 1957.

Bardhan, Pranab. *The Political Economy of Development in India.* Oxford: Basil Blackwell, 1984.

Bayly, C. A. "The Pre-History of 'Communalism'? Religious Conflict in India, 1700–1860." *Modern Asian Studies* 19, no. 2 (1985): 177–203.

———. *Indian Society and the Making of the British Empire.* The New Cambridge History of India, Part 2, vol. 1. Cambridge: Cambridge University Press, 1988.

Bhabha, Homi. "DissemiNation: Time, Narrative, and the Margins of the Modern Nation." In Bhabha, ed., *Nation and Narration,* pp. 291–322. London: Routledge, 1990.

Bhattacharya, J. N. *Hindu Castes and Sects*. 1896. Reprint. Calcutta: Editions Indian, 1973.

Borthwick, Meredith. *Keshub Chunder Sen: A Search for Cultural Synthesis*. Calcutta: Minerva Associates, 1977.

———. *The Changing Role of Women in Bengal, 1849–1905*. Princeton: Princeton University Press, 1984.

Bose, Nirmal Kumar. *The Structure of Hindu Society*. Translated by André Beteille. New Delhi: Orient Longman, 1975.

Broomfield, J. H. *Elite Conflict in a Plural Society: Twentieth-Century Bengal*. Berkeley and Los Angeles: University of California Press, 1968.

Buckland, C. E. *Bengal under the Lieutenant Governors*. 2 vols. 1901. Reprint. New Delhi: Deep, 1976.

Chakrabarty, Dipesh. *Rethinking Working-Class History: Bengal, 1890–1940*. Princeton: Princeton University Press, 1989.

———. "Postcoloniality and the Artifice of History: Who Speaks for 'Indian' Pasts?" *Representations* 37 (Winter 1992): 1–26.

Chakrabarty, Ramakanta. *Vaiṣṇavism in Bengal*. Calcutta: Sanskrit Pustak Bhandar, 1985.

Chakravarti, Tripurari. "The University and the Government: 1904–24." In Niharranjan Ray and Pratulchandra Gupta, eds., *Hundred Years of the University of Calcutta*, pp. 179–210. Calcutta: University of Calcutta, 1957.

Chakravarty, Sukhamoy. *Development Planning: The Indian Experience*. Oxford: Clarendon Press, 1987.

Chatterjee, Partha. *Bengal 1920–1947: The Land Question*. Calcutta: K. P. Bagchi, 1984.

———. *Nationalist Thought and the Colonial World: A Derivative Discourse?* London: Zed Books, 1986.

———. "On Gramsci's 'Fundamental Mistake.'" *Economic and Political Weekly: Review of Political Economy* 23, no. 5 (1988): PE19–23 and 24–26.

———. "Caste and Subaltern Consciousness." In Ranajit Guha, ed., *Subaltern Studies VI*, pp. 169–209. Delhi: Oxford University Press, 1989.

Chatterjee, Partha, and Gyanendra Pandey, eds. *Subaltern Studies VII*. Delhi: Oxford University Press, 1992.

Chatterjee, Satis Chandra. *Classical Indian Philosophies: Their Synthesis in the Philosophy of Sri Ramakrishna*. Calcutta: University of Calcutta, 1963.

Chattopadhyay, Raghabendra. "The Idea of Planning in India, 1930–1951." Ph.D. diss., Australian National University, Canberra, 1985.

Chaudhuri, Ajit. "From Hegemony to Counter-hegemony." *Economic and Political Weekly: Review of Political Economy* 23, no. 5 (1988): PE19–23.

Chetanananda, Swami. *They Lived with God: Life Stories of Some Devotees of Sri Ramakrishna*. St. Louis, Mo.: Vedanta Society of St. Louis, 1989.

Cohn, Bernard S. "The Census, Social Structure and Objectification in South Asia." In Cohn, *An Anthropologist among the Historians and Other Essays*, pp. 224–54. Delhi: Oxford University Press, 1987.

Cotton, H. E. A. *Calcutta Old and New*. 1909. Reprint. Calcutta: General Printers, 1980.

Das, Arvind Narayan. *Agrarian Unrest and Socio-economic Change, 1900–1980*. Delhi: Manohar, 1983.

Das Gupta, Sashibhusan. *Obscure Religious Cults.* Calcutta: Firma KLM, 1969.

Dasgupta, Uma. *Rise of an Indian Public: Impact of Official Policy, 1870–1880.* Calcutta: Rddhi India, 1977.

De, Sushil Kumar. *Early History of the Vaisnava Faith and Movement in Bengal.* Calcutta: Firma KLM, 1961.

Dirks, Nicholas B. *The Hollow Crown: Ethnohistory of an Indian Kingdom.* Cambridge: Cambridge University Press, 1987.

Dumont, Louis. *Homo Hierarchicus.* Translated by Mark Sainsbury. London: Paladin, 1970.

Elliot, H. M. *The History of India as Told by Its Own Historians: The Muhammadan Period.* Edited by John Dowson. 8 vols. London: Trübner, 1867–77.

Elphinstone, Mountstuart. *The History of India: The Hindu and Mahometan Periods.* 9th ed. London: John Murray, 1905.

Eribon, Didier. *Michel Foucault.* Translated by Betsy Wing. Cambridge: Harvard University Press, 1991.

Foucault, Michel. *Power/Knowledge: Selected Interviews and Other Writings, 1972–1977.* Edited by Colin Gordon. New York: Pantheon, 1980.

———. *Politics, Philosophy, Culture: Interviews and Other Writings, 1977–1984.* Translated by Alan Sheridan et al. New York: Routledge, 1988.

Galanter, Marc. *Competing Equalities: Law and the Backward Classes in India.* Delhi: Oxford University Press, 1984.

Gandhi, M. K. *The Collected Works of Mahatma Gandhi.* 90 vols. New Delhi: Publications Division, 1958–.

Gellner, Ernest. *Nations and Nationalism.* Oxford: Basil Blackwell, 1983.

Ghosh, Srabashi. " 'Birds in a Cage': Changes in Bengali Social Life as Recorded in Autobiographies by Women." *Economic and Political Weekly: Review of Women's Studies* 21 (October 1986): WS88–96.

Ghurye, G. S. *Caste and Class in India.* Bombay: Popular Prakashan, 1957.

Gopal, S. *British Policy in India, 1858–1905.* Cambridge: Cambridge University Press, 1965.

Gramsci, Antonio. *Selections from the Prison Notebooks.* Translated by Quintin Hoare and Geoffrey Nowell Smith. New York: International Publishers, 1971.

Grewal, J. S. *Muslim Rule in India: The Assessments of British Historians.* Calcutta: Oxford University Press, 1970.

Guha, Ranajit. "On Some Aspects of the Historiography of Colonial India." In Ranajit Guha, ed., *Subaltern Studies I,* pp. 1–8. Delhi: Oxford University Press, 1982.

———. *Elementary Aspects of Peasant Insurgency in Colonial India.* Delhi: Oxford University Press, 1983.

———. *An Indian Historiography of India: A Nineteenth-Century Agenda and Its Implications.* Calcutta: K. P. Bagchi, 1988.

———. "Discipline and Mobilize." In Partha Chatterjee and Gyanendra Pandey, eds., *Subaltern Studies VII* pp. 69–120. Delhi: Oxford University Press, 1992.

Guha, Ranajit, ed. *Subaltern Studies I–VI.* Delhi: Oxford University Press, 1982–90.

Guha-Thakurta, Tapati. *The Making of a New "Indian" Art: Artists, Aesthetics and Nationalism in Bengal, 1850–1920.* Cambridge: Cambridge University Press, 1992.

Gupta, Dipankar. "Continuous Hierarchies and Discrete Castes." *Economic and Political Weekly* 19, nos. 46–48 (17 and 24 November and 1 December 1984): 1955–58, 2003–5, 2049–53.

[Gupta, Mahendranath.] *The Gospel of Sri Ramakrishna*. Translated by Swami Nikhilananda. New York: Ramakrishna-Vivekananda Center, 1942.

Gusdorf, Georges. "Conditions and Limits of Autobiography." Translated by James Olney. In James Olney, ed. *Autobiography: Essays Theoretical and Critical*, pp. 28–48. Princeton: Princeton University Press, 1980.

Habermas, Jürgen. *The Philosophical Discourse of Modernity*. Translated by Frederick Lawrence. Cambridge: MIT Press, 1987.

———. *The Structural Transformation of the Public Sphere: An Inquiry into a Category of Bourgeois Society*. Translated by Thomas Burger. Cambridge: MIT Press, 1991.

Habib, Irfan. "The Peasant in Indian History." *Social Scientist* 11, no. 3 (March 1983): 21–64.

Habib, Muhammad. "An Introduction to the Study of Medieval India (A.D. 1000–1400)." In K. A. Nizami, ed., *Politics and Society during the Early Medieval Period: Collected Works of Professor Muhammad Habib*, pp. 3–32. New Delhi: People's Publishing House, 1974.

Haq, Muhammad Enamul. *A History of Sufi-ism in Bengal*. Dhaka: Asiatic Society of Bangladesh, 1975.

Hardiman, David. *Peasant Nationalists of Gujarat*. Delhi: Oxford University Press, 1984.

———. "The Bhils and Shahukars in Eastern Gujarat." In Ranajit Guha, ed., *Subaltern Studies V*, pp. 1–54. Delhi: Oxford University Press, 1987.

Harriss, John. *Capitalism and Peasant Farming: Agrarian Structure and Ideology in Northern Tamil Nadu*. Delhi: Oxford University Press, 1982.

Hartog, François. *The Mirror of Herodotus: The Representation of the Other in the Writing of History*. Translated by Janet Lloyd. Berkeley and Los Angeles: University of California Press, 1988.

Hegel, G. W. F. *Philosophy of Right*. Translated by T. M. Knox. 1952. Reprint. London: Oxford University Press, 1967.

———. *Encyclopaedia of the Philosophical Sciences*. Pt. 1. Translated by William Wallace. Oxford: Clarendon Press, 1975.

Hodivala, Shahpurshah Hormasji. *Studies in Indo-Muslim History: A Critical Commentary on Elliot and Dowson's "History of India as Told by Its Own Historians."* 2 vols. 1939. Reprint. Lahore: Islamic Book Service, 1979.

Inden, Ronald. *Imagining India*. Oxford: Basil Blackwell, 1990.

Isherwood, Christopher. *Ramakrishna and His Disciples*. New York: Simon and Schuster, 1965.

Jayawardena, Kumari. *Feminism and Nationalism in the Third World*. London: Zed Books, 1986.

Juergensmeyer, Mark. *Religion as Social Vision: The Movement against Untouchability in Twentieth-Century Punjab*. Berkeley and Los Angeles: University of California Press, 1982.

Kane, P. V. *History of Dharmasastra*. Vol. 2. Pt. 1. Poona: Bhandarkar Oriental Research Institute, 1974.

Karlekar, Malavika. "Kadambini and the Bhadralok: Early Debates over

Women's Education in Bengal." *Economic and Political Weekly: Review of Women's Studies* 21 (April 1986): WS25–31.

———. *Voices from Within: Early Personal Narratives of Bengali Women.* Delhi: Oxford University Press, 1991.

Karve, Irawati. *Hindu Society: An Interpretation.* Poona: Deccan College, 1961.

Kaviraj, Sudipta. "Bankimchandra and the Making of Nationalist Consciousness: I. Signs of Madness; II. The Self-Ironical Tradition; III. A Critique of Colonial Reason." Occasional Papers 108, 109, and 110. Calcutta: Centre for Studies in Social Sciences, 1989; "IV. Imaginary History." Manuscript.

———. "Signs of Madness: The Figure of Kamalakanta in the Work of Bankimchandra Chattopadhyay," *Journal of Arts and Ideas* 17–18 (June 1989): 9–32.

———. "The Imaginary Institution of India." In Partha Chatterjee and Gyanendra Pandey, eds., *Subaltern Studies VII*, pp. 1–39. Delhi: Oxford University Press, 1992.

Keith, Arthur Berriedale. *A Constitutional History of India, 1600–1935.* 1937. Reprint. New York: Barnes and Noble, 1969.

Khare, R. S. *The Untouchable as Himself: Ideology and Pragmatism among the Lucknow Chamars.* Cambridge: Cambridge University Press, 1983.

Kohli, Atul. *The State and Poverty in India: The Politics of Reform.* Cambridge: Cambridge University Press, 1987.

Kolenda, Pauline Mahar. "Religious Anxiety and Hindu Fate." *Journal of Asian Studies* 23 (1964): 71–82.

Kosambi, D. D. "Caste and Class in India." In A. J. Syed, ed., *D. D. Kosambi on History and Society: Problems of Interpretation*, pp. 127–32. Bombay: University of Bombay, 1985.

Laird, M. A. *Missionaries and Education in Bengal, 1793–1837.* Oxford : Clarendon Press, 1972.

Lejeune, Philippe. *On Autobiography.* Translated by Katherine Leary. Minneapolis: University of Minnesota Press, 1989.

Life of Ramakrishna Compiled from Various Authentic Sources. 1924. Reprint. Calcutta: Advaita Ashrama, 1964.

Lynch, Owen. *The Politics of Untouchability: Social Mobility and Social Change in a City of India.* New York: Columbia University Press, 1969.

MacIntyre, Alasdair. *After Virtue: A Study in Moral Theory.* London: Duckworth, 1981.

Mallick, A. R. "Modern Historical Writing in Bengali." In C. H. Philips, ed., *Historians of India, Pakistan and Ceylon*, pp. 446–60. London: Oxford University Press, 1961.

Mani, Lata. "The Production of an Official Discourse on *Sati* in Early Nineteenth-Century Bengal." *Economic and Political Weekly: Review of Women's Studies* 21 (April 1986): WS32–40.

———. "Contentious Traditions: The Debate on *Sati* in Colonial India." In Kumkum Sangari and Sudesh Vaid, eds., *Recasting Women: Essays in Colonial History*, pp. 88–126. New Delhi: Kali for Women, 1989.

Marx, Karl. *Capital.* Vol. 1. Translated by Samuel Moore and Edward Aveling. Moscow: Progress Publishers, 1971.

Mason, Mary G. "The Other Voice: Autobiographies of Women Writers." In

James Olney, ed., *Autobiography: Essays Theoretical and Critical*, pp. 207–35. Princeton: Princeton University Press, 1980.

Massie, J. W. *Continental India*. Vol. 2. London: Thomas Ward, 1839.

Metcalf, T. R. *The Aftermath of Revolt*. Princeton: Princeton University Press, 1964.

Misra, B. B. *The Bureaucracy in India: An Historical Analysis of Development up to 1947*. Delhi: Oxford University Press, 1977.

Mookerjee, Nanda, ed. *Sri Ramakrishna in the Eyes of Brahma and Christian Admirers*. Calcutta: Firma KLM, 1976.

Mozoomdar, P. C. *The Life and Teachings of Keshub Chunder Sen*. 1887. Reprint. Calcutta: Nababidhan Trust, 1931.

Mukherjee, Meenakshi. "The Unperceived Self: A Study of Five Nineteenth-Century Autobiographies." In Karuna Chanana, ed., *Socialisation, Education and Women: Explorations in Gender Identity*. New Delhi: Orient Longman, 1988.

Mukherjee, Mridula. "Peasant Resistance and Peasant Consciousness in Colonial India: 'Subaltern' and Beyond." *Economic and Political Weekly* 23, nos. 41, and 42 (8 and 15 October 1988): 2109–20 and 2174–85.

Mukhopadhyay, Govindagopal, and Gopikamohan Bhattacharya. *A Tri-lingual Dictionary*. Calcutta Sanskrit College Research Series 47, lexicon no. 1. Calcutta: Sanskrit College, 1966.

Mukhopadhyay, Subodh Kumar. "Evolution of Historiography in Bengali (1800–1947): A Study of the Pattern of Growth." In Tarasankar Banerjee, ed., *Historiography in Modern Indian Languages, 1800–1947*, pp. 29–42. Calcutta: Naya Prokash, 1987.

Murali, Atlury. "Civil Disobedience Movement in Andhra, 1920–1922: The Nature of Peasant Protest and the Methods of Congress Political Mobilization." In Kapil Kumar, ed., *Congress and Classes: Nationalism, Workers and Peasants*, pp. 152–216. New Delhi: Manohar, 1988.

Murshid, Ghulam. *Reluctant Debutante: Response of Bengali Women to Modernization, 1849–1905*. Rajshahi: Rajshahi University Press, 1983.

Nandy, Ashis. *The Intimate Enemy: Loss and Recovery of Self under Colonialism*. Delhi: Oxford University Press, 1983.

Nehru, Jawaharlal. *The Discovery of India*. New York: John Day, 1946.

———. *Jawaharlal Nehru's Speeches*. Vol 2. New Delhi: Publications Division, 1954.

O'Hanlon, Rosalind. *Caste, Conflict and Ideology: Mahatma Jotirao Phule and Low Caste Protest in Nineteenth-Century Western India*. Cambridge: Cambridge University Press, 1985.

———. "Recovering the Subject: *Subaltern Studies* and Histories of Resistance in Colonial South Asia." *Modern Asian Studies* 22, no. 1 (1988): 189–224.

Pal, Bipinchandra. *Memories of My Life and Times*. 1932. Reprint. Calcutta: Bipinchandra Pal Institute, 1973.

Pandey, Gyanendra. *The Ascendancy of the Congress in Uttar Pradesh, 1926–1934*. Delhi: Oxford University Press, 1978.

———. "Encounters and Calamities: The History of a North Indian *Qasba* in the Nineteenth Century." In Ranajit Guha, ed., *Subaltern Studies III*, pp. 231–70. Delhi: Oxford University Press, 1984.

Patnaik, Arun. "Gramsci's Concept of Hegemony: The Case of Development Administration in India." *Economic and Political Weekly: Review of Political Economy* 23, no. 5 (1988): PE 12–18.

Perlin, Frank. "Of White Whale and Countrymen in the Eighteenth-Century Maratha Deccan." *Journal of Peasant Studies* 5, no. 2 (January 1978): 172–237.

————. "Proto-Industrialization and Pre-Colonial South Asia." *Past and Present* 98 (February 1983): 30–95.

————. "State Formation Reconsidered." *Modern Asian Studies* 19, no. 3 (1985): 415–80.

Prakash, Gyan. "Writing Post-Orientalist Histories of the Third World: Perspectives from Indian Historiography." *Comparative Studies in Society and History* 32, no. 2 (April 1990): 383–408.

Pylee, M. V. *Constitutional History of India, 1600–1950.* Bombay: Asia, 1967.

Radhakrishnan, S. *Eastern Religions and Western Thought.* 1939. Reprint. New York: Oxford University Press, 1959.

Ray, Rajat K. *Social Conflict and Political Unrest in Bengal, 1875–1914.* Delhi: Oxford University Press, 1984.

Raychaudhuri, Tapan. *Europe Reconsidered: Perceptions of the West in Nineteenth-Century Bengal.* Delhi: Oxford University Press, 1988.

Risley, H. H. *The Tribes and Castes of Bengal.* Vol. 1. 1891. Reprint. Calcutta: Firma KLM, 1981.

Rudolph, Lloyd H., and Susanne Hoeber Rudolph. *In Search of Lakshmi: The Political Economy of the Indian State.* Chicago: University of Chicago Press, 1987.

Said, Edward W. "Identity, Negation and Violence." *New Left Review* 171 (1988): 46–60.

————. "Third World Intellectuals and Metropolitan Culture." *Raritan Quarterly* 9, no. 3 (Winter 1990): 27–50.

Sanyal, Hitesranjan. *Social Mobility in Bengal.* Calcutta: Papyrus, 1981.

————. "Trends of Change in the Bhakti Movement in Bengal." Occasional Paper 76 (July 1985). Calcutta: Centre for Studies in Social Sciences.

Saradananda, Swami. *Sri Ramakrishna the Great Master.* Translated by Swami Jagadananda. Madras: Sri Ramakrishna Math, 1952.

Sarkar, Sumit. *The Swadeshi Movement in Bengal.* New Delhi: People's Publishing House, 1973.

————. *A Critique of Colonial Reason.* Calcutta: Papyrus, 1985.

————. "'Kaliyuga,' 'Chakri' and 'Bhakti': Ramakrishna and His Times." *Economic and Political Weekly* 27, 29 (18 July 1992): 1543–66.

Sarkar, Tanika. "Jitu Santal's Movement in Malda, 1924–1932: A Study in Tribal Protest." In Ranajit Guha, ed., *Subaltern Studies IV*, pp. 136–64. Delhi: Oxford University Press, 1985.

Sastri, Sivanath. *History of the Brahmo Samaj.* 1911–12. Reprint. Calcutta: Sadharan Brahmo Samaj, 1974.

Scott, David C., ed., *Keshub Chunder Sen.* Madras: Christian Literature Society, 1979.

Scott, James. *Weapons of the Weak: Everyday Forms of Peasant Resistance.* New Haven, Conn.: Yale University Press, 1985.

272 BIBLIOGRAPHY

Seal, Anil. *The Emergence of Indian Nationalism*. Cambridge: Cambridge University Press, 1971.

Sen, Asok. "The Frontiers of the *Prison Notebooks*." *Economic and Political Weekly: Review of Political Economy* 23, no. 5 (1988): PE31–36.

[Sen, Keshabchandra.] *Keshub Chunder Sen in England: Diaries, Sermons, Addresses and Epistles*. 1871. Reprint. Calcutta: Writers Workshop, 1980.

Sen, Prosanto Kumar. *Keshub Chunder Sen*. Calcutta: Keshub Sen Birth Centenary Committee, 1938.

Siddiqi, Majid Hayat. *Agrarian Unrest in North India: The United Provinces, 1918–1922*. New Delhi: Vikas, 1978.

Sinha, Pradip. *Calcutta in Urban History*. Calcutta: Firma KLM, 1978.

Slater, T. E. *Keshab Chandra Sen and the Brahma Samàj*. Madras: Society for Promoting Christian Knowledge, 1884.

Smith, Vincent A. *Indian Constitutional Reform Viewed in the Light of History*. London: Humphrey Milford, 1919.

Spivak, Gayatri Chakravorty. "Subaltern Studies: Deconstructing Historiography." In Ranajit Guha, ed., *Subaltern Studies IV*, pp. 338–63. Delhi: Oxford University Press, 1985,

———. "Can the Subaltern Speak?" In Cary Nelson and Lawrence Grossberg, eds., *Marxism and the Interpretation of Culture*. Urbana: University of Illinois Press, 1988.

Srinivas, M. N. *Caste in Modern India and Other Essays*. Bombay: Asia, 1962.

———. *Social Change in Modern India*. Bombay: Allied, 1966.

Stein, Burton. "State Formation and Economy Reconsidered." *Modern Asian Studies*, 19, no. 3 (1985): 387–413.

Taylor, Charles. "Modes of Civil Society." *Public Culture* 3, no. 1 (Fall 1990): 102–19.

Thapar, Romila. "Communalism and the Writing of Ancient Indian History." In Romila Thapar, Harbans Mukhia, and Bipan Chandra, *Communalism and the Writing of Indian History*. Delhi: People's Publishing House, 1969.

Thompson, Edward, and G. T. Garratt. *Rise and Fulfilment of British Rule in India*. 1934. Reprint. Allahabad: Central Book Depot, 1962.

Tod, James. *Annals and Antiquities of Rajasthan, or the Central and Western Rajput States of India*. Edited by William Crooke. 1829–32. Reprint. London: Oxford University Press, 1920.

Washbrook, D. A. "Progress and Problems: South Asian Economic and Social History, c. 1720–1860." *Modern Asian Studies* 22, no. 1 (1988): 57–96.

Weber, Eugen. *Peasants into Frenchmen: The Modernization of Rural France, 1870–1914*. London: Chatto and Windus, 1979.

Index

Preface

I have long resisted the temptation to do a single-volume study of Indian politics, despite the fact that, over the years, many people have reminded me that this was entirely expected of me as an Indian political scientist. The reason for my reluctance was not that I did not take seriously my professional responsibilities towards the discipline to which I belonged. On the contrary, it was precisely because I took those responsibilities seriously that I hesitated to undertake the task. To put it plainly, the reason was that I did not know how to write such a book.

The problem as I saw it was one of defining my location in relation to the object of study: namely, the institutional structures and political processes of the Indian state. Since the beginning of my professional life in the early 1970s, I have been acutely conscious of the fragility of this relationship. Having reached adolescence in the restless decade of the 1960s, when every young mind in West Bengal was touched by the dream of liberation, I brought into my first academic exercises on contemporary politics a conceptual and analytical language that was derived — unabashedly — from Marx, Lenin and Mao Zedong. To use this language with conviction, one needed not just to glance from time to time at the image of an alternative state of the social world, but to possess and display that image as an object of one's own creation, and hence of proprietorship. One needed, in other words, to occupy that high ground of criticism from which one could match, claim for claim, argument for argument, evidence for evidence, the whole panoply of ruling doctrines; in short, to advance, on behalf of a class, an alliance or the people as a whole, a rival claim to rule. I do not know if in brandishing this language of power, I managed to sound convincing. What I do know, however, is that I had a certain degree of freedom to find my own way through that dense and fiercely contested doctrinal terrain; after all, I was not bound by any party line and did not need to have my writings screened for their ideological correctness. In any case, the years 1975–7 drastically realigned my relation to the study of Indian politics.

The declaration of Emergency in June 1975, its sudden lifting after a year and a half, and the elections of March 1977 confirmed for many of us what we thought were the characteristic properties of the structure of political rule in post-colonial India. We described these structural properties in terms of the balance between the constituent elements of the ruling class coalition. Electoral democracy, it was clear, was an important enabling condition for the working of this balance; the limits of electoral democracy too would be set by the requirements of maintaining the balance. What was new, however, in our understanding of Indian politics was the discovery, after 1977, that this particular structure of class rule, more sophisticated and effective than in many other post-colonial countries of the world, also afforded significant strategic opportunities for popular struggles for democracy. In time, with the rapid decline through the 1980s of the Congress as the principal political organization of India's ruling classes, the incorporation of the substantial part of the Left into the institutions of governance, and the new attempts in the 1990s of the Hindu Right to occupy the ground lost by the Congress, our description of the structure of class rule in India necessarily took on a much less unified and much more contingent quality.

There was no position I could truthfully occupy from which I might claim to provide a panoptic view of Indian politics. Nevertheless, I did continue to write on the subject — nearly once a week on an average — mainly at the behest of Samar Sen, editor of the Calcutta weekly, *Frontier*. I now know how enormously rewarding an experience this was, for I was required to write history as it happened; not as a journalist would, since I had neither the opportunity nor the skills of reporting, but as a critic trying to match structure to event, institution to process, claim to fact.

I offer this volume in place of the book on Indian politics that I will never write. It is constructed from my writings over the last twenty years, and includes a variety of genres — essays, reviews, polemics, editorial comments, and journal entries. I have selected and arranged this material so as to produce an account of structures in motion, described from shifting vantage points, sometimes with the advantage of historical hindsight, but often alongside the events themselves. I believe this gives a more engaged, rich and truthful account of my understanding of post-colonial politics than a more smoothly constructed synthetic volume.

I do think there is an overall theoretical concern that has emerged out of these twenty years of my engagement with the study of Indian politics. It is a concern with democratic politics — where democracy is not, as the republican cliché still proclaims, government of the people, but *the politics of the governed.* The perspective is oppositional, negative, resolutely critical. It is sceptical of all utopian talk — liberal, populist or socialist. Contrary to liberal preaching, it is conscious of the fact that the critical issue of governance in many post-colonial countries is increasingly being posed as the opposition between capitalist growth and democracy. At the same time, this perspective makes one wary of using a populist language of power, since it cannot intelligibly conceive of a state of the social world in which the masses will be anything other than objects of government. It is a perspective that has taught one to rely on one's own strength, to fight strategically and to dream within the realms of the possible.

As in the case of *The Present History of West Bengal,* the companion volume to this book, I must thank Timir Basu, editor of *Frontier,* for giving me permission to use many of my writings published in that journal. I am also grateful to Arup Mallik for letting me use a translated version of an article we had jointly authored in our youth. This manuscript was put together during the winter of 1995, which I spent at the International Institute of the University of Michigan at Ann Arbor: my thanks to my colleagues and students there. As always, I remain grateful to the staff of the Centre for Studies in Social Sciences, Calcutta, for their unstinting help. And finally, I thank Nitasha Devasar of Oxford University Press, Delhi, for making the fiftieth year of India's independence (which also happens to be the fiftieth year of my life) the occasion for the publication of this book.

Calcutta   PC
March 1997

Acknowledgements

Chapter 1: 'The Indian Big Bourgeoisie: Comprador or National', *Frontier*, Annual Number 1985, pp. 32–8.

Chapter 2: 'Jawaharlal Nehru and the Decade After Freedom', *Indian Historical Review*, 6, 1–2 (1979–80), pp. 237–45; 'The Last Years of Jawaharlal Nehru', *Frontier*, 17, 6–8 (Autumn 1984), pp. 28–34.

Chapter 3: (With Arup Mallik) 'Bhāratīya ganatantra o burjoyā pratikryā', *Anya artha*, 8 (March 1975), pp. 6–25. Translated from the Bengali.

Chapter 4: '1977: Reflections on the "Second Independence" '; paper presented at the Indian Political Science Conference, Bangalore, December 1977; previously unpublished.

Chapter 5: 'Caraṇ sim-er rājnīti prasaṅge', *Anīk*, 15 (September 1978), pp. 104–8. Translated from the Bengali.

Chapter 6: 'Bhārate saṃsadīya rajnītir kayekṭi prakryā prasaṅge', *Anīk*, 17, 3–5 (September 1980), pp. 9–10, 112–14. Translated from the Bengali.

Chapter 7: *Frontier*, 16, 15 (26 November 1983); 16, 20 (31 December 1983); 16, 22 (14 January 1984); 16, 40 (26 May 1984); 16, 44 (23 June 1984); 16, 48 (21 July 1984); 17, 2 (1 September 1984); 17, 9 (20 October 1984); 17, 11 (3 November 1984); 17, 12 (10 November 1984); 17, 14 (24 November 1984).

Chapter 8: 'The Writing on the Wall', *Frontier*, 17, 18 (22 December 1984), pp. 5–7.

Chapter 9: *Frontier*, 17, 28 (2 March 1985); 17, 39 (18 May 1985); 17, 40 (25 May 1985); 17, 42 (8 June 1985); 17, 44 (22 June 1985); 17, 50 (3 August 1985); 18, 2 (31 August 1985); 18, 7 (5 October 1985); 18, 19 (28 December 1985); 18, 27 (22 February 1986); 18, 30 (15 March 1986); 18, 38 (10 May 1986); 18, 40 (24

May 1986); 18, 43 (14 June 1986); 19, 5 (20 September 1986); 19, 12 (8 November 1986); 19, 14 (22 November 1986); 19, 16 (6 December 1986); 19, 18 (20 December 1986).

Chapter 10: 'The Politics of Appropriation', *Frontier*, 19, 8–10 (11–25 October 1986), pp. 30–6.

Chapter 11: *Frontier*, 19, 39 (16 May 1987); 19, 46 (4 July 1987); 19, 48 (18 July 1987); 20, 5 (19 September 1987); 20, 16 (5 December 1987); 20, 32 (26 March 1988); 20, 42 (4 June 1988); 20, 45 (25 June 1988); 21, 1 (20 August 1988); 21, 4 (10 September 1988); 21, 6 (24 September 1988); *Ānandabājār patrikā*, 27 October 1988, translated from the Bengali; *Frontier*, 21, 12 (5 November 1988); 21, 21 (7 January 1989); 21, 23 (21 January 1989); 21, 34 (8 April 1989); 21, 47 (8 July 1989); 21, 52 (12 August 1989); 22, 2 (26 August 1989); 22, 6 (23 September 1989); 22, 13 (11 November 1989); 22, 16 (2 December 1989).

Chapter 12: *Frontier*, 22, 19 (23 December 1989); 22, 48 (14 July 1990); 22, 50 (28 July 1990); *Ānandabājār patrikā*, 14 September 1990, translated from the Bengali; *Frontier*, 23, 14 (17 November 1990).

Chapter 13: *Frontier*, 23, 33 (30 March 1991); 23, 35 (13 April 1991); 23, 42 (1 June 1991); 23, 44 (15 June 1991); 23, 46 (29 June 1991); 23, 50 (27 July 1991); *Bāromās*, 18, 2 (April 1996), pp. 13–15, translated from the Bengali.

Chapter 14: 'Secularism and Toleration', *Economic and Political Weekly*, 29, 28 (9 July 1994), pp. 1768–77.

Chapter 15: 'Talking About Our Modernity in Two Languages', *Studies in Humanities and Social Sciences* (Shimla), 2 (1996), 2, pp. 153–69.

Contents

1

The Indian Big Bourgeoisie: Comprador or National?

Suniti Kumar Ghosh has written a serious and provocative book[1] which deserves to be widely discussed in political circles in India. It is a remarkable book in many respects. Suniti Ghosh does not write in the detached, academic style of professional social scientists pretending to produce 'objective, positive knowledge' for the consumption of anyone who has use for it. He writes as a partisan in the political struggle, judging historical issues from the standpoint of a committed political activist. And in this genre of political writing in India, his book is truly remarkable for the range and depth of research that has gone into the construction of its arguments. Undoubtedly, there will be much scope for debate about Ghosh's main argument, but by not shirking the laborious task of presenting a solid and well-informed thesis, he has ensured that the debate in Left circles on the character of the Indian bourgeoisie will henceforth be raised to a much higher level of theoretical precision and attention to factual details.

Ghosh's main thesis is that the Indian big bourgeoisie has been comprador in nature from its very birth. It was never hostile to foreign capital either before or after the transfer of power. It sought not independent capitalist development but development as a subordinate partner of imperialist monopolies. But in the course of arguing his case, Ghosh undertakes a wide-ranging survey of historical developments in India from the period immediately preceding British rule to the transfer of power in 1947.

In discussing the pre-British Indian economy, Ghosh uses the results of a lot of recent historical research to make an extremely useful contribution to the Marxist debate on the subject. There

[1] Suniti Kumar Ghosh, *The Indian Big Bourgeoisie: Its Genesis, Growth and Character* (Calcutta: Subarnarekha, 1985).

has been for long a great deal of confusion among Indian Marxists regarding the pre-British agrarian structure, the nature of the 'village community', the supposed 'stagnation' and 'unchangeable' nature of Indian society, and of course that inevitable problem of the Asiatic mode of production. Suniti Ghosh shows that it is grossly incorrect to assume that there were no forces of change in the economy and society before the colonial conquest. In fact, in many areas there was a considerable expansion of commodity production and the emergence of large manufacturing centres, a vast growth of internal trade and external commerce, the organization of commercial credit, a high degree of monetization of the supra-village economy, and 'an unmistakable trend towards the growth of private property in land'. Whether all these tendencies could have amounted to the creation of conditions sufficient for the historical transformation of Indian society is a question so speculative as to be virtually meaningless. Because surely, the sufficient conditions of revolutionary transformation are provided not just by structural movements in the economy, but also by the political configuration of the class struggle in the period of crisis. And on the latter question, there are no historically available means by which an answer might be attempted, because the imposition of colonial rule changed the fundamental political configuration.

But the significance of the finding that there were these tendencies of change in pre-colonial India is that it enables us to make a much clearer and unambiguous assessment of the consequences of British rule. On this, too, there has been a lot of hedging and prevarication among Indian Marxists; and, it cannot be denied, Marx himself contributed to the confusion by what he wrote in his early articles on India. In 1853, he had written:

England, it is true, in causing a social revolution in Hindostan, was actuated only by the vilest interests, and was stupid in her manner of enforcing them. But that is not the question. The question is, can mankind fulfil its destiny without a fundamental revolution in the social state of Asia? If not, whatever may have been the crimes of England, she was the unconscious tool of history in bringing about that revolution.[2]

This was a chief source of the ambivalent attitude of the

---

[2] Karl Marx, 'British Rule in India', in Karl Marx and Frederick Engels, *Collected Works*, vol. 12 (Moscow: Progress Publishers, 1979), pp. 125–33.

'progressive' intelligentsia in India about the historical necessity of colonial rule, and helped in perpetuating the myth about the dual role of British rule — its 'destructive' as well as its 'regenerative' effects.

Marx's writings on India in the 1850s show to what extent he was still imprisoned by the stereotypes of the European Enlightenment. But his later writings, beginning with the *Grundrisse* and *Capital*, and particularly his studies from 1871 to his death which have survived in the form of draft notes, show how seriously he struggled with these stereotypes; how till his last days he unceasingly groped for a framework of world history that would go beyond the Enlightenment notion of unilineal 'progress' towards 'the destiny of mankind', that would be more universal precisely by accounting for the specifically *different* possibilities of historical development in countries such as Russia or India or China. Suniti Ghosh has forcefully made the point regarding the significant changes in Marx's thinking about the effects of British rule in India. These late writings make it abundantly clear that Marx abandoned his earlier belief in the 'regenerative' role of colonialism. In fact, time and again, in his brief remarks in *Capital,* and most unambiguously in his *Ethnological Notebooks,* Marx pointed out how by its interventions in the agrarian and manufacturing economies and by its legal and administrative actions, the colonial state had, instead of unleashing new forces of transformation, only distorted and stultified the course of social development.[3] Ghosh's survey of the historical material on pre-British India brings him to the same conclusion:

The possibility of the transition from feudalism to capitalism was forestalled by colonial rule, which destroyed the progressive elements awakening to life within the old society, allied itself with all its reactionary and benighted forces, and gave rise to retarded, misshapen, lopsided economic and social structures. (p. 81)

Was Indian Society Feudal?

In his discussion of pre-colonial Indian society, however, Suniti Ghosh also makes a formulation which seems to ignore a rather

[3] Lawrence Krader, *The Ethnological Notebooks of Karl Marx* (Assen: Van Gorcum, 1974).

basic position that Marx continued to hold even in his last writings. Ghosh's argument is that the mode of production in pre-colonial India was feudal, not Asiatic (as Marx characterized it) nor 'tribute-paying' (in Samir Amin's recent formulation).[4] The state in India was the chief landlord; the form in which the surplus was extracted was a land tax, but this is only a formal difference from rent in European feudalism. Not only that:

India, at least certain parts of the subcontinent like Bengal, had entered a late feudal stage at the time of the advent of colonial rule. No doubt, feudalism was on the decline and a serious crisis afflicted every sphere of feudal life. (p. 77)

Ghosh seems to think that Marx's 'early characterization of the mode of production in pre-colonial India as Asiatic' was the result of his misplaced reliance on the writings of European travellers like Bernier and of British officials. But even in his later writings on India, in which he fundamentally revised his earlier assessment of the historical role of colonialism, Marx did not give up his identification of the crucial difference between European feudalism and the social formation in India. And here the charge of over-reliance on Bernier's accounts cannot be sustained, because Marx's jottings in the *Ethnological Notebooks* show how deeply he had familiarized himself with the workings of the land revenue system and the agrarian economy in British India, particularly Bengal, in the late nineteenth century. For Bengal in particular, Marx was perfectly aware of the consequences of the Permanent Settlement: the breakdown of the old *zamindaris,* the purchase of estates by 'comprador' traders, the growth of subinfeudation, the fragmentation of *zamindari* property, its sale and mortgage, even the differentiation among *raiyati* holders.[5] In other words, Marx was well aware of the evidence on which Ghosh bases his conclusion: 'Land became a commodity — alienable private property — and the peasant's traditional right of occupancy to land was abolished.' (p. 114) But Marx did not accept this formulation: in fact, he specifically criticized British officials such as James Phear for suggesting it.

[4] Samir Amin, *Le developpement inégal* (Paris: Edition de Minuit, 1973).
[5] See my introductory comments to the Bengali translation of the sections on John Phear in Marx's *Ethnological Notebooks*: 'Bāṅlār grāmsamāj prasaṅge kārl mārks', *Bāromās*, 9, 1 (September 1987), pp. 1–22.

Why? One must not forget that Marx's chief concern in inquiring into the dynamics of pre-capitalist formations was to identify the possibilities of transition to capitalism. And here, the fundamental structural condition for transition was the separation of a large proportion of direct producers from the means of production. Marx was certain that the overall conditions of reproduction of feudal relations of production in Europe were much more favourable for such a separation than the corresponding conditions in India. In particular, Marx identified two elements: first, the existence in feudal Europe of a notion of individual proprietorship of the lord over his estate (carried over from the concept of property in Roman law), which in turn implied an individuated notion of the bondage of a serf to his lord; and second, the network of a two-way flow of commodities between town and country in late medieval Europe, which implied that with commodity production the rural economy would in no way be insulated from its transformative consequences. Neither of these elements was in general present in pre-colonial India; and, crucial for Marx's argument, neither of them was unambiguously established even after one hundred years of British rule.

The implication of British land settlements in Bengal was not to introduce alienable private property in land, but rather to transform into a commodity the different sets of revenue-collecting rights. Marx made detailed notes on the way in which *zamindari* and intermediate tenure-holding property was being subdivided and transferred in Bengal, and he especially emphasized the fact that what was being bought and sold was a specific share at a particular rung of the revenue-collecting hierarchy. Besides, such a transfer would not necessarily affect the rights of others to the same piece of land. This was hardly an appropriate legal–political condition under which an emergent capitalist, or a landlord wishing to evict small tenants in order to lease out his land to a capitalist farmer, could exercise unrestricted and individuated private property rights in land. It was also not conducive for that drastic development which was a necessary precondition for generalized commodity production: the large-scale eviction of peasants completely dissociated from their ties with the land.

In fact, it was the very political conditions of colonial rule in the nineteenth century that forced the development of a highly fragmented and ambiguous notion of property rights in land. The Permanent Settlement did confer 'proprietary rights' on landlords; the *haptam* and *panjam* regulations did fortify this with arbitrary powers of distraint, etc. But the colonial state was unprepared to endanger the political conditions of colonial extraction by allowing large-scale eviction of tenants. Thus, it was forced to curb both the 'high landlordism' of the 1830s and 1840s and the depredations of English indigo planters, by successively limiting the 'proprietary' rights of landlords by protecting the 'occupancy' rights of certain sections of tenants. The result was not the generalization of bourgeois private property in land, but rather a half-baked and distorted structure of property rights.[6] In fact, this distorted legal–political form was a specific expression of the development in eastern India of those production relations which many have characterized as 'semi-feudal.'

Specificities of Asian Societies

The historical material which Suniti Ghosh uses in his discussion of the pre-colonial and early colonial economy should lead to a much more serious enquiry into the specific character of the social formation in India. First of all, there was considerable variation in the actual form of 'possession' of land within the village. The phenomenon of 'joint ownership' was quite rare. (Incidentally, Marx too was perfectly aware of this.) Second, there were differential rights over land within the village and certainly a fair amount of inequality in the size of holdings. Further, in most parts of India there existed a sizeable portion of the labouring population, comprising the lowest castes, who were denied all rights of possession of land. Consequently, there existed exploitative class relations not only between a state nobility and the direct producers in the village, but also between sections of the village population, in particular between upper castes and landless untouchables. (Here, Marx can be faulted for not recognizing the significance of the latter set of relations.) Yet, despite the existence of exploitative relations within the village, the conditions of reproduction were maintained by a

[6] For a longer discussion, see Partha Chatterjee, *Bengal 1920–1947: The Land Question* (Calcutta: K.P. Bagchi, 1985).

comprehensive cultural–ideological system — an ethical system — which emphasized the mutual dependence of different elements within the *jati* structure of division of labour. By emphasizing the *social* obligation of guaranteeing a subsistence for all, albeit a differential subsistence according to one's place in the caste hierarchy, the ideological structure of caste expressed the overall *social* unity of the labourer with his means of labour. It was in this sense that there existed a 'community', the social unity of a class-divided collective.

Marx was keenly aware of the strength and comprehensiveness of the collective framework of social relations in the Indian village. Hence, his emphasis on the difficulties of effecting a separation of a large section of producers from the means of production. Marx did not think that the producers in Indian villages were free, but their unfreedom was of a *collective* nature, very different from the individual unfreedom of the European serf. What Marx was relatively unaware of was the continued existence of elements of resistance within this comprehensive social structure — of ideologies which did not accept the Brahmanical code, of movements which sought to defy the rules of caste. How such elements were related to changes in the economy, to what extent they contained the possibilities of overturning the ideological framework of caste, why they failed in doing this, what changes occurred in the social structure because of the impact of these movements — these are problems to which Marxists in India have paid little attention. Yet they are vital for an understanding not only of the nature of pre-colonial society, or of the specific distortions which capitalist development brings under colonial rule, but also of the possibilities of transformation which exist today. The specific problems posed in countries such as India will not be resolved by arbitrary attempts to force Indian reality into the received moulds of European history.

It is worth remarking here that the question of 'feudalism' in China, from which many Marxists in India have drawn their analogies, is by no means unproblematic. In a recent collection of essays from the Chinese Academy of Social Sciences,[7] Wu Dakun of Beijing University has shown how many of Marx's arguments on the Asiatic mode conform to the facts of Chinese

---

[7] Su Shaozhi et al., *Marxism in China* (Nottingham: Spokesman, 1983).

history. Even more remarkable is his clarification that the term 'feudal' used in English translations of Mao's works is meant to be a rendering of the Chinese word *fengjian*, an old Chinese term whose meaning is fundamentally different from the English term 'feudal'. Perhaps we have all been misreading Mao in poor English translations!

The Big Bourgeoisie

Let us now come to Suniti Ghosh's main thesis about the origins and character of the Indian big bourgeoisie. His arguments are fundamentally aimed against nationalist historians, including 'Left nationalists', who seek to portray the Indian bourgeoisie as a whole as struggling singlemindedly against imperialist domination. But in doing this, Ghosh sets up a straw man, because he alleges that these historians are positing 'an irreconcilable contradiction' between the Indian capitalist class and foreign capital. Now, the more sophisticated among such historians would hardly do this; they would not deny that there was some degree of collaboration between the two. But, of course, their argument is that in the end the Indian bourgeoisie came around to the cause of 'national freedom'.

Suniti Ghosh does not deny that there was '*some* contradiction' (p. 177) between the Indian big bourgeoisie and imperialist capital. But his point is that 'such contradiction was over secondary issues . . . [they] could be resolved within the framework of the imperialist system itself'. Fundamentally, '*much* of the capitalist industry that developed in India did so not in the *strongest* contradiction with the policies of imperialism but *mostly* on a comprador basis'. (p. 215) Now, all the italicized terms above (my italics) are qualifications to Ghosh's main formulation which suggest a certain *quantitative* measure of the degree of comprador or national characteristics. Can such a measure be found? Or will such a mode of argument resolve the debate?

Let us turn Ghosh's argument around by beginning from the end. In the final sentence of his book, Ghosh quotes Mao to make the point that 'in the era of imperialism the road to *independent capitalist* development of a colony or semi-colony [is] blocked'. (p. 290) If that is so, then it is hardly surprising that the Indian big bourgeoisie, inasmuch as it still exists and flourishes as a dominant class in India, should not display the signs of an *independent* capitalist class.

But, on the other hand, Ghosh also quotes Lenin to argue that it is the characteristic of national movements to strive for 'the formation of national states' since they provide the best conditions for modern capitalism. Now, it is an undeniable fact of world history since World War II that formally independent national states have been created all over Asia and Africa in many of which the indigenous big bourgeoisie is in a dominant position. What then is our theoretical problem: to identify the specific character of this bourgeoisie which remains dependent on foreign capital and yet enjoys power in its particular national state, or to reassert the general proposition that the big bourgeoisie is not a truly independent capitalist class?

An Obsolete Problem

I think it is because Suniti Ghosh restricts himself to the second problem that he is unable to bring out the most significant implications of the historical material on the growth of Indian capitalism. It is because of this again that his case against nationalist historiography is not as strong as it could have been. He summarizes the fairly well-known facts about the close connections between early Indian industrial entrepreneurs and British capital as well as the colonial government. He traces the origins of the present big industrial houses in India in their role as brokers and suppliers of British managing agencies. He notes the fact that in the period up to the end of World War I, Indian capitalists accumulated vast wealth principally by collaborating with foreign capital and the colonial government. But in discussing the relation between the big bourgeoisie and the nationalist movement, Ghosh does not quite see the economic possibilities and political strategies which the leading Indian capitalists used to explore their prospects in a rapidly changing historical situation.

Once again, to turn his argument around, Ghosh recognizes that formal political independence has now given the Indian bourgeoisie the freedom to woo several imperialist powers instead of one, and to bargain between them. (p. 278) He also notes (pp. 130–4) that a formally independent state has given the bourgeoisie the added option of harnessing public resources in the cause of private accumulation by instituting a structure of state capitalism.

But all this *required* the creation of a formally independent state, and this was a principal political objective of the Indian big bourgeoisie, certainly by the late 1930s. Ghosh also ignores the fact that it was from this time that Indian capitalists, particularly those based in Calcutta, launched a major onslaught on British-owned companies in the jute and coal industries. They used their financial links with British capital to actually take over British companies, not in the way in which lackeys like the Maharaja of Burdwan or Lord Sinha or Sir B.P. Singh Roy would be made directors, but in the face of fierce opposition from British expatriate businessmen. (The evidence contained in the papers of Sir Edward Benthall is quite revealing on this point.) It is in this perspective that the ideas contained in the so-called 'Bombay Plan' can be understood. The state which the Indian big bourgeoisie visualized was not based on a revolutionary transformation of the colonial economy. It was a state which would in fact carry over almost wholesale the framework of colonial government; the changes it would bring about would be in small doses, in a reformist manner. But it would be *their* state.

Ghosh is not incorrect in stating that 'instead of coming into conflict with each other, British monopoly capital and Indian big capital looked forward to playing complementary roles in the post-war period'. (p. 234) But what is crucial is that Indian big capital was looking towards changing the *political terms* on which such bargaining and collaboration would be made. It was seeking to collaborate not under the aegis of a colonial state, but of an independent state operating in the world economy.

To a large extent, the old problem of comprador/national capital developed in the context of the pre-World War II situation is now obsolete. The political significance of the concepts at that time was to identify enemies and allies in a revolutionary struggle of national liberation. It was not presumed that this struggle would remain under the leadership of the bourgeoisie. For whatever historical reasons, the leadership of the national movement in India remained firmly in the hands of the bourgeoisie, and so have the central organs of the Indian state since independence. It is now futile to speculate on what might have happened if a genuine revolutionary force had seized the leadership of the national struggle, and whether in that case a section of the bourgeoisie might have been mobilized in the cause of independent capitalist development. Since that did not happen, simply to reassert the truism that the Indian big bourgeoisie remains dependent on foreign capital will not get us very far in understanding the specific forms of capitalist development in India or of the role and nature of the contemporary Indian state.

2

The Nehru Era

The Decade after Freedom

The publication of the first volume of Professor Gopal's
biography of Jawaharlal Nehru[1] was an important event in
the writing of the history of modern India. Despite the many
criticisms one could make of that book, there was no denying
the importance of the historical material presented in it, or the
unmistakable sensation of a massive turmoil overtaking the
leaders of the nation as they tried to make sense of those events
and to control them as best as they could. One was frequently
moved by the warmth and sensitivity of Gopal's portrayal of a
leader in the making, urged on by what was basically an intellectual appreciation of the ideals of national freedom on the
one hand and an unquestioning emotional loyalty to the Mahatma on the other; a man wanting desperately to plunge headlong
into the currents of mass upsurge, yet forced by his intellect
and temperament to remain aloof. Gopal's first volume on
Nehru was a sincere study of the hero in his youth, for those
were days of sacrifice and idealism. The many indecisions, vacil-
lations, irresolutions of purpose, the compromises on principles,
could with justification be ignored in the face of the overwhelming onward march of history.

Gopal's second volume[2] leaves much to be desired. In the
first place, it deals with a period that is less obviously dramatic.
It is a period of slow reconstruction, of long-range planning,
of a gradual evolution of relations and structures; a period in
the country's recent past which saw few open confrontations
in the political battlefield between the great forces of history.

[1] Sarvepalli Gopal, *Jawaharlal Nehru: A Biography*, volume 1, *1889–1947*
(Delhi: Oxford University Press, 1976).
[2] Sarvepalli Gopal, *Jawaharlal Nehru: A Biography*, volume 2, *1947–1956*
(Delhi: Oxford University Press, 1979).

It is a period that requires the cold ray of analysis to penetrate the deceptive layer of contemporary perceptions, and bring to light the more latent social processes which worked to change the various structures on which our society is built. If there is any drama at all in this history, it can only emerge out of an analysis of the interaction of those more imperceptible forces. Gopal, unfortunately, does not attempt this analysis. Secondly, because politics during these years could no longer be seen as the clash of great ideals, manoeuvres and machinations necessarily seem more naked, unabashedly prompted by narrow considerations of personal, sectarian, or organizational power. This was the sort of politics that must have been quite disasteful to Nehru himself, or at least to that part of him which was a Fabian liberal. Gandhi, too, was no mean practitioner of the art of realpolitik; yet a total clarity of commitment to his own ethical norms freed him completely from any feeling of guilt on this score. Nehru, on the other hand, is tormented by guilt. Again unfortunately, lacking the scientific apparatus to situate the activities of a political leader in the more impersonal context of structures and processes and thus, in a sense, to 'objectify' the problem, Gopal is hard put to it to explain Nehru's crisis. Much of what he says in the book by way of comments on Nehru's actions seems like special pleading.

I will suggest that both these shortcomings arise because of certain methodological problems inherent in the very project which Professor Gopal has set out for himself: namely, to write as biography the history of Indian politics in the very recent past, using the conventional techniques of the historian. Gopal uses Nehru's letters as his principal source. One result is that each event takes on a structure dictated by the contents and tone of the letters. This is not so much of a problem in the case of conventional histories which use the biographical form, for there the broad structural features of society or the basic historical processes are usually reasonably well understood and have already become part of the standard historical literature for the period. Biases, distortions or angularities in the biographical material can, therefore, be set against the more 'objective' constructions of the economic, political, or social histories of the period concerned. In fact, in the hands of a skilful historian, the distortions themselves can become material for the study of social ideology. This procedure, however, is not adequate for periods which are still, in important ways, contemporary. For here, our perceptions have not yet been sufficiently clarified by theoretical understanding; they are still subjects of current research and debate within the various social science disciplines. Biographical material in what these days is called 'contemporary history' must, therefore, be placed against these tentative findings of the social sciences and interpreted as best as possible in the context of their still-inconclusive debates.

Gopal, however, does not go beyond the conventional methods. The text is constructed very largely out of direct quotes from or paraphrases of Nehru's correspondence, with occasional references to contemporary newspapers and published reminiscences on Nehru. Even the narrative follows in the main a sequence determined by the letters. Nehru's views on the Soviet Union, to take one example, seem to undergo inexplicable changes. In September 1948, he thinks there is 'not the least chance of India lining up with the Soviet Union in war or peace'. (p. 45) In February 1949, he is 'anxious, despite Soviet criticism of his government and support for the Indian Communist Party, to be as friendly as possible and develop contacts in such non-political matters as exchange of films and cultural delegations, to continue talks on a possible trade agreement and offer to buy petrol'. (p. 57) In July 1950, 'his suspicions of the Soviet Union were unchanged . . . "we face today a vast and powerful Soviet group of nations, which tends to become a monolithic bloc, not only in pursuing a similar internal economic policy but a common foreign policy. That policy is an expansionist one. . . . It is expansionist not only in the normal political sense but also in encouraging internal trouble in other countries" '. (p. 102) In August 1957, however, Nehru is writing to Katju: "At the present moment, I would almost say that owing to various circumstances, we have rather undermined the Communist position in India." (p. 277) Nevertheless, during his Moscow visit in August 1955, he 'was concerned to put forward the case for the United States and to make clear that his independent thinking could not be submerged by cordiality and the current coincidence of his outlook with the Russians'. (p. 247) And yet, it is clear by this time that 'from the summer of 1954, the drift away from the United States and towards the

Communist Powers continued steadily'. (p. 226) From Gopal's account, it is quite impossible to know how one should interpret these sudden changes in Nehru's thinking. And as for the larger question of the reasons behind the slow but decisive shift in official Indian foreign policy, Gopal can find no explanation in his sources other than certain irritating communications from the US State Department.

To take another example of how the narrative is shaped by the contents of the Nehru papers, there occurs more than one digression on relations between Nehru and Krishna Menon. Menon, incidentally, comes off very poorly: 'fawning hysteria and plaintive self-pity' is Gopal's comment on Menon's attitude. (p. 142) But one can see no better reason for these extensive digressions than the existence of a few quotable letters.

To the extent Gopal uses any explanatory concepts at all, they are the usual poorly defined catch-all phrases of Indian political journalese, many of them used by Nehru himself to order his own thinking on politics and society. There is that ubiquitous force of communalism which seems to explain so much that is complicated and difficult in Indian politics. This, for instance, is how Gopal handles the Abdullah episode. To start with, Nehru has complete confidence in Abdullah, 'a close friend and comrade' from the days of the freedom struggle. 'The only person who can deliver the goods in Kashmir is Abdullah. . . . No satisfactory way out can be found in Kashmir except through him.' (p. 117) But then Abdullah begins to complain about Hindu communal forces in India who believed in surrendering Kashmir to Pakistan: ' . . . there are powerful influences at work in India,' wrote Abdullah to Nehru, 'who do not see eye to eye with you regarding your ideal of making the Union a truly secular state and your Kashmir policy.' (p. 119) Nehru plays down Abdullah's fears about Hindu communalism. Abdullah, remarks Gopal, is 'obsessed with Hindu communalism and the fantasy of independence'. (p. 124) Nehru sought to 'explain away' Abdullah's fears by saying: 'He is not a very clever thinker. . . . He is of course obsessed with the idea of meeting the challenge of Pakistan and keeping his own people from being influenced by Pakistan's propaganda.' (p. 117) But Nehru's efforts to support Abdullah are upset by a communalist combination of the Jana Sangh, Akali Dal, Hindu

Mahasabha and the RSS. There were communalists in the bureaucracy too: 'The Home Ministry was at this time in the hands of Kailas Nath Katju . . . and his doddering ineptitude was accentuated by the tardiness of many officials whose communal sympathies were barely concealed.' (p. 123) One thing led to another and the episode culminated in Abdullah's dismissal and arrest. One cannot but conclude from this that either Abdullah was fully justified in his alleged 'obsession' with the influence of Hindu communal forces, or else what shaped the course of these events were forces much more complex and variegated than what is suggested by the term 'communalism'.

Caesar?

The lack of theoretical reasoning in Gopal's presentation is particularly painful because there is a wealth of material in the Nehru correspondence quoted by Gopal which could be used to illuminate many crucial but not very well understood problems of Indian politics. Consider, for instance, the question of Nehru's role in the building up of the Congress party organization in a situation where the party was in power and had to remain in power by winning elections. From all that we know of this process, the role of a Caesarist leadership is vital; for, the delicate balancing of contending interests within the broad coalition of ruling forces requires a leader who is not identified with any specific group and yet has the charismatic power to reach the people directly. How far was Nehru this sort of a Caesarist leader? We have some clues in the correspondence which Gopal quotes. Nothing is more distasteful to Nehru than the business of selecting Congress candidates for the elections. That is where there is the most unbridled bickering and infighting among the various groups in the ruling party. But Nehru feels himself a complete outsider at these proceedings: 'I have felt recently as if I was in a den of wild animals.' (p. 161) When a whole spate of agitations break out in 1955–6 on the question of linguistic provinces, Nehru is at a complete loss to understand the reasons behind the trouble. 'This is a terrible job, and I do not see much light yet. Passions have been roused and old friends have fallen out.' He is hesitant, unsure of himself. He does not have a clear stand. As he stated:

I have been greatly distressed about the Bombay and Maharashtra matter and the fact that practically the entire people of Maharashtra feel almost unanimously and strongly on this subject, is rather an overwhelming one. Nobody can deny that there is a good deal of logic in what they say, although there is some logic for the other view too. Anyhow, we have landed ourselves in a position where we are doing something which intimately hurts the whole people of Maharashtra and their representatives. That is a bad position. (p. 269)

In all these squabbles about language, religion, caste, region, and such other parochial loyalties, Nehru is never a partisan; he is always the distant observer, quite alienated from all those concerns which to the rest of his colleagues in the party and to his countrymen are the very stuff of politics.

Yet it was not as though Nehru was not conscious of the need to gain organizational power within the party. He did not think of his own role as that of an outsider co-opted into the leadership. He worked with conscious deliberation towards acquiring a position of unchallenged personal authority in government as well as in the party. The most crucial episode here is that of Tandon's election to Congress presidentship and his subsequent resignation. Unfortunately, Gopal can see no more in this than Nehru's attempt to 'wage full war against all communal elements in the country'. (p. 155) The whole question of how Nehru succeeds in building, step by step, a complex and intricately balanced political structure so as to organize the power of the state within a political process of electoral democracy, is missed entirely.

There is a similar inability to see the crucial importance of socialist phrase-mongering in an ideology of populism which goes hand in hand with this kind of political structure and process. The questions of the electoral non-viability of an independent Socialist Party, and the appropriation of most parts of the Socialist platform by Nehru and his Congress, are reduced essentially to personal relations between Nehru and Jayaprakash Narayan (Jayaprakash was 'cross-grained, wolly-minded and exasperatingly self-righteous') (p. 66) or to the 'escapist mood' of the Socialists who 'had no positive alternative to offer and contented themselves by giving petty trouble on minor issues to the government'. (p. 68) No significance is attached to Nehru's persistent efforts to secure support for his programmes from the

Socialists, his employment of Kidwai for this purpose (p. 153), and his concern, despite all this, that the Socialists should maintain an independent organization outside the Congress. 'The resolution of the Congress in January 1955 to build a "socialistic pattern" of society,' Gopal himself notes, 'blurred differences between the Congress and left-wing parties. . . . Most Socialists felt there was now no basic reason why they should not return to the Congress fold, but Nehru dissuaded them. He claimed to have done so because of his belief that the Socialists still had a role to play as a responsible opposition party; but he was probably also influenced by the desire not to hurt Jayaprakash.' (p. 235) Rather a naive view of politics, this!

Take, again, the decision to retain the ICS cadres in the highest echelons of the bureaucratic machinery. This too was a vital decision in the construction of the new state apparatus under Nehru. It is the unbroken tradition of a colonial bureaucracy, originally built around intricate rules and procedures enshrining unfettered executive power, which provided in the governmental system of independent India an effective mechanism for country-wide control. It is above all the upper bureaucratic structure which protects, in a well-ordered, recurrent and continuous process, those sections of the ruling classes which have interests of an all-India character. Nehru took a conscious decision to retain the ICS. 'Before independence,' says Gopal, 'none had been severer than Nehru in criticism of these officials; but he did not, when the chance came, promptly retire them. Their retention was,' and this is Gopal's principal explanation, 'in a sense a concession to his basic generosity. . . . But perhaps also,' and this is a second, more contingent, explanation, 'in the pressure of post-partition events, there was no alternative to reliance on the Indian Civil Service if the administration was not to break down completely.' (p. 35) But Gopal does not stop here. The consequences of retaining the ICS were not entirely happy. These officers were 'conservative by training and temperament'; in course of time 'they gradually encroached on the making of policy'. But, of course, it was not Nehru who was at fault, because 'Nehru never, like Patel, became the unqualified champion of these officials . . . they were encouraged in this not only by Patel, who approved of their traditional attitudes, but also by Mountbatten, who though temperamentally close to Nehru, was in ideology akin to Patel'. It is true that the civil servants became increasingly powerful, despite Nehru. 'Nehru realized and regretted this; but he also recognized that there seemed little he could do about it. . . . It should have been easier to have changed the over-bureaucratized system of government at the time of the transfer of power, but the nature and context of that occasion had prevented it; and now the system, even though it lacked intrinsic strength, had succeeded in perpetuating itself.' (pp. 36–7)

Compromises

Substantial doubts also arise about the way Gopal has used secondary material to buttress his arguments at crucial points. Let me give just two instances which I have checked. On the question of Kashmir, Gopal is greatly concerned to show that what Nehru did had nothing to do with any romantic attachment he might have felt towards the land which his family had called home. As an argument, Gopal says that when the first request came from the Prime Minister of Kashmir for Indian troops, 'Nehru declined and was only persuaded by Patel and Abdullah to agree'. (p. 19) In support of this, Gopal cites M.C. Mahajan's account of this meeting in his memoirs.[3] Now, reading the relevant passage in Mahajan's book, one finds there were many more dimensions to the context in which this meeting took place than would warrant the rather straightforward conclusion that 'Nehru declined and was only persuaded by Patel and Abdullah to agree'. Mahajan, for instance, had only a few weeks earlier been appointed Prime Minister by the Maharaja of Kashmir with the clear intention of preventing Abdullah from staking a claim to that office. Nehru was always unenthusiastic about Mahajan's appointment because he wanted a popular government in Kashmir under Abdullah. It was at Patel's urging that Mahajan went to Kashmir.[4] Only the day before, Mahajan had rebuffed an emissary from the Pakistan government who was threatening him with dire consequences if Kashmir did not immediately join Pakistan, by telling him that such threats would 'throw the state

[3] M.C. Mahajan, *Looking Back* (Bombay: Asia Publishing House, 1963).
[4] Ibid., p. 127.

into the lap of India'.[5] The next day, Mahajan was in Delhi requesting Nehru for immediate military aid to save the town of Srinagar.

the Prime Minister said that even if the town was taken by the tribesmen, India was strong enough to retake it. Its recapture, however, could not have undone the damage that would have resulted. I, therefore, firmly but respectfully insisted on the acceptance of my request for immediate military aid. The Prime Minister observed that it was not easy on the spur of the moment to send troops as such an operation required considerable preparation and arrangement, and troops could not be moved without due deliberation merely on my demand. I was, however, adamant in my submission; the Prime Minister also was sticking to his own view. As a last resort I said, 'Give us the military force we need. Take the occasion and give whatever power you desire to the popular party. The army must fly to save Srinagar this evening or else I will go to Lahore and negotiate terms with Mr Jinnah.'

When I told the Prime Minister of India that I had orders to go to Pakistan in case immediate military aid was not given, he naturally became upset and in an angry tone said, 'Mahajan, go away.' I got up and was about to leave the room when Sardar Patel detained me by saying in my ear, 'Of course, Mahajan, you are not going to Pakistan.' Just then, a piece of paper was passed over to the Prime Minister. He read it and in a loud voice said, 'Sheikh Sahib also says the same thing.' It appeared that Sheikh Abdullah had been listening to all this talk while sitting in one of the bedrooms adjoining the drawing room where we were. He now strengthened my hands by telling the Prime Minister that military help must be sent immediately. This came as a timely help for the success of my mission to New Delhi. The Prime Minister's attitude changed on reading the slip.[6]

Take another instance. In course of describing Nehru's role in the making of the Constitution, Gopal says, 'Nehru had opposed the listing of the right to property among the fundamental rights, but had to give in.' (p. 79) He cites K.M. Munshi's description of this event.[7] Gopal then goes on to say:

From this arose the question of the right to compensation in case of

5 Ibid., p. 142.

6 Ibid., pp. 151– 2.

7 K.M. Munshi, *Indian Constitutional Documents, volume 1: Pilgrimage to Freedom (1902– 1950)* (Bombay: Bharatiya Vidya Bhavan, 1967), pp. 79–80.

expropriation of private property. . . . But Nehru, Pant and others who were eager to press forward with the abolition of the *zamindari* system wished to make it clear that it was for the legislature and not the courts to lay down the principles on which compensation should be paid. So Article 31 stipulated that the law must specify the compensation or the principles on which it should be paid. (pp. 79–80)

But in Munshi, the context is quite the opposite. The immediate context of discussion in the Advisory Committee was the issue of *zamindari* abolition. There was strong opposition to the draft clause on Fundamental Rights from 'the representatives from the U.P. and Bihar. . . . Govind Ballabh Pant, the Chief Minister of the U.P., led the attack on the right to property'. The issue was the question of fair compensation and who should decide what was fair. A large section, including Nehru, Pant and others, thought the legislatures should have unfettered discretion in this matter, while others, notably Munshi and T.T. Krishnamachari, argued for the right of property to be included in the Constitution so that the courts could act as final arbiter. As Munshi states:

Finally, the controversy came to a head at the Party meetings when the right to property (ultimately numbered Article 31) was being discussed. Jawaharlal Nehru thundered against its inclusion; he urged that in the history of man notions of property had changed from time to time; the right to property, therefore, should not be included as a Fundamental Right.

During the discussions, the final blow was struck in defence of the right to property by John Mathai, the then Finance Minister of the Union Government, who fought back vigorously. . . .

A compromise was ultimately effected. An amendment implementing the compromise formula was moved in the Assembly which stood in the name of Jawaharlal Nehru, Govind Ballabh Pant, Alladi Gopalaswamy Ayyangar and myself.

Clearly, then, the context was one of a generalized debate springing from the specific issue of *zamindari* abolition and payment of compensation, not an abstract philosophical position on the right to property giving rise to a specific debate. There were many others in the Congress leadership who shared Nehru's position on this matter all down the line. Yet, the subtle shift in context which occurs in the course of Gopal's use of this evidence produces the impression of a majestically lonely figure, wanting to stand firmly by his cherished principles of socialism, but forced by the pressure and machinations of those he must work with to compromise on each one of them.

The Unexamined Hero

This may seem like quibbling on minor matters, but it is not. It is closely related to the question of the difficulties of using the biographical method when writing 'contemporary history'. There is, for one thing, the matter of the historian's biases and prejudices, which can be intense as well as inconsistent when personalities from within one's own life-experience are involved. Gopal is particularly guilty on this score. His adulation of Nehru is frank. But his penchant for invective against those he does not like is equally unrestrained. We have already noted his remarks on Jayaprakash Narayan and Krishna Menon. Rajendra Prasad was a man 'of inferior intellectual quality and with a social outlook which belonged to the eighteenth century', (p. 77) Bidhan Roy was 'reactionary', (p. 72) but the choicest epithets are reserved for Nehru's special assistant, M.O. Mathai. In four long paragraphs towards the end of the book, Gopal lambasts Mathai, 'an illiterate upstart', 'disloyal, avaricious and opportunistic' who 'revived in Delhi the atmosphere of a decadent court'. (pp. 310–12)

But this matter of biases is not necessarily all that much of a shortcoming. In fact, there is much to be said in favour of the view that a good biography requires a sympathetic biographer, just as a good portrayal on stage or screen requires an actor who can empathize with the character he portrays. The important thing is to probe deeply into a personality, to search for those compelling inner motivations which keep a man going, to discover the logic and ideological consistencies of an active and imaginative mind, to see him in a certain social context, a context which moulds his life and personality, changes it with time, and which in turn is affected by his activities as a leader of society. One is not necessarily asking for a psycho-history, although some forays into the terrain of psychology are unavoidable for any biographer. In any case, the whole field of the working of the human mind, whether individual or collective, is still only vaguely charted by science, so that almost anything that an intelligent, sensitive and courageous writer — novelist, playright or biographer — may say on the subject is likely to be of some value.

The trouble with Professor Gopal as a biographer is that his courage seems to fail him whenever he comes up against the problematical or contradictory aspects of Nehru's personality. It is almost as though he is afraid of finding something unpleasant and so stops probing any further. Yet the contradictions in Nehru's personality are so fundamental and glaring that one cannot but ask: What kept the man going? Why didn't he chuck it all up? His disillusionment with what the Congress had become was acute.

If I chose according to my own inclination, I would like other people to carry on the business here and to be left free to do some other things that I consider very important. Yet with all modesty, I think that my leaving might well be in the nature of a disaster. No man is indispensable, but people do make a difference at a particular time. (p. 75)

This was not something Nehru wrote in a sudden fit of depression; quotes of this kind occur throughout Gopal's book.

I have an increasing feeling that such utility as I have had is lessening and I work more as an automaton in a routine way rather than as an active and living person. . . . Functioning in such a way ceases to have much meaning. Many of our policies, economic and other, leave a sense of grave uneasiness in me. I do not interfere partly because I am not wholly seized with the subject and partly because of myself being entangled in a web out of which it is difficult to emerge. . . .

I feel that if I have to be of any real use in the future, I must find my roots again. I do not think I can do so by continuing for much longer in my present routine of life. I am prepared to continue for a while, but not too long. I do not think that my days of useful work have ended, but I feel sure that my utility will grow less and less in existing circumstances. (pp. 158–9)

Yet he kept at it till the end of his life, 'putting in,' as Gopal testifies, 'a twenty-hour day with hardly even breakfast as a private meal.' (p. 309) What kept him going? An ideological commitment? A vision of the India of the future? Yet there is little to show that Nehru had clear ideas about what he wanted India to be in the years ahead. He wanted industrialization, modern technology, the building up of infrastructure on a massive scale. When the great river valley projects were inaugurated, Nehru wrote: ' . . . a sense of adventure seized me and I forgot for a while the many troubles that beset us.' (p. 35) Yet, four years later, 'a sight of the hovels in which the workers of Kanpur lived caused him such intense shame that he developed a sort of fever. "I have no need for any industrialization which degrades a human being and sullies his honour." ' (p. 199) Confusion? Or hypocrisy? Self-deception? He compromised repeatedly on his principles of socialism. When Jayaprakash pointed this out to him — 'You want to go towards socialism, but you want the capitalists to help in that. You want to build socialism with the help of capitalism. You are bound to fail in that' — his defence was: 'I cannot, by sheer force of circumstance, do everything that I would like to do. We are all of us in some measure prisoners of fate and circumstance.' (p. 67) The arrest and detention of Abdullah rankled in his conscience. He wrote to Abdullah: 'We, who are in charge of heavy responsibilities, have to deal with all kinds of forces at work and often they take their own shape. We see in the world today great statesmen, who imagine they are controlling the destinies of a nation, being pushed hither and thither by forces beyond their control.' (p. 303) Was there, underlying the moral conflicts, a compelling ruthlessness which pushed him repeatedly towards the decisive use of the instruments of power?

Professor Gopal unfortunately does not help us find an answer. In fact, the sad thing is that he seems to prefer not to know the answer.

The Last Years

For Nehru fans, the last five or six years of the hero's life clearly pose the greatest problems. In domestic politics, there was in those years a sudden resurgence of linguistic, regional and communal strife; the ruling party organization began to show signs of widespread corruption, ineptitude and factionalism; and of course there was the inglorious episode of the ouster of the communist ministry in Kerala. On the economic front, the heady enchantment of planning began to wear off and a massive crisis loomed on the horizon. Internationally, there was the inexplicable dithering on Goa, a growing resentment voiced by African countries over India's role in the Congo, isolation from her neighbours nearer home, prevarication over the very foundations of non-alignment, and above all the shattering experience of the China War. Clearly, the hero had lost his magic touch; he was old, tired, disillusioned, embittered, no longer in control of things. It is not an easy period for an admiring biographer to write about.

To be fair to Sarvepalli Gopal, he has faced up to the task with considerable courage.[8] He decided that he would criticize Nehru where criticism was due. He has also attempted a general stock-taking of the economic and political conditions in India at the end of the Nehru era, and has taken note of the many criticisms that have been made of Nehru's policies from positions entirely at variance with Nehru's own. And yet, it all ends up with a 'despite these drawbacks his achievements were substantial' kind of conclusion. The criticisms remain on the surface. They do not lead Gopal to ask questions about the very nature of the economy and polity in which a leader such as Nehru could flourish — and flounder — and whether that is necessarily the kind of economy and polity which the Indian people must have.

Besides this superficial readiness to be critical, Gopal's style remains much the same as in the two earlier volumes. The narrative is primarily built upon Nehru's correspondence and other official papers to which Gopal has had privileged access. For the main part, he proceeds by paraphrasing large chunks of Nehru's prose and recorded speech. This is not of very great advantage to him. There are long passages with sentences such as these:

Obviously every country should evolve its own policies to fit in with its own conditions, as the best of theoretical approaches might not fit with the objective situation . . . one should change with the times and not be the prisoner of phrases. Socialism for India was not just an emotional commitment or an ideological preference; it was the only scientific way of solving social problems, the pragmatic means of achieving quickly higher standards of living for all. . . . Such material progress could also be achieved without divorce from values if the

[8] Sarvepalli Gopal, *Jawaharlal Nehru: A Biography, volume 3, 1956–1964* (Delhi: Oxford University Press, 1984).

people absorbed the right ideals and acted up to them. India had thought a great deal about these values through hundreds and thousands of years and it would be a misfortune if she forgot them in the pursuit of material well-being. . . . (p. 116)

Such paragraphs go on and on, over and over again, endlessly. Whatever meaning these sentences may have carried in the 1950s has been washed away by years of Nehruvian didacticism; today it is frothy verbiage — long-winded, hollow and painfully boring.

To come to the main events, the one most easily disposed of is Goa. It has always been a mystery why Nehru took such an interminably long time to decide on what to do about the wholly anachronistic obduracy of Salazar's government on the subject of Goa. On cultural, political and moral grounds, India's case was as perfect as it could ever be. Nehru's hesitation was about the use of force, and not, as Gopal points out at several places, because of any basic moral qualm. Nehru was not, he asserts, a pacifist. (Rather, he was a 'pacificist', says Gopal on the basis of a quite trivial distinction picked up from a book review by the redoubtable A.J.P. Taylor — the argument is that Nehru was prepared to abandon peaceful methods 'in the last resort'.) (pp. 190–1) Specifically, Nehru was worried about what 'the friends of India' would say if she was to use force in liberating Goa. Which friends? Nobody in the colonial or post-colonial world, or in any of the socialist countries, was likely to raise an eyebrow. The friends Nehru was bothered about were in Britain, France and the United States, and Nehru 'boxed himself in' by preaching to them so often about the absolute sanctity of peaceful methods. After the Goa operation was finally over — with, as it turned out, virtually no bloodshed at all — these 'friends' came back at him with a vengeance, accusing him of hypocrisy and jingoism. Strangely enough, Gopal himself shows extraordinary sensitiveness towards these charges, and seems to suggest that it would have done Nehru's image a lot of good if he had been able somehow to avoid 'shocking' his friends in this manner. The agonies of the liberal soul are often beyond comprehension.

Kerala 1957–9

Kerala 1957–9 is a much trickier subject for Gopal to handle. He seems to concede in a roundabout sort of way that wrong was done. But there were, he argues, extenuating circumstances which justified Nehru's action. In the first place, the communists themselves were to blame by their hasty and dogmatic decisions which alienated a lot of powerful interests in Kerala. Gopal approvingly quotes Nehru's judgement that the 'bookishness' and 'extra-territorial loyalties' of the Indian communists made it difficult for them to 'fit into the Indian context'. (p. 53) (There is an element of the ridiculous in a Jawaharlal Nehru accusing E.M.S. Namboodiripad or A.K. Gopalan of failing to 'adapt themselves' to Indian conditions, but Gopal does not see this.) Second, the Congress in Kerala, and subsequently several important central leaders like Pant, Indira Gandhi and even Krishna Menon, were pushing Nehru to dismiss the communist ministry. The crucial swing in Nehru's thinking came in July 1958, following the execution of Imre Nagy in Hungary. Holidaying in Manali, he suddenly saw civilization as

mentally exhausted and unable to cope with the rapid pace of change in human life . . . Rationalism too seemed inadequate . . . Communism . . . ultimately failed partly because of its rigidity but even more because it ignored certain essential needs of human nature . . . India had to evolve her own peaceful approach . . . perhaps we might also keep in view the old Vedantic ideal of the life force which is the inner base of everything that exists. (pp. 61–2)

This flight into metaphysics acquired a somewhat macabre significance, because Nehru returned from Manali to deliver a virtual charge sheet on Namboodiripad. 'Against this Nehru,' Gopal writes, 'Namboodiripad had little chance.' (p. 62) Nehru had now ceased to listen, though the communist Chief Minister continued to plead with him until the day before his dismissal, expecting a 'non-partisan and rational approach'. In the end, Gopal's judgment is that

Nehru was driven into a decision by the communists who passed on the initiative to him so that they could appear as victims and by the Congress who looked for undeserved and undemocratic advantages from a contrived crisis. . . . It could be faulted in theory and could be interpreted as inspired by narrow party advantage; but it appeared to him to be required in the public interest. He finally arrived at a decision which he knew to be wrong for what he believed were the right reasons. (p. 73)

What were the implications of this decision for Indian politics? Gopal thinks that it tarnished Nehru's reputation with the Indian Left: 'This made it more difficult for him, in the penultimate stage of his career, to achieve the goals of his economic and social policies.' (p. 74) A dubious conclusion. On the contrary, what the experience of Kerala achieved — something that was subsequently confirmed by the experience of the two United Front governments in West Bengal in 1967 and 1969 — was to define within the Indian state system the limits of communist political activity. This was Nehru's political achievement on behalf of India's ruling classes. The communists' reading of this experience could conceivably have been quite different. The rulers had given them the rules of the game; they could have thrown them aside. As we know, however, the main part of the communist movement decided henceforth to play within the rules.

War with China

The boundary dispute and the war with China naturally take up the largest part of this volume. On this, the reader is placed in considerable difficulty. Gopal's account is almost entirely a reiteration of the official stand of the Nehru government (which is not surprising because Gopal himself played an important part in preparing the historical documentation on behalf of that government). Gopal's evidence on the history of the dispute, the course of negotiations, and the series of border clashes leading up to the war in October 1962 and the unilateral Chinese withdrawal in November are mainly based, apart from published accounts by various Indian generals, on Indian official sources to which the ordinary scholar has no access. It is therefore impossible to judge whether Gopal's construction of the case is fair. His main argument on the border dipute is that the Indian claim was based on the 'traditional' demarcation. He does not even consider the argument as to whether a government which had come to power after struggling against a colonial regime was right in attributing such overwhelming sanctity to a border clearly drawn up according to the strategic interests of an imperial power, in a virtually unpopulated area with no complicating ethnic or national questions. Gopal argues that while holding firmly to this 'traditional' claim, Nehru was prepared to negotiate, but the Chinese kept changing their demands. Once again, without access to the relevant documents, it is hard to judge whether Gopal is right.

Gopal's explanation for the war itself is, expectedly, Chinese ambition and perfidy. He quotes Nehru with approval in laying the blame squarely on China's 'tradition of expansionism and its conceit and faith in its mission of world domination by force and revolution'. Gopal even goes into an assessment of Mao's legacy to China:

A hard-headed nationalist, he was determined to regain for his country not only equality among nations but a prime position in Asia . . . the permanent legacy of Mao to his country has been not continuous social and economic upheaval but a powerful state and army. China has become, under Mao's inspiration, an ambitious nation and a skilled practitioner of realpolitik. . . . In this as in most other issues of world affairs demanding a long perspective, Nehru was among the clear-sighted statesmen of his time. (pp. 238–9)

Let us ignore the utter imbecility of this political judgement on Mao which would have done credit to Ronald Reagan's speech-writers. But 'China's traditional expansionism' strengthened by the resurgence of Chinese nationalism? Whose expansionism? Of the country? The nation? Its imperial rulers? Would it not be ridiculous to suggest, on the basis of Indian history for instance, that Uzbekistan or Afghanistan has a 'tradition of expansionism?'

What does emerge from Gopal's recounting of the events of 1961 and 1962 is a picture of utter confusion in the political handling of a military situation. It does not put Nehru in a very favourable light. Gopal explains this in terms of an 'incompatibility between character and role' (buttressed by a bizarre citation of a scholarly work on Shakespearean tragedy): 'Forced to lead his people in resistance to aggression, he did his best without enthusiasm and seeking always to secure India from the corruption of battle.' The much-discussed 'forward policy', (p. 227) for instance, was in Nehru's mind one of establishing patrols and posts as close to the border as possible, with intermediate and near bases to support the forward positions.

But in the orders issued by Army Headquarters in furtherance of

Nehru's decision, the stipulation about strong bases in the rear was omitted. No explanation for this lapse is available, though the later justification of General Thapar . . . suggests that the omission was deliberate . . . the decision to push ahead with patrols and posts without supporting bases clearly was a departure from Nehru's policy and apparently not known to him. (pp. 208–9)

Nehru, it seems, was content only to lay down broad policy.

However, the army commanders were unable to take the right decisions within the ambit of the broad policy laid down by the Prime Minister and to utilize properly the discretion which he had vested in them . . . the officers in local command produced a scheme for evicting the Chinese which, incredible as it sounds, was apparently a make-believe plan which was not intended to be taken seriously but on which Kaul seized as the appropriate tactics. (p. 220)

In fact, Gopal's account does not contradict the interpretation that the Chinese read these ham-handed military moves as signs of the aggressive intent of the Indian government. Whether Nehru is to be blamed for warmongering is not quite relevant; the fact that political control was lax enough to allow the 'considerable personal distrust' among the generals to get on top at such a critical moment points to a political failure, and the Prime Minister cannot be absolved of ultimate responsibility.

Request for US Aid

Gopal's account also produces one or two startling facts about Nehru's reaction to the crisis. After the fall of Bomdila on November 19, he wrote to Kennedy requesting the immediate despatch of American fighter squadrons manned by American personnel; but he did this on his own, without consulting his Cabinet, and when S.K. Patil asked him about this, Nehru blandly replied that no policy decision had been taken without reference to the Cabinet. Gopal's comment on this case, of a Prime Minister misleading his own Cabinet on a major question of foreign policy in the middle of a war, is a model of understatement: 'Clearly Nehru's memory was not at this time at its best.' (p. 228n) One also reads with astonishment about Nehru's correspondence with Mountbatten in January 1961 on whether a post of Chairman of Chiefs of Staff should be created, and the latter's suggestion that Thimayya would suit the job because he was 'one of the most outstanding generals that I have ever come across in any country'. (p. 132) The reason why Mountbatten's suggestion was rejected was not the obvious impropriety of a former Viceroy advising the Prime Minister of an independent republic about appointments in its army, but because Nehru at this time had developed a distrust of the officer corps as a whole and was apprehensive of a military coup!

Nehru's overtures to the United States in the wake of the China war clearly spelled doom for the much-vaunted policy of non-alignment. Gopal does a lot of hair-splitting about what the principles of non-alignment really mean: 'War has its own momentum, and non-alignment cannot be at the cost of national survival . . . ' and so on. As far as Nehru was concerned, he was much more forthright: there can be no non-alignment *vis-à-vis* China, he said. (p. 229) Ironically, it was the Chinese themselves who saved India's non-alignment from an inglorious death, by withdrawing unilaterally.

Economy and Polity

Gopal also spends some time discussing the economy and the policy of development. He agrees that 'after years of planning, development in India is associated as much with an overall increase in poverty, inequality and unemployment as with a steady growth. All the measures introduced by Nehru were found compatible with the maintenance of capitalist relations of production and the preservation of middle-class hegemony.' (pp. 295–6) But this is not how it was meant to happen. Nehru had visualized a private sector helping to increase the national wealth, but the public sector would expand and ultimately overwhelm private capitalism and establish a socialist society. 'A rich business class,' pronounces Gopal, 'nullified the intentions of the Government.' (p. 291) Is this not infantile? What did one expect the business class to do? Happily cooperate with a 'socialist' policy in order to dig its own grave?

Gopal also says a lot of things about Nehru's belated realization that something had to be done about agrarian reform. The scheme of village cooperatives and panchayati raj, says Gopal, was meant to be a revolutionary step — not a 'passive revolution' in Gramsci's sense, but 'an active, democratic revolution carried out by the masses themselves'. (p. 168) This is another instance of Gopal's inept use of theoretical concepts. Had he understood Gramsci's concept correctly, he would have identified Nehru's panchayati raj and village coperatives as a classic instrument of the passive revolution. In the end, Gopal would have us believe, the policy failed because of lack of support from the bureaucracy. If indeed it was an 'active' revolution launched by the people themselves, one wonders how the bureaucracy came to have anything to do with it.

In fact, as author of a major political biography such as this, Gopal's lack of any kind of systematic understanding of the nature of the Indian polity and its balancing processes is painfully obvious. On the significance of such a crucial event as the Kamaraj Plan, all Gopal does is quote Rajni Kothari's debatable proposition that in place of the Prime Minister's overarching authority, it gave more power to influential party bosses and weakened the central government. What Gopal has to add by way of his own comment is a flippant remark: the Kamaraj Plan had the effect of barring Morarji Desai from succeeding Nehru as Prime Minister, 'and who, having seen Desai in the office of Prime Minister many years later, can say that Nehru was wrong?' (p. 245)

In the end, Gopal continues to maintain an undiminished admiration for the personality of Nehru. He does not find it odd that someone who preached so much about the need to adapt to the real conditions of India, about being pragmatic and not dogmatic, should have felt so alienated in his intellectual make-up from the beliefs and practices of the people of his country. All his life, he never stopped complaining that the people were not behaving the way they should. When regional or communal riots broke out, he complained that people 'were forgetting major issues and getting excited over minor matters'. (p. 175) When the Nagpur resolution did not appear to rouse much enthusiasm about agrarian reform, he complained about 'the general sense of depression among our people'. (p. 117) When charges were made about corruption in high places, he complained about 'this kind of underground, over-ground and middle-ground propaganda of every type. . . . We are a gossipy people'. (p. 123) When caste and class differences appeared unlikely to vanish, he complained: 'What is wrong with us? We have no sense of equality?' (p. 280) During his momentous sojourn in Manali, he even thought the whole world was out of step with the kind of thinking that was required for the progress of human civilization. (p. 61)

Gopal finds in all this confirmation of the vast intellectual superiority of his hero:

... the Prime Minister was really looking far too ahead; and his images of maintaining and coordinating the rhythms of life between the individual and society and the past and the present and getting the Indian peasant in line with the rhythm of the modern world, all by means of the cooperatives, the panchayats and the schools, were well beyond the understanding, let alone the reach, of his officials and party men. (pp. 169–70)

He does not stop to consider the paradox of a 'pragmatic' leader, impatient of rigid theoretical schemes, always thinking 'far too ahead' of those who were meant to implement his policies, not to speak of those on whom they were to be implemented. Theoretically, Gopal tells us, Nehru shared a 'spirit of over-confident Benthamism'. (p. 280) Gopal admits that this showed a 'capacity for self-delusion,' even if not 'amounting almost to deliberate· self-deception.' Basically, we are told again, Nehru was 'in the line of William Morris;' his socialism, 'as that of the French socialists, Jaurès and Blum, was above all "a humanistic creed, placing its major emphasis on the fulfilment of the individual." ' (p. 285) Why this unprecedented amalgam of Benthamism, William Morris and French socialism should appear to anyone as being suited to Indian reality defies comprehension.

Finally, a minor point. Reviewing in his last chapter some of the arguments put forward by Nehru's critics, Gopal writes: 'The angry prejudice which insinuates that he was a hypocrite or no more than an ambitious politician does not merit serious treatment.' (p. 298) I read through the line and then the whole page until I discovered from the footnote at the bottom that Gopal was referring to a review I had written of the second volume of his book. I found it hard to believe that anything I had written on Nehru could be reduced to something as crass as this. I hunted up a reprint of the review and found that the offending lines were in the penultimate paragraph which ran as follows:

What kept him [Nehru] going? An ideological commitment? A vision of the India of the future? Yet there is little to show that Nehru had clear ideas about what he wanted India to be in the years ahead . . . Confusion? Or hypocrisy? Self-deception? He compromised repeatedly on his principle of socialism. When Jayaprakash pointed this out to him — 'You want to go towards socialism, but you want the capitalists to help in that. You want to build socialism with the help of capitalism. You are bound to fail in that' — his defence was: 'I cannot, by sheer force of circumstances, do everything that I would like to do. . . .' The arrest and detention of Abdullah rankled in the conscience . . . Was there, underlying the moral conflicts, a compelling ruthlessness which pushed him repeatedly towards the decisive use of the instruments of power?

That is what I wrote. Does this amount to an insinuation that 'he was a hypocrite or no more than an ambitious politician?' I do not have the temerity to question Professor Gopal's knowledge of the English language. Gopal has now conceded, in the final volume of his biography, Nehru's self-deception and the impossibility of building socialism with the help of capitalism. About the rest, what can one say except that Sarvepalli Gopal twists what he reads in order to suit his purpose, even to mislead?

Gopal's biography ends dramatically. Nehru, he announces, 'is India's once and — we may hope — future king.' (p. 302) No, Professor Gopal. The freedom of the Indian people lies in the steadfast rejection of all such pretenders to the throne.

3

Indian Democracy and Bourgeois Reaction*

There has been much talk in recent months about the rise of fascism in India. Some are arguing that the government, bent upon crushing the opposition movement by the use of 'semi-fascist' methods, is turning the country into a 'police state'. Others are claiming that it is not the government but various reactionary forces outside it that have launched a movement with a view to destroying democracy and installing a right-wing regime. All these discussions, however, seem to assume a notion of ideal bourgeois democracy at one extreme and of pure fascism at the other; the problem is seen to be one of judging how much Indian politics has moved away from the former and towards the latter. What is forgotten is that bourgeois reaction can take many different political forms. These forms depend upon the nature of the resistances which the bourgeoisie faces in its attempt to generalize its particular mode of production throughout society.

Consequently, before we decide how much we have deviated from the ideals of bourgeois democracy or what are the possibilities of fascism in India, we first need to have a clearer idea of the political resistances faced today by the Indian ruling classes. It is on the basis of their understanding of these resistances that the ruling classes will weigh the various economic strategies open to them. The specific choice of strategy, and the subsequent forms of political movement conducted by the opposition forces, will determine the kind of political regime the ruling classes will seek to impose.

In this essay, we will first present a brief description of the social conditions necessary for establishing bourgeois rule within

* This essay was written, jointly with Arup Mallik, three months before the declaration of internal Emergency in June 1975.

a democratic structure, i.e. the 'first way' of capitalist development. We will then discuss the historical possibilities of a 'second
way' of capitalism which dispenses with democracy.

Capitalism and Democracy

Three conditions are necessary for the 'pure' (or more precisely,
the English) way of capitalism. Following Adam Smith's classic
analysis, these can be enumerated as follows: (1) the abolition of
rent as the principal mode of surplus extraction from agriculture;
(2) small units of industrial production; and (3) a general preference for productive over unproductive labour. These conditions
make for a social dynamic leading towards an industrial revolution.

When a bourgeoisie generalizes its mode of production in
society, it establishes its leadership not only over the economy
but over all structures of society, including its ideological–cultural superstructure. Most notable here is the split between state
and civil society. Bourgeois social philosophy depicts the state as
an abstract and neutral arbiter situated above all social conflicts.
By doing this, the bourgeoisie can separate the sphere of production from the domain of the state, and can keep the state from
getting entangled in social conflicts emanating from the domain
of production. This is a major political significance of the doctrine of *laissez faire*.

Where the political state has achieved its full development, man leads
a double life, a heavenly and an earthly life, not only in thought or
consciousness but in *actuality*. In the *political community* he regards himself as a *communal being*; but in *civil society* he is active as a *private individual*,
treats other men as means, reduces himself to a means, and becomes
the plaything of alien powers. The political state is as spiritual in relation
to civil society as heaven is in relation to earth. . . . In the state where
he counts as a species-being . . . he is an imaginary member of an
imagined sovereignty, divested of his actual individual life and endowed
with an unactual universality.[1]

What is most significant about this process is not so much the
capture of state power, but rather the success of the bourgeoisie

[1] Karl Marx, 'On the Jewish Question', in Lloyd Easton and Kurt Guddat,
eds, *Writings of the Young Marx on Philosophy and Society* (Garden City, N.Y.:
Doubleday, 1967), pp. 225–6.

in diffusing its own world-view into the practices and beliefs of the overwhelming majority of the people. By abolishing the directly political character of civil society in feudalism, the bourgeoisie separates it from the state, and by achieving hegemony over civil society, legitimizes its political rule. The state, it can argue, is neutral; the state stands above all social conflicts. No single group or class has control over the state; even when particular governments come and go, the framework of the state remains unaltered.

By splitting man into public and private, and by granting public political rights to the individual as citizen, the bourgeoisie secures recognition of the private nature of the individual in civil society.

The state abolishes distinctions of *birth, rank, education* and *occupation* in its fashion when it declares them to be *non-political* distinctions, when it proclaims that every member of the community *equally* participates in popular sovereignty without regard to these distinctions, and when it deals with all elements of the actual life of the nation from the standpoint of the state. Nevertheless the state permits private property, education and occupation to *act* and manifest their *particular* nature as private property, education and occupation in their *own* ways. Far from overcoming these *factual* distinctions, the state exists only by presupposing them; it is aware of itself as a *political state* and makes its *universality* effective only in opposition to those elements.[2]

The bourgeoisie grants political liberty to all citizens, i.e. gives every citizen as a private individual the right to do anything which does not harm other private individuals. By granting this right of liberty, it secures the legitimation of the right of private property. By granting to each citizen the security of his person and property ('the supreme social concept of civil society, the concept of the police'), it guarantees the basic egoistic principle of bourgeois economy and law.

At the same time, the bourgeoisie, through various civil–social institutions — the family, the cultural associations, the communications media, and particularly the educational system which, in bourgeois society, becomes the most influential part of the ideological state apparatus — seeks to diffuse its own individualistic world-view over the rest of society; an individualistic world-view

2 Ibid., pp. 224–5.

which again seeks to de-emphasize cultural distinctions in the realm of political life. This ideological–cultural programme of bourgeois society is linked very closely with the process of universalization of the capitalist mode of production in first-way capitalism. For, this facilitates the creation, on the one hand, of a homogeneous consumer market with relatively similar tastes and cultural values; and on the other, of a free capital and labour market with relatively unrestricted movements of finance and population within the country. A uniform legal code and a gradually broadening education system through the medium of a common and popularly understood language creates the conditions for a relative cultural homogeneity among the peoples of the nation. Indeed, once these conditions are ensured and civil liberties are given universal recognition by the state, only to guarantee the continued existence of inequality and exploitation, the bourgeoisie can continue to grant political rights to the working class. It gives the working class the right to vote, and thereby legitimizes the false concept that by being able to express one's opinion as an individual one acquires a part of the popular sovereignty. It allows the workers the right to form unions, but the sway of the principles of egoism in civil society virtually ensures that these remain bogged down in the mire of economism.

It is worth noting that bourgeois democracy achieves its complete political form only *after* the bourgeois revolution, *after* the industrial revolution and *after* the conquest of social hegemony by the bourgeoisie. In the countries which were latecomers to capitalism, which were left behind in the race for overseas colonies, the conditions for 'normal', i.e. first-way capitalist development did not exist. In countries like Germany, the industrial bourgeoisie was weak as a social class, and it required an authoritarian state to take the initiative for capital accumulation and economic growth and thereby carry through the programme of industrialization. The state, by imposing protective tariffs, guaranteed the domestic market for German industrialists. The Prussian landlords emerged as capitalists in agriculture and the eviction of tenants from land supplied the industrial reserve army. With the expansion of productive capacity, the industrialists soon had to come up against a restricted domestic market; the solution to this problem was sought in increasing militarism and an aggressive foreign policy.

The second way of capitalist development thus requires from the start an absolutist, centralized and undemocratic state. The bourgeoisie there cannot afford to grant civil liberties — its programme of industrialization must be carried through with maximum speed and efficiency, involving a forced mobilization of resources imposed from above. Consequently, in second-way capitalism, because of the direct participation of the state in the system of production, the bourgeoisie is unable to achieve an effective separation between state and civil society.

We are now in a position to make two formulations for our subsequent discussion. In countries where the bourgeoisie is able to establish its hegemony in the classical form, it is possible for it to contain political opposition by using normal legal methods — such as, for instance, the police. Where the bourgeoisie does not exercise such hegemony, its authority can be so weak as to make it impossible for it to rule within the normal legal limits of coercive powers. In such cases, bourgeois reaction will take a different political form.

India: Economy and Polity

Before 1947, much of the industrial sector which existed around the metropolitan centres of India was dominated by foreign capital. However, particularly after World War I, indigenous Indian capitalism on a modern industrial scale developed significantly in engineering, textiles, cement, jute and paper. Nevertheless, this indigenous industry relied heavily on selling its products to government establishments and to foreign exporters and manufacturers. Even before independence, industrial capital in India tended to be highly monopolistic in character.[3] Apart from the bourgeoisie, urban life and politics in India were dominated by the upper petty bourgeoisie — successful professionals, Westernized, articulate. In their role as professionals, they had developed a range of interests that was all-India in scope: in this role, therefore, professionals from Bombay could associate with those from Calcutta or Madras or Allahabad in an all-India forum such as the Indian National Congress.

[3] On this, see Amiya Kumar Bagchi, *Private Investment in India, 1900–1939* (Cambridge: Cambridge University Press, 1972).

As far as the organization of agricultural production was concerned, this was where colonialism left its most crucial impact. Colonial revenue policies had the effect of forcing the peasant to produce cash crops; if he did not have adequate capital, or if his produce or its price was insufficient, he was forced to borrow. As a result, usury and speculative trading in cash crops became lucrative occupations for those who had any funds. One consequence was the rapid expansion in commercial crop production at the cost of food crop production.

The root of the problem of stagnation in Indian agriculture was lack of investment. With the introduction of commercialization in a labour-surplus economy with low levels of irrigation, it was decidedly more profitable for landlords to turn to rack-renting, usury and speculative trade than to invest in the improvement of the land or its output. Thus, while rent exploitation was extended over lands transferred from an immiserized peasantry, the landlords did not turn to intensive exploitation through capitalist farming. That remained the crux of the agrarian problem in colonial India.

The Legacy of the National Movement

The national movement as it developed during the first half of the present century was supported by the Indian business houses at the highest levels of the organizational structure of the movement. Clearly, the objective was to achieve an influence over the emerging national state-power in order to further expand and consolidate their monopolistic command over various sectors of domestic production and trading. However, as we have already mentioned, by the very nature of the commodities they produced, these industries were heavily dependent upon the foreign market and upon orders from the government at home. With the possible exception of textiles, which too were rapidly tending towards the manufacture of finer varieties, these monopolistic industries did not produce commodities of mass consumption. Their markets were consequently limited from the very beginning.

While the Indian industrial and commercial classes provided the bulk of the financial support to the national movement and sought to further their programmes through the Congress

organization, the personnel of the Congress came overwhelmingly from the urban middle classes. They usually manned the
various provincial Congress committees and many district committees as well, represented the Congress party in the provincial
legislatures, and were the acknowledged public leaders of the
party.

The mass organization of the Congress, however, brought
into the national movement much broader sections of the people.
From recent researches into the social bases of mass movements
led by the Congress,[4] it seems clear that these localized but
prolonged rural movements were invariably led by the upper and
middle strata of the *raiyat* peasantry. While the broader issues of
anti-imperialism and the Gandhian programme were always reiterated, it is also clear that what actually served to mobilize a
broad-based participation were local issues affecting the lot of
the common peasantry, issues that often had strong anti-landlord
or anti-moneylender overtones. In many cases, 'no-tax' campaigns of the Congress were pushed ahead towards a refusal to
pay rent to the *zamindar*. These local issues reflected clear, and
often quite specific, class demands, and thus succeeded in making
the Congress popular with large masses of the lower peasantry.

However, the notable feature of the organizational structure
of the national movement, especially that of the Congress, is
that it became differentiated into several levels. The leadership
at each territorial level — village, *thana* or *taluka,* subdivision,

[4] See, for instance, Hitesranjan Sanyal, ' Arāmbāger jātiyatābādī āndolan',
Anya Artha, 6 (September 1974) and 7 (November 1974); Hitesranjan Sanyal,
Bāṅkudā jelār jātiyatābādī āndolan', *Itihās*, 1975; Hitesranjan Sanyal, 'The
Sociopolitical Roots of Nationalism: A Case Study of Political Movements in
Eastern Medinipur', paper presented at the Indian History Congress, Chan-
digarh, 1973; Hitesranjan Sanyal and Barun De, 'Background of the 1942
Uprising in Eastern Medinipur', paper presented at the Indian History Con-
gress, Jadavpur, 1974; Gyanendra Pandey, 'A Rural Base for Congress: UP
1920–39', unpublished paper; Majid Hayat Siddiqi, 'Peasant Movements in
Western UP', paper presented at the Indian History Congress, Jadavpur, 1974.
[These researches, ongoing in early 1975, have since appeared as monographs
(in Hitesranjan Sanyal's case, posthumously): Hitesranjan Sanyal, *Svarājer
pathe* (Calcutta: Papyrus, 1995); Gyanendra Pandey, *The Ascendancy of the Congress in Uttar Pradesh, 1926–1934* (Delhi: Oxford University Press, 1978); Majid
Hayat Siddiqi, *Agrarian Unrest in North India: The United Provinces, 1918–1922*
(New Delhi: Vikas, 1978)].

district, province — enjoyed fairly large areas of relative autonomy, varying naturally with the strengths of the organization
at each level and locality, as also with the personalities involved.
However, this meant that while a broad-based mass support
could be achieved and maintained at the lower levels by means
of radical rhetoric and marginal concessions touching upon local
issues, the necessary political compromises could be made at
the higher levels of the political structure. There are numerous
instances again of the village and *taluka* Congress committees
carrying on vigorous propaganda against the local landlords or
moneylenders, while these same landlords and moneylenders
would make marginal concessions but still maintain a large
degree of political effectiveness by influencing the district or
provincial Congress committee. An appreciation of this differentiated and flexible structure of the Congress political organization is important for an understanding of how the later
ruling class alliance, based upon a major political compromise
and containing within itself several crucial contradictions, could
be forged and maintained for decades after independence.

Constraints on Indian Capitalist Development

Immediately after independence and during the framing of
the Constitution, the future ruling alliance was still in the
process of formation. The various constraints and social forces
to be reckoned with had still not clearly emerged. Domestic
capital, under the unquestioned domination of the big houses,
at this time made an effort to push forth its programme.
A crucial part of this programme was the integration of the
princely states with the Indian Union and the abolition of
zamindari. This programme was reflected quite clearly in Vallabhbhai Patel's speeches in the Constituent Assembly and in
his major political acts of the period.[5] Of course, the price
was the payment of compensation to landlords (which in fact
strengthened the concept of property in the legal institutions
of the country) and sizeable representation to princes and *zamindars* in the Constitutent Assembly. Nevertheless, an important

[5] On this point, see S.K. Chaube, *Constituent Assembly of India* (New Delhi:
People's Publishing House, 1973).

step towards clearing the ground for capitalist development was accomplished.

It was largely this programme which was pursued in the First Five-Year Plan. The First Plan was extremely modest in scope. It soon became apparent that any rapid capitalist development towards an independent industrial revolution was structurally impossible. The basic problem was one of increasing capital accumulation. None of the basic conditions for 'normal' capitalist development along English lines existed in post-colonial India. Theoretically, of course, there was a possibility of Indian capital using its newly gained control over the state apparatus to erect protective barriers against foreign competition, and then mopping up the surpluses from the agricultural sector to promote capitalist development along the 'second' way.[6] However, given the specific historical conditions, the second way was closed.

For one thing, capitalism in agriculture, even if it could be promoted over large areas of the country through government support policies, was unlikely to solve the marketable surplus problem in a land-scarce, labour-surplus economy like India's.[7] Further, the big bourgeoisie in India is not exactly comparable to its German counterpart. Though German industry developed under tariff protection, its ultimate aim was to compete with English and French industry in the international market: further ideological motivation was provided by the frenzy of *Weltpolitik*. This element of competition was the main stimulus for technical advancement. Coming in the post-colonial era when the historical gap between the developed and the underdeveloped world is enormous, Indian capitalists have neither the aspiration nor the ability to compete independently in the international market. On the contrary, they operate by borrowing obsolete foreign technology in the protected domestic market. Competition in the export market for sophisticated manufactured goods only takes them into further dependence on foreign technology. Even offical reports admit that Indian firms with foreign technical collaboration spend very little on research

[6] The theoretical conditions are outlined in Karl Marx, *Capital*, vol. 3, ch 20.

[7] Amiya Kumar Bagchi, 'Notes Towards a Theory of Underdevelopment: In Memoriam Michal Kalecki', *Economic and Political Weekly*, 6, 3–5 (January 1971).

and development activities with a view to future technological independence.[8]

These points of difference are crucial in understanding the different evolution of state capitalism and the associated political forms in the two situations. What was most important was that the new political structure of independent India was overtly based upon the principles of liberal bourgeois democracy, with unrestricted party competition at the elections, and universal adult suffrage. The consensus on these basic constitutional issues had been created in the minds of the nationalist leadership almost from the very beginning of the movement, and reflected the profound, though often purely formal, liberal ideology of the colonial upper petty bourgeoisie from which the leading personnel of the Congress party was drawn. The very form of the national struggle, with a very strong legal constitutional bias, made it virtually inevitable that a formal structure of electoral democracy be created under the new Constitution. In the absence of the necessary social bases, of course, the Constitution could never attain a true liberal democratic content. From the very start, therefore, the Indian bourgeoisie was faced with a challenge which no bourgeoisie in the world has ever tackled successfully: to make an industrial revolution under capitalism within a political structure of electoral democracy and universal adult suffrage.

As a consequence, any programme of rapid capitalist development with active intervention by the state presupposed the continued dominance of the bourgeoisie within the structure of state power, in a system which required periodic general elections. For this, an alliance with other powerful social forces was inevitable. The most crucial element in the coalition became the rural gentry, possessing varying amounts of landed property and wielding varying degrees of local political influence. The highly differentiated and flexible political organization of the Congress, developed during the period of the national movement, was now streamlined into an efficient vote-getting machinery. Again a measure of autonomy was granted to the leadership at each level of the Congress organization, and a tendency towards the maintenance of the status quo was thereby built into the structure of

---

[8] *Reserve Bank of India Bulletin* (June 1974).

the party. Given the socio-economic formation in post-colonial India, politics made it inevitable that only a class coalition would rule and that the interests of none of the constituents of this coalition would be seriously disturbed.

Nehru, Populism and State Capitalism

To appeal to the voters, however, it was clearly unwise for the Congress party to appear publicly as a party of the status quo; for it was evident that, to the overwhelming majority of the population, the status quo was intolerable. For an acceptable popular image, it was necessary for the ruling party and the government to appear to be responsive to the general popular desire for change, and not to appear to be too closely identified with any of the forces of exploitation in society. This was necessary not only to present a populist image to the mass of the peasantry, but also to pre-empt those issues on which the more organized opposition forces, that is to say, the working class and the lower petty bourgeoisie, could agitate.

It was Nehru who accomplished this facelift for the party. Patel's death perhaps facilitated the process, but Nehru assumed virtually dictatorial powers on all important policy matters within the government, and himself took over the office of Congress Presidentship by removing Purushottam Das Tandon. In economic policy, the Second Plan called for an ambitious programme of economic development through a strategy of partial state capitalism, and politically, slogans of 'socialism' were voiced with increased frequency and fervour. Nehru's image was suited to this populist role, wielding as he did enormous executive powers, yet appearing to stand above the mundane battle of classes to intervene decisively in favour of the weak and the oppressed.

Nehru's emergence at the helm of the government and the Congress party at this juncture was, in fact, an example of the classic phenomenon of Caesarism.

Caesarism can be said to express a situation in which the forces in conflict balance each other in a catastrophic manner; that is to say, they balance each other in such a way that a continuation of the conflict can only terminate in their reciprocal destruction. When the progressive force A struggles with the reactionary force B, not only may A defeat B or B defeat A, but it may happen that neither A nor B defeats the other — that they bleed each other mutually and then a third force C intervenes from outside, subjugating what is left of both A and B.[9]

In other words, the situation is one where neither of the principal contending forces is able to decisively clinch the issue in its favour. In such conditions, it is possible for a third force, or a great 'heroic' personality, professing to be independent of the main contenders, to emerge and take charge of the situation as a neutral party.

As in all such compromises, Nehru's assumption of the role of Caesar had mixed virtues. The Indian bourgeoisie was itself clearly in no position to assume complete control over state power. By the very nature of the existing structure of economic and political power, it was forced to accept a compromise. The legacy of the national movement dictated that the majority of the petty bourgeoisie be kept in the alliance. This meant an increased reliance on state capitalism in the programme for economic growth, an expansion of the governmental apparatus and continuance of formal liberal democracy. Insofar as the bourgeoisie was required by the circumstances to accept this compromise, it constituted (as it does in all Caesarist compromises) a progressive potential to be utilized by the progressive forces in this continuing war of position. On the other hand, the political process itself made the rural gentry a crucial element in the ruling party's electoral strategy, and this was clearly the element of restoration in the compromise. At the same time, the existence of universal franchise afforded some protection, however fragile, to peasant proprietorship; and in a land-scarce, labour-surplus economy, this constituted a progressive potential for resisting the pauperization of small peasants that would inevitably come in the wake of capitalism in agriculture.[10] Of course, the realization of this progressive potential in Nehru's populism depended entirely on a rational resolution of the agrarian question. Finally, the very

[9] Antonio Gramsci, *Selections from the Prison Notebooks*, tr. Quintin Hoare and Geoffrey Nowell-Smith (New York: International Publishers, 1971), p. 220.

[10] See in this connection, Lenin's evaluation of Sun Yat-sen's programme: V.I. Lenin, 'Democracy and Narodism in China', *Selected Works*, vol. 4 (London: Lawrence and Wishart, 1943), pp. 305–11.

strategy of state capitalism, coming up against the resource problem, made external assistance inevitable, thereby strengthening neocolonial interference in the economy.

The Second Plan emphasized the development of heavy industry. The linkage effects of the public investment programme were likely to create opportunities for the big capitalists. Besides, the growth of the public sector and the imposition of government controls expanded considerably the channels of profits from circulation. To the middle class, the Plan opened up new opportunities in areas of administration, education and white-collar employment. The landed gentry knew that the land reforms would not pose any serious threat to them: having retained or acquired considerable political power at the local level, they were sure to scuttle even the modest land reforms which were undertaken. Besides, the Plan also had a mass appeal in creating the impression that, by emphasizing the development of heavy industries first, India was following the socialist path of economic development.

In actual fact, of course, the policy followed with respect to the private sector was hardly unfavourable to it. In order to boost private investment, a multitude of credit institutions were opened to offer loans to the private sector at low rates of interest. This effectively helped in strengthening the grip of big business or monopoly houses over the economy. Their assets increased much faster than the growth in national income, while their own savings increased at a much slower rate. Needless to say, the development of monopoly or oligopoly capital is hardly consistent with socialism; there was not even a valid growth argument. The oligopolistic sellers increase their profit margins by charging a higher price in relation to cost of production. With investment of profits, however, the industry soon comes up against the constraint of the overall growth rate of the market. Indeed, it can be shown that oligopoly slows down the growth of the economy. This factor is, in fact, the most important in explaining the stagnation problem in mature capitalism.[11] The Indian government, by encouraging monopoly, brought into an economy at an early stage of capitalist development the problems of mature capitalism.

[11] Josef Steindl, *Maturity and Stagnation in American Capitalism* (New York: Monthly Review Press, 1978).

As the Plan progressed, the economy came up against bottlenecks which, in technical terms, are summed up under three heads: the savings gap, the foreign exchange gap and the food gap. The institutional factors behind these so-called gaps are now well known.[12] The main component of the economy's savings is government savings, for the fate of the private sector depends on the public investment programme. The amount of government investment depends on the sustainability of the drive to raise larger fiscal revenues and the proportion of capital formation expenditure in the government budget. The government cannot impose any tax on the rural gentry; it cannot introduce tax reform measures to plug the various loopholes through which the tax burden in evaded by the urban propertied classes.[13] The only instrument available to the government is a system of indirect taxes. On the expenditure side, the government cannot but continue high-level defence expenditure and a top-heavy education expenditure. The basic point, again, was that the progressive potential of public expenditure depended entirely on a corresponding broad-based expansion of the home market. Failing this, domestic industry was bound to retain its character of luxury commodity production for an extremely narrow market; even a prolonged period of public investment was not likely to change this 'enclaved' character of industrial production. But then a large-scale expansion of the home market could only follow a rational solution to the agrarian problem, and this the government could not attempt.

The argument that the public investment programme is at the root of the foreign exchange problem is not wholly correct. In

[12] A.K. Bagchi, 'Long-term Constraints on India's Industrial Growth, 1951–68', in E.A.G. Robinson and Michael Kidron, eds, *Economic Development and South Asia* (London: Macmillan, 1970), pp. 170–92; A.K. Bagchi, 'Aid Models and Inflows of Foreign Aid', *Economic and Political Weekly*, 5, 3–5 (January 1970); N.K. Chandra, 'Western Imperialism and India Today', *Economic and Political Weekly*, 8, 4–6 (February 1973); Ranjit Sau, *India's Economic Development: Constraints and Problems* (Madras: Orient Longman, 1974); Prabhat Patnaik, 'On the Political Economy of Underdevelopment', *Economic and Political Weekly*, 8, 4–6 (February 1973); Prabhat Patnaik, 'Imperialism and the Growth of Indian Capitalism', in Roger Owen and Bob Sutcliffe, eds, *Studies in the Theory of Imperialism* (London: Longman, 1972), pp. 210–29.

[13] Nicholas Kaldor, *Indian Tax Reform: Report of a Survey* (New Delhi: Ministry of Finance, Government of India, 1956).

India, the import intensity of consumption is high enough to cover 40 per cent of total imports.[14] Almost 40 per cent of these industrial consumption goods are consumed by the top 10 per cent of the rural and urban population. Most of this urban population is employed as unproductive labour. In line with the old colonial pattern, the rate of employment in the tertiary sector has been much greater than the rate of factory employment in independent India.

The problem of the food gap can be analysed from the supply as well as the demand side. The elimination of a few big *zamindars* did not mean that the rentier class and the semi-feudal mode vanished from rural India. In some of the areas previously under the Permanent Settlement, like West Bengal, even recent surveys reveal the proportion of sharecroppers in the agricultural labour force to be as high as 30 per cent.[15] In fact, as has been argued earlier, even capitalism in agriculture cannot be a solution in a land-scarce, labour-surplus economy. A possible solution might be to build up a broad base of small and middle peasants together with a public distribution scheme for the supply of agricultural inputs and the procurement of the output. But that obviously hurts the interest of the landed gentry, one of the chief components of the ruling coalition.

The food problem was aggravated by factors on the demand front also. In the period 1951–67, if everyone could be kept on a minimum nutritional requirement, India needed to import 20 million tons of foodgrain, whereas the actual imports were 60 million tons.[16] Here too, unproductive consumption played the crucial role.

In a framework of partial state capitalism, the real problems were: (1) how to solve the agrarian question in a land-scarce economy without hurting the landed gentry; (2) how to sustain accumulation and technical dynamism through the monopoly houses without ever hoping to become competitive in the international market; and (3) how to contain unproductive labour and provide for the urban middle classes at the same time.

[14] Bharat R. Hazàri, *The Structure of the Indian Economy: An Analysis* (Delhi: Macmillan, 1980), ch. 3, pp. 27–50.

[15] N. Banerjee, '*Bargadars* and Institutional Finance', Directorate of Land Records and Survey, Government of West Bengal, 1973.

[16] Chandra, 'Western Imperialism and India Today'.

The problems were beyond solution. Given the configuration of social forces and the relations between them, it was a foregone conclusion that a strategy of partial state capitalism which shied away from disturbing the existing political-economic structure was not going to produce a decisive breakthrough.

The weakness of state capitalism lay in the fact that the nature of the state, while apparently giving it enormous strength, made it fundamentally weak. While on the one hand it had to maintain the balance of the class coalition (by effectively curbing any constituent group that became too strong), and to make periodic concessions to the exploited, on the other hand it could not change the position of any constituent group too strongly, for that would affect the collective strength of the coalition. . . . The limits of state action were sharply drawn and any radical structural reform was ruled out.[17]

In the absence of radical structural reform, the Indian state did not possess the strength to mobilize sufficient resources internally. External aid, consequently, became inevitable for the development of state capitalism. The amount of aid nearly doubled in the Third Plan compared to the Second. Western aid, including aid from the World Bank, was sought and received in infrastructural projects, particularly fertilizers and seeds, and in the form of shipments of American agricultural surpluses, mainly wheat. At the same time, aid from the Soviet Union and the Eastern European countries also increased considerably. The high point of Western aid was reached around 1966 when virtually the entire IMF policy package to aid-receiving countries had to be accepted by India: the rupee was devalued in the hope of greater exports, imports were liberalized, agriculture was to be developed through the market mechanism, and for all practical purposes the five-year plan was suspended.

On the other hand, foreign private capital in the Indian economy increased phenomenally after independence — sixfold, from Rs 2,644 million in 1948 to Rs 15,428 million in 1968. Further, imperialist penetration of the Indian economy also increased in another form — foreign collaboration with Indian industries, which reached a peak in the early and mid-1960s, declined in 1968 and 1969 because of the recessionary situation, but shot up again after 1970.[18]

---

[17] Patnaik, 'Imperialism and the Growth of Indian Capitalism'.
[18] Chandra, 'Western Imperialism and India Today'.

The Restoration of Caesarism

Industrialization within a framework of partial state capitalism reached a virtual dead end by the second half of the 1960s. At the same time, the election reverses suffered by the Congress party in 1967 landed the ruling classes in a political crisis as well. The reverses were caused not so much by an actual fall in Congress votes, but rather by a series of effective electoral alliances between opposition parties. However, the Congress machinery had taken a highly oligarchic form in most states, and had become quite openly linked with its financiers and supporters among the business and landowning groups. On the other hand, in states like West Bengal, the ruling circles faced a more organic challenge in the form of the increased strength of the organized working class.

The Congress split of 1969 and the reorganization of the party machinery under Indira Gandhi represented a Caesarist restoration. In common with Nehruvian Caesarism, the tempo of socialist rhetoric was increased, and certain economic steps were taken to highlight the claim of a 'leftward' swing in official policy. The failure of the rightist policies of the mid-1960s, leading to the colossal dependence on Western aid even on the food front, reduced the dominance of the big bourgeoisie within the ruling alliance. This facilitated the apparent leftward swing, both in domestic policy and in international alignments involved in the new equilibrium.

However, the restoration also brought into the party certain new, and hitherto untapped, sources of support. As Gramsci has noted about modern Caesarist phenomena, they often 'shatter stifling and ossified state structures in the dominant camp as well, and introduce into national life and social activity a different and more numerous personnel'.[19] Particularly in those states where the bourgeoisie faced a more organic crisis of authority, the ruling party consciously sought to create activist cadres from among unemployed petty bourgeois youth and the backward sections of the working class. These were precisely the sections which, supported by the ample financial resources of the ruling party and unencumbered by fixed hours of work, could make use of illegal

[19] Gramsci, *Prison Notebooks*, p. 223.

means to strike at the cadres of the organized opposition, while the state itself could maintain its facade of legality. This is a feature peculiar to modern Caesarism.

In the period up to Napoleon III, the regular military forces or soldiers of the line were a decisive element in the advent of Caesarism and this came about through precise *coups d'état*, through military actions, etc. In the modern world, trade-union and political forces, with the limitless financial means which may be at the disposal of small groups of citizens, complicate the problem. The functionaries of the parties and economic unions can be corrupted or terrorised without any need for military action in the grand style — of the Caesar or 18 Brumaire type.[20]

This method of reactionary political warfare is unavoidable for a weak bourgeoisie operating within a fundamentally weak state structure. When the ruling classes lack legitimate authority in crucial sectors of society (as must be the case with a non-hegemonic bourgeoisie), the indiscriminate use of state power, i.e. the police or the military, can only erode its authority still further. The use of police methods must be selective, but where used, ruthless and decisive. Specifically, they are used to create divisions within the organized opposition and thereby to maintain their combined weakness.

. . . a social form 'always' has marginal possibilities for further development and organizational improvement, and in particular can count on the relative weakness of the rival progressive force as a result of its specific character and way of life. It is necessary for the dominant social form to preserve this weakness: that is why it has been asserted that modern Caesarism is more a police than a military system.[21]

If one compares the economic consequences of the present phase of Caesarism in India with the previous phase, certain differences are apparent. Agricultural production in the decade of the 1950s had increased mainly by bringing new lands under cultivation and through some improvements in irrigation. It is true that there were no significant efforts to mobilize the owner peasantry for cooperative ventures to increase production. Yet, it is also true that the destructive effects of the encroachment of capitalism in agriculture were to some extent resisted. Capitalism

---

[20] Ibid., p. 220.
[21] Ibid., p. 222.

of a sort made rapid inroads into Indian agriculture from around 1966 under the banner of the 'green revolution'. In spite of this much-heralded 'breakthrough', it turns out that per capita production of foodgrains grew at a slower rate in the 1960s than in the 1950s.[22] And whatever growth did occur was for a limited period (the output having reached a plateau in the years 1972–4 in Punjab and Haryana), in specific regions and among owners of large holdings. As a result, a major part of the marketable surplus of foodgrains in the country is now controlled by a few persons in a limited region of the country. Indeed, a convincing argument can be made that it is the uneven development of capitalism in agriculture, together with the government procurement policy, which is at the root of the chronic inflationary situation in India.[23]

Even without going into a complicated argument about the economics of the matter, it is quite obvious that following the 'green revolution', the political power of large landholders in certain states of India has increased phenomenally. It is the Punjab or the Haryana legislature that today witnesses the most stormy debates on land ceilings or the procurement price of foodgrains. The proportion of agriculturist members of the Congress party in Parliament has also increased significantly, from 18.2 per cent in 1952 to 27.2 per cent in 1962, 36.8 per cent in 1967 and 41 per cent in 1971. Correspondingly, the proportion of agriculturists among all Members of Parliament moved from 22.4 per cent in 1952 to 31.1 per cent in 1967.[24] The Indian capitalist class has always found it difficult to launch a serious attack on powerful landed interests in India. After the 'green revolution', it has become evident that Indian capitalism would have to find room for growth without any major shake-up of the agrarian system.

The final contrast with the earlier phase of Caesarism is that planned development through state capitalism has been virtually

[22] Ashok Mitra, 'Population and Foodgrain Output in India: A Note on Disparate Growth Rates', in Robinson and Kidron, *Economic Development*, pp. 21–8.

[23] See Prabhat Patnaik, 'Current Inflation in India', *Social Scientist*, 30–31 (1975).

[24] From figures compiled by Hung-chao Tai, *Land Reform and Policies: A Comparative Analysis* (Berkeley: University of California Press, 1974), p. 95.

abandoned since 1966. Yet state expenditure has not diminished. Official figures show that the overall expenditure on education and general administration has increased at a much faster rate than the 71 per cent increase in prices between 1960–1 and 1969–70.[25] Even in the private sector, salaries have risen much faster than wages. It is by this method of increasing the share of unproductive labour in both the private and public sectors that employment has been created. Again, by raising the purchasing power of a small number of people, a market has been created for industrial goods.

This phenomenon of 'institutionalized waste' is not new to the Indian economy. It is a continuation of the economic structure under colonialism, and was persisted with under the First and Second Five-Year Plans as well. It is not surprising then that, by taking advantage of this expansion in the unproductive waste sector, there was growth of industrial luxury goods in the 1960s. The trend has continued through the 1960s, as is shown by the fact that whereas the share of the agricultural sector in the aggregate national income declined between 1960–1 and 1971–2 from 51 per cent to 47.8 per cent, that of industry showed virtually no change at all (from 20.1 per cent to 20.8 per cent), whereas the share of trade and commerce went up from 14 per cent to 16 per cent and that of the tertiary sector from 14.9 per cent to 17.8 per cent.[26]

Ever since the scuttling of the Plans, therefore, it is the margin of institutionalized waste that has created the market for industrial goods in India. The viability of this 'enclaved' market was always very precarious: a sudden rise in food prices, for instance, could shatter it. Indeed, the constraint on domestic industrial growth is so severe that in the last few years we have seen the strange spectacle of an industrially underdeveloped and capital-poor country like India exporting steel and heavy engineering products. A new channel for industrial products is now being sought through exports, with active state suppport. In 1960–1, government expenditure on exports was nil; in 1965 it was Rs 198 million and in 1970 Rs 420 million. But the strategy

25 Reserve Bank of India, *Report on Currency and Finance, 1970–71.*

26 Central Statistical Organization, Government of India, *Estimates of National Product, Savings and Capital Formation, 1972–73.*

is fraught with the grave danger of substantially increased dependence on foreign technology.

Our comparison between the two phases of Caesarism in post-colonial India thus points to three significant features. First, the internal organization and style of the ruling party has changed. Second, after the 'green revolution', the Indian bourgeoisie now has to seek ways of continued accumulation only after making major concessions to the newly empowered group of large landowners. Third, with the abandonment of planned industrialization, increasing the margins of institutionalized waste has become the pre-eminent instrument for maintaining a home market for industrial manufactures.

Bourgeois Reaction and Indian Politics

Let us recapitulate. Only the first or classical way of capitalist development organically engenders a liberal democracy. The second way of capitalist development tends strongly to go against democracy. The problems of the second way ultimately led in Europe to the rise of fascism. The politics which in India wears the cloak of liberal democracy can be called Caesarism, which has passed through two distinct phases. The question now is: what are the similarities and differences between Caesarism and fascism?

The analysis presented by the Communist International in 1928 pointed out the following general features of fascism:

1. Fascism constructs an economic basis for the organizational unity of large capitalists, rural exploiters and the urban petty bourgeoisie.
2. Fascism rapidly adopts a foreign policy of militarism and imperialist aggression.
3. Taking advantage of the weaknesses of social democracy, fascism mobilizes an organized force of cadres from the urban petty bourgeoisie and the backward sections of the working class.
4. In the stage of seizure of power, fascism adopts populist slogans against capitalism, but soon after it captures power, it comes under the sway of big capital.
5. In place of liberal democracy, fascism establishes a structure of direct authoritarian rule.[27]

[27] Cited in Rajani Palme Dutt, *Fascism and Social Revolution* (Calcutta: National Book Agency, 1977, second Indian edition). There are many debates about this Comintern document on fascism and the strategies of antifascist

We have shown that in the second phase of Caesarism in India, a foundation has been laid for the alliance of monopoly capital, large landowners, the petty bourgeoisie and foreign capital. We have also pointed out that this second Caesarism achieved power by the use of anti-capitalist slogans and has changed the organization and style of functioning of the ruling party in order to deal more effectively with opposition forces. It is true, of course, that the Indian state is not militaristic in the same way that fascist powers in Europe were militaristic. But in the present state of international politics, there are only limited opportunities for the rulers of a country such as India to flex their muscles; those limited opportunities are, however, eagerly seized. Heavily militarized fascist regimes in Europe created, through the rapid expansion of a war economy, domestic markets for industrial manufactures. We have shown that in India under its second Caesarist regime, it is government expediture on unproductive labour that has become the chief instrument for maintaining a domestic market for industrial goods.

The only feature where Caesarism in India is sharply different from fascism in Europe is in the absence of direct authoritarian rule. All of our discussions today about a 'right-wing coup' or 'the rise of fascism' really hinge upon this one question: will electoral democracy survive in India? It should be clear from our above discussion that as far as the present ruling classes in India are concerned, it is not desirable for them, for structural reasons, to abandon electoral democracy. First of all, a complex but flexible political structure is highly suitable for maintaining the internal balance in the ruling class coalition and for creating an economy of institutionalized waste. Second, in the current state of world politics, it is advantageous for a Third-World country seeking various forms of international aid to project a democratic facade. Consequently, when official circles send out repeated warnings about the dangers of a 'right-wing coup' and when left-wing supporters of the government faithfully translate those

---

struggle. Trotskyists in particular reject this analysis as entirely mistaken. It would not be pertinent here to enter into a discussion on the merits of the Trotskyist analysis of fascism. We find ourselves largely in agreement with these general statements made in the 1928 Comintern document on European fascism. We are not making any claims regarding the acceptability of every resolution in that document.

warnings into complex theoretical analyses, one has reasons to suspect that a fictional spectre is being conjured up to hide the reactionary character of the present regime.

It seems obvious that until such time that opposition forces in India can hold out the threat of electorally defeating the ruling party at the centre, there will be no real pressure to completely jettison the structure of electoral democracy. If there are minor fears of losing elections, it is possible for the ruling powers to manipulate the electoral system in order to produce the desired result, as has been demonstrated several times in many parts of India, most recently in West Bengal in 1972. On the other hand, if there is a major electoral challenge, and if electoral democracy is indeed thrown aside, then the progressive forces can hardly meet that crisis solely by electoral means. Only an organized form of the revolutionary unity of the oppressed classes can resist that form of bourgeois reaction. In an underdeveloped, populous Asian country, such unity can only be built around the alliance of the working class and the peasantry. If the working class movement does not consciously seek unity with the peasantry, if it restricts itself merely to battles for increasing the salaries of the urban petty bourgeoisie, then the ruling classes will either use that movement to its own advantage within the present forms of politics, or crush it by unleashing its repressive forces — legal as well as illegal, both from within and from outside the state.

4

Nineteen Seventy-Seven

Economy and Polity: Structural Conditions

In a paper presented at the last session of this Conference[1], I had attempted to delineate what appeared to me the basic structural features of the Indian polity and its mechanisms for maintaining the stability of the system. I had pointed out that India's political economy, as it had emerged after two hundred years of direct colonial rule, was such that no single class in Indian society possessed the strength to rule the country on its own. Although industrial capitalism had grown, it was restricted to sectors of the economy which were dependent either upon the export market or upon the extremely narrow luxury consumption sector at home. Besides, in its ownership pattern, Indian industry already exhibited many of the features of monopoly and stagnation characteristic of capitalist economies at much higher stages of development. The horizons of capitalistic development in industry were severely restricted by the widespread prevalence of pre-capitalist forms of production and exploitation in the agricultural sector. The processes of surplus appropriation in agriculture under colonialism almost inevitably created and fostered semi-feudal relations of production and exploitation. In terms of the whole economy, this created a situation where, in spite of the introduction of commercialization, the agricultural sector remained essentially stagnant. This made it impossible to develop a growing home market on the basis of which domestic industry could break out of its ties of dependence with foreign capital and launch the economy on a path of independent capitalist development. The phase of the nationalist movement brought to the fore, at several critical junctures, this

[1] Partha Chatterjee, 'Stability and Change in the Indian Political System', *Political Science Review*, 16, 1 (January–March 1977), pp. 1–42 [largely incorporating Chapter 3 of this volume].

choice before the indigenous capitalist class: whether to go in for a thoroughgoing campaign to break pre-capitalist production relations in the countryside with a view to leading the economy on a path of self-reliant capitalist development, or whether to compromise with imperialism abroad and the entrenched landed interests at home. Every time the all-India capitalist class, unwilling to take large political risks, chose the latter option.

In the process, India after the transfer of power came to be ruled by a coalition of classes, of which the two most crucial were the big bourgeoisie, on the one hand, and the landed gentry, on the other. The literature on how the political economy of India has grown — or failed to grow — is now fairly sizeable, and the basic dimensions set out with some clarity.[2] It is also fairly well known how, and why, the economy is in a virtually endemic state of crisis, reflected from time to time in food shortages, lack of foreign exchange, inflation, large unsold stocks of industrial goods, excess capacity in basic industries and excess of foreign exchange.

Less studied, I think, are the instrumentalities of the political process by which this precarious balance of ruling class interests is maintained. In the paper mentioned earlier, I had attempted to present an analysis of this process, crucial in which were a ruling party organization; the division of powers between a centre and the states, both in government and in party affairs; a Caesarist leadership; and a populist ideology. We will discuss these features here only inasmuch as they are important in understanding what happened in Indian politics in the period 1975–7.

The organization of the Congress, of course, developed in the course of the movement for the country's independence, and the basic organizational mechanism for maintaining the class alliance

2 A few important readings on this subject are Prabhat Patnaik, 'On the Political Economy of Underdevelopment', *Economic and Political Weekly*, 8, 4–6 (February 1973); Patnaik, 'Imperialism and the Growth of Indian Capitalism', in Roger Owen and Bob Sutcliffe, eds, *Studies in the Theory of Imperialism* (London: Longman, 1972), pp. 210–29; A.K. Bagchi, 'Long-term Constraints on India's Industrial Growth, 1951–68', in E.A.G. Robinson and Michael Kidron, eds, *Economic Development and South Asia* (London: Macmillan, 1970), pp. 170–92; Ranjit Sau, *India's Economic Development: Constraints and Problems* (Madras: Orient Longman, 1974); Ashok Mitra, *Terms of Trade and Class Relations* (London: Frank Cass, 1977).

was evolved in the course of that movement. This took the form of a differentiated structure of the party, organized as it was at the village or union, *taluka* or *thana,* district, provincial and all-India levels. While the committee at each level was subject to the directives of the higher committee, each level also retained some measure of independence. The manipulative possibilities of this arrangement had important implications for the political process. As the Congress broadened its movement, for instance, campaigns on issues involving the demands of the broadest masses were conducted at the lowest levels of the organization; but the necessary political compromises could be made at the higher levels of the structure. The hierarchy of peasant, landlord and commercial interests were thus accommodated within this flexible and differentiated structure of the party.

It is important to note here that the interests of the peasantry, the landed gentry and much of the commercial classes were local or provincial. The one truly all-India ruling class was the indigenous industrial bourgeoisie, and allied to it the upper levels of the professional and salariat middle classes. The influence of the bourgeoisie on the Congress organization was understandably most marked at the all-India level (apart from provincial committees such as those of Bombay or Bengal). Thus, the structured differentiation of areas of relative autonomy within the Congress organization was also consonant with the respective areas of interest that concerned the different sections of the ruling classes.

This differentiated structure of interests was carried on to the sphere of government after the transfer of power. Industry and industrial policy became a subject with which the Union government was concerned; agriculture became a state subject. With large public expenditure going into an effort for the planned development of the economy, the Union government became the focus for various industrial and large commercial interests. There was a perceptible bias towards centralization, but state governments and legislatures were clearly more amenable to pressure and control by the rural gentry.

The populist ideology of the Congress, of course, also evolved from the days of the national movement — a product of the effort to create and foster a broad-based multi-class front against British imperialism. While the class demands of the poorer sections of the people had to be voiced, class conflict could not be allowed to be stressed too far. And all this took place, as we have already mentioned, within the broad political-economic framework of a ruling alliance of the bourgeoisie and the landed gentry. With the inauguration of a parliamentary system based on adult franchise, it was necessary for an acceptable popular image of the Congress to appear to be responsive to the general popular desire for change, and not to appear too closely identified with any of the forces of exploitation in society. This was necessary not only to present an acceptable popular image, but also to pre-empt the issues on which the more organized opposition forces in society — the working class and the lower petty bourgeoisie — could agitate.

It is in this context, of maintaining the rule of a class coalition within a framework of parliamentary democracy, that the role of a Caesarist leadership becomes crucial. Put very briefly, this role consists in a popular leader who can maintain the balance within the ruling class coalition by appearing to stand above any particular interest, and thereby, to present and execute governmental decisions in the interests of the 'people' or the 'nation'. Nehru performed this role in the first several years of the new polity, and then, after a short spell of instability, Indira Gandhi assumed this role after the reorganization of the Congress party in 1969.

The Political Crisis in 1975

There have been some attempts to explain the declaration of Emergency in terms of an economic crisis which defied a solution except through the intervention of an authoritarian state machinery. Such an explanation is not adequate at this level of analysis: it is relevant in delineating the broader context — the more long-term parameters — within which the Indian polity functions, but does not explain why at one particular point of time certain changes in the functioning of the political institutions were thought to be necessary. The evidence about the economic crisis only shows its endemic nature; there is nothing to indicate that the crisis was suddenly aggravated in any major way in the middle of 1975.

It was rather a political crisis which led to the declaration of Emergency. The accentuation of the economic crisis in 1972–4 had led to several agitations against the government, most notably in Gujarat and Bihar. But from all indications it appears that the strength of these movements was distinctly on the wane by April or May 1975.[3] The real crisis was precipitated by the judgement of the Allahabad High Court, for now the opposition was directed not so much against government policies, but against the person of the Caesarist leader. The immediate context of the declaration of Emergency was the attempt to preserve the position of Caesar and to scotch attempts by the opposition to jeopardize this position. If our characterization of the crucial role of a Caesarist leader in the Indian political system is correct, it goes a long way in explaining — a task not quite accomplished by merely labelling the entire political leadership of the Congress as servile or spineless — why such drastic measures were accepted, more or less without major protest, by the Congress party. After all, the most overwhelming vision of the aims of the Emergency was conjured up by that great political theorist D.K. Barooah in the aphorism 'India is Indira, Indira is India!'

The solution to the crisis resembled in many ways the classic examples of Bonapartism.[4] Indeed, it was a Bonapartist solution, relying heavily on centralized executive powers implemented through the bureaucracy and a huge establishment of police and paramilitary personnel. In the process, several essential elements of the earlier institutional structure of politics were given up.

In the first place, the organization of the party was made subordinate to the government, and more particularly the executive, like it had never been before. Secondly, the entire structure of a division of powers between the centre and the states, both in governmental and party affairs, was replaced by a virtually total centralization of all effective powers. Chief Ministers were changed at will, state ministries were shuffled and reshuffled on directives from the Centre, legislatures virtually became defunct, and even disputes in the state party organizations were referred to the Great Leader for arbitration.

As a result of this, an essential part of the institutional mechanism, by which the balance among the constituent parts of the

[3] Ghanshyam Shah, 'Revolution, Reform or Protest? A Study of the Bihar Movement', *Economic and Political Weekly*, 12, 15–17 (9, 16 and 23 April 1977).

[4] It is striking how often there were references and allusions to, and indeed straight reproductions of, Marx's *The Eighteenth Brumaire of Louis Bonaparte* in the opposition literature of the Emergency.

ruling class coalition was earlier maintained, was sacrificed. We will consider the implications of this in a moment.

The new opportunities of centralization were sought to be utilized by the one class which stood to gain most from centralization, namely, the industrial bourgeoisie. Not only did it extend effusive (and servile) support to the policies of the new regime, but it also attempted to provide a new direction to the economic policies of the Emergency. While most of the populist slogans of the 20-point programme merely defaced the walls of government offices, two points which required little effort to implement were a national permit scheme for road transport and the raising of the exemption limit on income tax. In September 1975, T.A. Pai, Minister for Industry and Civil Supplies, announced a plan for a 'national sector', whereby public sector units were to

throw open their shareholding to the public at large and . . . not remain exclusively government-owned. . . . The public sector units should be thrown open to the rough and tumble of market forces; they should neither claim, nor be given, any special privileges . . . the public sector will not in the future be allowed to pre-empt capacity in any particular fields.[5]

In November 1975, major reforms were announced in licensing policy: some fifteen export-oriented engineering industries were allowed automatic expansion of capacity — virtually all of them were marked by low average capacity utilization; blanket exemptions from licensing were granted to twenty-one industries in the medium sector, and unlimited expansion beyond the licensed capacity was allowed to foreign companies and large monopoly houses in thirty other important industries; the procedure for regularizing unauthorized capacity installed by monopoly houses and foreign companies was liberalized.[6]

The whole thrust of the new move was to find a way out for the stagnating industrial sector, mainly through a boost in exports. This required fairly capital-intensive and sophisticated technology, and little additional labour. In any case, a large part of the labour problem had been taken care of by the state of Emergency. There was now a virtual ban on labour agitation; the minimum bonus legislation had been withdrawn. Recent

[5] *Economic and Political Weekly*, 13 September 1975.
[6] *Economic and Political Weekly*, 22 November 1975.

estimates have revealed that the profits as well as the assets of large business went up in the period of the Emergency.[7]

This process of restoring, and indeed reversing, the balance between the big bourgeoisie and the landed interests, which had turned somewhat in favour of the latter in the early 1970s (revealed not only in the adverse terms of trade of industry with agriculture, but also in the significant rise in the proportion of agriculturists even among Members of Parliament), was sought to be pushed even further. The move towards centralization was constitutionally formalized in the 42nd Amendment through a strengthening of the Central executive *vis-à-vis* Parliament, *vis-à-vis* the judiciary and *vis-à-vis* the states. Education was taken out of the State List and put in the Concurrent List. And, most significantly, a move was made (in the proposals of the Swaran Singh Committee) to transfer agriculture from the State List to the Union List. The fact that the proposal had to be dropped only reveals the real political strength of the landed interests in the Indian polity.

The Collapse of the Emergency Regime

This was towards the end of 1976. By then, the difficulties of having to work with a political system lacking an effective mechanism for maintaining the internal balance in the ruling class coalition were becoming clear to its constituents, as was to be revealed so dramatically in March 1977.

In the first place, the vested interests in the agricultural sector had definite reasons to be unhappy with the Emergency regime. The suspension of the earlier system of division of power, and the centralization of effective control, deprived the landed interests of their access to governmental machinery which, as we have noted, was hitherto located in the state governments and the state party organizations. Landed interests in India, except for specially favoured areas such as Punjab or Haryana, are not so organized as to be able to lobby effectively in New Delhi. The attempts to translate the process of centralization into an attack against the position of the landed gentry in the economy

---

[7] Ranjit Sau, 'Indian Political Economy, 1967–77', *Economic and Political Weekly*, 12, 15 (9 April 1977).

undoubtedly brought home to them the dangerous potentialities of a centralized system of authoritarian government. It was, indeed, in a systemic sense that the basic class alliance between the bourgeoisie and the landed gentry was jeopardized by the regime of the Emergency.

Secondly, while the big monopoly houses, and perhaps the industrial bourgeoise as a whole, made the most significant gains from the imposition of authoritarian rule, even for this class the new machinery of popular administration was not entirely satisfactory. For, the centralization of executive power was not based on any rational system of impersonal bureaucratic procedure: it was overwhelmingly, and dangerously, arbitrary. The entire phenomenon of the 'caucus' or 'coterie' surrounding the residence of the Prime Minister and intervening in major and minor decisions of government policy or implementation at national, state and local levels, and even extending into the functioning of public undertakings and nationalized banks (as is now being revealed daily in the proceedings of the Shah Commission) marks the monstrous arbitrariness of this kind of centralization. Normal methods of legislative debate, bureau-cratic procedure, lobbying, public discussion, etc. had all been suspended. For organized industry, such arbitrary and irrational modes of bureaucratic behaviour were essentially antithetical to the requirements of large-scale business. True, the regime of the Emergency was beneficial to industry; but the benefits could be, and were, differential, and success or disaster depended very largely on the highly uncertain criterion of remaining in the good books of the 'coterie'.

Not only that, the 'coterie' also included within it and in its close peripheries several industrial and commercial entrepren-eurs with no capitalist pedigree but with aggressive ambitions, and arbitrary powers were wielded with complete lack of ration-ality or scruples in their favour. Latching on to these lumpen elements in the world of business were certain middle-range industrial concerns with ambitions of entering the closed world of the big monopoly houses. All this certainly worked against the long-term, if not the immediate, interests of big business.

Thirdly, the bureaucratic implementation of several schemes of the Emergency, and particularly the much-discussed urban resettlement and family planning programmes, brought home to a very large section of the masses of northern India the truly repressive force of the state machinery. It is particularly important to consider this aspect of Emergency rule, especially in view of the wholly unorganized and spontaneous nature of popular opposition expressed in the March elections in the northern Indian states. Large-scale demolition of houses or *nasbandi* were arbitrary acts; but they were not in any way extraneous to a system of centralized rule which, in the absence of appropriate organizational procedures even for maintaining the rule of the exploiting classes, was specifically characterized by arbitrariness. In such situations, it only requires a fanatical commander such as Dyer at Jallianwalla Bagh, or a pampered and power-hungry infant like our own Sanjay Gandhi, to drop the mask and reveal the true nature of an oppressive state machinery.

Peasant ideology is everywhere characterized by a distancing from the central organs of state power with which peasant life normally has little contact. It is also characterised by an innate sense of peasant democracy, which is quick to react against any tangible evidence of repressive state violence. Unorganized, it has little opportunity to combat the state, except through such sporadic and purely limited acts as the burning of government jeeps or physically attacking government personnel. But given the first chance of registering its protest, it is quick to do so. The elections in March 1977 gave the peasantry of northern India this opportunity, and the results are well-known.

We see, then, that the collapse of the 'Congress system' was fundamentally the result of the failure to preserve the crucial institutional mechanism by which the alliance of the ruling classes functioned. This failure not only alienated the landed gentry from the Emergency system, but even the industrial bourgeoisie had reasons to be unhappy with it and was not, therefore, totally threatened by the spectre of an alternative political leadership coming to power. The crucial act, of course, was provided by the north Indian masses who experienced the indiscriminate repressions of an authoritarian state machinery, so that virtually the entire peasantry and the urban poor turned against the Congress.

5

Charan Singh's Politics

The newspapers are full of stories about the disarray in the Janata Party at the Centre. Up in the cool climes of Shimla, a minister violates prohibitory orders and delivers a fiery speech against his party leaders; the Prime Minister threatens to punish him; this leads another minister to drop hints that he has enough material to nail the Prime Minister's son on charges of corruption; the Prime Minister immediately removes him from his ministry. Now we have statements, counter-statements, resignations, threats of resignation. No one knows who is with whom or who is against whom. And finally, the already muddied waters of the capital's politics have been further agitated by stories about the sex life of a minister's son.

On the other hand, the two Congress parties are in no better shape. In Maharashtra, the coalition ministry of the two Congresses has collapsed; one wing has now joined hands with the Janata Party to form a ministry. There has been a split in the powerful group of Indira Gandhi supporters in Vidharbha. In West Bengal too, factionalism is raising its head in the Congress(I). Stories are circulating about disagreements between Mrs Gandhi and her close associates Devraj Urs and Chenna Reddi over proposals to unite the two Congress parties.

Perhaps never since 1947 has the central political structure in India looked so unstable.

The Crisis of Rule[1]

What is the reason for this instability? Some are saying, 'This was only to be expected. When Indira Gandhi unexpectedly called for elections in early 1977, different·leaders from different parties, united by nothing else but the urge to form an electoral

[1] [The following paragraphs summarize two sections that largely reproduce the analysis given in Chapter 4.]

alliance against her, came together to set up the Janata Party. An assembly under a sign does not create a political party. The Janata leaders had neither organizational nor ideological unity. From the very beginning, it was a virtual certainty that as soon as it was sucked into the whirlpool of politics, the alliance would come apart.' Others are trying to bring the Janata leaders to reason, to remind them that their quarrels were only helping Indira Gandhi. If only they would rise above these petty squabbles, these friendly critics seem to be saying, and set their minds on the tasks of government, all would be well.

Although we frequently hear comments like these, even from important political circles, they do not help us in the least to understand the seriousness of the problem or its historical significance. Even in the heyday of its power, the Congress party was riddled with factions, internal rivalries and ideological disputes. Yet it managed to win election after election and to rule the country. How was it able to do this? Why did that structure collapse? Perhaps eighty per cent of the current leaders of the Janata Party were once in the Congress; it is there that they built up their bases of support. When they came to power in 1977, why were they unable to construct an effective structure of rule along the lines of the Congress in the Nehru era?

First, the structure of rule in the Nehru period was characterized by a flexible and differentiated hierarchy of power, in government as well as in the ruling party. Second, at its peak, the form of authority was Caesarist. Third, its ideology was a supra-class populism. Armed with this political apparatus, the ruling classes in India tried to lay the foundations of an industrialized economy. The attempt led to a severe economic crisis in the mid-1960s.

One of the main elements in the subsequent strategy that was adopted in order to get out of the crisis was the so-called 'green revolution'. Backed by huge state support, the strategy succeeded in raising foodgrain production in select regions of northern India. It also increased significantly the political power of large landowners in those regions. This could not but upset the balance of power within the coalition of ruling classes. A very interesting aspect of the many initiatives taken during the period of Emergency by the central executive power was the move to clip the wings of the new rich peasant lobby. That the Emergency regime collapsed because of the combined opposition of practically the entire rural population in northern India, from landlords down to poor peasants, was not in small part due to these moves to curtail the power of the dominant rural classes. This is an important part of the history of the rise to power of the Janata Party.

The Importance of being Charan Singh

Since the emergence of the Janata Party, the rich peasant interests in northern India, now seeking greater political power, are organized principally in the Akali Dal and the Bharatiya Lok Dal. The unquestioned ideological leader of this group is Charan Singh. There is a single political argument that frames Charan Singh's politics. The principal thrust of development in the Nehru years, this argument says, was towards big industry, modern science and technology and the cities. This direction has to be shifted. Now the emphasis must be on the rural economy: the larger part of development funds must be spent there. Not only must there be a ceiling on land ownership, but also a floor, so as to eliminate uneconomic small holdings. Government programmes must provide irrigation, electricity, fertilizers, seeds. With this support, the hardworking and enterprising *kisan* will transform the Indian countryside.

Anyone who knows a thing or two about the conditions in which the Indian economy works, situated as it is within the present structure of the global economy, will see that this is a pipe dream. There is no possibility of sustained development in a country like India along a path exclusively defined by the extension of capitalism in agriculture. Not surprisingly, this is the usual judgement one hears from economists and journalists in India on Charan Singh's proposals. But perhaps the real question is not whether Charan Singh is right or wrong. The more serious question is: is Charan Singh's politics likely to appeal to Indian peasants? If so, what are the probable consequences for the future course of Indian politics?

That it does indeed have an appeal has been shown quite clearly in the past year or so — in the new caste wars. The word has gone around in the north Indian countryside that all this time it was the urban, upper-caste, English-speaking classes that had cornered all of the government's funds. A few crumbs thrown to the Harijans had ensured their support. Now the time has come for the middle castes, the bulwark of the peasant communities, to get their due. They will not accept any more the dominance of the urban classes. Young men from the Jat, Yadav, Ahir, Kurmi and other middle castes have taken to the streets to demand education, employment and more funds for the villages. The new movement has identified two enemies: upper castes on the one side and Harijans on the other. This aggressive politics of the landed middle castes is not confined only to northern India, it has spread to Marathwada, Tamil Nadu, Karnataka and Andhra, all of which have witnessed in recent months a series of brutal killings of Harijans. A 'peasant organization' from Haryana has even put up a demonstration in New Delhi demanding that government land distributed to Harijans should now be given to 'real peasants'. When Charan Singh resigned, there was some talk of a central peasant rally in the capital: many were perturbed by the prospect, since it was clear to all who know the situation in the north Indian countryside that Charan Singh does indeed have the clout to assemble a massive show of force.

The uncertainty over the future of the Janata government has revealed one truth about the political process in India: if the economy is to grow under centralized command in accordance with the needs of big capital, then it is impossible, within the framework of a parliamentary democracy, to give in to the demand of rich peasants for greater political power. Where rapid industrialization is not even a remote possibility, to concede this demand will mean tilting the terms of trade between agriculture and industry even further against the latter. In addition, given the largely local relevance of peasant interests, the tendency will be continuously to take governmental power away from central executive control and devolve it at state and local levels. The owners of large industry and commerce and the all-India professional classes are, not surprisingly, alarmed by this prospect. Of the organized dominant interests, they are the principal opponents of Charan Singh's bid for power. This section of the ruling classes is now looking for a solution somewhat similar to that of the Caesarism of the Congress. In view of the experience of the Emergency, all that these interests will demand is that central executive command be strong, but that it avoid the arbitrariness of the Emergency regime, and that it impose discipline in general and virtually Emergency conditions in the factories in particular. The search is now on for a leader and a political organization that have the ability to reorganize the structure of power along these lines. Needless to say, this provides the greatest opportunity for the return of Indira Gandhi. News-reports indicate that the Soviet Union too will favour a solution of this kind. Even some so-called leftists are saying, 'Well, if the unity of the country is to be preserved and effective government restored, what other option do we have? Don't you see what mess this Janata government has put us in?'

On the other hand, the cry has gone up in some other leftist circles: 'To stop Indira, we must join Charan Singh. He is our ally in the fight to save democracy.'

The Dangers of Charan Singh's Politics

Whenever we are confronted by a formation that is not distinctly capitalist, we have a curious tendency to immediately identify it as feudal. Similarly, when we see an organization demonstrating against authoritarianism, we rush to embrace it because we think it must be deeply in love with democracy. Neither of these responses show that we have any skill with dialectical thinking.

When I say that Charan Singh's politics seeks the aggressive expansion of capitalism in agriculture and that it could pose a serious danger to the prospects of building real democracy and socialism in this country, I do not mean to suggest that feudalism has evaporated from the Indian countryside. Nor do I mean that the principal structural tendency is in the direction of a transition from feudalism to capitalism. Moments of crisis usually contain within them several possibilities of transition. The specific turn that history takes is decided on the battlefield of politics: the outcome depends on the relative effectiveness of the rival social forces in preparing their grounds of support and in creating, through ideology and organization, the possibility for the emergence of an alternative mode of production. Theoretical analysis can only describe an actual, historically given situation and indicate the several tendencies contained in it; it is the task of politics to direct the social forces towards the desired tendency.

What is unfortunate is that at the present moment of severe crisis in the ruling structure, none of the Left forces, and especially none of the communist parties, are succeeding in reaching the people with a credible programme for an alternative mode of productive organization. Nearly all of the parties which call themselves communist are identifying enemies and seeking friends from within the existing structure of organized power. The only concern seems to be the immediate gains and losses of the parties or factions and of their leaders; there is no vision here of pursuing any long-range political objectives.

What is dangerous is that, in the meantime, a clear political message is being sent out to a vast mass of the labouring people of India — the message of Charan Singh's politics. From rich farmers to subsistence peasants, owners of agricultural land are being told: make your demands to the government for grants, for subsidies, for appropriate laws, and the labour that you have put into your own lands from time immemorial will at last be justly rewarded; soon everyone will get rich. In the present state of the economy and of the class structure, this politics poses a grave danger. If this appeal succeeds in finding a stable home in peasant consciousness, it will be impossible at any future time to politically unite owner-peasants, large or small, with the landless. Never has this been done in any country in the world.

If the principles of an alternative structure of agrarian economy are not enunciated in the very near future through the political and economic programmes of the Left, the large bulk of the landowning peasantry will never again be brought around to the cause of socialism. Not only that, peasants could then easily come under the sway of some agrarian populist peddling dreams of *kisan raj*. That is the history of the rise of Mussolini in Italy. A movement of agrarian fascism will of course necessarily end up surrendering itself to big capital or to foreign powers. The ruling class coalition which now finds itself hamstrung within the complexities of parliamentary democracy could then discover an unforeseen opportunity for preserving its class dominance.

That is the danger represented by Charan Singh's politics. It will not do merely to restate the academic truism that no long-term solution to India's crisis will be found by strengthening private property and the means of individual profit. If this is something we believe to be true, we must shape our political programmes accordingly. Our economic struggles must be informed by our desire to establish the political means for an alternative mode of productive organization based on collective labour. We know that without a perspective of capture of political power, no fundamental change can be brought about in the mode of production. Today we should also remind ourselves that without the perspective of an alternative mode of production, the political struggle will be led astray.

6

Some New Elements in India's Parliamentary Democracy

There is enormous disarray and confusion today among those who rule India. When in January this year (1980) the Congress under Indira Gandhi returned to power with a huge majority, many had expected that the political order would regain some sort of stability. The previous five or six years had seen the parliamentary system in India go through severe strains: Jayaprakash's movement in 1974–5, the Emergency, the historic elections of 1977, the falling out among the leaders of the Janata Party, the collapse of the Janata government, the curious ministry headed by Charan Singh, and finally the elections of 1980. During all that time, the Indian ruling classes were searching — without success — for the means of stable political rule. It was not as though their dominance was ever challenged, notwithstanding the uncertainties in the political arena. But they were clearly unable to find an organizational means to balance their mutual relations within a coherent political order.

There is little doubt that the entire administrative apparatus is today on the verge of collapse. Take the institutions of the economy. For many years now, there has been a sense of crisis surrounding the economy, but all governments had somehow tried to muddle through. When Indira Gandhi returned to power earlier this year, many of her supporters thought that steps would now be taken to revive the economy. After all, they said, foodgrains production had been good for several years running, and the mayhem caused in the Janata years was largely the result of political incompetence. Whatever else might be the shortcomings of Indira Gandhi, lack of determined leadership was not one of them.

Yet this year has seen no improvement in the state of the economy. One of the major allegations of the Congress(I) against Charan Singh's government was the latter's failure to tackle inflation. But eight months after the Congress(I) was returned to power, the prices of essential commodities continue to rise. The hike in petroleum prices is one factor in this. Far more important, however, is the control exercised by a small group of traders over the supply of various commodities. Obviously, traders will, when the opportunity presents itself, restrict the supply of commodities in the hope of making larger profits. But how effectively, over which areas, and in which commodities traders will be able to make these speculative profits now depends to a very large extent on political conditions. One must remember that when the prices of mass consumption goods rise, while those who trade in those commodities make quick profits, the interests of industrial manufacturers are usually hurt, because rising prices mean rising costs of raw materials and demands for increased wages.

The most notable feature of the recent spate of rising prices is its direct connection with the process of parliamentary democracy. Many millions of rupees are spent in a general election in India. With the growing spread, intensity and sophistication of election campaigns, the costs too are rising rapidly. There are many ways, all of them outside the sphere of public accounting, of raising the funds to finance election campaigns. A recent method, for instance, is to charge a below-the-counter 'commission' on the many large transactions of state-owned corporations engaged in foreign trade, and on exports and imports carried out through agreements with foreign governments. A single transaction of this kind could bring several million rupees into the coffers of the party in power. Another method is to get the support of traders in agricultural commodities and raw materials. First of all, these are businesses which are still relatively 'unorganized' in terms of modern business practices, which means that they are less amenable to statutory controls and legal regulation. Secondly, these trade networks reach into the interiors of rural society and are therefore tied intimately with the economic life of a large section of peasant producers. The political influence of these traders is, therefore, not limited only to their role as contributors to the election funds of political parties, but arises out of their power over peasant producers in large areas of agricultural production. The local political influence of sugar traders in Uttar Pradesh, cotton traders in Maharashtra, oilseed traders in Gujarat, and tobacco traders in Andhra Pradesh are well known instances. This year saw an election to Parliament, and only a few months later, elections to several state assemblies: the rapid rise in the prices of agricultural commodities can be seen as an inevitable result of these political processes.

But the general sense of administrative breakdown cannot be attributed to the power of local economic interests. In the colonial period, of course, the administration was not limited by parliamentary representation of the subject population; the edifice of imperial rule was premised on the absolute supremacy of executive power. The very last years of British rule saw elected ministries in the provinces: many Congress leaders were first introduced to the business of state administration in the period between 1937 and 1947. It was in those years that many of the conventions regarding the relation between elected ministries and the permanent bureaucracy in India were shaped, within the overall framework of a colonial government. This framework was largely retained in the Nehru period. Many Congress ministers in those days, at the Centre as well as in the states, neither knew nor cared for the intricacies of British-style bureaucratic procedure. Once the overall policies had been determined at the political level, most ministers were content to leave the actual task of daily administration in the hands of the officers. It is fair to say that the general practice among Congress leaders of the Nehru era was to respect the experience and expertise of the permanent civil service, and even to rely upon it to maintain continuity of policy and administrative practice.

But with the rising intensity of party and factional competition, the use of administrative power to further narrow sectional interests became more and more common. As a result, from the central or state secretariat to the district or *taluk* or block, government officers became increasingly entangled in the web of party or factional loyalties. It became common practice for political leaders to exercise their clout by ordering officers to get things done for them and to transfer them if they did not comply. One of the first things that happen these days when a new member is elected to a state assembly is the transfer of administrative and police officers in the constituency. Frequent transfers on this scale clearly mean major problems for the accumulation of experience and expertise in the administration. Following the recent communal riots in Uttar Pradesh, for instance, a former inspector-general of police has written that even ten years ago, an officer appointed to a police station would use the first three months to get acquainted with the area in his jurisdiction. Each police station had a guidebook for this purpose in which every officer-in-charge would add his comments. Now, because of the frequent transfers, officers do not even bother to maintain the guidebooks. Apparently, an officer was seen at the time of the recent riots, accompanied by a team of armed police, asking local people for directions that might lead him to the hideouts of the culprits.

The question of administrative efficiency has varied implications for different constituents of the ruling class coalition. A rationally ordered, non-arbitrary and efficient administrative machinery is required above all for the purposes of a modern industrial economy. If there is laxity or corruption in the bureaucracy, especially at the upper levels and in its central structures, it is industrial capitalists who should be the ones to object first. Small traders, moneylenders or owners of rural property do not bother too much about bureaucratic niceties: in fact, the looser the procedures at the lower rungs of a centralized bureaucracy, the easier it is for these classes to exercise their local dominance.

One of the new features of parliamentary democracy in India in the last decade is the political rise of a rich peasant class following the 'green revolution'. After a subdued spell during the Emergency, this class was particularly prominent in the years of the Janata government. In those years, it attempted to consolidate its local dominance by using its influence over the district administration. One manifestation of this was the proliferation of arms at the local level. A recent estimate shows that there are at present as many as twenty thousand licensed firearms in the district of Moradabad alone. In the 1950s, this figure was less than two thousand. It is also said that for every licensed firearm there are usually three that are unlicensed. This means that in Moradabad alone there are some eighty thousand firearms. By comparison, all of Great Britain has a total of 75,000 licensed arms. There are reasons to suspect that in several districts of Bihar or Punjab, there are even larger quantities of arms in the hands of locally powerful groups. Many observers have been astonished by the extensive use of firearms in the recent communal riots in Uttar Pradesh. If we keep in mind some of the changes in the political process in the north Indian countryside in the last decade and a half, there should be less cause for surprise.

This does not mean, however, that in the central structures of state power in India, the power of rural landowners has increased in relation to that of industrial capitalists. No matter how much the local dominance of landlords or rich peasants, it has not been successfully transformed into an organized force that could stake its claim to state power at the central level. There is a history of the politics of the rich peasant in India, from its rise within the Congress movement in the 1930s, its presence at the local levels of electoral politics in the Nehru era, its visibility even in the central representative bodies in Indira Gandhi's reorganized Congress in the early 1970s, to its bid for central power under the leadership of Charan Singh. The bid failed. The failure signified, first, that the influence of industrial capital in the organized arena of state power is now pre-eminent, and second, that it is virtually impossible to translate the local dominance of the rural rich in the different parts of a country like India into a central force within the ruling coalition.

Nevertheless, the bourgeoisie in India cannot rule except by sharing power with other dominant classes. But in what form? Through which instruments? That has become the principal question of parliamentary democracy in India. There does not appear to be a political leadership with the ability to establish and maintain a new balancing mechanism for sharing power within the ruling classes. Every political party seems to have failed in this task.

We see, consequently, that the political agitations that have broken out in different parts of the country in recent months are eluding the influence of both ruling parties and parties of the opposition. The movement in Assam is the most obvious example. But the agitation against rising prices in Gujarat, the peasant agitation over irrigation waters in Karnataka, and the repeated clashes in Kashmir between the people and the armed forces show the same feature. On top of this, of course, are the endless episodes of communal violence in Uttar Pradesh. What is significant about these events is not only the growing signs of popular agitation, but the failure of every established political party to influence or control them.

When the ruling powers are in such disarray, there is, however, no significant organized political challenge to their rule; which is why the present political crisis could contain many dangerous possibilities. It remains to be seen, for instance, how long the industrial capitalists will endure the breakdown of administration and the lack of political direction. Many influential circles in India had been vocal in the recent past about getting rid of the baggage of parliamentary forms in order to set right the administrative apparatus and the public and private enterprises. Since the death of Sanjay Gandhi, those circles have been somewhat subdued. Perhaps that is the only reason why parliamentary democracy will survive for a while in this country. The largest democracy in the world appears to be hanging from a thread.

7

Indira Gandhi: The Final Year

21 November 1983: Of Monarchs and Democrats[1]

The Queen is in India. Not our Queen, of course. Thanks to the freedom movement and our Constitution, the British monarch no longer reigns in India. But there is nevertheless a special relationship of some kind, and the Queen is in India in connection with the meeting of the heads of governments of the Commonwealth, of which India is a member and the Queen the head.

It has been remarked that the visit of the British monarch has not aroused the same sort of enthusiasm among the people as did her visit to this country twenty-two years ago. Perhaps we have at long last shed our colonial legacy. The reports even say that the royal motorcade driving into Rashtrapati Bhavan had to be diverted, because Rajpath had been taken over by crowds celebrating the *Ekatmata Yajna* organized by the Vishwa Hindu Parishad. Surely such a defiant demonstration of our collective religious will would never have been allowed to interfere with a royal procession in the days of the Raj. We now live in a truly secular country, where the state does not meddle with religion, at least not when it suits its purpose. Perhaps we have also outgrown our juvenile fascination with monarchs and princes. We now live in a democracy where we ourselves elect the leaders of our government.

Or perhaps we have found an even cleverer solution, one which political theorists and constitutional experts have not yet dreamt of. Perhaps, unknown to all, we have quietly built up a system in which we can, to the accompaniment of the full fanfare of a democratic process, elect our own monarchs. Two weeks ago, the AICC(I) session concluded in Bombay with the

[1] *Frontier*, 16, 15 (26 November 1983).

investiture of a Crown Prince, one whom the party expected to be duly elected to the office of our democratic monarchy. The Prime Minister, speaking on the occasion, is reported to have explained with beguiling simplicity: 'I don't come from a royal family but we have acquired the status by our dedicated service to the nation, by sincerity of purpose and hard work.' One party leader after another took up the cue and asserted that it was only in the fitness of things and wholly in accordance with the wishes of the people that Mr Rajiv Gandhi should in due course take up the reins of government from his tired mother. Even Mr Priyaranjan Das Munshi, Congress firebrand and erstwhile rebel against Sanjay Gandhi's authoritarian ways, is said to have confessed his sins and asked to be forgiven: ' . . . like a mother she will forgive her errant son.'

One can ridicule and condemn such abject servility among those who claim to rule this country. But we must also pause to think why, despite the fact that the politics of the ruling party has been reduced to such a pathetic state, it continues to rule and in fact believes that the best way for it to seek another term in power is to project Rajiv Gandhi as the legitimate successor to the Prime Minister. One can argue endlessly about whose 'objective' interests Mrs Gandhi serves by being in power, but what is the sum and substance of her own politics today except to do whatever is necessary to secure, in some form or another, a dynastic succession? Individuals, one hears, play only a limited role in history. But sometimes they play crucial roles. Perhaps it will be individual ambitions and individual weaknesses which will bring about, in the next few months, a situation in this country pregnant with terrible dangers as well as far-reaching possibilities. One can only hope the people will find leaders bold enough to seize those historical opportunities.

In the meantime, Mrs Gandhi will probably envy the quiet graciousness of the British Queen. Being a constitutional monarch, the latter does not need to play at politics to make certain that her family continues to reign. On the other hand, one suspects that at the meeting of Commonwealth heads of governments, Queen Elizabeth too will face stiff competition in the business of regal demeanour. After all, one who thinks she is monarch by virtue of the dedicated services of her family to the nation has much to flaunt.

26 December 1983: Who Wins What?[2]

The results of the by-elections to three Lok Sabha and eleven Assembly seats in Haryana, Rajasthan, Uttar Pradesh, Bihar and West Bengal have come as something of a disappointment to those complacent optimists who had been talking for sometime now of the rapidly eroding electoral support for the Congress(I) all over northern India. The results have shown that, whatever may have been the popular mood a few months ago, the concerted propaganda campaign launched by Mrs Gandhi about the so-called threat to national unity and the imminence of a border war with Pakistan has enabled her, at least for the moment, to hold the opposition at bay. Not only that: by winning the prestige contest at Sonepat where the former Lok Dal and now Janata leader Devi Lal was soundly thrashed, the Congress(I) has come out of this round with a fair bit of advantage.

The results have shown in particular the failure of either of the two opposition combines to emerge as a clear and credible national alternative to the Congress(I). The BJP–Lok Dal combine has had two successes — in the Fazilnagar and Madhogarh Assembly seats, which it has taken away from the Congress(I) and the Janata respectively. But it has lost the Mandawa seat in Rajasthan. The Janata Party has scored one significant victory — in the Bulandshahr (U.P.) Lok Sabha contest — but has lost elsewhere. Maneka Gandhi's party has won the Pilibhit Assembly seat which has for long been her associate Akbar Ahmed's stronghold. The Bettia Lok Sobha seat has gone to the CPI.

The West Bengal results are even more significant because the CPI(M) has lost both seats that had fallen vacant. Admittedly, both Kaliachak (Malda) and Krishnaganj (Nadia) were marginal seats, but the fact remains that despite the pathetic organizational state of the Congress(I) in West Bengal, it has managed to improve its electoral image sufficiently to win those seats. Or perhaps the results are more indicative of a growing popular disenchantment with the Left Front — the inevitable consequence of the complete exhaustion of its narrow programmes of reform, and hence the increasingly strong impression of non-performance on virtually every aspect of government activity.

[2] *Frontier*, 16, 20 (31 December 1983).

Perhaps Mrs Gandhi will now be tempted to call an early election and cash in on the present confusion in the opposition ranks. The Left parties will in all likelihood continue to keep their options open. In recent weeks, every Left leader has uttered the litany about the threat to national unity and the imminent danger of a border war. They have all expressed their praise and support for the supposedly 'progressive' foreign policy of Mrs Gandhi. Mr E.M.S. Namboodiripad is even reported to have said that in the present context of national instability, a certain degree of centralization of power must be conceded; the task of the Left forces is to ensure that this centralization does not lead to authoritarian rule.

So the charade will continue in the next few weeks, each party counting its wins and losses and figuring out how best to respond to Mrs Gandhi's next move. What all this will show once again is the utter inability of the opposition leaders to look beyond the set patterns of electoral arithmetic, to conceive of this otherwise bewildering tactical game of moves and countermoves in the wider and much more real context of the daily struggle of the people for a more decent, more humane and more democratic social order.

9 January 1984: Conclave in Calcutta[3]

The winter's festivities continue this week in Calcutta with an international football tournament and the next round of talks among the all-India opposition parties. The former will be inaugurated by the Prime Minister who is paying her second visit to the city in two weeks, this time on what looks like an exclusively cultural mission. She for one seems bent on pushing to the fullest extent her latest political line on West Bengal: save Bengal's cultural heritage from the marauding Marxists!

Two days later, the West Bengal government will play host to the opposition conclave. The officially announced agenda for the closed-door sessions contains subjects that are both diverse and of varying importance. They cover matters like external debts, lockouts in factories and unemployment on the one hand, and electoral reforms and Congress(I) attempts to topple the

[3] *Frontier*, 16, 22 (14 January 1984).

governments in Jammu and Kashmir and Karnataka on the other. It is said that there is no official proposal to discuss the prospects for electoral unity among the opposition parties. Yet there is no doubt that whatever the subjects discussed and resolutions adopted, they will be read not so much for their actual content as for the signs they might disclose about the thinking of each party on the forthcoming general elections — whenever they are held — and about the possibilities of electoral adjustments.

Indeed, the conclave is coming at a particularly crucial time. The recent by-elections have produced very ambiguous results, with no one gaining any decisive advantage. But the signal is clear that if there is a broad oppositional unity, Mrs Gandhi will be put into considerable difficulties in northern India. Already the BJP has issued an appeal to the Janata-led combination for constructive talks on a common programme with a view to setting up a non-communist front. Mrs Gandhi will, of course, desperately try to keep the opposition divided. Already, she has made up her mind to sacrifice her traditional Muslim 'vote bank', play an adroit Hindu-communal line and direct the full firepower of government-sponsored propaganda against the 'anti-national' attitude of Farooq Abdullah and the National Conference. By this, she probably hopes to make the choice more difficult for the Janata group of parties: by coming together with the BJP–Lok Dal alliance, it could risk losing its newly acquired Muslim support. It is strange indeed that at a time when the Congress(I) has raised the bogey of an imminent attack from Pakistan, it is the BJP which is able most strongly to put this down as one more out of Mrs Gandhi's endless stock of vote-catching gimmicks.

But it is the Left which is truly in a quandary. The Soviets have made no secret of their wish that the so-called 'left and progressive forces' should support Mrs Gandhi. The CPI(M)'s central leadership has in recent weeks taken up the cue with great alacrity. But West Bengal is obviously a crucial factor in that party's electoral calculations, and the recent by-election results in Malda and Nadia have upset matters greatly. The Congress(I) in West Bengal has apparently been able to persuade Mrs Gandhi and her son that a sustained campaign against the CPI(M) in the state could earn them considerable electoral dividends. This seems to have unnerved the CPI(M)'s state leadership. Underlying its inept bunglings and indecisiveness on how to react to the Governor's action on the Vice-Chancellor issue, there is probably a groundswell of opinion within the party which would like, on the eve of the opposition conclave, to bind both its central leadership and a vacillating Chief Minister to a more uncompromisingly anti-Congress(I) position.

21 May 1984: Imperial Strategy[4]

From drift to decisive action. Or is it? The government is claiming that its latest attempts to clean up the Punjab mess are paying off and, slowly but surely, the situation is coming under control. Although terrorist actions by groups such as the Dashmesh Regiment continue to hit the headlines every day and most Punjab cities are under curfew, the police administration claims considerable success from its 'mopping up operations'. A statement by police chief P.S. Bhinder declares that in a series of raids in 359 villages in Amritsar district alone, nearly 250 people with 'terrorist connections' had been arrested and large amounts of arms and ammunition seized. On the other hand, Hindu communal bodies like the Rashtriya Hindu Suraksha Sena have already come into the forefront; they took a leading part in organizing the *bandh* following the murder of Ramesh Chandra, editor of a distinguished Jullundur daily.

In dealing with the Punjab situation, the government of Mrs Gandhi has adopted what looks like a classic imperial strategy. If you do not want a reasonable democratic solution of a political problem, allow the situation to drift, let the disaffection mount. Soon there will be some who will demand quick and extreme solutions. Allow them to put on the pressure, even pamper them for a while. The passions will rise, violence will spread, people — perhaps many people — will get killed. Do not get carried away, stick to your plan. For as soon as the 'extremists' will seem to have gained the upper hand, the moderates will be pushed into a corner. Then, and only then, will you strike a deal.

A classic imperial strategy. And Mrs Gandhi's government is playing it with a degree of insensitivity and ruthlessness which,

4 *Frontier*, 16, 40 (26 May 1984).

even after a decade and a half of her despotic career, is no less frightening. In a recent interview, she has reportedly stated that a solution of the Punjab problem has been within the realms of possibility for several months now, but every time 'some obstacles came in the way.' And now, after hundreds of deaths, complete disruption of the economic and social life of the people, and a deep entrenchment of feelings of mutual hostility and distrust, the armed forces are going ahead with their 'mopping up operations' and the moderate Akali leaders have been suddenly released from prison. Reports from New Delhi indicate that informal discussions are already under way with the Akali leadership and a 'deal' of some sort may well be in the offing. Perhaps Mrs Gandhi now feels that the wings of the moderates have been sufficiently clipped, so that a deal under these conditions, although its specific terms might easily have been acceptable several months ago, would not give them the credit of a political victory. Unless, of course, some new 'obstacle' comes in the way.

In the meantime, Punjab will live in fear and anguish. And many more will die. That, of course, is of little concern to those who have reduced the business of politics to a sordid game of self-interest and vanity.

19 June 1984: All This for What?[5]

Judging from the fever-pitch excitement now being whipped up by the government media and the all-India press, it would seem that organized public opinion in the towns and cities of India has been swept by a wave of nationalist hysteria. Never has there been such xenophobic fervour and such a frenzy of statolatry in this country except in times of war. All shades of political opinion, from the extreme Right to large sections of the Left, have lined up behind Mrs Gandhi and the Union government and have hailed the military action in Punjab as a bold, decisive and entirely necessary step in fighting 'the grave threat to the unity and security of the country'. The Prime Minister, it would seem, has once again performed one of her famous political tricks, perhaps her most dramatic since the Bangladesh war of 1971.

5 *Frontier*, 16, 44 (23 June 1984).

Everyone appears to be supporting her move — everyone except, of course, the Sikhs.

Not every Sikh in Punjab was a supporter of the extreme communalist politics of the now deceased Bhindranwale. Surely the overwhelming majority was hoping for an end to the violence, bloodshed and complete disruption of normal life in that state. But the few reports from Punjab that have been allowed to pass through the tight net of censorship regulations indicate a quite pervasive mood of sullen anger and bitterness among the Sikhs. The storming of the Golden Temple was not just a military operation. If the objective was simply to flush out 'terrorists', there were other means available. It was meant to be a symbolic act of high political drama, intended above all to impress upon the country as a whole that the government had acted with courage, determination, meticulous planning and bold execution. Yet in choosing this particular form of action, the Union government has inevitably alienated the Sikhs as a community. The Sikhs feel they have been accused as a community of being criminals and enemies of the nation, of harbouring secessionist sentiments and deserving punishment and humiliation. Every day now, responsible members of the community, not even remotely supporters of Bhindranwale, are coming out in public to express their sorrow and dismay at what has happened and to protest against the military action. Virtually the entire moderate Akali leadership is in prison, detained indefinitely under the National Security Act.

Most 'disturbing' perhaps are the signs of unrest among Sikh soldiers in the army. There have been mutinies in at least eight army camps in various parts of the country, the most serious being in Ramgarh in Bihar where the officially confirmed figure of desertions is over 500. Numerous mutineers have been killed in encounters with loyal troops; most seem to have been arrested and will doubtless be proceeded against according to normal military procedures.

All this for what? The Prime Minister has achieved her political objective. She had already decided that she would not make any political settlement on the issue of Centre–State relations in Punjab which would give the moderate Akali Dal leadership any electoral leverage. This was the primary reason why the abnormal situation there had dragged on for such a long time; for, the moderates, unable to clinch the issue, kept losing ground in the face of pressure from the extremist wing as well as the mounting threat from Hindu communal organizations. Now, having herself brought the situation to such a pass, the Prime Minister has acted 'decisively'. She has obviously decided that it was not worth her while trying to woo back the traditional minority vote. She needed something dramatic to swing the crucial Hindu vote in northern India. The Punjab situation gave her this chance, and she has seized it with her customary alacrity and ruthlessness.

16 July 1984: Stepping Up Repression[6]

The inevitable is happening. Having immersed itself in the quagmire of armed counter-insurgency operations in Punjab, the Union government is now taking increasingly repressive measures on a national scale. It has used the most blatantly undemocratic means to dismiss the government of Farooq Abdullah in Jammu and Kashmir, and has sought to justify this outrageous step in terms of the need to fight subversive and anti-national activities. And now it has come out with an ordinance empowering the Union government to declare any part of India a 'terrorist-affected' area and to set up special courts to try 'crimes against the country's security and integrity'. The powers given to the Union government under this ordinance are drastic, and fall little short of declaring an Emergency by other means. The offences which can be construed as anti-national and terrorist crimes include waging war against the state, abetting mutiny, promoting enmity between classes, assertion of imputations prejudicial to national integrity, and serious offences like murder, dacoity and hijacking.

The so-called White Paper is a classic document of official deception. It puts the whole blame for what happened in Punjab not, as one might have expected, on the extreme communalist section led by Jarnail Singh Bhindranwale or even on external sources, real or mythical, supporting 'separatist elements'. Rather, it lays the blame squarely on the Akali Dal as a whole for launching a movement which it could not

[6] *Frontier*, 16, 48 (21 July 1984).

control, and which provided a 'respectable cover for subversive and anti-national forces' as well as for the involvement of 'criminals, smugglers, antisocial elements and Naxalites'. The document alleges that it was the Akali Dal leadership which 'lacked the will to arrive at a settlement on the basis of any reasonable framework offered by government'. It refused to dissociate itself from the separatism of the extremist groups and ultimately allowed the initiative to pass out of its hands. The Union government, the White Paper asserts, had no alternative in the end but to take armed action. As the most damning sentence in the whole document puts it: 'The government have affirmed, in the only way open to them, the imperatives of national integrity against all forms of separatism.'

The White Paper, of course, is completely silent on the role of the Congress(I) leadership itself in systematically setting up Bhindranwale as a counter to the Akali Dal leadership in Punjab. It does not mention why Bhindranwale, at the time of his rise to prominence, was repeatedly given political protection despite several criminal cases being brought against him. It does not say that it was the Union government, and not the Akali Dal, which went back on its word on the eve of the Haryana elections in 1983 when it suddenly became apprehensive that a settlement with the Akalis might mean a loss of Hindu votes for the Congress(I) in Haryana. It does not mention the provocative role of Hindu communal bodies in Punjab and Haryana in aggravating the situation early this year. It does not mention Union Home Minister P.C. Sethi's infelicitous dithering on the eve of the final round of talks with the Akali Dal. The document, in other words, has nothing to say about the narrow, shortsighted and sectarian political calculations which guided the Union leadership into postponing a political settlement on the main issues concerning Centre–State relations which lay at the heart of the Akali demands. It was this, and not the intransigence of the extremists or the lack of will of the moderates, which finally brought about a situation in which the government could show that it had no alternative but to unleash armed violence on a massive scale.

Now repression will spread all over the country. What the forces of opposition will do to meet this challenge remains to be seen.

27 August 1984: A Decisive Moment[7]

The All-India Protest Day on 25 August has passed off peacefully. There was much greater response in the southern states and in West Bengal than in the rest of the country. In Andhra Pradesh, the deposed Chief Minister, Mr N.T. Rama Rao, despite his precarious health, began in Vijaywada a campaign to mobilize public resentment against the outrageous way in which he was ousted from office, and to demand his reinstatement. The crowds he is drawing are a fair indication of the massive and spontaneous feelings of the people of that state against the undemocratic actions of the Governor and the autocratic powers in New Delhi. The Governor, Mr Ram Lal, has apparently brought to a close a series of incidents at once disgraceful and farcical by announcing his resignation. Yet, at the moment of writing, there are no signs that the basic wrong will be undone by giving Mr Rama Rao a fair chance to prove his majority and come back to an office from which he was removed.

All this has, of course, suddenly galvanized the opposition into united action against Congress(I) misrule. After their speeches in Parliament and a deputation to the President failed to produce significant results, there was no course left but to launch a sustained countrywide agitation. The programmes taken so far have been cautious and limited. The Protest Day envisaged bandhs only in West Bengal, Kerala and Karnataka, while the leftist trade unions were asked to carry out industrial action wherever feasible. The opposition leaders do not appear to have too many ideas about how to sustain the agitation if Mrs Gandhi remains obdurate and chooses to bide her time. This time they do not have a Jayaprakash Narayan to lead them, and the leaders of the rightist and centrist opposition are not made of the kind of stuff that can pass through a prolonged, possibly bloody, period of struggle against a centralized, autocratic and thoroughly ruthless regime. All they are hoping for is to ride into power on the crest of a popular electoral wave; they cannot be expected to relish the prospects of a long spell of political turmoil. Already Mr Chandra Shekhar is reported to have expressed his anxiety that countrywide agitations might provoke Mrs Gandhi to declare an Emergency.

[7] *Frontier*, 17, 2 (1 September 1984).

Mrs Gandhi is obviously counting on the limited staying power of the opposition. She is reported to have decided to shift the elections from November 1984 to January 1985. By then, she hopes, the opposition will have run out of steam and the challenge withered away. Perhaps her new-found protégé Bhaskar Rao will find enough time and opportunity to buy up the requisite MLAs to prove his majority in the Andhra Assembly. If that fails, President's Rule could be declared in the state. Other issues might come up in the meantime, including foreign adventures in the southern seas. If her prospects do not improve by early-1985, she could make a move for drastic constitutional amendments or even an Emergency. The present opposition leadership does not seem prepared for such ordeals.

For the first time in many years, a historic opportunity has arisen in which the Left might be called upon to perform the role of leading a sustained phase of popular struggle on an issue that is national in scale. At such moments, the question is not so much the real limits, sectoral or regional, of organized strength. The question is that of the will and the ability to step into the breach, to lead the popular democratic cause through a phase where repression becomes harsh and the established leadership is found wanting. Mrs Gandhi's reluctance to abdicate power, even in the face of popular disapproval, may provide the Left with just such an opportunity to project itself as a truly national alternative. Will the Left be found wanting?

The signs are not entirely hopeful. Only two days before the All-India Protest Day, Mr E.M.S. Namboodiripad is reported to have made a statement that there is little chance of an electoral adjustment of the Left with parties like the BJP or even the Janata. He also added that the Left still supported the 'progressive' foreign policy of Mrs Gandhi. The timing of the statement is as significant as its content; for it indicates fear, a reluctance to seize the moment, and needless to say, an ingrained slavishness to the modes of parliamentary politics.

15 October 1984: Riots and Politics[8]

There have been a series of incidents in recent weeks involving violent Hindu–Muslim clashes. The distinctive feature of these

[8] *Frontier*, 17, 9 (20 October 1984).

incidents is that they have not been restricted to any one part of the country. Relations between the two communities in the cities of Hyderabad have been tense for several months, and things have flared up at least half-a-dozen times in the course of this year. In Maharashtra, after the terrible killings in Bombay and Bhiwandi a few months ago, we now have reports of riots in Malegaon — once again, a powerloom town. Communal violence also broke out at more or less the same time in Belgaum in Karnataka, Pulampur in Gujarat and Azamgarh in Uttar Pradesh. It has been suggested that the trouble has been caused by the fact that this year Muharram and Dusserah have coincided, and this sort of conjunction of Hindu and Muslim festivals always creates the possibility of conflict. This seems too facile an explanation. The coincidence of public festivals might mean additional problems for the civil administration in towns and districts, but there is no reason why it should necessarily cause antagonism and bitterness among ordinary people.

Much more plausible is the explanation that, this being election year, politicians of all grades and descriptions are seeking the opportunity of getting into the act, and any kind of public event is being drawn into the vortex of politics. Not necessarily is there a countrywide conspiracy or organization behind the series of communal disturbances in recent weeks. Local issues and local forces are enough to precipitate an incident that will make the news. The riots in Bombay and Bhiwandi a few months ago, and the more recent ones in Hyderabad, have shown quite clearly that a handful of well-organized and well-financed troublemakers can create havoc in densely-populated urban areas. There is not much doubt that much of what has happened in Malegaon or Belgaum or Azamgarh is the handiwork of such forces out to make quick political capital.

But that is not all. Two other things need to be remembered. First, the willing participation, or at least connivance, of the administration. Both in Bombay and in Hyderabad, the clear connivance of the police as well as the political leadership holding office at the time was responsible for the way in which rioters had a field day. If indeed it is true that many of these incidents are the handiwork of small groups of troublemakers, it is hardly likely that they would have either the courage or the ability to cause such large-scale destruction and killing if the administration was prompt and decisive in taking action. Moreover, the Congress(I) itself, in its bid to stave off the opposition in northern and western India, has created the clear impression that it will stop at nothing to win the so-called 'organized Hindu vote'.

The other important fact is that there is at the moment a general sense of political uncertainty in the country. The popular mood is restive; people feel that something ought to be done about their growing hardships. Yet the political scene does not offer any decisive hope of a national leadership willing or able to provide a credible alternative. That the people desire a change has been indicated over and over again. When this popular mood finds a worthwhile political cause, it can show, as it has done in Andhra, amazing determination and powers of resistance. Without such a cause and without genuine political leadership, such periods of uncertainty can create situations in which even small-time troublemakers can have a field day.

29 October 1984: Jockeying for Position[9]

Mr Charan Singh sprang a major surprise last week by declaring the formation of a new party. It will be called the Dalit Mazdoor Kisan Party (DMKP). With the growing profusion of splits and mergers among political parties, even their names are getting more and more cumbersome. The new party is the result of the coming together of the erstwhile Lok Dal, Mr Bahuguna's DSP, Mr Ratubhai Advani's Rashtriya Congress, and a significant section of Janata dissidents including Mr Devi Lal and, hopefully, Mr Karpoori Thakur. The new party, needless to add, will be headed by Charan Singh himself.

The impact of this latest move by the irrepressible old warhorse from Jatland will be felt most severely by the Janata Party, and by Chandra Shekhar in particular. For several days before Charan Singh's announcement, talks had been conducted with the intention of a merger between the Lok Dal and the Janata Party. It was even reported that a broad agreement on organizational unification had been reached: Charan Singh was to become president and Chandra Shekhar working president, and a joint parliamentary board was to be set up. But obviously, Charan

[9] *Frontier*, 17, 11 (3 November 1984).

Singh thought there were possibilities of a better bargain. Now he has virtually pulled the rug from under Chandra Shekhar's feet. With Devi Lal and Karpoori Thakur gone, and Satyendra Narayan Sinha already joining the Congress(I), the Janata Party will now be left with Karnataka as its only secure base. It is hardly surprising therefore that it has accused Charan Singh of the 'politics of piracy'.

Already, DMKP leaders have begun to air their expectations about how strongly the new party will perform in north India. Charan Singh is clearly a considerable force in Uttar Pradesh, but now with the addition of H.N. Bahuguna, backward caste leaders like Karpoori Thakur and the expected campaign support of Syed Mir Kasim and Farooq Abdullah, DMKP leaders are exuberant.

But everyone realizes that the chances of a decisive opposition victory lie crucially in its ability to prevent the splitting of anti-Congress(I) votes. Hence, the fielding of unanimous opposition candidates all over the country is something everyone agrees is a primary requirement. The trouble is that each party is also interested in getting as much as possible for itself out of a unanimous agreement. And this is pushing back the prospects of unanimity. It is not true, as Mrs Gandhi so frequently alleges, that the opposition has only a one-point programme — that of removing her from power. If it did, the opposition would have been united long ago.

With the brief flush of enthusiasm over Mr Rama Rao's ouster and reinstatement quickly receding into the distant past, Indian politics is now fully engaged in the electoral market place. It is certain that in the coming weeks there will be many more moves and countermoves, small and big bargains, splits and realignments, all with the objective of maximizing one's chances of a seat in Parliament. It will be incorrect to accuse, as Congress(I) leaders are sure to do, only the opposition leaders of such unprincipled politics. The ruling party itself is no haven of selfless servants of the people. The recent expulsions of F.M. Khan and J.R. Dhote are only a surface indication of the equally unscrupulous jockeying for position that is engaging the leaders of that party at the moment. The only difference, probably, is the cringing sycophancy which gives to Congress(I) politics the doubtful appearance of the passionate fervour of devotees at a shrine.

5 November 1984: Troubled Times[10]

The last week was one of the most momentous in the recent history of this accursed country — grim, harrowing and full of dark portents. Despite the cycle of violence into which Punjab had been drawn since early this year, and the dramatic escalation in its scale and intensity since the storming of the Golden Temple in Amritsar by the army and its continued operations in the countryside, the manner in which Mrs Indira Gandhi was assassinated was, and still remains, incredible. That there could be such an appalling failure of security and intelligence is a measure of the incompetence of the most vaunted and well-funded section of the administrative machinery.

And then, while people were still in a state of shock and disbelief at the outrageous act by two of the Prime Minister's bodyguards and perhaps a minuscule group of conspirators, still unidentified, who believed that this could be a solution to any of the country's problems, it was plunged into the worst communal holocaust since Partition. The full details of the carnage are still to come in, but what has already appeared in the press is horrible enough. From West Bengal to Haryana, across the whole stretch of central and northern India, virtually every town and city, particularly the capital, was in the grip of a mad orgy of murder, loot and arson. Although reports are still incomplete, the death toll is already being put at over 1000, and no one has yet attempted to estimate the losses of property. The overwhelming majority of those killed, maimed or plundered were completely innocent of any complicity in the act for which their assailants claimed they were taking revenge; it can hardly be believed that anyone other than a tiny minority even sympathized with Mrs Gandhi's murderers. It is far more likely, as is usually the case on such occasions, that groups of hoodlums at many places took advantage of a situation of uncertainty and panic; helped by the Hindu backlash, either on their own initiative or at the behest of others, they took the 'law' into their own hands.

At the time of writing, the situation appears to be slowly coming under some semblance of control. The army, incidentally, has been deployed over a wide area for peacekeeping

10 *Frontier*, 17, 12 (10 November 1984).

purposes, further boosting its image as our saviour, and numerous towns and cities are still under curfew. Whether there was a large-scale conspiracy and organization behind the disturbances over such a wide area will probably not be known for a long time, although the suddenness with which the pretext for the trouble appeared would seem to militate against the possibility of any prior planning. What is true is that the administration at most places was slow on the uptake, tardy in keeping pace with developments and hesitant about what to do. Here again the administrative lapses are a pointer to the political reality of a governing machine packed with sycophants and most obedient servants, always waiting for orders from the impervious top, neither able nor willing to act according to any interests other than the wishes of their masters.

Indira Gandhi, who of late made a series of political miscalculations on Sikkim, Kashmir, Punjab and Andhra Pradesh, has now been succeeded in office by her son Rajiv. For at least the last two years, this was known to be her personal mission — to install her son as Prime Minister. Given the extraordinary circumstances in which the succession has taken place, criticisms about the perpetuation of a dynastic rule have been somewhat muted. However, some opposition leaders have complained about the procedural impropriety of the way in which the President took it for granted that Mr Rajiv Gandhi's election as leader of the Congress(I) Parliamentary Party was virtually assured, and could be formalized as soon as things were a little more normal.

But the procedural point, although it is worth making, is not really the most serious malady which the succession signifies. Senior leaders of the Congress(I) realized immediately after Mrs Gandhi's death that their best chance of survival lay in installing her son as quickly and with as little acrimony as possible. For, the ruling party of India is not really a political party in the usual sense, and has not been so for at least a decade. It is a party whose organization, procedures, ideology, electoral support — in short, its very existence — has flowed from a single source, that of its supreme leader. In her absence, the only way the party can hold together is with the survival of a symbolic presence, a representation. And who better to perform this role than one who in his person and name is a living memory of that singular source of power and authority.

In all likelihood, the Congress(I) will now go in for parliamentary polls as soon as possible, in order to cash in on the post-assassination sentiments of shock and grief among the people whose memory of the terror of the Emergency and the killings of thousands — victims of state violence — in the past few years, has faded. The feelings of shock will undoubtedly be stoked in order to persuade the people of the dangers to the integrity of the country and the need to consolidate a strong centralized power. It is even possible that some elements of the opposition, who have until now cried themselves hoarse about the undemocratic implications of dynastic rule, will now be brought around to support Mr Rajiv Gandhi in this so-called 'hour of crisis'. The question is, how long will this appeal remain credible. The new Prime Minister's political acumen and ideological preferences are still very largely unknown factors. But even his most optimistic supporter will be hard put to it to deny that he will face a daunting task to simply hold his party together, with no resources to go on except the memory of the departed leader.

The most critical question today is the nature of the wound the polity has suffered as a result of the events of last week. Will it be allowed to fester and further breed deep-rooted feelings of hatred among the people? Such are the questions which must engage the immediate attention of politically conscious people today. And let us not forget for a moment that members of the hunted Sikh community form a large contingent of the armed forces. Punjab is the crucial factor. What happens there may determine what happens to India. Things are falling apart. Talk of the 'healing touch' after what has occurred in large areas of the country sounds like mockery. Not even the solemnity of the funeral procession in the presence of world leaders can compensate for the lapse into barbarism.

19 November 1984: Election Prospects[11]

The expected has happened, perhaps sooner than expected. Even before the endless ceremonies of a state mourning had been gone through, this time with the full ritual grandeur of a royal

[11] *Frontier*, 17, 14 (24 November 1984).

funeral in some ancient Hindu monarchy (recreated for television in a secular democracy), Congress members were eagerly talking about the great wave of sympathy that was rising in electoral waters all over the country. In death as in life, Indira Gandhi had acted as their saviour, miraculously transforming what looked like a precarious electoral prospect into one in which the ruling party had only to romp home to a new term in office. Barely three days after the mourning formalities were completed, the new Prime Minister announced that parliamentary elections would be held on 24 and 27 December, allowing only for the statutory minimum period of notice. No Congress member can complain that his new leader has failed, at least on this instance, to seize a political opportunity at its most favourable point.

The Congress(I)'s campaign strategy will be simple and straightforward. Indira Gandhi, it will tell the electorate, alone stood for that supreme political value — the unity and integrity of India. Relentlessly, to the last day of her life, she warned her countrymen of the grave danger to that unity, of the dark forces of regional separatism and communal divisiveness that were threatening to tear the nation apart. Support a strong central government, she had said, so that the unity of the country could be properly defended. And who was more willing or able to hold a strong Centre than the Congress(I)? Many had doubted her words then, claiming they were merely a clever ploy to justify her policy of concentration of power and her desire to perpetuate an authoritarian and possibly dynastic rule. Now, the Congress(I) campaigners will remind the voters, Indira Gandhi had paid the ultimate price to prove that she was right.

The Congress(I) will hope that in the face of a saturation campaign of glorification of the assassinated leader, coupled with patriotic fervour and a subtle undertone of Hindu chauvinism, the more unpleasant questions about the actual record of Congress(I) misrule will not be asked. Will the strategy succeed? It all depends on the effectiveness of the opposition campaign, for there are a great many unpleasant questions which can and should be asked. The so-called threat to the unity of the country, which has now acquired the dreadful forms of communal hatred and political assassination, is integrally and inseparably tied with the history of authoritarianism, mindless opportunism, corruption, and the extravagant use of state violence which were the hallmarks of Congress rule in the last decade and a half. It is no secret that the seeds of communal extremism of the Bhindranwale kind were sown with the active connivance of the Congress(I), in the years when its sole political objective was to discredit and disunite its electoral opponents in Punjab. Its pretensions to a democratic political process were shown to be a complete sham as recently as four months ago — in the series of government topplings in Sikkim, Kashmir and Andhra. Despite the much-vaunted achievements in high technology and the hosting of international sporting events, its economic policies have led, in the last few years and perhaps more decisively than ever before, to a rapid sharpening of income differences between a top crust of luxury consumers and a huge substratum of the poor and dispossessed, reeling under the impact of ever-increasing inflation. About the administrative competence or moral integrity of the present leaders of the ruling gentry, the less said the better — the cases of A.R. Antulay and Ramrao Adik have temporarily receded from the front pages of national dailies, but they cannot be forgotten, for they were by no means exceptional cases. And as to cohesiveness and mutual trust within the party itself, the cracks have only just been papered over by organizing a lightning succession to the highest office and presenting Congress members with a *fait accompli*; the cracks will reappear as soon as tickets are distributed for the coming elections.

Despite the presumed wave in favour of the Congress(I) in the northern states, the talk of a landslide Congress victory is not wholly credible. In the last Lok Sabha, the Congress(I) had won a huge majority of seats from the south — 42 out of 42 in Andhra, 27 out of 28 in Karnataka. It may now lose most of those seats. In Maharashtra, Gujarat, Rajasthan, Haryana, Uttar Pradesh, Madhya Pradesh and Bihar, most seats were won by narrow pluralities, and only because the opposition votes were more or less evenly split between two contending candidates. A reasonable degree of opposition unity can still make things extremely difficult for the Congress(I), even assuming that a certain wind of sympathy will blow in its favour in the northern states. But perhaps the petty ambitions, greed, shortsightedness and unprincipled opportunism that has characterized so much of opposition politics in recent years will prevail. That is surely what the computer boys at 1, Akbar Road are counting on. If they are proved right, they will then embark on their cherished project of giving a new look to India's economy and polity. For the vast majority of the people of this country, that can only be a change for the worse.

8

The Writing on the Wall

There is much talk these days about a national crisis. The year 1984 had opened for us with a smug dismissal of George Orwell's apocalyptic predictions. Little did we know then that the year would have in store some of the most harrowing experiences in our country's recent history. As 1984 comes to a close, a feeling of anxiety and uncertainty has gripped every segment of political opinion in India.

The crisis this time is not immediately an economic one, although there are crucial economic questions which are tied to it at a more basic level. Viewed from the standpoint of the ruling classes, particularly that of big capital, 1984 has been a relatively comfortable year; and with the new emphasis on high technology, import liberalization and relaxation of controls having taken a quite definite shape, Indian industrialists were looking forward to a period of relatively rapid expansion and accumulation. This is why the present crisis has emerged even more sharply in its purely political form.

Essentially, it is a very deep crisis in the political organization of the Indian ruling class. Never since 1947 has the structure of political rule in India faced such terrible possibilities of rupture and disintegration. In fact, one might even argue that never since the 1930s, when the Congress acquired its fully developed form as an organization of national power, have the Indian ruling classes been brought face to face with such a crisis of organized political leadership. It is not simply a question of the absence of national leaders — personalities possessing the requisite authority to speak on behalf of 'the nation', whether in the ruling Congress party or in the opposition. This absence is symptomatic of a much more fundamental problem of political organization. It is there that the crisis truly lies.

How has this situation come about? Recall the 'bright' days of the post-colonial state in India. The Nehru era saw this state in full blossom — not because of what it was able to achieve in improving the conditions in which the Indian people live and work (the so-called 'progressive' aspects of Nehru's politics, over which our present generation of 'progressive' intellectuals wax so eloquent), but because it represented the fullest development yet of what this state was meant to be as a viable machinery of power exercised by the ruling classes. It was an elaborate system of balances, structured hierarchically as well as over geographical regions, providing for a reasonable degree of autonomy at each level. This process of balancing between the different sectional interests within the ruling class alliance was sustained by a federally structured party organization, led and managed by local, regional and national leaders enjoying considerable popular support on their own, and each having a recognized area of legitimate operation. Above it all was the charismatic personality of Nehru himself, standing above all sectional interests, his power not despotic but rather that of a supreme arbiter and guide. A Caesarist leadership and an interventionist state, but within a complex political organization which ensured the rule of a not necessarily harmonious alliance of dominant classes in a system of electoral democracy.

This 'golden' age could not survive the repeated crises of the 1960s. After the many uncertainties of the mid-1960s, caused by the massive food crisis, devaluation, the two wars with China and Pakistan and the shock of the Congress defeats in several states in 1967, the polity was reorganized on a new basis after the split in the ruling party. Indira Gandhi's Congress was never the same as Nehru's Congress, and the longer she exercised power the more different it became. The basic accent was now on the centralizing of executive power, and with it, the centralizing of the balancing mechanism. Thus, the representational function of the ruling party, which was earlier diffused and layered across different levels and regions, was now concentrated in the fountainhead of all representation — the person of the Prime Minister who, beyond all political divides, loyalties, interest groups, etc., supposedly stood in a direct relationship with the nation. The consequences for the polity were: concentration of executive power in the central cabinet and bureaucracy; the devaluation of Parliament and the legislative organs; the virtual elimination of internal democracy and federalism within the Congress party;

and hence, the vast accumulation of arbitrary power in the hands of a small leadership, which took upon itself the ultimate responsibility of maintaining the delicate balances between the different power groups, regional interests, sectional lobbies and so on that make up, in concrete terms, the ruling class alliance.

To be sure, this centralizing tendency, and an increasing reliance on state violence to meet oppositional moves, was itself a response to growing unrest, and to agitational movements by the oppressed classes as well as by disaffected sections from within the ruling alliance. As is usual for such politics, concentration itself aggravates divisive tendencies, and these in turn are met by still more centralization.

The Emergency and After

The difficulties of this system as a viable representative machinery for the exercise of power became clear during the Emergency period. If nothing else, the Emergency showed the inherent difficulties of an undemocratic and centralized system in maintaining the balance between different sections of the bourgeoisie and the powerful landed interests divided up regionally and locally. It also showed how massive the information gap could become between the governing authority and the state of popular opinion.

Mrs Gandhi's return to power in 1980 did not alter these tendencies. The Indian ruling classes, it seemed, had no option but to go along with Indira Gandhi's political organization; no other viable organization of class rule seemed available after the rapid break-up of the Janata alliance.

The critical dangers of the system have now been revealed. In fact, the signs were appearing in the last two or three years. In the sphere of the economy, a shift in direction was asked for and accomplished. Thus, the opening up of the Indian economy, relaxation of controls, import of high technology, and greater access to foreign funds for investment have all now become established policy in the sphere of industrial development. But the nexus between government decision-making and corporate funding of powerful political groups, at their current levels of operation, had dangerous possibilities of arbitrariness and manipulation for narrow political interests. The Swraj Paul–Escorts affair has sent shock waves through Indian big industry, and such tremendous concentration of arbitrary power in the hands of a political leadership can never be conducive to the maintenance of a stable climate which the big bourgeoisie desire.

Even more than this, Assam, Punjab and Andhra showed that the ruling Congress(I) leadership in Mrs Gandhi's last year no longer had the political acumen to manage the polity even as a machinery of class rule. The problem was not the sudden 'emergence' of regional and sectarian tendencies. Such tendencies are inherent in India's multinational polity. The point of an effective ruling machinery is precisely to manage the contrary tendencies within a viable state order. It is not that there were no linguistic or religious movements in India in the 1950s or 1960s — some of these movements, such as in Andhra, Maharashtra, Telengana, or even Punjab — were no less massive than the recent movements in Assam and Punjab. The problem is that the present ruling party fundamentally lacks the means to contain, defuse and finally appropriate these movements within itself. This is the state to which Mrs Gandhi's politics has reduced every organ of legitimate class rule in India. She reduced the ruling party to a shambles, and left behind a bureaucracy ridden by corruption and factional loyalties. The country's economic institutions have been rendered subservient and impotent, and finally, after Operation Blue Star, even the army is suffering from an unprecedented crisis in morale. It is a terrible historical irony that Indira Gandhi, who always spoke of the need for a strong state under firm and determined central leadership, finally failed the Indian ruling classes on whose behalf she was meant to rule.

Fundamental Crisis

This is the most significant dimension of the present crisis. It is a fundamental crisis of the state. There are few alternatives which are open. Perhaps many are hoping that Rajiv Gandhi will win a substantial majority in the forthcoming elections and renew the ruling organization under a legitimate and viable leadership. But the signs are not hopeful, not only because the election prospects themselves remain uncertain, but because the political acumen of the new leadership — its appalling inexperience, a distressing narrowness of political vision and the apprehensions of 'coterie rule' — is highly suspect. It is now well known that the fiasco of N.T. Rama Rao's abortive ouster, the farcical attempt to set up Santa Singh as the representative voice of the Sikh people, and the widespread dissatisfaction with the distribution of tickets for the Lok Sabha elections — only partially mitigated after Kamalapati Tripathi's threatened revolt — were all results of the inept political acts of the coterie. The present campaign of falsehood, vilification, barely concealed Hindu communalism and obtuse hostility against the opposition being carried out by Rajiv Gandhi himself will not raise hopes that the new leadership will be able the reorganize a legitimate and popular basis for the exercise of class rule. Besides, the situation within the ruling party itself is such that there is no guarantee that even a sizeable majority in Parliament will ensure a stable Congress government at the Centre.

No Viable Organization

That then is the writing on the wall. The ruling classes in India no longer have a viable political organization of class rule. And they have very few options left. This is why the indecision and immobility on the part of the Left becomes still more significant. True enough, there is no realistic basis today to claim that the Left in India can itself step into the breach and immediately take up the mantle of a national alternative, although there are many instances in history where even more dramatic transformations have occurred. But the Left must face this fundamental crisis of the state, and work out in its campaigns and programmes the outlines of an alternative. This cannot be done if slogans such as national unity, secularism, divisive tendencies, etc. are adopted by the Left on the same basis and in the same terms as those laid down by the ruling classes. For, today these are precisely the slogans which offer the Left the opportunity to launch a fundamental critique of the Indian Constitution and the Indian state order as it exists now. Unfortunately, the electoral Left is shying away from this task. Instead, we hear 'progressive' intellectuals shamelessly pleading for support to Rajiv Gandhi in order to 'protect the unity, integrity and progressive development' of the country. Or else, we see the two communist parties criticizing the failures of the Congress(I) and speculating on the relative merits of possible opposition candidates for the Prime Minister's office, but stopping short of analysing the consequences of a prolonged period of governmental instability at the Centre.

There can be no doubt that the foremost electoral task today is to defeat the Congress(I). But the crucial political task is to educate the people that an unstable structure of central power is proof that the ruling classes are unable to rule India, and that instead of this being a cause for fear and anxiety, it offers wholly new opportunities for popular mobilization and radical transformation.

9

Rajiv's Regime: The Rise

25 February 1985: Wanted Another Mandate[1]

It is the final wiping of the slate. After this, everything will begin afresh. Or that at least is what the new rulers of the country have sought to convey to the electorate. The Assembly elections on 2 and 5 March 1985 in eleven states and the Union Territory of Pondicherry must put the final stamp of popular approval on the new project before the nation: to do away with the corrupt and inefficient system of old and bring in a fresh, clean, dynamic and forward-looking system of administration. And the indications are that, except in Andhra Pradesh and Karnataka, Rajiv Gandhi's Congress(I) will coast through to comfortable margins of victory. This is despite the fact that traditionally the Congress has done worse at Assembly elections than in elections to the Lok Sabha, and despite the possibility that the very expectation of easy victory will mean a low turnout and a drop in the winning margins.

Once again it is Rajiv Gandhi's election. The new government has done remarkably well in its first two months in giving the impression of undertaking wholesale changes in policy without actually doing anything. Every now and then, one has heard announcements — from the Prime Minister himself or from some of those reputed to be among his close advisers — that there will be a completely new policy on taxes, industry, foreign trade, education, administrative recruitment and numerous other areas; but except for vague professions of intent, nothing tangible has emerged so far. Even Punjab and Assam, which were said to have been top priorities in the new government's agenda of problems that needed immediate solution, remain in exactly the same state as they were before the Lok Sabha elections. On some

---

[1] *Frontier*, 17, 28 (2 March 1985).

of these issues, Rajiv Gandhi's position seems to be that the best way to solve these problems is to deny altogether that they exist. On the Delhi riots, for instance, he has gone on record as saying that commissions of inquiry or prosecutions would only reopen old wounds, which would not be in the interests of the security of the Sikhs, and that therefore, it was best to treat the riots as a thing of the past. And so the perpetrators of one of the worst communal holocausts in independent India have been given a clean chit by a Prime Minister whose main promise is 'clean' government.

The cleansing operations have, of course, been carried out with much fanfare in the Congress(I) stables. Drastic changes were made in the lists of nominations to the various Assembly constituencies. Between 25 and 50 per cent of sitting Congress MLAs in different states, including a large number of ministers, were dropped from the lists because of charges of corruption, casteism or inefficiency. As a result, practically every established power group or faction within the Congress(I) has been hurt. In many cases, the disaffected power lobbies have put up rebel candidates. There are, of course, many snags in this so-called cleaning-up operation; detailed studies of the lists have revealed many names with not-so-saintly reputations that have somehow passed through the sieve, and what is more, a very large number who are close relatives of people who are supposed to have been axed. But the intentions behind the operations are clear: Rajiv Gandhi would like to have a party of his own, but more than that, he would like to keep alive for as long as possible the impression that he is changing things. It is of course a dangerous game in the uncertain world of electoral politics to keep raising popular expectations to such high levels without actually having concrete ideas on how to achieve them; but he has so far ridden the crest of a wave, and surely wishes to stay there as long as possible.

His task has been made easier by the pathetic condition of the opposition. Except for Andhra Pradesh, where N.T. Rama Rao and his Telugu Desam are aiming to repeat their 1983 and 1984 victories, and Karnataka, where despite the breakdown of the alliance between the Janata and the BJP, Ramakrishna Hegde will at least be fighting hard to retain his government, the opposition in every other state is yet to recover from a state of shock.

The real test will begin after the polls — when the rulers try to match up to the claims they have themselves made about their intentions and capabilities. The Indian electorate, they will remember, does not deny a serious claimant to power a fair chance; but it is cruel to those who let it down.

13 May 1985: The Century and After[2]

Public celebrations to mark the centenary of the birth of the Indian National Congress began in New Delhi last week under the auspices of the Congress(I), with the full complement of official media coverage. Yet neither among Congress members nor among the general public was there any noticeable enthusiasm. The immediate political objective was to firmly install Rajiv Gandhi as unquestioned leader of the party. To go by appearances, this objective was achieved, to the accompaniment of the usual panoply of obsequious display and sycophantic verbiage. More than ever before in its hundred-year history, the Congress today looks like a dynastic institution; and every time its glorious heritage is recalled, the obligatory names are Motilal, Jawaharlal and Indira — and now Rajiv to take us into the twenty-first century.

Given the state of activity in the party in recent weeks, marked as it has been by abject surrender to the dictates of the ruling caucus around the Prime Minister, no one was expecting any political controversy at the AICC session immediately preceding the public celebrations. Yet it did show up, perhaps not quite a controversy, but at least an inkling of certain underlying tensions, with ideological as well as organizational overtones. The economic resolutions adopted by the AICC reaffirmed 'unequivocally its commitment to socialism'; socialism was the goal 'because in India's social and economic conditions, no other way was conceivable for solving the problems of the people'. This statement, it transpired, was a major departure from the original draft proposed by V.P. Singh, the Union Finance Minister. The drafting committee for the AICC's economic resolution apparently became the forum for a significant discussion on the policies of the present government. Apart from emphasizing the continued

2 *Frontier*, 17, 39 (18 May 1985).

relevance of Jawaharlal's socialistic orientation, the committee insisted on several other changes to V.P. Singh's draft, including complete deletion of any reference to the introduction of modern technology, and inclusion of a paragraph expressing concern at 'the unwarranted upward trend in the prices of some commodities'. As Congress resolutions go, there was nothing particularly striking in these statements; but such has been the tone of the recent pronouncements of the Prime Minister and his economic pundits in residence, that the note of discord sounded in the AICC could hardly be missed.

There is emerging, it would seem, a considerable hiatus between the economic dreams of the present rulers and the political compulsions of ruling the country. Rajiv Gandhi and his cronies speak of bringing in modern technology, giving greater incentives to the private corporate sector, inviting foreign investors, and removing the inefficiencies of the public sector as the solution to the poverty and stagnation of the country. Whether this is naive ideology or an astonishingly narrow class interest, one cannot tell; perhaps it is a bit of both. It is this brand of thinking that was reflected in the recent budget proposals.

But the political compulsions of ruling within a framework of electoral democracy impose an entirely different set of constraints on economic policy. The implications of the budget for the common man have become apparent in a dramatically short time, with a whopping 2.3 per cent price rise in five weeks. Taken together with the recent by-election reverses, it is hardly surprising that many Congress members have become worried about how they will keep their constituents quiet. The message from the AICC to the new leadership is clear: tread cautiously.

For the moment at least, Rajiv Gandhi seems to have read the message. At the public sessions, he dutifully mouthed all the obligatory slogans about socialism, the public sector and anti-poverty programmes. This has worried his supporters in the business world, who have seen in this an unexpected and entirely undesirable buckling under pressure. Of course, the framers of India's economic programme for the twenty-first century have hardly given up; after all, they have only just begun. But the signs are clear that their plans will not go through without a considerable political struggle, even within the ruling power bloc.

For a hundred years, the Congress has served its historical

role as the principal political organization of the Indian ruling classes. As such, it has also reflected on its surface the many contradictions among those classes. No matter how impatient the party's new leader may be with the slow and contentious process of political bargaining which has characterized the way the organization has functioned over these years, he is unlikely to succeed in keeping together a viable coalition of ruling class interests if he chooses to bypass the organization altogether. And senior Congress members are trying to explain to their inexperienced prince the lesson of one hundred years of politics; without a viable ruling class coalition, you cannot beat back the challenge of those you have to rule!

20 May 1985: Another Black Act[3]

The Union government has seemingly exhausted its political resources in trying to produce a settlement in Punjab. The brief spell of attempts at negotiation was shattered in early May by the series of bomb explosions in various north Indian towns. Now the government seems to have decided once again to 'get tough'. Among the many measures being adopted is a new piece of legislation giving it sweeping powers to deal with 'terrorism'.

The Terrorist and Disruptive Activities (Prevention) Bill was tabled in Parliament on 18 May 1985, and at the time of writing it has yet to be debated and passed. But the provisions are clear enough. The Bill gives a detailed definition of what constitute 'terrorist acts' and 'disruptive activities', provides a maximum punishment of death for such offences, and empowers the government to set up 'designated courts' for the speedy trial of such cases.

A 'terrorist act' is now defined as involving the use of bombs or other explosives, inflammable substances, firearms or other lethal weapons, poisons, noxious gases or other chemicals, in order to cause death or injury to persons or destruction of property or disruption of essential services, the intention being to overawe the government or to strike terror in the people or to adversely affect the harmony among different sections of the people. Whoever commits a 'terrorist act' will now be punishable

[3] *Frontier*, 17, 40 (25 May 1985).

by death. Even if such an act does not kill, the offender will be imprisoned for a minimum of five years, extendable to life.

These provisions are, of course, for explicitly violent acts of terrorism. But even more wide-ranging are the powers claimed by the government to contain 'disruptive activities'. Such activities are defined to include 'any action taken, whether by act or by speech or song or ballad or verse or words or by any book, pamphlet, paper, writing, record, tape, video cassette, drawing, painting, representation or in any manner whatsoever which questions, disrupts or is intended to disrupt, whether directly or indirectly, the sovereignty and territorial integrity of India or which is intended to bring about or support any claim, whether directly or indirectly, for the cession of any part of India or the secession of any part of India from the Union'.

Further, any act which 'advocates, advises, suggests, incites, predicts, prophesies, pronounces or otherwise expresses, in such a manner as to incite, advise, suggest or prompt' the killing of any public servant will be deemed a disruptive activity. The minimum period of imprisonment for such an offence will be three years, and the maximum, for life.

These provisions are ostensibly intended to deal with inflammatory and secessionist propaganda. But the terms are so broad that virtually any kind of oppositional agitation can be brought under its sway (note the very redundancy of the items listed as offences). Besides, the Bill gives the Union government immense administrative powers to deal with 'terrorist and disruptive activities'. These include censorship, entry into any place suspected of harbouring terrorists, prohibiting meetings and processions, demolition of buildings, preventing circulation of reports likely to promote hatred between different classes of people, and the right to compel any person to comply with any scheme for the prevention of terrorist acts.

Once again, therefore, the government is claiming extraordinary powers to deal with internal political instability. No one will dispute the need to take active security measures to protect state dignitaries, or disagree that the outrageous tactics of bomb attacks on unsuspecting people in buses, trains and public places need to be foiled. It is also quite clear that as far as Punjab is concerned, the so-called moderate Akalis have shown a pathetic political ineptitude in dealing with threats from the 'extremist' sections. Yet there can be no gainsaying the fact that it is the Union government which, through its actions over the last few years, is primarily responsible for creating the appalling mess which is Punjab today. And now it is claiming extraordinary powers to deal with 'terrorist and disruptive activities'.

It is one more proof, if proof is needed, of the utter incompetence of the law enforcement agencies of the state, including the police and the intelligence services, to do their job within the normal ambit of the law. The greater their failure, the more they clamour for extraordinary powers. The latest legislation to deal with 'terrorism' is tantamount to giving the administration the powers to act as in times of Emergency, without actually declaring it. And who are being entrusted with these extraordinary powers in the belief that they will use them with discretion? A bureaucracy which has distinguished itself by selling official secrets for bottles of whiskey, and a police which only the other day went on a rampage in Ahmedabad because the newspapers had complained about them.

The pretext for claiming greater and more arbitrary executive powers has been carefully prepared. Now the claim has been made. And more is being promised in the form of an Anti-Sedition Bill in the next session of Parliament.

3 June 1985: No Peace in Sight[4]

Amidst massive security arrangements and the full blast of media publicity, the country has been made to await with much anxiety the course of events during what the press is referring to in a perfectly matter-of-fact way as 'genocide week'. The first of June was the day when 'Operation Blue Star' was launched, and this is the first anniversary of those fateful days when the Golden Temple in Amritsar was stormed by the Indian armed forces. After the series of bomb blasts in several north Indian towns a few weeks ago, which effectively scuttled for the time being the various inchoate moves towards a negotiated solution to the Punjab crisis, it was widely apprehended that there would be more trouble in the first week of June. Security arrangements were made on a quite unprecedented scale. All road, rail and air

[4] *Frontier*, 17, 42 (8 June 1985).

traffic proceeding to and from the north of Delhi have been subjected to meticulous security checks. The border with Pakistan has been sealed off, ostensibly to block the smuggling of arms and personnel across the border. Police and intelligence forces in most north Indian cities are on full alert. Thousands of people suspected of having 'terrorist' connections have been arrested. And in Punjab itself, the armed forces have been deployed on a massive scale. Until the time of writing, however, no major incident has been reported from anywhere in the country.

In the meantime, the prospects of any solution to the immediate problem in Punjab seem as elusive as ever. It appears that the possibility of a settlement with the Longowal group in the Akali Dal has been given up: not only because of the factionally inspired impediments put up by the Tohra and Badal groups, but also in recognition of the plain fact that Harcharan Singh Longowal does not possess the credibility and moral authority to make a settlement which would be acceptable to the various sections of organized opinion among the Sikh people. There is no doubt that those who are described as 'extremists' enjoy considerable prestige and popular support. This section has now found a new symbol of public identity in the person of Baba Joginder Singh, father of the deceased Bhindranwale. There are speculations that the government is looking for a suitable opportunity to strike a deal with at least a sizeable section of the 'extremists' through Joginder Singh. If this is so, it would not be surprising if the venerable Baba feels it necessary to start by making a lot of defiant noises.

In objective terms, the government is counting on the fact that the most important organized interests which are said to be behind the recent spate of agitations in Punjab, would certainly prefer a solution which gives them more power within the framework of the Indian Union. Once again, objectively, this would demand a more broad-based and democratic devolution of power at the regional and local levels of government. The difficulty is that in the course of the last decade and a half, the Indian ruling classes and their political leaders have continuously undermined those very political institutions which could have made such a solution possible. Pushed into a crisis by its own political incompetence, the government must now rely on the armed forces to suppress the people while the bureaucrats fumble their way in search of a negotiated solution. No one has the moral authority to make a settlement stick. No one can claim that he has control over his own supporters. Even the government is not sure how the Congress(I) politicians in Punjab, or in neighbouring Haryana, Himachal Pradesh, Jammu and Kashmir or Western UP, will take to a negotiated settlement with the Akalis. And so the stalemate continues, broken periodically by sudden bursts of insane violence and the no-less-disagreeable ordeal of a peace enforced by armed strength.

17 June 1985: Gujarat Still in Flames[5]

It is already being called the longest 'riot' since independence, having continued for over four months. Is it a riot? A series of riots? A civil war? Or is it society breaking apart, a war of all against all? The labels do not matter any more, and as political observers and social analysts spout one new 'theory' after another on the Gujarat phenomenon, each explanation seems as true or as unenlightening as the next.

In terms of the immediate political situation, it is evident that all semblance of legitimate authority in the form of a civil administration has virtually evaporated from the towns and cities of Gujarat. If the eruptions of violence seem to die down from time to time, it is either out of sheer exhaustion or because of the heavy deployment of armed troops in the troubled areas. And soon after, the violence explodes somewhere else. The immediate issue which sparked off the trouble was the question of reserved seats in educational institutions for 'backward castes' in addition to the statutory quotas for 'scheduled castes and tribes'. The Madhavsingh Solanki government was thought to be 'pampering' the backward castes, particularly the Kshatriyas, for electoral reasons. The upper castes got together under the banner of the anti-reservation campaign, ostensibly to fight for equality and merit. As always, the first target of the agitation was the government and its law-enforcement agencies. The police retaliated with unseemly arbitrariness and complete disregard for the processes of law. The floodgates were

[5] *Frontier*, 17, 44 (22 June 1985).

opened. Every interest seemed to require its own instruments of armed protection. Criminals had a field day, offering their services for the technical organization of civil violence. Targets proliferated, offence and defence blurred into a medley of organized armed clashes between upper castes and backward castes, backward castes and scheduled castes, Hindus and Muslims, until no one knew any more the precise lines of alliance and antagonism.

The 'causes' of the continuing violence are now a subject of much discussion. The very proliferation of 'theories' on the subject is an indication that, in a quite fundamental sense, the processes of change now under way in India's economy and society are eluding the comprehension of policymakers as well as their critics. It is certain that the spread of capitalism in agriculture in the last two decades, the eviction from the land of large sections of the rural poor, the growing economic and political aspirations of the regional and local bourgeoisie spawned by this process, the rapid and seemingly irreversible obsolescence of the traditional sectors of Indian big industry, the rapid spread of an underpaid and unorganized 'informal' industrial sector, the increasing insecurity of the literati and urban middle classes — all of these have something to do with what is happening today in Punjab or Assam or Gujarat. The question is not simply one of the intrinsic theoretical or ethical merits of the case for 'reservations for the uplift of the socially disprivileged castes'. The more crucial problem is the inability of the political process either to constrain the new forces and antagonisms within a framework of legitimacy and order, or to channelize them into an organized struggle for revolutionary change. Thus, both the defence of privilege and the demands for an end to privilege remain sectional, fragmented, open to manipulation and, in an atmosphere of pervasive violence, to criminalization.

The irony is that the greater the proliferation of sectionally organized and criminally inspired violence, the stronger the claims of the government for extraordinary powers to maintain 'law and order', and the feebler the will and the ability of the parliamentary opposition to resist those claims. We have seen this happen in the case of the Anti-Terrorist Act as a sequel to the Punjab events.

30 July 1985: The Punjab Pact[6]

What is the accord? It is perhaps the first-ever formal 'accord'
signed between a Prime Minister of India and the leaders of
an opposition agitation. What does that indicate? The gravity
of the Punjab problem? Its unprecedented nature? A new
style of leadership which Rajiv Gandhi wishes to foster? Or
perhaps, sheer thoughtlessness about the implications of such
a precedent for the future governance of such a large and
variegated political entity as India?

What are the terms of the accord? Eleven points were agreed
upon, of which three — the territorial claims of Punjab to Chandigarh and of Haryana to the Hindi-speaking areas of Punjab,
the dispute over the sharing of the Ravi–Beas waters between
Punjab, Haryana and Rajasthan, and the Akali Dal demand for
revision of Centre–State relations — have been on the agenda
for several years now. Of the others, those relating to an enquiry
into the November 1984 riots, rehabilitation of army deserters,
the disposal of cases in special courts in Punjab, and compensation for property damaged in agitations and armed action, arose
in the course of events following upon the army action in Punjab
in June 1984. The government has conceded the demand for a
judicial enquiry into the riots in Delhi as well as in Bokaro and
Kanpur. The cases under the Armed Forces Special Powers Act
will be withdrawn. Only those charged with waging war and
hijacking will be tried at special courts; all other cases will be
transferred to ordinary courts. People whose property has been
damaged 'in agitation or any action after 1 August 1982' will be
compensated. Deserters will not be taken back into the army, but
will be provided 'gainful employment'.

Of the more long-standing demands, the agreement on the
disputes over territory and river waters had been available for
a long time. The obvious argument can be made that if the
fundamental points had been sorted out as late as early-1984,
the tragedy of Punjab could well have been avoided. What
prevented such an agreement? Disunity and indecision among
the Akalis, the unwillingness of the Congress(I) to concede a
'victory' to the Akali Dal, and the fear of loss of Hindu support

[6] *Frontier*, 17, 50 (3 August 1985).

in Haryana, western UP and Rajasthan. Have these calculations changed now, after a bloody army action, a Prime Minister assassinated, and the worst communal carnage in post-independence India? That is what the publicists would have us believe. But the proof is still to come. Three months ago they were saying that an agreement with the Akalis was impossible because they had no credible leaders. Now, suddenly, Sant Longowal has emerged as the universally accepted leader of the Sikhs. The transformation is hardly credible. It is still to be seen to what extent the Sant can carry, not just the faction-ridden band of *jathedars,* but the Sikh masses among whom a sense of injury and injustice has deepened far more in the last year or so than disputes over river waters. On the other side of the fence, it is obvious that all is not well with the 'Hindu vote bank' in Haryana and Rajasthan. For the time being, New Delhi has been able to muzzle the anxieties of Congress(I) leaders in those states, but the opposition can hardly be expected to let such a juicy agitational opportunity slip by. How local Congress members react to such an agitation needs to be watched. In other words, Rajiv Gandhi and his chief adviser on this matter — Arjun Singh, Governor of Punjab — have sought to use the accord with Sant Longowal to signal a dramatic change of scene, but it is not at all clear that the underlying political and organizational conditions have changed all that much.

Even more interesting is the question of Centre–State relations and the Anandpur Sahib resolution. During the December 1984 elections, Mr Gandhi had flogged the resolution for its 'anti-national and secessionist' overtones and castigated every opposition party for not having opposed it. Now, apparently, he is satisfied by the assurance of Sant Longowal that the resolution is 'within the framework of the Indian Constitution', and has agreed to refer it to the Sarkaria Commission. Most observers, including opposition leaders, have chosen to ignore this doublespeak. But this is perhaps the most crucial issue of the Indian polity which the Punjab events have brought to the surface — not the specific reference to the Sarkaria Commission, but the general problem of centralization of powers at the top of the structure, and the contrary tendency of the rise of 'regional power blocs'. Indira Gandhi had managed one sort of accommodation with the Tamil Nadu power bloc. Her son, after last year's fiascos over the attempted ouster of Mr Rama Rao, is attempting much the same sort of thing in Andhra. But Punjab is much closer to the centres of power, the emotional pitch of the dispute is much higher, and the people there have recently had much more direct exposure to 'great' political happenings. It is hardly likely that a power-sharing formula between a few Akali factions and the Congress(I) will resolve the fundamental tensions that are emerging in India's politics.

26 August 1985: The Gift Turns Sour[7]

The Punjab agony continues. Sant Harcharan Singh Longowal, once vilified by the Congress(I) for his inability to face up to the extremist threat, and in recent weeks hailed by the national press for his courage in taking the most decisive step so far in bringing peace to Punjab, has now been removed from the scene. Despite the proclamations of the Prime Minister, the future remains as uncertain as ever in that hapless part of the country.

Did the Sant's death have something to do with the sudden announcement of the decision to go in for immediate elections, despite the warnings of every opposition party including the Akali Dal itself? Was not an attempt on his life a virtual certainty? Looking back on events relating to Punjab in the last few weeks, the answer is a very definite 'yes'. And a review of these developments also brings out the utterly cynical calculations which lay behind the decisions taken by the rulers in New Delhi. The 'accord' was meant to signify their readiness to end a period of confrontation by coming to some arrangement of sharing power with the agitating groups in Punjab. After many explorations and experiments, they finally settled on Sant Longowal as the most acceptable partner with whom to strike this agreement. Immediately, there began an orchestrated media campaign celebrating the Prime Minister's youthful dynamism ('a government that works faster' is the latest slogan) and wisdom in seizing the right opportunity to bring peace to Punjab. The accord had been universally acclaimed in that state, and the 'extremists' were

[7] *Frontier*, 18, 2 (31 August 1985).

completely isolated — or so at least the media would have had us believe.

However, G.S. Tohra and Prakash Singh Badal, both of whom are far more adept at manipulative power-sharing politics than the late Sant Longowal, scrupulously dissociated themselves from the Sant as soon as the accord was announced. Underlying the mood of euphoria, the political realities in Punjab were far more complicated. This became clear from the unwillingness of every major political party in Punjab, except the Congress(I), to go in for elections. A competitive campaign for votes at this stage would only reopen the wounds, they said. The electorate could not but be split along communal lines, and with the tempo rising, the slogans would get more and more extreme on either side of the communal divide. Besides, the terrorist groups would surely try their best to scuttle the elections, by whatever means available.

New Delhi read these warnings as signs of the electoral weakness and organizational disarray of the opposition groups. The going was good, the rulers thought, for a quick Congress(I) victory in Punjab; or failing that, even a coalition with the Longowal group. Hasty calculations were made about how the Hindu vote or the Mazhabi Sikh vote would break, and how much abstention there was likely to be among Sikh voters because of extremist propaganda to boycott the elections. And then, in an amazing act of thoughtlessness, the Union government announced that elections would be held by 22 September 1985. Within three days, the Sant was dead.

What happens in Punjab now? The Prime Minister has reiterated that elections must be held; not to do so would be to surrender to the terrorists. The opposition parties — including a leaderless Akali Dal — are still, at the time of writing, pleading with New Delhi to postpone the elections. The terrorists have flexed their muscles once; everyone seems to be apprehending more trouble. The sense of relief has evaporated rapidly. It is true, perhaps, that terrorist acts of this sort enjoy very little active support among the people. But the wounds in Punjab are deep and still festering. It is significant that extremist groups are reported to have openly celebrated Sant Longowal's death in several cities in Punjab. Now the nation awaits with trepidation the next round of trouble.

30 September 1985: New Phase in Punjab[8]

The Akali Dal (Longowal group) has won an unprecedented victory in the Punjab elections. Taking as many as 29 seats away from the Congress(I), it has come out victorious in 73 of the 100 seats it contested, winning a clear majority in a house of 117. It has also won 7 of the 13 Lok Sabha seats from the state. An Akali ministry under the leadership of Surjit Singh Barnala has also been sworn in. Never in the history of Punjab has the Akali Dal formed a ministry on its own. In fact, a common saying in Punjab was that it never could, given the very small majority of Sikhs in the religious break-up of the state's population. It is ironical that the most bitterly communalist phase of Punjab's history since independence should end with such a sweeping victory for the Akali Dal, and that the victory should be greeted with such a widespread sense of relief.

Once again, the meticulous electoral arithmetic based on religion, caste, patronage, etc. has been thrown by the wayside in a massive swing of votes away from the Congress(I) and in favour of the Akali Dal. The Dal itself could hardly go into these elections with anything like its normal organizational preparedness. The Union government, by unilaterally declaring elections with only the minimum statutory period of notice, did not give any of the political parties — particularly the Akali Dal — time to recover and reorganize after nearly two years of extremely abnormal political conditions. On top of that, the tragic assassination of Sant Longowal, who until the day of his death was urging a postponement of elections, threw the party into still greater trouble. Mr Barnala appeared as the successor to the Sant, but his influence over such important faction leaders as Mr Badal and Mr Tohra seemed questionable. Yet, despite these organizational shortcomings (reflected in the fact that the Dal was finally able to put up candidates in only 100 of the 115 seats for which elections were held this time), it has won a victory which no political analyst of Punjab would have thought possible before the series of incidents that began with 'Operation Blue Star'.

News-reports indicate a much sharper polarization of votes along communal lines than ever before. The fundamental strategy

[8] *Frontier*, 18, 7 (5 October 1985).

of the Congress in previous elections in Punjab had been to split the Sikh vote, especially by winning over the large scheduled-caste Mazhabi Sikh electorate. This time, it appears, the Mazhabi vote has uniformly gone in favour of the Akali Dal — such has been the emotional impact of the events following the storming of the Golden Temple, including the assassination of Sant Longowal. In some pockets, even Hindus have voted for the Dal as the best guarantee of peace in the state.

The popular verdict has proved, not what the bourgeois press is now claiming — that extreme communalist politics has no place in our present political system — but rather that extreme and violent communalism is allowed to raise its head when it becomes an instrument in the squabbles among the dominant class interests, and that the people are allowed to say 'no' to it only after a power-sharing arrangement has been worked out at the top. Organized terrorism of the kind practised in Punjab or Delhi, or financed and masterminded by extremist groups operating from abroad, does not require and never had a large popular support. This is indicated by the defeat in two constituencies of the widow of Beant Singh, one of those who killed Mrs Gandhi and was lionized by extremists and even moderates. As such, a popularly elected ministry in Punjab is no guarantee that such groups will cease to operate. Whether they will still have the support of powerful people in key positions is, of course, another matter.

The commercial and state media, in their usual fawning manner, have also showered praise on the Prime Minister for his 'wisdom' in sticking to his decision to hold the elections in Punjab, despite the pleadings of virtually every opposition party including the Akali Dal. The fact that the elections have gone through without much trouble is proof, they say, of Rajiv Gandhi's foresight and perspicacity. They have, of course, conveniently forgotten the fact that the run-up to these elections saw the killing of one of the foremost political leaders of Punjab, Sant Harcharan Singh Longowal, without whose cooperation there would have been no 'accord' and no election. Also not mentioned is the unprecedented, massive mobilization of security forces at the time of the elections.

Finally, what indeed will happen to the 'Punjab problem?' The Union government is said to be operating in terms of the so-called 'Tamil Nadu model', of allowing regionally dominant

class forces to come to power in the state while working out a
political alliance at the Centre. But in many ways, the Punjab
case is quite different. For one thing, the dominant agrarian
interests in Punjab are much more intimately linked with the
all-India foodgrains economy. There has also been a massive
accumulation of wealth in the hands of small and medium entrepreneurs in Punjab who are seeking to enter the world of all-
India commerce. These forces cannot easily be accommodated
within the present structure of the Indian economy without
jeopardizing established monopoly interests. It is by no means
certain, therefore, that the more basic dimensions of the 'Punjab
problem' have been resolved in any significant way.

23 December 1985: The No-win Choice[9]

By-elections, it is said, usually turn out badly for the ruling party.
People with even minor grievances go out and vote against the
government, knowing fully well that the result can only shake
things up a little; no major convulsion will be caused. That at
least is how Congress(I) spokesmen are trying to explain the
results of the latest by-polls. But even their supporters appear to
be sceptical.

For, the signs of waning public support are clear. Of the Lok
Sabha seats outside Assam, the Congress(I) has lost three important contests: Kishanganj in Bihar to the Janata (a seat the Con-
gress(I) had held previously), Bolpur to the CPI(M), and
Kendrapara also to the Janata. It has held four other seats — Churu
in Rajasthan, Bijnaur in U.P., Banka in Bihar, and South Delhi
— but all with considerably reduced majorities. Of the Assembly
by-polls, the significant results are from Jullundur in Punjab
where the BJP has won two urban and presumably predominantly
Hindu seats, and from West Bengal where the CPI(M) has retained the Nanur seat in Birbhum despite much organizational
embarrassment over the Banamali Das affair. Besides, the CPI(M)
almost managed to snatch away the Aurangabad seat in Murshidabad, a traditionally Congress seat.

These signs emanating from various parts of the country do
not, therefore, look good for the Congress(I). They cannot be

[9] *Frontier*, 18, 19 (28 December 1985).

explained away merely in terms of mid-term electoral impatience. First of all, it is only a year since the party under the new leadership of Rajiv Gandhi was swept into power under extraordinary circumstances. Those elections held a year ago were by no means normal, run-of-the-mill elections; and the new government, over the last year, has used every available opportunity to drive it into our heads that it is bent on making a clean break with the past. There has indeed been a conscious effort to bring in a change of style. Even so, the latest results show, if not a rejection, at least evidence that voters in different parts of the country have not been particularly impressed by the new style. It is now being said quite openly in Congress(I) circles that the new Prime Minister's clean-cut, modern-management style of functioning is not proving to be an effective vote-catching strategy among the larger electorate. And if a member of the Nehru family is not going to be a vote-catcher for the Congress, why have him at the top anyway?

These rumblings of discontent and dissension within the Congress(I) have grown louder with the decisive defeat of the party in Assam. Disproving every prediction, the newly formed Asom Gana Parishad, organizational successor to the movement which in the last six years has so often made Assam front-page news in the national dailies, has won an absolute majority. At the time of writing, it is set to form only the second non-Congress government in Assam since independence. The AGP virtually swept the Assamese vote, and was able to win a majority of seats despite the fact that it did not even contest in some 15 per cent of seats. On the other hand, the Congress(I) lost its traditional support among the minority and tribal populations of the state. The Bengali-speaking and Muslim voters flocked to support the newly constituted United Minorities Front, while the Plains Tribal Council has won more seats this time than ever before. The result is that the Congress(I) has ended up with a paltry 25 seats in a house of 125.

As far as election results go, the Assam results are decisive, for the AGP will have the chance to make its own government and to carry out its own programmes. As far as those programmes go, however, the portents are dire. The last several years saw a campaign against Bengali-speaking and predominantly Muslim 'immigrants' whom the movement leaders designated as 'foreigners'. That movement directed itself against the Union government and the Congress(I), principally because the Congress(I) in Assam was thought to be protecting minority interests for electoral purposes. Indira Gandhi had no qualms about using such divisive ploys for electoral gains: the outcome was the Nellie massacre and the farcical elections of 1983. Rajiv Gandhi, zealously setting out to 'solve' one after the other the 'problems' left behind by his mother, signed an 'accord' on Assam in the same way that he had on Punjab, and at one stroke signed away any viable electoral strategy for the Congress(I). For, the accord began to be flaunted by the protagonists of the Assam movement as their historic victory, whereas the minorities, made ever more insecure, felt they had been betrayed by the Congress(I). The polarization of votes was virtually complete: the Congress(I) became the loser on both sides.

Having won the elections, the AGP leaders are now trying to assuage the minorities by declaring that those who are 'genuine' Indian nationals have nothing to fear. Of their broader socio-economic programmes, nothing is known because nothing has been thought of. The AGP, after all, is an organization born out of a one-point movement. How far the new leadership will be able to control its hordes of overenthusiastic and chauvinistic supporters is anybody's guess. There is no doubt that the minorities in Assam will now carefully watch every move of the new government. The decisive electoral result has thus heightened the tension and anxieties in Assam, not resolved them.

At the all-India plane, Assam becomes the eighth state with a non-Congress government, not counting Tamil Nadu where the ruling party is an electoral ally of the Congress(I). Already, the discrepancy between the massive Congress(I) majority in Parliament and its lack of support in the states is becoming stark. More fundamentally, the strategy of the new leadership under Mr Gandhi seems to be to contain regional forces by allowing them a measure of power at the state level: not in the old way by absorbing them within the Congress, but by retaining their autonomous identity. Bureaucratically, the strategy might seem viable, because as long as the real powers rest with the central executive, it matters little if regional parties run the government in some of the states. The problem lies at the level of the ruling political party, for this strategy appears to have spelt doom for the state-level Congress leadership everywhere. And without nurturing support at this level, where will the central leadership find the popular support to sustain its new bureaucratic endeavours?

17 February 1986: Mosque or Temple?[10]

It seems like a throwback to the days of the Raj. A local dispute involving the conflicting claims of the 'Hindoo' and 'Moslem' communities; the judicial wing of the state called upon to pronounce its judgement by looking at the 'historical and other' evidence on the matter; a decision of the court which leads to open clashes 'between the two communities'. That is what we have witnessed in the last few weeks following an order of the district and sessions judge of Faizabad in Uttar Pradesh, directing the government to 'open forthwith' the gates of a place of worship in Ayodhya which for at least four hundred years has been known as the Babari mosque, but which some local Hindus claim was the site of a 2000-year-old temple which was converted into a mosque in Mughal times. The order was 'greeted with massive victory celebrations' by Hindu organizations in different U.P. towns, while Muslim organizations have launched a 'country-wide agitation' to demand the restoration of the Babari mosque. The tension is still building up, but already there has been a serious communal clash in Old Delhi and several minor incidents in different places in the country.

The history of the dispute itself reads like a history of Indian communalism in miniature. For more than three centuries, the particular premises in Ayodhya town had been a mosque, said to have been established by the first Mughal emperor. But stories had survived of its once having been a temple, built by none other than Emperor Vikramaditya, on the site of the birthplace of Rama. The recent spate of conflicts had its roots in the middle of the last century, when there was a series of Hindu–Muslim clashes all over northern India. That was a period of large-scale change, turmoil and realignment of power relations in the wake of the spread and consolidation of British rule in that region. It was then that wealthy and powerful

---

[10] *Frontier*, 18, 27 (22 February 1986).

Hindus in the area demanded that the status of the site as a place of worship of Rama be recognized. Sometime in the late 19th century, British administrators permitted both Hindus and Muslims to use the place for religious purposes in separate parts of the building. The latest phase of the dispute dates back to 1949, when a Hindu group forcibly entered the premises, installed idols of Rama and Sita, and declared it the Rama Janmabhumi temple. The matter went to court and had been lying there for the last thirty-six years, with numerous claims being made not only on the matter of the specific religious status of the building, but also on which particular group or individuals had rights of ownership over it. Now, on 31 January 1986, the district court has passed an order: not on the whole series of disputes before it, but simply clarifying a 1950 directive, to say that the premises should be unlocked to allow devotees to perform puja. This has been read as a sign of 'victory' by organizations such as the Vishwa Hindu Parishad and the RSS, and correspondingly by Muslim organizations as yet another violation of minority rights.

The matter is no longer something to do with the local history of a small town in U.P. It has been drawn into the vortex of communalist politics in India today. All-India Muslim bodies such as the Majlis-e-Mushawarat have launched campaigns throughout the country to mobilize Muslim opinion on the issue. The communal situation in India today is very delicately poised, and this has to do with the general feeling of crisis and uncertainty that has crept into political life given the continued intractability of the Punjab problem, the demise of familiar leaders and parties, and the sudden talk of rapid change without anyone being sure of where exactly we are heading. In a situation like this, minor matters can become major irritants, and there is no dearth of people and organizations who will do their utmost to exploit any available issue to make their voices heard. Besides, religion is good business, especially when associated with no less a personage than Lord Rama and the place of his birth. Behind the talk of ancient tradition and spirituality, there are hard-headed, money-minded people who are already fighting over the possible spoils of a Rama Janmabhumi temple made suddenly famous by being 'liberated' from the hands of the Muslims. And the ruling political order, having chosen to function within exactly the same legal and administrative framework as the British colonial state, can only pronounce upon the comparative merits of 'Hindu' and 'Muslim' claims, and then send out the police to maintain 'law and order'.

10 March 1986: Walling Off Women?[11]

While the opposition to the proposed Muslim Women (Protection of Rights on Divorce) Bill has gained in strength over the last two or three weeks, the government still seems bent upon pushing it through Parliament in the current session. The reasons which suddenly prompted the Prime Minister and his advisers to decide to conciliate Muslim fundamentalist opinion were unconvincing from the very beginning, even from a purely pragmatic standpoint. Now opinion against the move is mounting, and is being voiced openly even within the Congress Parliamentary Party: the men who rule are now having to use the whip to silence the dissenters, and to persuade the doubters that the Prime Minister's political prestige is involved in the matter, for which reason they must vote in favour of the Bill. Why the Prime Minister should have allowed himself to get caught in a jam entirely of his own making is of course a question that is being politely avoided.

If one attempts to unravel the reasoning behind the government's move, the point to begin is the Supreme Court judgement last year on the Shah Bano case. The Court had ruled that when a Muslim woman is divorced, the responsibility of the husband to provide maintenance was not restricted only to the so-called *iddat* period of three months, and that the *mehr* promised at the time of the wedding was not an adequate compensation for divorce. It further ruled that if there was a conflict between sections 125 and 127 of the Criminal Procedure Code and the relevant sections of the Muslim Personal Law, the former must prevail. This judgement was hailed in progressive circles as an extremely bold move to defend the rights of Muslim women, who normally do not have the means to demand even the minimal rights given to them under the *shari'a* but are burdened with all the deprivation enjoined upon them by a harsh medieval

[11] *Frontier*, 18, 30 (15 March 1986).

religious code. Not surprisingly, the judgement led to protests from various conservative Muslim bodies. This was inevitable; but at least the signs were clear that the debate within the Muslim intelligentsia in India on matters of religious reform had reached a qualitatively new stage.

It is here that the thoughtlessness of Rajiv Gandhi's advisers altered the situation completely. With the economy not behaving in the way they had ordered, the Punjab problem — once believed to have been 'solved' — suddenly bouncing back with unexpected severity, and a series of by-election upsets, the ruling clique in New Delhi suddenly discovered that the people were no longer loving their rule the way they had a year ago. The advisers rummaged through their computer printouts, went into a huddle, and came up with the brilliant suggestion that the one electoral group which needed immediate conciliation was the Muslims. They seemed to be agitated by the Shah Bano judgement. Do something to please them, and that would ensure the support of a crucial minority group!

Thus came the Muslim Divorce Bill. It was drafted, the Prime Minister said, after consultation with 'Muslim opinion'. This could only have been the most conservative opinion going. The tactic was to get the Bill through Parliament as quickly as possible, without allowing much time for a debate to develop on the issue. But the opposition in Parliament succeeded in stalling the introduction of the Bill by a vital two days. In that time, a memorandum was submitted to the Prime Minister with an impressive list of signatures of Muslim intellectuals, including several who are not only known to be supporters of the Congress(I) but are closely associated with the present government. This gave the lie to the Prime Minister's claim that Muslim opinion had been consulted. Several women's organizations, including those of Muslim women, also protested against the Bill. Finally, the government's credibility was damaged beyond repair when Arif Mohammed Khan, Minister of State for Energy in the Union government, resigned from Rajiv Gandhi's ministry.

Reports indicate that there is considerable resistance to the Bill even within the solid phalanx of Congress(I) Members of Parliament. Much of this opposition, of course, comes not from any progressive appreciation of the role of the state in matters of religion. The new regime had played its Hindu-communal card with unconcealed glee in the days following the assassination of Indira Gandhi; and a large bulk of its supporters, firmly wedded to the dominant ideology of the 'cow belt', are now rejoicing at the so-called 'liberation' of the Ram Janmabhumi temple in Ayodhya. These are the people whom Rajiv Gandhi's aides are now finding it difficult to keep in line. On the other hand, the Congress has historically drawn towards it the support of much of the progressive opinion among Muslims. This section the government has now chosen to ignore. As a result, the regime finds itself in a mess.

5 May 1986: Right on Target[12]

Until a few days ago, it would have seemed to an outside observer that the terrorist groups in Punjab were on their last legs. Their actions were becoming indiscriminate and desperate. They were finding it far more difficult than before to get cover, and their reckless killings were turning them away from the very people they were supposed to be fighting for. The Akali Dal government under Surjit Singh Barnala seemed to be in control. Nevertheless, the situation seemed favourable enough for New Delhi to take decisive and firm 'police action' against the terrorist groups with the full support of the Barnala government.

Then, on 29 April 1986, came a 'declaration' from the so-called Panthic Committee that 'Khalistan' had been established in Punjab, and that a 'parallel government' was operating from the Golden Temple in Amritsar. It also made the extravagant declaration that ultimately Delhi would be the capital of Khalistan, and that the *Kesari* flag would fly on top of the Red Fort.

It was a farcical claim, and the government need not have taken it with greater seriousness than the many so-called 'governments in exile' which dissident Sikh groups have been running in Britain and Canada for several years now. But almost on cue, security measures were stepped up around the Golden Temple complex. Mr Barnala was in Delhi holding consultations with the central leadership. Twenty-four hours later, men of the CRP and the Punjab Police, along with a group of commandos, entered the Golden Temple, supposedly

12 *Frontier*, 18, 38 (10 May 1986).

to round up the members of the 'parallel government'. Surprisingly, the police found not a single political activist of note.

There are strong indications that New Delhi, now represented in Chandigarh by the redoubtable Mr Siddhartha Shankar Ray and the new police chief Mr Ribeiro, was waiting for an opportunity to enter the Golden Temple complex which, despite the many splits and counter-splits in the ranks of the 'extremists' (many of them undoubtedly engineered by the government), was still functioning as the political headquarters of the rebels. Whether the 'Khalistan declaration' itself was part of the preparations for such a move is still a matter of speculation.

The police action in the temple has turned the situation against the Barnala government. Now he has been made to appear a complete stooge of Delhi, ordering the police into the precincts of the temple for no reason at all. It also appears that, while Mr Barnala discussed in general terms the subject of stronger steps against terrorism with his cabinet colleagues on the eve of the police action of April 30, he did not take specific clearance for the move.

The reaction set in within a few hours of the incident. There were four resignations from the Akali Dal ministry, and Mr P.S. Badal and Mr G.S. Tohra publicly dissociated themselves from Mr Barnala. Now as many as twenty-nine MLAs of the Akali Dal have reportedly signed a statement criticizing the police action. Even more significant are reports of widespread popular reaction among Sikhs, who are seeing the police action as a pointless desecration of the temple. Suddenly, Mr Barnala now seems friendless and isolated. His political predicament is not being helped by the declarations of support for him from the opposition groups in the Punjab Assembly. If the Barnala government has to survive with the help of the Congress(I), it will only strengthen the claim of his critics that he is a puppet acting at the behest of New Delhi.

19 May 1986: Retooling Democracy[13]

When the Congress(I) under Rajiv Gandhi won the elections barely a year and a half ago with the largest ever majority in the

[13] *Frontier*, 18, 40 (24 May 1986).

Lok Sabha, he had promised to give the country a clean, efficient and open government. Many at the time had greeted the announcement as a welcome change from the secretive and thoroughly despotic style of rule practised in his mother's time. They also thought that the fact that the government enjoyed such an unassailable majority in Parliament would help in bringing about this change. Rid of the constant anxiety about retaining support in the House, the new government, it was thought, could well afford to permit free flow of information and a certain degree of internal criticism. Parliamentary illusions die hard.

Nothing of the sort has happened. It took very little time for the euphoria to vanish. With that, it has become clear that the massive parliamentary majority, artificially propped up by the Anti-Defection Act, is devoid of all substance. Now the government seems jittery about any discussions in Parliament, not so much because of what the opposition would say, but because it is unsure of what its own party members might do. The recent Muslim Divorce Bill was rammed through the House after care was taken to gag potential critics in the Treasury benches — something one would have thought entirely unnecessary for a party which has more than three-fourths of the seats in the Lok Sabha.

And now it seems the government is keen to avoid Parliament as far as possible. It is resorting more and more to that familiar technique already perfected in many Congress(I)-ruled states: namely, rule by ordinance. But last week's ordinance on commissions of enquiry must go down as one of the crowning achievements of fraud and duplicity in the field of democratic government.

Barely two days after the closing of the budget session of Parliament, the government has announced that it will not be bound to place before Parliament, and hence before the people, the report of any commission of enquiry if it feels that its publication will jeopardize 'the national interest'. It is, of course, the executive branch of government which has been given the power to assess whether something in the report would harm the national interest, and therefore, whether it should be kept away from the prying eyes of the elected representatives of the people.

The fact that this latest edict of secret governance deals with commissions of enquiry makes the assault on even our so-called democracy doubly blatant. And the unscrupulousness and cynicism of the present bunch of rulers is made even clearer because the immediate pretext for the ordinance is also known. It appears that the report of the Thakkar Commission of Enquiry to probe into the assassination of Indira Gandhi has already been submitted, while that of the Ranganath Mishra Commission on communal killings in Delhi immediately following the assassination is on its way. Both events have been of monumental significance in the recent history of the country. And the second commission in question was set up after persistent demands from civil rights groups and opposition parties. In fact, the provision for setting up commissions of enquiry is justified by the need for an authoritative and impartial probe into the conduct of government officials and police functionaries, so that the people are satisfied that those who rule them do so in a fair and legitimate way. To say that commissions may be set up (at the cost of the public exchequer) to enquire into incidents in which the actions or motives of government personnel have been called to question, but that their findings may not be made public if the government so decides, is fraud of the worst kind imaginable.

There is rampant speculation about the exact reasons why those who are in power have felt it necessary to keep the findings of the Thakkar Commission a secret. Were important people implicated in the conspiracy to murder Mrs Gandhi? Whom are the rulers trying to protect?

9 June 1986: Tinkering Again[14]

New Delhi seems to be tying itself up in knots tackling that intractable problem of Punjab. In a mystifying move last week, the Haryana Chief Minister, Bhajan Lal, was asked to quit; and Bansi Lal, Union Defence Minister, sent to Chandigarh to head the Congress(I) government in Haryana. Bhajan Lal, faced with an angry popular mood skilfully fomented by the wily opposition leader Devi Lal, had made no secret of his lack of enthusiasm about the implementation of the Punjab accord. Now, New Delhi has seen it fit to send in the indestructible Bansi Lal to ram the unpopular accord down the throats of unwilling Haryana politicians.

[14] *Frontier*, 18, 43 (14 June 1986).

The decision appeared to have taken most people by surprise. Bhajan Lal, it is reported, was prepared to answer the summons from New Delhi by organizing a large-scale resignation of Congress(I) MLAs were he asked to resign. In the end, he did nothing of the sort. Whether he was persuaded to desist from open revolt by promises of further personal advancement or by threats of dire consequences is not known. He accepted the decision of the High Command with apparent equanimity, and handed over his charge to Bansi Lal. The new Chief Minister immediately pronounced that the people of Haryana should be prepared to accept the unpalatable fact of the transfer of Chandigarh to Punjab, because it was 'in the overall national interest'. However, he immediately added that while Punjab would have formal jurisdiction over Chandigarh, the city would continue to serve as Haryana's capital for another five years or until such time as a new capital is built for Haryana. The argument was odd, because that has been precisely the ground on which Chandigarh has served as a dual capital for the last twenty years — ever since Indira Gandhi's agreement with Sant Fateh Singh on the terms of the Punjab–Haryana partition. So what is new in Bansi Lal's sincere resolve to implement the Punjab accord? One wonders whether Mrs Gandhi's trusted hatchet man was celebrating his return to Chandigarh by pulling yet another fast one 'in the national interest'.

There is another line of speculation which suggests that this sudden move has little to do with the transfer of Chandigarh, or the impending decision of the Venkatramaiah Commission on demarcating the Hindi-speaking regions of Punjab which should go to Haryana. Rather, the calculations range over a slightly longer time-frame to cover the Haryana Assembly elections early next year. Bhajan Lal, it is said, would have been unable to ensure a Congress(I) victory, because in an atmosphere of general resentment in Haryana over the events in Punjab, he would have had no means of finding any support from the formidable Jat lobby which has virtually ruled that state ever since its creation. Hence, the decision to send Haryana's most celebrated Jat politician Bansi Lal to Chandigarh, to try and recoup the Congress(I)'s electoral chances in his home base.

Whichever be the real reason behind the latest change of *subedars* in India's new imperial system, it is intimately connected with the continued intractability of the so-called Punjab problem. The Punjab accord has not been the magic solution it was claimed to be. Instead, it has led to further complications: a series of boundary commissions and political instability in Haryana being the most important of them. A vigorous attempt to tackle the 'extremists' in Punjab by massive use of state violence has not yielded any significant results. Despite the much-publicized appointment of Siddhartha Ray as the new Governor and the blank cheque give to the new police chief Ribeiro, all that has been accomplished is widespread state terror, a predictable rise in 'encounter deaths', and overflowing prisons. The spate of terrorist killings has not diminished, and a daily average of fifteen to twenty civilian deaths has become a routine affair. Insecurity, fear and a sense of hopelessness have struck deep roots in Punjab, and mutual distrust and antipathy between communities has reached a quite unprecedented level. Even the Punjab Chief Minister, Mr Barnala, has been forced to recognize the magnitude of the problem of migration of non-Sikh residents out of Punjab. In the midst of such a massive churning of the social set-up, with no apparent purpose except the spreading of hatred and mistrust among the people, the tinkering of the rulers in New Delhi with Governors, Chief Ministers and police chiefs cannot but seem somewhat puerile.

15 September 1986: Valley of Intrigues[15]

The political situation in Jammu and Kashmir continues to hang in a limbo with President's Rule being imposed on the state. Constitutionally, this is a slightly different procedure from Governor's Rule, a provision that exists only for Kashmir and which is how Mr Jagmohan, the present Governor, had been exercising his highly personalized rule over the valley. But there was no constitutional provision for extending Governor's Rule any further, and the rumour was rife that there would be some moves towards installing a popular government. Obviously, these moves have not yielded any results yet, or at least not results that would be satisfactory to the rulers in Delhi. Hence, central administration will continue in Jammu

15 *Frontier*, 19, 5 (20 September 1986).

and Kashmir under the more familiar procedures of President's Rule.

What has caused much greater sensation in Kashmir, however, is the story of an impending rapprochement between Farooq Abdullah and Rajiv Gandhi. Dr Abdullah has been, of course, in the frontline of the anti-Congress(I) forces in Kashmir ever since he was unceremoniously removed from power nearly three years ago, by the Congress(I) in league with G.M. Shah. But suddenly in the last few months, there seemed to appear signs that the leadership in New Delhi was searching for other alternatives, the experiment with the unpopular Shah government having failed miserably. And the strongest alternative was a coming to terms with Dr Abdullah. There was indeed a series of meetings between the Prime Minister and Dr Abdullah, in which the former is said to have suggested a coalition government between the Abdullah-led National Conference and the Congress(I). This suggestion Dr Abdullah rejected. But the efforts did not cease, and the ebullient successor to Sheikh Abdullah was appointed official leader of the Indian delegation to the Haj in Mecca. This Dr Abdullah accepted. Ever since his return from Mecca a few days ago, speculations have gained ground that new terms are being discussed.

The effects of these rumours in Kashmir cannot have gladdened Dr Abdullah's heart. There is said to be a 'whisper campaign' warning of a sell-out to Delhi. There are growing murmurs of discontent within the National Conference. Dr Abdullah's popularity in recent years has been no less due to his opposition to the Congress(I) and the halo of martyrdom at having been unfairly ousted from power by the machinations of New Delhi, than to his claim to be the real successor to Sheikh Abdullah's political legacy. Any hint of compromise on that position is bound to cost him dearly.

On the other hand, given the constraints imposed by New Delhi, and especially now in view of the continued instability in neighbouring Punjab and all the hullabaloo about security on the Pakistan borders, Dr Abdullah seems to have little alternative but to come to some kind of understanding with the central power. He is said to be insisting on fresh elections before the installation of any ministry in Jammu and Kashmir. He has also made strong public assertions rejecting any suggestion of a 'political sell-out'.

But he has also warned of the dangers posed by Muslim fundamentalist forces operating in the valley. There is no doubt that speculations on Dr Abdullah's secret confabulations with Mr Gandhi are grist to the propaganda mill of these fundamentalist forces.

New Delhi, as always, is viewing all this from the only standpoint it knows — the immediate costs and benefits. It had to do something in a hurry because Governor's Rule' could not be extended any further. It tried the option of installing a coalition ministry with Farooq Abdullah. But this would have been political suicide for the latter. Delhi was then left with the only option of imposing President's Rule and delaying a long-term solution. At this moment, it cannot accept the risks of fresh elections in Jammu and Kashmir. But without it, any agreement with Dr Abdullah will cut at the roots of his political support in the valley. What will emerge victorious from all this are precisely those forces which the Prime Minister daily warns his countrymen against — those of religious fundamentalism and disruption.

3 November 1986: The Regional Dimension[16]

The 'accords' continue. As more and more power concentrates in the hands of the central executive, and particularly the office of the Prime Minister, the principal method to contain the opposing force of what is called 'regionalism' has become one where the chief executive personally negotiates a settlement with the regional leader by offering him a legitimate share of provincial power. This was done with the late Mr Longowal in Punjab, with Mr Prafulla Mahanta in Assam, and with Mr Laldenga in Mizoram. The same method has now been followed with Dr Farooq Abdullah in Jammu and Kashmir. It seems a somewhat new phenomenon in Indian politics. As a matter of fact, however, it is a rather old technique, received from the days when Hindustan was a sprawling empire, where provincial rebels who could not be put down by force were simply incorporated into the imperial structure of government by recognizing them as regional satraps. Indian democracy is, in more senses than one, a system of imperial rule.

[16] *Frontier*, 19, 12 (8 November 1986).

What is called regionalism is not a recent product. There was a massive spell of regional movements in the 1950s and 1960s, which basically demanded the redrawing of the administrative boundaries of the states according to a linguistic principle. In the main, this demand was conceded. Thus we had the formation, after intense mass movements, of the states of Andhra, Gujarat, Maharashtra, Punjab and Haryana. In all these cases, the movements were at first directed against the ruling group in Delhi. In each case, however, once the main demand was conceded, the bulk of popular support was reintegrated into the ruling Congress party. This was accomplished not by an 'accord' with the rebel leaders, but rather by accommodating the principal content of the regional demand within the overall constitutional framework of federal rule. Thus, the very existence of a distinct regional political movement was made redundant, and the locally dominant forces found it far more profitable to insert themselves into the countrywide structure of the ruling Congress party. The relatively flexible and decentralized structure of the party itself made this possible in the 1950s and 1960s.

Both the framework of the Congress party and the process of governmental rule have changed fundamentally in the last two decades. The ruling party is now openly recognized as more or less the personal staff of its supreme leader — the Prime Minister. And the governmental structure has its centre in the Prime Minister's office, a few chosen advisers, and the topmost levels of the Union bureaucracy. The regional movements today have few specific demands. Whatever the nature of their leadership and whatever the particular issues on which they express themselves (and these vary from straightforward separatism as with the Khalistanis, to protection of Assamese identity with the AGP, to the restoration of Telugu honour in the case of Mr Rama Rao, to what is it now with the AIADMK?), the basis on which they draw their political support is a vague sense of disaffection with a system of government where the centre of power lies at a great distance from the people, and which seems to threaten their immediate and familiar cultural identities. All regional movements in recent years have been built around the question of cultural identity, and all have posed their demands in relation to the central power structure located in New Delhi.

Rajiv Gandhi, it is true, inherited these problems; he did not create them. He has proceeded to solve them by giving the regionalist leadership a legitimate share of governmental power. Thus far, the formula seems to have worked in Assam; Mizoram is too recent to enable one to make a judgement. It has clearly failed in Punjab. The government of Mr Barnala has been caught in the unenviable position of being regarded by the extremists as a stooge of New Delhi and by New Delhi as being soft on the extremists. Given the harrowing experience of daily violence on the people perpetrated both by terrorists and government forces, it cannot be said that the central framework of governmental rule has been validated in any way in the popular mind of Punjab.

It could well be argued that a similar scenario will unfold in the Kashmir valley. Farooq Abdullah was a champion of the popular opinion in Kashmir as long as he was seen as an implacable opponent of New Delhi. Now that he has taken, after much prevarication, the final step of entering into a coalition government with the Congress(I) without seeking a popular mandate at a general election, he is more likely than not to lose that basis of popular support. Perhaps there will be splits in the National Conference. The greater cause for apprehension is the definite possibility of the rise of communal tensions. The politics of ethnic loyalties is fertile ground for the play of reactionary politicians of all sorts, whether they operate from the citadels of power in New Delhi or whether they roam around the streets and bazaars in small provincial towns.

17 November 1986: Managing Congress[17]

Not so long ago, it was being said that the new Prime Minister would dismantle the decrepit structure of arbitrary authority built up in the days of his mother and bring in a whole new era of dynamic, democratic politics. Soon afterwards, we heard complaints that the Prime Minister was being manipulated by a small coterie of his friends: it was they who were running the show. Before, it was said that the new regime was youthful and forward-looking, not tied down by custom or protocol. Now we hear that this government acts first, thinks later. People have apparently had a lot of difficulty in deciding what

17 *Frontier*, 19, 14 (22 November 1986).

Rajiv Gandhi's regime is all about. Who runs it? To what ends?

Speculations of this sort took a new turn last week when Kamalapati Tripathi announced his resignation from the post of working president of the Congress(I), and the general secretaries of the AICC were removed. What was the Prime Minister up to this time? The Tripathi resignation was not surprising in itself. After his abortive rebellion earlier this year, when his letter to the Prime Minister complaining bitterly about the goings-on in the Congress was released to the press, Mr Tripathi was more or less serving time, pending settlement of his post-retirement benefits. These matters have apparently been sorted out now to the satisfaction of all concerned, and Mr Tripathi has bid good-bye, wishing the Prime Minister well and pledging to support him come what may.

It is the removal of the general secretaries that has given the impression that the Prime Minister, who is also the President of the Congress(I) party, now intends to clear the deck and refurbish the party in his own image. This was on the agenda for some time. Rajiv Gandhi after all began his political career, brief though it may have been, not in the government but in the Congress party. It was believed that in association with Arun Nehru, Rajiv Gandhi was particularly keen to infuse fresh blood into the party, beginning from below. There was apparently a grand plan to induct dynamic, young, forward-looking and competent young men and women at the district level Congress organizations. These people would be politically and ideologically committed to the new regime, and through them an organizational base would be built which could replace the old and corrupt system of support based on the discredited power-brokers.

The plan has been under way for some time, and there have been more organization-building activities in the Youth Congress, the Congress Seva Dal and the various district Congress levels than at any time in the recent past. Most of these have been run like management training programmes. The other part of this grand plan was to hold organizational elections in the Congress throughout the country, and use this democratic machinery to wipe out the regime of the power-brokers of the past. That is where the plan faltered. The old guards proved far too wily and well-entrenched, and Kamalapati Tripathi's sudden outburst about bogus membership in the party electoral list was only one example of the enormous difficulties of replacing the Congress structure from the top.

Now Rajiv Gandhi seems to have changed tracks. He has openly broken with his former friend and comrade, Arun Nehru. Neither Arun Singh nor Arjun Singh figure any more among his closest political advisers. He has come to terms with the opposition in Jammu and Kashmir by clinching an agreement with Farooq Abdullah, to the intense displeasure of the Kashmir Congress(I). An agreement with Sharad Pawar of Congress(S) is in the offing in Maharashtra: what his reward will be is still not clear, although the larger plan of a wholesale merger of the Congress(S) with the Congress(I) may not come through. Perhaps another agreement with Jagannath Mishra is on the cards, and this may mean a change of government in Bihar. Possibly, what all this means is that Mr Gandhi has decided that to take on the much despised power-brokers as a body would prove too much for him, and that it is better to come to an arrangement with those among them who could be relied upon to keep their own regions in order. In the meantime, it is goodbye to organizational elections within the Congress. The leader must first have enough time to make up his own mind: party democracy can wait. Perhaps by then we will have a sufficient number of PCC resolutions urging Mrs Sonia Gandhi to become Congress President!

1 December 1986: Gorbachev's Visit[18]

Despite an unprecedented media blitz calculated to produce the impression of a 'historic' occasion, Mikhail Gorbachev's visit to New Delhi contained virtually no surprises. Nothing new or significant transpired in the course of three days of protocol-signing and press conferences. There were, of course, a few ceremonial firsts, like a special red carpet at Rashtrapati Bhavan and the use of the Ashoka Hall in that building for a joint press conference by Mr Gorbachev and Mr Gandhi. These privileges, the country was told, had never before been extended to any visiting dignitary, not even to the Queen of

---

[18] *Frontier*, 19, 16 (6 December 1986).

England. We were left to draw our own conclusions from that regarding the 'historic' nature of the visit.

That word was repeated endlessly on radio and television, as official hacks worked overtime waffling away on the everlasting friendship between India and the Soviet Union. For five days, Doordarshan was virtually taken over by the huge Soviet delegation, and there was no escaping the inevitable scenes of dignitaries sitting down to a banquet or the interminable translations of interminable speeches from Russian into English and vice versa. The press was around, but kept at a distance by the heavy security arrangements. Still, they dutifully reported what Mrs Gorbachev wore and what she bought.

Amidst all this fanfare, stage-managed to the very end, what is it that has materialized? Very little, it would seem. The official high point was the so-called Delhi Declaration which Mr Gorbachev described as a 'unique and extraordinary document'. In it, the Soviet and Indian governments have jointly called for a ban on the use or threat of use of nuclear weapons. Apart from this specific declaration, the rest of the document is an exercise in redundancy and hyperbole. It is understandable that after the failure at Reykjavik, Mr Gorbachev should wish to push ahead with his propaganda advantage in the 'peace war' with President Reagan. It was only to be expected, therefore, that he would enlist Indian support in some new and dramatic peace offensive. Yet the document produced has succeeded in recording nothing more concrete than homilies like 'human life must be recognized as supreme', 'understanding and trust must replace fear and suspicion', 'conditions must be guaranteed for the individual's harmonious development', and so on. This by itself is telling evidence of the immense gulf that separates the genuine desire of the people of the world for nuclear disarmament and peace, and the strategic calculations of the nuclear powers themselves.

On the economic front, there has been an agreement for a Rs 23,000 million credit by the Soviet Union for projects such as the construction of the Tehri hydroelectric complex, the modernization of the Bokaro steel plant, the opening of new coal mines in Jharia, and the exploration of oil and natural gas sources in West Bengal. Nothing concrete has been achieved on the trade front, which has been sagging of late, except a pious wish to increase trade between the two countries by two-and-a-half times in the next five years. How this is to be done is still not clear, and Mr Gandhi was cautious enough to say in his press conference that this would have to be left for 'experts' to decide. He has learnt that the compulsions of regional dominance and world politics make it imperative for his government to depend on Soviet political and military support, but that is no reason to restrict one's options in the matter of trade and economic relations. Mr Gorbachev also made a proposal for an international space research centre in India for the training of astronauts and the launching of spacecraft. Mr Gandhi did not seem overly enthusiastic.

The visit underlined once again the fact that, in the international context in which the Indian ruling classes hold and exercise their power in this country, the strategic relation to the Soviet Union is more or less invariant. This was shown earlier in the brief period of Janata rule, when professedly anti-Soviet politicians, after suddenly coming to power in the 1977 elections, found themselves having to sign agreements with Moscow. Rajiv Gandhi too was said to have pro-Western sympathies, and the European and American press made much of this in the first few months of his regime. Now they know better.

Even the parliamentary Left in India, having now been fully appropriated into the structure of ruling power, has fitted into this scheme of things. In the last few years, there has been little difference between the CPI and the CPI(M) in their arguments on the Soviet Union. This fact, it seems, has been recognized by the Soviets as well, because this time Mr Gorbachev officially met separate delegations from the two parties. Another 'historic' first, but only confirming what has been well known for a long time.

15 December 1986: Congress Culture[19]

'There is now only one Congress,' Sharad Pawar declared in Aurangabad last week. Gone are the days when one had to search for the correct letter in the alphabet to insert in parentheses, in order to describe a particular fragment of the Congress party. Most of the tiny splinters had vanished anyway, readmitted

[19] *Frontier*, 19, 18 (20 December 1986).

into the Congress(I) by Indira Gandhi in a sudden spell of generosity and forgiveness in the last year of her life. A few organizations had died with the death of their leaders who gave them their distinctive names. The Congress(S) was, of course, the major opposition group which still claimed to be the real Congress. Its early stalwarts were either dead or back in the Congress(I). Younger firebrands like A.K. Anthony and P.R. Das Munshi had undergone the elaborate ritual of repentance, and having shed their image as rebels with a cause, had been readmitted into the ruling party. Sharad Pawar remained the only leader of any consequence in the Congress(S), and with most people having forgotten what the (S) originally stood for, had often lent his own name to describe the organization.

Now that his prolonged efforts to establish a formal rapport with Rajiv Gandhi have finally succeeded, Mr Pawar feels that it is he who deserves the credit for having reunited the Congress. This is a historic moment, he thinks. Not only is there a crisis in the country which requires all Congress members to come together, but the fact that there is really only a single 'Congress culture and ethos', born out of the long history of the party, makes the erstwhile divisions in the ranks of Congress members wholly artificial. There were no real ideological grounds for these divisions. Now, says Mr Pawar, when 'the leader of the nation and the Congress(I) party', Rajiv Gandhi, is bringing in 'a new spirit of reconciliation' (meaning presumably that he is not as tough on party dissidents as his mother was), there is no point in wasting one's time sitting in the opposition. In other words, now is the time to seize the opportunity and get a share of real power.

The Congress(I)–Congress(S) merger had been on the cards for some time now. And as expected, the merger has not been entirely smooth, because a few notable leaders like T. Unnikrishnan of Kerala and Sarat Chandra Sinha of Assam have refused to accept it. But, of course, as an organization of any electoral consequence, the Congress(S) existed only in Maharashtra where it was by far the largest opposition party in the Assembly. Mr Pawar's prize, it is being said, is the chief ministership, although the person concerned is still being very coy about this. It is also said that the industrialists of Maharashtra, who have always regarded Mr Pawar as a reliable and effective political representative, have quietly persuaded him to take this decisive step. There may be many subtle implications in this well-known tie-up between Mr Pawar and the Bombay businessmen. He may be expected to deliver the goods either as Chief Minister of Maharashtra, or perhaps at an even higher level — may be as a check to the unpredictable and troublesome V.P. Singh: who knows?

All this may also be part of Rajiv Gandhi's grand plan for building a new ruling party. He has systematically weeded out from his organization the closest associates of Indira Gandhi. And in one sudden swoop last month, he dismissed both the working president Kamalapati Tripathi and the entire secretariat of the party. Mr Gandhi has thus far given no inkling as to what he intends to do after this; and at the moment at least, the ruling party exists and functions (so far as it is required to function) without an executive body. All that is apparent is that the Prime Minister is seeking to build bridges with people who have independent sources of electoral support in the regions — Dr Abdullah in Kashmir and now Mr Pawar in Maharashtra. This is a style quite different from that of his mother. Whether it develops into a clear and consistent policy is still to be seen. After all, whatever may be Rajiv Gandhi's qualities, clarity and consistency do not figure in that list.

10

The Politics of Appropriation

It is as old as the history of bourgeois politics in this country — of bourgeois politics seeking to forge the solid edifice of a bourgeois state. As the contours begin to take shape and each little part is brought to bear a definite relation to the whole, the cracks are neatly papered over; all the signs of friction, of hindrance and resistance, carefully erased from public view. And for those particularly stubborn marks of dissension which refuse to go away — well, they are simply made part of the structure itself, as if they were meant to be there all along. Thus the myth is built up of the bourgeois state as the great reconciler of differences, so representative that it is virtually one with the nation itself.

That is the story of the appropriation of opposition politics in India. It can be seen in the ways in which the state has, from time to time, sought to usurp the politics based on the economic demands of various exploited classes: by the creation of high-wage islands within the working class; the fixing of procurement prices for agricultural products; the poverty-eradication programmes; and a variety of special schemes for backward or scheduled castes, and for the tribes. But nowhere is this process more dramatic than in the state's handling of the 'national question' in India, for that is where every expression of opposition involves, whether implicitly or explicitly, the questioning of the very territorial basis of the state and of how power is distributed over that territory.

For reasons of space, we will not go too far back into history, although there is a lot there that is relevant to the present discussion. Let it suffice to say that the Congress-led national movement only met the question halfway. The antagonism between colonialism and the 'Indian nation' was ideologically posed in the pre-Gandhian era of bourgeois politics in India, without however discovering any practical means by which to politically organize the masses for the struggle to create a national state. Those means were developed in the period since 1919–20. One of the basic organizational innovations was the formation of the provincial Congress committees based on more or less homogeneous linguistic units, ignoring the existing administrative demarcation of provinces by the colonial state in India. These provincial committees were the main organizing foci of the mass movements of the Congress. It was at this level that the democratic demands of the people, voiced through the various movements at the localities and districts, were organized and coordinated — in the language of the people and in conformity with regional economic and cultural specificities. It was also at this level that the all-India leaders of the Congress sought to assert their control over the organization of the national movement throughout the country.

Two Tendencies

The provincial level of the Congress was, one might say, the site where two tendencies in the Indian national movement met. One was the tendency of opening the movement towards the democratic aspirations of the masses against the domination exercised by alien rule. As with all bourgeois-democratic movements of nationality, this tendency accompanied or followed the development of certain cultural forms, which could become the standard for emulation by all classes and strata within the linguistic community. In the Indian case, this tendency found its true home in the large linguistic communities formed by the modern Indian languages, and these were in the main the domain of the provincial organization of the Congress. The other tendency was towards the consolidation, through this process of popular struggle against colonial rule, of the interests of the all-India bourgeoisie, including within it the big bourgeoisie as well as the top strata of the professional middle classes. In political terms, this tendency always preferred the relative centralization of governmental powers and the containment of democratic mass movements within limits that conformed with these all-India interests.

This inherent conflict between the two historical tendencies was not resolved in the period of the national movement. The history of the post-colonial state in India shows that the conflict has still not been resolved within the framework of the Indian

Constitution. In the colonial period, the democratic content of the movements of the nationalities found relatively free expression precisely in the periods of the mass movements launched by the Congress. Then, when these mass movements were sought to be contained, we notice the assertion of the organizational dominance of an all-India Congress leadership, and the emergence of many regionally-based factional groupings within the Congress.

Centralization

After the formation of the independent Indian state, the conflict between the two tendencies came to a head in the 1950s. The Constitution sought to strike a compromise between the two tendencies by laying down a federal structure of government, without however recognizing the existence of 'nationalities'. This diplomatic silence on the part of the Constitution-makers did not pass muster, because strong demands began to be voiced from different parts of India for the reorganization of states on a linguistic basis. Implicitly, these demands only represented the normal bourgeois-democratic aspirations of nationality. In the Indian case, the specific demand was that the federating units of the Indian Union should in fact be the linguistic nationalities. This was, as we have said before, the implicit assumption of the Congress organization at least since 1919–20. Now, however, important sections within the all-India state leadership, including Jawaharlal Nehru himself, began to raise doubts about the desirability of such a reorganizaton of states. They argued that to recognize the linguistic principle would mean sowing the seeds of destruction of the political unity of India. Their argument, in fact, implied the belief that India could only be effectively ruled in the administrative style of centralized empires, by concentrating power in the capital and dividing up the basis for democratic solidarity in the provinces.

In this particular period, the centralizing tendency had to retreat in the face of massive popular movements in Andhra, Maharashtra–Gujarat and Punjab–Haryana. The States Reorganization Commission accepted with qualifications the linguistic principle for demarcating states. But the problems were not necessarily resolved, because the principle of the matter was never clinched. The Indian state always took the position that there was only one nation — India — and its territorial sovereignty was unitary and inviolate. All matters of formation and demarcation of states (or Union Territories) were a matter of 'practicality': no firm principle was ever laid down or accepted. On certain occasions, demands for the redrawing of state boundaries were conceded; on others, they were denied. The ground was laid, therefore, for the play of pressure politics of the most unprincipled sort. It became evident that if you could put enough pressure on the government, your demand stood a good chance of being conceded. Quite obviously, this also created room for the manipulative politics of the central state power itself: it could employ the carrot-and-stick policy, both to contain democratic movements of the nationalities and to appropriate their results. The most dramatic example of this has been the handling of the nationalities question in the north-eastern regions of India, the latest episode in that story being the 'accord' with Mr Laldenga in Mizoram.

The Communist Stand

The communist movement had for a long time theoretically accepted the principle of linguistic nationalities in India. In the early 1940s, this principle was sought to be twisted in the so-called Adhikari thesis to justify the demand for Pakistan, but this was soon regarded as a mistake. After 1947, the communist movement theoretically identified the Indian state as multinational in character, although it was not very forthright on the question of 'the right of secession' (for entirely valid reasons, one might argue, because except for the case of the north-eastern region, this was not yet a serious political issue).

But with the incorporation of the bulk of the communist movement into the exclusive form of parliamentary politics, the theoretical principle on the question of the Indian nationalities has now been totally abandoned in favour of the criterion of 'practicality'. In the 1950s, communists were in the forefront of the movement for a separate state of Andhra Pradesh. They supported the division of Bombay into Maharashtra and Gujarat, and of Punjab into Punjab and Haryana. They virtually led the movement against B.C. Roy's proposal in 1954 to merge West

Bengal and Bihar into a single state. All this was in accordance with the principle that the component units of the Indian Union were linguistic nationalities which had a right to separate political existence within the federation. Today we read reports of an incredible statement from Benoy Chowdhury, one of the senior-most CPI(M) leaders, accusing the Congress of having started the process of disintegration of the country by creating states on a linguistic basis!

What is it that has happened in the last decade or so to bring about this remarkable transformation in communist politics? We need not recount here what the CPI and the CPI(M) have or have not said on the recent controversies over Punjab, Assam, Mizoram or the so-called Gorkhaland movement. Any questions on these matters will, we know, be answered essentially by an appeal to 'practicality'. There will be one set of criteria used to assert the 'democratic' content of moderate Akali politics in Punjab and the 'anti-national' character of the demand for Khalistan; and quite a different set of criteria to condemn as 'chauvinistic' the politics of the AGP in Assam. And no one among the CPI(M) leaders is more forthright in his adherence to 'practicality' than Jyoti Basu, self-proclaimed propagator of 'commonsense' Marxism in India. Helped by his deep-seated contempt for 'theoretical' debate, it is Mr Basu who has now supplied us with a ground rule for understanding the CPI(M)'s new politics. We must, he says, give up the whole line of thinking on the nationalities question based on the right of self-determination of nations, because Lenin's arguments on this matter are inapplicable to Indian conditions.

What, we may well ask, are these specific variations in socio-historical conditions in the Indian case that make Lenin's arguments inapplicable? Mr Basu has not given us the benefit of a detailed presentation of his thinking on the subject: he, after all, is a 'practical' man who has little time for the luxuries of theoretical rumination. But let us, for the sake of argument, construct a case for Mr Basu.

No Oppressor Nationality

He would, we presume, point out above all the absence of an oppressor nationality in India, which would make the political

question of the self-determination of nationalities wholly irrelevant. Where, he would ask, is the alien national body from
which the so-called Indian nationalities must seek their separation? With the ending of British rule and the founding of an
independent Indian state, this matter has been settled.

Has it? The answer would depend on what we make of the
story of Indian independence and the place of the nationalities
within the new Indian state. The CPI(M) argues, and we still do
not know of any change in this position, that the dominant power
in the state structure is held by the Indian big bourgeoisie which
rules in alliance with the owners of large landed property. The
big bourgeoisie, it further argues, is incapable of completing the
bourgeois-democratic revolution in India because, first, it is dependent on foreign capital; second, it is politically incapable of
abolishing pre-capitalist forms of exploitation in the countryside;
and third, because it necessarily impedes the development of
small capital which exists in the local and regional markets. It
would follow from this that the organized interest which would
most strongly favour the centralization of governmental power
in the Indian state structure is the Indian big bourgeoisie.

Now this big bourgeoisie also has an 'all-India' character, inasmuch as it cannot be identified as belonging exclusively, or even
predominantly, to any particular ethnic community. Its members
hail from different parts of India and its 'home market' is spread
all across the country. It exploits the mass of the Indian people,
but its oppression cannot be identified as that of an oppressor
nationality. Does this mean then that the Indian big bourgeoisie
has succeeded in unifying the people into the bourgeois-democratic framework of a single nation? That cannot be the case, for
then we would have to regard the bourgeois-democratic revolution in India as something that has been largely completed.

What, then, is the specific socio-historical form which enables
the Indian big bourgeoisie to rule through an independent
'nation–state' without actually completing the historical task of
forming a single bourgeois-democratic nation?

The All-India Sector

It was Lenin who in 1914 had cited with approval Kautsky's
proposition that 'the multinational state represents

backwardness'.[1] It is in fact the historical backwardness of Indian capitalism which gives the present Indian state its multinational character. Yet it is not the same kind of multinational state as Czarist Russia was in its last years, for here we do not have capitalist development based on the cultural unification of an oppressor nationality — Russia — imposing its oppression on other subjugated nationalities. But we must be careful here. Indian Marxists have generally agreed on the origins of the big bourgeoisie in this country, in its role as subordinate collaborators of British colonial capital, however much they may differ on the characterization of its subsequent role in the later phase of the national movement and in the post-colonial era. It was colonial capital and the British colonial state which created an 'all-India' market for the operation of big capital, whether commercial, financial or industrial. It was this 'all-India' market which the Indian big bourgeoisie subsequently took over and consolidated.

This market is spread all over India, but it does not incorporate the whole demographic mass of the country. It only skims off a thin top layer of consumers from all the regions, and constitutes itself as an 'all-India' market. This layer, thin as it is in comparison with the whole population, nevertheless includes not only the bourgeoisie, but also most of the middle classes, the richer landed classes and even a section of the relatively better-paid working class. The big bourgeoisie does indeed seek to build homogeneous cultural patterns within this market — in the print medium, principally by the adoption of the English language as the practical language for 'all-India' communication; but more effectively in the audiovisual media (radio, cinema, and now television), through the propagation of a peculiarly neutral, aseptic and non-literary brand of Hindi, purged of all the richness of idiom and nuance of a vital cultural tradition. The cultural homogeneity which big capital in India has imposed on this 'all-India' market through its management of the consumer media, is now being consolidated by the state through its new policies on education and the management of television programming.

But the important feature of this 'all-India' market is that it

[1] V.I. Lenin, 'The Right of Nations to Self-determination', in Lenin, *Selected Works*, vol. 1 (Moscow: Progress Publishers, 1970), pp. 597–647. The reference to Kautsky is on p. 599.

does not even attempt to include within it the whole of the Indian people. Consumerism in India, which is the 'growth sector' on which Indian monopoly capital banks for continuing its process of accumulation, is a phenomenon restricted only to something like the top 10 or 15 per cent of the total population of the country. The rest are outside the pale of the 'all-India' market, and can *never* be incorporated into it unless the full historical process of a bourgeois-democratic revolution can be completed. Perhaps the big bourgeoisie does not even need to include, in its effective market, this vast mass of people with little income to spend on industrial commodities. For, even with 15 per cent of the population, this 'all-India' market is already larger in demographic size than the home markets of most European capitalist countries. We thus have the makings of a nation within the nation: a privileged minority of consumers economically and culturally integrated into a capitalist home market, and increasingly separated from the majority of the people of the country.

It is in that vast peripheral mass that the sense of oppression takes on the form of the cultural aspirations of oppressed nationalities. This is most unambiguous in the case of communities which contain no significant stratum that is incorporated into the 'all-India' sector — in particular, various tribal communities in the north-eastern and central parts of India. But even for the rest of the population, the signs of cultural oppression are evident in the aspirations for political identity of linguistic communities all over the country. These are not only marks of the necessary incompleteness of the bourgeois-democratic revolution carried out under the auspices of the all-India big bourgeoisie, but also of the historical necessity of extending and deepening the bases of democratic politics in this country.

Relevance of Lenin

The fact that there is no identifiable oppressor nationality in India does not mean that nationalities in this country are not oppressed. They *are* oppressed ·by what has come to be called the 'all-India' sector of capitalism. The difficulty is that the movements of the nationalities cannot direct their struggle against an easily identifiable target. That, in fact, is the greatest strategic strength of the Indian big bourgeoisie — its oppression

cannot be identified as one carried out by an oppressor nationality. This is why we have so much ambiguity and confusion
in the movements of the nationalities, with the Nepali-speaking
people of Darjeeling being led to believe that it is the Bengalis
as a whole who oppress them, or the Sikh peasants of Punjab
that it is the Hindus. The closest the nationalities ever get
to their real target is when they vaguely point to 'Delhi' as
the source of their oppression, but that too is a misconception.
Only a consistent bourgeois-democratic programme, recognizing the reality of the oppression of the nationalities and
aimed against the economic domination and cultural privileges
of the 'all-India' agglomeration, can harness the general democratic content of these popular aspirations towards a historically
progressive movement.

This, therefore, is the question: whether the bourgeois-democratic revolution in India will be allowed to ossify in its present
form, of an all-India monopoly bourgeoisie ruling over a 'sovereign' India which excludes the vast mass of the peoples of India
from any participation in sovereignty; or whether the battle for
a truly federal democracy will be carried on, by locating its bases
in the democratic aspirations of the nationalities. As long as
Marxists agree that this is a matter of principle and not of 'practicality', Lenin's discussion on the right of self-determination of
nations will remain vitally relevant.

It is by succumbing to considerations of 'practicality' that
the parliamentary communists in India have allowed their politics to be appropriated by the Indian state. They have been
trapped in the bourgeois game of practicality, as the CPI(M)
has now been trapped in relation to the demands of the Nepali-
speaking people of the hill areas of Darjeeling. For a long time,
and for entirely principled reasons, the CPI(M) had supported
the political and cultural demands of these people, whose very
status as Indian citizens is not clearly recognized by the Indian
state. Whether the CPI(M) had done enough to fulfil those
demands is another matter. Now, when a rival leadership —
clearly instigated or at least tacitly supported by the ruling powers
in Delhi — threatens to take the wind out of the CPI(M)'s
sails, and the West Bengal Congress and the all-India press
accuse the communists of having sown the seeds of separatism
by supporting the Nepali demands all this time, the CPI(M)

responds by prevaricating on its principled stand. The 'practical' constraints of running a government and winning elections force it to backtrack. Tomorrow, if there is a movement to protect minority rights in Assam, and the ruling party in Delhi chooses to manipulate it to its electoral advantage (as it undoubtedly will), the CPI(M) would be hard put to declare its support for the minorities in Assam without inviting the charge of supporting 'separatism'. That is how bourgeois politics entraps and appropriates the politics of the opposition.

It was Lenin who strongly asserted that the party of the proletariat must not in any event succumb to the bourgeois demand for 'practicality' on the national question. He said that the proletariat would refuse to give a categorical 'yes' or 'no' answer to the question of secession by any nation. The proletariat, he said, will support the right to self-determination without giving any guarantees or privileges to any nation.[2] Now, in India, we are witnessing the remarkable spectacle of the CPI(M), which claims to be the party of the proletariat, asking the ruling party in New Delhi for a categorical answer to the question: 'Does or does not the Government of India regard the GNLF as a secessionist movement?' One can hardly imagine a more farcical example of a communist party trying to be more nationalistic than the nationalists themselves.

2 Ibid., especially pp. 608–13.

11

Rajiv's Regime: The Fall

11 May 1987: Hour of Trial[1]

A cloud of uncertainty still hangs over New Delhi. Everybody, whether in government or in the opposition, seems jittery; and every day seems to hold the possibility of some dramatic event. It is a measure of the utter exhaustion of the strength of our political system that, with an unprecedented majority in Parliament, Rajiv Gandhi's government should still consider so seriously the danger of being toppled by some sort of parliamentary coup.

As soon as the Fairfax affair was pushed away from the glare of controversy by the appointment of a commission of inquiry, and the nasty questions about the purchase of military equipment from a Swedish company led to the ouster of V.P. Singh from the Union Cabinet, Congress MPs seemed to rally round the present leadership in a way not seen before at any time during the two-and-a-half years the government has been in power. Their calculations were clear and wholly cynical. They had been elected to Parliament on the expectation that they would be there for at least five years before they were required to face the electorate again. Factional rivalries within the ruling party over sharing the fruits of power were permissible, as long as there was no question about remaining in power. But if the future of the government itself was in jeopardy, Congress members would instinctively declare their faith in their leaders. Indeed, the lower the credibility of the government, the less the chances of Congress members being re-elected in any mid-term election, and hence the greater their loyalty to the incumbent regime. It was this chain of political reasoning that was in evidence in New Delhi immediately after V.P. Singh's resignation.

[1] *Frontier*, 19, 39 (16 May 1987).

But doubts about the inner strength of the regime persisted. A lot of hue and cry was raised about the combination of external and internal forces trying to destabilize the country. The argument was specious in the extreme. It seemed to say that whatever be the sins of the government, and of the law-breakers who were flourishing under the protection of the government, any criticism of their activities would threaten the stability of the regime and hence add support to the efforts of the 'destabilizers'. Similar noises had of course been made before in Indian politics, most notably during the time of Indira Gandhi. What was curious this time was the reason why, with an unchallengeable majority in Parliament, the government should feel it necessary to woo the support of opposition groups, particularly the Left parties.

The uncertainties continued, with growing speculation — assiduously cultivated from within ruling party circles — that the President was contemplating dismissal of the government. Constitutionally, this is absurd, and virtually everybody has said so. And yet, doubts about the future actions of Giani Zail Singh have not been removed. The Union Cabinet last week took the unprecedented step of writing collectively to the President, telling him that he had no right to demand information about the working of the government (the immediate issue being the Bofors deal), and that the Cabinet would only give him as much information as it deemed necessary. Now there are rumours (it is remarkable how much of the 'news' emanating from Delhi these days consists of a listing of the rumours circulating in the capital) that the President might resign, or do something equally dramatic, before nominations for the next Presidential elections are made at the end of this month (i.e. May 1987). For this reason, Parliament, it is said, will be kept in session until that time.

The other side of this picture is the uncertainty surrounding V.P. Singh. The expression of loyalty in Rajiv's leadership has been matched by widespread condemnation by Congress MPs of the 'treacherous' role of V.P. Singh. But the top leadership has been undecided about how strongly they should move against this maverick U.P. politician, for his ouster has made him a hero in much of northern India. The indecision is compounded by the impending elections to the Haryana Assembly in June. That, by all counts, will prove a crucial test to the present regime.

And yet, no matter how low the public credibility of Rajiv

Gandhi's government, it is difficult to foresee how any change can be brought about from within the Congress party. There is no focus that has emerged for an alternative leadership. The attempt to perpetuate the Nehru dynasty has eroded every shred of democratic vitality in the Congress. Nothing is more telling than the present occupation of the Prime Minister and his advisers (whoever they are), which consists of running from one fire-fighting job to another. Only sheer political ineptitude can reduce a government with such a huge majority in Parliament to such a state in a matter of two-and-a-half years.

30 June 1987: Democracy, Indian Style[2]

After much drama and suspense, the nominees for the next Presidential elections have been finally announced. It will be, for all practical purposes, a straight contest between the Congress(I) candidate, Mr Venkataraman, and the joint opposition choice, Mr Krishna Iyer. A third candidate, Mr Mithilesh Kumar, has managed to get himself proposed by ten independent MLAs from Bihar, which is an achievement in itself; but he is unlikely to have any effect on the final outcome of the presidential race.

Mr Venkataraman had been the most likely choice as Congress(I) candidate for a long time. He is the Vice-President of the country; also, he is from the south, which satisfies the unwritten Congress convention that while Prime Ministers must come from Uttar Pradesh (preferably from Allahabad), Presidents should alternate between the north and south of the country. He would have been an automatic choice had not Mr Gandhi become unnerved by the real or imaginary pranks played by Mr Zail Singh. There was talk of the President dismissing the government, and of running for a second term, if need be as an opposition candidate. Coming on top of the successive electoral defeats and the growing din about the Bofors scandal, Mr Gandhi for a while seemed uncertain about the intentions of Mr Zail Singh, and even about the prospects of victory of the Congress(I) candidate. He was the one who broached the possibility of a 'unanimous' candidate, and even went through the whole gamut of talks with individual

2 *Frontier*, 19, 46 (4 July 1987).

opposition parties on this matter. In the end, nothing came of it and Mr Venkataraman's name was announced as the Congress(I) candidate.

The drama, as always, was far more intense in the opposition camp. A three-member committee, consisting of Mr N.T. Rama Rao, Mr Chandra Sekhar and Mr E.M.S. Namboodiripad, had been set up to suggest names of possible candidates. Mr Namboodiripad was keen on Mr Krishna Iyer, who had served on his first ministry in Kerala, later went on to become a judge of the Supreme Court, and after retirement has devoted himself energetically to various civil rights causes. Other names, such as those of Mr P.N. Bhagwati, Mr Ramakrishna Hegde and Mr V.M. Tarkunde were also mentioned. The real drama began with the suggestion that Mr Zail Singh might be agreeable to being sponsored by the opposition. Mr Namboodiripad suddenly threw a fit, walked out of the opposition meeting and issued a press statement dissociating himself from such machinations. The issue was settled by Mr Zail Singh himself, who let it be known that he would not be a party 'to a losing game'. Apparently, the President was waiting for a signal that a sizeable section of Congress MPs would come out openly in his support. This was obviously not forthcoming; and those in the opposition who were waiting to seize this opportunity to split the Congress(I) and bring down Rajiv Gandhi along with it, were bitterly disappointed. Mr Namboodiripad finally won the day.

There is still much acrimony over whether the Left, and the CPI(M) in particular, was up to a devious game to save Mr Gandhi. The 'inside story', if there is any, may not be known for some time. The plain fact, however, is that Congress MPs, once having been elected, are unwilling to go for a mid-term poll. It must be clear as daylight to most members of the ruling party that with their present leader, despite his immaculate dynastic credentials, they have little certainty of winning the next general elections due in 1989. Yet, while they must be looking for a change in leadership, they will desperately seek a way of doing this without splitting the party — a way that has not been found as yet. In such circumstances, it was unlikely that a large number of Congress legislators would have come out openly to support Zail Singh as a rebel candidate. The shrewd politician from Punjab, who has been through the rough and tumble of Congress politics in Indira Gandhi's time, knew that this was not the best way to secure his future. He withdrew from the race, and saved Mr Namboodiripad from having to defend his action against the rest of the opposition. He may also have provided Rajiv Gandhi a temporary reprieve, because given the party strengths, Mr Venkataraman should now win comfortably. But Mr Gandhi's fate does not depend on the President. It depends on the fickle and entirely mercenary loyalties of his partymen, whom he has treated for so long with utter contempt.

13 July 1987: Fever Pitch[3]

As legislators all over the country prepare to elect a new President for the republic, all of northern India remains a seething cauldron of hatred, distrust, insecurity and panic. The Punjab terrorists struck again — with the mindless killing of bus passengers in Punjab, and then in Haryana where a new government has just come into power on a platform that was sharply critical of the Congress handling of the Punjab situation. The political objectives of those who can hold up and shoot down in cold blood an entire busload of helpless travellers are as clear as they ever were: to spread terror and panic, provoke a communal backlash, precipitate conditions for what would virtually be a civil war, and thus ingrain in the popular mind the belief that the only hope for peace is to concede to the demands of the extremists. It is a maddening strategy, absurd in its simplicity and naïveté, and one which any political regime with solid foundations of legitimate authority would have defeated with ease. And yet, such is the ineptitude and brittleness of our present rulers in Delhi that even this absurd campaign of terrorism seems to be succeeding. About ten weeks ago, when the Barnala government in Punjab was dismissed and President's Rule clamped down, the Prime Minister had admitted that things were 'back to square one'. He did not mention that, in politics, there is never an exact return to the same position; historical processes are not reversible. Superficially, things were back to the days of Operation Blue Star. The Union government had swept aside the complications of parliamentary politics in Punjab,

---

[3] *Frontier*, 19, 48 (18 July 1987).

and was concentrating on the security aspects of trapping down and eliminating the terrorists. The men in charge included a Governor who boasted of his 'success' in dealing with 'Naxalites' in West Bengal, and a police chief whose exploits had earned him an award for the 'Most Notable Indian of the Year'. And yet, the crucial difference now is that a whole phase of political experiment with popular government, initially supported by a massive expression of goodwill from people of all communities in Punjab, has now been swept into the dustbin. Failure to tackle the law-and-order situation at this juncture — and failure seems inevitable — cannot be redeemed by another spell of popular government. The political options have been closed off.

This is why the mood in northern India seems to get more and more desperate every day. Helplessness breeds panic. It also breeds extreme political reactions, like urging the government to stop at nothing in taking 'strong measures' against the terrorists. It also induces people to take it upon themselves to protect their lives and property, since the government cannot be trusted to do this adequately. That is precisely the condition which precipitates civil strife. The Punjab terrorists wish to provoke riots between Hindus and Sikhs in Delhi and Haryana. Yet a crisis of authority could well give rise to Hindu–Muslim riots elsewhere in northern India, where tensions and suspicions have reached a quite unprecedented level in recent months. While Punjab has gone from bad to worse, the present crisis of political authority could lead to far more dangerous and destructive events, of which Meerut is probably only a curtain-raiser.

Our rulers in the meantime have just returned from a 'goodwill mission' to Moscow, sufficiently fortified to get down to the task of demonstrating their political loyalties in the forthcoming Presidential election.

14 September 1987: Left Right Left[4]

While it may be all right for Kanu Sanyal of the Communist Organization of India (Marxist–Leninist) to issue a call to 'opposition parties of every hue' to join in ousting the corrupt government of Rajiv Gandhi and not to shirk from using 'extra-parliamentary

---

[4] *Frontier*, 20, 5 (19 September 1987).

means' to achieve this end, the parliamentary Left has other things to worry about. Its main problem at the moment is V.P. Singh. E.M.S. Namboodiripad has urged Mr Singh to 'make up his mind', which is the surest indication that the Left parties, with the CPI(M) in the forefront, are finding it increasingly difficult to make up *their* minds.

The situation has arisen time and time again in the history of the Indian Left. Whenever the principal party organization of the ruling classes in India has found itself in a quandary — weak, internally divided, often leaderless — the Left has suddenly woken up to the fact that the situation called for its intervention. And every time, its attempted intervention has taken the form of picking out a set of so-called 'progressive and left-oriented' Congress members — sometimes a single leader — and latching on to them in a bid to provide a 'leftist thrust' to the policies of the Indian state. The results have not been a success, judging by the present strength of the Left even in terms of parliamentary seats.

The present problem arises because the Left is yet to decide whether V.P. Singh is indeed a 'progressive and left-minded' Congress leader. Following the revelations about improprieties and kickbacks in various arms deals, V.P. Singh has emerged as the leading figure in the campaign against Rajiv Gandhi in northern India, and is being looked upon as the most credible alternative leader around whom disgruntled Congress members can rally. Whether an alternative leadership will mean alternative policies is of course a moot question. Congress leaders have had little qualms about advertising their commitment to whatever policies seem to suit the mood of the day; yet, regardless of the slogans emblazoned under the tricolour, the state runs the same way as ever. V.P. Singh, it may be presumed, will be no exception. At the present moment, he has refused to commit himself to anything other than his one-point campaign against the corruption of the Rajiv Gandhi government. This is precisely what is to be expected, since that is the issue which has thrown him to the top of the popularity chart in the Hindi belt; and he is unlikely to do anything that might confuse the picture. His aim at the moment is to build the largest possible coalition of those opposed to Rajiv Gandhi, and to present himself to those Congress members who are still sitting on the fence as the most likely leader of a viable alternative government.

The parliamentary Left's dilemma stems from the fact that it does not know whether a change will necessarily further its own electoral interests. While V.P. Singh keeps repeating his disingenuous platitude that the people must focus on issues and not on heroes, the Left unfortunately is able to present neither. Ever since its conclave politics was aborted three years ago, the CPI(M) and its allies in the Left have continuously talked of the building of a left and democratic front on a national scale, but have failed to come up with a credible set of programmes on which such a campaign might be launched. Their own strength is localized in a few regional pockets; and while they rejoice at the fact that nearly half the states in India today are ruled by non-Congress governments, they have yet to come up with the sorts of issues around which the growing resentment of the people all over the country can be mobilized, in the direction of an assault upon the existing structures of state power. A popular rejection of the Congress only seems to mean the installation of a few more Rama Raos and Devi Lals in various state capitals. Like it or not, therefore, the only political choice before the parliamentary Left is to decide on whether, and how far, it will follow the popular hero of the day. That is precisely the problem which V.P. Singh has posed to the Left.

And so the Left finds itself in a quandary. Its call to all Congress members to take 'a bold stand' and to demand a new government still stands. It invites V.P. Singh to address a seminar organized by its student wing. At the same time, it disapproves of Mr Singh's unwillingness to discard the BJP, or his eagerness in accepting the title of 'Raj Rishi' awarded him by the venerable Brahmins of Banaras. It is a waiting game on all sides; nobody is willing to commit too much.

1 December 1987: Pushing for Peace?[5]

The Union Minister of Defence, K.C. Pant, has rejected the suggestion from certain opposition parties that the Indian government open negotiations with the LTTE for an end to the hostilities in Sri Lanka. He has said that the government is determined to implement the Indo-Sri Lanka accord, which

[5] *Frontier*, 20, 16 (5 December 1987).

presumably means that the Indian 'peacekeeping' forces will continue their present operations in Sri Lanka until the LTTE has been completely crushed. At the same time, however, with Indian casualties from sniper attacks continuing to mount in the Jaffna peninsula, the government has also offered a set of 'incentives' to the Tamil Tigers — including free food and shelter, a monthly stipend, educational facilities and employment — in exchange for the immediate surrender of their arms. In short, then, Rajiv Gandhi's government is now fully engaged in fighting a protracted civil war on foreign soil, in a way which the Sinhalese hardliners could not have imagined in their wildest dreams when they had first protested against Mr Jayawardene's signing the accord. They have realized once again, but this time with pleasure, that their President is a wily customer indeed.

The military situation has not changed very much in the last two weeks, and is unlikely to shift decisively either way. Having mobilized an overwhelmingly superior force, some 30,000 Indian troops are now in the unenviable situation of an army of occupation facing a hostile civilian population. The stories coming out of Jaffna have all the classic marks: professionally trained foreign soldiers losing their way in unfamiliar territory, urban guerrillas suddenly encircling an Indian unit and shooting from all sides, little boys moving around with automatic weapons, house-to-house searches by the occupying troops who are afraid that even women and children might shoot them in the back. How long will all this continue? Quite simply, if the melancholy history of similar campaigns in different parts of the world in the last two decades is any indication, it can continue indefinitely, with rising body counts and burning hatred on both sides. There has never been a purely military solution to such campaigns before, and one cannot see how there will be one this time.

It is clear now that the Rajiv–Jayawardene accord did not resolve any of the fundamental conflicts which lay at the bottom of the ethnic problem in Sri Lanka. It only opened a new chapter in the political alignments and armed hostilities based on those conflicts. When Indian troops first went into Sri Lanka, they were ostensibly going there to protect the Tamils from the official Sinhalese forces. But clearly the Tamil guerrillas, and the LTTE in particular, were unwilling to take Rajiv Gandhi's word that once they had surrendered their arms and the Indian forces were out, they would not be at the mercy of the Sinhalese hardliners. It was at this point that the Indian government, bullied by an irate Sri Lanka President, decided to adopt a tough line and landed its own troops in this unprecedented mess.

The hardliners in Jayawardene's party are unlikely to relinquish this opportunity of getting the Indians to finish, once and for all, the military resistance of the Tamils. Already the Sri Lanka press is clamouring about 'secret deals' between the absconding LTTE chief Mr Prabhakaran and the Indian government. The campaign against the guerrillas, it says, must not be halted. 'If India did not play the role of godfather to the terrorists, Indian jawans need not die in the sands of Jaffna.' And rounding off this macabre and yet perfectly logical argument, it has concluded: 'Nations which aspire to the status of great powers and have taken upon difficult tasks have to implement them in the manner of great nations.' One can hardly fail to hear in this, echoes of the Saigon press exhorting Johnson or Nixon to send more troops to fight the 'Viet Cong'.

21 March 1988: At Odds[6]

Even bad dreams unfold in phases. Last week, Punjab moved into yet another phase of its continuing nightmare. The 59th Constitutional Amendment Bill has now empowered the Union government to declare an Emergency in Punjab on grounds of internal disturbances. The Bill also allows the Centre to continue President's Rule in Punjab beyond 11 May 1988, when the present sanction of Parliament to the Siddhartha Shankar Ray–Ribeiro dyarchy is due to expire. Despite the vociferous protests of virtually the entire opposition, the ruling party used its whip to push through the Bill in both houses, only condescending to make a minor change in the wording of the Bill specifying that its provisions would apply only to Punjab. In sum, the Amendment has restored to the Constitution the criterion of 'internal disturbances' as a ground for the imposition of Emergency. This was precisely the reason Indira Gandhi cited when she declared her Emergency in 1975; and one of the few lasting achievements of the short-lived Janata government was to have this phrase

[6] *Frontier*, 20, 32 (26 March 1988).

struck off the Constitution when it passed the 45th Amendment in 1978. Now her son has proceeded to restore all of those legal conditions for authoritarian rule.

It was significant that the Constitutional Amendment Bill was passed in Parliament on the very day the opposition parties had called for a *Bharat bandh* demanding the resignation of Rajiv Gandhi. If AIR and Doordarshan are to be believed, the general strike on 15 March 1988 was a complete flop. A more careful reading of the news, however, suggests a quite different interpretation of the mood of the people. In West Bengal, Kerala and Karnataka, where the opposition parties are quite firmly in the saddle, the *bandh* was more or less total. In Andhra, the Telugu Desam has already lost control, largely because of its own failings: whatever else might be its qualities, Mr Rama Rao's government can have little credibility in the matter of civil liberties or in the campaign against corruption. Tamil Nadu is under President's Rule, and the quite massive repression and arrests on the day of the *bandh* in that state were more closely connected with the continuing battle over MGR's legacy than with questions of all-India politics. In Bihar and Orissa, on the other hand, the positive response to the opposition call was significant. Not so, however, in the crucial northern belt of U.P. and Haryana, where the unresolved tangle of alliance politics which plagues the opposition today was painfully apparent. Neither the BJP nor the Bahuguna-led Lok Dal was particularly keen to join the call to demand Rajiv Gandhi's resignation. And V.P. Singh, who still retains a position of crucial importance in U.P. politics despite his relatively low profile in recent weeks, is apparently determined to bide his time until the forthcoming by-election in Allahabad. If there is a groundswell of antipathy to Rajiv Gandhi's follies in northern India, the *Bharat bandh* did not show it because there was no one to channelize the popular disapproval into the forms of organized protest.

The experience of the *bandh* should suggest a quite obvious course of action to the Prime Minister's political advisers, whoever they may be. Keep the seeds of divisive movements alive, for they provide the best pretext for claiming greater executive powers and continuity of leadership. Prepare the institutional grounds for assuming extraordinary powers should the occasion arise. Keep the opposition divided by selective rewards and punishments. And when it is time for the next general elections, who can say that a change of regime will mean a better government! It is the same strategy which Indira Gandhi followed when she was in power; and her son can only be thankful to the opposition parties that they have not required him to learn anything new.

31 May 1988: The Foreign Hand[7]

With the Lok Sabha by-elections round the corner and the option of an early dissolution of Parliament not entirely ruled out, it is time for New Delhi to step up the hue and cry about the ubiquitous 'foreign hand'. Over the last month or so, official 'leaks' have virtually flooded the media with stories of how Pakistan is arming itself with the latest weapons developed in U.S. defence laboratories. The most sensational report was the one culled from an American daily, suggesting that Pakistan had managed to develop and test a missile capable of carrying nuclear warheads that could reach New Delhi or Bombay. The report suggested that the missile had been developed with Chinese assistance, but the whole matter was confused by the speculation that the missile closely resembled a well-known Soviet short-range missile: it was suggested that the Pakistanis had somehow managed to procure some of these Soviet missiles and develop them for their own use with Chinese help. The Indian government has officially denied any knowledge of such a nuclear delivery system possessed by Pakistan, but of course the point of the whole matter is not to make an official allegation, but rather to allow the seeds of suspicion and fear to be sown in the mind of the electorate.

There is much at stake. It is clear that the by-elections two weeks from now will not see the end of the controversy about defence purchases, their propriety and the manner in which these deals are struck. It is also clear that, besides mucking up the trail of hush-hush deals and below-the-counter payments, one of the strongest arguments on the government side, will be the age-old appeal to protect and strengthen the country's defence forces. The greater the atmosphere of threat and insecurity, the stronger the government's case that all this talk of

[7] *Frontier*, 20, 42 (4 June 1988).

irregular defence purchases is merely the ploy of subversive forces to weaken the country's security programme.

The other area in which the Pakistani hand has been rediscovered is that of 'internal destablization'. Once again, we have had a series of official disclosures — incontrovertible evidence, we are told, that Pakistan has been both the brain and the brawn behind the Khalistani insurgency in Punjab. Supposedly, these are discoveries made after interrogating arrested Khalistani terrorists. It seems that from 1985, Sikh terrorists have been recruited from Canada, Britain and the United States, brought to Pakistan, 'indoctrinated in the Khalistan ideology', trained in the techniques of terrorist violence and subversion, supplied with arms, and sent across the border into India. The 'evidence' trotted out repeatedly speaks of something that can hardly cause any surprise — that Sikh terrorists have procured and stocked arms in various places in Pakistan, and that these have been smuggled across the border into India. Most insurgent movements today seek out safe places across the country's borders in order to acquire arms, regroup forces, train cadres, and so on. The Tamil insurgents did this for years on end on Indian soil. If the Indian government has officially denied having actively helped in arming and training these groups, it cannot but accept the fact that it was unable to prevent them from using Indian territory as their base until it became politically necessary — after the Rajiv–Jayawardene accord — for the Indian government to move in against the Tamil insurgents. Surely, something very similar has been going on in Pakistan; and it does not need much 'evidence' in the form of garbled reports of 'interrogation' sessions to prove that Khalistani activists have been using the borders as a crucial element in their strategy of insurgency.

The problem surely does not lie in the very existence of borders, although that would seem to be the last resort in the Indian government's argument about its failure to resolve the Punjab situation. Now we are being told that it was Pakistan (what, we may ask, is this entity called 'Pakistan' — its government, some of its officials, certain elements in its population?) which forced upon a reluctant group of disgruntled Sikhs the very 'ideology of Khalistan', coaxed and badgered them into making the 'Khalistan declaration' in exchange for arms and training. As if, without the proximity of Pakistan, the Punjab problem would simply vanish. It is the last ploy of an incompetent and discredited state apparatus to explain away its failure to resolve, through a political process, the conflicting demands within the body politic. Every step in the long and bloody history of Punjab has been a move from one depth of short-sightedness and incompetence to another.

20 June 1988: The By-Elections[8]

From the very beginning, there was something prefigurative about the Allahabad by-election, like the trailer of a new film yet to be released. First, it was Mr V.P. Singh who threw down a challenge to Amitabh Bachchan, declaring that he would fight the superstar and no one else. But, of course, it was not the screen hero who was the real object of his campaign: it was the Prime Minister himself, and his coterie of ambitious money-grabbing young men among whom was included Ajitabh Bachchan, charged with laundering the illegal kickbacks from the defence purchases of the government. Faced with this challenge, the Rajiv cohort prevaricated. Amitabh Bachchan had put up a show of injured pride by resigning his Lok Sabha seat as soon as the charges of financial impropriety were made against his brother. This would have been a good opportunity for him to take his case to the electorate and clear his name; and with it, the cloud of suspicion that had gathered around the Prime Minister. But the risks were too great. Clearly, the high command knew enough about the popular mood in northern India to decide, finally, that a contest between V.P. Singh and Amitabh Bachchan in Allahabad would inevitably build up into a proxy war for the next general elections. The rulers of New Delhi developed cold feet; but resorting to a level of low cunning that has characterized so much of Congress politics in recent years, they kept up the pretence of renominating the film hero until the very last moment, in order to keep an obdurate V.P. Singh in the field. In the end, they sought to precipitate an anticlimax by choosing Sunil Shastri, a political lightweight uninvolved in any way with the notorious circle of Rajiv Gandhi.

Despite every effort by the Congress(I) to downplay the

8 *Frontier*, 20, 45 (25 June 1988).

significance of the by-elections, the central issue could not be kept under cover. All over northern India, the Lok Sabha by-elections turned into a referendum on the probity of the Rajiv government. As it turned out, except for the Pali seat in Rajasthan, the Congress(I) was unable to retain four seats in U.P., Gujarat, Jammu and Haryana. The polling was suspended in Faridabad because of violence, but everyone expects the Congress(I) to lose there anyway. The only other seat which the Congress(I) was able to win was in Meghalaya where the redoubtable Williamson Sangma, who wins elections on his own, now happens to be in that party.

All in all, the Lok Sabha by-election results are a clear pointer to the main direction in which politics will move in the next year and a half. Beyond doubt, there is strong suspicion in the popular mind of the worthlessness and corruption of the Rajiv Gandhi government. This feeling is more or less generalized, and cuts across the usual segmentations of the electorate by election managers and forecasters. It is also clear that the opposition knows that it is in with a very good chance of actually winning the next election, if it can stay united. A very prominent feature of these by-elections was the agreement of all opposition parties on a common candidate in every Lok Sabha seat. The results are clear; where the opposition has won, it has done so by huge margins. Kanshi Ram's candidature in Allahabad was double-edged; as the results show, his strong support among scheduled-caste voters probably cost the Congress(I) a significant portion of its traditional votes. What is also clear by now is that V.P. Singh will be the strongest candidate as opposition leader. Questions of programmatic unity, the position of the BJP, and the ever-enigmatic role of the parliamentary Left are of course matters that will not be settled in a day. But the scent of victory is the strongest unifier in opposition politics in India, and that is something which will now keep the opposition going until the next general elections.

Far more problematic is the question of what happens in the Congress(I). The threat of dissension, and even of a split, will keep hanging over Congress politics. Nothing dramatic may happen in the near future; but by winning Allahabad with such a large margin, V.P. Singh has fought back all attempts to silence and marginalize him, and has consolidated his position as the rival centre to which Congress members, disgruntled or disillusioned with the electoral prospects of Rajiv Gandhi, can flock. This fact will now remain unaltered until the next general elections. What Rajiv Gandhi will now do to build up a more reliable party organization or a more populist image for the government remains to be seen. But then, this young man's stock of political ideas, never plentiful, seems to have reached rock-bottom.

16 August 1988: Alliance-Making[9]

The first steps were taken last week in setting up the electoral alternative to the Rajiv Congress. This time, there was not the drama of eleven years ago, when a collective experience in India's prisons cemented the virtually spontaneous coming together of an opposition tormented by the Emergency regime. Nor was there the saintly hand of a patriarch-renouncer like J.P., keeping everybody in line, pushing below the surface the petty conflicts and jealousies that always threatened to erupt, and generally reminding the leaders of their responsibilities to the people. This time there has been a much more mundane process of alliance-making, involving a long series of negotiations and deals. The result — the National Front or Rashtriya Morcha of seven opposition parties — is perhaps a more realistic expression of the possibilities of opposition politics today, but it is also much less dramatic in its impact.

Three constituents of the Front are the Lok Dal, the Janata Party and the Jan Morcha. These parties have been riding the crest of the widespread disenchantment with the Rajiv Congress that appears to be sweeping across the northern regions of the country. The recent electoral reverses suffered by the Congress(I) have generally been at the hands of these parties. It is not so much what they represent in themselves that has made them the principal spokesmen of the opposition in northern India. It is rather their position as a counter-force to the Rajiv Congress that has given them their recent impetus. Initially, it was Devi Lal's resounding victory in Haryana last year. Then there was the series of by-election victories by insignificant Janata Party candidates in several Assembly and Parliamentary constituencies in U.P. and Bihar. And finally, of course, there

9 *Frontier*, 21, 1 (20 August 1988).

was V.P. Singh's dramatic win in Allahabad two months ago. There is no doubt that the northern Indian component of the new Front is sensing a large-scale 'wave' in the Hindi belt, and it is this above all else which will keep the alliance going until the next general elections.

The other components are the Congress(S), the DMK, the Asom Gana Parishad and the Telugu Desam. Of these, the first does not count for much, now that Sharad Pawar has been co-opted with full honours in the Congress(I) in Maharashtra. The DMK has undoubtedly received a new lease of life with the demise of its seemingly invincible enemy M.G.R., and the subsequent squabbles between the two women claiming his legacy. The AGP and the Telugu Desam are still the principal political forces in their regional bases and will, for that reason, have an important participation in the Front. Besides, N.T. Rama Rao has sought to play the role of elder statesman in the alliance-making exercises, and has been named as chairman of the Front. There is, of course, a southern component of the Janata Party as well, but its supremacy in Karnataka has been recently damaged — perhaps irreparably — by Ramakrishna Hegde's troubles in containing the factionalism within his own party. Now that he has chosen to quit the Chief Ministership, Mr Hegde may well play a more active part in the national politics of the Front: whether this will be an element of strength or weakness remains to be seen.

No serious analyst will believe that the National Front, as it has come into being, is a credible alternative — in the sense of a politically viable organization with a feasible alternative programme. Relations between its own constituents are lacking in harmony — as reflected in the continued vagueness as to who is to be the parliamentary leader of the Front, and in persistent rumours that people like H.N. Bahuguna may be taken back into the Congress(I). Also, there is still no certainty about the relations between the Front and the two other principal segments of the opposition: namely, the BJP and the Left. If electoral calculations predominate, as they seem to be doing at the moment, an alliance with the Left may seem more profitable. This is because the anti-Rajiv 'wave' in the Hindi belt, if it does rise, may be expected to hold irrespective of whether the BJP joins the Front or not, whereas the support of the Left will mean several additional parliamentary seats in West Bengal and Kerala. But then, the Left still remains undecided in this matter. In principle, the CPI(M) has declared itself in favour of an opposition alliance excluding the BJP. But in the days to come, it is certainly going to be wooed by the Congress(I) and asked to stay out of such an alliance. On the other hand, there is also an opinion within the Left which says that the overthrow of the Rajiv regime is the principal parliamentary task, and the broadest possible opposition alliance is the order of the day. Since programmes, policies and ideology have taken a backseat anyway, it is the calculation of votes and seats which will finally decide the matter.

5 September 1988: Gagging the Press[10]

The secrecy in which the Defamation Bill was drafted, the haste with which it was sought to be cleared through Parliament, the utter incompetence of its phraseology, the contempt it showed for the most elementary principles of law, the juvenile malice with which it sought vengeance upon its enemy — the press — and finally, the unprecedented political mess in which it has landed those that it tried to protect — all this can only be described as the doings of men who have taken leave of their senses.

To follow the phraseology of the Bill itself, what are the 'facts of the matter'? The first fact is that there has been, in recent months, a spate of revelations in the press about the illegal doings of the handful of men and women who are at the helm of affairs in New Delhi today. The second fact is that, in spite of the strenuous and successful efforts of all government agencies to see to it that these revelations are not followed up by legal proceedings in court, there are clear signs that the people — meaning, a vast majority of the electorate — are sufficiently convinced that their present rulers are so crooked that they can no longer be trusted with the reins of government. These two basic facts have combined to produce the insane reaction called the Defamation Bill, 1988.

It is now clear that the Bill was drafted, both in secrecy and in haste, perhaps within the space of a week. It seems that it was not even discussed in the Cabinet before P. Chidambaram, the

[10] *Frontier*, 21, 4 (10 September 1988).

Minister of State for Home, sought to move the Bill in the Lok Sabha, with only a few hours' notice. As the provisions of the Bill became known, the members of the House, and soon the entire nation, were astounded by the conceit of those who thought that they could push through a law so glaringly inconsistent with every principle of freedom of speech.

The Bill introduces in the existing law of defamation a new concept called 'criminal imputation'. Under this, if a person makes an imputation 'falsely alleging' that someone has committed an offence, the aggrieved party can go to court, but the onus of establishing that the imputation is true will be on the accused. A criminal imputation will incur a punishment, 'in the case of the first offence', of imprisonment up to one year and a fine up to Rs 2000, and for 'a second or subsequent offence', of imprisonment up to two years and a fine up to Rs 5000.

The implications of this provision for the freedom of the press are obvious: they amount to its obliteration. For the Bill takes away the right of fair comment, which is the soul of press freedom. The new Bill, if it were to become law, would mean that one would have to have evidence sufficient to prove a person guilty in a court of law before one could make a fair comment on his or her activities. It would mean, in effect, that those who are guilty of paying or accepting commissions and kickbacks would first have to be brought to trial and convicted, before the press could gain the right to talk about the Bofors scandal. It would also mean that the printer or publisher of a newspaper, if once convicted of defamation, would subsequently be liable to the higher penalty if there is 'criminal imputation' in a second, completely unrelated, case. Anyone who has any knowledge of how newspapers work will realize that this would mean that most papers of any standing would simply have to close shop.

Mr Chidambaram defended his new Bill with a series of statements beginning 'Truth is . . .' and 'Truth is not . . .' But he was unable to persuade anybody that the Bill was not meant to destroy the freedom of the press in order to protect corrupt persons in authority. In fact, much to the dismay of Rajiv Gandhi, not only the members of the opposition, but even the stalwarts of the establishment media were forced to throw up their hands and say that this was too much. Every organ of the press, including the venerable Editors' Guild, declared its opposition to the Bill, threatening an all-India newspaper strike on 6 September 1988. Faced with this un-precedented — and by all accounts, unanticipated — opposition, Rajiv Gandhi has finally deferred the motion of the Bill in the Rajya Sabha, and has constituted a ministerial committee to discuss 'the misgivings' of the press.

There is, of course, nothing to discuss. The 'fact of the matter' is as clear as daylight and we all know it. Rajiv Gandhi and his cronies are now a frightened lot. They have been unnerved by the spate of news items that have cast far more than reasonable doubt on their probity as public servants. They are dreading the prospect of more revelations.

19 September 1988: The Limits of Power[11]

The seven-party National Front of the opposition which was formally launched last week at a huge rally on Marina Beach, Madras, has declared that one of its first concerns will be the discrimination by the Centre against non-Congress(I)-ruled states. Opposition politics in India has always moved through instant reactions to instant issues. Undoubtedly, N.T. Rama Rao, a leading star of the National Front, had in mind the recent attack by the Prime Minister's security men on Telugu Desam legislators when he said that the federal polity had been 'twisted and warped for the aggrandizement of the Centre', and that 'the states had been reduced to beggary'. The allegation is wholly true, but although opposition politicians tend to see the matter as simply a case of discrimination against non-Congress(I)-ruled states, it is in fact an expression of a much more fundamental malady.

Take the Congress(I)-ruled states. Is the situation any dif-ferent? If some of them at certain points of time seem to enjoy the special favours of fund-dispensing authorities in New Delhi, one can be sure that has to do with the immediate electoral or factional concerns of the ruling power group at the Centre. But there will be as many occasions when Congress(I)-ruled states have been discriminated against, when Congress(I) chief min-isters have been thrown out and replaced with such casualness

11 *Frontier*, 21, 6 (24 September 1988).

that one would think the chief minister was a member of the Prime Minister's personal staff and not the elected leader of the people of the state. It was the people's realization of their collective non-existence as a state within the Indian Union, that brought about the groundswell which threw men like Rama Rao or Prafulla Mahanta into power. The lathi blows on Telugu Desam MLAs may have been particularly humiliating, or the delay in sending flood relief to Assam particularly crass, but there is no reason to think that the people in other states, in their collective role as constituent units of a federal union, are any better off.

The fact is not only that the original framework of federalism in India has been distorted beyond recognition. Just as there has been a consistent tendency towards the centralization of powers in the last twenty years, so also has there been the growth of entirely new forces and aspirations among the people of this country. An innocent call for a return to the days of Jawaharlal Nehru will not be the answer. The plain fact is that the original structure of federalism, as thought of by the makers of the Indian Constitution, is incapable of accommodating the entirely genuine desires of the peoples of this country to maintain their distinct identities as well as to live together. It is high time that those who claim to voice the resentment of the people against Congress(I) misrule give more thought to this fundamental malady. The need of the day is a call for a new federalism.

Already we have had experiments and innovations — entirely ad hoc and piecemeal — within the old structure that point to an entirely different arrangement. The Hill Council in Darjeeling, which has just been created as a result of the Gorkhaland agitation, has the legal stamp of the present provisions of the Constitution; but its content is wholly new, because for all practical purposes it introduces the concept of a state within a state. No matter how much Subrata Mukherjee may shout about the injured pride of Bengalis, there is nothing to despair in this. On the contrary, it is an innovation wholly to be welcomed, and worked upon, improved, and developed. This may in fact give us the forms of a multi-tiered federal structure, which may be the most useful way of giving to the aspirations of many recently developed cultural identities in India their legitimate and constructive place within the union of the Indian peoples.

Those to whom political power only means the pompous stamp of sovereignty and the iron rod of bureaucracy will of course see in this the signs of a loss of 'national integrity'. It is the duty of those who claim to be the opposition to see that a new and more flexible federal structure will strengthen rather than weaken the unity of our people. The real tragedy is that those who lead opposition politics today cannot see beyond their noses.

20 October 1988: Satanic? Or the Surrender of the Modern?[12]

Is the Government of India seeking directly to interfere with the right of free speech? Is it trying to control what will be written and what will be read? Is it trying to create a climate where no uncomfortable question or dangerous thought will raise its head?

On the face of it, this must be the explanation behind the decision by the government to ban Salman Rushdie's novel. The book was banned as soon as it was published, before most people had a chance to read it. In other words, even before its literary or other qualities could be judged, an executive fiat declared the book unfit to be bought or read. If this decision is accepted without protest, it will be tantamount to a death warrant on artists, writers and scientists in this country.

Who decides on the quality of a serious literary work? Who is to pronounce judgement on a writer's social or political views? The literary readership, or a political leader or bureaucrat? By banning *The Satanic Verses*, the Government of India has declared that if there is sufficient political opposition, a literary work, irrespective of its artistic merits, will not reach its intended readership.

The menace contained in this move hardly requires explication. Yet, this virtual truism now has to be stated afresh. This is because the principal argument that is being offered in support of the government's decision, is political realism. It is the old argument about a situation of emergency: the times are dangerous,

[12] *Ānandabājār patrikā*, 27 October 1988 (translated from the Bengali).

there are too many risks of outbreak of violence. At such times, one must above all be practical. There will be occasions in future for the pure contemplation of moral principles; now, one must tackle the immediate situation, if necessary even by conceding a little bit to the enemy. Those journalists — official hacks — who only a few days ago were forced to shut up when faced with the storm of protest over the Defamation Bill, are now declaiming on the principles of political realism. And listening to these lectures on the intricate methods of determining the volatility of a political situation, even many of the progressives have been left without an answer. Publicly, they are silent about the ban; in private, they will confess their anxieties: 'You never know, these communal matters are highly inflammable. It's best to stay out of them.'

The ban is not part of a planned authoritarian assault. It is the sign of extreme insecurity, when rulers appeal to realism and practicality to cover up their weakness. This politics of immediate solutions to immediate problems is shortsighted and vacuous, and more dangerous because it would have everyone ignore the consequences. It is being argued that if Rushdie's book had been allowed to be sold, there would have been riots. Interestingly, none of those who demanded the ban or imposed it had read the book. Syed Shahabuddin has made the weighty pronouncement that to tell that a drain is a drain, one does not need to jump into it. In his case, of course, the task was simple. He had heard it being said: 'Here is a drain.' Where did he hear it? From some time before *The Satanic Verses* was actually published, there were stories about it in the papers. Not literary reviews, but news stories: that is to say, sensational speculations, half-truths and assorted misrepresentations. That was sufficient grist to Shahabuddin's mill. His politics consists of sniffing around for drains. As soon as he finds one, he shouts: 'There it is, it's polluting everything. Clean it up.' Looking for impurities and cleaning them up: that is the politics of fundamentalism. No matter what the religion or ideology, it thrives on an obsessive and intolerant search for polluting influences. Shahabuddin needed a drain; he found it. If it hadn't been this one, he would have found something else. The cry went up immediately: 'We will not tolerate this satanic conspiracy. Ban the book.' The demand found a few supporters from among that group whose only identity in democratic India is that of being 'secular Muslims'. 'Secular', and hence part of the so-called nationalist mainstream, yet 'Muslim', and hence different. They have tried all these years to keep their distinct identity intact while swimming with the mainstream — with pathetic results. Of course, being the trusted advisers of the government on Muslim matters, their sense of political realism is especially sharp. They were the ones who persuaded the government that the communal situation in northern India was so serious that with the impending general elections, etc., etc. . . .

I have read *The Satanic Verses.* I was fortunate in having bought a copy soon after the book appeared, not knowing at that time, of course, that it would be banned the next day. Having begun reading it, I could not put it down. I pushed aside all other work and read the book at a stretch over three days. Soon, I will read it once more. A narrative that is meticulously crafted, that shows unparalleled skills in the use of language, that has a complex structure, that does not sweep one away in a flood of emotion but ignites one's intelligence, that conceals at every turn the possibility of discovering some unexpected meaning: I like reading books such as this. Needless to say, the work of an author like Rushdie, steeped in the traditions of Western literary modernism and with skills virtually unsurpassed today in the innovative use of English prose, is exceedingly sophisticated. Woven into the dramatic twists and turns of the narrative is Rushdie's running conversation with other authors — comments, debates with Goethe, Dickens, Tolstoy, Joyce, Brecht, Borges, Marquez: I am sure I will notice many more when I read the book again. This is a serious book written with much effort and care: it deserves care and effort on the part of the reader.

Those who say that the book is meant to defame Prophet Muhammad are either lying (because they have not read the book), or they are being deceitful, or else they are plain ignorant. The subject of the novel is not the life of Prophet Muhammad; the subject is Salman Rushdie himself. One of the two principal characters of the story is Saladin Chamchawalla. Born in Bombay, his nationalist Congress-supporting father, like many others of his generation, believed that now that the sahibs had left, his son would become a sahib and run the country. The boy Saladin was sent off to England, to study in the sahibs' school. His effort to become a sahib was earnest. He thought he would churn the ocean of European civilization and drink the pure nectar of freethinking modernity, and in the process wipe out his inherited marks of race, nationality and culture. The other character is Gibreel Farishta. He is a superstar, known all over India for his roles in blockbuster mythologicals. He is in love with the good life, with luxury and modern technology, addicted in equal measure to Scotch whisky and the company of white women. But his words are pure *swadeshi*, reflecting his unshakeable conviction about the decay and imminent destruction of a shallow, materialistic, spiritually vacuous Western civilization.

Gibreel and Saladin are two sides of the same self — two sides of Indian modernity, the one inseparable from the other. Suddenly, by a stroke of providence, Gibreel acquires the powers of an angel, while the hapless Saladin becomes the embodiment of Satan. Now, Saladin is made to see through the facade of British liberalism and discover the reality of racial discrimination in the land of his dreams. He sees that in London neighbourhoods torn by race riots, he is just one of a thousand other Indians, Pakistanis, Bangladeshis, Caribbeans. And Gibreel? He decides to take his new role as an angel seriously. He proceeds to redeem Western society from its million sins. Gibreel, angel of god, is slowly transformed into Azreel, the angel of death. In his mad desire to purify the world, he ignites a devastating fire of violence, hatred and destruction.

Needless to say, this is not the whole story of *The Satanic Verses*. It is narrative that sustains this massive book of 547 pages, and even two long paragraphs cannot provide a summary. The section that has caused such an uproar actually occupies a small portion of the book. Both Gibreel and Saladin are Muslim. Having been reborn, they ask themselves, 'What is religion? What is truth? What is the good?' Buried for so long under the layers of their consciousness, the words of the Koran are now interrogated afresh. If the Mahound described in this novel is the Prophet Muhammad, I have to say that in Rushdie's telling of his story he appears as a political figure of immense nobility: noble, but human, tortured by doubt, uncertain about the complex claims of right and wrong, courageous enough to admit his mistakes. The twelve prostitutes over whom there is so much protest are, in the novel, hardly the 'wives' of the Mahound; they are just prostitutes. It is the vengeful Salman Farsi and the poet Baal who, seeking to bring Muhammad to disrepute, spread the rumour that they might be the wives of the Prophet. And of course, it is the madam of the brothel who seeks to make a little business out of religion. Mahound, who is otherwise forgiving even in his moment of triumph, cannot forgive these transgressors. Waiting for his execution, Baal, the eternal unbeliever (one can hardly fail to recognize here the hero of Brecht's first play), says to Muhammad: 'Whores and writers. We are the people you can't forgive.' Muhammad replies, 'Writers and whores. I see no difference here.'

The Satanic Verses is a story of the contradictions, anxieties and crisis of a rationalist consciousness in independent India. This consciousness is touched by the magical certainty of folk belief, but it can never accept folk religion as its own. (One can hear Rushdie's debate with Marquez on this subject.) The days of divine revelation are past. Whether awake or in our dreams, never again will we hear another prophet. At least, not unless we deceive ourselves. And if we do, there are two choices. We could, like Saladin Chamcha, shut our eyes and say, 'It's fine the way it is, don't upset things too much.' This is the deception of political realism. Or else, we could make a prophetic declaration that the world will have to be cleansed of the pollution of evil, and like Gibreel Farishta, send thousands of innocent people to their doom. This is the deception of fundamentalism. Two sides of the same self: the two sides of Indian modernity, the one inseparable from the other.

I have heard a few 'secular Muslims' complaining about why the minorities were being singled out as being overly sensitive. If a book like this had been written about Hinduism, they ask, would Hindus have tolerated it? The complaint is justified. Among the frightened and cowardly adherents of modernity in India, there are no differences between Hindus and Muslims. If today, a man called Michael Madhusudan Dutt were to write a book called *Meghnādbadh* and declare, 'I despise Rama and his rabble,' I have no doubt the book would be proscribed. It is the good fortune of Bengali literature that the colonial state of the nineteenth century banned books only when they went against colonial interests, and not at the request of their native subjects.

1 November 1988: Looking Back[13]

A small piece of news tucked away in a corner: an additional sessions judge in New Delhi has sentenced six persons to rigorous life terms for killing four people in the Delhi riots of November 1984. This is the first significant judicial verdict in what remains perhaps the worst incident of communal violence in independent India. What was more interesting was the judge's observation that he was awarding the minimum punishment for murder, since the assassination of Mrs Gandhi 'had sent shock waves across the country, causing anger and anguish and resulting in the clogging of a sense of proportion and rationale in the common masses.'

'Clogging' of a sense of proportion is an adequate, if somewhat infelicitous, metaphor to describe much of what is happening today in our politics, although whether 'the common masses' are the only ones to suffer from the malady is debatable. Four years have passed since the riots in Delhi, and the government still insists that there is no need to inquire into why and how they were caused and who were responsible: as though the wounds will heal simply by refusing to recognize that they are there. The fact remains, of course, that the wounds have not healed. They have multiplied and bled, and the events in Punjab, Haryana and Delhi in the last four years are ample reminder that, no matter how desperately those in power might wish, the people do not simply forgive and forget. Fear and insecurity have become for them part of the daily business of survival, and they simply do not trust the sweet, reassuring platitudes of those who claim to run the state. The people know that it is not simply 'anger and anguish' which can lead to the sort of organized killings that swept the capital in those bloody days in November 1984. They also know that the real culprits are being sheltered by those who are in power.

If there is anything which can characterize the mood of the 'common masses' in northern India today, it is a pervasive feeling of insecurity and distrust. Authority and legitimate leadership have virtually vanished. Nothing can be taken at face value and nobody taken on his word. A wave of communal violence is sweeping the towns of Uttar Pradesh, from Muzaf-farnagar through Aligarh, Khatauli, Faizabad to Bahraich. Since no one can trust the authorities of the law to maintain order and protect lives, the rule is: 'each for himself as best as he can'. Every street and *muhalla* in the U.P. towns is armed and organized to defend, retaliate and attack in a warfare of the most elemental kind. And the state is keeping itself busy by banning demonstrations, imposing curfews, sending in more and more armed policemen over whom it has less and less control, while pretending that the problem will go away if only people can be stopped from talking about it. What we are witnessing in Uttar Pradesh today is a farcical illustration — farcical and horrific at the same time — of the 'withering away' of the state!

2 January 1989: All Options Open[14]

In the end, all the speculations about an open conflict over the party line and a change in the top leadership proved to be futile. The Party Congress of the CPI(M) ended last week in Trivan-drum after confirming both E.M.S. Namboodiripad as general secretary and his supposedly controversial line as the agreed line of the party. Mr Namboodiripad held up his line as one of unbroken continuity since the party's foundation in 1964, and demonstrated its correctness by pointing out such diverse events as the presence in the Party Congress of fraternal delegations from both the Soviet and Chinese parties (the first time this has happened in the party's history), the recent cordiality in the meetings between Prime Minister Rajiv Gandhi and the Chinese leaders (which, said E.M.S., only confirmed the CPI(M)'s posi-tion in 1964 on the border dispute), and the realization by the CPI that the Congress(I) was a force to be opposed and CPI(M) an ally. Continuity is a virtue which most communist parties treasure, particularly a party which has had a completely un-changed leadership since the death of Jawaharlal Nehru.

But despite the assertion of continuity and consensus, the speeches and resolutions at the Party Congress bear clear signs of a papering over of differences. There is no doubt that the

[14] *Frontier*, 21, 21 (7 January 1989).

disagreement over electoral strategy has not been sorted out: it has merely been shelved for the time being. The main political resolution proclaims the party's intention to forge a broad unity of the 'left, democratic and secular' forces in the country in order to oust the Congress(I) government. However, a lot of persuasion is still going on within the party to assure members that this line is not going to become an instrument to prop up the Rajiv government, should it fall in a crisis. This is revealed by the fact that the inclusion of 'secular' needed to be tied with an explanation that the communal forces in India were directly serving the interests of imperialist powers, and matched with the declaration that the Congress(I) was nevertheless the principal enemy of the Indian people. Clearly, many members are not completely reassured; and Mr Namboodiripad not only had to explain the differences between the situation in 1977–9 when the Janata came to power and the situation prevailing today when a purely secular opposition stands the chance of replacing the Congress(I), but he also had B.T. Ranadive chide the delegates from West Bengal for not appreciating the dangers of the communal forces in the country. In the end, the resolution adopted basically concedes that the specific question of electoral alliances will be taken up as and when the situation demands. In other words, all opinions within the party may argue that its options have been left open.

It is interesting that, whereas the Akali Dal and Telugu Desam are regarded by the CPI(M) as solidly secular allies in the fight for an alternative to the Congress(I) based on a socio-economic programme, and while there is much soul-searching about the failure of a Left advance in northern India, the only radical movement which has made the most significant headway into the heart of the Bihar countryside in recent years — against the fiercest opposition from both landlords and the state administration — has been officially declared by the CPI(M) as an 'enemy of the Left'. Perhaps this is the true indicator of the seriousness with which the terms 'left', 'secular', 'democratic', etc. are taken by the parliamentary communists. These terms have come to bear entirely different meanings for them, and are used as signals for identifying, in Aesopian language, the specific electoral parties with which open or secret understandings may be arrived at for electoral purposes. If there are sections among the CPI(M) members who are still suspicious about the intentions of their leaders and about the significance of their newly adopted political line, they have good reasons for their suspicion.

16 January 1989: Unite to Divide[15]

While public attention is now focused on Tamil Nadu where the election campaign is hotting up, there were other signs last week of the endless tangles in which opposition politics has found itself. All this time the assumption was that the National Front led by V.P. Singh would be the principal alliance around which the opposition would organize itself in order to oust the government of Rajiv Gandhi. Of course, a spanner was thrown into the works early on by Chandra Shekhar, who refused to go along with the decision to merge some of the party identities in order to go into the Front. But no one takes Chandra Shekhar seriously these days, and although his intransigence did mean some problems for the Janata government in Karnataka, this was never seen as an insurmountable problem for opposition alliance-making.

The problem was not with the middle, but with the two extremes of the opposition — the BJP on the one side and the Left on the other. V.P. Singh has been trying his utmost to have both sides go along with the National Front. He has offered all sorts of formulae so that both could contribute their respective electoral advantages to the Front, without unduly compromising on their publicly declared hostility towards each other. The calculations for the National Front are simple. Having the Left with it may not immediately contribute very much in terms of winning seats in Parliament, because in the areas where the Left has electoral strength — especially in West Bengal and Kerala — it will win or lose on its own, without gaining very much from the alliance. The advantage to the Front is rather in terms of keeping the Left away from the Congress(I), and of neutralizing any attempt the latter might make to project a 'left' image in its campaign. It has been clear for some time that Rajiv Gandhi's advisers have rediscovered

15 *Frontier*, 21, 23 (21 January 1989).

the electoral usefulness of a left-leaning campaign, something which his mother had used with such deadly perfection. On the other hand, the BJP is a very significant electoral force in a lot of parliamentary seats in northern India, and the existence or otherwise of an electoral understanding with it may decide the fate of at least fifty seats in four or five states in the Hindi belt. Mr Singh, it seems, has tried out several methods to have the Front retain both advantages, including seat adjustments on a state-by-state basis so that the Left need not be seen as running on the same platform with the BJP in those states where the latter has strength.

But the CPI(M) in particular, having recently adopted in its Party Congress a political resolution which pronounced communalism to be at least as grave a danger to the country as the misrule of the Congress(I), took a leading part last week in a move to launch a 'national campaign for a left democratic programme'. Along with the CPI, the RSP, and the Forward Bloc, the CPI(M) leaders teamed up with the indestructible H.N. Bahuguna to remind the nation that politics is not simply about winning elections but about ideology and programmes. The object of the 'campaign', these leaders said, was not to set up another front but to 'radicalize the national political situation' by drawing attention to the question of 'national unity' and to the crucial issue of India's foreign policy. They criticized the National Front, and its leader V.P. Singh, for not taking these two issues seriously. Naturally enough, they also singled out the BJP as an enemy of this 'left democratic programme' and said categorically that there was no question this time of reviving 'the spirit of 1977'.

It is curious that whenever Mr Bahuguna is down and out, he suddenly reappears as bearing the conscience of the Left. That has been his method of finding his way back into favour with the Congress(I). For the CPI(M), the double game played by its all-India leaders has been clear for some time. While its rank and file is largely committed to the struggle against a corrupt and brutal regime, exemplified so tragically by the murder of Safdar Hashmi, its national leaders are jockeying for bargaining advantage in the horse race for power. In Tamil Nadu, they have teamed up with the DMK and a faction of the Muslim League, while at the national level they talk endlessly of the great communal danger and of the infinite wisdom of Rajiv Gandhi's foreign policy. While the new 'national campaign' was so forthright in its criticism of V.P. Singh's ideological vagueness, Jyoti Basu declared in Calcutta that, come what may, the Left would in the end support the National Front in the next elections. All in all, therefore, the scenario remains unclear. And doubtless, Rajiv Gandhi and his advisers will spare no effort to keep the opposition as confused as ever.

3 April 1989: Conceal and Be Damned[16]

The Thakkar Commission report as placed before Parliament has been called a damp squib. It is, and it isn't. True, it contains virtually no sensational disclosures apart from the references to R.K. Dhawan already published in the *Indian Express* report which, of course, was what started the entire hullabaloo anyway. The reasons for Justice Thakkar's damning observation that the 'needle of suspicion' pointed towards Mr Dhawan have not been elaborated with any substantive evidence beyond what was already known from the extracts leaked out earlier. It was clear even then that the insinuations levelled against Mrs Gandhi's confidential secretary by Justice Thakkar did not, notwithstanding the honourable judge's florid prose, add up to a credible indictment; it is still clear that there is a great deal of mystery about the former Prime Minister's assassination that has hardly been touched upon.

Justice Thakkar had recommended that Mr Dhawan's role be thoroughly investigated. After the Commission's report was tabled in Parliament, Mr Buta Singh announced that this had in fact been done, and that the special investigation team had cleared Mr Dhawan of all suspicions of complicity in the crime or in the conspiracy. Curiously, however, Justice Thakkar's own evidence, on the basis of which he had identified the 'needle of suspicion', had come from earlier interrogations of Mr Dhawan conducted by the same investigation team headed by S. Anandaram. The special investigation team's later report, which has supposedly discounted all of Justice Thakkar's suspicions, has not been made public.

16 *Frontier*, 21, 34 (8 April 1989).

Not only that: despite Rajiv Gandhi's boastful announcement that the entire report of the Commission would be placed before Parliament and thoroughly discussed so that 'the truth would be out', it now turns out that only two of the five volumes of the original report have seen the light of day. When this was pointed out by opposition members, the government resorted to the old plea that the remaining portions of the report could not be made public for 'reasons of national security'. It was, of course, under the same plea that a law had been pushed through Parliament to prevent publication of the report; and it was only after the furore caused by the *Indian Express* leak three weeks ago that the government had relented. Now it is clear that the government has many more things to hide.

Pushed into a corner by the countrywide uproar over the leaked extracts of the report, Rajiv Gandhi's attempt to come clean has boomeranged. The suspicion has deepened in the public mind that the story of Mrs Gandhi's assassination did not end with the executions of Satwant and Beant Singh, and that there was a much more deep-rooted conspiracy whose details Rajiv Gandhi's government is at pains to conceal. The matter has been made even murkier by the government's indecisive, indeed panicky, handling of the consequences of the *Indian Express* story. After three days of heavy-handed attempts by the government to throttle the demands of the opposition and to manipulate the rumour mill in order to identify the person who may have leaked the report, the Prime Minister suddenly announced — apparently without even consulting his ministers — that the report would be published in full. Now that this promise has been breached, even the strongest Rajiv Gandhi loyalists are at a loss to defend their position.

In the meantime, Mr Dhawan continues to occupy his new official position among Mr Gandhi's advisers, while no formal move has yet been made against any of Mrs Gandhi's former security chiefs whose lapses Justice Thakkar had forcefully, and quite predictably, condemned.

Since politics in the nation's capital has for long assumed the character of medieval palace intrigue, rumours, speculations, insinuations and innuendos have become the very stuff of politics. But despite their fleeting existence, rumours also leave a deep residue of conviction in the popular mind, and this has nothing to do with the tenability or otherwise of specific suspicions or accusations. The full details of the conspiracy behind Mrs Gandhi's assassination may not be revealed for a long time to come; but the people of this country have already formed their judgement on the utter falsity of the present government's pretensions to probity, cleanliness and efficiency in public life.

3 July 1989: Cynical Moves[17]

Early in the morning on 25 June 1988, terrorists fired into a public gathering of the local RSS *shakha* in Moga town in Punjab and killed 25 people. The day before, in different parts of Punjab, some 24 people were killed in terrorist actions, including the Superintendent of Police of Tarn Taran. A few days before that, a massive bomb blast in a crowded waiting hall at New Delhi railway station killed another 30 people. So what is new? People have become inured to incidents such as these. Punjab is not a subject that provokes any serious discussion any more, because everything that anyone had to say has been said. This is the classic situation of a permanent state of siege: a permanent insurgency pitted against a permanent counter-insurgency.

The government, of course, keeps making its periodic claims of 'success'. The government, in this case, means the triumvirate of the Governor S.S. Ray, the Union Home Minister Buta Singh and the Prime Minister. A police state is best run by a small political leadership who bear no popular responsibility. An apparent lull in terrorist incidents, or a set of 'encounter deaths' or the capture of a 'dreaded terrorist' by security forces, immediately prompts a government claim that the back of terrorism has been broken. If the terrorists strike in Delhi, the government claims that they are on the run and are only hitting out in desperation. When they strike back in Punjab, the government issues a sobering reminder that the stamping out of terrorism takes years, even decades.

Opposition responses too have by now fallen into a set pattern. Blame the government for its failures, praise the people for their courage and good sense, remind everyone that nothing can be

[17] *Frontier*, 21, 47 (8 July 1989).

set right without a 'political solution'. In the five years that have passed since Operation Blue Star, it is of course the political solution that has been promised time and again. It is that solution which now seems more distant than ever.

In the meantime, the last hope for a negotiated settlement — the Unified Akali Dal President Simranjit Singh Mann — is now appearing daily in a New Delhi courtroom, facing charges of conspiracy to assassinate Indira Gandhi. The series of rumours about an impending change in the Governorship of Punjab has also abated. Nothing new, it seems, is likely to happen in Punjab in the next few months, except a repetition of the same hopeless pattern.

All of this points to the true significance of a recent announcement by a senior Congress member, that Punjab will be the main issue in the forthcoming general elections. Rajiv Gandhi in his recent speeches has taken to screeching, and one of the things he has been screeching is an accusation that the entire opposition is in league with the Khalistanis. Punjab, it seems, will be allowed to bleed for some time longer, only to enable it to become a credible example for the Congress(I) campaign that the nation is still in danger. The utter cynicism which runs through ruling class politics in India today is best exemplified by the speculation, seriously debated in supposedly 'informed' circles, that the elections for a new Parliament will be held on the fifth anniversary of Indira Gandhi's death!

7 August 1989: Getting Organized?[18]

When the cause has a moral fervour, even the dullest foot-dragger can turn out a brilliant tactician. So many times in the last three years, the opposition has seemed little more than a rag-tag bunch of factious old men, mouthing antiquated slogans and moved only by petty jealousies. And then, all of a sudden, some particularly heinous injustice committed by Rajiv Gandhi's government — and there have been many such crimes — has galvanized them into unity and action. The effect of the mass resignations by opposition members of the Lok Sabha two weeks ago was electrifying, throwing the ruling party into panic and

[18] *Frontier*, 21, 52 (12 August 1989).

confusion. Now the time has come to consolidate and prepare for the next round, which is where the opposition finds the going much tougher.

The official campaign machinery of the government and the ruling party has, of course, swung into action. If the opposition to Rajiv Gandhi has a one-point programme — opposition to Rajiv Gandhi — so does the official campaign have a one-point programme, namely to hammer home the argument that the opposition can never unite. It is a tactic which the ruling Congress party has always used. For, the simple arithmetic of parliamentary elections in India is that if the opposition does unite across the board, the Congress can never hope to win a majority of seats and form a government. The opposition knows this, and so all talk of unity ultimately boils down to a simple question: can the opposition agree enough to put up just one candidate for each seat?

No matter what the media pundits might say, there is little doubt that the opposition this time has had a much longer spell of preparations and talking-among-themselves than at any previous general election in India. Their principal point of moral criticism against the Rajiv Gandhi government, sharpened through a long period of public debate, has now been focused on one simple and well-known issue: corruption in high places. After all, the great turnaround elections always hinge on questions of ethical judgement. Unlike previous elections, and especially unlike 1977, it now also has an unquestioned candidate for the post of Prime Minister. The question of alliances and seat adjustments has been considered off and on for a long time, and since everyone knows that will be the crucial arithmetic that will decide their fate, the discussions in the matter have been conducted on a level of hard-nosed realism. On all these counts, it would appear that the opposition is, in a fundamental sense, far better prepared to face the next elections than it has ever been before.

The question that is being asked is: can this unity last? That is the question which Rajiv Gandhi's media minions are throwing at the public. Surprisingly, the same question is not asked of the Congress(I) itself. Has there been unity in the Congress(I)? How has it been achieved? In the states where it is out of power, the disunity and factiousness in its ranks are so stark that they do not even have to be pointed out. Where it is in power, the same disunity and factiousness make the life of every Congress(I) chief minister as anxious and painful as a spell in purgatory. Even at the Centre, there have been more changes in ministerial positions in the last four years than anyone can remember. And even a monumental majority in Parliament has had to be artificially kept in place by the enactment of an anti-defection law. So what unity are we talking about anyway?

The Indian voters have now been hardened enough by experience not to ask for the moon. They seem to know very well what elections can and cannot achieve. The continuity in government policy, which in essence means continuity in the conditions of power for the ruling classes, is not fundamentally affected by changes in governments and ministers. What the people do wish to assert is their right to say, 'We have had enough of you lot.'

21 August 1989: Gohpur Again[19]

No trick is too low for today's cynical practitioners of the political game of squeezing the last drop out of a corrupt and cynical system. This is most apparent in the contentious field of centre–state relations. The players in this particular game consist not only of the Union and state governments, but also of groups and movements claiming to represent the aspirations to statehood of peoples who do not have a distinct political identity within the Indian federation. Given all that has happened over this issue in the last few years — in Punjab, Assam, Darjeeling, Jharkhand, to name only the most well-known cases — one would have thought the time had come for all those who claim to lead our nation to put their heads together to devise a suitable political framework for the proper working out of Indian federalism. That the present constitutional order is grossly inadequate to provide for the aspirations to autonomy of new cultural solidarities and nationalities has never been more obvious.

Yet what we are witnessing is a sickening display of unscrupulous manipulation and low cunning. The incidents over the last two weeks in the remote area of Gohpur on the Assam–Arunachal border constitute a particularly unsavoury instance.

[19] *Frontier*, 22, 2 (26 August 1989).

What first attracted national headlines was an announcement from Itanagar that the Arunachal police, with the help of the CRP, had recovered more than a hundred bodies of victims of group clashes at Gohpur in Assam, bordering Arunachal Pradesh. The report added that most of the victims were Bodo women and children, and that the death figures were probably much higher. The scale of violence seemed very large, and immediately the official propaganda machinery orchestrated from New Delhi went into full swing. Another instance of 'Assamese chauvinism', the chorus went up. Further proof of the incompetence of the AGP government! The AICC even made an official demand to the Prime Minister that the Assam government be dismissed and President's Rule declared in the state.

It gradually transpired that the event in question was of a different order altogether. Gohpur has been a sensitive place for ethnic relations for a long time. It was the scene of considerable violence in February 1983, at the time of the disputed Assam Assembly elections. The incidents this time were precipitated, it appears, with the killing of a non-tribal by an alleged Bodo militant. The total number of those killed in the ethnic clashes that followed was somewhere around fifteen, and most of the victims were non-tribals. It was the overenthusiastic Arunachal Chief Minister Gegong Apang who was mainly responsible for distorting and exaggerating the incident out of all proportion and creating a first-rate crisis. He was undoubtedly emboldened by the postures of his senior party leaders in New Delhi, led by the Prime Minister himself, to create as much trouble as possible for the non-Congress(I) state governments in the run-up to the next general elections. A further compulsion was introduced by the forthcoming talks on 28 August 1989 between representatives of the All Bodo Students Union and the Assam government, supervised by the Union government. Since the leaders in Delhi have shown that they are prepared to concede to all parties who can create the maximum trouble, especially if a non-Congress(I) government can be cut down to size in the process, one can hardly blame the Bodo agitators for choosing the tactics they have adopted. The fact that thousands of innocent people are being rendered homeless, their properties burnt or looted, and that dozens are being killed every week simply to keep up the tempo of the agitation bothers nobody at all. It does not take too much skill in political analysis to predict that a lot more blood will flow in Assam in the next few months before anything like a 'solution' to the Bodo problem is found. When the very existence of a 'problem' serves the purpose, who wants a solution?

18 September 1989: Dirty Game[20]

As the general elections draw nearer, a great number of issues that would otherwise have been regarded as of merely regional importance are increasingly becoming entangled in the cobweb of national politics. No part of the country is free of this process. In the non-Congress(I) states, for instance, the Union government, along with whatever help it can get from the Governors, the local Congress(I) machinery, and of course its own captive media, is out to create as much trouble as possible. A relentless campaign is on against Devi Lal for one. The plot to buy up a number of Janata Dal MLAs in Haryana having failed, it was Siddhartha Ray who stepped in with a series of letters charging Devi Lal with having interfered with the functioning of the Punjab government on the occasion of the *Bharat bandh*. In Assam, the Bodo agitation seems to have the silent, and not-so-silent, blessings of New Delhi. In Andhra Pradesh, Mr Rama Rao is being pressurized from all possible quarters. In West Bengal, several Congress(I) leaders have demanded that President's Rule be imposed in view of a threatening law and order situation. In Tamil Nadu, there were alarming reports that the Congress(I) was preparing for a major show of violence against the DMK on the day of the *bandh*: fortunately nothing happened, perhaps only because of the advance publicity.

This is not to say, of course, that the non-Congress(I) governments have nothing to answer for. Whether it is Haryana or West Bengal or Andhra Pradesh, there is much in the way these states are being ruled that smacks of inefficiency, arbitrariness, sectarianism, corruption and the authoritarian use of governmental and party power. The point is, however, that the criticism of these injustices and failings, inasmuch as it is being taken up by the Congress(I), is motivated exclusively by considerations that

[20] *Frontier*, 22, 6 (23 September 1989).

have to do with the next general elections, with a general helping
hand being provided by the dirty tricks department of the central
government. Corruption and autocratic functioning being the
central issues threatening the future of the Rajiv Gandhi regime,
the attitude seems to be to proclaim: 'We are not the only ones;
everybody else is just as bad.'

Turning to the Congress(I)-ruled states, the situation is
similar. In Jammu and Kashmir, where Farooq Abdullah rules
as a pliable proxy for the Congress(I), what was previously a
vast reservoir of regional grievances on which Mr Abdullah's
father had thrived despite the machinations of New Delhi, is
now being rapidly channelized into a purely communal politics.
Once Mr Abdullah decided to abandon his natural constituency
for what he thought was a comfortable sinecure offered to him
by Delhi, this was virtually a foregone conclusion. In other
states, like U.P. or Bihar or Madhya Pradesh, the political picture
is dominated by the jockeying for positions within the Con-
gress(I). Many forces are at work here. There are first the
calculations of which groups will get what share of the nominations for the parliamentary elections. Following upon that, there
is the need to demonstrate one's indispensability for the Con-
gress(I)'s electoral success in the state. Finally, there is a subtle
but nonetheless perceptible calculation, which is weighing the
options and probabilities of a Congress(I) disaster in the general
elections, and thus opening up avenues of communication with
'the other side'.

While all this is likely to continue in the next couple of
months — the period of preparation — it is by no means
certain that this will have any necessary bearing upon the
results of the next elections. There have been in recent years
several occasions when the voters have, without any obvious
prompting, acted collectively to produce a 'wave'. There are
many reasons to believe that the forthcoming elections might
become one where the one exclusive issue will be a referendum
on Rajiv Gandhi. If that does turn out to be the case, regional
calculations will not figure in the minds of the voter at all.
The only question which he or she will want to answer is:
'Do we want to give Rajiv Gandhi another term as Prime
Minister?' No matter what the opinion polls say, perhaps most
people have already decided.

6 November 1989: From Despair to Hope[21]

When Rajiv Gandhi announced to his startled Cabinet colleagues that he had decided to call the general elections ahead of schedule, he is said to have explained that the campaign arrangements were already complete. Two weeks later, it is now clear that what he meant was that his ad boys had finalized the plans for the media blitz now sweeping the country, exhorting voters to count the number of times their hearts beat for India. One more example, if example was indeed required, of the sources of political authority and wisdom from which the Prime Minister draws sustenance for his rule: they lie not in his party or in the democratic processes of national life, but in his inner circle of family, schoolboy network and assorted conmen. With a little more than two weeks to go for the elections, the ruling Congress(I) has not yet managed to release its election manifesto. But then, what is the use of a party manifesto when the ad men have decided that the only way to secure votes for the Congress(I) is to strike terror in the hearts of the voters?

Terror there is in abundance. Not only in the full-page ads in national dailies and in the millions of posters, hoardings and audio-visual presentations that will soon flood the length and breadth of the country, but also in the actual course of events on the political scene.

The daily killings continue in Punjab and Kashmir, as they have for so many months. In the rest of northern India, the communal situation is on the edge of a precipice. After a series of sparks in different towns of U.P., Rajasthan and Madhya Pradesh, the fire was lit in Bhagalpur in Bihar; and after some forty deaths in cold-blooded rioting, the area still continues to be under curfew. The Vishwa Hindu Parishad is going ahead with its highly provocative programme of the *Ramshila yajna* on 9 November, and the Union government has refused to take a clear position in the matter. There are reports of secret negotiations between the Union Home Minister Buta Singh and the VHP organizers — offering, it seems, covert encouragement. V.P. Singh, after having warned at least a month ago that the Congress(I) would engineer communal riots all over the country

21 *Frontier*, 22, 13 (11 November 1989).

before seeking a fresh mandate, is desperately appealing to the VHP to withdraw its programme, but to no avail. If one follows the basic principle of criminal investigation and looks for the party which has the most to gain from a crime, there can be no doubt about which one is the strongest suspect in this grisly and cynical story of political criminality. And yet, notwithstanding the atmosphere of surcharged communal tension, Rajiv Gandhi had no compunctions about inaugurating his election campaign in Ayodhya, 'the birth place of Rama' as he proudly announced, and promising to lead the struggle for *Ram Rajya*.

The silver lining is that despite these cold-blooded and cynical manipulations of base passions, the Congress(I) has been seriously frustrated in its attempt to establish an early lead in the campaign race. If the motive behind the sudden announcement of elections was to catch the opposition napping, the move has clearly failed. For once, the opposition has shown itself able to sort out its differences, arrive at workable understandings, and put up common candidates against the Congress(I) for most of the seats. There has been no alliance between the National Front and the BJP — in fact, the political differences have been clearly marked — but this has not pushed them into the obvious trap laid by the ruling party, of putting candidates against each other and dividing the opposition votes. What has come to the surface most dramatically is the state of discord and uncertainty in the Congress(I) ranks, expressed most surprisingly in the refusal by K.C. Pant, the Defence Minister, to accept the nominations offered to him by the party. There are even stronger indications that senior leaders of the party are only biding their time, hoping to catch their Prime Minister at a vulnerable moment.

The most hopeful sign is the steady assertion of a popular mood, strong enough, it seems, to openly proclaim its rejection of an arbitrary, corrupt, wilful and utterly unprincipled regime.

28 November 1989: Promises and Anxieties[22]

The similarities with 1977 are close enough to be uncanny. In three-fourths of the country, from Gujarat in the west to Haryana and Delhi in the north to West Bengal and Orissa in the east,

[22] *Frontier*, 22, 16 (2 December 1989).

the Congress(I) has been virtually routed. In the four southern states, not only has this wave been resisted, it has been reversed. The result is that the Congress(I), having enjoyed an unprecedented 400-plus bonanza in the previous Lok Sabha, is now down to about 200 seats, leaving it with virtually no chance of forming a government even with the help of its electoral allies. From three-fourths of the country, the verdict of the electorate has been clear: it is an emphatic defeat of the Congress(I).

The political activity will in the meantime shift to New Delhi where the President, Mr Venkataraman, will have to make the momentous decision in a situation which has been unprecedented at the national level in this country: how to form a workable government out of a hung Parliament? Two small differences from 1977 have produced this unprecedented situation: first, the Congress rout is not as complete in the north as it was in 1977, so that it has secured about forty additional seats; and second, what is now the BJP had merged with the Janata Party in 1977, so that, taken together, the Janata Party then had an absolute majority on its own. This time, the non-Congress Members of Parliament are divided into three distinct blocs — the National Front (which is now virtually identical with the Janata Dal as far as the Lok Sabha is concerned), the BJP and the Left. The only possibility for a government now seems to be a National Front government supported from outside by both the BJP and the Left. The initial responses from the leaders of all three blocs suggest that they are in fact working towards this course of action.

The election results have now produced another opportunity — only the second time in Indian history — for a non-Congress government at the Centre. The earlier experience was bitterly disappointing, and it has taken the electorate ten years to be persuaded that the opposition deserves to be given another chance. The responsibility that has been bestowed upon the three non-Congress blocs in Parliament is huge. The ideological differences between them have been many, but in so far as they have been thrown together in common criticism of Congress(I) misrule, it now devolves upon them to work out a common programme on which basis a National Front government might work. The possibility for this is not as remote as is often made out. After all, the entire opposition had agreed over the last five,

years that the evils of the Rajiv Gandhi regime lay not so much
in its declared policies, whether on internal or external matters,
but in the excessive over-centralization of powers, the arbitrariness of a coterie rule, the unwillingness to make itself account-
able to the people, and the cynical manipulation of people and
of issues by the use of money, muscle-power and the media.
These evils provide a large enough target for any non-Congress
government to work upon. A more effective federal system, a
more open style of government, greater responsiveness to popular demands, and the cleansing of political institutions of the
squalid atmosphere of sycophancy, corruption and highhandedness that has resulted from despotic dynastic rule — these goals
can well form the immediate programme of such a government.
It is therefore not true that nothing can be done on which the
entire non-Congress spectrum in Indian politics can agree. The
people seem to have placed, even if cautiously, this trust in the
anti-Congress parties. It is now up to them to fulfil this trust.

The issue of communalism has dominated the scene, at least
in northern India, in the weeks preceding the general elections.
Unless one takes an utterly cynical view of politics and asserts
that the Indian people are inherently communal-minded, or
that they are mere playthings in the hands of communal agitators, there can be only one interpretation of the north Indian
results. The people have expressed their condemnation of the
way in which the Congress(I) has handled the communalism
issue. Here too they have placed their trust in the opposition.
The new government, even if it has to depend for its survival
on the two opposed groups — the BJP and the Left — will
enjoy a great deal of goodwill from the people, at least in the
initial phase. This will probably be the first major test which
will prove whether or not a non-Congress government can
really work in Indian politics.

The people have demonstrated that they, at least, are not afraid
to take risks for the sake of change. Whether the political leaders
will do the same remains to be seen.

12

The National Front and After

18 December 1989: Taking Over[1]

V.P. Singh's first press conference as Prime Minister was predictably undramatic. He did not make any startling revelations either on policy or on personnel matters. He was careful in his choice of words and eager to avoid any unnecessary controversy. In a way, it was indicative of the mood of cautious optimism in which the new government has begun its work.

No doubt, on the home front, Mr Singh made a significant gesture on Punjab by choosing to visit Amritsar and take a trip through the city streets in an open jeep. The spontaneous good-will he was clearly successful in eliciting from the people makes for a new beginning. More than any specific political demands, it is the feeling of distrust and alienation among the people of Punjab which has made peace in that part of the country seem like an impossible dream. The Prime Minister has begun by using the occasion of a change of regimes in Delhi to send out the signal that the new government is prepared to begin afresh. The change of governors in Punjab, the all-party meeting on 17 December and the appointment of Air Chief Marshal Arjan Singh as Lieutenant-Governor of Delhi are all part of that exercise. It is true that nothing concrete has emerged yet, and it would be foolhardy to think that the conflicting political trends and leadership tussles among different sections of the Akali movement will vanish simply by virtue of the electoral victories of the Mann group. Nevertheless, a new chapter has certainly opened in what has so far been the grim story of Punjab.

On Kashmir, however, the auguries are far more disquieting. The appointment of Mufti Muhammad Sayeed as Union Home Minister was immediately greeted by the kidnapping of his

[1] *Frontier*, 22, 19 (23 December 1989).

daughter in Srinagar. After several days of tense negotiations, an exchange was arranged in which five activists of the Jammu and Kashmir Liberation Front were released from prison. What the incid'nt showed was the depth of popular animosity about 'Indian' rule in Kashmir, and the extent to which, by aligning itself with the Congress(I), the regime of Farooq Abdullah had alienated itself from its historical legacy of being the true voice of the people of Kashmir. Clearly, the northern-most state of India will rank high among the 'problems' which Mr Singh's government has inherited from Rajiv Gandhi.

On the economy, too, the prognostics are grim. The budget exercise is being prolonged, and Madhu Dandavate, the Union Finance Minister, has already announced that there will be a vote on account until such time as the new government is prepared with a statement on the overall condition of the economy. Given the mindless spending spree in which Rajiv Gandhi and his men had indulged, the state of public finances, both domestic and external, is critical. The new government is in an unenviable position. It cannot simply tighten up and say that we cannot spend until our finances are in better shape: the political expectations are too pressing. It will have to be a complicated balancing act.

The silver lining is that as far as the 'support from outside' factor is concerned, neither the BJP nor the Left parties have so far said or done anytl 'g that might embarrass the government. For some time at least, V.P. Singh will have the support and goodwill of a large section of political opinion in the country. For how long will depend on the performance of the government.

9 July 1990: The Politics of Economics[2]

With Kashmir going the way of Punjab, no one expects the National Front government to produce any dramatic results any more. It seems to have been taken for granted that yet another part of the country will now fester and bleed, with nobody knowing what to do with it. Kashmir having been relegated to the inside pages, the news from the capital last

2 *Frontier*, 22, 48 (14 July 1990).

week was dominated by economics. Shorn of jargon, it was really politics by another means.

The issue was the government's new industrial policy, which was discussed and apparently adopted by the Cabinet. When the Industries Minister Ajit Singh announced the policy a few weeks ago, there was considerable confusion, since it seemed to run in an opposite direction from the new Planning Commission's thinking. The Congress(I) was, of course, quick to pounce on the issue, declaring that the National Front government was preparing to sell the country to the multinationals. The stand was hardly credible, since the new policy seemed to follow with perfect consistency the direction taken by Rajiv Gandhi's government during its own term in office.

More dramatic opposition came, however, from the irrepressible Chandra Shekhar. He criticized the new policy as one calculated to please the World Bank and the multinationals. It would not ease the foreign currency situation at all, but exacerbate it. It would bring in wasteful and unhealthy investment by the multinationals in the luxury sector. He was particularly critical of the lessening of importance of the public sector, which he said had to be revived and strengthened, not abandoned, if self-reliance was to be achieved.

Chandra Sekhar's arguments immediately received the support of the CPI and the CPI(M). Even the BJP seemed to echo his sentiments about the undesirable entry of multinationals. More interesting was the support he received from Devi Lal, then recuperating in Bangalore. This too seemed to follow the expected alignments within the Janata Dal. Curiously, however, the unpredictable patriarch of Haryana did a sudden *volte-face*, claiming two days later that the policy was not as disastrous as Chandra Shekhar was making it out to be, that in fact it was the best possible move in the present circumstances.

Devi Lal has now queered the pitch. No one knows how he plans to move when he returns to Delhi next week. The confusion over this was compounded by his statement on Ramakrishna Hegde's resignation from the Planning Commission. This in itself was a tortuous affair, although it had nothing to do with the controversy over economic policy. Mr Hegde offered to resign because he had apparently been censured by the Kuldip Singh Commission, appointed by the previous government to investigate the telephone tapping affair in Bangalore. V.P. Singh first asked Mr Hegde to continue. Then, on second thoughts, he accepted his resignation.

It is possible that there will be factional realignments within the Janata Dal in the next few weeks. New general secretaries are to be chosen, and Om Prakash Chauthala, disgraced and ousted from his seat in Haryana despite his father Devi Lal's clout, is in the running. The outside supporters of the Dal, without whose cooperation the National Front government cannot survive, are also becoming restive. The BJP, unhappy with the removal of Jagmohan from Kashmir, has begun to threaten the government for its 'anti-Hindu' policy over the Ayodhya issue. The Left has been particularly critical over the economic policy of the government. While the policy itself was approved by the Cabinet, differences of opinion seem to persist, since old-time socialists like George Fernandes and Sharad Yadav do not share the views of liberalizers like Ajit Singh and Arun Nehru.

23 July 1990: Stronger, but Weaker[3]

It had to be the irrepressible Devi Lal who would do it. Ever since the National Front government took office, it has been clear that the danger to its stability lay not where minority governments usually flounder — the uncertain support of allied parties outside the government. Rather, this government was most likely to be endangered from within. Initially, it had seemed that the truculent Chandra Shekhar, who had kept himself out of a ministerial position in a fit of pique, was the danger man. Only two weeks ago, it was Chandra Shekhar who launched the major attack against the new industrial policy of the government. At the time, Devi Lal was undergoing treatment in a clinic in Bangalore.

Immediately on his return to Delhi, however, Devi Lal got going. When he first came to Delhi in November 1989, persuading himself that as Deputy Prime Minister he would supervise the affairs of the new government as a sort of senior statesman and father-figure, he arranged to hand over his satrapy in Haryana to his son Om Prakash Chauthala. There was a great deal of eyebrow-raising about this in the press as well as within the Janata Dal, because talk of 'dynastic rule' was still very much in the air. But to the patriarch from Haryana this seemed the most natural procedure of transfer of power. The real difficulty arose when Mr Chauthala, seeking election to the Haryana Assembly in order to meet the basic legal qualification to continue as Chief Minister (another needless encumbrance invented by effete urban minds, Devi Lal surely thought), perpetrated the most ham-handed attempt at rigging an election in recent electoral history. The hue and cry was so strong that Devi Lal had to concede that Chauthala must step down until investigations into the Meham poll violence were completed.

Most people underestimated how much of a personal blow this was to the senior citizen from Haryana. It was, so to speak, a challenge to the very core of his authority. The investigations, as usual, were slow to get off the ground. Mr Chauthala, in the meantime, became a candidate in another by-election and won a seat in the Assembly. Devi Lal, impatient in his efforts to secure a legitimate political position for his son, interceded with the Prime Minister to make him a general secretary of the Janata Dal. If there were any other agreements at this meeting, they will perhaps long remain secrets. Immediately after this, in a swift stroke of political organization, the Haryana MLAs met in Delhi, elected Mr Chauthala their leader, the current Chief Minister resigned, and Devi Lal's son was sworn in again as Chief Minister.

All hell broke loose after this. Beginning with Arun Nehru and Arif Mohammed Khan, as many as sixteen ministers sent in their resignations from the Union Cabinet. Finally, to take the crisis to its peak, V.P. Singh himself sent in a letter of resignation to the party president. For three days, the capital was on tenterhooks, fearing the collapse of the government. Devi Lal, intractable as ever, refused to budge. In the end, the truth of the matter was forced to come out in the open. The entire spectrum of opinion and personalities in the National Front, including such sworn enemies as Chandra Shekhar, had to declare that V.P. Singh must stay and Chauthala resign. There could have been no other solution, and after two days of recalcitrance Devi Lal had to give way.

V.P. Singh has now established what should have been obvious from the very beginning: that the political credibility of this government will stand or fall with the credibility of V.P. Singh. By precipitating the drama of his resignation, he has now proved to all his indispensability. There are fears, of course, that Devi Lal will strike back. Chandra Shekhar, never reconciled to the reality of V.P. Singh's pre-eminence, is probably only biding his time. The question of Arun Nehru and Arif Mohammed Khan has now become a new element in the complex calculations of political viability, for their loyalty to the present leadership has come under a cloud. But the crisis has proved that the true centre of stability is the Prime Minister himself.

What is thus a strength is also, not surprisingly, the principal weakness of this government. It is not ideology or organization or an agreement on policy that keeps the government going. There will be constant jerks and irritations in its wayward journey. Above all, it will be the quality of leadership of one man which will decide whether this experiment in non-Congress government will succeed or flounder.

10 September 1990: We Have Heard This Before[4]

When the interests of dominant minorities are threatened, the reactions are always the same.

A hundred years ago, when the demand was made that, to enable Indians to sit for the examinations to the Indian Civil Service, the age limit of applicants be raised and arrangements be made for examinations to be held in India, British civil servants were aghast. 'That would bring disaster,' they said. 'We could never maintain the efficiency of the service. Indians cannot have the same abilities as graduates of British universities. Besides, these jobs will be cornered by a tiny elite among Indians. What good will that do to the vast majority?' Historians today consider these opinions as reflecting the racial prejudices of the then rulers of India.

Fifty years ago, when the demand to abolish *zamindari* was being debated, landlords raised similar arguments. The demand was discriminatory, they said. First, to take property away from one class and give it to another violated the universal right of property. Second, not all *zamindars* were wealthy or oppressive. There were many who were owners of small landed property whose incomes

4 *Ānandabājār patrikā*, 14 September 1990 (translated from the Bengali).

barely provided them with a livelihood. The only class that would profit from the abolition of *zamindari* was the rich peasantry. This class was poorly educated, with no tradition of assuming social leadership or responsibility. If they had power, rich peasants would be far more oppressive than *zamindars* ever were. The poor peasant would hardly be better off. Third, the demand was politically motivated. It would produce conflict between classes and hatred and disorder in society. If the anti-reservationists of today take a look at the debates in the provincial legislatures of Bengal, Bihar or U.P. half a century ago, they will be astonished. Whether they will be embarrassed as well, I cannot tell.

It is often true that the more substantial peasants were the ones who gained the most from the abolition of *zamindari*. It is also true that they are the ones who have in many regions become the oppressive rich farmers of today. But we do not for that reason claim that the abolition of *zamindari* was wrong. On the contrary, we often condemn the Congress governments of the time for having paid compensation to *zamindars,* and for allowing the loopholes in law which enabled landlords to retain their hold over much of their possessions. Of course, we forget which classes of the future were to profit from those loopholes.

The same arguments are now being repeated in the debate over reservation of jobs for backward castes in the Central government services. Three objections have been raised to the proposal. First, disregarding the criterion of merit, jobs are being reserved for one section of applicants: this is both discriminatory and harmful to administrative efficiency. Second, it is not true that everyone from the upper castes is privileged or that everyone from the lower castes is disadvantaged. If jobs are reserved by caste, the better-off among the lower castes will grab them; those who are truly disadvantaged will not gain in any way. If jobs have to be reserved, it should be done by economic criteria, not by caste. Third, a politically motivated move such as this will only create new conflicts between castes. Unlike education or land reforms which are the real answers to caste discrimination, this proposal will only increase disparities, not remove them.

The same arguments, but in different contexts. The debate must therefore be carried out all over again.

Take first the question of merit. It does not require much knowledge of economic theory to see that under conditions of free competition, those who have greater initial endowments will in the end capture the market. The observation holds for the education market too. Where recruitment is by open competitive examination, if it is found that successful applicants come predominantly from a small section of society, then surely the conclusion cannot be that their merit is a natural gift. There must be social reasons for systematic disparities in 'merit'. The report of the Mandal Commission shows that of Class I positions in the Central services, only 7.14 per cent are held by those from the scheduled castes or tribes (despite a reservation for them of 22.5 per cent). Other backward castes hold 2.59 per cent. Of Class II posts, scheduled castes and tribes have only 13.66 per cent. Of Class III and IV jobs, however, they hold 31 per cent, well above the reserved quota. Obviously, the upper castes are not particularly interested in these lowly jobs. Hence, the division of labour in the administrative apparatus of our modern state looks much like that recommended by the *varna* system of the scriptures.

Yet this is a division of labour produced by an assessment of educational merit. And it is not as if we do not know why such a result has been produced. Yes, there has been an expansion of secondary and higher education in independent India, but this expansion has brought into existence two separate educational systems. The more the educated upper castes have been ousted from landed property and turned themselves into the urban middle classes, the more strenuously have they built up their own institutions for producing professionals with 'merit'. The consequence has been that the system of public education catering to the rest of the population has been entirely dissociated from the production of 'merit'. This disparity has been less the result of state patronage and more that of the enterprise, expenditure and infinite energy of the urban middle classes. Every city and town in India is now part of this structure, beginning with nursery schools. These institutions have better teaching, better facilities; the costs are also much higher. Needless to say, there is also far greater homogeneity in the class backgrounds of students. Every urban resident in India knows that if one can manage to put one's child into one of these 'English-medium' schools, he or she would get a headstart in the race to acquire 'merit'. Disparities in educational achievement, therefore, begin from the primary stage of schooling.

Where there is such extreme disparity in access to education, it is easy to see what open competitive examinations will perpetuate. If educational achievement is the only merit that will be tested, surely those who come from educated middle class families and who have had the privilege of going into the elite schools will be the ones to qualify. Others will not stand a chance. If the criterion of merit is to be applied fairly, there should not only be expansion of education but also equalization of educational opportunities, at least up to the secondary level. In every country of the world where there is universal secondary education, the principle is not only that every child must go to school, but that, with rare exceptions, they will go to the same *kind* of school. This is not some coercive diktat of socialist regimes. Even the United States follows exactly the same system. Except for a handful who go to private or denominational schools, all children in that holy land of modern capitalism and meritocracy are educated through a universal system of public schooling. If in India today it is ruled that all children, irrespective of class, will have to attend their neighbourhood schools, I suppose middle-class parents in their despair will decide to renounce the world and retire to monastic life. There is no political force in the country which can bring about such a democratic revolution in education.

If jobs are reserved for those from socially and educationally backward castes, it is obvious that they will go to the relatively better-off sections among those castes. What else could we expect? Only those from relatively prosperous lower caste families will have the minimum educational qualifications for getting even the reserved places in the Class I and II services, over which there is so much competition. The alternative proposal of reservation by economic criteria is entirely irrelevant to the problem of caste discrimination. If that proposal is aimed at reserving places for those who, irrespective of caste, fall below a certain level of income, then we are hardly likely to find many who will be from a backward caste, from a low-income family, and at the same have the minimum educational qualifications for the job. Clearly, these reserved positions will then go overwhelmingly to low-income upper-caste applicants. That will only reinforce the present caste imbalance in the professional middle class; the lower castes will again be denied entry into that exclusive circle.

Hidden behind the cloud of political slogans is a very simple fact. Is it at all correct to say that the demand for reservations is the result of the lack of spread of education' or the incompleteness of land reforms? To me, the truth seems to be the exact opposite. It is in fact because of the spread, however tardy, of education in rural areas and of land reforms, no matter how inadequate, that there has now grown a class of prosperous peasants in the countryside. They have even acquired some economic and political power at the local levels. Their children are now making a bid to find a place among the urban middle classes which inhabit the central institutions of power in society. This has nothing to do with the removal of poverty in the country at large. The Central government services, over which there is such conflict today, actually comprise only about ten per cent of the total employment in the organized sector of the economy. If one takes the Class I and II positions, they account for less than five per cent. Not even an idiot will claim that by distributing these jobs the problem of poverty will be affected in any way. It is in fact the class differentiation among the peasantry and among the middle castes, brought about in the rural areas in the last few decades by economic changes and the expansion of education, that is now producing the assault on the citadels occupied for so long by the educated urban middle classes. The real question is: will the institutions of administrative, professional and cultural power remain under the dominance of the upper castes, or will others have to be given a place? That is what the fight is all about.

It is apparent that caste conflicts will grow. Those who were complaining the most about the possibility of conflict are the ones who have now taken to violence. This is a conflict that took place in the south of the country a few decades ago. In most parts of southern India, the social dominance of the upper castes has crumbled. The conflict has now emerged in a big way in the north. To complain of political motives in this connection is strange, to say the least. Could any decision of such consequence for the structures of power in the country have been taken without strong political motivations? Were there no political motives behind the fact that the Mandal Commission report had only gathered dust in the last ten years? In terms of politics, the truth is that the National Front government has taken a daring risk. It is a tough task indeed to incur the wrath of the urban upper and middle classes and still remain in power.

The expressions of wrath are frightening. There are few things more ugly than the flaunting of the cultural superiority of dominant minorities. I am no longer surprised when I hear of the parents of anti-reservationist student agitators waxing nostalgic about the golden age of the ICS. I can see in front of my eyes the first political movement in independent India whose campaign is in English, whose slogans are in English, whose ideology too, I presume, is articulated in English. I can also see despicable vulgarities of which only the privileged are capable, from ridiculing the Chief Minister of Bihar on the size of his family to shining shoes for the benefit of news photographers. These are perhaps the most sublime examples of the perversities of a merit-producing education.

There is no doubt that there will be conflict. There is also no doubt that no political party and no elected government in India will ever succeed in overturning the recent decision to reserve government jobs for backward castes. Of course, there will now appear innumerable loopholes in the regulations: in whose interest, it hardly needs to be elaborated. And it is my presumption that future historians will judge the anti-reservationists of today in exactly the same way that present-day historians judge British imperialists or Indian *zamindars*. It may be that I am being excessively optimistic. Only the future acts of the present generation of educated youth can decide whether my presumption will prove to be correct.

10 November 1990: The People Betrayed[5]

There are times when the perversities of the parliamentary system can produce results that are completely contradictory even to the electorally expressed wishes of the people. Such a time has now come with the installation of Chandra Shekhar's government.

The withdrawal of support by the BJP immediately after Mr Advani's burlesque act was stopped, had sealed the fate of the National Front government. If V.P. Singh still insisted that he would test his majority in the Lok Sabha, it was because he wished, in effect, to use the occasion to open his campaign for the next elections. With V.P. Singh's government gone, the only options would seem to have been a Congress(I) minority government or fresh elections. The Congress(I), however, chose an even more roundabout way to get back the reins of power without actually taking the responsibility of running a government. It chose to rule by proxy.

Mr Chandra Shekhar's allergy towards V.P. Singh was never concealed: it was written on his face. He agreed with expected alacrity to be the pawn in Rajiv Gandhi's game. Projected by the Congress(I) as the one man who could save the country from going into another general election within a year, Chandra Shekhar, in association with the ever-unpredictable Devi Lal, first attempted to effect a change in the leadership of the Janata Dal. When that attempt failed, they chose to form a breakaway group which would stake its claim to government with Congress(I) support. A rehearsal was carried out in Gujarat where the Chimanbhai Patel ministry had also lost its majority after the withdrawal of BJP support. Chimanbhai was given support by the Congress(I). The same pattern has now been repeated in New Delhi.

There is something grotesque in the sight of a breakaway group of uncertain status, comprising barely one-tenth of the members of the Lok Sabha, forming a government with the outside support of the largest single party in the House. What is even more ridiculous is that all the members in Chandra Shekhar's group had been elected only a year ago on an expressly anti-Congress(I) platform. Rajiv Gandhi has managed to satisfy all his needs at present. Having made delightfully vague utterances right through the political crisis of the last two months and not having taken the responsibility of a decisive intervention, he now finds that he cannot afford to go into elections even after the collapse of the latest experiment with a non-Congress government. Yet it is necessary for him to gain some control over the administrative apparatus before the elections finally come. He will now be able to do this without actually bearing any responsibility for the performance of this ramshackle government.

It is curious that the first legislative move of Rajiv Gandhi immediately after he was elected to power in 1984 was to bring an anti-defection law. He has now resorted precisely to the well-tested means of engineering defections in order to instal his proxy government. Whatever the technical considerations in the application of the anti-defection law — and these will probably be contested for some time in the case of the Janata Dal split — there is no doubt that it is the author of the anti-defection law who has now flouted its very spirit in order to gain his own objectives.

No one believes that the Chandra Shekhar government will stay for any length of time. The BJP has demanded immediate elections: clearly, it wishes to cash in on the *Hindutva* madness for whatever it is worth. V.P. Singh's Janata Dal has announced its programme of 'going to the people' on the issues that brought about its fall. The Left, having stayed with V.P. Singh despite a few mild flutters, is for the moment resolved to make anti-communalism and social justice the main issues for a national campaign. The Congress(I) knows that this government will not last. Its problem is to decide when it will be ready to face the electorate: a volatile atmosphere in which basic political issues are being debated is not a congenial condition in which Rajiv Gandhi's skills can flourish.

The uncertainty will therefore continue. The people will have to press on for some more time before they are given a chance to make a decision.

13

The Centre Crumbles

25 March 1991: Business Or Politics?[1]

Perhaps the most significant index of the professionalization of political careers in India today was provided by one of the last acts of this short-lived Parliament. When it became clear to all that there was no alternative but to go back and face the electorate all over again, the esteemed Members of our Parliament rushed through in record time a Bill to secure for themselves a lifelong pension and other perquisites. A.K. Roy, the Marxist Coordination Council member from Dhanbad, did try and remind the so-called leaders of the people that they were using, for purely personal gratification, the powers given to them by the Constitution to supervise the finances of the government. But Mr Roy was peremptorily silenced by virtually every other member of the House.

For many, politics is now a business, like speculating in the share markets. It is a risky business where you can go bust all of a sudden, but where you can also make a fortune if things go all right. The purely individualized fortune-hunting political career is best exemplified by that disreputable bunch that styled itself the Janata Dal (Socialist). Backroom manoeuvres and deals had brought them to power under the most extraordinary circumstances. When Chandra Shekhar decided to turn a patently impossible situation into a moral victory, the Janata Dal(S) members, disappointed at having their days in power cut short, did not however give up on their attempts to pursue their business. Om Prakash Chauthala, in one of those incredible two-hour performances, reclaimed the Chief Minister's chair in Haryana for the third time in a year and a half. Chimanbhai Patel and Mulayam Singh Yadav have made it known that they

1 *Frontier*, 23, 33 (30 March 1991).

will strike a deal with anybody and on any terms to stay in power in Gujarat and Uttar Pradesh. And Chandra Shekhar himself has said that since 'everything is possible in politics', no alliances and agreements can be ruled out. It is said that Chandra Shekhar's strategy is to have as many of his people elected as possible, no matter which parties they happen to join or seek support from. Should the numbers game become important in the next Parliament, he would then be in a position once again to strike a bargain.

There is a very strong opinion in the ruling establishments in the country that this is what politics should be. Avoid issues, avoid political debate, avoid popular movements. Politics is a matter of bargains and compromises between organized interests. The Congress(I), which represents more than any other party the dominant ethos of the ruling classes, has stated this very clearly in its revived slogan of 'stability'. This party has no stand on the Ayodhya dispute, nor does it have a clear position on the question of reservations. It decries the fact that so much heat should be generated in political controversy. Why don't you let Rajiv Gandhi's bright boys run the government? The fact is, of course, that there is nothing stable about the Congress(I) except its supreme leader, which position is hereditary. At every other rung of the leadership, the situation is as unstable as can be. There have been more changes of ministers and chief ministers — all the result of factional intrigue and court politics — in Congress(I) governments than anywhere else. What the Congress(I) means by stability and orderly government is simply that the politics be taken out of politics.

The issues of communalism and reservations are likely to be the most strongly discussed topics in the next elections. It must be said that no matter how limited or distorted the form, certain basic questions about power and justice have once again emerged in popular consciousness. The value in terms of the power of the people to intervene in the political process is considerable. No matter how much the backroom strategists may decry such populist politics, mobilization of the people around issues is the only way to keep the polity from falling entirely into the clutches of self-seeking and unprincipled political speculators.

8 April 1991: What Stability?[2]

It is a major paradox of Indian politics since 1979 that the more strident the cry of 'stability', the more pronounced have been the tendencies towards regionalism. The Congress(I), which took over in that year of collapse of the Janata experiment the role of the principal political organization of the all-India ruling classes, fought and won the general elections on the slogan of 'stability'. This was Indira Gandhi in a new incarnation; for, ten years before when she first took the hustings by storm, her cry was not stability but 'change'. From her fight against the 'Syndicate' to the 20-point programme, she managed to give to her politics the edge of a radical rhetoric. In the process she also created a new centre.

From 1980, it is this new centre which the all-India political establishment has sought to protect. Right through that decade, the Congress(I) dynasty — mother and son — brought about a concentration of power unparalleled in the history of India. On the one hand, it was a decade of selective economic liberalization — selective in its choice of targets, now breaking the power of this monopoly house, now favouring that monopoly house. On the other hand, the political institutions of representative democracy were systematically destroyed. Even the ruling party, the Congress(I), virtually ceased to have any effective centre of power anywhere other than at the very top. Congress chief ministers were appointed and dismissed at the whim of the Gandhis. All Congress candidates for Parliament, assemblies, or even local bodies were selected in Delhi. The institution of the state Governor was reduced to that of a police agent appointed from New Delhi. Federalism was in a shambles.

It was in the 1980s again that the new regionalism also began. Punjab and Assam were the most dramatic examples, followed by Jammu and Kashmir. They have all reached a stage where the normal processes of democratic politics seem to have been suspended permanently. But there were other examples. Regional parties came to power in Andhra and Assam, while Tamil Nadu has for a long time developed its own local party system. As the Andhra and Tamil Nadu cases show, whether in or out of power, a regional party is a permanently viable entity, surviving on local

2 *Frontier*, 23, 35 (13 April 1991).

interests and solidarities but making suitable alliances with all-India organizations. The Left groups in Kerala, West Bengal and Tripura are again at core similar groupings of regional interests.

The topsy-turvy politics of the last year has brought this paradox even more sharply into prominence. The Congress(I) is once again shouting 'stability'. But having split the opposition Janata Dal once, it is now trying to strike deals with the fragments of the Janata(S). In Gujarat, Chimanbhai Patel has floated a new regional party simply to keep his alliance going with the Congress(I). The same might have happened in U.P., but Mulayam Singh Yadav showed once again that in the game of conmanship Rajiv's bright boys are still novices. In Haryana, it was Bansi Lal yesterday, it is Bhajan Lal today, it may be Devi Lal tomorrow. In the north-eastern states, the Congress(I) has changed its chief ministers so often that no one can be sure which local force is actually with the all-India party. In Tamil Nadu, the Congress(I)'s seat-sharing arrangement is a matter of formal agreement. So what is this stability that the Congress(I) talks about? It too is only an unstable collection of regional forces.

The issue of real federalism should have emerged as a major question in the forthcoming elections. Some of the most positive — although incomplete and half-hearted — steps taken in the brief period of the National Front government related to the creation of some new procedures to give more effective powers to the federal units. The irony is that the Left is all for more federalism when it suits its party interest, but is for central rule and 'stability' when it goes against it, as it does at the moment in Punjab. It is such unprincipled opposition politics which continues to give sustenance to the Congress(I) slogan of 'stability'.

27 May 1991: Waiting Game[3]

There is no end to the bizarre curiosities Indian democracy is capable of producing. The swearing-in of Rajiv Gandhi after the assassination of his mother was one of the most unbelievable confirmations of the fact that a monarchical mode of political leadership can develop even within what is ostensibly a republic. The attempt by the Congress leaders to persuade Mrs Sonia

3 *Frontier*, 23, 42 (1 June 1991).

Gandhi to succeed her assassinated husband is only further confirmation of this trend. Paradoxically, however, the shocking death of Rajiv Gandhi has also produced the circumstances in which this extra-constitutional monarchical system can be buried once for all.

The successive tragedies that have befallen the Nehru–Gandhi family are not unrelated to the fact that the Congress system since the era of Indira Gandhi has consistently emulated the form of monarchical rule. It is not only that the real exercise of power in both party and government was centralized; the very style of rule sought to produce the impression that power flowed only from one source. Even the most trivial policy decision required approval from the top; every state programme was packaged as a special gift of benevolence of the supreme leader. Within the hierarchy of power, it produced the most abject protestations of feudal loyalty and sycophancy.

It is curious that the Nehru–Gandhi family, whose legitimacy within the Indian elite rests on its claims to a thoroughly modernist social vision and lifestyle, should have become willing accomplices if not the actual perpetrators of a system of political leadership which is totally contradictory to the modern forms of exercise of power. The superiority of the modern state — its institutions of representative politics and rational bureaucracy — consists in the fact that power does not flow from one source. Rather, it is distributed over the entire field of social life. This is how the exercise of power is made economic and efficient.

It was a corollary of the monarchical form of power that the violence of the Indian state — a systematic and often brutal violence of the state machinery — should have been perceived as a violence carried out personally by Indira or Rajiv Gandhi. Their assassinations were also personalized acts of violent retribution. The real tragedy of their deaths lay in the surrender by the ruling Congress party of all the efficiencies and advantages of the modern institutions of power which it had built up over a hundred years. Now, with the sudden death of Rajiv Gandhi, the total bankruptcy of its organization is staring the party in the face.

The fact that the assassination has taken place in the middle of the parliamentary elections has made the task doubly difficult for the Congress. On the one hand, there is unconcealed glee that the party will actually gain from its tragedy by drawing upon the 'sympathy' of the voters. On the other hand, there is the fear that unless it can put its own house in order in a very short time, the voters may not be persuaded that the Congress is still in business. The two contradictory pulls have, at the time of writing, landed the Congress in a state of paralysis.

The two other elements on the national political scene — the BJP and the National Front–Left alliance — are waiting for the Congress to make its move. And Mr Chandra Shekhar, who thrives on political confusion, is undoubtedly hoping that the next Parliament will be even more confused than the last one so that his considerable skills at manipulative politics will find fresh pastures.

10 June 1991: Getting Along With Panic[4]

The immediate aftermath of the assassination of Rajiv Gandhi saw attacks by Congress(I) supporters all over the country on the party's political opponents. In Kerala, their target was the Left Front, in Tamil Nadu the DMK, in Andhra the Telugu Desam, in West Bengal and Tripura the CPI(M), in northern India it was the BJP and the Janata Dal. Part of the frustration of Congress(I) supporters could have stemmed from the mystery surrounding the identity of Rajiv Gandhi's killers. But the situation was made far worse by dozens of irresponsible statements from senior Congress(I) leaders, accusing opposition politicians and parties by name and charging them with the responsibility for the murder. The most serious consequences of these acts of political vandalism were in Andhra and Tripura: in the former state, N.T. Rama Rao went on a hunger strike which was forcibly and hamhandedly broken by the Congress(I) government, while in the latter the CPI(M) has withdrawn from the Lok Sabha elections alleging widespread violence and terrorization by the Congress(I).

One institution which has contributed a great deal to the uncertainties and confusion is the Election Commission itself. The very appointment of T.N. Seshan to the post had raised eyebrows. The pomposity and highhandedness of his methods became apparent almost as soon as the election process went

[4] *Frontier*, 23, 44 (15 June 1991).

under way. Following Rajiv Gandhi's death, the Election Commission announced the next morning a postponement of elections by three weeks. No political parties were consulted. Mr Seshan then went on to take a series of unprecedented decisions — the countermanding of elections in six Lok Sabha constituencies, and the ordering of re-polls a full two weeks after polling had taken place. There are now open allegations by a number of political parties that the Election Commission is acting at the behest of the Congress(I) and some ministers of the Chandra Shekhar government.

If panic and confusion have marked the Congress(I) and its supporters, those who make tall claims about responsible and serious politics have not entirely escaped either. A few days after Rajiv Gandhi's death, the CPI(M) leader E.M.S. Namboodiripad wrote an open letter to the Congress(I) suggesting that it rethink its attitude towards the Left. Other leaders of the CPI(M) had to rush in to clarify that the Left was still aligned with the National Front and was going to remain faithful to that alliance. What prompted the veteran communist to do what he did will probably never be known, but whether it was panic or a 'shrewd tactical move', all it has achieved is further confusion about alignment and principles.

Perhaps the most panicky reactions have come from those sinecurist members of the country's political establishment — the national communists. The real possibility of the end of the Nehru–Gandhi dynasty has hit them with such a terrible shock that some have suggested immediate cancellation of elections and the formation of a national government; others have called for wholesale changes in the Constitution. The most piquant has been the observation by several of these students of political physiognomy that Priyanka's jaw shows the same boldness and determination as Indira's did. Why blame only the Indian peasant for nourishing a fondness for kings and princesses?

24 June 1991: Ten Parliaments[5]

A Congress(I) ministry has assumed office in New Delhi. It was not a particularly smooth affair. Apart from the fact that it is a

5 *Frontier*, 23, 46 (29 June 1991).

minority government which does not have an explicit promise of support from any quarter, the manner in which it decided upon the Prime Minister and the unseemly delays in distributing portfolios do not augur well for the cohesiveness of the ministry. At the time of writing, certain important departments such as Defence and Industry are without a minister, and all seems to have been held up for Mr Sharad Pawar's striking an agreement with Mr Narasimha Rao.

Perhaps the most significant aspect of the ministry-making exercise has been the demonstration of the continued grip of the so-called 'Rajiv coterie' on the Congress(I). Belying predictions of the emergence of a new 'syndicate' consisting of powerful regional bosses, the coterie not only managed to overwhelm Sharad Pawar's much-advertised attempt to force an election of the party leader but also imposed itself on the new Cabinet. M.L. Fotedar, Ghulam Nabi Azad and Sitaram Kesri, none of them members of the Lok Sabha, have now occupied senior Cabinet-rank posts, and Sharad Pawar is still out in the cold.

One effect of the coterie's reassertion has been the fizzling out of all speculations about coalitions and alliances. Namboodiripad, Surjeet and Basu are now looking downright silly after their panicky protestations of support; the coteric-ruled Congress(I) has now made it clear that it is not terribly worried about support and will go ahead with its owns plans; no one has the courage now to bring down the government and take the blame for precipitating yet another mid-term election.

The plans are also emerging bit by bit. In Punjab and Kashmir, it will be more of the same: continued occupation by the security forces, continued killings, continued recriminations against 'hostile forces across the border' and no political initiative. On the economy, not merely the IMF loan with the full range of 'conditionalities' but a host of relaxations of legal and bureaucratic controls on direct foreign investment. There is no doubt that this moment is going to be seized by all the proponents of 'new industrialization'; and the bitter pill of devaluation, expenditure-cutting and inflation will be given the sugar coating of export-led growth and foreign investments. It will be a pretty sight indeed to see Nehruvians, Lohiaites and public-sector Marxists voting to usher in the full range of World Bank–IMF sponsored economic reforms.

In domestic politics, no matter how hard the Congress(I) may wish that the problem will simply go away, the mosque–temple issue will remain the single most divisive dispute. The BJP, having been swept into power in India's most populous state on the promise of building the temple at the very spot where Rama is alleged to have been born, is unlikely to kill the goose which laid the golden egg. It is a most convenient issue which will now acquire all the overtones of a centre–state confrontation; and we may now hear the BJP speak from Lucknow in the same language that the CPI(M) speaks in Calcutta.

The new Parliament will certainly be one of the most interesting in the history of post-independence India.

22 July 1991: Coup[6]

It is nothing short of a *coup d'état*. Whatever the composition of the circle which is now running the country, it has managed to hijack the central organs of government and is hurtling India on a course which would never have been approved of if the normal procedures of democracy had been allowed to function. But that is often the characteristic of representative democracies — to produce 'democratic' results which are totally contradictory to the balance of democratic opinion.

The plan unfolded in the last days of the Chandra Shekhar government, when the cry went up that the economy was facing a crisis. In fact, it was then that the announcement was made that there was no alternative to the IMF loan. The period of the elections and the subsequent formation of the Narasimha Rao ministry is still dotted with many mysteries, including the assassination of Rajiv Gandhi, the attempts by the President to form a 'national government', and the victory of Narasimha Rao over Sharad Pawar.

Immediately after the inauguration of the government, the question of the economy took centre stage. Manmohan Singh, a government economist who has held key advisory positions since Mrs Gandhi's days in the 1970s, was chosen to be Finance Minister; and the people who were said to be negotiating with

6 *Frontier*, 23, 50 (27 July 1991).

the IMF during Yashwant Sinha's brief tenure were kept on. Indeed, it seemed as if the small group of government economists who were said to comprise the 'liberalization' lobby in government had taken complete charge, and had found new allies among former left-wingers including the new Finance Minister himself.

The campaign was now taken up in right earnest by the media. The crisis of the economy and the inevitability of an IMF loan was the principal theme, but the need for 'hard decisions' and a complete restructuring of an 'outmoded' system was the refrain. It soon transpired that the 'structural reforms' would be an unavoidable part of the conditions the IMF would demand, and since the decision had already been made that the IMF loan was inevitable, there was no way the 'reforms' could be avoided either. A series of policy decisions and pronouncements, beginning with a two-stage (three-stage?) devaluation of the rupee and a new trade policy, was followed by warnings that the new fiscal policy would cut down government expenditure and subsidies and the new industrial policy would mean a removal of government controls and an invitation to direct foreign investment.

It is a strange negotiating tactic which first announces that we have no alternative to the IMF loan and then proceeds to negotiate. What is left to negotiate? The more credible answer is that there is a lobby in the ruling establishment which has made the balance of payments crisis a pretext to ram through massive changes in the institutional structure of the Indian economy. These are changes which have no sanction in democratic opinion.

The point about 'reforms' of this kind is, of course, that there is no going back. Once institutional changes of such far-reaching magnitude are initiated, they will have to be continued. There are almost no previous instances of these kinds of changes being implemented in a liberal democracy. Given a peculiar set of circumstances, a coup has taken place in Indian democracy. If the democratic procedures assert themselves, whether inside or outside Parliament, there could be more serious attempts to subvert the democratic institutions altogether. After all, the announcement has already been made by the leaders of the coup: 'We have no choice.'

25 March 1996: Of Obsolete Modernities and Unborn Democracies[7]

Given the virtual certainty of a hung Parliament after the forth-coming general elections, a general sense of panic appears to have seized the country. There are, of course, many reasons for anxiety. Many seem to believe that without a stable govern-ment at the Centre, the financial, administrative and defence systems of the country will collapse. Others are worried that if no party gets a majority in Parliament, the sordid game of party-splitting and buying MPs could reach such unplumbed depths that government in general would lose all moral auth-ority. Indeed, if the events at the time of the fall of the V.P. Singh government and the formation of the Chandra Shekhar regime are any precedent, and if the process of the Rao govern-ment transforming itself from a minority to a majority in Par-liament is kept in mind, there is much reason to be apprehensive about what might happen in New Delhi after these elections. Some commentators have also reminded us of what happened after the 1991 elections: an unstable government with uncertain control over the economy will provide yet another opportunity for the international financial institutions to ram their medicines down the throat of the Indian economy.

On the other hand, it is also not clear that we will have a stable government of acceptable quality, even if one of the three contending forces in national politics manages to get a majority in Parliament. If the Congress gets a majority, it will only mean a worsening of all the processes of decay that had seized the central political structures of Indian politics in the last five years. The Congress as an all-India political organization is now daily crumbling from the inside. There is no reason to think that a victory in these elections will arrest that process of disintegration. As for the Bharatiya Janata Party, the prospect of its winning a majority and forming a government at the Centre is like a nightmare for a large section of the Indian people. And as far as the National Front–Left Front combination is concerned, the elements of agreement within this 'third force ˹re so narrow

---

[7] Bātil ādhunikatā, anāgata gaṇatantra', *Bāromās*, 17, 2 (April 1996), pp. 13–15 (translated from the Bengali).

and weak that, apart from the slogan of 'social justice', there seems to be little that will convince anyone that this assortment of parties could run a government on the basis of a credible minimum programme.

It is this general sense of uncertainty among voters all over the country that is reflected in the prospects of a hung Parliament. There is simply no party today that can command the confidence of a majority of the people of India. It is noticeable that whereas in earlier elections, anyone trying to make a casual prediction of the number of seats the various parties might win would usually end up with a total of 600 or more seats, this time no one seems to be able to account for more than 350 or 400 seats.

If one studies the recent history of Indian politics a little closely, it will become clear that this state of uncertainty has not emerged overnight. In the days of Rajiv Gandhi's rule, it might have seemed as though the political centre, with the government enjoying a huge majority and the chain of command ending up in a tightly focused centre of authority, was strong and fully in control. In actual fact, the countrywide organization of the Congress as the all-India ruling party was already in an advanced stage of decay. This process had started as early as the first phase of Indira Gandhi's dominance after the 1971 elections. In her successful attempt to re-establish Congress hegemony, she had embarked on a policy of centralization of powers, both in government and in the party organization. As a result, the space that had existed in the Nehru era for relatively independent exercise of power by Congress leaders at state and district levels was now completely taken away from them. The differentiated and flexible structure of both government and party organization, with powerful Congress leaders ruling at state and district levels — which was so much a characteristic of the old Congress system — now disappeared under Indira Gandhi, and after her, under her son. Every time a Congress leader had differences with the central leadership, he or she would now either leave the party or go into the political wilderness. This process has now reached a stage where even though the Congress is in power at the Centre, it does not rule in most of the states of India.

At this moment, there is no clear or stable pattern in the central structures of party politics in India. It is not the case that if the

Congress fails to win a majority, some other party or alliance will make a smooth entry into power. The two-party structure which is supposed to characterize a parliamentary system of the British type is at present completely absent in all-India politics. It is this absence that is being read as a sign of general political instability.

If one looks at the states, on the other hand, the picture is very different. In most states, a two-party or two-front system has attained a fair degree of permanence. If one party loses, the other gains a majority and forms the government. In most of the states of India, there is not a trace of the kind of uncertainty that hangs over New Delhi.

What is the significance of this fact? My interpretation is that the centre of gravity of Indian politics has decisively shifted from the central level to that of the states. The negotiations between various class and group interests, which are the stuff of democratic politics, are now most effectively conducted in the states. Each state has now developed, after five decades of electoral democracy, its own party structure that fits the effective structures of power as they exist in that state. Indeed, regions that have their own political identities but which do not have the status of separate states — such as the various regions of Uttar Pradesh or the Jharkhand region, or the Darjeeling hills in West Bengal — have also developed their own distinct party systems.

If one considers the nature of democratic politics, there is nothing surprising about these developments. Fifty years ago, when a new structure of electoral democracy was created in this country, the actual proportion of the country's population which effectively participated in it was extremely small. Today, there are numerous groups that are able to make their demands heard in the democratic arena: groups which, even twenty years ago, would have gone entirely unnoticed. The more the processes of democracy have deepened in India, the more has its centre of gravity moved downwards.

One can cite several kinds of evidence in support of this observation. At one time, it was virtually a truism to say that state policy in India in relation to large industry was laid down by the central government. Today, it has become clear that in the matter of new industrial investments, not only by domestic capital but also by foreign investors, a great deal depends on the enterprise and resourcefulness of the state governments. For several years now, state governments have taken the initiative in attracting investments, even by sending delegations abroad. And yet, on paper it is still the central government which lays down policy for large industry. That things are somewhat different in reality is not because of any constitutional or administrative change. It is because those who make industrial investments have discovered that their projects will effectively work only when they have managed to steer them through the ground-level realities at the state and local levels. Their practical sense for business tells them that effective political power is now so structured that it must be negotiated at those lower levels.

There is no doubt that this democratization of the political institutions has pushed many of the older institutions of civil society into a tight corner. We have heard persistent complaints for some time that the modern institutions of civic life that were built in India since the days of British rule are now in a state of collapse; that party and caste politics has brought ruin to our schools, colleges and universities, our cultural institutions, our voluntary organizations, our hospitals, our sporting clubs. These sentiments are widespread in educated middle-class circles in India today. This is the reason why, when an Election Commissioner or a judge of the Supreme Court declares that he will rid the public institutions of this country of the muck and grime of politics and turn the walls of Indian cities into sparkling and sanitized suburban facades, he is enthusiastically applauded by the educated.

The question is: can our civic institutions be revived by whitewashing the walls of our cities? Or will it only strengthen the anti-democratic prejudices of our elite? I believe this conflict has sharpened in recent years — on the one hand, the decay of our old institutions of modernity in the face of the growing demands of democratic politics; and, on the other, the attempt, in the name of institutional modernization, to erect fortifications against democracy.

There is much reason to be concerned about the way in which anti-democratic attitudes have slowly and almost imperceptibly seeped into the country's most articulate, conscious and well-educated circles. These sentiments had erupted at the time of the agitations against the Mandal Commission recommendations. But there are many other symptoms of this phenomenon. It can be seen in one aspect of that collective malady called *Hindutva* — not the one which charged, pickaxe and shovel in hand and 'Jai Sri Ram' in their voices, to break the mosque in Ayodhya, but rather the one which explains in rational and sophisticated words its impatient dream of turning India into a world power. It is, as I said, among the articulate and educated that the anti-democratic attitudes are the stongest. Similar sentiments also seem to be building up among those who are frustrated by what they see as unwarranted political obstacles to their project of rapid economic liberalization.

Of course, it is not the case that the effects of democratization are always desirable or acceptable. It is also true that institutional reform is necessary. The question is: can we bring about these reforms only by beating the breast over the collapse of moral values, or wallowing in nostalgia for some long-lost golden age? Listening these days to many political analysts on the Left, it almost seems as though the Nehru era was a utopia of self-reliance, secularism and even socialism. They have forgotten that at that time the Leftists were — I believe, for entirely justified reasons — Nehru's most trenchant critics.

Faced with the political uncertainties of the present, many do not want to admit that those institutions which are now facing collapse have actually exhausted their vitality and usefulness. They can never be revived by trying to go back to the old ways. Rather, the task for tomorrow is to build new civic institutions that are consonant with the demands of an expanding democracy. It seems reasonable to suppose that such institutions will first evolve at local and regional levels. Perhaps even at this moment, such institutions are actually taking shape in various parts of the country. It may take a long time for a new structure of democratic institutions to assume clear forms at the central level of Indian politics. Perhaps what we now refer to as the 'central level' may be very differently organized and located under the new democratic arrangements. Until then, we will simply have to put up with the laments, the breast-beating and the snivels of nostalgia.

14

Secularism and Toleration

There is little doubt that in the last two or three years, we have seen a genuine renewal of both thinking and activism among left-democratic forces in India on the question of the fight for secularism. An important element of the new thinking is the re-examination of the theoretical and historical foundations of the liberal-democratic state in India, and of its relation to the history and theory of the modern state in Europe and the Americas.

An interesting point of entry into the problem is provided by the parallels recently drawn between the rise of fascism in Europe in the 1920s and 1930s, and that of the Hindu right in India in the last few years. Sumit Sarkar, among others, has noted some of the chilling similarities.[1] But a more careful look at precisely this comparison will, I think, lead us to ask a basic and somewhat unsettling question: is secularism an adequate, or even appropriate, ground on which to meet the political challenge of Hindu majoritarianism?

The Nazi campaigns against Jews and other minority groups did not call for an abandonment of the secular principles of the state in Germany. If anything, Nazi rule was accompanied by an attempt to de-Christianize public life and to undermine the influence of the Catholic as well as the various Protestant Churches. Fascist ideology did not seek the union of state and religion in Italy, where the presence of a large peasant population and the hold of Catholicism might be supposed to have provided an opportune condition for such a demand — and this despite the virtually open collaboration of the Roman Church with Mussolini's regime. Nazi Germany and fascist Italy are, of course, only two examples of a feature that has been noticed many times in

[1] Sumit Sarkar, 'The Fascism of the Sangh Parivar', *Economic and Political Weekly*, 30 January 1993, pp. 163–7; Jan Breman, 'The Hindu Right: Comparisons with Nazi Germany', *Times of India*, 15 March 1993.

the career of the modern state in many countries of the world: namely, that state policies of religious intolerance, or of discrimination against religious and other ethnic minorities, do not necessarily require the collapsing of state and religion, nor do they presuppose the existence of theocratic institutions.

The point is relevant in the context of the current politics of the Hindu right in India. It is necessary to ask why the political leadership of that movement chooses so meticulously to describe its adversaries as 'pseudo-secularists', conceding thereby its approval of the ideal as such of the secular state. None of the serious political statements made by that leadership contains any advocacy of theocratic institutions; and, notwithstanding the exuberance of a few sadhus celebrating their sudden rise to political prominence, it is unlikely that a conception of the 'Hindu Rashtra' will be seriously propagated which will include, for instance, a principle that the laws of the state be in conformity with this or that *saṃhitā* or even with the general spirit of the *Dharmaśāstra*. In this sense, the leading element in the current movement of the Hindu right can be said to have undergone a considerable shift in position from, let us say, that of the Hindu Mahasabha at the time of the debate over the Hindu Code Bill some forty years ago. Its position is also quite unlike that of most contemporary Islamic fundamentalist movements, which explicitly reject the theoretical separation of state and religion as 'western' and un-Islamic. It is similarly unlike the fundamentalist strand within the Sikh movements in recent years. The majoritarianism of the Hindu right, it seems to me, is perfectly at peace with the institutional procedures of the 'western' or 'modern' state.

Indeed, the mature, and most formidable, statement of the new political conception of 'Hindutva' is unlikely to pit itself at all against the idea of the secular state. The persuasive power, and even the emotional charge, that the Hindutva campaign appears to have gained in recent years does not depend on its demanding legislative enforcement of ritual or scriptural injunctions, a role for religious institutions in legislative or judicial processes, compulsory religious instruction, state support for religious bodies, censorship of science, literature and art in order to safeguard religious dogma, or any other similar demand undermining the secular character of the existing Indian state. This is not to say that in the frenzied mêlée produced by the Hindutva brigade such noises would not be made; the point is that anti-secular demands of this type are not crucial to the political thrust, or even the public appeal, of the campaign.

Indeed, in its most sophisticated forms, the campaign of the Hindu right often seeks to mobilize on its behalf the will of an interventionist modernizing state, in order to erase the presence of religious or ethnic particularisms from the domains of law or public life, and to supply, in the name of 'national culture', a homogenized content to the notion of citizenship. In this role, the Hindu right in fact seeks to project itself as a principled modernist critic of Islamic or Sikh fundamentalism, and to accuse the 'pseudo-secularists' of preaching tolerance for religious obscurantism and bigotry. The most recent example of this is the Allahabad High Court pronouncement on divorce practices among Muslims by a judge well known for his views on the constitutional sanctity of Lord Rama.

Thus, the comparison with fascism in Europe points to the very real possibility of a Hindu right locating itself quite firmly within the domain of the modernizing state, and using all of the ideological resources of that state to lead the charge against people who do not conform to its version of the 'national culture'. From this position, the Hindu right can not only deflect accusations of being anti-secular, but can even use the arguments for interventionist secularization to promote intolerance and violence against minorities.

As a matter of fact, the comparison with Nazi Germany also extends to the exact point that provides the Hindutva campaign with its venomous charge: as Sarkar notes, ' . . . the Muslim here becomes the near exact equivalent of the Jew.' The very fact of belonging to this minority religious community is sufficient to put a question mark against the status of a Muslim as a citizen of India. The term 'communal', in this twisted language, is reserved for the Muslim, whereas the 'pseudo-secular' is the Hindu who defends the right of the Muslim citizen. (Note once more that the term 'secular' itself is not made a target of attack.) Similarly, on the vexed question of migrants from Bangladesh, the Hindu immigrant is by definition a 'refugee' while the Muslim is an 'infiltrator'. A whole series of stereotypical features, now sickeningly familiar in their repetitiveness, are then adduced in order to declare as dubious the historical, civil and political status of the

Muslim within the Indian state. In short, the current campaign of the Hindu right is directed not against the principle of the secular state, but rather towards mobilizing the legal powers of that state in order to systematically persecute and terrorize a specific religious minority within its population.

The question then is as follows: is the defence of secularism an appropriate ground for meeting the challenge of the Hindu right? Or should it be fought where the attack is being made, i.e. should the response be a defence of the duty of the democratic state to ensure policies of religious toleration? The question is important because it reminds us that not all aggressive major-itarianisms pose the same sort of problem in the context of the democratic state: Islamic fundamentalism in Pakistan or Bangla-desh, or Sinhala chauvinism in Sri Lanka do not necessarily have available to them the same political strategies as the majoritarian politics of the Hindu right in India. It also warns us of the very real theoretical possibility that secularization and religious tolera-tion may sometimes work at cross-purposes.[2] It is necessary therefore to be clear about what is implied by these concepts.

Meaning of Secularism

At the very outset, let us face up to a point that will be invariably made in any discussion on 'secularism' in India: namely that in the Indian context the word has very different meanings from

---

[2] Ashis Nandy makes a distinction between religion-as-faith, by which he means a way of life that is operationally plural and tolerant, and religion-as-ideology which identifies and enumerates populations of followers fighting for non-religious, usually political and economic, interests. He then suggests, quite correctly, that the politics of secularism is part of the same process of formation of modern state practices which promotes religion-as-ideology. Nandy's con-clusion is that rather than relying on secularism of a modernized elite we should 'explore the philosophy, the symbolism and the theology of tolerance in the various faiths of the citizens and hope that the state systems in South Asia may learn something about religious tolerance from everyday Hinduism, Islam, Buddhism, and/or Sikhism. . . . ': 'The Politics of Secularism and the Recovery of Religious Tolerance', in Veena Das, ed., *Mirrors of Violence: Communities, Riots and Survivors in South Asia* (Delhi: Oxford University Press, 1990), pp. 69–93. I am raising the same doubt about whether secularism necessarily ensures toleration, but, unlike Nandy, I am here looking for political possibilities *within* the domain of the modern state institutions as they now exist in India.

its standard use in the English language. This fact is sometimes cited as confirmation of the 'inevitable' difference in the meanings of a concept in two dissimilar cultures. ('India is not Europe: secularism in India cannot mean the same thing as it does in Europe.') At other times, it is used to underline the 'inevitable' shortcomings of the modern state in India. ('There cannot be a secular state in India because Indians have an incorrect concept of secularism.')

Of course, it could also be argued that this comparison with European conceptions is irrelevant if our purpose is to intervene in the Indian debate on the subject. What does it matter if secularism means something else in European and American political discourse? As long as there are reasonably clear and commonly agreed referents for the word in the Indian context, we should go ahead and address ourselves to the specifically Indian meaning of secularism.

Unfortunately, the matter cannot be settled that easily. The Indian meanings of secularism did not emerge in ignorance of the European or American meanings of the word. I also think that in its current usage in India, with apparently well-defined 'Indian' referents, the loud and often acrimonious Indian debate on secularism is never entirely innocent of its Western genealogies. To pretend that the Indian meaning of secularism has marked out a conceptual world all of its own, untroubled by its differences with Western secularism, is to take an ideological position which refuses either to recognize or to justify its own grounds.

In fact, I wish to make an even stronger argument. Commenting upon Raymond Williams's justly famous *Keywords*, Quentin Skinner has pointed out that a concept takes on a new meaning not when (as one would usually suppose) arguments that it should be applied to a new circumstance succeed, but rather when such arguments fail.[3] Thus, if one is to consider the 'new' meaning acquired by the word 'secularism' in India, it is not as though the plea of the advocates of secularism that the concept bears application to modern Indian state and society

[3] Quentin Skinner, 'Language and Political Change', in Terence Ball, James Farr and Russell L. Hanson, eds, *Political Innovation and Conceptual Change* (Cambridge: Cambridge University Press, 1989), pp. 6–23.

has won general acceptance, and that the concept has thereby taken on a new meaning. If that had been the case, the 'original' meaning of the word as understood in its standard sense in the West would have remained unmutilated; it would only have widened its range of referents by including within it the specific circumstances of the Indian situation. The reason why arguments have to be made about 'secularism' having a new *meaning* in India is because there are serious difficulties in applying the standard meaning of the word to the Indian circumstances. The 'original' concept, in other words, will not easily admit the Indian case within its range of referents.

This, of course, could be a good pretext for insisting that Indians have their own concept of secularism which is different from the Western concept bearing the same name; that, it could be argued, is exactly why the Western concept cannot be applied to the Indian case. The argument then would be about a difference in concepts: if the concept is different, the question of referential equivalence cannot be a very crucial issue. At the most, it would be a matter of family resemblances, but conceptually Western secularism and Indian secularism would inhabit entirely autonomous discursive domains.

That, it is needless to say, is hardly the case. We could begin by asking why, in all recent discussions in India on the relation between religion and the state, the central concept is named by the English words 'secular' and 'secularism', or in the Indian languages, by neologisms such as *dharma-nirapeksatā* which are translations of those English words and are clearly meant to refer to the range of meanings indicated by the English terms. As far as I know, there does not exist in any Indian language a term for 'secular' or 'secularism' which is standardly used in talking about the role of religion in the modern state and society, and whose meaning can be immediately explicated without having recourse to the English terms.

What this implies is that although the use of *dharma* in *dharma-nirapeksatā* or *mazhab* in *ghair-mazhabi* might open up conceptual or referential possibilities in Indian discourse which were unavailable to the concept of secularism in the West, the continued use of an awkward neologism, besides of course the continued use of the English term itself, indicates that the more stable and well-defined reference for the concept lies in the Western political discourse about the modern state.[4] In fact, it is clear from the discussions among the Indian political and intellectual elite at least from the 1920s that the proponents of the secular state in India never had any doubt at all about the meaning of the concept of secularism; all the doubts were about whether that concept would find a congenial field of application in the Indian social and political context. The continued use of the term 'secularism' is, it seems to me, an expression of the desire of the modernizing elite to see the 'original' meaning of the concept actualized in India. The resort to 'new meanings' is, to invoke Skinner's point once more, a mark of the failure of this attempt.

It might prove instructive to do a 'history of ideas' exercise for the use of the word 'secularism' in Indian political discourse in the last hundred years, but this is not the place for it. What is important for our purposes is a discussion of how the nationalist project of putting an end to colonial rule and inaugurating an independent nation-state became implicated, from its very birth, in a contradictory movement with regard to the modernist mission of secularization.

British Rule, Nationalism, and the Separation of State and Religion

Ignoring the details of a complicated history, it would not be widely off the mark to say that by the latter half of the nineteenth century, the British power in India had arrived at a reasonably firm policy of not involving the state in matters of religion. It tried to keep neutral on disputes over religion, and was particularly careful not to be seen as promoting Christianity. Immediately after the assumption of power by the Crown in 1858, the most significant step was taken in instituting equality before the law

---

[4] Even in the mid-1960s, Ziya-ul Hasan Faruqi was complaining about the use of *ghair-mazhabi* and *la-dini*. '*Ghayr mazhabi* means something contrary to religious commandments and *la dini* is irreligious or atheistic. . . . The common man was very easily led to conclude that the Indian state was against religion. It is, however, gratifying to see that the Urdu papers have started to transliterate the word "secular" . . .': 'Indian Muslims and the Ideology of the Secular State', in Donald Eugene Smith, ed., *South Asian Politics and Religion* (Princeton: Princeton University Press, 1966), pp. 138–49.

by enacting uniform codes of civil and criminal law. The area left out, however, was that of personal law which continued to be governed by the respective religious laws as recognized and interpreted by the courts. The reason why personal law was not brought within the scope of a uniform civil code was, precisely, the reluctance of the colonial state to intervene in matters close to the very heart of religious doctrine and practice. In the matter of religious endowments, while the British power in its early years took over many of the functions of patronage and administration previously carried out by Indian rulers, by the middle of the nineteenth century it largely renounced those responsibilities and handed them over to local trusts and committees.

As far as the modernizing efforts of the Indian elite are concerned, the nineteenth-century attempts at 'social reform' by soliciting the legal intervention of the colonial state are well known. In the second half of the nineteenth century, however, the rise of nationalism led to a refusal on the part of the Indian elite to let the colonial state enter into areas that were regarded as crucial to the cultural identity of the nation. This did not mean a halt to the project of 'reform': all it meant was a shift in the agency of reform — from the legal authority of the colonial state to the moral authority of the national community.[5] This shift is crucial: not so much because of its apparent coincidence with the policy of non-intervention of the colonial state in matters of religion in the late nineteenth century, but because of the underlying assumption in nationalist thinking about the role of state legislation in religion — legal intervention in the cause of religious reform was not undesirable *per se*, but it was undesirable when the state was colonial.

As it happened, there was considerable change in the social beliefs and practices of the sections that came to constitute the new middle class in the period leading up to independence in 1947. Not only was there change in the actual practices surrounding family and personal relations, and even in many religious practices, without there being any significant change in the laws of the state, but, perhaps more important, there was an overwhelming tide in the dominant attitudes among these sections

---

[5] I have discussed the point more elaborately in *The Nation and its Fragments: Colonial and Postcolonial Histories* (Princeton: Princeton University Press, 1993).

in favour of the legitimacy of 'social reform'. These reformist opinions affected the educated sections in virtually all parts of the country, and found a voice in most religious and caste communities.

One of the dramatic results of this cumulation of reformist desire within the nationalist middle class was the sudden spate of new legislation on religious and social matters immediately after independence. This is actually an extremely significant episode in the development of the nation-state in India, and its deeply problematic nature has been seldom noticed in the current debates over secularism. It needs to be described in some detail.

Religious Reform and the Nation-State

Even as the provisions of the new Constitution of India were being discussed in the Constituent Assembly, some of the provincial legislatures had begun to enact laws for the reform of religious institutions and practices. One of the most significant of these was the Madras *Devadasis* (Prevention of Dedication) Act, 1947, which outlawed the institution of dedicating young girls to temple deities, and prohibited 'dancing by a woman . . . in the precincts of any temple or other religious institution, or in any procession of a Hindu deity, idol or object of worship. . . .'[6] Equally important was the Madras Temple Entry Authorization Act, 1947, which made it a punishable offence to prevent any person on the ground of untouchability from entering or worshipping in a Hindu temple. This act was immediately followed by similar legislation in the Central Provinces, Bihar, Bombay and other provinces, and finally by the temple entry provisions in the Constitution of India.

Although in the course of the debates over these enactments, views were often expressed about the need to 'remove a blot on the Hindu religion', it was clearly possible to justify some of the laws on purely secular grounds. Thus, the *devadasi* system could be declared unlawful on the ground that it was a form of bondage or of enforced prostitution. Similarly, 'temple entry' was sometimes defended by extending the argument that the denial of

---

[6] Cited in Donald Eugene Smith, *India as a Secular State* (Princeton: Princeton University Press, 1963), p. 239.

access to public places on the ground of untouchability was unlawful. However, a contradiction appeared in this 'civil rights' argument since all places of worship were not necessarily thrown open to all citizens; only Hindu temples were declared open for all Hindus, and non-Hindus could be, and actually still are, denied entry. But even more problematically, the right of worship 'of all classes and sections of Hindus' at 'Hindu religious institutions of public character', as Article 25(2) of the Constitution has it, necessarily implies that the state has to take up the onus of interpreting even doctrinal and ritual injunctions in order to assert the *religious* legitimacy of forms of worship that would not be discriminatory in terms of caste.[7]

Still more difficult to justify on non-religious grounds was a reformist law like the Madras Animal and Bird Sacrifices Abolition Act, 1950. The view that animal sacrifices were repugnant and represented a primitive form of worship was clearly the product of a very specific religious interpretation of *religious* ritual, and could be described as a sectional opinion even among Hindus. (It might even be described as a view that was biased against the religious practices of the lower castes, especially in southern India.) Yet in bringing about this 'purification' of the Hindu religion, the legislative wing of the state was seen as the appropriate instrument.

The period after independence also saw, apart from reformist legislation of this kind, an enormous increase in the involvement of the state administration in the management of the affairs of Hindu temples. The most significant enabling legislation in this regard was the Madras Hindu Religious and Charitable Endowments Act, 1951, which created an entire department of government devoted to the administration of Hindu religious

---

[7] In fact, the courts, recognizing that the right of a religious denomination 'to manage its own affairs in matters of religion' [Article 26(b)] could come into conflict with the right of the state to throw open Hindu temples to all classes of Hindus [Article 25(2)(b)], have had to come up with ingenious, and often extremely arbitrary, arrangements in order to strike a compromise between the two provisions. Some of these judgements are referred to in Smith, *India as a Secular State*, pp. 242–3. For a detailed account of a case illustrating the extent of judicial involvement in the interpretation of religious doctrine and ritual, see Arjun Appadurai, *Worship and Conflict under Colonial Rule: A South Indian Case* (Cambridge: Cambridge University Press, 1981), pp. 36–50.

endowments.[8] The legal argument here is, of course, that the religious denomination concerned still retains the right to manage its own affairs in matters of religion, while the secular matters concerned with the management of the property of the endowment is taken over by the state. But this is a separation of functions that is impossible to maintain in practice. Thus, if the administrators choose to spend the endowment funds on opening hospitals or universities rather than on more elaborate ceremonies or on religious instruction, then the choice will affect the way in which the religious affairs of the endowment are managed. The issue has given rise to several disputes in court about the specific demarcation between the religious and the secular functions, and to further legislation, in Madras as well as in other parts of India. The resulting situation led one commentator in the early 1960s to remark that 'the commissioner for Hindu religious endowments, a public servant of the secular state, today exercises far greater authority over Hindu religion in Madras state than the Archbishop of Canterbury does over the Church of England.'[9]

Once again, it is possible to provide a non-religious ground for state intervention in the administration of religious establishments, namely prevention of misappropriation of endowment funds and ensuring the proper supervision of what is after all a public property. But what has been envisaged and actually

---

[8] Actually, the increased role of the government in controlling the administration of Hindu temples in Madras began with the Religious Endowments Acts of 1925 and 1927. It is interesting to note that there was nationalist opposition to the move at the time: S. Satyamurthi said during the debates in the provincial legislature in 1923 that 'the blighting hand of this Government will also fall tight on our temples and *maths*, with the result that they will also become part of the great machinery which the Hon'ble Minister and his colleagues are blackening every day.' During the debates preceding the 1951 Act, on the other hand, T.S.S. Rajan, the Law Minister, said: ' . . . the fear of interfering with religious institutions has always been there with an alien Government but with us it is very different. Ours may be called a secular Government, and so it is. But it does not absolve us from protecting the funds of the institutions which are meant for the service of the people.' For an account of these changes in law, see Chandra Y. Mudaliar, *The Secular State and Religious Institutions in India: A Study of the Administration of Hindu Public Religious Trusts in Madras* (Wiesbaden: Fritz Steiner Verlag, 1974).

[9] Smith, *India as a Secular State*, p. 246.

practised since independence goes well beyond this strictly negative role of the state. Clearly, the prevailing views about the reform of Hindu religion saw it as entirely fitting that the representative and administrative wings of the state should take up the responsibility of managing Hindu temples in, as it were, the 'public interest' of the general body of Hindus.

The reformist agenda was, of course, carried out most comprehensively during the making of the Constitution and subsequently in the enactment in 1955 of what is known as the Hindu Code Bill.[10] During the discussions, objections were raised that in seeking to change personal law, the state was encroaching upon an area protected by the right to religious freedom. B.R. Ambedkar's reply to these objections summed up the general attitude of the reformist leadership:

The religious conceptions in this country are so vast that they cover every aspect of life from birth to death. There is nothing which is not religion and if personal law is to be saved I am sure about it that in social matters we will come to a standstill . . . There is nothing extraordinary in saying that we ought to strive hereafter to limit the definition of religion in such a manner that we shall not extend it beyond beliefs and such rituals as may be connected with ceremonials which are essentially religious. It is not necessary that the sort of laws, for instance, laws relating to tenancy or laws relating to succession, should be governed by religion. . . . I personally do not understand why religion should be given this vast expansive jurisdiction so as to cover the whole of life and to prevent the legislature from encroaching upon that field.[11]

Impelled by this reformist urge, the Indian Parliament proceeded to cut through the immensely complicated web of local and sectarian variations that enveloped the corpus known as 'Hindu law' as it had emerged through the colonial courts, and to lay down a single code of personal law for all Hindu citizens. Many of the new provisions were far-reaching in their departure from traditional brahmanical principles. Thus, the new code legalized inter-caste marriage; it legalized divorce and prohibited

[10] Actually, a series of laws called the Hindu Marriage Bill, the Hindu Succession Bill, the Hindu Minority and Guardianship Bill and the Hindu Adoptions and Maintenance Bill.

[11] *Constituent Assembly Debates* (New Delhi: Government of India, 1946–50), vol. 7, p. 781.

polygamy; it gave to the daughter the same rights of inheritance as the son, and permitted the adoption of daughters as well as of sons. In justifying these changes, the proponents of reform not only made the argument that 'tradition' could not remain stagnant and needed to be reinterpreted in the light of changing conditions, but they also had to engage in the exercise of deciding what was or was not essential to 'Hindu religion'. Once again, the anomaly has provoked comments from critical observers: 'An official of the secular state [the law minister] became an interpreter of Hindu religion, quoting and expounding the ancient Sanskrit scriptures in defence of his bills.'[12]

Clearly, it is necessary here to understand the force and internal consistency of the nationalist-modernist project which sought, in one and the same move, to rationalize the domain of religious discourse and to secularize the public domain of personal law. It would be little more than reactionary to rail against the 'western-educated Hindu' who is scandalized by the profusion of avaricious and corrupt priests at Hindu temples, and who, influenced by Christian ideas of service and piety, rides roughshod over the 'traditional Hindu notions' that a religious gift was never made for any specific purpose; that the priest entrusted with the management of a temple could for all practical purposes treat the property and its proceeds as matters within his personal jurisdiction; and that, unlike the Christian church, a temple was a place 'in which the idol condescends to receive visitors, who are expected to bring offerings with them, like subjects presenting themselves before a maharaja.'[13] More serious, of course, is the criticism that by using the state as the agency of what was very often only religious reform, the political leadership of the new nation-state flagrantly violated the principle of separation of state and religion.[14] This is a matter we will now consider in

---

[12] Smith, *India as a Secular State*, pp. 281–2.

[13] See, for instance, J. Duncan M. Derrett, 'The Reform of Hindu Religious Endowments', in Smith, ed., *South Asian Politics and Religion*, pp. 311–36.

[14] The two most comprehensive studies on the subject of the secular state in India make this point. V.P. Luthera in *The Concept of the Secular State and India* (Calcutta: Oxford University Press, 1964) concludes that India should not properly be regarded as a secular state. D.E. Smith in *India as a Secular State* disagrees, arguing that Luthera bases his conclusion on too narrow a definition of the secular state, but nevertheless points out the numerous anomalies in the current situation.

detail, but it is nevertheless necessary to point out that the violation of this principle of the secular state was justified precisely by the desire to secularize.

Anomalies of the Secular State

What are the characteristics of the secular state? Three principles are usually mentioned in the liberal-democratic doctrine on this subject.[15] The first is the principle of *liberty* which requires that the state permit the practice of any religion, within the limits set by certain other basic rights which the state is also required to protect. The second is the principle of *equality* which requires that the state not give preference to one religion over another. The third is the principle of *neutrality* which is best described as the requirement that the state not give preference to the religious over the non-religious, and which leads, in combination with the liberty and equality principles, to what is known in US constitutional law as the 'wall of separation' doctrine: namely, that the state not involve itself with religious affairs or organizations.[16]

Looking now at the doctrine of the secular state as it has evolved in practice in India, it is clear that whereas all three principles have been invoked to justify the secular state, their application has been contradictory and has led to major anomalies. The principle of liberty, which implies a right of freedom of religion, has been incorporated in the Constitution which gives to every citizen — subject to public order, morality and health — not only the equal right to freedom of conscience but

[15] For a recent exchange on this matter, see Robert Audi, 'The Separation of Church and State and the Obligations of Citizenship', *Philosophy and Public Affairs*, 18, 3 (Summer 1989), pp. 259–96; Paul J. Weithman, 'Separation of Church and State: Some Questions for Professor Audi', *Philosophy and Public Affairs*, 20, 1 (Winter 1991), pp. 52–65; Robert Audi, 'Religious Commitment and Secular Reason: A Reply to Professor Weithman', *Philosophy and Public Affairs*, 20, 1 (Winter 1991), pp. 66–76.

[16] The US Supreme Court defined the doctrine as follows: 'Neither a state nor the federal government can set up a church. Neither can pass laws which aid one religion, aid all religions, or prefer one religion over another. . . . Neither a state nor the federal government can, openly or secretly, participate in the affairs of any religious organization or groups and vice versa.' *Everson* v. *Board of Education*. 330 U.S. 1 (1947), cited in Smith, *India as a Secular State*, pp. 125–6.

also, quite specifically, 'the right freely to profess, practise and propagate religion'. It also gives 'to every religious denomination or any section thereof' certain collective rights of religion. Besides, it specifically mentions the right of 'all minorities, whether based on religion or language', to establish and administer their own educational institutions. Limiting these rights of freedom of religion, however, is the right of the state to regulate 'any economic, financial, political or other secular activity which may be associated with religious practice', to provide for social welfare and reform and to throw open Hindu religious institutions to all sections of Hindus. This limit to the liberty principle is what enabled the extensive reform under state auspices of Hindu personal law, and of the administration of Hindu temples.

The liberal-democratic doctrine of freedom of religion does recognize, of course, that this right will be limited by other basic human rights. Thus, for instance, it would be perfectly justified for the state to deny that — let us say — human sacrifice or causing injury to human beings, or as we have already noted in the case of *devadasis*, enforced servitude to a deity or temple, constitutes permissible religious practice. However, it is also recognized that there are many grey areas where it is difficult to lay down the limit. A case very often cited in this connection is the legal prohibition of polygamy even when it may be sanctioned by a particular religion: the argument that polygamy necessarily violates other basic human rights is often thought of as problematical.

But no matter where this limit is drawn, it is surely required by the idea of the secular state that the liberty principle be limited only by the need to protect some other *universal* basic right, and not by appeal to a particular interpretation of religious doctrine. This, as we have mentioned before, has not been possible in India. The urge to undertake by legislation the reform of Hindu personal law and Hindu religious institutions made it difficult for the state not to transgress into the area of religious reform itself. Both the legislature and the courts were led into the exercise of interpreting religious doctrine on religious grounds. Thus, in deciding the legally permissible limits of state regulation of religious institutions, it became necessary to identify those practices that were *essentially* of a religious character; but, in accordance with the judicial procedures of a modern state, this decision could not be left to the religious denomination itself but had to be determined 'as an objective question' by the courts.[17] It can be easily seen that this could lead to the entanglement of the state in a series of disputes that are mainly religious in character.

It could, of course, be argued that given the dual character of personal law — inherited from the colonial period as religious law that had been recognized and codified as the laws of the state — and in the absence of appropriate institutions of the Hindu religion through which religious reform could be organized and carried out outside the arena of the state, there was no alternative to state intervention in this matter. Which other agency was there with the requisite power and legitimacy to undertake the reform of religious practices? The force and persuasiveness of this argument for the modernist leadership of independent India can hardly be overstated. The desire was in fact to initiate a process of rational interpretation of religious doctrine, and to find a representative and credible institutional process for the reform of religious practice. That the use of state legislation to achieve this modernist purpose must come into conflict with another modernist principle, of the freedom of religion, is one of the anomalies of the secular state in India.

The second principle — that of equality — is also explicitly recognized in the Indian Constitution which prohibits the state from discriminating against any citizen on the basis only of religion or caste, except when it makes special provisions for the advancement of socially and educationally backward classes or for scheduled castes and scheduled tribes. Such special provisions in the form of reserved quotas in employment and education, or of reserved seats in representative bodies, have of course led to much controversy in India in the last few decades. But these disputes about the validity of positive discrimination in favour of underprivileged castes or tribes have almost never taken the form of a dispute about equality on the ground of religion. Indeed, although the institution of caste itself is supposed to derive its basis from the doctrines of the brahmanical religion, the recent debates in the political arena about caste discrimination usually do not make any appeals at all to religious doctrines. There is only one significant way in which the question of

[17] *Durgah Committee* v. *Hussain, A.* 1961 S.C. 1402 *(1415)*, cited in Durga Das Basu, *Constitutional Law of India* (New Delhi: Prentice-Hall of India, 1977), p. 84.

positive discrimination in favour of scheduled castes is circumscribed by religion: in order to qualify as a member of a scheduled
caste, a person must profess to be either Hindu or Sikh; a public
declaration of the adoption of any other religion would lead to
disqualification. However, in some recent provisions relating to
'other backward classes', especially in the much-disputed recommendations of the Mandal Commission, attempts have been
made to go beyond this limitation.

The problem with the equality principle which concerns us
more directly is the way in which it has been affected by the
project of reforming Hindu religion by state legislation. All the
legislative and administrative measures we have mentioned before concern the institutions and practices of the Hindus, including the reform of personal laws and of religious endowments.
That this was discriminatory was argued in the 1950s by the
socially conservative sections of Hindu opinion, and by political
parties like the Hindu Mahasabha which were opposed to the
idea of reform itself. But the fact that the use of state legislation
to bring about reforms in only the religion of the majority was
creating a serious anomaly in the very notion of equal citizenship,
was pointed out by only a few lone voices within the progressive
sections. One such belonged to J.B. Kripalani, the socialist leader,
who argued: 'If we are a democratic state, I submit we must make
laws not for one community alone. . . . It is not the Mahasabhites
who alone are communal: it is the government also that is communal, whatever it may say.' Elaborating, he said,

If they [the Members of Parliament] single out the Hindu community
for their reforming zeal, they cannot escape the charge of being communalists in the sense that they favour the Hindu community and are
indifferent to the good of the Muslim community or the Catholic community. . . . Whether the marriage bill favours the Hindu community
or places it at a disadvantage, both ways, it becomes a communal
measure.[18]

The basic problem here was obvious. If it was accepted that
the state could intervene in religious institutions or practices in
order to protect other social and economic rights, then what was
the ground for intervening only in the affairs of one religious
community and not of others? Clearly, the first principle — that

18 Cited in Smith, *India as a Secular State*, pp. 286, 288.

of freedom of religion — could not be invoked here only for the minority communities when it had been set aside in the case of the majority community.

The problem has been got around by resorting to what is essentially a pragmatic argument. It is suggested that, for historical reasons, there is a certain lag in the readiness of the different communities to accept reforms intended to rationalize the domain of personal law. In any case, if equality of citizenship is what is desired, it already stands compromised by the very system of religion-based personal laws inherited from colonial times. What should be done, therefore, is to first declare the desirability of replacing the separate personal laws by a uniform civil code; but to proceed towards this objective in a pragmatic way, respecting the sensitivity of the religious communities about their freedom of religion, and going ahead with state-sponsored reforms only when the communities themselves are ready to accept them. Accordingly, there is an item in the non-justiciable Directive Principles of the Constitution which declares that the state should endeavour to provide a uniform civil code for all citizens. On the other hand, those claiming to speak on behalf of the minority communities tend to take a firm stand in the freedom of religion principle, and to deny that the state should have any right at all to interfere in their religious affairs. The anomaly has, in the last few years, provided some of the most potent ammunition to the Hindu right in its campaign against what it describes as the 'appeasement' of minorities.

It would not be irrelevant to mention here that there have also occurred, among the minority religious communities in India, not entirely dissimilar movements for the reform of religious laws and institutions. In the earlier decades of this century, there were organized attempts, for instance, to put an end to local customary practices among Muslim communities in various parts of India and replace them with a uniform Muslim personal law. This campaign, led in particular by the Jamiyat al-ulama-i Hind of Deoband — well known for its closeness to the Indian National Congress — was directed against the recognition by the courts of special marriage and inheritance practices among communities such as the Mapilla of southern India, the Memon of western India, and various groups in Rajasthan and Punjab. The argument given was not only that such practices were 'un-Islamic'; specific criticisms were also made about how these customs were backward and iniquitous, especially in the matter of the treatment of women. The preamble to a Bill to change the customary succession law of the Mapilla, for instance, said, using a rhetoric not unlike what would be used later for the reform of Hindu law, 'The Muhammadan community now feels the incongruity of the usage and looks upon the prevailing custom as a discredit to their religion and to their community.'[19]

The reform campaigns led to a series of new laws in various provinces and in the central legislature, such as the Mapilla Succession Act 1918, the Cutchi Memons Act 1920 and 1938, and the NWFP Muslim Personal Law (Shari'at) Application Act 1935 (which was the first time that the terms 'Muslim personal law' and Shari'at were used interchangeably in law). The culmination of these campaigns for a uniform set of personal laws for all Muslims in India was reached with the passing of the so-called Shari'at Act by the Central legislature in 1937. Interestingly, it was because of the persistent efforts of Muhammad Ali Jinnah, whose political standing was in this case exceeded by his prestige as a legal luminary, that only certain sections of this Act were required to be applied compulsorily to all Muslims; on other matters its provisions were optional.

The logic of completing the process of uniform application of Muslim personal law has continued in independent India. The optional clauses in the 1937 Act have been removed. The Act has been applied to areas that were earlier excluded: especially the princely states that merged with India after 1947, the latest in that series being Cooch Behar where the local customary law for Muslims was superseded by the Shari'at laws through legislation by the Left Front government of West Bengal in 1980.

Thus, even while resisting the idea of a uniform civil code on the ground that this would be a fundamental encroachment on the freedom of religion and destructive of the cultural identity of religious minorities, the Muslim leadership in India has not shunned state intervention altogether. One notices, in fact, the same attempt to seek rationalization and uniformity as one sees in the case of Hindu personal law or Hindu religious institutions.

[19] Cited in Tahir Mahmood, *Muslim Personal Law: Role of the State in the Indian Subcontinent* (Nagpur: All India Reporter, 1983), p. 21.

The crucial difference after 1947 is, of course, that unlike the majority community, the minorities are unwilling to grant to a legislature elected by universal suffrage the power to legislate the reform of their religions. On the other hand, there do not exist any other institutions which have the representative legitimacy to supervise such a process of reform. That, to put it in a nutshell, is the present impasse on the equality principle.

The third principle we have mentioned of the secular state — that of the separation of state and religion — has also been recognized in the Constitution, which declares that there shall be no official state religion, no religious instruction in state schools, and no taxes to support any particular religion. But, as we have seen, the state has become entangled in the affairs of religion in numerous ways. This was the case even in colonial times; but the degree and extent of the entanglement, paradoxically, has increased since independence. Nor is this involvement limited only to the sorts of cases we have mentioned before, which were the results of state-sponsored religious reform. Many of the older systems of state patronage of religious institutions, carried out by the colonial government or by the princely states, still continue under the present regime. Thus, Article 290A of the Constitution makes a specific provision of money to be paid every year by the governments of Kerala and Tamil Nadu to the Travancore Devaswom Fund. Article 28(2) says that although there will be no religious instruction in educational institutions wholly maintained out of state funds, this would not apply to those institutions where the original endowment or trust requires that religious instruction be given. Under this provision, Benaras Hindu University and Aligarh Muslim University, both central universities, do impart religious instruction. Besides, there are numerous educational institutions all over the country run by religious denominations which receive state financial aid.

The conclusion is inescapable that the 'wall of separation' doctrine of US constitutional law can hardly be applied to the present Indian situation (as indeed it cannot in the case of many European democracies; but there at least it could be argued that the entanglements are politically insignificant, and often obsolete remnants of older legal conventions). This is precisely the ground on which the argument is sometimes made that 'Indian secularism' has to have a different meaning from 'Western secularism'.

What is suggested in fact is that the cultural and historical realities of the Indian situation call for a *different* relationship between state and civil society than what is regarded as normative in Western political discourse, at least in the matter of religion. Sometimes it is said that in Indian conditions, the neutrality principle cannot apply; the state will necessarily have to involve itself in the affairs of religion. What must be regarded as normative here is an extension of the equality principle, i.e. that the state should favour all religions equally. This argument, however, cannot offer a defence for the selective intervention of the state in reforming the personal laws only of the majority community. On the other hand, arguments are also made about secularism having 'many meanings',[20] suggesting thereby that a democratic state must be expected to protect cultural diversity and the right of people to follow their own culture. The difficulty is that this demand cannot be easily squared with the homogenizing secular desire for, let us say, a uniform civil code.

Where we end up then is a quandary. The desire for a secular state must concede defeat even as it claims to have discovered new meanings of secularism. On the other hand, the respect for cultural diversity and different ways of life finds it impossible to articulate itself in the unitary rationalism of the language of rights. It seems to me that there is no viable way out of this problem within the given contours of liberal-democratic theory, which must define the relation between the relatively autonomous domains of state and civil society always in terms of individual rights. As has been noticed for many other aspects of the emerging forms of non-Western modernity, this is one more instance where the supposedly universal forms of the modern state turn out to be inadequate for the post-colonial world.

To reconfigure the problem posed by the career of the secular state in India, we will need to locate it on a somewhat different conceptual ground. In the remainder of this paper, I will suggest the outlines of an alternative theoretical argument which holds the promise of taking us outside the dilemmas of the secular-modernist discourse. In this, I will not take the easy route of appealing to an 'Indian exception'. In other words, I will not trot out yet another version of the 'new meaning of secularism'

[20] Sumit Sarkar, 'The Fascism of the Sangh Parivar'.

argument. But to avoid that route, I must locate my problem on a ground which will include, at one and the same time, the history of the rise of the modern state in both its Western and non-Western forms. I will attempt to do this by invoking Michel Foucault.

Liberal-Democratic Conundrum

But before I do that, let me briefly refer to the current state of the debate over minority rights in liberal political theory, and why I think the problem posed by the Indian situation will not find any satisfactory answers within the terms of that debate. A reference to this theoretical corpus is necessary because, first, left-democratic thinking in India on secularism and minority rights shares many of its premises with liberal-democratic thought; and second, the legally instituted processes of the state and the public domain in India have clearly avowed affiliations to the conceptual world of liberal political theory. Pointing out the limits of liberal thought will also allow me, then, to make the suggestion that political practice in India must seek to develop new institutional sites that cut across the divide between state sovereignty on the one hand and people's rights on the other.

To begin with, liberal political theory in its strict sense cannot recognize the validity of any collective rights of cultural groups. Liberalism must hold as a fundamental principle the idea that the state, and indeed all public institutions, will treat all citizens equally, regardless of race, sex, religion or other cultural particularities. It is only when everyone is treated equally, liberals will argue, that the basic needs of people, shared universally by all, can be adequately and fairly satisfied. These universal needs will include not only 'material' goods such as livelihood, health care or education, but also 'cultural' goods such as religious freedom, free speech, free association, etc. But in order to guarantee freedom and equality at the same time, the locus of rights must be the individual citizen, the bearer of universal needs; to recognize rights that belong only to particular cultural groups within the body of citizens is to destroy both equality and freedom.

Needless to say, this purist version of the liberal doctrine is regarded as unduly rigid and narrow by many who otherwise identify with the values of liberal-democratic politics. But the attempts to make room, within the doctrines of liberalism, for some recognition of collective cultural identities have not yielded solutions that enjoy wide acceptance. I cannot enter here into the details of this controversy which, spurred on by the challenge -of 'multiculturalism' in many Western countries, has emerged as perhaps the liveliest area of debate in contemporary liberal philosophy. A mention only of the principal modes of argument, insofar as they are relevant to the problems posed by the Indian situation, will have to suffice.

One response to the problem of fundamental moral disagreements caused by a plurality of conflicting — and sometimes incommensurable — cultural values, is to seek an extension of the principle of neutrality in order to preclude such conflicts from the political arena. The argument here is that, just as in the case of religion, the existence of fundamentally divergent moral values in society would imply that there is no rational way in which reasonable people might resolve the dispute; and since the state should not arbitrarily favour one set of beliefs over another, it must not be asked to intervene in such conflicts. John Rawls and Thomas Nagel, among others, have made arguments of this kind, seeking thereby to extend the notions of state impartiality and religious toleration to other areas of moral disagreement.[21]

Not all liberals, however, like the deep scepticism and 'epistemic abstinence' implied in this view.[22] More relevant for us, however, is the criticism made from within liberal theory that these attempts to cope with diversity by taking the disputes off the political agenda are 'increasingly evasive. They offer a false impartiality in place of social recognition of the persistence of fundamental conflicts of value in our society.'[23] If this is a judgement that can be made for societies where the 'wall of separation' doctrine is solidly established, the remoteness of

---

[21] John Rawls, 'Justice as Fairness: Political not Metaphysical', *Philosophy and Public Affairs*, 14 (1985), pp. 248–51; John Rawls, 'The Priority of the Right and Ideas of the Good', *Philosophy and Public Affairs*, 17 (1988), pp. 260–4; Thomas Nagel, 'Moral Conflict and Political Legitimacy', *Philosophy and Public Affairs*, 16(1987), pp. 218–40.

[22] For instance, Joseph Raz, 'Facing Diversity: The Case of Epistemic Abstinence', *Philosophy and Public Affairs*, 19 (1990), pp. 3–46.

[23] Amy Gutmann and Dennis Thompson, 'Moral Conflict and Political Consensus', *Ethics*, 101 (October 1990), pp. 64–88.

these arguments from the realities of the Indian situation hardly needs to emphasized.

However, rather than evade the question of cultural diversity, some theorists have attempted to take up the 'justice as fairness' idea developed by liberals such as John Rawls and Ronald Dworkin, and extend it to cultural groups. Justice, according to this argument, requires that undeserved or 'morally arbitrary' disadvantages should be removed or compensated for. If such disadvantages attach to persons because they were born into particular minority cultural groups, then liberal equality itself must demand that individual rights be differentially allocated on the basis of culture. Will Kymlicka has made such a case for the recognition of the rights of cultural minorities whose very survival as distinct groups is in question.[24]

We should note, of course, that the examples usually given in this liberal literature to illustrate the need for minority cultural rights are those of the indigenous peoples of North America and Australia. But in principle there is no reason why the argument about 'being disadvantaged' should be restricted only to such indubitable cases of endangered cultural groups; it should apply to any group that can be reasonably defined as a cultural minority within a given political entity. And this is where its problems as a liberal theory become insuperable. Could a collective cultural right be used as an instrument to perpetuate thoroughly illiberal practices within the group? Would individual members of such groups have the right to leave the group? If an individual right of exit is granted, would that not in effect undermine the right of the group to preserve its identity? On the other hand, if a right of exit is denied, would we still have a liberal society?[25]

Clearly, it is extremely hard to justify the granting of substantively different collective rights to cultural groups on the basis of liberalism's commitment to procedural equality and universal citizenship. Several recent attempts to make a case for special rights for cultural minorities and oppressed groups, have

[24] Will Kymlicka, *Liberalism, Community and Culture* (Oxford: Oxford University Press, 1989).

[25] See, for example, the following exchange: Chandran Kukathas, 'Are there any Cultural Rights?' and Will Kymlicka, 'The Rights of Minority Cultures', *Political Theory*, 20, 1 (February 1992), pp. 105–46; Kukathas, 'Cultural Rights Again', *Political Theory*, 20, 4 (November 1992), pp. 674–80.

consequently gone on to question the idea of universal citizenship itself: in doing this, the arguments come fairly close to upholding some sort of cultural relativism. The charge that is made against universal citizenship is not merely that it forces everyone into a single homogeneous cultural mould, thus threatening the distinct identities of minority groups; but that the homogeneous mould itself is by no means a neutral one, being invariably the culture of the dominant group, so that it is not everybody but only the minorities and the disadvantaged who are forced to forego their cultural identities. That being the case, neither universalism nor neutrality can have any moral priority over the rights of cultural groups to protect their autonomous existence.

Once again, arguments such as this go well beyond the recognized limits of the liberal doctrine; and even those who are sympathetic to the demands for the protection of plural cultural identities feel compelled to assert that the recognition of difference cannot mean the abandonment of all commitment to a universalist framework of reason.[26] Usually, therefore, the 'challenge of multiculturalism' is sought to be met by asserting the value of diversity itself for the flowering of culture, and making room for divergent ways of life *within* a fundamentally agreed set of universalist values. Even when one expects recognition of one's 'right to culture', therefore, one must always be prepared to act within a culture of rights and thus give reasons for insisting on being different.[27]

None of these liberal arguments seems to have enough strength to come to grips with the problems posed by the Indian situation. Apart from resorting to platitudes about the value of diversity, respect for other ways of life, and the need for furthering understanding between different cultures, they do not provide any means for relocating the institutions of

[26] See, for example, Charles Taylor, *Multiculturalism and 'The Politics of Recognition'* (Princeton: Princeton University Press, 1992); Amy Gutmann, 'The Challenge of Multiculturalism in Political Ethics', *Philosophy and Public Affairs*, 22 (1993), pp. 73–206.

[27] Rajeev Bhargava has sought to make the case for the rights of minorities in India in these terms. See 'The Right to Culture', in K.N. Panikkar, ed., *Communalism in India: History, Politics and Culture* (New Delhi: Manohar, 1991), pp. 165–72.

rights or refashioning the practices of identity in order to get out of what often appears to be a political impasse.

Governmentality

I make use of Foucault's idea of governmentality not because I think it is conceptually neat or free of difficulties. Nor is the way in which I will use the idea here one that, as far as I know, Foucault has advanced himself. I could have, therefore, gone on from the preceding paragraph to set out my own scheme for re-problematizing the issue of secularism in India, without making this gesture towards Foucault. The reason I think the reference is necessary, however, is that by invoking Foucault I will be better able to emphasize the need to shift our focus from the rigid framework laid out by the concepts of sovereignty and right, to the constantly shifting *strategic* locations of the politics of identity and difference.

Foucault's idea of governmentality[28] reminds us, first, that cutting across the liberal divide between state and civil society there is a very specific form of power that entrenches itself in modern society, having as its goal the well-being of a population, its mode of reasoning a certain instrumental notion of economy, and its apparatus an elaborate network of surveillance. True, there have been other attempts at conceptualizing this ubiquitous form of modern power: most notably in Max Weber's theory of rationalization and bureaucracy, or more recently in the writings of the Frankfurt School, and in our own time in those of Jürgen Habermas. However, unlike Weberian sociology, Foucault's idea of governmentality does not lend itself to appropriation by a liberal doctrine characterizing the state as a domain of coercion ('monopoly of legitimate violence') and civil society as the zone of freedom. The idea of governmentality — and this is its second important feature — insists that by exercising itself through forms of representation, and hence by offering itself as an aspect of the self-disciplining of the very population over which it is

---

[28] See, in particular, Michel Foucault, 'Governmentality', in Graham Burchell, Colin Gordon and Peter Miller, eds, *The Foucault Effect: Studies in Governmentality* (Chicago: University of Chicago Press, 1991), pp. 87–104; and 'Politics and Reason', in Foucault, *Politics, Philosophy, Culture: Interviews and Other Writings 1977–1984* (New York: Routledge, 1988), pp. 57–85.

exercised, the modern form of power, whether inside or outside the domain of the state, is capable of allowing for an immensely flexible braiding of coercion and consent.

If we bear in mind these features of the modern regime of power, it will be easier for us to grasp what is at stake in the politics of secularization. It is naive to think of secularization as simply the onward march of rationality, devoid of coercion and power struggles. Even if secularization as a process of the decreasing significance of religion in public life is connected with such 'objective' social processes as mechanization or the segmentation of social relationships (as sociologists such as Bryan Wilson have argued),[29] it does not necessarily evoke a uniform set of responses from all groups. Indeed, contrary phenomena such as religious revivalism, fundamentalism, and the rise of new cults have sometimes also been explained as the consequence of the same processes of mechanization or segmentation. Similarly, arguments about the need to hold on to a universalist framework of reason even as one acknowledges the fact of difference ('deliberative universalism' or 'discourse ethics') tend to sound like pious homilies because they ignore the strategic context of power in which identity or difference is often asserted.

The limit of liberal-rationalist theory is reached when one is forced to acknowledge that, within the specific strategic configuration of a power contestation, what is asserted in a collective cultural right is in fact *the right not to offer a reason for being different.* Thus, when a minority group demands a cultural right, it in fact says, 'We have our own reasons for doing things the way we do, but since you don't share the fundamentals of our world-view, you will never come to understand or appreciate those reasons. Therefore, leave us alone and let us mind our own business.' If this demand is admitted, it amounts in effect to a concession to cultural relativism.

But the matter does not necessarily end there. Foucault's notion of governmentality leads us to examine the other aspect of this strategic contestation. Why is the demand made in the language of rights? Why are the ideas of autonomy and freedom invoked? Even

[29] Bryan Wilson, *Religion in Secular Society* (London: Watts, 1966); Wilson, *Religion in Sociological Perspective* (Oxford: Oxford University Press, 1982). Also, David Martin, *A General Theory of Secularization* (Oxford: Basil Blackwell, 1978).

as one asserts a basic incommensurability in frameworks of reason, why does one nevertheless say, 'We have our own reasons'?

Consider then the two aspects of the process that Foucault describes as the 'governmentalization of the state': juridical sovereignty on the one hand, governmental technology on the other. In his account of this process in Western Europe since the eighteenth century, Foucault tends to suggest that the second aspect completely envelops and contains the first.[30] That is to say, in distributing itself throughout the social body by means of the technologies of governmental power, the modern regime no longer retains a distinct aspect of sovereignty. I do not think, however, that this is a necessary implication of Foucault's argument. On the contrary, I find it more useful — especially of course in situations where the sway of governmental power is far from general — to look for a disjuncture between the two aspects, and thus to identify the sites of application of power where governmentality is unable to successfully encompass sovereignty.

The assertion of minority cultural rights occurs on precisely such a site. It is because of a contestation on the ground of sovereignty that the right is asserted *against governmentality*. To say 'We will not give reasons for not being like you' is to resist entering that deliberative or discursive space where the technologies of governmentality operate. But then, in a situation like this, the only way to resist submitting to the powers of sovereignty is literally to declare oneself unreasonable.

Toleration and Democracy

It is necessary for me to clarify here that in the remainder of this paper, I will be concerned exclusively with finding a defensible argument for minority cultural rights in the given legal–political

30 'Maybe what is really important for our modernity — that is, for our present — is not so much the *étatisation* of society, as the "governmentalization" of the state. . . . This governmentalization of the state is a singularly paradoxical phenomenon, since if in fact the problems of governmentality and the techniques of government have become the only political issue, the only real space for political struggle and contestation, this is because the governmentalization of the state is at the same time what has permitted the state to survive, and it is possible to suppose that if the state is what it is today, this is so precisely thanks to this governmentality, which is at once internal and external to the state . . . ': Foucault, 'Governmentality', p. 103.

situation prevailing in India. I am not therefore proposing an abstract institutional scheme for the protection of minority rights in general. Nor will I be concerned with hypothetical questions such as: 'If your proposal is put into practice, what will happen to national unity?' I am not arguing from the position of the state; consequently, the problem as I see it, is not what the state, or those who think and act on behalf on the state, can grant to the minorities. My problem is to find a defensible ground for a strategic politics, both within and outside the field defined by the institutions of the state, in which a minority group, or one who is prepared to think from the position of a minority group, can engage in India today.

When a group asserts a right against governmentality, i.e. a right not to offer reasons for being different, can it expect others to respect its autonomy and be tolerant of its 'unreasonable' ways? The liberal understanding of toleration will have serious problems with such a request. If toleration is the willing acceptance of something of which one disapproves, then it is usually justified on one of three grounds: a contractualist argument (persons entering into the social contract cannot know beforehand which religion they will end up having, and hence will agree to mutual toleration),[31] a consequentialist argument (the consequences of acting tolerantly are better than those of acting intolerantly),[32] or an argument about respect for persons.[33] We have already pointed out the inappropriateness of a contractualist solution to the problems posed by the Indian situation. The consequentialist argument is precisely what is used when it is said that one must go slow on the universal civil code. But this is only a pragmatic argument for toleration, based on a tactical consideration about the costs of imposing what is otherwise the right thing to do. As such, it always remains vulnerable to righteous moral attack.

The principle of respect for persons does provide a moral

[31] The most well known such argument is in John Rawls, *A Theory of Justice* (London: Oxford University Press, 1971), pp. 205–21.

[32] See, for instance, Preston King, *Toleration* (London: George, Allen and Unwin, 1976); D.D. Raphael, 'The Intolerable', in Susan Mendus, ed., *Justifying Toleration: Conceptual and Historical Perspectives* (Cambridge: Cambridge University Press, 1988), pp. 137–53.

[33] For instance, Joseph Raz, 'Autonomy, Toleration and the Harm Principle', in Mendus, ed., *Justifying Toleration*, pp. 155–75.

argument for toleration. It acknowledges the right of the tolerated, and construes toleration as something that can be claimed
as an entitlement. It also sets limits to toleration and thereby
resolves the problem of justifying something of which one disapproves: toleration is required by the principle of respect for
persons, but practices which fail to show respect for persons need
not be tolerated. Applying this principle to the case of minority
cultural rights, one can easily see where the difficulty will arise.
If a group is intolerant towards its own members and shows
inadequate respect for persons, how can it claim tolerance from
others? If indeed the group chooses not to enter into a reasonable
dialogue with others on the validity of its practices, how can it
claim respect for its ways?

Once again, I think that the strategic location of the contestation over cultural rights is crucial. The assertion of a right to be
different does not exhaust all of the points where the contestation
is grounded. Equally important is the other half of the assertion:
'We have our own reasons for doing things the way we do.' This
implies the existence of a field of reasons, of processes through
which reasons can be exchanged and validated, even if such processes are open only to those who share the viewpoint of the
group. The existence of this autonomous discursive field may
only be implied and not activated, but the implication is a necessary part of the assertion of cultural autonomy as a matter of *right*.[34]

The liberal doctrine tends to treat the question of collective
rights of cultural minorities from a position of externality. Thus,
its usual stand on tolerating cultural groups with illiberal practices
is to advocate some sort of right of exit for individual dissident
members. (One is reminded of the insistence of the liberal Jinnah
that not all sections of the Shari'at Bill should apply compulsorily

[34] In some ways, this is the obverse of the implication which Ashis Nandy
derives from his Gandhian conception of tolerance. His 'religious' conception
of tolerance 'must impute to other faiths the same spirit of tolerance. Whether
a large enough proportion of those belonging to the other religious traditions
show in practice and at a particular point of time and place the same tolerance
or not is a secondary matter. Because it is the imputation or presumption of
tolerance in others, not its existence, which defines one's own tolerance. . . .'
Nandy, 'The Politics of Secularism'. My search is in the other direction. I am
looking for a 'political' conception of tolerance which will set out the practical
conditions I must meet in order to demand and expect tolerance from others.

to all Muslims.) The argument I am advancing would, however, give a very different construction to the concept of toleration. Toleration here would require one to accept that there will be political contexts where a group could insist on its right not to give reasons for doing things differently, provided it explains itself adequately in its own chosen forum. In other words, toleration here would be premised on autonomy and respect for persons, but it would be sensitive to the varying political salience of the institutional contexts in which reasons are debated.

To return to the specificities of the Indian situation, then, my approach would not call for any axiomatic approval to a uniform civil code for all citizens. Rather, it would start from the historically given reality of separate religion-based personal laws and the intricate involvement of state agencies in the affairs of religious institutions. Here, equal citizenship already stands qualified by the legal recognition of religious differences; the 'wall of separation' doctrine cannot be strictly applied either. Given the inapplicability of the neutrality principle, therefore, it becomes necessary to find a criterion by which state involvement, when it occurs in the domain of religion, can appear to the members of a religious group as both legitimate and fair. It seems to me that toleration, as described above, can supply us with this criterion.

Let us construct an argument for someone who is prepared to defend the cultural rights of minority religious groups in India. The 'minority group', she will say, is not the invention of some perverse sectarian imagination: it is an actually existing category of Indian citizenship — constitutionally defined, legally administered and politically invoked at every opportunity. Some people in India happen to be born into minority groups; a few others choose to enter them by conversion. In either case, many aspects of the status of such people as legal and political subjects are defined by the fact that they belong to minority groups. If there is any perversity in this, our advocate will point out, it lies in the specific compulsion of the history of the Indian state and its nationalist politics. That being so, one could not fairly be asked to simply forget one's status as belonging to a minority. What must be conceded instead is one's right to negotiate that status in the public arena.

Addressing the general body of citizens from her position

within the minority group, then, our advocate will demand toleration for the beliefs of the group. On the other hand, addressing other members of her group, she will demand that the group publicly seek and obtain from its members consent for its practices, insofar as those practices have regulative power over the members. She will point out that if the group was to demand and expect toleration from others, it would have to satisfy the condition of representativeness. Our advocate will therefore demand more open and democratic debate within her community. Even if it is true, she will say, that the validity of the practices of the religious group can be discussed and judged only in its own forums, those institutions must satisfy the same criteria of publicity and representativeness that members of the group demand of all public institutions having regulatory functions. That, she will insist, is a necessary implication of engaging in the politics of collective rights.

She will not of course claim to have a blueprint of the form of representative institutions which her community might develop, and she will certainly resist any attempt by the state to legislate into existence representative bodies for minority groups as prerequisites for the protection of minority rights. The appropriate representative bodies, she will know, could only achieve their actual form through a political process carried out primarily within each minority group. But by resisting, on the one hand, the normalizing attempt of the national state to define, classify and fix the identity of minorities on their behalf (the minorities, while constituting a legally distinct category of citizens, can only be acted upon by the general body of citizens; they cannot represent themselves), and demanding, on the other, that regulative powers within the community be established on a more democratic and internally representative basis, our protagonist will try to engage in a strategic politics that is neither integrationist nor separatist. She will in fact locate herself precisely at that cusp where she can face, on the one side, the assimilationist powers of governmental technology and resist, on the grounds of autonomy and self-representation, its universalist idea of citizenship; and, on the other side, struggle, once again on the grounds of autonomy and self-representation, for the emergence of more representative public institutions and practices within her community.

Needless to say, there will be many objections to her politics, even from her own comrades. Would not her disavowal of the idea of universal citizenship mean a splitting up of national society into mutually exclusive and rigidly separated ethnic groups? To this question, our protagonist could give the abstract answer that universal citizenship is merely the form offered by the bourgeois-liberal state to ensure the legal–political conditions for the deployment and exploitation of differences in civil society; universal citizenship normalizes the reproduction of differences by pretending that everyone is the same. More concretely, she could point out that nowhere has the sway of universal citizenship meant the end of either ethnic difference or discrimination on cultural grounds. The lines of difference and discrimination dissolve at some points, only to reappear at others. What is problematic here is not so much the existence of bounded categories of population, which the classificatory devices of modern governmental technologies will inevitably impose, but rather the inability of people to negotiate, through a continuous and democratic process of self-representation, the actual content of those categories. That is the new politics that one must try to initiate within the old forms of the modern state.

She will also be asked whether, by discounting universal citizenship, she is not throwing away the possibility of using the emancipatory potential of the ideas of liberty and equality. After all, does not the liberal-secular idea of equal rights still hold out the most powerful ideological means to fight against unjust and often tyrannical practices within many religious communities, especially regarding the treatment of women? To this, the answer will be that it is not a choice of one or the other. To pursue a strategic politics of demanding toleration, one would not need to oppose the liberal-secular principles of the modern state. One would, however, need to rearrange one's strategic priorities. One would be rather more sceptical of the promise that an interventionist secular state would, by legislation or judicial decisions, bring about progressive reform within minority religious groups. Instead, one would tend to favour the harder option, which rests on the belief that if the struggle is for progressive change in social practices sanctioned by religion, then that struggle must be launched and won within the religious communities themselves. There are no historical short-cuts here.

A strategic politics of demanding toleration does not require one to regurgitate the tired slogans about the universality of discursive reason. Instead, it takes seriously the possibility that at particular conjunctures and on specific issues, there could occur an honest refusal to engage in reasonable discourse. But it does not, for that reason, need to fully subscribe to a theory of cultural relativism. Indeed, it could claim to be agnostic in this matter. All it needs to do is to locate itself at those specific points where universal discourse is resisted (remembering that those points could not exhaust the whole field of politics: e.g. those who will refuse to discuss their rules of marriage or inheritance in a general legislative body might be perfectly willing to debate in that forum the rates of income tax or the policy of public health); and then engage in a two-fold struggle — resist homogenization from the outside, and push for democratization inside. That, in brief, would be a strategic politics of toleration.

Contrary to the apprehensions of many who think of minority religious groups as inherently authoritarian and opposed to the democratization of their religious institutions, it is unlikely, I think, that the principal impediment to the opening of such processes within the religious communities will come from the minority groups themselves. There is considerable historical evidence to suggest that when collective cultural rights have been asserted on behalf of minority religious groups in India, they have often been backed by the claim of popular consent through democratic processes. Thus, the campaign in the 1920s for reform in the management of Sikh gurdwaras was accompanied by the Akali demand that Sikh shrines and religious establishments be handed over to elected bodies. Indeed, the campaign was successful in forcing a reluctant colonial government to provide, in the Sikh Gurdwaras and Shrines Bill 1925, for a committee elected by all adult Sikhs, men and women, to take over the management of Sikh religious places.[35] The Shiromani Gurdwara Prabandhak Committee was perhaps the first legally constituted public body in colonial India for which the principle of universal suffrage was recognized. It is also important to note that the so-called 'traditional' *ulema* in India,

[35] For this history, see Mohinder Singh, *The Akali Movement* (Delhi: Macmillan, 1978).

when campaigning in the 1920s for the reform of Muslim religious institutions, demanded from the colonial government that officially appointed bodies such as Wakf committees be replaced by representative bodies elected by local Muslims.[36] The persuasive force of the claim for representativeness is often irresistible in the politics of collective rights.

The more serious opposition to this proposal is likely to come from those who will see in the representative public institutions of the religious communities, a threat to the sovereign powers of the state. If such institutions are to be given any role in the regulation of the lives and activities of its members, then their very stature as elected bodies representative of their constituents will be construed as diminishing the sovereignty of the state. I can hear the murmurs already: 'Remember how the SGPC was used to provide legitimacy to Sikh separatism? Imagine what will happen if Muslims get their own parliament!' The deadweight of juridical sovereignty cannot be easily pushed aside even by those who otherwise subscribe to ideas of autonomy and self-regulating civil social institutions.

I do not, therefore, make these proposals for a reconfiguration of the problem of secularism in India and a redefinition of the concept of toleration with any degree of optimism. All I can hope for is that, faced with a potentially disastrous political impasse, some at least will prefer to err on the side of democracy.

---

36 Tahir Mahmood, *Muslim Personal Law*, pp. 66–7.

15

Talking about our Modernity
in Two Languages

I had promised the editors that I would do an English version
of something I had written in Bengali. Here it is. But I cannot
offer it without considerable qualification.

In September 1994 I delivered in Calcutta a public lecture in
memory of a student of mine who had died the year before of
an incurable kidney ailment. The subject of that talk was 'Our
Modernity'.[1] Needless to say, my intention was to problematize
the much-talked-about notion of modernity by focusing on the
pronoun 'our'. One implication of using the pronoun was to
suggest that there might be modernities that were not ours. If
we could have 'our' modernity, then others could just as well
have 'their' modernities. It could be the case, I said, that what
others think of as modern, we have found unacceptable, whereas
what we have cherished as valuable elements of our modernity,
others do not consider to be modern at all. By playing upon the
distinction between 'us' and 'them', I was hoping to lead the
discussion into an area where I could question commonsensical
notions about the existence of certain universally held values of
modernity, and suggest that modernity was a contextually located
and enormously contested idea.

In that lecture I did not go into any explicit discussion of
whom I meant when I said 'our'. I had assumed that when I
played with the range of meanings available to the terms 'we' and
'they' in the particular context in which I was talking, my Calcutta
audience would follow me the whole way. When I said 'our', we
— I and my audience — would have meant, depending on the

---

[1] The Srijnan Halder Memorial Lecture, 1994, delivered in Bengali in
Calcutta on 3 September 1994. Published as 'Āmāder ādhunikatā', *Yogasūtra*,
October 1994, pp. 71–86. English translation published in *The Present History
of West Bengal: Essays in Political Criticism*, chapter 12, pp. 193–210.

context, Indians, or Bengalis, or perhaps more specifically the Indian or the Bengali middle class, or perhaps in an even more limited sense the literati or intelligentsia of the last hundred years or so a group possessing an articulate historical consciousness of being modern, and what is more, of being modern in a way that was, in significant ways, different from 'their' modernity. By 'them', there could have been little ambiguity about what we meant. We meant the modern West, sometimes more specifically modern Europe. We were aware of course of the many debates and disagreements within Western thought about the meanings of modernity; we also knew that not everything in contemporary Western society was necessarily modern. But we nevertheless felt it meaningful to hold on to a certain notion of Western modernity as something that was 'theirs', with reference to which we needed to define 'our' modernity.

In assuming this complicity between me and my audience, I was not being unjustifiably hopeful. There was, I knew, a fairly well established tradition of talking about 'ours' and 'theirs' in exactly this way in the immediate intellectual tradition to which both I and most of my audience belonged. This was, of course, the nationalist tradition of social and historical thinking that had emerged, in Bengal along with other parts of India, over more than a hundred years; a tradition built up for the most part by bilingual intellectuals who were conversant with the rhetorics and modes of thought of the modern West as well of their own indigenous cultures. Speaking as I was to a roomful of listeners having practically the same intellectual background as myself — most of them being teachers and researchers in the social sciences, and many of them indeed being my colleagues or former students — I had no doubt that my gesture of inclusiveness would easily draw my audience into a comfortable enclosure of shared texts, shared memories and shared languages.

I propose now to give my readers in English a glimpse of that space, and to let them hear some of those conversations. For a substantial part of this lecture, now, you will have to imagine yourself transported to an uncomfortably warm September evening in Calcutta, looking into a somewhat dingy room crammed with nearly a hundred people, and listening — let us say — to a simultaneous English translation of my Bengali lecture. After you have heard me out in this way, I will pose to you a problem for which I have no answer.

Conceptualizing Our Modernity

I began my talk that evening by going directly into a nineteenth century account of the consequences of modernity.

In 1873, Rajnarayan Basu had attempted a comparative evaluation of *Se kāl ār e kāl* [Those Days and These Days].[2] By 'those days' and 'these days', he meant the period before and after the full-fledged introduction of English education in India. The word *ādhunik*, in the sense in which we now use it in Bengali to mean 'modern' was not in use in the nineteenth century. The word then used was *nabya* [new]: the 'new' was that which was inextricably linked to Western education and thought. The other word that was much in use was *unnati*, an equivalent of the nineteenth-century European concept of 'improvement' or 'progress', an idea we will today designate by the word *pragati*.

Rajnarayan Basu, needless to say, was educated in the *nabya* or new manner; he was a social reformer and very much in favour of modern ideas. Comparing 'those days' with 'these days', he spoke of seven areas where there had been either improvement or decline. These seven areas were health, education, livelihood, social life, virtue, polity and religion. His discussion on these seven subjects is marked by the recurrence of some familiar themes. Thus, for instance, the notion that whereas people of 'those days' were simple, caring, compassionate and genuinely religious, religion now is mere festivity and pomp, and people have become cunning, devious, selfish and ungrateful:

Talking to people nowadays, it is hard to decide what their true feelings are . . . Before, if there was a guest in the house, people were eager to have him stay a few days more. Before, people even pawned their belongings in order to be hospitable to their guests. Nowadays, guests look for the first opportunity to leave. (Basu, p. 82)

Rajnarayan gives several such examples of changes in the quality of sociability.

But the subject on which Rajnarayan spends the longest time

---

[2] Rajnarayan Basu, *Se kāl ār e kāl*, Brajendranath Bandyopadhyay and Sajanikanta Das, eds (Calcutta: Bangiya Sahitya Parishat, 1956).

in comparing 'those days' with 'these days' is that of the *śarīr*, the body. I wish to present this matter a little elaborately, because in it lies a rather curious aspect of our modernity.

Ask anyone and he will say, 'My father and grandfather were very strong men.' Compared with men of those days, men now have virtually no strength at all . . . If people who were alive a hundred years ago were to come back today, they would certainly be surprised to see how short in stature we have become. We used to hear in our childhood of women who chased away bandits. These days, leave alone women, we do not even hear of men with such courage. Men these days cannot even chase away a jackal. (Basu, pp. 37–8)

On the whole, people — and Rajnarayan adds here, 'especially *bhadralok*', respectable people — have now become feeble, sickly and short-lived.

Let us pause for a minute to consider what this means. If by 'these days' we mean the modern age, the age of a new civilization inaugurated under English rule, then is the consequence of that modernity a decline in the health of the people? On ethics, religion, sociability and such other spiritual matters, there could conceivably be some scope for argument. But how could the thought occur to someone that in that most mundane of worldly matters — our biological existence — people of the present age have become weaker and more short-lived than people of an earlier age?

If my historian friends are awake at this moment, they will of course point out straightaway that we are talking here of 1873, when modern medicine and health services in British India were still confined to the narrow limits of the European expatriate community and the army, and had not even begun to reach out towards the larger population. How could Rajnarayan be expected in 1873 to make a judgement on the miraculous advances of modern medicine in the twentieth century?

If this be the objection, then let us look at a few more examples. Addressing the All-India Sanitary Conference in 1912, Motilal Ghosh, founder of the famous nationalist daily, the *Amrita Bazar Patrika*, said that sixty years ago — that is to say, more or less at the time Rajnarayan referred to as 'these days' — the Bengal countryside of his childhood was almost entirely free from disease. The only illnesses were common fevers which could be cured in a few days by an appropriate diet. Typhoid was rare and cholera had not been heard of. Smallpox occurred from time to time, but indigenous inoculators using their traditional techniques were able to cure their patients without much difficulty. There was no shortage of clean drinking water. Food was abundant and villages 'teemed with healthy, happy and robust people, who spent their days in manly sports'.[3] I can produce more recent examples. Reminiscing in 1982 on her childhood in Barisal, Manikuntala Sen, the communist leader, writes: 'The thought brings tears to my eyes. Oh Allah, why did you give us this technological civilization? Weren't we content then with our rice and *ḍāl*, fish and milk? Now I hear there is no hilsa fish in all of Barisal!' Even more recently, Kalyani Datta in her *Thoḍ baḍi khāḍā* published in 1992 tells so many stories from her childhood about food and eating habits, that the people Rajnarayan Basu talks of as having lived in the late eighteenth century seem to have been very much around in the inner precincts of Calcutta houses in the 1930s. After having a full meal, she says, people would often eat thirty or forty mangoes as dessert.[4]

Examples can be easily multiplied. In fact, if I had suitably dressed up Rajnarayan's words and passed them off as the comments of one of our contemporary writers, none of you would have suspected anything, because we ourselves talk all the time about how people of an earlier generation were so much stronger and healthier than ourselves.

The question is: why have we held on to this factually baseless idea for the last hundred years? Or could it be the case that we have been trying all along to say something about the historical experience of our modernity which does not appear in the statistical facts of demography? Well, let us turn to the reasons that Rajnarayan gives for the decline in health from 'those days' to 'these days'.

The first reason, Rajnarayan says, is change in the environment.

---

[3] Cited in David Arnold, *Colonizing the Body: State Medicine and Epidemic Disease in Nineteenth-Century India* (Berkeley: University of California Press, 1993), pp. 282–3.

[4] Manikuntala Sen, Sediner Kathā (Calcutta: Nobapatra, 1982), p. 10. Kalyani Datta, *Thoḍ baḍi khāḍā* (Calcutta: Thema, 1992), esp. pp. 26–48.

Before, people would travel from Calcutta to Tribeni, Santipur and
other villages for a change. Now those places have become unhealthy
because of the miasma known as malaria . . . For various reasons it
appears that there is a massive environmental change taking place in
India today. That such change will be reflected in the physical strength
of the people is hardly surprising. (Basu, pp. 38–9)

The second reason is food: lack of nutritious food, consumption of adulterated and harmful food, and excess of drinking. 'We have seen and heard in our childhood of numerous examples of how much people could eat in those days. They cannot do so now.'

The third reason is labour: excess of labour, untimely labour and the lack of physical exercise.

There is no doubt that with the advent of English civilization in our
country, the need to labour has increased tremendously. We cannot
labour in the same way as the English; yet the English want us to do
so. English labour is not suited to this country . . . The routine now
enforced by our rulers of working from ten to four is in no way suitable
for the conditions of this country. (Basu, p. 39)

The fourth reason is the change in the way of life. In the past, people had few wants, which is why they were able to live happily. Today there is no end to our worries and anxieties. 'Now the European civilization has entered our country, and with it European wants, European needs and European luxuries. Yet the European way of fulfilling those wants and desires, namely, industry and trade, is not being adopted.' Rajnarayan here makes a comparison between two old men, one a 'vernacular old man', the other an 'anglicized old man'.

The anglicized old man has aged early. The vernacular old man wakes
up when it is still dark. Waking up, he lies in bed and sings religious
songs: how this delights his heart! Getting up from bed, he has a bath:
how healthy a habit! Finishing his bath, he goes to the garden to pick
flowers: how beneficial the fragrance of flowers for the body! Having
gathered flowers, he sits down to pray: this delights the mind and
strengthens both body and spirit . . . The anglicized old man, on the
other hand, has dinner and brandy at night and sleeps late; he has never
seen a sunrise and has never breathed the fresh morning air. Rising late
in the morning, he has difficulty in performing even the simple task of
opening his eyelids. His body feels wretched, he has a hangover, things

look like getting even worse! In this way, subjected to English food and drink and other English manners, the anglicized old man's body becomes the home of many diseases. (Basu, pp. 49–50)

Rajnarayan himself admits that this comparison is exaggerated. But there is one persistent complaint in all of the reasons he cites for the decline in health from the earlier to the present age: not all of the particular means we have adopted for becoming modern are suitable for us. Yet, by imitating uncritically the forms of English modernity, we are bringing upon us environmental degradation, food shortages, illnesses caused by excessive labour and an uncoordinated and undisciplined way of life. Rajnarayan gives many instances of uncritical imitation of English manners, as for instance the following story about the lack of nutritious food.

Two Bengali gentlemen were once dining at Wilson's Hotel. One of them was especially addicted to beef. He asked the waiter, 'Do you have veal?' The waiter replied, 'I'm afraid not, sir.' The gentleman asked again, 'Do you have beef steak?' The waiter replied, 'Not that either, sir.' The gentleman asked again, 'Do you have ox tongue?' The waiter replied, 'Not that either, sir.' The gentleman asked again, 'Do you have calf's foot jelly?' The waiter replied, 'Not that either, sir.' The gentleman said, 'Don't you have anything from a cow?' Hearing this, the second gentleman, who was not so partial to beef, said with some irritation, 'Well, if you have nothing else from a cow, why not get him some dung?' (Basu, p. 44)

The point which this story is supposed to illustrate is that 'beef is much too heat-producing and unhealthy for the people of this country'. On the other hand, the food that is much more suitable and healthy, namely, milk, has become scarce: English officials, Muslims and a few beef-eating Bengalis 'have eaten the cows, which is why milk is so dear'.

Many of Rajnarayan's examples and explanations will seem laughable to us now. But there is nothing laughable about his main project, which is to prove that there cannot be just one modernity irrespective of geography, time, environment or social conditions. The forms of modernity will have to vary between different countries depending upon specific circumstances and social practices. We could in fact stretch Rajnarayan's comments a bit further to assert that true modernity consists in determining the particular forms of modernity that are suitable in particular circumstances; that is, applying the methods of reason to identify or invent the specific technologies of modernity that are appropriate for our purposes. Or, to put this another way, if there is any universal or universally acceptable definition of modernity, it is this: that by teaching us to employ the methods of reason, universal modernity enables us to identify the forms of our own particular modernity.

Western Modernity Representing Itself

How is one to employ one's powers of reason and judgement to decide what to do? Let us listen to the reply given to this question by Western modernity itself. In 1784, Immanuel Kant wrote a short essay on *Aufklärung*, which we know in English as the Enlightenment, i.e. *ālokprāpti*.[5] According to Kant, to be enlightened is to become mature, to reach adulthood, to stop being dependent on the authority of others, to become free and assume responsibility for one's own actions. When man is not enlightened, he does not employ his own powers of reasoning but rather accepts the guardianship of others and does as he is told. He does not feel the need to acquire knowledge about the world, because everything is written in the holy books. He does not attempt to make his own judgements about right and wrong; he follows the advice of his pastor. He even leaves it to his doctor to decide what he should or should not eat. Most men in all periods of history have been, in this sense, immature. And those who have acted as guardians of society have wanted it that way; it was in their interest that most people should prefer to remain dependent on them rather than become self-reliant. It is in the present age that, for the first time, the need for self-reliance has been generally acknowledged. It is also now that for the first time it is agreed that the primary condition for putting an end to our self-imposed dependence is freedom, especially civil freedoms. This does not mean that everyone in the present age is enlightened, or that we are now living in an enlightened age. We should rather say that our age is the age of enlightenment.

The French philosopher Michel Foucault has an interesting

5 Immanuel Kant, *On History*, Lewis White Beck, ed. (Indianapolis: Bobbs–Merrill, 1963), pp. 1–10.

discussion on this essay by Kant.[6] What is it that is new in the way in which Kant describes the Enlightenment? The novelty lies, Foucault says, in the fact that for the first time we have a philosopher making the attempt to relate his philosophical inquiry to his own age, and concluding that it is because the times are propitious that his inquiries have become possible. In other words, this is the first time that a philosopher makes the character of his own age a subject of philosophical investigation, the first time that someone tries from within his own age to identify the social conditions favourable for the pursuit of knowledge.

What are the features that Kant points out as characteristic of the present age? Foucault says that this is where the new thinking is so distinctive. In marking out the present, Kant is not referring to some revolutionary event which ends the earlier age and inaugurates the age of enlightenment. Nor is he reading in the characteristics of the present age the signs of some future revolutionary event in the making. Nor indeed is he looking at the present as a transition from the past to some future age that has not yet arrived. All of these strategies of describing the present in historical terms have been in use in European thought a long time before Kant — from at least the Greek age — and their use has not ceased since the age of Kant. What is remarkable about Kant's criteria of the present is that they are all negative. Enlightenment means an exit, an escape: escape from tutelage, coming out of dependence. Here, Kant is not talking about the origins of the Enlightenment, or about its sources, or its historical evolution. Nor indeed is he talking about the historical goal of the Enlightenment. He is concerned only with the present in itself, with those exclusive properties that define the present as different from the past. Kant is looking for the definition of enlightenment, or more broadly, of modernity, in the difference posed by the present.

Let us underline this statement and set it aside for the moment; I will return to it later. Let us now turn to another interesting aspect of Foucault's essay. Suppose we agree on the fact that autonomy and self-reliance have become generally accepted norms. Let us also grant that freedom of thought and speech is

[6] Michel Foucault, 'What is Enlightenment?', in Paul Rabinow, ed., *The Foucault Reader* (New York: Pantheon, 1984), pp. 32–50.

acknowledged as the necessary condition for self-reliance. But freedom of thought does not mean that people are free to do just as they please at every moment and in every act of daily life. To admit that would be to deny the need for social regulation, and to call for total anarchy. Obviously, the philosophers of the Enlightenment could not have meant this. While demanding individual autonomy and freedom of thought, they also had to specify those areas of personal and social living where freedom of thought would operate, and those other areas where, irrespective of individual opinions, the directives or regulations of the recognized authority would have to prevail. In his essay 'What is Enlightenment?' Kant did specify these areas.

The way he proceeds to do this is by separating two spheres of the exercise of reason. One of these Kant calls 'public', where matters of general concern are discussed and where reason is not mobilized for the pursuit of an individual interest or for the support of a particular group. The other is the sphere of the 'private' use of reason, which relates to the pursuit of individual or particular interests. In the former sphere, freedom of thought and speech is essential; in the second, it is not desirable at all. Illustrating the argument, Kant says that when there is a 'public' debate on the government's revenue policy, those who are knowledgeable in that subject must be given the freedom to express their opinions. But as a 'private' individual, I cannot claim that since I disagree with the government's fiscal policy I must have the freedom not to pay taxes. If there is a 'public' discussion on military organization or war strategy, even a soldier could participate; but on the battlefield his duty is not to express his free opinions but to follow orders. In a 'public' debate on religion, I may, even as a member of a religious denomination, criticize the practices and beliefs of my order; but in my 'private' capacity as a pastor, my duty is to preach the authorized doctrines of my sect and to observe its authorized practices. There cannot be any freedom of speech in the 'private' domain.

This particular use by Kant of the notions of 'public' and 'private' did not gain much currency in later discussions. On the contrary, the usual consensus in liberal social philosophy is that it is in the 'private' or personal sphere that there should be unrestricted freedom of conscience, opinion and behaviour, whereas the sphere of 'public' or social interaction should be subject to recognized norms and regulations that must be respected by all. But no matter how unusual Kant's use of the public/private distinction, it is not difficult for us to understand his argument. When my activities concern a domain in which I as an individual am only a part of a larger social organization or system, a mere cog in the social wheel, there my duty is to abide by regulations and to follow the directives of the recognized authority. But there is another domain of the exercise of reason which is not restricted by these particular or individual interests, a domain that is free and universal. That is the proper place for free thought, for the cultivation of science and art — the proper place, in one word, for 'enlightenment'.

It is worth pointing out that in this universal domain of the pursuit of knowledge — the domain which Kant calls 'public' — it is the individual who is the subject. The condition for true enlightenment is freedom of thought. When the individual in search of knowledge seeks to rise above his particular social location and participate in the universal domain of discourse, his right to freedom of thought and opinion must be unhindered. He must also have the full authority to form his own beliefs and opinions, just as he must bear the full responsibility for expressing them. There is no doubt that Kant is here claiming the right of free speech only for those who have the requisite qualifications for engaging in the exercise of reason and the pursuit of knowledge, and those who can use that freedom in a responsible manner. In discussing Kant's essay, Foucault does not raise this point; although he might well have done so, given the relevance of this theme in Foucault's own work. It is the theme of the rise of experts and the ubiquitous authority of specialists, a phenomenon which appears alongside the general social acceptance of the principle of unrestricted entry into education and learning. We say, on the one hand, that it is wrong to exclude any individual or group from access to education or the practice of knowledge, on grounds of religion or any other social prejudice. On the other hand, we also insist that the opinion of such and such a person is more acceptable because he is an expert in the field. In other words, just as we have meant by enlightenment an unrestricted and universal field for the exercise of reason, so have we built up an intricately differentiated structure of authorities which specifies who has the right to say what on which subjects. As markers of this authority, we have distributed examinations, degrees, titles, insignia of all sorts. Just think how many different kinds of experts we have to allow to guide us through our daily lives — from birth, indeed from before birth, to death and even afterwards. In many areas, in fact, it is illegal to act without expert advice. If I do not myself have a medical degree or licence, I cannot walk into a pharmacy and say, 'I hope you know that there is unrestricted access to knowledge, because I have read all the medical books and I think I need these drugs.' In countries with universal schooling, it is mandatory that children go to officially recognized schools; I could not insist that I would educate my children at home. There are also fairly precise identifications of who is an expert in which subject. At this particular meeting today, for instance, I am talking on history, social philosophy and related subjects, and you have come here to listen to me, either out of interest or out of plain courtesy. If I had announced that I would be speaking on radiation in the ionosphere or the DNA molecule, I would most definitely have had to speak to an empty room, and some of my well-wishers would probably have run to consult experts on mental disorders.

Needless to say, the writings of Michel Foucault have in recent years taught us to look at the relation between the practices of knowledge and the technologies of power from a very new angle. Kant's answer two hundred years ago to the question, 'What is Enlightenment?' might seem at first sight to be an early statement of the most commonplace self-representation of modern social philosophy. And yet, now we can see embedded in that statement the not-very-well-acknowledged ideas of differential access to discourse, the specialized authority of experts, and the use of the instruments of knowledge for the exercise of power. The irresistible enthusiasm that one notices in the writings of Western philosophers of the Enlightenment, about a modernity that would bring in the era of universal reason and emancipation, does not seem to us (witness to the many barbarities of world history in the last two hundred years — and I say this with due apologies to the great Immanuel Kant) as mature in the least. Today our doubts about the claims of modernity are out in the open.

A Modernity that is National

But I have not yet given you an adequate answer to the question with which I began this discussion. Why is it the case that, for more than a hundred years, the foremost proponents of our modernity have been so vocal about the signs of social decline rather than of progress? Surely, when Rajnarayan Basu spoke about the decline in health, education, sociability or virtue, he did not do so out of some post-modern sense of irony. There must be something in the very process of our becoming modern that continues to lead us, even in our acceptance of modernity, to a certain scepticism about its values and consequences.

My argument is that because of the way in which the history of our modernity has been intertwined with the history of colonialism, we have never quite been able to believe that there exists a universal domain of free discourse, unfettered by differences of race or nationality. Somehow, from the very beginning, we had made a shrewd guess that given the close complicity between modern knowledge and modern regimes of power, we would for ever remain consumers of universal modernity; never would we be taken seriously as its producers. It is for this reason that we have tried, for over a hundred years, to take our eyes away from this chimera of universal modernity and clear up a space where we might become the creators of our own modernity.

Let us take an example from history. One of the earliest learned societies in India devoted to the pursuit of modern knowledge was the Society for the Acquisition of General Knowledge, founded in Calcutta in 1838 by some former students of Hindu College. Several of them had been members of 'Young Bengal', that celebrated circle of radicals that had formed in the 1820s around the free-thinking rationalist Henry Derozio. In 1843, at a meeting of the Society held at Hindu College, a paper was being read on 'The Present State of the East India Company's Criminal Judicature and Police'. D.L. Richardson, a well-known teacher of English literature at Hindu College, got up angrily and, according to the Proceedings, complained that

to stand up in a hall which the Government had erected and in the heart of a city which was the focus of enlightenment, and there to denounce, as oppressors and robbers, the men who governed the country, did in his opinion, amount to treason . . . The College would never have been in existence, but for the solicitude the Government felt in the mental improvement of the natives of India. He could not permit it, therefore, to be converted into a den of treason, and must close the doors against all such meetings.

At this, Tarachand Chakrabarti, himself a former student of Hindu College, who was chairing the meeting, rebuked Richardson:

I consider your conduct as an insult to the society . . . if you do not retract what you have said and make due apology, we shall represent the matter to the Committee of the Hindoo College, and if necessary to the Government itself. We have obtained the use of this public hall, by leave applied for and received from the Committee, and not through your personal favour. You are only a visitor on this occasion, and possess no right to interrupt a member of this society in the utterance of his opinions.[7]

This episode is usually recounted in the standard histories as an example of early nationalist feelings among the new intelligentsia of Bengal. Not that there is no truth in this observation, but it does not lie in the obvious drama of an educated Indian confronting his British teacher. Rather, what is significant is the separation between the domain of government and that of 'this society', and the insistence that as long as the required procedures had been followed, the rights of the members of the society to express their opinions, no matter how critical of government, could not be violated. We could say that at this founding moment of modernity, we did genuinely want to believe that in the new public domain of free discourse there were no bars of colour or of the political status of one's nationality; that if one could produce proof of one's competence in the subjects under discussion, one had an unrestricted right to voice one's opinions.

It did not take long for the disillusionment to set in. By the second half of the nineteenth century, we see the emergence of 'national' societies for the pursuit of modern knowledge. The learned societies of the earlier era had both European and

<hr />

[7] A report on this meeting that appeared in the *Bengal Hurkaru*, 13 February 1843, is reprinted in Goutam Chattopadhyay, ed., *Awakening in Bengal in Early Nineteenth Century (Select Documents)*, vol. 1 (Calcutta: Progressive Publishers, 1965), pp. 389–99.

Indian members. The new institutions were exclusively for Indian members, and devoted to the cultivation and spread of the modern sciences and arts among Indians — if possible, in the Indian languages. They were, in other words, institutions for the 'nationalization' of modern knowledge, located in a space somewhat set apart from the field of universal discourse, a space where discourse would be modern, and yet 'national'.

This is a project that is still being pursued today. Its success varies from field to field. But unless we can state why the project was at all considered feasible and what conditions governed its feasibility, we will not be able to answer the question I had asked at the beginning of this talk about the peculiarities of our modernity. We could take as an example our experience with practising any one of the branches of modern knowledge. Since I began this talk with a discussion on the body and its health, let me tell you the story of our acquaintance with the modern science of medicine.

In 1851, a Bengali section was opened at the Calcutta Medical College in order to train Indian students in Western medicine without requiring them first to go through a course of secondary education in English. The Licentiate and Apothecary courses in Bengali were a great success. Beginning with a mere twenty-two students in its first year, this section overtook the English section in 1864, and in 1873 it had 772 students compared to 445 in the English section. Largely because of the demand from students, nearly seven hundred medical books were published in Bengali between 1867 and 1900.[8]

But while the courses remained popular, complaints began to be heard from around the 1870s about the quality of training given to the students in the vernacular sections. It was alleged that their lack of facility in English made them unsuitable for positions of assistants to European doctors in public hospitals. This was the time when a hospital system had begun to be put in place in Bengal, and professional controls were being enforced in the form of supervision by the General Medical Council of London. From the turn of the century, with the institutionalization of the professional practices of medicine in the form of

---

[8] Computed from list supplied by Binaybhusan Ray, *Uṇiś śataker bāṅglāy bijñān sādhanā* (Calcutta: Subarnarekha, 1987), pp. 252–77.

hospitals, medical councils and patented drugs, the Bengali section in the medical school died a quick death. From 1916 all medical education in our country has been exclusively in English.

But the story does not end there. Curiously, this was also the time when organized efforts were on, propelled by nationalist concerns, to give to the indigenous Ayurvedic and *Unani* systems of medicine a new disciplinary form. The All India Ayurveda Mahasammelan, which is still the apex body of ayurvedic practitioners, was set up in 1907. The movement which this organization represented sought to systematize the knowledge of ayurvedic clinical methods, mainly by producing standard editions of classical and recent texts; to institutionalize the methods of training by formalizing, in place of the traditional family-based apprenticeship, a college system consisting of lectures, textbooks, syllabuses, examinations and degrees; and to standardize the medicines and even promote the commercial production of standard drugs by pharmaceutical manufacturers. There have been debates within the movement about the extent and form of adoption of Western medicine within the curricula of ayurvedic training, but even the purists now admit that the course should have 'the benefit of equipment or the methods used by other systems of medicine . . . since, consistent with its fundamental principles, no system of medicine can ever be morally debarred from drawing upon any other branch of science . . . unless one denies the universal nature of scientific truths.'[9]

The very idea of the universality of science is being used here to carve out a separate space for ayurvedic medicine, defined according to the principles of a 'pure' tradition, and yet reorganized as a modern scientific and professional discipline. The claim here is not that the field of knowledge is marked out into separate domains by the fact of cultural difference; it is not being suggested that ayurveda is the appropriate system of medicine for 'Indian diseases'. It is rather a claim for an alternative science directed at the same objects of knowledge.

We have of course seen many attempts of this sort in the fields

[9] *Report of the Shuddha Ayurvedic Education Committee* (Delhi, 1963), cited in Paul R. Brass, 'Politics of Ayurvedic Education: A Case Study of Revivalism and Modernization in India', in Susanne Hoeber Rudolph and Lloyd I. Rudolph, eds, *Education and Politics in India* (Cambridge, Mass.: Harvard University Press, 1972), pp. 342–71.

of literature and the arts to construct a modernity that is different. Indeed, we might say that this is precisely the cultural project of nationalism: to produce a distinctly national modernity. Obviously, there is no general rule that determines which should be the elements of modernity and which the emblems of difference. There have been many experiments in many fields; they continue even today. My argument was that these efforts have not been restricted only to the supposedly cultural domains of religion, literature or the arts. The attempt to find a different modernity has been carried out even in the presumably universal field of science. We should remember that a scientist of the standing of Prafulla Chandra Ray, a Fellow of the Royal Society, thought it worth his while to write *A History of Hindu Chemistry*, while Jagadis Chandra Bose, also an FRS, believed that the researches he carried out in the latter part of his career were derived from insights he had obtained from Indian philosophy. In particular, he believed that he had found a field of scientific research that was uniquely suited to an Indian scientist. These researches of Jagadis Bose did not get much recognition in the scientific community. But it seems me to that if we grasp what it was that led him to think of a project such as this, we will get an idea of the principal driving force of our modernity.

Present History in the Age of Globalization

Whenever I think of enlightenment, I am reminded of the unforgettable first lines of Kamalkumar Majumdar's novel *Antarjali yātrā*:[10]

Light appears gradually. The sky is a frosty violet, like the colour of pomegranate. In a few moments from now, redness will come to prevail and we, the plebeians of this earth, will once more be blessed by the warmth of flowers. Gradually, the light appears. (p. 1)

Modernity is the first social philosophy which conjures up, in the minds of the most ordinary people, dreams of independence and self-rule. The regime of power in modern societies prefers to work not through the commands of a supreme sovereign, but through the disciplinary practices that each individual imposes on his or her own behaviour on the basis of the dictates of reason.

[10] Kamalkumar Majumdar, *Antarjali yātrā* (Calcutta: Kathasilpa, 1962).

And yet, no matter how adroitly the fabric of reason might cloak the reality of power, the desire for autonomy continues to range itself against power; power is resisted. Let us remind ourselves that there was a time when modernity was put forward as the strongest argument in favour of the continued colonial subjection of India: foreign rule was necessary, we were told, because Indians must first become enlightened. And then it was the same logic of modernity which one day led us to the discovery that imperialism was illegitimate; independence was our desired goal. The burden of reason, dreams of freedom; the desire for power, resistance to power: all of these are elements of modernity. There is no promised land of modernity outside the network of power. Hence one cannot be for or against modernity; one can only devise strategies for coping with it. These strategies are sometimes beneficial, often destructive; sometimes they are tolerant, perhaps all too often they are fierce and violent. We have, as I said before, long had to abandon the simple faith that because something was modern and rational, it must necessarily be for the good.

At the end of Kamalkumar's novel, a fearsome flood, like the unstoppable hand of destiny, sweeps away a decadent Hindu society. With it, it also takes that which was alive, beautiful, affectionate, kind. The untouchable plebeian cannot save her, because he is not entitled to touch that which is sacred and pure.

A single eye, like the eye mirrored on hemlock, kept looking at her, the bride seeking her first taste of love. The eye is wooden, because it is painted on the side of a boat; but it is painted in vermilion, and it has on it drops of water from the waves now breaking gently against the boat. The wooden eye is capable of shedding tears. Somewhere, therefore, there remains a sense of attachment. (p. 216)

This sense of attachment is the driving force of our modernity. We would be unjust to ourselves if we think of it as backward-looking, as a sign of resistance to change. On the contrary, it is our attachment to the past which gives birth to the feeling that the present needs to be changed, that it is our task to change it. We must remember that in the world arena of modernity, we are outcastes, untouchables. Modernity for us is like a supermarket of foreign goods, displayed on the shelves: pay up and take away what you like. No one there believes that we could be producers of modernity. The bitter truth about our present is our subjection, our inability to be subjects in our own right. And yet, it is because we want to be modern that our desire to be independent and creative is transposed on to our past. It is superfluous to call this an imagined past, because pasts are always imagined. At the opposite end from 'these days' marked by incompleteness and lack of fulfilment, we construct a picture of 'those days' when there was beauty, prosperity and a healthy sociability, and which was, above all, our own creation. 'Those days' for us is not a historical past; we construct it only to mark the difference posed by the present. All that needs to be noticed is that whereas Kant, speaking at the founding moment of Western modernity, looks at the present as the site of one's escape from the past, for us it is precisely the present from which we feel we must escape. This makes the very modality of our coping with modernity radically different from the historically evolved modes of Western modernity.

Ours is the modernity of the once-colonized. The same historical process that has taught us the value of modernity has also made us the victims of modernity. Our attitude to modernity, therefore, cannot but be deeply ambiguous. This is reflected in the way we have described our experiences with modernity in the last century and a half, from Rajnarayan Basu to our contemporaries today. But this ambiguity does not stem from any uncertainty about whether to be for or against modernity. Rather, the uncertainty is because we know that to fashion the forms of our own modernity, we need to have the courage at times to reject the modernities established by others. In the age of nationalism, there were many such efforts which reflected both courage and inventiveness. Not all were, of course, equally successful. Today, in the age of globalization, perhaps the time has come once more to mobilize that courage. Perhaps we need to think now about 'those days' and 'these days' of our modernity.

The Bilingual Predicament

This is where I ended my lecture that warm September evening in Calcutta. Four months later, when I began to think of trying out the same ideas on an English-reading public, it immediately struck me that a mere translation would not do. The shift was not just one of language; I would in fact need to indicate a shift in the very terrain of discourse.

Let me therefore point out first what it is that remains the same. It was possible for me, as you would have noticed, to talk about Kant and Foucault in terms that would be entirely familiar to practitioners of the social sciences in modern academies the world over. This was possible precisely because of the success of the struggle carried out by bilingual intellectuals in the last hundred years to 'nationalize' modern knowledge by creating and constantly invigorating a field of modern social-scientific discourse in the Indian languages. On the other hand, even as I spoke of Kant and Foucault from texts that were familiar — were at least in principle accessible — to my audience, I was marking them out as situated at some distance from 'us'. These texts, we knew, were produced in a domain that was accessible to us; their results were available for us to use in ways that were authorized in the land of their emergence, so long as we chose to remain within the precincts of the modern academy. But there was no way in which we could count ourselves as belonging to the community of producers of that discourse. The distance was marked in the very language I was using.

On the other hand, lodged in the interstices of my Bengali prose were many figures and allusions that referred to texts and to practices whose meanings could only be available to those who were, like me and most of my Calcutta audience, daily practitioners of contemporary literary Bengali. Even as I tried, in translating for you the text of my lecture, to gloss those terms that were particularly significant for the texture of my argument, I was acutely aware of how much meaning I was losing. For instance, when I translate the binary opposition that recurs throughout my text as 'those days'/'these days', I know I have failed to convey the possibility of the meaning of *se kāl* varying with the age of the speaker: for someone affecting the wisdom of old age it could mean 'those good old days', whereas in the impatient voice of a youthful speaker the adjective *sekele* would refer to that which is outdated and no longer suitable for the present. Given the convenient fact that my own age is somewhere in between those two extremes, and with some skilful positioning of my voice between that of the hoary interpreter of tradition and the zealous prophet of modernity, I had tried, in my attempt to problematize the idea

of the present, to gain maximum mileage from the deep ambiguities that have accumulated around the very dimension of
time in the contemporary Indian languages. I know that in my
translation I have lost that mileage.

Perhaps the most obvious, and in some ways the most crucial
loss, is my inability to translate several of those terms that are
in use in contemporary Bengali which carry a rich load of
conceptual meaning derived from various systems of philosophical and religious discourse in India, but around which have also
accreted a range of meanings borrowed from related concepts
in Western philosophy and social sciences. When I said 'plebeians of the earth' in my quotation from Kamal Majumdar's
novel, I was not displeased at the implied invocation of some
of the rhetoric of modern European socialism. But of course
the meaning *prākṛtajan* in the original was heavily loaded with
the language of a caste-divided society. *Prākṛta* therefore would
mean not just the populace, but specifically the lowly, the un-
refined, the vulgar. But not only that; *prākṛta* also carries with
it the sense of that which is primordial, natural, close to the
earth. The rhetorical gesture of counting oneself as one of the
prākṛtajan, therefore, was a move to identify with the lowly and
downtrodden, as well as to invoke a human collectivity that is
primary and hence in some ways closer to reality.

I have also spoken here about 'attachment to the past'. In
Kamal Majumdar's novel, the word is *māyā*. Some of you will
know of the enormous philosophical and religious baggage that
this word carries, and I have to say that there was much conceit
in my use, within a modernist social science discourse, of this
word as a description of our relation to the past. *Māyā* not only
means attachment, but in some metaphysical systems an attachment that is illusory; to valorize *māyā*, in opposition to that
metaphysics, is therefore also to humanize. But in this sense, of
course, *māyā* would mean not just attachment, but also affection,
compassion, tenderness. When I said that the driving force of
our modernity was our *māyā* for the past, I knew that I would
get my Bengali audience to sit up and take notice. I am certain
that I have failed to convey the rather startling effect of that
formulation when I say it in English.

Much has been said in recent years about the hybridity of
post-colonial intellectuals. It can hardly be denied that this recent

self-awareness has been immensely productive. No one who was not acutely aware of the sheer pain of an existential location that was always between cultures and never within any one of them, could produce the power that Salman Rushdie does when he writes of the ropes around his neck: 'I have them to this day, pulling me this way and that, East and West, the nooses tightening, commanding, *choose choose* . . . Ropes, I do not choose between you. Lassoes, lariats, I choose neither of you, and both. Do you hear? I refuse to choose.'[11]

But perhaps there is another figure that is far more ubiquitous in the history of non-Western modernities: that of the bilingual intellectual who is sometimes on one discursive terrain, sometimes on another, but never in between. He or she does not necessarily feel commanded to choose. When he is in the Western academy, he abides by the institutional rules of that academy. But he brings to it a set of intellectual concerns that have emerged somewhere else. Those concerns put him or her in an uneasy and intensely contestatory position in relation to the prevailing disciplinary norms of those institutions. There is no comfortable normalized position for the bilingual intellectual in the Western academy.

On the other hand, when the same person is a participant in an intellectual arena shaped by a modern non-European language, he or she is conscious of being an active agent in the forming of the disciplines in that arena, far more so than would be the case with him or her in the Western academy. But this role in the non-Western intellectual field is, paradoxically, premised on one's membership in the Western academy. Whichever way one looks at it, therefore, the relation between the intellectual and the academy in the two cases is not symmetrical.

One could, of course, say that the bilingual intellectual, operating as a full member in two different academic arenas, has a uniquely advantageous position of being interpretative and critical in both. This undoubtedly is what legitimizes his or her role. In that case, it must follow that what the bilingual intellectual does is actively reproduce the unequal relationship between the two academic arenas. On the other hand, if struggling with the act of translation, whether in this arena or that, is the very stuff

11 Salman Rushdie, *East, West* (London: Jonathan Cape, 1994), p. 211.

of what the bilingual intellectual does, then even in the knowledge that there must always remain an untranslated residue, a loss of meaning, one would still be entitled to the belief that translation is an act of transformation — changing not only that which is being translated but also that to which the translation is a contribution. And if, as would be the case with many bilinguals, the act of translation works in both directions, then one might be entitled to the further supposition that in spite of the asymmetry between the two intellectual arenas of modernity I have talked about — the Western claiming to be the universal and the national aspiring to be different — one is contributing to the critical transformation of both. But how exactly that might happen, I am unable to tell you. That, as I said at the beginning, is a problem to which I do not have an answer. I can only invite you to ponder upon my predicament.

Index